COLORADO

9th Edition

**Where to Stay and Eat
for All Budgets**

**Must-See Sights
and Local Secrets**

Ratings You Can Trust

Fodor's Travel Publications   New York, Toronto, London, Sydney, Auckland
www.fodors.com

FODOR'S COLORADO
Editor: Cate Starmer

Editorial Contributors: Barbara Colligan, Jad Davenport, Carrie Miner, Lois Friedland, Martha Schindler Connors, Kyle Wagner

Production Editor: Astrid deRidder
Maps & Illustrations: Mark Stroud and Henry Colomb, Moon Street Cartography; David Lindroth; Ed Jacobus, *cartographers;* Bob Blake, Rebecca Baer, *map editors;* William Wu, *information graphics*
Design: Fabrizio La Rocca, *creative director;* Guido Caroti, Siobhan O'Hare, *art directors;* Tina Malaney, Chie Ushio, Ann McBride, Jessica Walsh, *designers;* Melanie Marin, *senior picture editor*
Cover Photo: Cumbres and Toltec Railroad: Ron Ruhoff/Index Stock/Photolibrary
Production Manager: Amanda Bullock

COPYRIGHT
Copyright © 2010 by Fodor's Travel, a division of Random House, Inc.

Fodor's is a registered trademark of Random House, Inc.

All rights reserved. Published in the United States by Fodor's Travel, a division of Random House, Inc., and simultaneously in Canada by Random House of Canada, Limited, Toronto. Distributed by Random House, Inc., New York.

No maps, illustrations, or other portions of this book may be reproduced in any form without written permission from the publisher.

9th Edition

ISBN 978-1-4000-0415-7

ISSN 2769018

SPECIAL SALES
This book is available at special discounts for bulk purchases for sales promotions or premiums. Special editions, including personalized covers, excerpts of existing books, and corporate imprints, can be created in large quantities for special needs. For more information, write to Special Markets/Premium Sales, 1745 Broadway, MD 6-2, New York, New York 10019, or e-mail specialmarkets@randomhouse.com.

AN IMPORTANT TIP & AN INVITATION
Although all prices, opening times, and other details in this book are based on information supplied to us at press time, changes occur all the time in the travel world, and Fodor's cannot accept responsibility for facts that become outdated or for inadvertent errors or omissions. So **always confirm information when it matters,** especially if you're making a detour to visit a specific place. Your experiences—positive and negative— matter to us. If we have missed or misstated something, **please write to us.** We follow up on all suggestions. Contact the Colorado editor at editors@fodors.com or c/o Fodor's at 1745 Broadway, New York, NY 10019.

PRINTED IN THE UNITED STATES OF AMERICA

10 9 8 7 6 5 4 3 2 1

Be a Fodor's Correspondent

Your opinion matters. It matters to us. It matters to your fellow Fodor's travelers, too. And we'd like to hear it. In fact, we need to hear it.

When you share your experiences and opinions, you become an active member of the Fodor's community. That means we'll not only use your feedback to make our books better, but we'll publish your names and comments whenever possible. Throughout our guides, look for "Word of Mouth," excerpts of your unvarnished feedback.

Here's how you can help improve Fodor's for all of us.

Tell us when we're right. We rely on local writers to give you an insider's perspective. But our writers and staff editors—who are the best in the business—depend on you. Your positive feedback is a vote to renew our recommendations for the next edition.

Tell us when we're wrong. We're proud that we update most of our guides every year. But we're not perfect. Things change. Hotels cut services. Museums change hours. Charming cafés lose charm. If our writer didn't quite capture the essence of a place, tell us how you'd do it differently. If any of our descriptions are inaccurate or inadequate, we'll incorporate your changes in the next edition and will correct factual errors at fodors.com immediately.

Tell us what to include. You probably have had fantastic travel experiences that aren't yet in Fodor's. Why not share them with a community of like-minded travelers? Maybe you chanced upon a beach or bistro or B&B that you don't want to keep to yourself. Tell us why we should include it. And share your discoveries and experiences with everyone directly at fodors.com. Your input may lead us to add a new listing or highlight a place we cover with a "Highly Recommended" star or with our highest rating, "Fodor's Choice."

Give us your opinion instantly at our feedback center at www.fodors.com/feedback. You may also e-mail editors@fodors.com with the subject line "Colorado Editor." Or send your nominations, comments, and complaints by mail to Colorado Editor, Fodor's, 1745 Broadway, New York, NY 10019.

You and travelers like you are the heart of the Fodor's community. Make our community richer by sharing your experiences. Be a Fodor's correspondent.

Tim Jarrell, Publisher

CONTENTS

MAPS

ABOUT THIS BOOK

Our Ratings

Sometimes you find terrific travel experiences and sometimes they just find you. But usually the burden is on you to select the right combination of experiences. That's where our ratings come in.

As travelers we've all discovered a place so wonderful that its worthiness is obvious. And sometimes that place is so unique that superlatives don't do it justice: you just have to be there to know. These sights, properties, and experiences get our highest rating, **Fodor's Choice**, indicated by orange stars throughout this book.

Black stars highlight sights and properties we deem **Highly Recommended**, places that our writers, editors, and readers praise again and again for consistency and excellence.

By default, there's another category: any place we include in this book is by definition worth your time, unless we say otherwise. And we will.

Disagree with any of our choices? Care to nominate a place or suggest that we rate one more highly? Visit our feedback center at *www. fodors.com/feedback.*

Budget Well

Hotel and restaurant price categories from ¢ to $$$$ are defined in the opening pages of each chapter. For attractions, we always give standard adult admission fees; reductions are usually available for children, students, and senior citizens. **AE, D, DC, MC, V** following restaurant and hotel listings indicate whether American Express, Discover, Diners Club, MasterCard, and Visa are accepted.

Restaurants

Unless we state otherwise, restaurants are open for lunch and dinner daily. We mention dress only when there's a specific requirement and reservations only when they're essential or not accepted—it's always best to book ahead.

Hotels

Hotels have private bath, phone, TV, and air-conditioning and operate on the European Plan (aka EP, meaning without meals), unless we specify that they use the Continental Plan (CP, with a Continental breakfast), Breakfast Plan (BP, with a full breakfast), or Modified American Plan (MAP, with breakfast and dinner), or are all-inclusive (AI, including all meals and most activities). We always list facilities but not

whether you'll be charged an extra fee to use them, so when pricing accommodations, find out what's included.

Many Listings
★ Fodor's Choice
★ Highly recommended
⊠ Physical address
↔ Directions or Map coordinates
⬦ Mailing address
☎ Telephone
🖶 Fax
⊕ On the Web
🖅 E-mail
🎟 Admission fee
☉ Open/closed times
Ⓜ Metro stations
🚌 Credit cards

Hotels & Restaurants
🏨 Hotel
🛏 Number of rooms
⚸ Facilities
🍽 Meal plans
✕ Restaurant
🖎 Reservations
🛆 Dress code
🚭 Smoking
🎵 BYOB

Outdoors
🏌 Golf
⛺ Camping

Other
🅒 Family-friendly
⇨ See also
⊠ Branch address
☞ Take note

Experience Colorado

WORD OF MOUTH

"Put on those hiking boots or sneakers, some layers to add or subtract, a water bottle and snack bar and go on any trail in Rocky Mountain National Park or any trail near Boulder. If you haven't seen it, Red Rocks Amphitheatre in Morrison is unique and there are dinosaur tracks nearby. Go west to Breckenridge, go southwest to Leadville and the Collegiate Peaks, but wherever you go, get out of the car!"

—39N105W7800Ft

WHAT'S WHERE

The following numbers refer to chapters.

2 Denver. Colorado's capital and largest city, Denver is unmatched in its combination of urban pleasures and easy access to outdoor recreation.

3 The Rockies near Denver. Scenic highway I–70 ascends into the foothills through historic towns Idaho Springs and Georgetown. Feeling lucky? Try the gambling at Central City and Black Hawk.

4 Summit County. The ski resorts of Keystone, Breckenridge, Copper Mountain, and Arapahoe Basin cluster near I–70 as it rises in the Rockies. Lake Dillon and its port towns attract summer visitors.

5 Vail Valley. Vail, the world's largest single-mountain ski resort, sits in a narrow corridor bounded by steep peaks. Also in the valley: upscale ski area Beaver Creek and sleepy Minturn.

6 Aspen and the Roaring Fork Valley. Glitzy Aspen is a serious skiing draw. Farther west, Victorian charmer Glenwood Springs centers on a massive hot springs pool.

7 Boulder and North Central Colorado. College town Boulder balances high-tech with bohemia. Estes Park abuts Rocky Mountain National Park's eastern entrance, while Grand Lake is its quieter western gateway.

8 Rocky Mountain National Park. The wilderness and alpine tundra here welcome wildlife and outdoor enthusiasts year-round.

9 Northwest Colorado and Steamboat Springs. Where the Rockies transition into an arid desert, Grand Junction is the region's hub. Nearby are the Colorado and Dinosaur National Monuments. Steamboat Springs offers skiing with cowboy charm.

10 Southwest Colorado.
Evergreen-clad peaks and red desert beckon outdoor nuts to mountain-biking birthplace Crested Butte, Black Canyon of the Gunnison, idyllic Telluride, and historic Durango.

11 Mesa Verde National Park. Designated a park in 1906, this protected series of canyons provides a peek into the lives of the Ancestral Puebloan people who made their homes among the cliffs.

12 South Central Colorado.
Next to Pikes Peak, Colorado Springs' mineral waters still flow. Cañon City is a rafting hub; Buena Vista and Salida are two artists' colonies. To the south, explore Great Sand Dunes National Park.

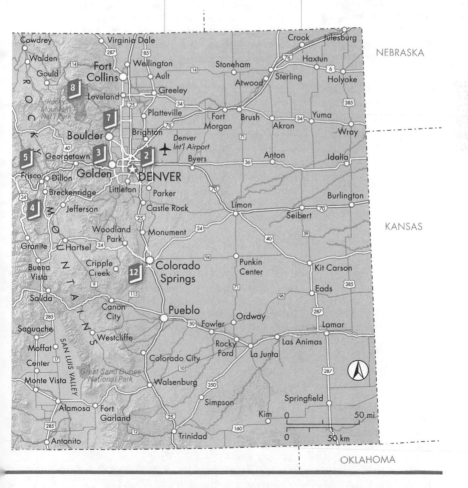

COLORADO PLANNER

What to Bring?

Colorado is famous for its "Rocky Mountain formal" dress code, which means cowboy attire is accepted everywhere, even in the fanciest restaurants, so bring your jeans and leave your formalwear at home. It's wise to be prepared for rapidly changing weather, however, as well as cooler nights (even when daytime temperatures hit summer highs).

If your plans include outdoor activities such as golf, skiing, or mountain biking, most major towns and cities have rental equipment available.

High Altitude Tips

The three things to consider with high-altitude travel are altitude sickness, dehydration, and sunburn.

■If you are coming from sea level and plan to visit the mountains, it's worth taking a day or two in Denver or other lower-elevation area to acclimate. Either way, take it easier than usual.

■Drink plenty of water and avoid alcohol.

■Always wear sunscreen and protective clothing. Sunglasses and a hat also are must-haves at higher elevation.

When to Go

The Colorado you experience will depend on the season you visit. Summer is a busy time. Hotels in tourist destinations book up early, especially in July and August, and hikers crowd the backcountry. Ski resorts buzz from December to early April, especially around Christmas and Presidents' Day. Many big resorts are popular summer destinations.

If you don't mind capricious weather, rates drop and crowds are nonexistent in spring and fall. Spring's pleasures are somewhat limited, since snow usually blocks the high country—and mountain-pass roads—well into June. But spring is a good time for fishing, rafting, birding, and wildlife-viewing. In fall, aspens splash the mountainsides with gold, wildlife comes down to lower elevations, and the angling is excellent.

How's the Weather?

Summer in the Rocky Mountains begins in late June or early July. Days are warm, with highs often in the 80s; nighttime temperatures fall to the 40s and 50s. Afternoon thunderstorms are common over the higher peaks. Fall begins in September; Winter creeps in during November, and deep snows arrive by December. Temperatures usually hover near freezing by day, thanks to the warm mountain sun, and drop overnight, occasionally as low as -60°F. Winter tapers off in March, though snow lingers into April on valley bottoms and into July on mountain passes.

At lower elevations (Denver, the eastern plains, and the southwestern corner of the state), summertime highs above 100°F are not uncommon, and winters are still cold, with highs in the 20s and 30s. The entire state sees snowy winters, even on the plains.

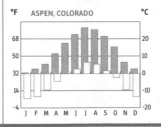

°F   ASPEN, COLORADO   °C

68   20
50   10
32   0
14   -10
-4   -20
    J F M A M J J A S O N D

1

Getting Here and Around

For more detailed information, see Travel Smart Colorado.

Modern and busy, **Denver International Airport (DEN)**
☎ *800/247-2336* ⊕ *www.flydenver.com*) moves travelers
in and out efficiently. There's also **Colorado Springs Airport**
(COS ☎ *719/550-1900* ⊕ *www.flycos.com*) and a number of smaller airports near resorts—Steamboat Springs,
Aspen, and Telluride.

In Denver some of the hotels provide free shuttles, and the
free Mall shuttle and light rail make it easy to get around
the metro area. You can travel to some major ski areas
by pre-arranged shuttle van. **Amtrak** (☎ *303/534-2812*
⊕ *www.amtrak.com*) has stops in Denver, Winter Park,
Glenwood Springs, Grand Junction, Trinidad, and La Junta.

Any other travel, however, makes a car an absolute necessity. Always check on road conditions, as the weather in
the foothills and mountains can be unpredictable. **Colorado
Road Condition Hotline** (☎ *303/639-1111 near Denver,
303/639-1234 statewide* ⊕ *www.cotrip.org*).

Dining and Lodging

Dining in Colorado has evolved over the past decade and
there are now more upscale and varied options than ever.
However, the dress code remains casual. Reservations are
recommended in most areas except rural communities, and
are essential in the high country, especially during the winter ski season and in places where golf, mountain biking,
and water sports are popular during the summer.

Plan well ahead for lodging in mountain areas and resort
towns, particularly during ski season and midsummer,
when festivals dominate. Condos can be a value in those
places during high season, especially if you have a group
or family, because you can save money on dining or share
expenses. While ski-area lodges can offer the closest access, they also will be the most expensive.

DINING AND LODGING PRICE CATEGORIES

	¢	$	$$	$$$	$$$$
Restaurants	under $8	$8-$12	$13-$18	$19-$25	over $25
Hotels	under $80	$80-$120	$121-$170	$171-$230	over $230

Restaurant prices are for a main course at dinner, excluding tax. Hotel
prices are for two people in a standard double room in high season,
excluding service charges and tax.

Festivals and Events

Summer in Colorado is full of
food and culture celebrations.
Here are some highlights:

**June Telluride Bluegrass
Festival.** The top acts in bluegrass take the music to new
levels in a stunning setting.
☎ *800/624-2422* ⊕ *www.blue-
grass.com.*

Country Jam. The likes of Keith
Urban and Alan Jackson party
in Grand Junction. ☎ *800/780-
0526* ⊕ *www.countryjam.com.*

**June-Aug. Bravo! Vail Val-
ley Music Festival.** A parade
of national orchestras around
the Valley. ☎ *877/812-5700*
⊕ *www.vailmusicfestival.org.*

**Strings in the Mountains
Music Festival.** Chamber music,
jazz, rock, and country in Steamboat Springs. ☎ *970/879-5056*
⊕ *www.stringsinthemountains.
org.*

**July-Aug. Crested Butte Music
Festival.** A variety of genres
played among the wildflowers. ☎ *970/349-0619* ⊕ *www.
crestedbuttemusicfestival.com.*

**Aug. Vail International Dance
Festival.** All types of dance
are presented in this series
at the beautiful Vilar Center.
☎ *970/949-1999* ⊕ *www.vvf.
org.*

**Sept. Telluride Film Festi-
val.** Premieres, workshops,
and the chance to rub elbows
with celebs. ☎ *510/665-9494*
⊕ *www.telluridefilmfestival.com.*

COLORADO
TOP ATTRACTIONS

Pikes Peak
(A) There are 54 peaks topping 14,000 feet in Colorado, but only here can you drive the switchbacks or take the Cog Railway to the top. The inspiration for Katharine Bates' song "America the Beautiful," Pikes Peak looms a few miles west of Colorado Springs.

Rocky Mountain National Park and Estes Park
(B) Estes Park is the gateway town to Rocky Mountain National Park, full of lush forests, high-alpine lakes, snow-capped peaks, wildflower-covered meadows, and 355 mi of trails. Abundant wildlife like black bear, elk, and bighorn sheep, and even more abundant crowds are drawn to this year-round paradise.

Mile High Denver
(C) The state's capital and largest city, Denver boasts of a diverse population with a rich mix of cultural offerings, and most of the 2.7 million metro area residents are intense sports fans and serious outdoors enthusiasts. The lively downtown area has a baseball stadium, an amusement park, historic neighborhoods, and a vast park system. Denver also claims the Denver Art Museum, the Denver Museum of Nature & Science, and the Denver Performing Arts Complex.

Boulder
(D) A college town with dramatic environs nestled up against the Flatirons, Boulder has a reputation for being the most outdoors-oriented of all of Colorado towns. With its commitment to preserving open space and wilderness, the city abuts so many nonurbanized zones that you can be on a trail to a mountain peak in no time. Terrific restaurants and a vibrant arts scene add to the allure.

Aspen and Glenwood Springs

(E) Stop by Glenwood Springs for a rejuvenating dip in the mineral springs–fed pool before continuing on to the glitzy-but-relaxing scene that is Aspen. The historic mining town has top-notch dining, the beautiful Maroon Bells mountains, and unparalleled skiing.

Mesa Verde National Park

(F) Home to the Ancestral Puebloans more than 700 years ago, Mesa Verde allows visitors to walk among the mesmerizing cliff dwellings built into alcoves perched hundreds of feet above and below level ground. Drive through the 80-square-mi park, stopping along the way to climb down into the dwellings, which tuck into the dramatic sandstone formations.

Summit County

(G) One of Colorado's premier giant playgrounds, Summit County is a year-round destination. Choose from a number of ski resorts—Copper Mountain, Keystone, Breckenridge, or local favorite Arapahoe Basin. The towns of Dillon, Silverthorne, and Frisco cluster around Dillon Reservoir, connected by an extensive paved bike path and rimmed by the looming peaks of the Continental Divide that border the east and south of the county. The old mining town of Leadville, with its exceptional greenway and historic buildings, has become a destination for families.

Black Canyon of the Gunnison National Park

(H) It's hard to say who appreciates this natural wonder more: fishermen, river rafters, hikers, or photographers. All are drawn to the glorious narrow canyon with its dramatic, jagged walls and enormous surrounding recreation area.

QUINTESSENTIAL COLORADO

The Great Outdoors

Colorado gets more than 300 sunny days per year, and that's a big part of why the natives get restless when forced to spend too much time inside. On any given day you'll find folks figuring out ways to get out there, from biking to work along the intricate veins of multiuse paths to hiking with the dog around expanses of open space, to soccer and jogging at the well-planned parks scattered around cities. In fact, Coloradans talk about the outdoors the way some people elsewhere talk about meals. They want to know where you just skied, hiked, biked, or rafted, and then, while they're in the middle of those adventures themselves, they'll discuss in-depth the next places on the list.

Hot Springs

In the late 1800s people came to Colorado not for gold or skiing, but for the legendary restorative powers of the mineral-rich hot springs that had been discovered all over the state. Doc Holliday was one such patient. Suffering from consumption, he spent his final days breathing the sulfurous fumes in Glenwood Springs. To this day there are nearly two-dozen commercial hot-springs resorts, most with lodging or other activities attached, and many more pools have been identified where people can hike in for the private backcountry experience. Some hot springs have been left in their natural state, while others are channeled into Olympic-size swimming pools and hot tubs. Either way, they have become destinations for all who long to take advantage of their therapeutic benefits.

Summits Without the Sweat

As fanatic as the famous "14ers" bunch can be—folks who have climbed or are in the process of "bagging" or summiting all 54 of the state's 14,000-foot peaks—not everyone is as enthusiastic about spending entire days to get the good views. The

Colorado is famous as one big playground, from snowcapped ski resorts and biking and hiking trails to white-water rivers and hot springs.

good news is that there are other ways to get, well, if not to 14,000 feet, then at least Rocky Mountain high enough to see something spectacular. In the summer a ride on the gondola in Telluride between town and Mountain Village is free and provides magnificent views. Any road trip through the Rockies will give you great views. You can drive to the tops of Mount Evans and Pikes Peak or take the Pikes Peak Cog Railway to the summit, or take a road trip to Aspen and drive the route over Independence Pass. Another terrific drive is Shrine Pass—Exit 180 off I–70 toward Vail Pass—especially in the fall, which allows you to see the Mount of the Holy Cross and the Tenmile, Gore, and Sawatch ranges.

Land of the Lost

Colorado definitely has a thing for dinosaurs—no surprise, considering that the state sits on prime dino real estate, with plenty of sandstone and shale perfect for preservation and the Rocky Mountains pushing the fossils closer to the surface for easier discovery. Dinosaur Ridge, close to Morrison, features a trail where you can see, touch, and easily photograph Jurassic-period bones and Cretaceous footprints and participate in a simulated dig. Both the Denver Museum of Nature and Science and the University of Colorado Museum of Natural History have extensive collections of fossil specimens, the former offering views into its working laboratory where volunteers process fossil specimens. Other attractions, such as the Denver Botanic Gardens and Red Rocks Amphitheatre, offer regular dino-themed events. There's even a town called Dinosaur, which sits near Dinosaur National Monument in the southwest part of the state, and Parfet Prehistoric Reserve east of Golden and Picketwire Canyonlands south of La Junta have hiking trails with extensive sets of dinosaur tracks.

OUTDOOR ADVENTURES

HORSEBACK RIDING

Horseback riding in the Rocky Mountains can mean a quick trot on a paved trail through craggy red rocks or a week-long stay at a working dude ranch, where guests rise at dawn and herd cattle from one mountain range to another.

Horse-pack trips are great ways to visit the backcountry, since horses can travel distances and carry supplies that would be impossible for hikers. Although horsemanship isn't required for most trips, it's helpful, and even an experienced rider can expect to be a little sore for the first few days. Clothing requirements are minimal. A sturdy pair of pants, a wide-brim sun hat, and outerwear to protect against rain are about the only necessities. Ask your outfitter for a list of things you'll need. June through August is the peak period for horse-pack trips.

Dude ranches fall roughly into two categories: working ranches and guest ranches. Working ranches, where you participate in such activities as roundups and cattle movements, sometimes require experienced horsemanship. Guest ranches offer a wide range of activities in addition to horseback riding, including fishing, four-wheeling, spa services, and cooking classes. At a typical dude ranch you stay in log cabins and are served meals family style in a lodge or ranch house; some ranches now have upscale restaurants on-site, too. For winter, many ranches have now added snow-oriented amenities.

When choosing a ranch, consider whether the place is family-oriented or adults only, and check on the length-of-stay requirements and what gear, if any, you are expected to bring. Working ranches plan around the needs of the business, and thus often require full-week stays for a fixed price, while regular guest ranches operate more like hotels.

Contacts Colorado Dude Ranch Association (⊕ *www.coloradoranch.com*).

Best Riding

■ **Academy Riding Stables, Colorado Springs.** Ideal for visitors who have only a short time in the area but long to do a half-day trail ride, Academy brings red-rock country up close at the Garden of the Gods, with pony rides for kids and hay wagon or stagecoach rides for groups.

■ **C Lazy U Guest Ranch, Granby.** One of the finest ranches in the state, C Lazy U offers a relaxing upscale experience, from daily horseback rides with a horse chosen for the duration of the visit to supervised kids' activities and chef-prepared meals, deluxe accommodations, a spring-fed pool, and an on-site spa.

■ **Colorado Cattle Company & Guest Ranch, New Raymer (near Fort Collins).** The real deal, the adults-only Colorado Cattle Company is two hours from Denver International Airport and seconds from turning you on to a true Western experience, with continual cattle drives, branding, fencing, and roping on a 7,000-acre ranch with 1,000 head of cattle.

■ **Devil's Thumb Ranch, Tabernash (near Winter Park).** Their commitment to the environment, use of renewable resources, and focus on the finest quality, from the organic ingredients in the restaurant to the luxurious bed linens in the rustic yet upscale cabins, make Suzanne and Bob Fanch's spread a deluxe getaway. They continue to update the ranch, with a new spa and lodge added to the superior horseback-riding, cross-country skiing, and ice-skating programs already in place.

SKIING AND SNOWBOARDING

The champagne powder of the Rocky Mountains can be a revelation for new-comers. Forget treacherous sheets of rock-hard ice, single-note hills where the bottom can be seen from the top, and mountains that offer only one kind of terrain from every angle. In the Rockies the snow builds up quickly, leaving a solid base that hangs tough all season, only to be layered upon by thick, fluffy powder that holds an edge, ready to be groomed into rippling corduroy or left in giddy stashes along the sides and through the trees. Volkswagen-size moguls and half-pipe–studded terrain parks are the norm, not the special attractions.

The added bonus of Rocky Mountain terrain is that many resorts have a wide variety of terrain at all levels, from beginner (green circle) to expert (double black diamond). Turn yourself over to the rental shops, which provide expert help in planning your day and outfitting you with the right equipment. Renting is also a great chance for experienced skiers and snowboarders to sample the latest technology.

Shop around for lift tickets before you leave home. Look for package deals, multiple-day passes, and online discounts. The traditional ski season usually runs from mid-December until early April, with Christmas, New Year's, and the month of March being the busiest times at the resorts.

Skiing the Rockies means preparing for all kinds of weather, sometimes in the same day, because the high altitudes can start a day off sunny and bright but kick in a blizzard by afternoon. Layers help, as well as plenty of polypropylene to wick away sweat in the sun, and a water-resistant outer layer to keep off the powdery wet-ness that's sure to accumulate—especially if you're a beginner snowboarder certain to spend time on the ground. Must-haves: plenty of sunscreen, because the sun is closer than you think, and a helmet, because so are the trees.

Contacts Colorado Ski (⊕ *www.coloradoski.com*). **Colorado Association of Ski Towns** (⊕ *www.coloradoskitowns.org*).

Best Skiing and Snowboarding

■ **Aspen.** Part "Lifestyles of the Rich and Famous" and part sleepy ski town, picturesque Aspen offers four mountains of widely varied terrain within easy access and some of the best dining in the state.

■ **Breckenridge.** Four terrain parks, each designed to target a skill level and promote advancement, give snowboarders the edge at this hip resort, which manages to make skiers feel just as welcome on its big, exposed bowls.

■ **Keystone.** The family that does winter sports together stays together at Keystone, which is small enough to navigate easily. Near Breckenridge and Copper Mountain, Keystone has a high percentage of beginner and intermediate offerings.

■ **Vail.** Those looking for the big-resort experience head to Vail, where modern comforts and multiple bowls mean a dizzying variety of runs and every possible convenience, all laid out in a series of contemporary European-style villages.

■ **Winter Park.** Winter Park has retained the laid-back vibe of a locals' mountain, and is still one of the better values on the Front Range. Mary Jane offers a mogul a minute, while the gentler Winter Park side gives cruisers a run for their money.

HIKING

Hiking is easily the least expensive and most accessible recreational pursuit. Sure, you could spend a few hundred dollars on high-tech hiking boots, a so-called personal hydration system, and a collapsible walking staff made of space-age materials, but there's no need for such expenditure. All that's really essential are sturdy athletic shoes, water, and the desire to see the landscape under your own power.

Hiking in the Rockies is a three-season sport that extends as far into fall as you're willing to tromp through snow, though in the arid desert regions it's possible to hike year-round without snowshoes. One of the greatest aspects of this region is the wide range of hiking terrain, from high-alpine scrambles that require stamina to flowered meadows that invite a relaxed pace to confining slot canyons where flash floods are a real danger.

There are few real hazards to hiking, but a little preparedness goes a long way. Know your limits, and make sure the terrain you are about to embark on does not exceed your abilities. It's a good idea to check the elevation change on a trail before you set out—a 1-mi trail might sound easy, until you realize how steep it is—and be careful not to get caught on exposed trails at elevation during afternoon thunderstorms in summer. Bring layers of clothing to accommodate changing weather, and always carry enough drinking water. Make sure someone knows where you're going and when to expect your return.

Contacts Colorado MountainClub (⊕ *www.cmc.org*).

Best Hiking

■ **Bear Lake Road, Rocky Mountain National Park.** A network of trails threads past alpine lakes, waterfalls, aspens, and pines. Stroll 1 mi to Sprague Lake on a wheelchair-accessible path, or take a four-hour hike past two waterfalls to Mills Lake, with its views of mighty Longs Peak.

■ **Black Canyon of the Gunnison National Park.** These are serious trails for serious hikers. There are six routes down into the canyon, which can be hot and slippery, and super steep. But the payoff is stunning: a rare look into canyon's heart and the fast-moving Gunnison River.

■ **Chautauqua Park, Boulder.** Meet the locals (and their dogs) as you head up into the mountains to look back down at the city or to get up close and personal with the Flatirons. There's even a grassy slope perfect for a picnic.

■ **Colorado National Monument, Grand Junction.** Breathe in the smell of sagebrush and juniper as you wander amid red-rock cliffs, canyons, and monoliths.

■ **The Colorado Trail.** The beauty of this epic hike, which starts just north of Durango and goes 500 mi all the way to Denver, is that you can do it all or just pieces of it.

■ **Green Mountain Trail, Lakewood.** Part of Jefferson County Open Space, the easy, mostly exposed trail affords panoramic views of downtown Denver, Table Mesa, Pikes Peak, and the Continental Divide from the top. You must share with bikers and dogs, as well as other critters.

■ **Maroon Bells, Aspen.** Bring your camera and take your shot at the twin, mineral-streaked peaks that are one of the most-photographed spots in the state.

BIKING

The Rockies are a favorite destination for bikers. Wide-open roads with great gains and losses in elevation test (and form) the stamina for road cyclists, while riders who prefer pedaling fat tires have plenty of mountain and desert trails to test their skills. Many bicyclers travel between towns (or backcountry huts or campsites) in summer. Unmatched views often make it difficult to keep your eyes on the road.

Thanks to the popularity of the sport here, it's usually easy to find a place that rents bicycles, both entry-level and high-end. Bike shops are also a good bet for information on local rides and group tours.

Most streets in the larger cities have bike lanes and separated bike paths, and Denver, Boulder, Fort Collins, Durango, Crested Butte, and Colorado Springs are especially bike-friendly. Cities and biking organizations often offer free maps.

On the road, watch for trucks and stay as close as possible to the side of the road, in single file. On the trail, ride within your limits and keep your eyes peeled for hikers and horses (both of which have the right of way), as well as dogs. Always wear a helmet and carry plenty of water.

Contacts Bicycle Colorado (☎ *303/417–1544* ⊕ *bicyclecolo.org*).

Best Biking

■ **Breckenridge.** Groups of mixed-skill level bikers make for Summit County, where beginners stick to the paved paths, the buff take on Vail Pass, and single-track types test their technical muscles in the backcountry.

■ **Cherry Creek Bike Path, LoDo, and Cherry Creek.** The ultimate urban trek, the paved trail along the burbling creek is part of 400 mi of linked Denver greenway.

■ **Crested Butte.** Pearl Pass is the storied birthplace of mountain-biking (check out the museum devoted to it in town). If your legs are not quite ready for that 40-mi, 12,700-foot challenge, there are plenty of paths more suitable to mere mortals.

■ **Durango.** Bikes seem to be more popular than cars in Durango, another fabled biking center. You can bike around town or into the mountains with equal ease.

■ **Grand Junction/Fruita.** With epic rides such as Over the Edge and Kokopelli Trail, these areas beckon single-track fanatics with their wavy-gravy loop-de-loops and screaming downhill payoffs. Beware: The heat can be intense.

■ **Keystone.** Serious downhillers head to Keystone's Drop Zone, the resort's expert section packed with rock gardens and high-speed jumps. Don't like the grunt-filled climb? Hop on a chairlift and smile away the sweet downhill.

■ **Rangely.** From the Raven Rims, you can see the town from nearly every point along this fun mountain-bike ride that starts in the corrals at Chase Draw.

■ **Steamboat Springs.** Yes, it is a cowboy town. But the backcountry is also laced with miles of jeep trails and single-track perfect for the solitude-seeking cyclist.

■ **Winter Park.** Home to the fabled Fat Tire Classic bike ride, Winter Park features tree-lined single-track trails that vary from gentle, meandering jaunts to screaming roller-coaster rides.

■ **Matthews/Winters Park, Golden.** With expansive views of the Red Rocks Park, the moderate to challenging combination of double-track and single-track mountain biking is crowded at sunrise and sunset.

RAFTING

Rafting brings on emotions as varied as the calm induced by flat waters surrounded with stunning scenery and wildlife and the thrill and excitement of charging a raging torrent of foam.

Dozens of tour companies have relatively mundane floats ranging from one hour to one day starting at $20. Others fulfill the needs of adventure tourists content only with chills, potential spills, and the occasional wall of water striking them smack-dab in the chest. Beginners and novices should use guides, but experienced rafters may rent watercraft.

Seasoned outfitters know their routes and their waters as well as you know the road between home and work. Many guides offer multiday trips in which they do everything, including searing your steak and rolling out your sleeping bag. Waters are ranked from Class I (the easiest) to Class VI (think Niagara Falls).

Select an outfitter based on recommendations from the local chamber, experience, and word of mouth. Ask your guide about the rating on your route before you book. Remember, ratings can vary greatly throughout the season due to runoff and weather events.

"Raft" can mean any of a number of things: an inflated raft in which passengers do the paddling; an inflated raft or wooden dory in which a licensed professional does the work; a motorized raft on which some oar work might be required. Be sure you know what kind of raft you'll be riding—or paddling—before booking.

Wear a swimsuit or shorts and sandals and bring along sunscreen and sunglasses. Outfitters are required to supply a life jacket for each passenger that must be worn. Most have moved to requiring helmets, as well. Early summer, when the water is highest, is the ideal time to raft, although many outfitters stretch the season, particularly on calmer routes.

Contacts Colorado River Outfitters Association (☎ 303/229–6075 ⊕ www.croa.org).

Best Rafting

■ **Animas River, Durango.** Even at high water, the Lower Animas stays at Class III, which makes for a great way to see the Durango area. Meanwhile, the Upper Animas runs between Class III and Class IV, hits a few at V, and gives little time to appreciate the mountain scenery and canyon views that race by.

■ **Arkansas River, Buena Vista, and Salida.** The Arkansas rages as a Class V or murmurs as a Class II, depending on the season. It's *the* white-water rafting destination in the state.

■ **Blue River, Silverthorne.** The Class I–III stretches of the Blue that run between Silverthorne and Columbine Landing are ideal for first-time paddlers. Be sure to check the flows; there is a short season.

■ **Colorado River in Glenwood Canyon, Glenwood Springs.** Choose a wild ride through the Shoshone Rapids (up to Class IV) or a mellow float down the lower Colorado.

■ **Gunnison River, north of Black Canyon of the Gunnison National Monument.** Packhorses carry your equipment into this wild area that leads into Gunnison Gorge, where Class I–III waters take you past granite walls while bald eagles fly overhead.

■ **Yampa and Green Rivers, Grand Junction.** Ride the Yampa and Green rivers through the remote, rugged canyons of Dinosaur National Monument.

FISHING

Trout do not live in ugly places.

And so it is in Colorado, where you'll discover unbridled beauty, towering pines, rippling mountain streams, and bottomless pools. It's here that blue-ribbon trout streams remain much as they were when Native American tribes, French fur trappers, and a few thousand faceless miners, muleskinners, and sodbusters first placed a muddy footprint along their banks.

Those early-day settlers had one advantage that you won't—time. To make the best use of that limited vacation, consider hiring a guide. You could spend days locating a great fishing spot, learning the water currents and fish behavior, and determining what flies, lures, or bait the fish are following. A good guide will cut through the options, get you into fish, and turn your excursion into an adventure complete with a full creel.

If you're comfortable with your fishing gear, bring it along, though most guides loan or rent equipment. Bring a rod and reel, waders, vest, hat, sunglasses, net, tackle, hemostats, and sunscreen. Fishing licenses, available at tackle shops and a variety of stores, are required in Colorado for anyone over the age of 16.

If you're not inclined to fork over the $250-plus that most quality guides charge per day for two anglers and a boat, your best bet is a stop at a reputable fly shop. They'll shorten your learning curve, tell you where the fish are, what they're biting on, and whether you should be "skittering" your dry fly on top of the water or "dead-drifting" a nymph.

Famed fisherman Lee Wolff wrote that "catching fish is a sport. Eating fish is not a sport." Most anglers practice "catch and release" to maintain productive fisheries and to protect native species.

A few streams are considered "private," in that they are stocked by a local club; other rivers are fly-fishing or catch-and-release only, so be sure you know the rules before making your first cast.

The season is always a concern when fishing. Spring runoffs can cloud the waters; summer droughts may reduce stream flows; and fall weather can be unpredictable. But as many fishing guides will attest, the best time to come and wet a line is whenever you can make it.

Contacts Colorado Division of Wildlife (☎ 303/297–1192 ⊕ www.wildlife.state. co.us).

Best Fishing

■ **Arkansas River, Buena Vista.** Fly-fish for brown or rainbow trout through Browns or Bighorn Sheep Canyon, or combine white-water rafting with fishing by floating on a raft through the Royal Gorge.

■ **Gunnison River, Almont.** In a tiny hamlet near Crested Butte and, more importantly, near the headwaters of the Gunnison, they *live* fly-fishing.

■ **Lake Dillon, Dillon.** Pick your spot along 26 mi of shoreline and cast away for brown and rainbow trout and kokanee salmon. The marina has rental boats and a fully stocked store.

■ **Lake Granby, Grand Lake.** Can't wait for summer? Try ice fishing on Lake Granby, on the western side of the Rockies.

■ **Roaring Fork River, Aspen.** Uninterrupted by dams from its headwaters to its junction with the Colorado, the Roaring Fork is one of the last free-flowing rivers in the state, plus it has a healthy population of 12- to 18-inch trout.

FLAVORS OF COLORADO

Despite a short growing season in much of the state, Colorado enjoys a strong culinary reputation for its commitment to organic, sustainable farming practices, farmers markets, and chef-fueled focus on buying and dining locally. Locally produced microbrews and wine, a robust agricultural foundation, and a continual roster of food-themed festivals make it easy for the traveler to snag a taste of Colorado while passing through. The region also is known for its many steak houses that keep the state's reputation as cattle country thriving.

Festivals of Local Bounty

Nearly every region of Colorado has some kind of fruit or vegetable that grows so well it makes a name for itself—which inevitably leads to a festival. The alternating swathes of high altitude and low valley are credited with providing a head start or a late blast of sun that in turn pumps that produce with extra flavor.

■ **Peach Festival, Palisade.** The small town of Palisade, which also is blessed with a climate ideal for growing wine grapes, is noted for several types of fruits, including their famous peaches.

■ **Wild Mushroom Festival, Crested Butte.** The climate above 9,000 feet in Crested Butte is just right for fungi, which leads to a celebration of the result every August.

Stream-Raised and Grass-Fed

Colorado is famous for its trout, beef, bison, and lamb, so much so that vegetarian restaurants have been slower in proliferating than in other parts of the country. The state also offers visitors the chance to pluck the trout right from its many rivers and lakes—rainbow, cutthroat, brook, brown and, of course, lake—although so many get shipped out that it's as likely to be frozen as not at restaurants—be sure

to ask. Meanwhile, whether or not the beef and bison seen grazing across the West are natural (meaning no hormones, steroids, or antibiotics), every town, large or small, boasts a steak house. And it's the grasses in their mountain diet that have been credited with the superior flavor and texture of the Colorado lamb.

■ **Buckhorn Exchange, Denver.** More than 500 pairs of eyes stare down at you during the meal, but it's what's on your plate that will keep your attention: dry-aged, prime-grade Colorado steaks served with hearty sides. Since 1893 this has been one of the state's game-meat specialists, as well.

■ **The Fort Restaurant, Morrison.** Bison is a particular specialty at this replica of Bent's Fort, a former Colorado fur-trade mecca, but the steaks, trout, elk, and other meats are delicious, as well.

■ **Game Creek Club, Vail.** With the word "game" in the name, it's not hard to imagine that the tony eatery does a good job with meats. The Bavarian-style lodge is open to the public for dinner.

Green Chile

Not the pepper itself but a gravylike stew is what Coloradans refer to when they talk about *chile verde,* the heady mixture that migrated with families who made their way from Mexico up through New Mexico and Texas and over from California to settle the high country. Its recipes vary as much across the state as minestrone does across Italy and pot-au-feu across France, but you can usually count on a pork-based concoction with jalapeños, sometimes tomatoes, and maybe tomatillos, the heat ranging from mellow to sinus-clearing. Green chile can smother just about anything—from enchiladas to huevos—but a plain bowlful with

a warmed tortilla is all the purist requires, and it's the best hangover cure ever.

■ **Blue Bonnet Café and Lounge, Denver.** The crowds are out the door at peak dining times to get at this longtime eatery's hearty, pork-based green chile, which comes on a wide variety of reasonably priced combination plates.

■ **Dos Hombres, Grand Junction.** The regular green chile at this cheerful spot is tomato-based, with a variety of chilies and pork for a thick, colorful mixture. They also offer milder, vegetarian, and New Mexican-style versions.

■ **Fiesta Jalisco, Frisco.** Light on chilies but packed with pork, the green here is medium-spicy and perfect on a burrito. The margaritas are special, too.

Topical Microbrews

Although fancy cocktails and wine continue to make headway against beer elsewhere in the country, Colorado is still the land of microbrews. Pool tables, multiple televisions for sports viewing, and live music make the brewpub an essential part of the weekend scene in most major cities and towns. Many of the best Denver brewpubs are in LoDo, or lower downtown. These offer tasting flights much like wineries, served with food that runs the gamut from pub grub to upscale. Many microbreweries also have tasting rooms open to the public, where growlers (half gallon glass jugs) of fresh beer can be purchased for takeout, perfect for picnics and tailgate parties.

■ **Boulder Beer Company, Boulder.** Colorado's first microbrewery (it started in 1979) offers a British-style ale, amber, pale, golden, and India pale ales and a stout, to name a few—and has a pub attached that offers s solid roster of grub.

■ **New Belgium Brewing Company, Fort Collins.** Fat Tire Amber Ale resonates with Coloradans because of its mountain-biking history, and is this microbrewery's most popular beer. It's readily available around the state, but a visit to the 100% wind-powered brewery is the best way to check it out.

■ **Wynkoop Brewing Co. Denver.** You can see part of the brewing operation through large glass windows at this popular brewpub in LoDo. The Railyard Ale is one of the signature beers, but the spicy chile beer is a local favorite.

Local Wines

Microbrews may rule, but Colorado's wine country continues to get kudos for producing reasonably priced, award-winning vino. The wines run the gamut, from lightweight whites to heavy-duty reds, and Colorado varietals as well as wines made from California grapes that don't grow well in the short season (such as red zinfandel). Cabernet sauvignon, merlot, and chardonnay are the most popular, but the viognier and Riesling offerings have gotten good press, too. Another of Colorado's best-kept secrets is its winery tours through Palisade and Grand Junction, great ways to see how your favorite wine goes from vineyard to glass.

■ **Trail Ridge Winery, Fort Collins.** In an atmospheric feed-and-grain barn, the tasting room for Trail Ridge sets out sips of their spicy Gewürztraminer, buttery chardonnays, oakey merlots, creamy Rieslings, and smooth cabernet sauvignons.

■ **Two Rivers Winery & Chateau, Grand Junction.** With its setting evocative of rural France, this inn set among the vines is the ideal spot for a sip of Burgundian-style chardonnay after a tour of the Colorado national monuments.

GREAT ITINERARIES

CONNECTING THE DOTS IN COLORFUL COLORADO

Arriving in Denver

Denver is filled with folks who stopped to visit and never left. After a few days in the Mile High City and surrounding metro area it's easy to see why: Colorado's capital has much to recommend it, including a thriving cultural scene, restaurants representing every ethnicity, plenty of sunshine, outdoor options galore, and snowcapped peaks for visual variety.

The Old West still holds sway in visitors' imaginations, and there are plenty of throwback trappings to check out, but the reality is that Denver is a modern metropolis that offers cosmopolitan amenities and state-of-the-art amusements.

Logistics: There are myriad well-marked ground transportation options near baggage claim at the sprawling Denver International Airport (DEN). Head to the taxi stand to pay about $55 to get downtown, or visit the RTD desk for bus schedules (SkyRide operates multiple routes starting at $8 one-way). Several independent companies operate shuttles from desks within the airport for about $19 one-way, and many hotels have complimentary shuttles for their guests.

All of the major car-rental companies operate at DEN. The rental-car counters that you see in the main terminal are there merely to point you toward the shuttles that take you to the car-rental center. Depending on time of day and traffic, it will take 30 minutes to an hour to reach downtown Denver and another 30 minutes for Boulder and the foothills.

DAYS 1-2: DENVER AND BOULDER

Option 1: Metro Denver

After you've settled into your hotel, head downtown, or if you're already staying there—always a good option to truly explore the city—make your way to Lower Downtown, or LoDo. The historic district is home to many of the city's famous brewpubs, art galleries, and Coors Field, as well as popular restaurants and some of the area's oldest architecture.

Hop on the free MallRide, the shuttle bus run by RTD, to head up the 16th Street Mall, a pedestrian-friendly, shopping-oriented strip that runs through the center of downtown. From there you can walk to Larimer Square for more shopping and restaurants, as well as the Denver Art Museum, the Colorado History Museum, the Colorado State Capitol, the Molly Brown House, and the U.S. Mint.

Logistics: Vending machines at each station for TheRide, Denver's light-rail, show destinations and calculate your fare ($1.50–$2.75 depending on the number of zones crossed). The machines accept bills of $20 or less and any coin except pennies. Children under age 5 ride free when accompanied by a fare-paying adult. RTD buses also provide an excellent way to get around; schedules are posted inside shelters and are available at Civic Center Station at the south end of the 16th Street Mall and Market Street Station toward the north end. Fares are $1.50 one-way.

Option 2: Boulder

Boulder takes its fair share of ribbing for being a Birkenstock-wearing, tofu-eating, latter-day hippie kind of town, but the truth is that it is one healthy, wealthy area, exceedingly popular and rapidly

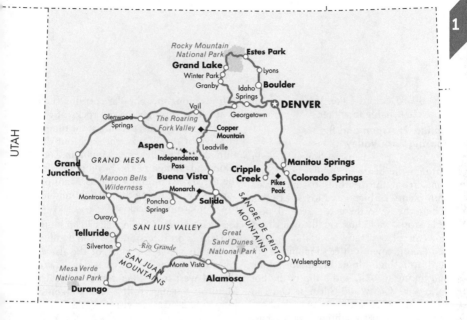

heading toward overdevelopment. For now, though, it's still a groovy place to visit. Stroll along the Pearl Street Mall and sample the excellent restaurants and shops, catching one of the dozens of street performers; or head just outside the city to tour Celestial Seasonings, the tea manufacturer; or to Chautauqua Park to hike in the shadow of the dramatic Flatiron Mountains. In winter, Eldora Mountain Resort is a 21-mi jaunt up a steep, switchback-laden road with no lift lines as payoff. The University of Colorado campus here means there is a high hip quotient in much of the nightlife.

Logistics: You can take an RTD bus to Boulder from Denver, but it's just as easy to drive up U.S. 36, and if you're going to go beyond the Pearl Street Mall, it's nice to have a car once you're there. Parking, though, can be quite tight.

DAYS 3–7: THE ROCKIES

Option 1: Estes Park, Rocky Mountain National Park, and Grand Lake

Rocky Mountain National Park (RMNP) is a year-round marvel, a park for every season: summer's hiking, fall's elk-mating ritual, winter's snowcapped peaks, and spring's wildflowers. Estes Park is the gateway to RMNP but a worthwhile destination itself, a small town swelling to a large one with the tourists who flock to its Western-theme shops and art galleries. The alpine-surrounded Grand Lake is a rustic charmer, a mecca for the sports person, and an idyllic locale for a family vacation.

Logistics: Estes Park is a hop-skip from Denver and Boulder, about 65 mi northwest of Denver via Interstate 25 and then CO–66 and U.S. 36. To get to RMNP, simply take U.S. 34 or U.S. 36 into the park. Grand Lake is on the other side of RMNP via U.S. 34, or from Denver, it's 100 mi by taking Interstate 70 to U.S. 40 over Berthoud Pass through Winter Park, Fraser, and Granby, and then turning onto

U.S. 34 to Grand Lake. It can be a bit more challenging in winter.

Option 2: Aspen and the Roaring Fork Valley

The drive to Aspen sends you straight through the heart of the Rocky Mountains, from the foothills to the peaks, with plenty of highs and lows between. Along the way there are several possible stops, including small-town diversions in places such as Idaho Springs and Georgetown, outlet shopping in Silverthorne, high-alpine mountain biking and hiking in Vail, and a dip in the hot springs in Glenwood Springs. Once in Aspen, world-class dining, upscale shopping, and celebrity-sighting await, while, depending on the season, the slopes will serve up wildflower-covered meadows or some of the best skiing in North America. Do not miss a pilgrimage to the Maroon Bells Wilderness area for a glimpse of the famous peaks.

Logistics: There are several flights in and out of Aspen/Pitkin County Airport daily, most routing through Denver. Many travelers drive to Aspen, however, making the 220-mi journey west on I–70 from Denver to Glenwood Springs, then taking U.S. 82 to Aspen. From May until about mid-October, Independence Pass, a more scenic option, is open; from I–70 take U.S. 91 at Copper Mountain south through Leadville to U.S. 82 and then use Independence Pass.

Option 3: Colorado Springs, Manitou Springs, and Cripple Creek

The Pikes Peak area may be dominated by 14,115-foot Pikes Peak itself—long ago the inspiration for "America the Beautiful"—and certainly getting to its summit, whether by cog railway, foot, or car, is a worthy goal. But there are other options along this popular corridor, such as strolling through the red rocks of the Garden of the Gods, peeking at the tunnel in Cave of the Winds, checking out the animals at the Cheyenne Mountain Zoo, taking advantage of the healing vibes in the artists' community that is Manitou Springs, or exploring the old gold-mining town of Cripple Creek.

Logistics: Colorado Springs sits 70 mi south of Denver on Interstate 25. You'll enjoy mountain views on most of the drive; Pikes Peak is visible on clear days. Take U.S. 24 west from Interstate 25 to reach Manitou Springs; follow CO–67 south from U.S. 24 west to visit Cripple Creek.

DAYS 8–14: THE SOUTHWEST

Option 1: Salida and Buena Vista

The way the Collegiate Peaks open up in magnificent panorama as you come around the bend on U.S. 285 is only one of the draws of a trip from Denver to Buena Vista and Salida. The plethora of outdoor activities available in this mountain- and river-rich region adds to the appeal. Salida has become a haven for its bevy of artists making a national name for their Western-oriented themes and grassroots sensibilities, and the banana-belt weather makes it all the more alluring.

Logistics: Take U.S. 285 south to Buena Vista. To reach Salida, continue on to Poncha Springs, then follow U.S. 50 east. Winter sports enthusiasts will want to make a side trip to Monarch Mountain, while mountain bikers won't want to miss the Monarch Crest Trail at Monarch Pass, both about 18 mi west of Salida on U.S. 50.

Option 2: Alamosa, San Luis Valley, and Great Sand Dunes National Park

The sand dunes dominate this sleepy, agriculturally abundant area, though they are only one of the natural playgrounds available to visitors. Alamosa National Wildlife Refuge is famous for its crane migrations, the fishing is superior in the Rio Grande, and the Sangre de Cristo Wilderness has its peaks and trails. Hop aboard the Cumbres & Toltec Scenic Railroad for a 64-mi trip back in time; the area, not to mention the train itself, has changed little since the 1880s.

Logistics: The round-trip is a worthwhile excursion alone, because the corridor between the Sangre de Cristo Mountains and the San Juans is one of the largest intermountain valleys in the world. Take Interstate 25 south to Walsenburg, then head west on U.S. 160 to Alamosa and north on CO–150.

Option 3: Telluride, Mesa Verde, and Durango

Durango is about an eight-hour drive from Denver, and well worth the effort. Mountain bikers make it a mission to try their mettle on the tough trails, and the Old West feel and small-town charm put this energetic spot high on the list for tourists. Telluride, though second home to several notable celebrities and famous for its film festival and other national events, presents a less glitzy face than other ski resorts like Aspen; and the San Juan Skyway, a 236-mi loop that connects Durango, Telluride, Ouray, and Silverton, is a gloriously scenic tour of mountains, alpine forests, and wildflower meadows. Mesa Verde National Park, meanwhile, safeguards the 1,400-year-old cliff dwellings of the Ancestral Puebloans.

> **TIPS**
>
> ■ Guard against the effects of altitude. Drink lots of water, slather on the sunscreen, and watch your alcohol intake. And pace yourself, especially when hiking or engaging in other outdoor pursuits.
>
> ■ Pack a lunch for your day in Rocky Mountain National Park. You'll have your pick of jaw-droppingly gorgeous spots for a picnic.
>
> ■ For the night in Aspen, consider reserving a room down-valley in Basalt or Carbondale if the rates in Aspen proper look too steep.
>
> ■ Denver and Aspen are the places to splurge on meals.
>
> ■ If you have a morning flight, consider staying the final night in Denver.

Logistics: To go straight to Durango, take U.S. 285 southwest to Monte Vista and then head west on U.S. 160. Mesa Verde is a 1½-hour drive from Durango, heading west on U.S. 160. For Telluride, take I–70 to Grand Junction and go south on U.S. 50 to Montrose; continue south on CO–550 to Ridgway, then turn right onto CO–62. Follow this to CO–145 and turn left. Follow the signs into Telluride. Telluride and Durango also have regional airports with limited service from major carriers.

MOUNTAIN FINDER

To help you decide which of Colorado's ski slopes are best for you, we've rated each major mountain according to several categories. To give some sense of cost, we have included the price of a peak-season one-day adult lift ticket at the time of this writing, as well as a category that covers affordable lodging options. Don't think this chart is only for winter visitors though—we'e also rated the mountain areas on their summer offerings. You should also consult the regional chapters and Outdoor Adventures.

	LIFT TICKET COST	VARIETY OF TERRAIN	SNOWBOARDER FRIENDLY	OTHER SNOW SPORTS	FAMILY FRIENDLY	DINING VARIETY	NIGHTLIFE	AFFORDABLE LODGING	OFF-SLOPE ACTIVITIES	SUMMER ACTIVITIES	CONVENIENCE FACTOR
Arapahoe Basin	$65	◓	●	○	◓	○	○	●	○	○	●
Aspen	$96	●	◓	●	◓	●	●	●	●	●	◒
Beaver Creek	$97	◓	◓	◒	●	◓	◒	●	◒	◒	◓
Breckenridge	$92	◓	●	●	●	◓	◓	◓	●	●	◓
Copper Mountain	$92	●	●	◒	●	◒	◓	◓	◓	○	◒
Crested Butte	$87	◓	●	◒	●	○	◒	●	◒	◓	○
Purgatory at Durango	$65	◒	◓	●	◓	○	○	●	○	○	○
Eldora	$65	◒	●	○	◓	○	○	●	○	○	●
Keystone	$96	●	◓	◓	●	◓	◓	◓	●	◒	◒
Loveland	$56	◒	●	○	●	○	○	●	○	○	●
Monarch	$54	◓	◓	○	●	○	○	●	○	○	○
Ski Cooper	$42	○	◓	○	●	○	○	●	○	○	◒
Snowmass	$96	◓	◓	◓	●	◒	◒	●	●	◓	◒
Steamboat	$91	◓	●	●	●	◒	◒	◓	●	●	◒
Telluride	$92	◓	◓	◓	◓	◓	◓	◒	◓	●	○
Vail	$97	●	◓	◓	●	●	●	◒	◒	●	◓
Winter Park	$92	●	●	◒	●	○	○	●	○	◒	●
Wolf Creek	$52	◓	◓	○	●	○	○	●	○	○	○

KEY: ○ few or none   ◒ moderate   ◓ substantial   ● noteworthy

Denver

WORD OF MOUTH

"The Art Museum is a great idea. The Botanic Gardens are wonderful also. The area around the stadium is fun—full of bars and restaurants. Go a bit further down toward town to LoDo for some nice shopping. There is a wonderful book store—The Tattered Cover. Some good food to be had . . . I have not seen many ballparks, but I do think Coors Field is gorgeous."

—Gretchen

"You've never been to Denver? There are lots of things to do for your weekend. You will not be bored . . . People in Denver are extraordinarily friendly (I'm biased), and will be happy to help you."

—PeaceOut

Updated by
Kyle Wagner

You can tell from its skyline alone that Denver is a major metropolis, with a Major League Baseball stadium at one end of downtown and the State Capitol building at the other. But look to the west to see where Denver distinguishes itself in the majestic Rocky Mountains, snow-peaked and breath-takingly huge, looming in the distance. This combination of urban sprawl and proximity to nature is what gives the city character and sets it apart as a destination.

Throughout the 1960s and '70s, when the city mushroomed on a huge surge of oil and energy revenues, Denver worked on the transition from Old West "cowtown" to a comfortable, modern place to live. The city demolished its large downtown "Skid Row" area, paving the way for developments such as the Tabor Center and the Auraria multicollege campus. In the early '90s mayors Federico Peña and Wellington Webb championed a massive new airport to replace the rickety Stapleton. Then the city lured major-league baseball, in the form of the purple-and-black Colorado Rockies, and built Coors Field in the heart of downtown. Around the stadium, planners developed LoDo, a business-and-shopping area including hip nightclubs, Larimer Square boutiques, and bike and walking paths.

Since the mid-1990s Denver has caught the attention of several major national corporations looking to move their operations to a thriving city that enjoys a relatively stable economy and a healthy business cli-mate. The fact that the Democratic National Party chose Denver for the 2008 national convention made it clear that the city had finally arrived. And win or lose, the sports teams continue to imbue the city with a sense of pride.

Many Denverites are unabashed nature lovers who can also enjoy the outdoors within the city limits, walking along the park-lined river paths downtown. (Perhaps as a result of their active lifestyle, Denverites are the "thinnest" city residents in the United States, with only 20% of the adult population overweight.) For Denverites, preserving the environ-ment and the city's rich mining and ranching heritage are of equally vital importance to the quality of life. LoDo buzzes with jazz clubs, restaurants, and art galleries housed in carefully restored century-old buildings. The culturally diverse populace avidly supports the Denver Art Museum, the Denver Museum of Nature & Science, the Colorado History Museum, and the Museo de las Americas. The Denver Perform-ing Arts Complex is the nation's second-largest theatrical venue, bested in capacity only by New York's Lincoln Center. An excellent public transportation system, including a popular, growing light-rail system and 400 mi of bike paths, makes getting around easy.

TOP REASONS TO GO

Denver Art Museum: Visitors are treated to Asian, pre-Columbian, and Spanish Colonial works along with a world-famous collection of Native American pieces.

Red Rocks Park and Amphitheatre: Even if you aren't attending a concert, the awe-inspiring red rocks of this formation-turned-venue are worth a look and there are hiking trails nearby.

Denver Botanic Gardens: Creatively arranged displays of more than 15,000 plant species from

around the world draw garden enthusiasts year-round.

Larimer Square: Specialty stores, superior people-watching, and some of the city's top restaurants and nightlife bring tourists and locals alike to the city's oldest street.

LoDo: Lower downtown's appeal lies in its proximity to Coors Field and the convenient and free 16th Street Mall shuttle. Shops and galleries are busy during the day, and it's also a hot spot at night.

ORIENTATION AND PLANNING

GETTING ORIENTED

Denver's downtown is laid out at a 45-degree angle to the rest of the metro area. Interstate 25 bisects Denver north to south, and Interstate 70 runs east to west. University Boulevard is a major north–south road and Speer Boulevard is a busy diagonal street. Most Denverites are tied to their vehicles, but the light-rail works well if you're going to certain areas.

If you're staying downtown, you can visit LoDo, Capitol Hill, and Larimer Square by walking or using light-rail or the free Mall shuttle. The Central Platte Valley can be accessed by taking the Mall shuttle all the way north to the end and then walking across the pedestrian-only Millennium Bridge. You will need a car to get to Cherry Creek or City Park, however, but once there, those sections also are easy to explore on foot.

Downtown. With its pedestrian-friendly numbered streets, free Mall shuttle, and plethora of restaurants, galleries, and museums within easy walking distance, downtown is a logical starting point for exploring.

Central Platte Valley. Just west of downtown, the Central Platte Valley is a destination for daytime activities along the Platte River and evening pursuits such as dining, music, and dancing.

City Park and Environs. East of downtown, the 370-acre oasis that is City Park also serves as a jumping-off point for the Denver Zoo and the Denver Museum of Nature & Science.

PLANNING

WHEN TO GO

Denver defies easy weather predictions. Although its blizzards are infamous, snowstorms are often followed by beautiful spring weather just a day or two later. Ski resorts are packed from roughly October to April, and Denver itself often bears the traffic. Summers are festival-happy, with a rock-concert slate at nearby Red Rocks Park and Amphitheatre and big names at the tent-covered Universal Lending Pavilion (also known as CityLights), in the parking lot outside the Pepsi Center downtown. Perhaps the best times to visit, though, are spring and fall, when the heat isn't so intense, the snow isn't so plentiful, and crowds are relatively thin. Ski resorts are still as scenic, but less expensive.

GETTING HERE AND AROUND

AIR TRAVEL

Denver International Airport (DEN) is 15 mi northeast of downtown, but it usually takes about a half-hour to 45 minutes to travel between them, depending on time of day. It's served by most major domestic carriers and many international ones. Arrive at the airport with plenty of time before your flight, preferably two hours; the airport's check-in and security-check lines are particularly long.

TRANSFERS   Between the airport and downtown, Super Shuttle makes door-to-door trips. The region's public bus service, Regional Transportation District (RTD), runs SkyRide to and from the airport; the trip takes 50 minutes, and the fare is $8–$12 each way. There's a transportation center in the airport just outside baggage claim. A taxi ride to downtown costs $55–$60.

Airport Denver International Airport (DEN) (📠 800/247–2336 ⊕ www. flydenver.com).

Airport Transfers Regional Transportation District/SkyRide (📠 303/299–6000 for route and schedule information ⊕ www.rtd-denver.com). **Super Shuttle** (📠 303/370–1300 ⊕ www.supershuttle.com).

BUS TRAVEL

In downtown Denver free shuttle-bus service operates about every 10 minutes until 1 AM, running the length of the 16th Street Mall (which bisects downtown) and stopping at two-block intervals. If you plan to spend much time outside downtown, a car is advised, although Denver has one of the best city bus systems in the country.

The region's public bus service, RTD, is comprehensive, with routes throughout the metropolitan area. The service also links Denver to outlying towns such as Boulder, Longmont, and Nederland. You can buy bus tokens at grocery stores or pay with exact change on the bus. Fares vary according to time and zone. Within the city limits, buses cost $2.

Bus Contacts RTD (📠 303/299–6000 or 800/366–7433 ⊕ www.rtd-denver.com).

CAR TRAVEL

Rental-car companies include Advantage, Alamo, Avis, Budget, Dollar, Enterprise, Hertz, and National. All have airport and downtown representatives.

2

Reaching Denver by car is fairly easy, except during rush hour. Interstate highways 70 and 25 intersect near downtown; an entrance to I–70 is just outside the airport.

■ **TIP→ When you're looking for an address within Denver, make sure you know whether it's a street or avenue.** Speer Boulevard runs alongside Cherry Creek from northwest to southeast through downtown; numbered streets run parallel to Speer and most are one-way. Colfax Avenue (U.S. 287) runs east–west through downtown; numbered avenues run parallel to Colfax. Broadway runs north–south. Other main thoroughfares include Colorado Boulevard (north–south) and Alameda Avenue (east–west). Try to avoid driving in the area during rush hour, when traffic gets heavy. Interstates 25 and 225 are particularly slow during those times; although the Transportation Expansion Project (T-REX) added extra lanes, a light-rail system along the highways, bicycle lanes, and other improvements, expansion in the metro area outpaced the project.

PARKING Finding an open meter has become increasingly difficult in downtown Denver, especially during peak times such as Rockies games and weekend nights. Additionally, most meters have two-hour limits until 10 PM, and at 25¢ for 10 minutes in some downtown areas, parking in Denver is currently more expensive than in New York or Chicago. However, there's no shortage of pay lots for $5 to $25 per day.

TAXI TRAVEL

Taxis can be costly and difficult to simply flag down as in some major metropolitan areas; instead, you usually must call ahead to arrange for one. Cabs are $2.50 minimum, $1.80–$2.25 per mile depending on the company. However, at peak times—during major events, and at 2 AM when the bars close—taxis are very hard to come by.

Taxi Companies Freedom Cab (☎ 303/292–8900). **Metro Taxi** (☎ 303/333–3333). **Yellow Cab** (☎ 303/777–7777).

TRAIN TRAVEL

Union Station, a comfortable old building in the heart of downtown filled with vending machines and video games, has Amtrak service.

RTD's Light Rail service's 5.3-mi track links southwest, southern, and northeast Denver to downtown. The peak fare is $2 within the city limits.

Contacts Amtrak (☎ 800/872–7245 ⊕ www.amtrak.com). **RTD Light Rail** (☎ 303/299–6000 ⊕ www.rtd-denver.com). **Union Station** (✉ 1701 Wynkoop St., at 17th Ave., LoDo ☎ 303/534–2812).

SAFETY

Although Denver is a generally peaceful city, the crime rate has increased slightly in recent years as the population has boomed. There are a few shadier areas on the outskirts of downtown, but violent crimes are few and far between. As always, paying attention to your surroundings is your best defense.

VISITOR AND TOUR INFO

The Denver Metro Convention and Visitors Bureau, open weekdays 9–5 and Saturday 9–2, is downtown above the Wolf Camera store on California Street. They also have self-guided walking-tour brochures and offer free guided walking tours at 9:30 AM on Thursday and Saturday June–August.

The Denver Microbrew Tour is a guided walking tour in LoDo that includes beer sampling at several microbreweries and a comprehensive history of local beer-making as well as Denver's history. Fees are $20–$25. Denver History Tours runs guided tours of historic Denver for $20.

Gray Line Colorado runs the usual expansive and exhaustive coach tours of anything and everything, from shopping in Cherry Creek to visiting Rocky Mountain National Park. Fees range from $35 to $100.

Tours Denver History Tours (☎ 720/234-7929 ⊕ www.denverhistorytours.com). **Denver Microbrew Tour** (☎ 719/238-5363 ⊕ denvermicrobrewtour.com). **Gray Line** (☎ 800/348-6877 ⊕ grayline.com).

Visitor Info Lower Downtown District, Inc. (☎ 303/628-5428). **Denver Metro Convention and Visitors Bureau** (✉ 1555 California St., LoDo ☎ 303/892-1112 or 800/393-8559 ⊕ www.denver.org).

EXPLORING DENVER

For many out-of-state travelers Denver is a gateway city, a transitional stop before heading into the nearby Rocky Mountains. Often, visitors will simply fly into Denver International Airport, rent a car, ask for directions to I–70, and head west into the mountains. But it's worth scheduling an extra few days, or even a few hours, to delve into the city itself. The city is a fairly easy place to maneuver, with prominent hotels such as the Brown Palace, excellent shopping at Cherry Creek and Larimer Square, sporting events ranging from the fabulous Avalanche to the ever-improving Nuggets, and plenty of (expensive) parking.

DOWNTOWN

Denver's downtown is an intriguing mix of well-preserved monuments from the state's frontier past and modern high-tech marvels. You'll often catch the reflection of an elegant Victorian building in the mirrored glass of a skyscraper. Hundreds of millions of dollars were poured into the city in the '90s in such projects as Coors Field, the downtown home of Denver's baseball Rockies; the relocation of Elitch Gardens, the first amusement park in the country to move into a downtown urban area; and an expansion of the light-rail system to run from downtown into the southern suburbs. Lower downtown, or LoDo, is a Victorian warehouse district revitalized by the ballpark, loft condominiums, and numerous brewpubs, nightclubs, and restaurants.

TIMING Downtown is remarkably compact, and can be toured on foot in an hour or less, but a car is recommended for exploring outside of downtown proper. The Denver Art Museum merits at least two to three hours, and the Colorado History Museum can be covered in an hour or two. Save some time for browsing and people-watching along the 16th Street Mall and Larimer Square. LoDo is a 30-block-square area that takes a few hours to meander through.

Numbers in the margin correspond to numbers in the margin and on the Downtown Denver map.

2

TOP ATTRACTIONS

❾ **Denver Art Museum.** Unique displays of Asian, pre-Columbian, Spanish
Fodor's Choice Colonial, and Native American art are the hallmarks of this model
★ of museum design. Among the museum's regular holdings are John
☾ DeAndrea's sexy, soothing, life-size polyvinyl painting *Linda* (1983); Claude Monet's dreamy flowerscape *Le Bassin des Nympheas* (1904); and Charles Deas's red-cowboy-on-horseback *Long Jakes, The Rocky Mountain Man* (1844). The works are thoughtfully lighted, though dazzling mountain views through hallway windows sometimes steal your attention. Imaginative hands-on exhibits, game and puzzle-filled Family Backpacks, and video corners will appeal to children; the Adventures in Art Center has hands-on art classes and exploration for children and adults. With the 2007 opening of the Frederic C. Hamilton building, the museum doubled in size. Designed by architect Daniel Libeskind, the 146,000-square-foot addition prompts debate: Some say the glass and titanium design has ruined the view, while others think the building is a work of art in its own right. To the east of the museum is an outdoor plaza—you'll know it by the huge orange metal sculpture—that leads to the Denver Public Library next door. ⊠ *100 W. 14th Ave. Pkwy., Civic Center* ☎ *720/865–5000* ⊕ *www.denverartmuseum.org* ⊠ *$13* ☾ *Tues., Thurs., Sat. 10–5; Fri. 10–10; Sun. noon–5.*

QUICK BITES

The Denver Art Museum's restaurant, **Palettes** (⊠ *100 W. 14th Ave. Pkwy.* ☎ *303/534–0889*), is the product of another kind of artist. Chef Kevin Taylor, a local fixture who also runs Prima Ristorante, fills the menu with colorful dishes like fruit-stuffed pork and flash-fried calamari. There's also a coffee shop, **Novo Coffee**, on the second floor of the museum, as well as **Mad Greens Inspired Eats**, a sandwich and salad spot on Martin Plaza across from the museum's main entrance, with outdoor tables on the plaza between the museum and the Denver Public Library.

❸ **Larimer Square.** Larimer Square is on the oldest street in the city, immor-
Fodor's Choice talized by Jack Kerouac in his seminal book *On the Road*. It was saved
★ from the wrecker's ball by a determined preservationist in the 1960s, when the city went demolition-crazy in its eagerness to present a more youthful image. Much has changed since Kerouac's wanderings; Larimer Square's rough edges have been cleaned up in favor of upscale retail and chic restaurants. The Square has become a serious late-night party district thanks to spillover from the expanded LoDo neighborhood and Rockies fans flowing out from the baseball stadium. Shops line the arched redbrick courtyards of **Writer Square**, Denver's most charming shopping district. ⊠ *Larimer and 15th Sts., LoDo* ☎ *303/685–8143* ⊕ *www.larimersquare.com.*

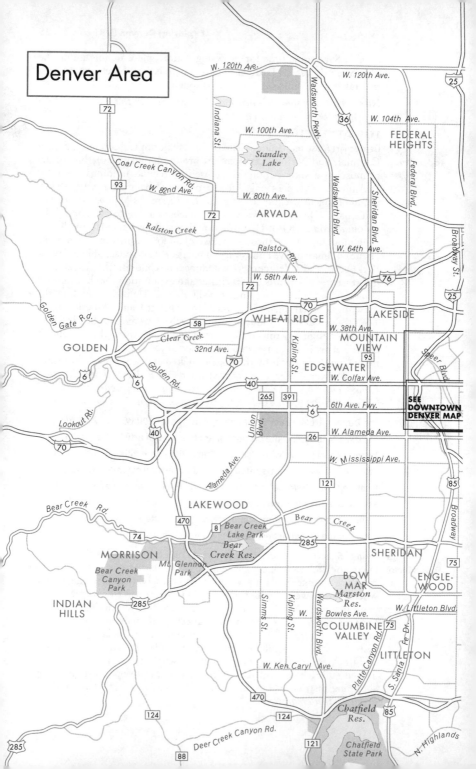

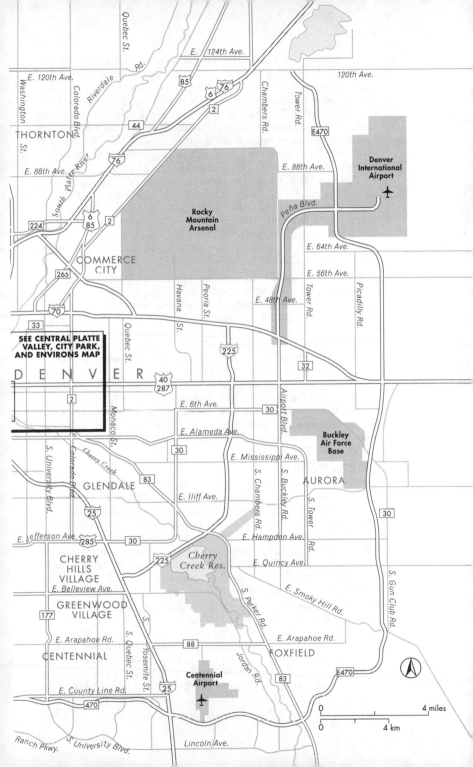

❶ LoDo. ★ Officially the Lower Downtown Historic District, the 25-plus square-block area that was the site of the original 1858 settlement of Denver City, is nicknamed LoDo. It's home to art galleries, chic shops, nightclubs, and restaurants ranging from Denver's most upscale to its most down-home. This part of town was once the city's thriving retail center, then it fell into disuse and slid into slums. Since the early 1990s LoDo has metamorphosed into the city's cultural center, thanks to its resident avant-garde artists, retailers, and loft dwellers who have taken over the old warehouses and redbricks. The handsome **Coors Field** (⊠ *Blake and 20th Sts., LoDo*), home of baseball's Colorado Rockies, has further galvanized the area. Its old-fashioned brick and grillwork facade was designed to blend in with the surrounding Victorian warehouses. As with cuddly Wrigley Field, on the north side of Chicago, Coors Field has engendered a nightlife scene of sports bars, restaurants, and dance clubs. ⊠ *From Larimer St. to South Platte River, between 14th and 22nd Sts., LoDo* ⊕ *www.lodo.org.*

★ **16th Street Mall.** Outdoor cafés and tempting shops line this pedestrians-only 12-block thoroughfare, shaded by red-oak and locust trees. The Mall's businesses run the entire socioeconomic range. There are popular meeting spots for business types at places like the Irish pub Katie Mullen's in the Sheraton Hotel; great people-watching from the sidewalk patio at the Paramount Cafe, around the corner from the Paramount Theatre; and plenty of fast-food chains. Although some Denverites swear by the higher-end Cherry Cheek Shopping District, the 16th Street Mall covers every retail area and is a more affordable, diverse experience. You can find Denver's best people-watching here. ■ **TIP→ Catch one of the free shuttle buses here that run the length of downtown.** Pay attention when you're wandering across the street, as the walking area and bus lanes are the same color and are hard to distinguish. ⊠ *From Broadway to Wynkoop St., LoDo.*

WORTH NOTING

❺ Brown Palace. The grande dame of Denver hotels was built in 1892, and is still considered the city's most prestigious address. Famous guests have included President Dwight D. Eisenhower, Winston Churchill, and Beyoncé. Even if you aren't staying here, the Brown Palace lobby is a great place to sit on comfortable old couches, drink tea, and listen to piano standards (or harp, during afternoon tea). Reputedly this was the first atrium hotel in the United States; its ornate lobby and nine stories are crowned by a Tiffany stained-glass window. ⊠ *321 17th St., LoDo* ☎ *303/297–3111* ⊕ *www.brownpalace.com.*

❿ Byers-Evans House Museum. Sprawling and detailed, red and black, this elaborate Victorian went up in 1883 as the home of *Rocky Mountain News* publisher William Byers. Restored to its pre–World War I condition, the historic landmark has occasional exhibitions and regular tours. Its main appeal is the glimpse it provides into Denver's past, specifically 1912 through 1924. The furnishings are those the Evans family acquired over the 80-some years they lived here. ⊠ *1310 Bannock St., Civic Center* ☎ *303/620–4933* ⊕ *www.coloradohistory.org* ⊠ *$5* ☉ *Tues.–Sun. 11–3.*

8 **Civic Center.** A peaceful respite awaits in this three-block park in the cultural heart of downtown, site of the State Capitol. A 1919 Greek amphitheater is in the middle of one of the city's largest flower gardens. Two of the park's statues, *Bronco Buster* and *On the War Trail,* depicting a cowboy and an Indian on horseback, were commissioned in the '20s. Festivals such as Cinco de Mayo, Taste of Colorado, and the People's Fair keep things lively here in spring and summer. The park was born in 1906, when Mayor Robert Speer asked New York architect Charles Robinson to expand on his vision of a "Paris on the Platte." ⊠ *Bannock St. to Broadway south of Colfax Ave. and north of 14th Ave., Civic Center.*

12 **Colorado History Museum.** The state's frontier past is vibrantly depicted in this flagship of the Colorado Historical Society. Changing exhibits highlight eras from the days before white settlers arrived to the boom periods of mining. General exhibit themes include the growth of historic preservation and black cowboys in the American West. Permanent displays include Conestoga wagons, old touring cars, and an extraordinary time line called "The Colorado Chronicle 1800–1950," which covers the state's history in amazing detail. The museum is easy to spot by its huge, colorful mural of Native Americans, miners, and red rocks. The large brick area outside the front door, complete with grassy strip, is a great place to relax if you're walking through downtown. ⊠ *1300 Broadway, Civic Center* ☎ *303/866–3682* ⊕ *www.coloradohistory.org* 🎟 *$7* ⊙ *Mon.–Sat. 10–5, Sun. noon–5.*

4 **Daniels and Fisher Tower.** This 330-foot-high, 20-floor structure emulates the campanile of St. Mark's Cathedral in Venice, and it was the tallest building west of the Mississippi when it was built in 1909. William Cooke Daniels originally commissioned the tower to stand adjacent to his five-story department store. Today it's an office building and the city's most convenient clock tower, and is particularly striking—the clock is 16 feet high—when viewed in concert with the fountains in the adjacent Skyline Park. ⊠ *1601 Arapahoe St., at 16th St., LoDo.*

6 **Denver Firefighters Museum.** Denver's first firehouse was built in 1909 and now serves as a museum where original items of the trade are on view, including uniforms, nets, fire carts and trucks, bells, and switchboards. Artifacts and photos document the progression of firefighting machinery from horses and carriages in the early 1900s to the flashy red-and-white trucks of today. ⊠ *1326 Tremont Pl., LoDo* ☎ *303/892–1436* ⊕ *www. denverfirefightersmuseum.org* 🎟 *$6* ⊙ *Mon.–Sat. 10–4.*

11 **Denver Public Library's Central Library.** A life-size horse on a 20-foot-tall chair and other sculptures decorate the expansive lawn of this sprawling complex with round towers and tall, oblong windows. Built in the mid-'50s, the Central Library underwent a massive, Michael Graves–designed renovation in 1995. The map and manuscript rooms, Gates Western History Reading Room (with amazing views of the mountains), and Schlessman Hall (with its three-story atrium) merit a visit. The library houses a world-renowned collection of books, photographs, and newspapers that chronicle the American West, as well as original paintings by Remington, Russell, Audubon, and Bierstadt. The children's library is notable for its captivating design and its unique, child-

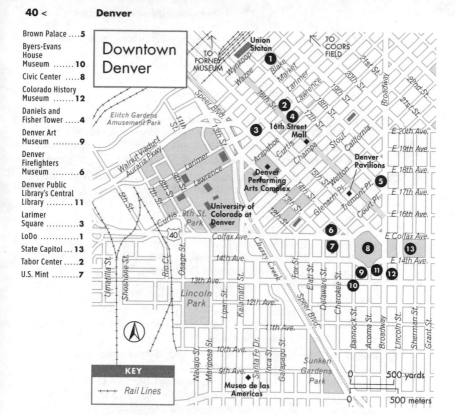

friendly multimedia computer catalog. ⊠ *10 W. 14th Ave. Pkwy., Civic Center* ☎ *720/865–1111* ⊕ *www.denver.lib.co.us* ☯ *Mon. and Tues. 10–8, Wed.–Fri. 10–6, Sat. 9–5, Sun. 1–5.*

**OFF THE
BEATEN
PATH**

Forney Museum of Transportation. Inside a converted warehouse are an 1898 Renault coupe, Amelia Earhart's immaculately maintained "Gold-bug," and a Big Boy steam locomotive, among other former vehicles. Other exhibits in this eccentric museum consist of antique bicycles, cable cars, and even experimental car-planes. This trivia-laden show-case is outside of the downtown loop: Go north on Brighton Boule-vard; the museum is adjacent to the Denver Coliseum on the south side of I–70. ⊠ *4303 Brighton Blvd., Globeville* ☎ *303/297–1113* ⊕ *www. forneymuseum.org* ⊠ *$7* ☯ *Mon.–Sat. 10–4.*

**OFF THE
BEATEN
PATH**

Museo de las Americas. The region's first museum dedicated to the achievements of Latinos in the Americas has a permanent collection as well as rotating exhibits that cover everything from Hispanics in the state legislature to Latin American women artists in the 20th century. Among the permanent pieces are the oil painting *Virgin of Solitude* (circa 1730) and a Mayan polychrome jar (circa 650–950), in addi-tion to contemporary works. Admission is free the first Friday of each month. ⊠ *861 Santa Fe Dr., Lincoln Park* ☎ *303/571–4401* ⊕ *www. museo.org* ⊠ *$5* ☯ *Tues.–Fri. 10–5, weekends noon–5.*

⓭ State Capitol. Built in 1886, the capitol was constructed mostly of materials indigenous to Colorado, including marble, granite, and rose onyx. Especially inspiring is the gold-leaf dome, a reminder of the state's mining heritage. The dome is open for tours by appointment only weekdays 9 AM–2 PM every hour on the hour; 30 people at a time can go to the top (using a 99-step staircase from the third floor) to enjoy the 360-degree view of the Rockies. Outside, multiple markers have been placed over the past century and found to be incorrect in identifying the exact location of exactly 1 mi high (above sea level); in 2003 the 13th step was designated as such. The legislature is generally in session from January through May, and visitors are welcome to sit in third-floor viewing galleries above the House and Senate chambers. ⊠ *200 E. Colfax Ave., Capitol Hill* ☎ *303/866–2604, 303/866–3834 for dome tours* ⊕ *www.state.co.us/gov* ⊠ *Free* ☉ *Bldg. weekdays 7–5:30. Tours Sept.–May, weekdays 9–2:30; June–Aug., weekdays 9–3:30.*

➋ Tabor Center. This festive shopping mall has about 55 stores and attractions, including fast-food eateries, strolling troubadours, jugglers and fire-eaters, and splashing fountains. A concierge desk at the Lawrence Street entrance is staffed with friendly people who lead free walking tours around the city. ⊠ *1200 17th St., LoDo* ☎ *303/572–6868* ⊕ *www.taborcenter.com.*

➐ U.S. Mint. Tour this facility to catch a glimpse of the coin-making process, as presses spit out thousands of coins a minute. There are also exhibits on the history of money and a restored version of Denver's original mint prior to numerous expansions. More than 14 billion coins are minted yearly, and the nation's second-largest hoard of gold is stashed away here. ■ **TIP→ To schedule a tour and prepare for your visit (there are strict security guidelines) visit the Mint's Web site.** Same-day walk-up tours on a limited space-available basis weekdays 8–2. The gift shop, which sells authentic coins and currency, is in the Tremont Center, across Colfax Avenue from the Mint. ⊠ *320 W. Colfax Ave., Civic Center* ☎ *303/405–4761* ⊕ *www.usmint.gov/mint_tours/* ⊠ *Free* ☉ *Gift shop, weekdays 9–3:30, tours by reservation only*

CENTRAL PLATTE VALLEY

Less than a mile west of downtown is the booming Central Platte Valley. Once the cluttered heart of Denver's railroad system, it's now overflowing with attractions. The imposing glass facade of the NFL Broncos' Invesco Field at Mile High, the stately Pepsi Center sports arena, the Downtown Aquarium, and the flagship REI outdoors store are but four more crowd-pleasers to add to the growing list in Denver. New restaurants, a couple of coffeehouses, and a few small, locally owned shops, including some that sell sporting goods and a wine boutique, make it appealing to wander around. The sights in this area are so popular that the city plans to complete a light-rail line that will connect the attractions with downtown by the end of the decade.

The South Platte River valley concrete path, which extends several miles from downtown to the east and west, snakes along the water through out-of-the-way parks and trails. The 15th Street Bridge is particularly

Central Platte Valley, City Park, and Environs

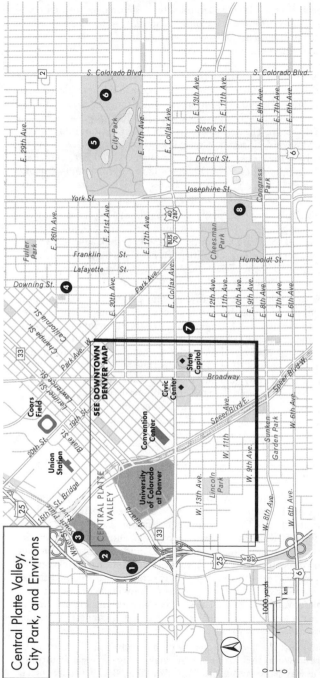

Central Platte Valley ▶

Children's Museum of
Denver **1**
Downtown Aquarium **3**
Elitch Gardens **2**

City Park and Environs ▶

Black American
West Museum **4**
Denver Botanic
Gardens **8**

Denver Museum ▶
of Nature and Science **6**
Denver Zoo **5**
Molly Brown House **7**

cyclist- and pedestrian-friendly, connecting LoDo with growing northwest Denver in a seamless way. The most relaxed, and easiest, way to see the area is on one of the half-hour or hour-long tours on the **Platte Valley Trolley** (☎ *303/458–6255* ⊕ *www.denvertrolley.org* ⊠ *$2*), which can be accessed by parking at the Children's Museum and catching the streetcar east of the lot by the river.

TIMING   You can easily spend a full day in this area, especially if you have kids or would like to explore the Greenway. Older kids tend to blaze through the Children's Museum in a morning or afternoon, but the under-6 set can spend all day here. The Aquarium can make a good four to six-hour stop. If you want to do both the Elitch Garden water park and main park, plan on spending a full day there.

Numbers in the margin correspond to the Central Platte Valley, City Park, and Environs map.

TOP ATTRACTIONS

❶ **Children's Museum of Denver.** This is one of the finest museums of its
☺ kind in North America, with constantly changing hands-on exhibits that
★ engage children up to about age 8 in discovery. The Maze-eum is a walkthrough musical maze. Children can build a car on an assembly line and send it careening down a test ramp at the Inventions display. One of the biggest attractions is the Center for the Young Child, a 3,700-square-foot playscape aimed at newborns through four-year-olds and their caregivers. ⊠ *2121 Children's Museum Dr., off Exit 211 of I-25, Jefferson Park* ☎ *303/433–7444* ⊕ *www.mychildsmuseum.org* ⊠ *$7.50* ☉ *Weekdays 9–4, Wed. open until 7:30, weekends 10–5.*

❸ **Downtown Aquarium.** On the north side of the South Platte across from
☺ Elitch Gardens, this is the only million-gallon aquarium between Chi-
★ cago and the West Coast. It has four sections that show aquatic life in all its forms, from the seas to the river's headwaters in the Colorado mountains. The 250-seat Aquarium Restaurant surrounds a 150,000-gallon tank filled with sharks and fish. Other highlights include an expanded stingray touch pool, a gold-panning area, animatronic creatures, and an interactive shipwreck. The aquarium also has a lounge with a weeknight happy hour. ⊠ *700 Water St., off Exit 211 of I-25, Jefferson Park* ☎ *303/561–4450* ⊕ *www.downtownaquariumdenver.com* ⊠ *$14.95; $9.95 after 6* PM ☉ *Sun.–Thurs. 10–9, Fri. and Sat. 10–9:30.*

❷ **Elitch Gardens.** This elaborate and thrilling park was a Denver family tradi-
☺ tion long before its 1995 relocation from northwest Denver to its current
★ home on the outskirts of downtown. The park's highlights include hair-raising roller coasters and thrill rides; for younger kids and squeamish parents there are also plenty of gentler, Bugs Bunny–hosted attractions. Twister II, an update of the classic, wooden Mister Twister, is from the original Elitch Gardens, as is a 100-foot-high Ferris wheel that provides sensational views of downtown. A 10-acre water-adventure park is included in the standard entry fee. You can spend a whole day at either the water park or the main park. Locker and stroller rentals are available; discounted tickets are available online. ⊠ *I-25 and Speer Blvd., Auraria* ☎ *303/595–4386* ⊕ *www.elitchgardens.com* ⊠ *$44.99 unlimited-ride pass* ☉ *June–Aug., daily; Apr., May, Sept., and Oct., Fri.–Sun.; hrs vary so call ahead.*

WORTH NOTING

Platte River Greenway. Just behind the REI flagship store, this serene park is at the center of the South Platte River valley path. Its rocks and rapids are especially attractive in summer for kayakers, bicyclists, and hikers. Sidewalks extend down the South Platte to the east toward the suburbs and west toward Invesco Field at Mile High. A pathway in yet another direction leads to LoDo. From the park it's about a 20-minute walk to the 16th Street Mall and Coors Field, which makes it a healthy way to sightsee when the weather is good. You can rent a kayak from nearby **Confluence Kayaks** (☎ 303/433–3676 ⊕ www.confluencekayaks.com) and take a quick lesson before paddling yourself down the river. ⊠ 1615 Platte St., Jefferson Park.

QUICK BITES

Down the street from the REI store, along the bicycle path on 15th Street, **My Brother's Bar** (⊠ 2376 15th St. ☎ 303/455–9991) is a homey neighborhood tavern that serves different microbrews, burgers—buffalo and beef—and sandwiches of all kinds until 1:30 AM. The bar's name isn't on the facade, so look for the street number.

CITY PARK AND ENVIRONS

Acquired by the city in 1881, City Park, Denver's largest public space (370 acres), contains rose gardens, lakes, a golf course, tennis courts, and a huge playground. A shuttle runs between two of the city's most popular attractions: the Denver Zoo and the Denver Museum of Nature & Science, both on the site. City Park is east of downtown Denver, and runs from East 17th Avenue to East 26th Avenue, between York Street and Colorado Boulevard.

TIMING If you have children or are an animal lover, you could easily spend half a day in City Park. Plan to arrive early on weekends, as parking can be difficult to obtain (it's free at the attractions, but goes fast), and in warm-weather months pack a picnic, as the park itself is a delightful daytime rest area, with plenty of room to stretch.

Numbers in the margin correspond to the Central Platte Valley, City Park, and Environs map.

TOP ATTRACTIONS

❻
©
Fodor'sChoice
★

Denver Museum of Nature & Science. Founded in 1900, the museum has amassed more than 775,000 objects, making it the largest natural history museum in the western United States. It houses a rich combination of traditional collections—dinosaur remains, animal dioramas, a mineralogy display, an Egyptology wing—and intriguing hands-on exhibits. In the Hall of Life you can test your health and fitness on a variety of contraptions and receive a personalized health profile. The Prehistoric Journey exhibit covers the seven stages of earth's development. The massive complex also includes an IMAX movie theater and a planetarium whose Space Odyssey exhibit simulates a trip to Mars. An impressive eating-and-relaxation area has a full-window panoramic view of the Rocky Mountains. ⊠ 2001 Colorado Blvd., City Park ☎ 303/322–7009 or 800/925–2250 ⊕ www.dmns.org ⊠ Museum

2

DENVER INVENTIONS

Every city likes to claim inventions, and Denver is no different. At the top of the city's list of accomplishments is the cheeseburger, for which resident Louis Ballast received a patent in 1935 after he accidentally spilled cheddar on his grill at the Humpty-Dumpty Drive-In on Speer Boulevard. The Denver boot, a bright yellow lock that attaches to a car tire and can only be removed with a special key, was invented by Frank Marugg as a way to keep people from stealing tires during World War II, when rubber snagged big bucks; in 1955 the boot came back to halt scofflaws. The Barnes Dance, a way for pedestrians to cross a four-way street diagonally, was named after Denver traffic engineer Henry Barnes in the 1930s, and although he didn't invent it, he was the first to use it on a large scale. And the Denver omelet, with green peppers, onions, and diced ham, has so many theories of inception it's almost impossible to track, but the best explanation is its evolution from the Western sandwich, with similar ingredients slapped inside bread by Chinese cooks who translated egg foo yong while working on the railroads.

$11, IMAX $8; $16 for combined pass (IMAX or planetarium) ⊙ Daily 9–5, IMAX showtimes vary.

QUICK BITES

An old-fashioned greasy-spoon diner that specializes in huge pancakes and spicy huevos rancheros, Pete's Kitchen (⊠ *1962 E. Colfax Ave. 80206* ☏ *303/321–3139*) is a short drive from the Denver Museum of Nature & Science. It's often packed, particularly on Sunday mornings.

❽ ★ Denver Botanic Gardens. The horticultural displays in thoughtfully laid-out theme gardens—more than 15,000 plant species from Australia, South Africa, and the Himalayas, and especially the western United States—are at their peak in July and August, when garden enthusiasts could spend half a day here. The tropical conservatory alone is worth an hour's visit in the off-season. Spring brings a brilliant display of wildflowers to the world-renowned rock alpine garden, primarily in late May and early June. The new OmniGlobe simulates the climate and atmospheric changes on earth; other environmental additions include a "green roof" atop the new bistro. Tea ceremonies take place some summer weekends in the tranquil Japanese garden, and artists such as folk–rocker Richard Thompson, singer–songwriter Jewel, and bluegrassy jazzman Bela Fleck have performed as part of the summer concert series. ⊠ *1005 York St., Cheesman Park* ☎ *720/865–3500* ⊕ *www.botanicgardens.org* ⊠ *$12.50 mid-May–Sept., $11.50 Sept.–mid-May* ⊙ *May–mid-Sept., Sat.–Tues. 9–8, Wed.–Fri. 9–5; mid-Sept.–May, daily 9–5.*

❺ ★ Denver Zoo. A bright peacock greets you at the door to the state's most popular cultural attraction, whose best-known exhibit showcases man-eating Komodo dragons in a lush re-creation of a cavernous riverbank. The **Conservation Carousel** ($2) rotates in the center of the 80-acre zoo, with handcrafted endangered species as mounts. A 7-acre Primate Panorama houses 31 species of primates in state-of-the-art environments that simulate the animals' natural habitats. Other highlights include a nursery for baby animals; seal shows; the world's only painting rhinoceros, Mshindi; the electric Safari Shuttle, which snakes through the property as you are treated to a lesson on the zoo's inhabitants; and the usual lions, tigers, bears, giraffes, and monkeys, and one extremely hairy elephant. The exhibits are spaced far apart along sprawling concrete paths, so build in enough time to visit everything. ⊠ *2300 Steele St. City Park* ☎ *303/376–4800* ⊕ *www.denverzoo.org* ✉ *$9 Nov.–Feb., $12 Mar.–Nov.* ⊙ *Nov.–Feb., daily 10–4; Mar.–Nov., daily 9–5.*

WORTH NOTING

❹ **Black American West Museum.** The revealing documents and artifacts here depict the vast contributions that African-Americans made to opening up the West. Nearly a third of the cowboys and many pioneer teachers and doctors were African-Americans. One floor is devoted to black cowboys; another to military troops such as the Buffalo Soldiers. Changing exhibits focus on topics such as the history of black churches in the West. ⊠ *3091 California St., Five Points* ☎ *303/482–2242* ⊕ *www. blackamericanwestmuseum.com* ✉ *$8* ⊙ *Sept.–May, Tues.–Sat. 10–2; June–Aug., Tues.–Sat. 10–5.*

❼ **Molly Brown House.** This Victorian celebrates the life and times of the scandalous, "unsinkable" Molly Brown. The heroine of the *Titanic* courageously saved several lives and continued to provide assistance to survivors back on terra firma. Costumed guides and period furnishings in the museum, including flamboyant gilt-edge wallpaper, lace curtains, tile fireplaces, and tapestries, evoke bygone days. The museum collects and displays artifacts that belonged to Brown, as well as period items dating to 1894–1912, when the Browns lived in the house. Tours run every half-hour; you won't need much more than that to see the whole place. ⊠ *1340 Pennsylvania St., Capitol Hill* ☎ *303/832–4092* ⊕ *www. mollybrown.org* ✉ *$8* ⊙ *June–Aug., Mon.–Sat. 10–3:30, Sun. noon– 3:30; Sept.–May, Tues.–Sat. 10–3:30, Sun. noon–3:30.*

SPORTS AND THE OUTDOORS

Denver is a city that can consistently, enthusiastically support three professional sports teams. Unfortunately, it has more than that—the Colorado Rockies, Colorado Avalanche, Denver Broncos, Denver Nuggets, and Colorado Rapids (soccer). Until recently, the Nuggets and Rapids had been the odd teams out, as the Rockies, Avalanche, and Broncos have all reached or won championships in their respective sports. But the Nuggets may be about to catch up, given their nucleus of hungry new young players.

What's great about Denverites is that most aren't just spectators. After a game, they go out and do stuff—hiking, bicycling, kayaking, and, yes, playing the team sports themselves. The city and its proximity to outdoor pursuits encourage a fit lifestyle.

BASEBALL

The Colorado Rockies, Denver's National League baseball team, play April–October in **Coors Field** (⊠ *2001 Blake St., LoDo* ☎ *303/292–0200 or 800/388–7625* ⊕ *www.coloradorockies.com*). Because of high altitude

CLOSE UP

National Western Stock Show

Thousands of cowpokes retrieve their string ties and worn boots and indulge in two weeks of hootin', hollerin', and celebratin' the beef industry during the **National Western Stock Show** (⊕ www.nationalwestern.com) every January.

Whether you're a professional rancher or bull rider, or just plan to show up for the people-watching, the Stock Show is a rich, colorful glimpse of Western culture. The pros arrive to make industry connections, show off their livestock, and perhaps land a few sales. The entertainment involves nightly rodeo events, presentations of prized cattle (some going for thousands of dollars), and "Mutton Bustin'." The latter is one of those rowdy rodeo

concepts that usually has no place in a genteel metropolis like Denver: kids, six years old and younger, don huge hockey-goalie helmets and hold for dear life on to the backs of bucking baby sheep. At the trade show you can buy hats and boots, but also yards of beef jerky and quirky gift items.

The yearly event is held at the **Denver Coliseum** (✉ *4655 Humboldt St., east of I–25 on I–70 Elyria* ☎ *303/297–1166 Ext. 810*). Just be sure to call first and ask for directions; although parking is plentiful, the Coliseum, usually home of straightforward sporting and entertainment events, becomes a labyrinth of lots and shuttles during the Stock Show.

and thin air, the park is among the hardest in the major leagues for pitchers—and the Rockies have had a tough time preserving young arms. But each year they manage to finish on a high enough note to bring the fans back into the stands the next season.

BASKETBALL
The Denver Nuggets of the National Basketball Association have been the ugly duckling in Denver's professional-sports scene for years. However, they continue to raise expectations with top-draft picks and exciting young players. From November to April the Nuggets play at the **Pepsi Center** (✉ *1000 Chopper Circle, Auraria* ☎ *303/405–8555* ⊕ *www.nba.com/nuggets*). The 19,000-seat arena, which opened in 1999, is also the primary spot in town for large musical acts such as Bruce Springsteen and Miley Cyrus.

BICYCLING AND JOGGING
The **Denver Parks Department** (☎ *720/913–0696* ⊕ *www.denvergov.org/parks*) has suggestions for bicycling and jogging paths throughout the metropolitan area's 250 parks, including the popular Cherry Creek and Chatfield Reservoir State Recreation areas. With more than 400 mi of off-road paths in and around the city, cyclists can move easily between urban and rural settings.

Just south of downtown, the **Bicycle Doctor/Edgeworks** (✉ *860 Broadway, Golden Triangle* ☎ *303/831–7228 or 877/245–3362* ⊕ *www.bicycledr.com*) repairs street and mountain bikes, and rents them for $15 to $50 a day.

The well-kept **Cherry Creek Bike Path** (⊠ *Cherry Creek, LoDo*) runs from Cherry Creek Shopping Center to Larimer Square downtown alongside the peaceful creek of its name. The scenic **Highline Canal** (⊠ *Auraria, Cherry Creek, LoDo*) has 70 mi of mostly dirt paths through the metro area running at almost completely level grade. **Platte River Greenway** (⊠ *Auraria, Cherry Creek and LoDo*) is a 20-mi-long path for in-line skating, bicycling, and jogging that runs alongside Cherry Creek and the South Platte River. Much of it runs through downtown Denver. There are 12 mi of paved paths along the **South Platte River** (⊠ *Central Platte Valley, LoDo*) heading into downtown. West of the city, paved paths wind through **Matthews/Winters Park** (⊠ *South of I–70 on CO 26, Golden*) near both Golden and Morrison. It's dotted with plaintive pioneer graves amid the sun-bleached grasses, thistle, and columbine. The **Deer Creek Canyon** (⊠ *Littleton* ⊕ *www.co.jefferson.co.us/openspace*) trail system is popular with mountain bikers, running through forested foothills southwest of Denver near the intersection of C–470 and Wadsworth Avenue.

FOOTBALL

The National Football League's Denver Broncos play September–December at **Invesco Field at Mile High** (⊠ *1701 Bryant St., Exit 210B off I–25, Sun Valley* ☎ *720/258–3000* ⊕ *www.denverbroncos.com*). Every game has sold out for 30 years, so tickets are not easy to come by, despite the Broncos' tepid success in the post–John Elway world.

GOLF

With their sprawling layouts and impressively appointed greens, these four private clubs merit a special look over their city-operated counterparts simply because of their more rural settings. On any Denver-area course, though, out-of-town golfers should keep in mind that the high altitude affects golf balls like it does baseballs—which is why the Rockies have so many more home runs when they bat at home. It's generally agreed that your golf ball will go about 10%–15% farther in the thin air here than it would at sea level.

Arrowhead Golf Club. Designed by Robert Trent Jones Jr., this course is set impressively among red sandstone spires. It's 45 minutes from downtown in Roxborough State Park, which means that any members of your group who don't want to golf can hike nearby. ⊠ *10850 W. Sundown Trail, Littleton* ☎ *303/973–9614* ⊕ *www.arrowheadcolorado.com* ⚑ *18 holes. Yards: 6,682/5,465. Par: 70/72. Green fee: $50/$140.*

Buffalo Run. A Keith Foster–designed course and the site for the 2004 Denver Open, the bargain-priced Buffalo Run counts wide-open views of the plains surrounding its lake-studded course among its charms, which also include streams running through it and the Bison Grill Restaurant. ⊠ *15700 E. 112th Ave., Commerce City* ☎ *303/289–1500* ⊕ *www.buffalorungolfcourse.com* ⚑ *18 holes. Yards: 7,411/5,277. Par: 72/71. Green fee: $27/$44.*

Ridge at Castle Pines North. Tom Weiskopf designed this 18-hole course with great mountain views and dramatic elevation changes. It's ranked among the nation's top 100 public courses. It's in Castle Rock, about 45 minutes south of Denver on I–25. ⊠ *1414 Castle Pines Pkwy., Castle*

Rock ☎ *303/688–0100* ⊕ *www.theridgecpn.com* ⚲ *Reservations essential* ⚑. *18 holes. Yards: 7,013/5,001. Par: 71/71. Green fee: $60/$115.*

Riverdale Golf Courses. It's two golf courses in one: Riverdale has the Dunes, a Scottish-style links course designed by Pete and Perry Dye that sits on the South Platte River and offers railroad ties, plenty of bunkers, and water, while the Knolls has a more-gnarly, park-inspired layout. Both courses are shaded by plenty of trees, and you can't beat the greens fees. ⊠ *13300 Riverdale Rd., Brighton* ☎ *303/659–6700* ⊕ *www.riverdalegolf.com* ⚑. *Knolls: 18 holes. Yards: 6,771/5,891. Par: 71/72. Dunes: 18 holes. Yards: 7,064/4,903. Par: 73/70. Green fee: $25/$46.*

Seven courses—City Park, Harvard Gulch, Evergreen, Kennedy, Overland Park, Wellshire, and Willis Case—are operated by the City of Denver and are open to the public. Green fees for all range from $15 to $33. For advance reservations golfers must use the **City of Denver Golf Reservation System** (☎ *303/784–4000* ⊕ *www.cityofdenvergolf.com*) up to three days in advance. For same-day tee times you can call the starters at an individual course (*City Park* ⊠ *2500 York St.* ☎ *303/295–2096; Evergreen* ⊠ *29614 Upper Bear Creek Rd.* ☎ *303/674–6351; Harvard Gulch* ⊠ *660 Iliff Ave.* ☎ *303/698–4078; Kennedy* ⊠ *10500 East Hampden Ave.* ☎ *303/751–0311; Overland Park* ⊠ *1801 S. Huron St.* ☎ *303/698–4975; Wellshire* ⊠ *3333 S. Colorado Blvd.* ☎ *303/692–5636; Willis Case* ⊠ *4999 Vrain St.* ☎ *303/458–4877*).

HIKING

Mount Falcon Park looks down on Denver and across at Red Rocks. It's amazingly tranquil, laced with meadows and streams, and shaded by conifers. The trails are well marked. ⊠ *Off Rte. 8, Morrison exit, or U.S. 285, Parmalee exit, Aurora.*

Fodor'sChoice ★ Fifteen miles southwest of Denver, **Red Rocks Park and Amphitheatre** is a breathtaking, 70-million-year-old wonderland of vaulting oxblood-and-cinnamon-color sandstone spires. The outdoor music stage is in a natural 9,000-seat amphitheater (with perfect acoustics, as only nature could have designed). Just want a look? The 5-mile scenic drive offers a glorious glimpse of the 868 acres of sandstone, and there are picnic and parking areas along the way for photos and a rest. If you're feeling particularly spunky, follow the locals' lead and run the steps for a real workout. The Trading Post loop hiking trail, at 6,280 feet, is 1.4 mi long and quite narrow with drop-offs and steep grades. The trail closes one-half hour before sunset. The park is open from 5 AM to 11 PM daily. ⊠ *17598 W. Alameda Pkwy., Morrison, I–70 west to Exit 259, turn left to park entrance* ⊕ *www.redrocksonline.com.*

Roxborough State Park has an easy 2-mi loop trail through rugged rock formations, offering striking vistas and a unique look at metro Denver and the plains. This trail is wheelchair accessible. ⊠ *Littleton, I–25 south to Santa Fe exit, take Santa Fe Blvd. south to Titan Rd., turn right and follow signs.*

Green Mountain is the first named foothill as you head west from Denver toward the mountains. Part of Jefferson County Open Space and a piece of William Frederick Hayden Park (City of Lakewood), the easy, mostly exposed trail affords panoramic views of downtown Denver, Table Mesa, Pikes Peak, and the Continental Divide from the top (895 feet in elevation gain). You must share with bikers and dogs, as well as other critters. There are multiple trails from several trailheads, including a 6.4-mi loop and a 3.1-mi loop. Open 5 AM to 10 PM daily. ⊠ *Lakewood, I–70 west to CO 470 to W. Alameda Pkwy., turn left to trailhead entrance* ⊕ *www.lakewood.org.*

HOCKEY

The **Colorado Avalanche** of the National Hockey League are wildly popular in Denver; the team won the Stanley Cup in 1996 and beat the New Jersey Devils for an encore in 2001. Although they've been relatively disappointing since, and legendary goalie Patrick Roy retired after the 2003 season, the still-exciting team plays October to April at the 19,000-seat Pepsi Center arena (⊠ *1000 Chopper Pl., Auraria* ☎ *303/405–8555* ⊕ *www.coloradoavalanche.com*).

WHERE TO EAT

As befits a multiethnic crossroads, Denver lays out a dizzying range of eateries. Head for LoDo, 32nd Avenue in the Highland District, or south of the city for the more inventive kitchens. Try Federal Street for cheap ethnic eats—especially Mexican and Vietnamese—and expect more authentic takes on classic Italian, French, and Asian cuisines than the city has offered in the past. Throughout Denver, menus at trendy restaurants are pairing international flavors with regional products in unique ways; Denver's top chefs are gaining the attention of national food magazines and winning culinary competitions. Also look for Quick Bites boxes that list great refueling stops in Exploring.

WHAT IT COSTS					
	¢	$	$$	$$$	$$$$
Restaurants	under $8	$8–$12	$13–$18	$19–$25	over $25

Prices are per person for a main course, excluding 8.22% tax.

Use the coordinate (✛ B2) at the end of each listing to locate a site on the corresponding map.

LODO

$$$–$$$$ ✕ **Denver ChopHouse & Brewery.** This is the best of the LoDo brewpubs
STEAK   and restaurants surrounding the Coors Field ballpark. Housed in the old Union Pacific Railroad warehouse, the restaurant, similar to the ones in Washington, D.C., Cleveland, and Boulder, is clubby, with dark-wood paneling and exposed brick. The food is basic American, and there's plenty of it: steaks, seafood, pizzas, and chicken served with hot corn bread and honey butter, and "bottomless" salads tossed at the table. ⊠ *1735 19th St., LoDo* ☎ *303/296–0800* ⊕ *www.chophouse.com* ▭ *AE, DC, MC, V* ✛ *B4.*

2

BEST BETS FOR DENVER DINING

Fodor's Choice	$$	Highland's Garden Café, p. 61
LoLa Mexican Seafood, p. 61	Domo, p.60	Mizuna, p. 61
Mizuna, p. 61	Little India, p. 60	**Best by Cuisine**
Restaurant Kevin Taylor, p. 57	New Saigon, p. 64	
Sushi Den, p. 63	Olivéa, p. 58	MEXICAN
The Fort, p. 64	Sushi Den, p. 63	LoLa, p. 61
		Jack–n–Grill, p. 62
Best by Price	$$$	
	Fruition, p. 60	STEAK
¢	LoLa Mexican Seafood, p. 61	Elway's, p. 62
	Panzano, p. 56	Capital Grille, p. 55
Spicy Pickle Sub Shop, p. 57	Restaurant Kevin Taylor, p. 57	Sullivan's, p. 54
Anthony's Pizza, p. 56	Rioja, p. 55	NEW AMERICAN
$	$$$$	Fruition, p. 60
		Highland's Garden Café, p. 61
Sam's No. 3, p. 57	Elway's, p. 62	Mizuna, p. 61
Jack–n–Grill, p. 62	The Fort, p. 64	Potager, p. 58
WaterCourse, p. 59		Vesta Dipping Grill, p.54

$$–$$$ ✕ **India House.** Diners get to see their food being prepared in the tandoor
INDIAN in this handsome space complete with luxurious wall treatments, comfy
upholstery, and interesting art. The spicing is gentle, and the preparations are skillful on the lengthy, well-chosen menu, which includes
vegetarian options. A local favorite is the *shahi sabz*, vegetables in a nut-
strewn cream sauce, and the house-made ice creams are delicious. The
market-price lobster dishes are standouts, too. ⊠ *1514 Blake St., LoDo*
☎ *303/595–0680* ⊕ *www.indiahouse.us* ▤ *AE, D, DC, MC, V* ✛ *A5.*

$$–$$$ ✕ **Jax Fish House.** A popular oyster bar serves as the foyer to the ever-
SEAFOOD busy Jax, whose brick-lined back dining room packs in the crowds,
especially when there's a ball game at Coors Field three blocks away.
A dozen different types of oysters are freshly shucked each day, and
they can be paired with one of the house-made, fruit-infused vod-
kas or chili-fired shooters. Main courses make use of fresh catches
flown in from both coasts such as ahi tuna, scallops, snapper, and
shrimp, and although there are a couple of meat dishes, only the truly
fish-phobic should not go there. The sides are fun, too: beignets, succotash, frittatas. ⊠ *1539 17th St., LoDo* ☎ *303/292–5767* ⊕ *www.*
jaxfishhousedenver.com ⚑ *Reservations essential* ▤ *AE, DC, MC, V*
☾ *No lunch* ✛ *A5.*

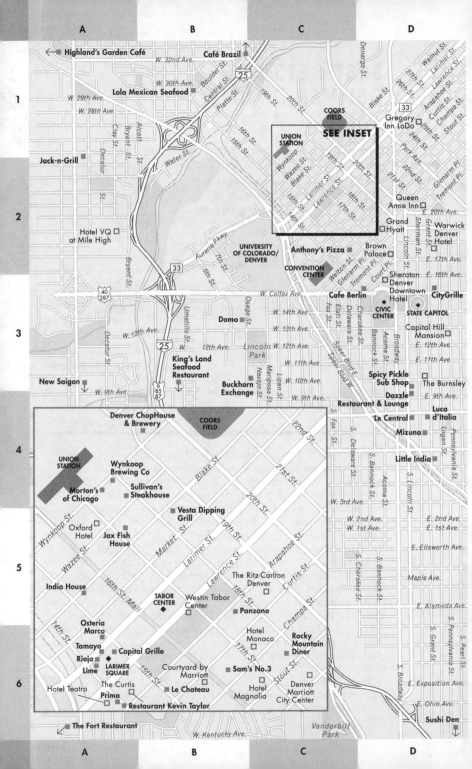

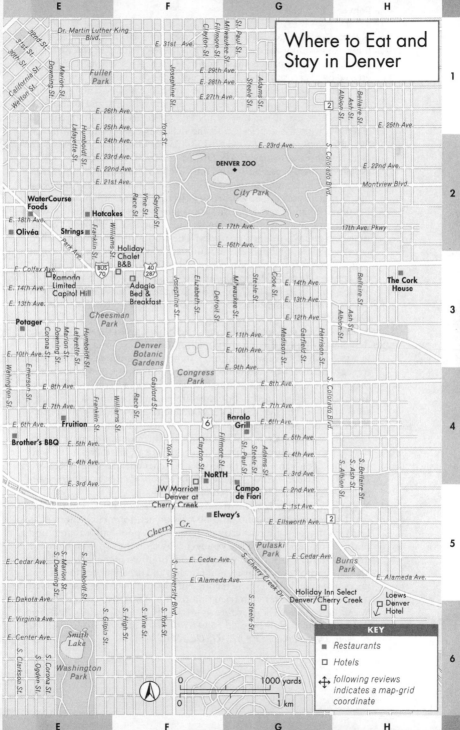

Where to Eat and Stay in Denver

KEY

■ Restaurants

□ Hotels

⊕ following reviews indicates a map-grid coordinate

0 — 1000 yards

0 — 1 km

$$$$
STEAK

✕ **Morton's of Chicago.** The Denver outpost of this nationally revered steak house is as swanky and overwhelming as the rest, with dark woods, white linens, and the signature steak knives at each place setting. Diners are greeted by expert staff wielding the cuts of the day and their accompaniments, and once choices are made the experience is almost always seamless. The steaks themselves are superb—prime, well aged, and unadorned. All sides cost extra, but they're big enough to feed two or three. The extensive wine list is pricey, and the delicious desserts are enormous. ✉ *1710 Wynkoop St., LoDo* ☎ *303/825–3353* ⊕ *www.mortons.com* ⌲ *Reservations essential* ▤ *AE, DC, MC, V* ☾ *No lunch* ✚ *A4.*

$$$$
STEAK

✕ **Sullivan's Steakhouse.** Sullivan's bills itself as a more affordable steak house, and although technically that may be true, it's easy to spend just as much here as at any other top-tier steak joint. Still, it's worth it, because the hand-carved, aged Black Angus beef is of high quality, well grilled, and accompanied by stellar sides such as grill-greasy onion rings and chunky mashed potatoes. The wood-lined barroom is filled with high tables and makes for a fun gathering place, especially when there's live jazz. It's reminiscent of a 1940s club. Swing by early for the reasonably priced happy-hour prix-fixe menu before 6 PM. ✉ *1745 Wazee St., LoDo* ☎ *303/295–2664* ⊕ *www.sullivanssteakhouse.com* ⌲ *Reservations essential* ▤ *AE, D, DC, MC, V* ☾ *No lunch weekends* ✚ *A4.*

$$$
NEW AMERICAN

✕ **Vesta Dipping Grill.** Both the remodeled building and the interior space designed to house this modern grill, named after Vesta, the Roman hearth goddess, have won national architectural awards, and it's easy to see why: the sensual swirls of fabric and copper throughout the room make diners feel as though they're inside a giant work of art, and the clever, secluded banquettes are among the most sought-after seats in town. The menu is clever, too, and the competent grill masters in the kitchen put out expertly cooked meats, fish, and vegetables, all of which can be paired with some of the three dozen dipping sauces that get their inspiration from chutneys, salsas, mother sauces, and barbecue. The wine list is as cool as the clientele. ✉ *1822 Blake St., LoDo* ☎ *303/296–1970* ⊕ *www.vestagrill.com* ⌲ *Reservations essential* ▤ *AE, D, DC, MC, V* ☾ *No lunch* ✚ *B5.*

$–$$
AMERICAN

✕ **Wynkoop Brewing Co.** This trendy yet unpretentious local institution was Denver's first brewpub, and now its owner, John Hickenlooper, is Denver's mayor. Different crowds frequent its pool-hall, cabaret, and dining-room levels—with the younger crowd on the top floor enjoying drinks and bar snacks during happy hour or down in the lower cabaret level for improv or live music, and families and urban professionals dining on the main level. Try the terrific buffalo meatloaf or venison served over mashed potatoes with fried onions. Wash it down with one of the Wynkoop's trademark microbrews—try either the exemplary Railyard Ale or the spicy chili beer. ✉ *1634 18th St., LoDo* ☎ *303/297–2700* ⊕ *www.wynkoop.com* ▤ *AE, D, DC, MC, V* ✚ *A4.*

LARIMER SQUARE

$$$$
STEAK

✕ **Capital Grille.** In a town that loves its steaks, the Rhode Island–based chain was taking a chance moving in and pretending to offer anything different from the other high-end big-boy steak houses. That said, Capital Grille—housed in a dark, noisy, broodingly decorated room typical of the genre—has much to recommend it, including a drop-dead Delmonico, textbook French onion soup, and terrific skin-on mashed potatoes. If you were ever to try steak tartare, this would be the place to do it, and the lobster is one of the best in town. The wine list is long, important, and expensive, but the service is remarkably fresh-faced and eager to please. ✉ *1450 Larimer St., LoDo* ☎ *303/539–2500* ⊕ *www.thecapitalgrille.com* ⌱ *Reservations essential* ▤ *AE, D, DC, MC, V* ☺ *No lunch Sat., Sun.* ✛ *A6.*

$
MEXICAN

✕ **Lime.** Hidden at basement-level, ultracasual Lime is always happening, especially for the younger, hipper crowd whose pockets aren't deep enough for more upscale LoDo spots. The made-to-order deep-fried tortilla chips arrive at the table when you do, and the salsas are zippy and well crafted. Imbibers are treated to a half-shot in a lime shell, and the Mighty Margarita is the only way to go from there. Shrimp stuffed with jalapeños and cream cheese—two of these "scorpions" can be added to any plate for $4—the tamales, and chiles rellenos are all winners, and the green-and-white bar is a fun place for late-night snacking. ✉ *1424-C Larimer St., Larimer Square* ☎ *303/893–5463* ⊕ *www.eatatlime.com* ▤ *AE, MC, V* ☺ *Closed Sun. No lunch* ✛ *A6.*

$$$
ITALIAN

✕ **Osteria Marco.** The Bonannos, whose Mizuna and Luca d'Italia are among the best restaurants in town, continue their success with this reasonably priced, casual eatery. High-backed wooden booths, dish towels as napkins, and exposed-brick walls provide a hip, urban setting below street level for wood-fired pizzas topped with Frank Bonanno's homemade or imported cheeses and house-cured meats. Or try one of the sampler trays from the formaggi and salumi (fresh cheese and meats) bar, the Italian version of an artisan deli that greets you at the entrance. Salads are large enough to eat as entrées. The mostly locally sourced meat dishes shine—especially Sunday night's roast suckling pig special. ✉ *1453 Larimer St., Larimer Square* ☎ *303/534–5855* ⊕ *www.osteriamarco.com* ⌱ *Reservations essential* ▤ *AE, DC, MC, V* ✛ *A6.*

$$$
MEDITERRANEAN

✕ **Rioja.** Chef Jennifer Jasinski's intense attention to detail is evident in her tribute to Mediterranean food with contemporary flair. Formerly of Panzano, she partners in this venture with two other women: Beth Gruitch runs the front of the house while sous chef Dana Rodriguez helps in the back, and together this trio makes intriguing and compelling combinations like paella gnocchi and crispy pork belly with Hawaiian blue prawns and green papaya salad. The restaurant is hip and artsy, with exposed brick and blown-glass lighting, arched doorways, and textured draperies. The wine list presents riojas galore, and is well priced for Larimer Square. ✉ *1431 Larimer St., Larimer Square* ☎ *303/820–2282* ⊕ *www.riojadenver.com* ⌱ *Reservations essential* ▤ *AE, DC, MC, V* ☺ *No lunch Mon., Tues.* ✛ *A6.*

$$$ ✕ **Tamayo.** Chef–owner Richard Sandoval brought his popular concept
MEXICAN of modern, upscale Mexican cuisine from New York to Denver, and it's just as welcome here. The food is classic Mexican with a twist, such as seafood tacos, *huitlacoche* (edible fungus) soup, elaborate moles, and chocolate tamales for dessert. The tequila flights are a favorite at the large, inviting bar, which is highlighted by a mural made of semiprecious stones made by artist and restaurant namesake Rufino Tamayo. Screens made from blond wood and Spanish art fill the interior, and in season the outdoor patio supplies a rare view of the mountains. ⊠ *1400 Larimer St., Larimer Square* ☎ *720/946–1433* ⊕ *www.modernmexican.com* ⌖ *Reservations essential* ▤ *AE, MC, V* ⊗ *No lunch weekends* ✛ *A6.*

DOWNTOWN

¢ ✕ **Anthony's Pizza & Pasta.** This two-story dive, with a standing counter
PIZZA as well as a sit-down dining area upstairs crammed with ramshackle chairs and tables in various stages of disrepair, is the closest Denver gets to a New York slice. Fold each triangle in half, tilt it to let it drip, and inhale. Sweet-and-spicy-sauced spaghetti with a side of meatballs offers an alternative for those who don't want pizza. ⊠ *1550 California St., Downtown* ☎ *303/573–6236* ⊕ *www.anthonyspizzaandpasta.com* ▤ *MC, V* ⊗ *Closed Sun.* ✛ *C2.*

$$ ✕ **Cafe Berlin.** New owners and a new location have transformed this
GERMAN beloved German eatery into an even more inviting spot, with an updated, somewhat contemporary feel and a small bar. But the traditional German fare remains the same. No fake beer-house stuff here: the potato pancakes taste like your (German) grandma made them, and the liver pâté and homemade German bread are as authentic as it gets. The kitchen attempts to lighten up heavy items such as dumplings, spaetzle, and Wiener schnitzel, and the sweet-and-sour cabbage is amazing. Check out the German beer roster, and finish off with an apple strudel. ⊠ *323 14th St., Downtown* ☎ *303/377–5896* ⊕ *www.cafeberlin.com* ▤ *D, MC, V* ⊗ *Closed Mon. No lunch weekends* ✛ *D3.*

$$$ ✕ **Le Chateau.** The former La Fondue has been transformed into a bright,
FRENCH open, airy space that works well for pre-theater dining. The pre-theater prix-fixe menu is always $52.80 per duo and includes salad, two entrée choices, and dessert, but some of the favorites are from the appetizer menu: plump crabcakes draped in a light, saffron-kissed butter sauce, tender calamari served with a pear-sweetened, spicy tomato sauce, and mussels in a garlicky broth ideal for bread-dipping. Fondue is still a menu favorite, but leave plenty of time for this experience. Service is snappy, and the valet will hold your car until after the show. ⊠ *1040 15th St., Downtown* ☎ *303/534–0404* ⊕ *www.lechateaudenver.com* ⌖ *Reservations essential* ▤ *AE, D, DC, MC, V* ⊗ *No lunch* ✛ *B6.*

$$$ ✕ **Panzano.** This dining room in Hotel Monaco is filled with fresh flow-
ITALIAN ers and windows that let in natural light, making the space cheerful and bright. Three meals a day are served, but it's lunch and dinner that focus on true Italian cuisine. Everything on the menu is multilayered, such as white-asparagus salad with basil aioli, watercress, and endive; or risotto made with an ever-changing and ever-pleasing variety of cheeses and fresh produce. The breads are baked in-house. The superior service

and accommodating staff make for a pleasant dining experience. The large, roomy bar is available for dining, too. ⊠ *909 17th St., Downtown* ☎ *303/296–3525* ⊕ *www.panzano-denver.com* ⌓ *Reservations essential* ⊟ *AE, D, DC, MC, V* ✢ *B5.*

$$$
ITALIAN

✕ **Prima.** The less expensive, whimsically decorated little sister of the upscale Restaurant Kevin Taylor also resides in the Hotel Teatro. With its Italian opera prints, curvaceous mezzanine, and black-granite bar, Prima appeals to lovers of modern Italian fare. The menu focuses on upscale renditions of contemporary classics, such as rare ahi tuna with lemon-artichoke relish and crispy game hen with Gorgonzola potatoes, and theatergoers love the one-block proximity to the Denver Performing Arts Complex. The weekend champagne brunch, which begins with a full line of crudo and continues through an astounding selection of northern Italian specialties such as soft egg ravioli with truffle butter, draws a crowd. ⊠ *1106 14th St., Downtown* ☎ *303/228–0770* ⊕ *www. ktrg.net* ⌓ *Reservations essential* ⊟ *AE, DC, MC, V* ✢ *A6.*

$$$$
MEDITERRANEAN
Fodor'sChoice
★

✕ **Restaurant Kevin Taylor.** Elegant doesn't do justice to this restaurant's dining room, a classy, soothing space done in tones of gold and hunter green. Exclusive upholstery, flatware, and dishes add to the upscale attitude, as does the formal service style and a top-shelf wine list. The contemporary menu has an updated Mediterranean bent underscored by French techniques, with such classics as Kobe rib eye sharing space with bison rib strudel and piquillo pepper fritters. The tasting menu, geared to theatergoers heading to the Denver Performing Arts Complex a block away, provides a rare chance to try chef Taylor's eclectic creations, and the stone-lined wine cellar makes for intimate private dining. ⊠ *1106 14th St., Downtown* ☎ *303/820–2600* ⊕ *www.ktrg.com* ⌓ *Reservations essential* ⊟ *AE, DC, MC, V* ☺ *Closed Sun. No lunch* ✢ *A6.*

$–$$
☺
DINER

✕ **Rocky Mountain Diner.** In the heart of the downtown business district you can come in to this Western-theme diner, complete with cigar store Indian, plenty of horse paraphernalia, and red-and-white checked napkins, and sample all-American fill-ups of cowboy steak, pan-charred rib eye served with crisp onions, or the very popular buffalo meat loaf. Don't miss the real mashed potatoes, gravy, and all the fixings. ⊠ *800 18th St., Downtown* ☎ *303/293–8383* ⊕ *www.rockymountaindiner. com* ⌓ *Reservations not accepted* ⊟ *AE, D, DC, MC, V* ✢ *C6.*

$
☺
DINER

✕ **Sam's No. 3.** Greek immigrant Sam Armatas opened his first eatery in Denver in 1927, and his three sons use the same recipes Pop did in their updated version of his all-American diner, from the famous red and green chiles to the Coney Island–style hot dogs and the creamy rice pudding. The room is a combination of retro diner and a fancy Denny's, and the bar is crowded with theatergoers and hipsters after dark. Good luck choosing: the menu is 10 pages long, with Greek and Mexican favorites as well as diner classics. The chunky mashed potatoes rule, and breakfast, which is served all day, comes fast. ⊠ *1500 Curtis St., Downtown* ☎ *303/534–1927* ⊕ *www.samsno3.com* ⌓ *Reservations not accepted* ⊟ *AE, D, DC, MC, V* ✢ *B6.*

¢
☺
CAFE

✕ **Spicy Pickle Sub Shop.** A spicy pickle does indeed come with every order at this hopping deli, which makes giant subs and panini, all filled with Boar's Head meats and house-made spreads. The breads are baked locally, and the side salads are good quality. Sit and eat in the casual space or take it to go. Come for lunch or an early dinner; they are open until 7 Monday to Thursday and 6 Friday to Sunday. Other locations are scattered around the Denver area. ⊠ *988 Lincoln St., Downtown* ☎ *303/860–0730* ⊕ *www. spicypickle.com* ⚲ *Reservations not accepted* ⊟ *AE, MC, V* ⊹ *D3.*

CAPITOL HILL

$ ✕ **CityGrille.** Politicians and construction workers rub shoulders while
AMERICAN   chowing down on the well-crafted sandwiches, soups, and salads at this casual eatery across the street from the State Capitol. CityGrille has earned national attention for both the burger, a half-pounder of ground sirloin, and the chile, a gringo stew of pork, jalapeños, and tomatoes that's spicy and addictive. The three-martini lunch lives on in this power-packed spot, and you can get a meal here until 11 PM (midnight on weekends). ⊠ *321 E. Colfax Ave., Capitol Hill* ☎ *303/861–0726* ⊕ *www.citygrille.com* ⊟ *AE, DC, MC, V* ⊹ *D3.*

¢   ✕ **Hotcakes Diner.** This jumping Capitol Hill spot is a breakfast and lunch
DINER   hangout. Weekend brunch draws crowds of bicyclists and newspaper readers in search of the croissant French toast, "health nut" pancakes, and colossal omelets. Even bigger are the scrumptious one-dish skillets; a popular one tops grilled pork chops with home fries, chile, cheddar, and eggs. They're open weekdays at 6 AM and weekends at 7 AM; closed each day at 2 PM. ⊠ *1400 E. 18th Ave., Capitol Hill* ☎ *303/832–4351* ⊕ *www.hcdiner.com* ⊟ *D, MC, V* ⊘ *No dinner* ⊹ *E2.*

$$ ✕ **Olivéa.** A group of veteran Denver restaurateurs took over the former
MEDITERRANEAN   Aix space in May 2009, causing the Uptown corridor to rejoice over the casual but cozy eatery's Mediterranean menu filled with affordable and memorable dishes. Start with a tasting plate of charcuterie—$16 for three such tidbits as lamb sausage, duck liver mousse, and boudin blanc (white sausage)—then try the gnocchi with short-rib sugo (an Italian gravy) or the duck meatballs with creamy polenta as an entrée. It's hard to save room for dessert, but it's equally hard to choose between the elegant concoctions and the housemade ice creams and sorbets. Service is friendly but snappy, and while the wine list is short, it's filled with well-chosen low-priced bottles. Still, it's the innovative happy-hour cocktails that truly have the town talking, along with the elaborate weekend brunches. ⊠ *719 E. 17th Ave., Capitol Hill* ☎ *303/861–5050* ⊕ *www.olivearestaurant.com* ⚲ *Reservations essential* ⊟ *AE, MC, V* ⊘ *No lunch* ⊹ *E2.*

$$$ ✕ **Potager.** The menu changes monthly at this industrial-designed res-
NEW AMERICAN   taurant, whose name, French for "kitchen garden," refers to the herb-rimmed back patio. Exposed ducts and a high ceiling make for a trendy dining room, and the floor-to-ceiling front windows allow the hip to be seen and the twinkling lights outside and in to be reflected for a warm glow. The menu always includes a risotto of the day along with fish dishes and the ever-popular goat-cheese soufflé. The wine list is all over the map but well priced, and the servers are among the most savvy in town. ⊠ *1109 Ogden St., Capitol Hill* ☎ *303/832–5788* ⊕ *www. potagerrestaurant.com* ⚲ *Reservations not accepted* ⊟ *AE, MC, V* ⊘ *Closed Sun. and Mon. No lunch* ⊹ *E3.*

$$$ ✕ **Strings.** This light, airy restaurant with its wide-open kitchen resembles
NEW AMERICAN   an artist's loft. It's a preferred hangout for Denver's movers and shakers
as well as for visiting celebs, whose autographs on head shots, napkins,
and program notes hang on the walls. The specialties include seafood
dishes such as seared sea scallops in a Meyer lemon emulsion and pasta
such as the popular mac-n-cheese with smoked chicken, and the desserts
are amazingly intricate and well crafted. ✉ *1700 Humboldt St., Capi-
tol Hill* ☎ *303/831–7310* ⊕ *www.stringsrestaurant.com* ♲ *Reservations
essential* ▤ *AE, D, DC, MC, V* ☽ *No lunch weekends* ✛ *E2.*

$ ✕ **WaterCourse Foods.** In a town known for its beef, WaterCourse stands
VEGETARIAN   out as a devoted vegetarian eatery in spacious digs uptown. This casual,
low-key place serves herbivores three meals a day, most of which are
based on fruits, vegetables, whole grains, and meatlike soy substitutes.
There are vegan and macrobiotic dishes available, along with choices
for those who eat cheese and eggs. The Reuben, with sauerkraut, porto-
bellos, and Swiss on grilled rye, is amazing. ✉ *837 E. 17th Ave., Capitol
Hill* ☎ *303/832–7313* ⊕ *www.watercoursefoods.com* ▤ *MC, V* ✛ *E2.*

CENTRAL DENVER

$$$ ✕ **Barolo Grill.** This restaurant looks like a chichi Italian farmhouse, with
ITALIAN   dried flowers in brass urns, hand-painted porcelain, and straw baskets
everywhere. The food isn't pretentious in the least, however. It's more
like Santa Monica meets San Stefano—bold yet classic, healthful yet
flavorful. Duckling stewed in red wine; fresh pastas, including spaghetti
tossed with shrimp, octopus, and arugula; and gnocchi with ricotta,
kalamata olives, and fresh basil, are all well made and fairly priced. The
reasonably priced five-course tasting menu is a smart way to sample
more of the kitchen's talents; although adding the wine pairings ups the
cost, it also improves the value. ✉ *3030 E. 6th Ave., Central Denver*
☎ *303/393–1040* ⊕ *www.barologrilldenver.com* ♲ *Reservations essential* ▤ *AE, D, DC, MC, V* ☽ *Closed Sun. and Mon. No lunch* ✛ *G4.*

$ ✕ **Brother's BBQ.** Two brothers from England traveled the southern United
SOUTHERN   States on a quest to learn everything there is to know about barbecue,
and they decided to share the information with Denver. The result is some
of the best 'cue in town, from St. Louis–style ribs to beef brisket, pulled
pork, and chicken. The sauces are a mishmash of their favorites, including
a vinegary one and a sweet one, and the baked beans use their smoked
meats for extra flavor. Eat at one of the metal tables amid license plates
and knickknacks from the boys' travels, or get it packed up nicely to go.
✉ *568 N. Washington St., Central Denver* ☎ *720/570–4227* ⊕ *www.
brothers-bbq.com* ♲ *Reservations not accepted* ▤ *MC, V* ✛ *E4.*

$$$$ ✕ **Buckhorn Exchange.** If hunting makes you queasy, don't enter this Den-
STEAK   ver landmark and taxidermy shrine, where 500 pairs of eyes stare down
at you from the walls. The handsome men's-club look—with pressed-
tin ceilings, burgundy walls, red-checker tablecloths, rodeo photos,
shotguns, and those trophies—probably hasn't changed much since the
Buckhorn first opened in 1893. Rumor has it that Buffalo Bill was to
the Buckhorn what Norm Peterson was to *Cheers.* The dry-aged, prime-
grade Colorado steaks are huge, juicy, and magnificent, as is the game.
Try the smoked buffalo sausage or navy-bean soup to start. ✉ *1000*

Osage St., Central Denver ☎ *303/534–9505* ⊕ *www.buckhornexchange. com* ▤ *AE, D, DC, MC, V* ☺ *No lunch weekends* ✢ *C3.*

$$
AMERICAN
✕**Dazzle Restaurant and Lounge.** If it's martinis and jazz you're after, come to this Art Deco space that allows for a groovy bar scene on one side and groovy dining on the other. The menu is as retro as the atmosphere, with an emphasis on comfort foods with a twist (check out the updated macaroni and cheese or the baked casserole dips), and live music most nights makes this a laid-back spot. The cocktail roster, printed inside old jazz albums, is one of the most intricate around, and the Sunday jazz brunch swings. ⊠ *930 Lincoln St., Central Denver* ☎ *303/839–5100* ⊕ *www.dazzlejazz.com* ▤ *AE, DC, MC, V* ☺ *No lunch Mon.–Thurs.* ✢ *D4.*

$$
JAPANESE
✕**Domo.** Domo's owners pride themselves on fresh flavors and the painstaking preparation of Japanese country foods, as well as one of the largest sake selections in town. Everything is prepared to order, and it's worth the wait: this is where you can find some of Denver's best seafood, curry dishes, and vegetarian fare. The house specialty is *wankosushi*—three to five courses of sushi accompanied by rice, soup, and six of Domo's tantalizing side dishes. The restaurant also houses a cultural-education center, a museum, and a Japanese garden. ⊠ *1365 Osage St., Central Denver* ☎ *303/595–3666* ⊕ *www.domorestaurant. com* ▤ *MC, V* ☺ *Closed Sun.* ✢ *B3.*

$$$
NEW AMERICAN
✕**Fruition.** Well-crafted, elegant comfort food made from seasonal ingredients is served in compelling combinations, like grilled pork chops with yellow corn spoonbread and pan-roasted ostrich loin with black-fig salad. A nightly offering of two courses of delightful dishes includes many vegetarian options, but many diners choose to make a meal from the amazing appetizer roster. The two small but nicely spaced dining rooms are gently lighted for a warm-toned atmosphere that fades into the background, allowing the evening to focus on the food and the expertly chosen and fairly priced wine list. ⊠ *1313 E. 6th Ave., Central Denver* ☎ *303/831–1962* ⊕ *www.fruitionrestaurant.com* ▤ *AE, D, MC, V* ☺ *No lunch* ✢ *E4.*

$$
FRENCH
✕**Le Central.** A real find, this homey bistro serves excellent mussel dishes and provincial French specialties, including beef bourguignonne (braised in red wine and garnished with mushrooms and onions), salmon *en croûte* (wrapped in pastry and baked), and steak au poivre. You can depend on Le Central for fabulous food, great service, and a surprisingly low tab. Weekend brunch is a big favorite. ⊠ *112 E. 8th Ave., Central Denver* ☎ *303/863–8094* ⊕ *www.lecentral.com* ▤ *AE, D, DC, MC, V* ✢ *D4.*

$$
INDIAN
✕**Little India.** The all-you-can-eat lunch buffet ($8.99), with dozens of well-prepared Indian dishes, is the big draw for Denverites at this casually elegant restaurant between downtown and Cherry Creek. Little India's menu has nearly 100 items, but it specializes in curries, vindaloos, and *biryanis,* all of which are expertly spiced. Be sure to try one of the specialty naans (tandoori-baked flat bread). The sweet mango *lassi,* a yogurt drink, is delightfully rich. ⊠ *330 E. 6th Ave., Central Denver* ☎ *303/871–9777* ⊕ *www.littleindiadenver.com* ▤ *MC, V* ✢ *D4.*

$$$$ ✗ **Luca d'Italia.** The restaurant's steel-gray, orange-and-red contemporary
ITALIAN   decor belies the fact that it's one of the most authentic Italian restaurants in the city. Chef-owner Frank Bonanno summons the memory of
his Italian grandmother to re-create small-town Italy through wild boar
with pappardelle, duck liver–stuffed ravioli, and house-cured capocollo
and homemade cheeses. His tiramisu and chocolate sorbet have to be
tasted to be believed. Service, overseen by Jacqueline Bonanno, is as
impeccable as at Bonanno's other restaurants, Mizuna and Osteria
Marco, and the wine list is agreeably priced and heavy on interesting
Italians. ☒ *711 Grant St., Central Denver* ☎ *303/832–6600* ⊕ *www.
lucadenver.com* ⌕ *Reservations essential* ▤ *AE, MC, V* ⊘ *Closed Sun.
and Mon. No lunch* ✛ *D4.*

$$$$ ✗ **Mizuna.** Chef-owner Frank Bonanno knows how to transform butter
NEW AMERICAN   and cream into comforting masterpieces at this cozy eatery with warm
Fodor's Choice   colors and intimate seating. His menu is reminiscent of California's
★   French Laundry, with quirky dishes such as "liver and onions" (foie
gras and a sweet-onion tart), and his Italian heritage has given him
the ability to work wonders with red sauce, such as in his inimitable
ragout. Be sure to try the griddle cakes for dessert, and expect to be
served by the most professional staff, trained by Jacqueline Bonanno,
in town. ☒ *225 E. 7th Ave., Central Denver* ☎ *303/832–4778* ⊕ *www.
mizunadenver.com* ⌕ *Reservations essential* ▤ *AE, MC, V* ⊘ *Closed
Sun. and Mon. No lunch* ✛ *D4.*

HIGHLAND

$$–$$$ ✗ **Café Brazil.** This always-packed spot is worth the trip to Highland
BRAZILIAN   for shrimp and scallops sautéed with fresh herbs, coconut milk, and
hot chilies; *feijoda completa,* the Brazilian national dish of black-bean
stew and smoked meats, accompanied with fried bananas; or grilled
chicken breast in a sauce of palm oil, red chile, shallots, and coconut
milk. There's a party style in this festive café with its vivid paintings and
colorful traditional masks, and it's frequented by locals in the know.
☒ *4408 Lowell Blvd., Highland* ☎ *303/480–1877* ⌕ *Reservations essential* ▤ *MC, V* ⊘ *Closed Sun. and Mon. No lunch* ✛ *B1.*

$$$$ ✗ **Highland's Garden Café.** Chef-owner Pat Perry follows the philosophy
NEW AMERICAN   of Alice Waters and her famous Chez Panisse: Use what's fresh that day.
The result is an ever-changing menu that takes advantage of Colorado's
unique produce and meats, and Perry puts them together in interesting and refreshing ways, as in her grilled quail with spring cherries
and grouper with wasabi cream. And as the name implies, the outdoor
patio is surrounded by elaborate gardens, and the inside dining rooms,
which occupy two Victorian houses, are painted with trompe-l'oeil views
into gardens as well. ☒ *3927 W. 32nd Ave., Highland* ☎ *303/458–5920*
⊕ *www.highlandsgardencafe.com* ⌕ *Reservations essential* ▤ *AE, D,
DC, MC, V* ⊘ *Closed Mon.* ✛ *A1.*

$$$ ✗ **LoLa Mexican Seafood.** This casual seafood eatery brings in a young,
MEXICAN   hip clientele, and provides a spectacular view of the city skyline from
Fodor's Choice   most of the sunny dining room, the bar, and the patio. Tableside gua-
★   camole, more than 90 tequilas, superior margaritas, and a clever, glass-
lined bar area are just a few of the reasons the lovely LoLa remains a

locals' hangout. The food is modern Mexican, with fresh seafood in *escabeche* (marinated, poached fish), *ceviche* (lime-cooked fish), and salads, as well as smoked rib eye and chicken *frito* (fried chicken). A Mexican-style brunch is served Saturday and Sunday. ⊠ *1575 Boulder St., Highland* ☎ *720/570–8686* ⊕ *www.loladenver.com* ⌔ *Reservations essential* ⊟ *AE, DC, MC, V* ⊗ *No lunch* ✢ *B1.*

NORTH DENVER

$ ✕ **Jack-n-Grill.** The friendly family that runs this small, pepper-decorated
☺   place moved to Denver from New Mexico, and they brought their
MEXICAN   love of chiles with them. The green chile is fire-breathing spicy, and the red is a smoky, complex brew. The best item, though, is the plate of chicken or beef *vaquero* tacos, slathered with a sticky-sweet barbecue sauce and served on buttery tortillas. Get it with a bowl of freshly roasted corn off the cob. Lunch is always packed, so arrive early, and don't be afraid to tackle a gigantic breakfast burrito, either. There's a mean margarita and there are cervesas, too. ⊠ *2424 Federal Blvd., North Denver* ☎ *303/964–9544* ⊕ *www.jackngrill.com* ⌔ *Reservations essential* ⊟ *MC, V* ✢ *A1.*

CHERRY CREEK

$$$ ✕ **Campo de Fiori.** As bright and airy as the marketplace this Italian eat-
ITALIAN   ery is named for, Campo serves fresh cuisine from northern Italy that makes it one of the busiest spots in town. Some come for the spacious, see-and-be-seen bar scene, some for the simple but flavorful fare, but all are treated well by the experienced staff. The food includes fried calamari, bruschetta, and grilled fresh vegetables as starters, and the entrées are a mix of pastas and grilled meats. The room is filled with tile-top tables and surrounded by wall murals evocative of the Italian countryside. ⊠ *300 Fillmore St., Cherry Creek North* ☎ *303/377–7887* ⊕ *www.campodefiori.net* ⌔ *Reservations essential* ⊟ *AE, DC, MC, V* ⊗ *Closed Sun., Mon. No lunch* ✢ *G4.*

$$$$ ✕ **Elway's.** You won't see the big guy here very often—or at the newer
STEAK   Ritz-Carlton-Denver location, either—but that doesn't keep hopeful sports fans from packing it in. But when the toothy-grinned former Broncos QB John Elway doesn't show, diners console themselves with some of the best steak-house fare in town, particularly the porterhouse (big enough for half a football team) and the huge side of chunky-creamy Yukon gold mashed potatoes. While you eat, ease back into the intimately set-up, camel-color suede booths and watch waterfalls cascade over granite slabs, choose from the pricey but appealing wine list, and save room for make-your-own s'mores. There's a second location in the Ritz-Carlton. ⊠ *2500 E. 1st Ave., Cherry Creek* ☎ *303/399–5353* ⊕ *www.elways.com* ⌔ *Reservations essential* ⊟ *AE, D, DC, MC, V* ✢ *F4.*

$$$ ✕ **NoRTH.** The beautiful people of Cherry Creek, young and old, flock
ITALIAN   to this jazzy space, the entire front of which opens to the sidewalk in nice weather. The space is decorated in what sound like food-themed Crayola colors: vanilla-white and sherbet-orange, lime-green and cocoa-

brown, all setting diners up for a parade of savory dishes. Start with the paper-thin zucca chips—faintly oily, addictively crispy, deep-fried zucchini—and then move on to an entrée; pasta, fish, and meat are each kissed with just the right amounts of Mediterranean herbs and sauces. The staff is smiley and reflects the cheerful exuberance of the atmosphere, and the lively bar is usually packed three deep. ⊠ *190 Clayton La., Cherry Creek* ☎ *720/941–7700* ⊕ *www.foxrc.com* ⌂ *Reservations essential* ⊟ *AE, D, DC, MC, V* ✛ *F4.*

SOUTH DENVER

$$$ ✕ **Sushi Den.** With a sister restaurant in Japan and owners who import
JAPANESE sushi-grade seafood to the United States, it's easy to see why this chic
Fodor's Choice sushi bar is the one Denverites count on to provide the best quality
★ available. The sushi chefs here can meet your every request, and the cooked dishes are just as well prepared—don't miss the steamed fish baskets. Check out the tony crowd and feast your eyes on the luxurious fabrics and well-designed furniture. There's almost always a wait to get in, and parking can be a hassle, but for serious sushi-heads this is the place to be. From Sunday through Thursday they'll accept a reservation for parties of five or more. ⊠ *1487 S. Pearl St., South Denver* ☎ *303/777–0826* ⊕ *www.sushiden.net* ⊟ *AE, D, MC, V* ⊗ *No lunch weekends* ✛ *D6.*

EAST DENVER

$$$ ✕ **Cork House.** Two veteran Denver restaurateurs took over the beloved,
ECLECTIC 30-year-old Tante Louise and turned it into a popular small-plate place (they also serve plenty of large plates, too), gently renovating it into a slightly-more-contemporary space that invites snacking with a glass of wine from the lengthy, well-priced roster. The wine bar offers 25 to 30 cheeses a night, with fresh breads, pâtés, and other appetizers, and the staff is adept at matching the international vino with the eclectic victuals. Weekend brunch is a lovely way to relax, with a variety of hearty egg dishes. ⊠ *4900 E. Colfax Ave., East Denver* ☎ *303/355–4488* ⊕ *www.corkhousedenver.com* ⊟ *AE, D, MC, V* ⊗ *No lunch* ✛ *H3.*

WEST DENVER

$$ ✕ **King's Land Seafood Restaurant.** Like a Chinese eatery in New York or
CHINESE San Francisco, King's Land does dim sum to perfection, serving it daily during the week for lunch and during their crazy, jam-packed weekends. Choose from dozens of dumplings, buns, and steamed dishes that are wheeled to you on carts, or go with the regular menu, also available at night, which includes delectable duck and seafood specialties. The dining room is huge and always noisy, and the staff doesn't speak much English. Just close your eyes and point. Reservations are accepted for parties of six or more. ⊠ *2200 W. Alameda Ave., West Denver* ☎ *303/975–2399* ⊟ *AE, MC, V* ✛ *B3.*

$$ **✗ New Saigon.** Denver's best Vietnamese, New Saigon is always crowded
VIETNAMESE   with folks trying to get at their crispy egg rolls, shrimp-filled spring
rolls, and cheap but hefty noodle bowls. With nearly 200 dishes on the
menu, this vast, avocado-color eatery has everything Vietnamese cov-
ered, including 30-some vegetarian dishes and 10 with succulent frogs'
legs. Service can be spotty, and not much English is spoken, but the staff
goes overboard trying to help and never steers anyone wrong. It's best
to go at off times to ensure a seat. Reservations are accepted for parties
of six or more. ⊠ *630 S. Federal Blvd., West Denver* ☎ *303/936–4954*
⊕ *www.newsaigon.com* ▭ *MC, V* ⊗ *Closed Mon.* ✛ *A3.*

MORRISON

$$$$ **✗ The Fort Restaurant.** This adobe structure, complete with flickering
STEAK   luminarias and a pinyon-pine bonfire in the courtyard, is a perfect
Fodor's Choice   reproduction of Bent's Fort, a Colorado fur-trade center. Buffalo meat
★   and game are the specialties; the elk with huckleberry sauce and tequila-
marinated quail are especially good. Intrepid eaters might try the buf-
falo bone-marrow appetizer, peanut-butter–stuffed jalapeños, or Rocky
Mountain oysters. Costumed characters from the fur trade wander the
restaurant, playing the mandolin and telling tall tales. ⊠ *19192 Hwy.
8, Morrison* ☎ *303/697–4771* ⊕ *www.thefort.com* ▭ *AE, D, DC, MC,
V* ⊗ *No lunch.*

WHERE TO STAY

Denver's lodging choices include the stately Brown Palace, bed-and-
breakfasts, and business hotels. Unless you're planning a quick escape
to the mountains, consider staying in or around downtown, where
most of the city's attractions are within walking distance. Many of
the hotels cater to business travelers, with accordingly lower rates on
weekends—many establishments slash their rates in half on Friday and
Saturday. The three hotels in the vicinity of Cherry Creek are about a
10- to 15-minute drive from downtown.

WHAT IT COSTS				
	¢	$	$$	$$$	$$$$
FOR TWO PEOPLE	under $80	$80–$120	$121–$170	$171–$230	over $230

Prices are for two people in a standard double room in high season, excluding
service charges and 14.85% tax.

*Use the coordinate (✛ B2) at the end of each listing to locate a site on
the corresponding map.*

DOWNTOWN

$–$$ 🖭 **Adagio Bed & Breakfast.** The music room of this 1892 Victorian mansion has a grand piano, and rooms are named after composers. The
theme continues with breakfast, served *adagio*—or at your leisure.

2

Guest rooms have lace-trim linens, period furniture, and different color schemes and special amenities; the Copland Suite has a living room, a working gas fireplace with original mantel, and a whirlpool bath. Between downtown and Cherry Creek, this B&B also stands out because of modern conveniences such as in-room Wi-Fi and cable television. The hired chef is restaurant quality, and you can choose a full-meal plan for an additional cost. **Pros:** breakfast available when you want it; pretty, cozy rooms; within driving distance of major attractions. **Cons:** not within walking distance of downtown or Cherry Creek; limited amenities due to size. ⊠ *1430 Race St., Capitol Hill,* ☎ *303/370–6911 or 800/533–3241* ⊕ *www.adagiobb.com* ⌨ *6 rooms, 1 suite* ⚏ *In-room: Internet, Wi-Fi. In-hotel: public Wi-Fi* ☰ *AE, MC, V* ⦿ *BP, MAP* ⊹ *F3.*

$$$$
Fodor's Choice
★
🖫 **Brown Palace.** This grande dame of Colorado lodging has hosted public figures from President Eisenhower to the Beatles since it first opened its doors in 1892. The details are exquisite: a dramatic nine-story lobby is topped with a glorious stained-glass ceiling, and the Victorian rooms have sophisticated wainscoting and Art Deco fixtures. The hotel pays equal attention to some modern necessities, such as high-speed Web access and cordless telephones. The formal Palace Arms is the in-house restaurant; the Churchill cigar bar sells rare cigars and single-malt scotches. A full-service spa has Swiss showers and a natural-rock waterfall that draws from the hotel's artesian well. **Pros:** sleeping here feels like being part of history; exceptional service; spacious and comfortable rooms. **Cons:** one of the most expensive hotels in Denver; parking costs extra. ⊠ *321 17th St., Downtown,* ☎ *303/297–3111 or 800/321–2599* ⊕ *www.brownpalace.com* ⌨ *205 rooms, 36 suites* ⚏ *In-room: refrigerator (some), Internet. In-hotel: 4 restaurants, room service, bars, gym, spa, concierge, laundry service, public Wi-Fi, parking (paid)* ☰ *AE, D, DC, MC, V* ⊹ *D2.*

$$$
☾
🖫 **The Burnsley.** This 16-story Bauhaus-style tower is a haven for visitors seeking peace and quiet; it's a few blocks south of the State Capitol. Spacious and private rooms attract executives and families to this all-suites hotel. The tastefully appointed suites have balconies and full kitchens, many have a sofa bed. Marble foyers and old-fashioned riding prints decorate the rooms. The swooningly romantic restaurant is a perfect place to pop the question. **Pros:** family-friendly; good for business travelers; convenient location. **Cons:** rooms are somewhat plain. ⊠ *1000 Grant St., Downtown,* ☎ *303/830–1000 or 800/231–3915* ⊕ *www. burnsley.com* ⌨ *80 suites* ⚏ *In-room: kitchen, Internet. In-hotel: restaurant, room service, bar, pool, concierge, laundry service, public Internet, parking (free), some pets allowed* ☰ *AE, D, DC, MC, V* ⊹ *D3.*

$$
🖫 **Capitol Hill Mansion Bed & Breakfast Inn.** The dramatic turret and intense rust color of this Richardson Romanesque Victorian mansion built in 1891 is enough to draw you in. Inside are eight elegantly appointed rooms done in varying themes, such as Rocky Mountain, Victorian, and Colonial. The Gold Banner suite is cheerfully yellow, with a separate sitting room and gas-log fireplace, and it, along with two other rooms, has a view of the Rockies. Breakfast and afternoon refreshments are included, along with samplings of Colorado wines. **Pros:** welcoming

hosts; inviting rooms. **Cons:** walls are thin; place feels remote compared to rest of downtown. ✉ *1207 Pennsylvania St., Capitol Hill,* ☏ *303/839–5221 or 800/839–9329* ⊕ *www.capitolhillmansion.com* ➹ *8 rooms, 3 suites* ⚴ *In-room: refrigerator, Internet, Wi-Fi. In-hotel: public Wi-Fi* ☐ *AE, D, DC, MC, V* ⦿| *BP* ✛ *D3.*

$$$ 🖭 **Courtyard by Marriott.** This stunning building (it used to be Joslins Department Store) sits right on the 16th Street Mall, which means everything downtown is a few blocks or a free Mall shuttle away. The lobbies and public spaces are modern Western in theme, and the cream-color, sparsely decorated rooms have city and mountain views. There's a Starbucks on-site. **Pros:** great location and views; deluxe rooms have sofabeds. **Cons:** pricey; rooms nothing fancy. ✉ *934 16th St., Downtown,* ☏ *303/571–1114 or 888/249–1810* ⊕ *www.marriott.com* ➹ *166 rooms, 11 suites* ⚴ *In-room: Internet, Wi-Fi. In-hotel: restaurant, room service, bar, pool, gym, concierge, laundry service, parking (paid), public Wi-Fi* ☐ *AE, D, DC, MC, V* ✛ *B6.*

$$ 🖭 **The Curtis.** Each floor here has a pop-culture theme, from classic cars
☼ to TV to science fiction. Don't be surprised when the elevator doors close and you feel like you are in a shark cage—the space is decorated like one. A robot roams the hallways and bubbly music plays in the background. Rooms are spacious and groovy, with speakers for your MP3 player and comfy, mod furnishings. The Corner Office Restaurant and Martini Lounge ($$) is a retro eatery and popular local happy-hour joint that serves comfort food with a twist such as lobster mac 'n' cheese and even Captain Crunch (yes, for dinner). The Oceanaire ($$$) is a tonier seafood restaurant. **Pros:** across the street from Denver Performing Arts Complex; kid-friendly; reasonably priced for location. **Cons:** can be noisy; high-traffic area; staff not always helpful. ✉ *1405 Curtis St., Downtown,* ☏ *303/571–0300 or 800/525–6651* ⊕ *www. thecurtis.com* ➹ *334 rooms, 2 suites* ⚴ *In-room: Internet, Wi-Fi. In-hotel: 2 restaurants, room service, bar, pool, concierge, laundry service, public Wi-Fi, parking (paid), some pets allowed (fee)* ☐ *AE, D, DC, MC, V* ✛ *B6.*

$$$$ 🖭 **Denver Marriott City Center.** The Denver Marriott is definitely geared toward the business traveler; it's a three-block walk from the Denver Convention Complex and has 25,000 square feet of meeting space of its own. Rooms are small but classy, with a strong "executive" look—many stripes, much leather—and recently updated (and comfier) bedding. The casual D-Spot Pub & Grill and Allies American Grille are worthwhile whether you have an expense account or not. The indoor pool is nice, and the fitness center contains enough equipment to provide a well-rounded workout. **Pros:** nice gym and pool; close to the convention center. **Cons:** not much maneuvering space in the rooms; prices have gone up. ✉ *1701 California St., Downtown,* ☏ *303/297–1300 or 800/228–9290* ⊕ *www.denvermarriott.com* ➹ *601 rooms, 14 suites* ⚴ *In-room: Internet, Wi-Fi. In-hotel: restaurant, room service, bar, pool, gym, spa, concierge, laundry service, public Wi-Fi, parking (paid)* ☐ *AE, D, DC, MC, V* ✛ *C6.*

$$$ 🖭 **Grand Hyatt.** Close to Larimer Square, the theaters, the 16th Street
☼ Mall, and the Colorado Convention Center—downtown locations don't

2

get much better than this. A stone fireplace makes for an inviting lobby, and the roomy quarters are done in beige and violet tones with black accents. The Colorado-theme eatery 1876—named for the year Colorado became a state—is decorated in wrought iron and cherrywood and serves contemporary Front Range favorites. The fitness center is one of the best-equipped of any hotel in town. **Pros:** great views from top floors; prime location; top-notch gym; lavish concierge lounge services. **Cons:** restaurants inconsistent. ✉ *1750 Welton St., Downtown,* ☎ *303/295–1234 or 800/233–1234* ⊕ *www.grandhyattdenver.com* � *513 rooms, 43 suites* ♿ *In-room: Internet. In-hotel: 2 restaurants, room service, pool, gym, concierge, laundry service, public Internet, parking (paid)* ⊟ *AE, D, DC, MC, V* ✚ *D2.*

$$$ 🏨 **Gregory Inn LoDo.** Decorated to resemble an old English inn, the Gregory in the Curtis Park neighborhood captures Old World charm through the use of mossy colors and exquisite linens and accents. All rooms, each distinctive and luxurious, have private baths, and many have small sitting rooms. There's also a sumptuous carriage house, which contains a full kitchen, washer and dryer, and dining and living areas. Breakfast is served each morning in the dimly lighted, soothing Gathering Room. **Pros:** a few blocks removed from downtown's bustle; inviting setting; excellent breakfasts. **Cons:** extra blocks from downtown center mean more walking; no young children. ✉ *2500 Arapahoe St., LoDo,* ☎ *303/295–6570 or 800/925–6570* ⊕ *www.gregoryinn. com* ➠ *8 rooms, 1 suite* ♿ *In-room: refrigerator, Wi-Fi. In-hotel: public Wi-Fi, no kids under 12* ⊟ *AE, D, DC, MC, V* ✚ *D1.*

$ 🏨 **Holiday Chalet B&B.** Stained-glass windows and homey accents throughout make this 1896 Victorian brownstone exceptionally appealing. It's also in Capitol Hill, the neighborhood immediately east of downtown. Many of the rooms have overstuffed Victorian armchairs and such historic touches as furniture once owned by Baby Doe Tabor. Some units have tile fireplaces, others have small sitting rooms. Each room has a full kitchen, a holdover from the building's days as an apartment building, and full breakfast is included. Across a serene courtyard, the B&B serves a light lunch with tea Thursday through Sunday. **Pros:** welcoming staff; delightful teas; enchanting style. **Cons:** parking can be a challenge. ✉ *1820 F. Colfax Ave., Capitol Hill,* ☎ *303/437–8245* ⊕ *www.denver-bed-breakfast.com* ➠ *10 rooms* ♿ *In-room: kitchen, Internet, Wi-Fi. In-hotel: public Wi-Fi, some pets allowed* ⊟ *AE, D, DC, MC, V* ❉❏ *BP* ✚ *F3.*

$$$ 🏨 **Hotel Monaco.** Celebrities and business travelers check into this hip property, which occupies the historic 1917 Railway Exchange Building and the 1937 Art Moderne Title Building, for the modern perks and Art Deco–meets–classic French style. The unabashedly colorful guest rooms, in vivid reds and yellows, have original art, custom headboards, glass-front armoires, and CD players. The service is similarly a cut above: room service is available around the clock; pets are welcome, and if you check-in without one you'll be given the complimentary company of a goldfish. The hotel's mascot, a Shih Tzu named Hercules, hangs out in the lobby during the day. **Pros:** one of the pet-friendliest hotels in town; welcoming complimentary wine hour; central location.

Cons: may be too pet-friendly; pricier than nearby options. ✉ *1717 Champa St., Downtown,* ☎ *303/296–1717 or 800/990–1303* ⊕ *www. monaco-denver.com* ☞ *157 rooms, 32 suites* ⚲ *In-room: refrigerator, Internet, Wi-Fi. In-hotel: restaurant, room service, bar, gym, spa, concierge, laundry service, public Internet, parking (paid), some pets allowed* ⊟ *AE, D, DC, MC, V* ✛ *C6.*

$$$ ⌃ **Hotel Teatro.** Black-and-white photographs, costumes, and scenery
★ from plays that were staged in the Denver Performing Arts Complex across the street decorate the grand public areas of this hotel. With 12-foot ceilings, the earth-tone rooms are sleek and stylish, featuring Frette linens, the latest technology, and spacious bathrooms with soaking tubs and rain forest showers, as well as televisions. The ninth-floor rooms have balconies. The two restaurants here—contemporary and elegant Restaurant Kevin Taylor and its casual Italian kid sister Prima—are both highly regarded. **Pros:** great location for theater and other downtown pursuits; excellent restaurants; lovely rooms and hotel spaces. **Cons:** noisy and chaotic area; costly parking; some rooms are tiny. ✉ *1100 14th St., Downtown,* ☎ *303/228–1100 or 888/727–1200* ⊕ *www.hotelteatro.com* ☞ *110 rooms, 6 suites* ⚲ *In-room: Internet, Wi-Fi. In-hotel: 2 restaurants, room service, bar, gym, concierge, laundry service, parking (paid)* ⊟ *AE, D, DC, MC, V* ✛ *A6.*

$ ⌃ **Hotel VQ at Mile High.** A stone's throw from Invesco Field at Mile High, the Hotel VQ took over the space vacated by the Red Lion and continues to provide free parking and complimentary shuttles to downtown, half a mile away. Visitors and locals alike hang out at the Skybox Grill and Sports Bar on the 14th floor, which has a panoramic view of the Denver skyline and surrounding attractions. No major remodeling was done, so the rooms are still red, white, and warm-yellows, with plenty of space to maneuver and an oversize desk. **Pros:** reasonable rates; easy highway access; spacious rooms. **Cons:** rooms feel dated; traffic during rush hours can be a nightmare. ✉ *1975 Mile High Stadium Cir., West Denver,* ☎ *303/433–8331 or 800/388–5381* ⊕ *www.redliondenverdowntown. com* ☞ *169 rooms* ⚲ *In-room: Wi-Fi. In-hotel: restaurant, room service, bar, pool, gym, concierge, laundry service, parking (free)* ⊟ *AE, D, DC, MC, V* ✛ *A2.*

$$$$ ⌃ **Magnolia Hotel.** The Denver outpost of this Texas-based chain has spacious, elegant rooms with sophisticated furnishings—some with fireplaces—and warm colors, all built within the confines of the 1906 former American Bank Building. Breakfast is included, as is an evening guest reception; drink coupons for the jazzy, retro-hip Harry's Bar; and late-night cookies and milk. One block off the 16th Street Mall, the Magnolia is convenient to downtown and LoDo. There's also an on-site Starbucks. **Pros:** pretty, comfortable rooms; nice complimentary breakfast buffet; good restaurants. **Cons:** although classy, can feel like a generic chain hotel. ✉ *818 17th St., Downtown,* ☎ *303/607–9000 or 888/915–1110* ⊕ *www.magnoliahoteldenver.com* ☞ *246 rooms, 119 suites* ⚲ *In-room: Internet, Wi-Fi. In-hotel: room service, bar, gym, concierge, laundry service, public Wi-Fi, parking (paid)* ⊟ *AE, D, DC, MC, V* ⦿ *BP* ✛ *C6.*

2

$$$
Fodor's Choice
★
⊞**Oxford Hotel.** During the Victorian era this hotel was an elegant fixture on the Denver landscape, and civilized touches like complimentary shoe shines, afternoon sherry, and morning coffee remain. Comfortable rooms are furnished with French and English period antiques, and the Cruise Room bar re-creates an Art Deco ocean liner. Art galleries are nearby. The popular McCormicks Restaurant ($$$) serves excellent seafood and a delicious Sunday brunch. **Pros:** prime LoDo location, gorgeous historic setting, great restaurants on-site and nearby. **Cons:** noisy ballpark crowds in-season turn LoDo area into a big party. ⊠ *1600 17th St., LoDo,* ☎ *303/628–5400 or 800/228–5838* ⊕ *www. theoxfordhotel.com* ⇥ *80 rooms* ☖ *In-room: Internet, Wi-Fi. In-hotel: restaurant, room service, bars, gym, spa, public Wi-Fi, parking (paid)* ⊟ *AE, D, DC, MC, V* ⊹ *A5.*

$$
⊞**Queen Anne Inn.** Just north of downtown in the regentrified Clements historic district (some of the neighboring blocks have yet to be reclaimed), this inn made up of adjacent Victorians is a delightful, romantic getaway. Both houses have handsome oak wainscoting and balustrades, vaulted ceilings, numerous bay or stained-glass windows, and period furnishings like brass and canopy beds, cherry and pine armoires, and oak rocking chairs. The best accommodations are the four "gallery suites" dedicated to Audubon, Rockwell, Calder, and Remington. A full breakfast and afternoon tastings of Colorado wines are offered daily. **Pros:** lovely rooms; welcoming hosts; hearty fare. **Cons:** not right downtown. ⊠ *2147 Tremont Pl., Central Denver,* ☎ *303/296–6666 or 800/432–4667* ⊕ *www.queenannebnb.com* ⇥ *10 rooms, 4 suites* ☖ *In-room: Internet. In-hotel: public Wi-Fi* ⊟ *AE, D, DC, MC, V* |◎| *BP* ⊹ *D2.*

$
⊞**Ramada Limited Capitol Hill.** As the name suggests, this Ramada is within walking distance of the State Capitol, as well as nine blocks east of downtown and the 16th Street Mall. A Southwestern flair pervades the leather couch–dominated Western-style lobby and lounge area. The somewhat dated but reasonably spacious rooms have dark carpeting and beige, red, and rose colors. There's also a pool and a small but serviceable fitness center. **Pros:** very reasonable rates; easy to get downtown. **Cons:** not the safest part of Colfax Avenue late at night. ⊠ *1150 E. Colfax Ave., Capitol Hill,* ☎ *303/831–7700 or 800/272–6232* ⊕ *www. ramada.com* ⇥ *143 rooms, 8 suites* ☖ *In-room: safe, Internet, Wi-Fi. In-hotel: restaurant, room service, bar, pool, gym, laundry service, parking (free)* ⊟ *AE, D, DC, MC, V* ⊹ *E3.*

$$$$
⊞**The Ritz-Carlton, Denver.** No trace of the former Embassy Suites remains in this beautifully renovated property with warm woods, elaborate glass fixtures, and luxurious details. Though it's only two blocks from the 16th Street Mall, the Ritz makes it tough to leave the sumptuous rooms, with their buttery leather furniture, featherbeds, oversize baths, and espresso machines. The independent, state-of-the-art fitness center is complimentary; the spa is almost too pretty, and has a full-range of treatments emphasizing natural products. Elway's restaurant ($$$)— a second outpost of the original in Cherry Creek—serves superb steaks and seafood. **Pros:** gracious service; room-service fare delicious and prompt; inviting public spaces. **Cons:** fitness-center staff not as service-

oriented as hotel's; pricey. ✉ *1881 Curtis St., Downtown* ☎ *303/312–3800* ⊕ *www.ritzcarlton.com* ⤳ *155 rooms, 47 suites* ⚥ *In-room: safe, refrigerator, Wi-Fi. In-hotel: restaurant, room service, bar, pool, gym, spa, laundry service, Internet terminal, Wi-Fi, parking (fee/no fee), some pets allowed* ▤ *AE, D, DC, MC, V* ✛ *B5.*

$$$$	⌸ **Sheraton Denver Downtown Hotel.** After a major remodel, the former Adam's Mark is looking pretty spiffy. Guest rooms are roomy and streamlined, with less fussy furniture and nice workstations that will appeal to the business traveler. Nothing was spared a redesign, from the lobby, which was made more cheerful and appealing for folks to simply relax in or stop by the updated business center, to the meeting and banquet rooms, which had desperately needed brightening and modernizing. Three restaurants serve a variety of tastes—the Irish pub Katie Mullen's ($$), the fine-dining spot 1550 Restaurant ($$–$$$), and a sports bar called Players ($)—and both the fitness center and heated outdoor pool are modernized. **Pros:** great location; many amenities; much nicer and more accommodating staff than the Adam's Mark's. **Cons:** restaurant food could be better; front area where cars come in still chaos central; rising prices. ✉ *1550 Court Pl., Downtown,* ☎ *303/893–3333 or 866/716–8134* ⊕ *www.sheratondenverhotel.com* ⤳ *1,231 rooms, 82 suites* ⚥ *In-room: Internet. In-hotel: 3 restaurants, room service, bars, pool, gym, concierge, laundry service, public Wi-Fi, parking (paid)* ▤ *AE, D, DC, MC, V* ✛ *D3.*

$$$	⌸ **Warwick Denver Hotel.** This stylish midsize business hotel is ideally located on the edge of downtown. The rooms and suites are some of the most spacious in town, with brass and mahogany furnishings and the latest in high-tech perks. All rooms contain wet bars and private terraces with exceptional city views. The restaurant, Randolph's, serves contemporary American cuisine three meals daily. **Pros:** reasonable rates; friendly staff; oversize rooms. **Cons:** food at Randolph's inconsistent; more than walking distance from the business district. ✉ *1776 Grant St., Downtown,* ☎ *303/861–2000 or 800/525–2888* ⊕ *www. warwickdenver.com* ⤳ *161 rooms, 58 suites* ⚥ *In-room: safe, Wi-Fi. In-hotel: restaurant, room service, bars, pool, gym, concierge, public Wi-Fi, parking (paid), some pets allowed* ▤ *AE, D, DC, MC, V* ✛ *D2.*

$$$$	⌸ **Westin Tabor Center.** This sleek, luxurious high-rise opens right onto
★	the 16th Street Mall and all the downtown action. Rooms are oversize and done in grays and taupes, with white duvets, piles of cushy pillows, and contemporary prints on the walls. The fourth-floor pool has one of the best views of the Rockies in all of downtown. The hotel buys blocks of tickets for weekend shows at the Denver Performing Arts Complex for guests' exclusive use. The Palm, a branch of the Manhattan-based steak house, is a favorite eating and drinking spot for local luminaries. **Pros:** convenient location on Mall; contemporary rooms; nice pool with great city view. **Cons:** the Palm is pricey; breakfast options are also expensive. ✉ *1672 Lawrence St., Downtown,* ☎ *303/572–9100 or 800/937–8461* ⊕ *www.westin.com* ⤳ *430 rooms* ⚥ *In-room: Internet. In-hotel: 2 restaurants, room service, bars, pool, gym, concierge, laundry service, public Internet, parking (paid)* ▤ *AE, D, DC, MC, V* ✛ *B5.*

AROUND CHERRY CREEK

$$ ⊡ **Holiday Inn Select Denver/Cherry Creek.** The Cherry Creek shopping district is 4 mi away, and the major museums and the zoo a five-minute drive from this bustling hotel, which provides coveted mountain views from many of its rooms. The entrance is impressive, with stone-supported pillars and Southwestern effects, whereas the rooms are decorated in autumn tones with velvety upholstery and leather chairs. At night Olives Martini Bar brings in Denverites, as well. **Pros:** good for business travelers, Starbucks on-site, location bridges gap for folks who want both museums and downtown. **Cons:** not walking distance to any attractions; far from downtown. ⊠ *455 S. Colorado Blvd., Cherry Creek,* ☎ *303/388–5561 or 888/388–6129* ⊕ *www.cherrycreekhoteldenver.com* ⤳ *276 rooms, 7 suites* ⌂ *In-room: Internet. In-hotel: restaurant, room service, bar, pool, gym, concierge, laundry service, parking (free)* ⊟ *AE, D, DC, MC, V* ✛ *G6.*

$$$$ ⊡ **JW Marriott Denver at Cherry Creek.** The hip atmosphere and location smack in the middle of Cherry Creek's shopping district has made this upscale outpost of the Marriott family popular with tourists and locals alike. Hotel rooms are done in autumn colors, with soft linens and cozy sofas, and the bathrooms are set up for comfort and well stocked with amenities. The groovy in-house restaurant, Second Home Kitchen and Bar ($$), serves three meals daily. The Spa at Cherry Creek, while expensive, is one of the most sought-after in town, and offers a gorgeous relaxation area and treatment rooms. **Pros:** friendly staff; great location for shopping; bus to downtown a block away. **Cons:** feels very much like a chain; restaurant inconsistent. ⊠ *150 Clayton La., Cherry Creek* ☎ *303/316–2700* ⊕ *www.marriott.com* ⤳ *191 rooms, 5 suites* ⌂ *In-room: safe, refrigerator, DVD, Internet, Wi-Fi. In-hotel: restaurant, room service, bar, pool, gym, spa, laundry facilities, laundry service, Internet, Wi-Fi, parking (paid), some pets allowed* ⊟ *AE, DC, MC, V* ✛ *F4.*

$$$ ⊡ **Loews Denver Hotel.** The 12-story steel-and-black-glass facade conceals the unexpected and delightful Italian baroque motif within. Spacious rooms are done in earth tones and blond wood and garnished with fresh flowers, fruit baskets, and Renaissance-style portraits. The formal Tuscany restaurant ($$$) serves sumptuous Italian cuisine. Use of a nearby health club and a Continental breakfast are included. If downtown or the Denver Tech Center are your primary destinations, this location is a drawback, but Cherry Creek fans will find its proximity a plus. **Pros:** gorgeous rooms and public spaces; wonderful restaurant; gracious staff. **Cons:** not near downtown; eatery pricey. ⊠ *4150 E. Mississippi Ave., Southeast Denver,* ☎ *303/782–9300 or 800/345–9172* ⊕ *www.loewshotels.com* ⤳ *183 rooms, 17 suites* ⌂ *In-room: safe, Internet. In-hotel: restaurant, room service, bar, gym, concierge, laundry service, public Internet, parking (free)* ⊟ *AE, D, DC, MC, V* |◎| *CP* ✛ *H6.*

NIGHTLIFE AND THE ARTS

Friday's *Denver Post* (⊕ *www.denverpost.com*) publishes a calendar of the week's events, as does the slightly alternative *Westword* (⊕ *www.westword.com*), which is free and published on Thursday. Downtown and LoDo are where most Denverites go at night. Downtown has more mainstream entertainment, whereas LoDo is home to fun, funky rock clubs and small theaters. Remember that Denver's altitude can intensify your reaction to alcohol.

The ubiquitous **TicketMaster** (☎ *303/830–8497* ⊕ *ticketmaster.com*) is Denver's prime agency, selling tickets to almost all concerts, sporting events, and plays that take place in the Denver area. On the theatrical side of the spectrum, the doubledecker **Ticket Bus**, on the 16th Street Mall at Curtis Street, sells tickets from 10 until 6 weekdays, and half-price tickets on the day of the performance.

THE ARTS

PERFORMANCE VENUES

★ The **Denver Performing Arts Complex** is a huge, impressively high-tech group of theaters connected by a soaring glass archway to a futuristic symphony hall. The complex, which occupies a four-block area, hosts more events than any other performing arts center in the world. Run by the Denver Center for the Performing Arts since 1972, the complex's anchors are the round, relaxing Temple Hoyne Buell Theatre, built in 1991, and the more impressive, ornate Auditorium Theatre, built in 1908. Both host large events, from classical orchestras to comedian Jerry Seinfeld to country singer Lyle Lovett. Some of the other five theaters include the small Garner Galleria Theatre, where the comedy *I Love You, You're Perfect, Now Change* once packed the house for more than four years running, and the midsize Space Theatre. Both the ballet and opera have their seasons here. Guided tours for groups of five or more are available by appointment only. ⊠ *Box office, 1101 13th St., LoDo* ☎ *303/893–4000* ⊕ *www.denvercenter.org.*

Downtown, the **Paramount Theatre** (⊠ *1631 Glenarm Pl., LoDo* ☎ *303/623–0106* ⊕ *www.theparamount.net*) is the venue for large-scale rock concerts. Designed by renowned local architect Temple H. Buell in the Art Deco style in 1930, the lovingly maintained Paramount is both an elegant place to see shows and a rowdy, beer-serving party location for rock fans.

Fodor's Choice ★ The exquisite 9,000-seat **Red Rocks Amphitheatre** (⊠ *17598 W. Alameda Pkwy., Morrison, off U.S. 285 or I–70* ☎ *303/640–2637* ⊕ *www.redrocksonline.com*), amid majestic geological formations in nearby Morrison, is renowned for its natural acoustics, which have awed the likes of Leopold Stokowski and the Beatles. Although Red Rocks is one of the best places in the country to hear live music, be sure to leave extra time when visiting—parking is sparse, crowds are thick, paths are long and extremely uphill, and seating is usually general admission.

SYMPHONY, OPERA, AND DANCE

Colorado's premier orchestra, opera company, and ballet company are all in residence at the Denver Performing Arts Complex.

The **Colorado Symphony Orchestra** performs September to June in the Boettcher Concert Hall (⊠ *13th and Curtis Sts., LoDo* ☎ *303/640–2862* ⊕ *www.coloradosymphony.org*).

Opera Colorado (☎ *303/778–1500* ⊕ *www.operacolorado.org*) has a spring season, often with internationally renowned artists, in the magnificent Ellie Caulkins Opera House in the renovated Newton Auditorium. Already world-renowned for its superior acoustics and a Figaro seat-back titling system that allows attendees to follow the text of the opera, the cherrywood-accented theater has red-velvet seating and a lyre shape, ideal for full-bodied sound travel.

The **Colorado Ballet** (☎ *303/837–8888* ⊕ *www.coloradoballet.org*) specializes in the classics with performances from September to April.

THEATER

The **Bug Theatre Company** (⊠ *3654 Navajo St., Highland* ☎ *303/477–9984*) produces primarily cutting-edge, original works in Denver's Highland neighborhood. **Denver Center Attractions** (⊠ *14th and Curtis Sts., at DPCA's Temple Hoyne Buell and Auditorium theaters, LoDo* ☎ *303/893–4100*) brings Broadway road companies to town. The **Denver Center Theater Company** (⊠ *14th and Curtis Sts., LoDo* ☎ *303/893–4100*) presents high-caliber repertory theater, including new works by promising playwrights, at the Bonfils Theatre Complex, part of the Denver Performing Arts Complex. **El Centro Su Teatro** (⊠ *4725 High St., Elyria* ☎ *303/296–0219*) is a Latino-Chicano company that puts on mostly original works and festivals during its May to September season. **Hunger Artists Ensemble Theater** (⊠ *Vintage Theatre, 2119 E. 17th Ave., City Park* ☎ *303/839–1361*) presents dramas, comedies, and adaptations of works from the likes of Shakespeare, James Joyce, and Tom Stoppard.

NIGHTLIFE

BARS AND BREWPUBS

The **Denver ChopHouse & Brewery** (⊠ *1735 19th St., LoDo* ☎ *303/296–0800* ⊕ *www.chophouse.com*) is a high-end microbrewery on the site of the old Union Pacific Railroad headhouse—with the train paraphernalia to prove it. It's a bit expensive for a brewpub, but if you hang out after Broncos games you might encounter local sports celebrities celebrating or commiserating. **Mynt Mojito Lounge** (⊠ *1424 Market St., LoDo* ☎ *303/825–6968* ⊕ *www.myntmojitolounge.com*) has established a chichi reputation with its namesake mojitos, Miami-style pastel colors, and fruity martinis—try the Strawberry Banana. Considered by some Denverites as the best bar in town, the laid-back, casual, slightly divey **PS Lounge** (⊠ *3416 E. Colfax Ave., Capitol Hill* ☎ *303/320–1200*) has a well-stocked jukebox and an owner, known to all simply as Pete, who hands out a free shot to anyone who behaves and seems to be having a good time. **Rock Bottom Brewery** (⊠ *1001 16th St., LoDo* ☎ *303/534–7616* ⊕ *www.rockbottom.com*) is a perennial favorite, thanks to its rotating special brews and reasonably priced pub grub. A vintage-style poolroom is just one reason to stop by the beloved **Skylark Lounge** (✉ *140 S. Broadway, South Denver* ☎ *303/722–7844* ⊕ *www.skylarklounge.com*), which counts live music, pinball machines, comfortable seating, and friendly staffers among its many charms. The **Wynkoop Brewing Co.** (✉ *1634 18th St., LoDo* ☎ *303/297–2700* ⊕ *www.wynkoop.com*) is now more famous for its founder—Denver Mayor John Hickenlooper—than for its brews, food, or ambience. But it remains one of the city's best-known bars—a relaxing, slightly upscale, two-story joint filled with halfway-decent bar food, the usual pool tables, and games and beers of all types. It has anchored LoDo since it was a pre-Coors Field warehouse district.

> ## BEERDRINKER OF THE YEAR
>
> Though it's a title many have tried to usurp, only one person (at a time) can truly be the Beerdrinker of the Year, as determined by Wynkoop Brewing Company and its panel of local and national judges, who wear British wigs and robes during the finals. Begun in 1997 by then-owner and current Denver mayor John Hickenlooper, the annual event draws contestants from all over the country, who are required to submit beer résumés and undergo a rigorous battery of tests and contests to determine their beery worthiness. Winners receive free beer for life at Wynkoop, not to mention bragging rights.

COMEDY CLUBS

Three area improv groups make their home at **Bovine Metropolis Theater** (✉ *1527 Champa St., LoDo* ☎ *303/758–4722* ⊕ *www.bovinemetropolis. com*), which also stages satirical productions. Denver comics have honed their skills at **Comedy Works** (✉ *1226 15th St., LoDo* ☎ *303/595–3637* ⊕ *www.comedyworks.com*) for more than 20 years. Well-known performers often drop by. Downstairs in the Wynkoop brewpub, at the **Impulse Theater** (✉ *1634 18th St., LoDo* ☎ *303/297–2111* ⊕ *www. impulsetheater.com*), the audience is invited to participate in interactive improv comedy and theater, and touring stand-up comics and local acts provide entertainment through physical comedy and other routines.

COUNTRY MUSIC CLUBS

The **Grizzly Rose** (✉ *5450 N. Valley Hwy., I–25 at Exit 215, Globeville* ☎ *303/295–1330* ⊕ *www.grizzlyrose.com*) has miles of dance floor, national bands, and gives two-step dancing lessons—and sells plenty of Western wear, from cowboy boots to spurs. Classic-rock bands are big, in addition to country acts big and small. The suburban **Stampede Grill & Dance Emporium** (✉ *2430 S. Havana St., Aurora* ☎ *303/696–7986* ⊕ *www.stampedeclub.net*) is another cavernous boot-scooting spot, with dance lessons and a restaurant.

DANCE CLUBS

The **Funky Buddha Lounge** (✉ *776 Lincoln St., Capitol Hill* ☎ *303/832–5075*) distinguishes itself with the Ginger Bar, an upstairs outdoor dance area with live DJs six nights a week. **La Rumba** (✉ *99 W. 9th Ave., Golden Triangle* ☎ *303/572–8006* ⊕ *www.larumba-denver.com*) offers up "Lipgloss," a DJ-spun frenzy of Brit-pop, soul, and rock on Friday nights in its cavernous industrial space, while Thursday and Saturday nights find salsa, meringue, and other Mambo King moves happening. The venerable dance club the **Snake Pit** (✉ *614 E. 13th Ave., Capitol Hill* ☎ *303/831–1234*) caters to a highly varied crowd.

GAY BARS

Charlie's (✉ *900 E. Colfax Ave., Capitol Hill* ☎ *303/839–8890* ⊕ *www. charliesdenver.com*) has country-western atmosphere and music. **JR's Bar & Grill** (✉ *777 E. 17th Ave., Central Denver* ☎ *303/831–0459*) features theme nights like retro and trivia, a raucous atmosphere, and a huge, long patio—with neighborhood people-watching—in nice weather.

JAZZ CLUBS

El Chapultepec (✉ *1962 Market St., LoDo* ☎ *303/295–9126*) is a cramped, fluorescent-lighted, bargain-basement Mexican dive. Still, the limos parked outside hint at its enduring popularity: this is where Ol' Blue Eyes used to pop in, and where visiting musicians, including the Marsalis brothers, continue to jam after hours. **Dazzle Restaurant and Lounge** (✉ *930 Lincoln St., Central Denver* ☎ *303/839–5100* ⊕ *www.dazzlejazz.com*) is a cozy, casual spot for nightly live jazz in the Golden Triangle. *Downbeat* magazine has named it one of the 100 best jazz clubs in the world; it offers acoustically treated walls in the dining room and the lounge, where the audience is up close and personal with the musicians. Hidden in the back of a parking lot, the hipster favorite **Herb's Hideout** (✉ *2057 Larimer St., LoDo* ☎ *303/299–9555* ⊕ *www.herbsbar.com*) is a gloriously nostalgic bar with dim lighting and checkerboard floors.

ROCK CLUBS

Of Denver's numerous smoky hangouts, the most popular is the regally restored **Bluebird Theater** (✉ *3317 E. Colfax Ave., Capitol Hill* ☎ *303/377–1666* ⊕ *www.bluebirdtheater.net*), which showcases local and national acts, emphasizing rock, hip-hop, ambient, and the occasional evening of cinema. The **Fillmore Auditorium** (✉ *1510 Clarkson St., Capitol Hill* ☎ *303/837–1482* ⊕ *www.livenation.com*), Denver's classic San Francisco concert hall spin-off, looks dumpy on the outside but is elegant and impressive inside. Before catching a big-name act such as Coldplay, LL Cool J, or Snoop Dogg, scan the walls for color photographs of past club performers.

The **Gothic Theatre** (✉ *3263 S. Broadway, Englewood* ☎ *303/788–0984* ⊕ *www.gothictheatre.com*) came of age in the early '90s, with a steady stream of soon-to-be-famous alternative-rock acts such as Nirvana and the Red Hot Chili Peppers. It has since reinvented itself as a community venue for theater, music, and charity events, and sits south of downtown. Down-home **Herman's Hideaway** (✉ *1578 S. Broadway, Overland* ☎ *303/777–5840* ⊕ *www.hermanshideaway.com*) showcases mostly local rock in a south Denver neighborhood, with a smattering of reggae and blues thrown in. The **Hi-Dive** (✉ *7 S. Broadway, Capitol Hill* ☎ *720/570–4500* ⊕ *www.hi-dive.com*) is an energetic, hip club that books a diverse and eclectic range of talent. The crowd is young, likes Red Bull, and tends to revel in the discovery of obscure underground music. The **Lions Lair** (✉ *2022 E. Colfax Ave., Capitol*

Denver Rock History

Colorado's moments of pop-music history have been spectacular. Many happened at Red Rocks Amphitheatre, where the Beatles performed in 1964 and U2's Bono made his famous "this song is not a rebel song—this song is 'Sunday Bloody Sunday'" speech in 1983. The Denver–Boulder area was a huge hub for country-rock in the '70s, and members of the Eagles, Poco, Firefall, and others lived here, at least briefly. Some of the most famous spots have closed, but rock fans can tour the hallowed ground—Ebbets Field, where Steve Martin and Lynyrd Skynyrd made early-career appearances in the '70s, at 15th and Curtis; and the original Auditorium Theatre, where Led Zeppelin performed its first U.S. show in 1968, at 14th and Curtis. The local scene remains strong, with the Samples, Big Head Todd and the Monsters, Leftover Salmon, String Cheese Incident, Apples In Stereo, and Dressy Bessy attracting audiences. Check *Westword* or *The Denver Post* for show listings.

Hill ☎ 303/320–9200) is a dive where punk-rock bands and occasional name acts like British rocker Graham Parker perform on a tiny stage just above a huge, square, central bar. The **Mercury Café** (✉ 2199 *California St., Five Points* ☎ 303/294–9281 ⊕ *www.mercurycafe.com*) triples as a health-food restaurant with sublime tofu fettuccine, fringe theater, and rock club in a downtown neighborhood specializing in acoustic sets, progressive, and newer wave music. The **Ogden Theatre** (✉ 935 *E. Colfax Ave., Capitol Hill* ☎ 303/832–1874 ⊕ *www.ogdentheatre.net*) is a classic old theater that showcases alternative-rock acts such as the Breeders and the Flaming Lips.

SHOPPING

Denver may be the best place in the country for shopping for recreational gear. Sporting-goods stores hold legendary ski sales around Labor Day. The city's selection of books and Western fashion is also noteworthy.

MALLS AND SHOPPING DISTRICTS

The **Denver Pavilions** (✉ 16th *St. Mall between Tremont and Welton Sts., LoDo* ☎ 303/260–6000 ⊕ *www.denverpavilions.com*) is downtown Denver's newest shopping and entertainment complex, a three-story, open-air structure that houses national chain stores like Barnes & Noble, NikeTown, Ann Taylor, and Talbot's. There are also restaurants, including Denver's Hard Rock Cafe, and a 15-screen movie theater, the UA Denver Pavilions. Don't expect distinctive local flavor, but it's a practical complement to Larimer Square a few blocks away.

Historic **Larimer Square** (✉ 14th *and Larimer Sts., LoDo* ⊕ *www. larimersquare.com*) houses distinctive shops and restaurants. Some of the square's retail highlights are Dog Savvy, a boutique devoted to pets complete with spa treatments; Cry Baby Ranch, which specializes in all things Western and cowboy-nostalgic; and John Atencio Designer Jewelry. **Tabor Center** (✉ *16th St. Mall, LoDo* ⊕ *www.taborcenter.com*) is a light-filled atrium whose 20 specialty shops and restaurants include the ESPN Zone–theme restaurant and the Shirt Broker. **Writer Square** (✉ *1512 Larimer St., LoDo* ⊕ *www.wsdenver.com*) has Tiny Town— a doll-size village inhabited by Michael Garman's inimitable figurines— as well as shops and restaurants.

In a pleasant, predominantly residential neighborhood 2 mi from downtown, the **Cherry Creek** shopping district has retail blocks and an enclosed mall. At Milwaukee Street, the granite-and-glass behemoth **Cherry Creek Shopping Mall** (✉ *3000 E. 1st Ave., Cherry Creek* ☎ *303/388–3900* ⊕ *www.shopcherrycreek.com*) holds some of the nation's top retailers. Its 160 stores include Abercrombie & Fitch, Banana Republic, Burberry's, Tiffany & Co., Louis Vuitton, Neiman Marcus, and Saks Fifth Avenue. Just north of the Cherry Creek Shopping Mall is the district **Cherry Creek North** (✉ *Between 1st and 3rd Aves. from University Blvd. to Steele St., Cherry Creek* ☎ *303/394– 2904*), an open-air development of tree-lined streets and shady plazas with art galleries, specialty shops, and fashionable restaurants.

The upscale **Park Meadows** (✉ *I–25, 5 mi south of Denver at County Line Rd., Littleton* ⊕ *www.parkmeadows.com*) is a mall designed to resemble a ski resort, with a 120-foot-high log-beam ceiling anchored by two massive stone fireplaces. The center includes more than 100 specialty shops. On snowy days "ambassadors" scrape your windshield while free hot chocolate is served inside.

SPECIALTY SHOPS

ANTIQUES
South Broadway between 1st Avenue and Evans Street, as well as the surrounding side streets, is chockablock with dusty antiques stores.

Antique Mall of Lakewood. More than 80 dealer showrooms make for one-stop shopping. ✉ *9635 W. Colfax Ave., Lakewood* ☎ *303/238–6940*.

BOOKSTORES
Fodor'sChoice **Tattered Cover.** A must for all bibliophiles, the Tattered Cover may be ★ the best bookstore in the United States, not only for the near-endless selection (more than 400,000 books on two floors at the newer Colfax Avenue location and 300,000 in LoDo) and helpful, knowledgeable staff, but also for the incomparably refined atmosphere. Treat yourself to the overstuffed armchairs, reading nooks, and afternoon readings and lectures, but be prepared for a less cozy environment at the Capitol Hill site in the renovated historic Lowenstein Theater than at the original Cherry Creek location. ✉ *2526 E. Colfax Ave., Capitol Hill* ☎ *303/322–7727* ✉ *1628 16th St., LoDo* ☎ *303/436–1070* ⊕ *www.tatteredcover.com*.

CRAFTS AND ART GALLERIES
LoDo has the trendiest galleries, many in splendidly and stylishly restored Victorian warehouses.

Camera Obscura Gallery. One of the oldest and best photography galleries between the East and West coasts, Camera Obscura carries both contemporary and vintage images. ☒ *1309 Bannock St., Capitol Hill* ☎ *303/623–4059* ⊕ *www.cameraobscuragallery.com.*

David Cook. David Cook specializes in historic Native American art and regional paintings, particularly Santa Fe modernists. ☒ *1637 Wazee St., LoDo* ☎ *303/623–8181* ⊕ *www.davidcookfineart.com.*

Mudhead Gallery. This gallery sells museum-quality Southwestern art, with an especially fine selection of Santa Clara and San Ildefonso pottery and Hopi kachinas. ☒ *555 17th St., across from the Hyatt, LoDo* ☎ *303/293–0007* ⊕ *www.mudheadgallery.net*

Native American Trading Company. The collection of crafts, jewelry, and regional paintings is outstanding. ☒ *213 W. 13th Ave., Golden Triangle* ☎ *303/534–0771* ⊕ *www.nativeamericantradingco.com.*

Old Santa Fe Pottery. The 20 rooms are crammed with Mexican masks, pottery, and rustic Mexican furniture—and there's even a chip dip and salsa room. ☒ *2485 S. Santa Fe Dr., Overland* ☎ *303/871–9434* ⊕ *www.oldsantafepottery.com.*

Pismo. Cherry Creek has its share of chic galleries, including Pismo, which showcases exquisite handblown-glass art. ☒ *235 Fillmore St., Cherry Creek* ☎ *303/333–2879* ⊕ *www.pismoglass.com.*

SPORTING GOODS

★ **REI.** Denver's REI flagship store, one of three such shops in the country, is yet another testament to the city's adventurous spirit. The store's 94,000 square feet are packed with all stripes of outdoors gear and some special extras: a climbing wall, a mountain-bike track, a whitewater chute, and a "cold room" for gauging the protection provided by coats and sleeping bags. There's also a Starbucks inside. Behind the store is the Platte River Greenway, a park path and water area that's accessible to dogs, kids, and kayakers. ☒ *1416 Platte St., Jefferson Park* ☎ *303/756–3100* ⊕ *www.rei.com.*

Sports Authority. At this huge, multistory shrine to Colorado's love of the outdoors, entire floors are given over to a single sport. There are other branches throughout Denver. ☒ *1000 Broadway, Civic Center* ☎ *303/861–1122* ⊕ *www.sportsauthority.com.*

WESTERN PARAPHERNALIA

Cry Baby Ranch. This rambunctious assortment of 1940s and '50s cowboy kitsch is at Larimer Square. ☒ *1421 Larimer St., LoDo* ☎ *303/623–3979* ⊕ *www.crybabyranch.com.*

The Rockies Near Denver

3

WORD OF MOUTH

"Georgetown is my favorite mountain town in Colorado. The main street has such great shops, and there are really nice restaurants. The train is tons of fun for kids. Be sure to get a good seat in one of the open cars—but not near the front of the train, or your face will be black from all the soot!"

—happy train

"Winter Park has lots of blue [intermediate] cruisers, and even Mary Jane has some—Edelweiss, Bluebell, and another I can't remember. I like the way some blues are groomed only on one side, so that you can try tougher skiing without committing to a whole run of it, and people of different ability levels can ski together."

—abram

Updated by
Lois Friedland

If you ever wondered why folks living along the Front Range—as the area west of Denver and east of the Continental Divide is known—continually brag about their lifestyles, you need only look at the western horizon where the peaks of snow-capped Rocky Mountains rise just a 35-minute drive from downtown. For those drawn to the Front Range, a morning workout might mean an hour-long single-track mountain-bike ride at Winter Park, a half-hour kayak session in Golden's Clear Creek, or a 40-minute hike in Mount Falcon Park.

The allure of this area, which rises from the red-rock foothills cloaked in lodgepole pine and white-barked aspens to the steep mountainsides draped with the occasional summer snowfields, has brought increasing recreational pressures as mountain bikers, equestrians, hikers, dog lovers, hunters, and conservationists all vie for real estate that is increasingly gobbled up by McMansion sprawl. On the Front Range the days of the elitist "Native" bumper stickers are long since gone; almost everyone here is from somewhere else. Finding an outdoor paddling, climbing, or skiing partner is about as difficult as saying hello to the next person you meet on the trail.

ORIENTATION AND PLANNING

GETTING ORIENTED

The Front Range Mountains, the easternmost mountains in Colorado, stretch more than 180 mi from the Wyoming border to Cañon City. The Continental Divide flows along much of the northern portion of this spine, which includes several "Fourteeners," 14,000-foot or higher peaks. A boon for high-country lovers, the Rockies Near Denver are easily accessed from the metro area via Interstate 70, Colorado's major east–west interstate, or Colorado Highway 285, the major route heading southwest into the mountains toward Fairplay in the now infamous South Park, one of the largest high-altitude valleys in the country. (Trey Parker, co-creator of the animated sit-com South Park went to Evergreen high school.) I–70 stitches together Denver, Golden, Idaho Springs, and Georgetown before crossing the Continental Divide through the Eisenhower Tunnel, right next to Loveland Ski Resort.

Foothills Near Denver. Less than 40 minutes from the city's heart, there are fast, cooling escapes in the mountain towns of Golden, Morrison, and Evergreen. Try your luck at the gaming towns of Central City and Black Hawk, or explore the former mining town of Idaho Springs.

TOP REASONS TO GO

Explore the Rockies: This section of mountains butts up against the Denver metro area, so it's easy to explore interesting towns and enjoy the mountain lifestyle.

Tour the MillerCoors Brewery: An entertaining (and free) tour ends in a sudsy stop at the end for an informal tasting. You'll see the steeping, roasting, and milling of the barley, then tour the Brew House where the "malt mash" is cooked in massive copper kettles.

Ride the Georgetown Loop Railroad: Peering out the window at the raw, steep mountainside and the rickety trestle bridge on the vintage train ride from Georgetown to Silverplume provides an eye-opening lesson in 1800s transportation.

Hit the slopes at Winter Park Resort: There's a blocked-off area for beginners, an outstanding children's program, and chutes and inbounds off piste–style terrain for experts.

Continental Divide Area. Colorado's gold and silver mining heritage is the highlight of Georgetown, within an hour's drive of Denver along I–70. Highway 40 climbs northwest from I–70, west of Idaho Springs, making a switchback ascent up Berthoud Pass before dropping into the resort town of Winter Park.

PLANNING

WHEN TO GO

Summers are hot in the city, but when you go higher up in the Front Range the days may be warm but the nights are cool. It's a time of year when many hikers and bikers head for the higher peaks. Heavy traffic on I–70 during weekends and holidays has become a sad fact of life for those wanting to explore the Front Range and Colorado's High Country. Slowdowns peak on Friday and Sunday afternoons when stop-and-go jams are the norm, particularly around Idaho Springs and Georgetown. Winter weekend and holiday traffic fares little better, with regular slowdowns in the morning rush to the Summit County ski resorts and afternoon returns. Many locals claim that the best seasons in Colorado are the spring and fall "mud seasons," when the tourists are gone and the trails are empty. In spring the Front Range mountains are carpeted with fresh new growth, while late September brings the shimmering gold of turning aspens. The interstate is well maintained. It's rare, but atop the mountain passes and at the Eisenhower Tunnel it's possible to see a bit of snow during the summer.

GETTING HERE AND AROUND

AIR TRAVEL

Denver International Airport is east of Denver, about a 35 -minute taxi ride from the city center and a 1-hour-and-55-minute drive from the Continental Divide when the roads are clear and traffic is normal.

Airport Denver International Airport (DEN) (☎ 800/247–2336 ⊕ www.flydenver.com).

Airport Transfers Home James (☎ *800/359–7503 shuttle service from Denver International Airport to Winter Park and Grand County* ⊕ *www.ridehj.com*).

CAR TRAVEL

The most convenient place to rent a car is at Denver International Airport. You can save money if you rent from the other offices of major car companies, but you'll have to take a shuttle or taxi to the city locations.

The hardest part about driving in the High Rockies is keeping your eyes on the road, what with canyons, mountain ridges, and animals to distract your attention. Some of the most scenic routes aren't necessarily the most direct, like the spectacular Loveland Pass.

Although it is often severely overcrowded on weekends and holidays, I–70 is still the quickest and most direct route from Denver to the High Rockies. It slices through the state, separating it into northern and southern halves. Idaho Springs is along I–70. Winter Park is north of I–70, on U.S. 40 and over Berthoud Pass, which is has gorgeous views but also has several hairpin turns. Highway 285 is the southwest route to Buena Vista, Salida, and the High Rockies. Any mountain road or highway can be treacherous when a winter storm blows in. Drive defensively, especially downhill to Denver and Dillon where runaway truck ramps see a fair bit of use.

Gasoline is readily available along I–70 and Highway 285, but not so in more-remote areas like Mount Evans and Guanella Pass. Blinding snowstorms can appear out of nowhere on the high passes at any time of the year. In the fall, winter, and early spring, it's a good idea to bring chains and a shovel along. Road reports and signage on the highways will indicate whether chains or four-wheel-drive vehicles are required. Keep your eyes peeled for wildlife, especially along the stretch of I–70 from Idaho Springs to the Eisenhower Tunnel. Bighorn sheep, elk, and deer frequently graze along the north side of the highway.

TRAIN TRAVEL

Amtrak has service from Denver's Union Station to Fraser, where shuttles to the Winter Park Ski Area are available.

VISITOR INFO
PARKS AND RECREATION AREAS

Most recreational lands in the foothills west of Denver are protected by **Jefferson County Open Space Parks** (☎ *303/271–5925* ⊕ *www.co.jefferson. co.us/openspace/index.htm*). These relatively small county parks are heavily used and have excellent hiking, mountain-biking, and horse-riding trails. **Golden Gate Canyon State Park** (☎ *303/582–3707* ⊕ *www. parks.state.co.us*), just west of Golden, has great hiking and wildlife-viewing. For Class II to IV rafting and kayaking, try **Clear Creek** (☎ *800/353–9901* ⊕ *www.clearcreekrafting.com*), which offers rafting on Clear Creek near Idaho Springs and on the Arkansas during the early spring snowmelt season and throughout the summer.

Much of the northern Front Range region is within **Arapaho-Roosevelt National Forest** (☎ *303/541–2500* ⊕ *www.fs.fed.us*). The **Indian Peaks Wilderness Area** is northwest of Denver and encompasses a rugged area of permanent snowfields, alpine lakes, and peaks reaching 13,000-foot and higher. It's a popular wilderness area for Denver and Front Range residents because it's easily reachable for overnight trips. Some of the trailheads on the eastern side are about one hour from Boulder and almost two hours from Denver. Because 90% of the people enter from the east side of the forests, visitors entering from the west side will find more solitude. *For more information about the Indian Peaks, see the Boulder and North Central Colorado section.*

RESTAURANTS

Front Range dining draws primarily from the Denver metro area; you'll find standard chains, mom-and-pop restaurants, upscale dining, and good ethnic food choices like Mexican and Thai with the occasional Middle Eastern restaurant thrown in.

HOTELS

In summertime, out-of-state and regional visitors flock to Georgetown and Idaho Springs to explore the rustic ambience, tour a mine, and hike or mountain bike on trails that thread the mountainsides; or to Golden to tour the MillerCoors Brewery. You won't find megaresorts or grand old lodges; but there are bed-and-breakfasts, condominiums, a few nice hotels in Golden, and some chain properties. Winter Park Resort has a mix of hotels and motels, plus a few upscale ranches. In Black Hawk and Central City, where gambling is allowed, there are several big hotels with casinos on the main floor, plus a few smaller casinos tucked into historical storefronts.

WHAT IT COSTS				
	¢	$	$$	$$$	$$$$
Restaurants	under $8	$8–$12	$13–$18	$19–$25	over $25
Hotels	under $80	$80–$120	$121–$170	$171–$230	over $230

Restaurant prices are for a main course at dinner, excluding 7.1%–8.9% tax. Hotel prices are for two people in a standard double room in high season, excluding service charges and 8.9% tax.

Contacts Chamber and Tourism Bureau of Clear Creek County (*Box 100, Idaho Springs 80452* ☎ *303/567–4660 or 866/674–9237* ⊕ *www.clearcreekcounty.org*).

FOOTHILLS NEAR DENVER

If you want to head into the High Country for a few hours, take the MillerCoors tour in Golden, then head up to the Buffalo Bill Museum. If you want to climb even higher, take a walk around the lake in the center of Evergreen and visit some of the local shops in the tiny downtown area.

GOLDEN

15 mi west of Denver via I–70 or U.S. 6 (W. 6th Ave.).

Golden was once the territorial capital of Colorado. City residents have smarted ever since losing that distinction to Denver by "dubious" vote in 1867, but in 1994 then-Governor Roy Romer restored "ceremonial" territorial-capital status to Golden. Today it is one of Colorado's fastest-growing cities, boosted by the high-tech industry as well as MillerCoors Brewery and Colorado School of Mines. Locals love to kayak along Clear Creek as it runs through Golden; there's even a racecourse on the water.

GETTING HERE AND AROUND

Golden is a 30-minute drive from downtown Denver via Colorado Highway 6. Downtown Golden is compact and easily walkable. You may want to drive to the Colorado School of Mines area of town, it's about a mile away from the downtown area, and you'll want a car to reach the Buffalo Bill Museum, which is several miles away. The parking area for the MillerCoors tours is within walking distance of downtown.

TIMING

You can explore downtown and tour the MillerCoors Brewery in three hours or so.

ESSENTIALS

Visitor Info Greater Golden Chamber of Commerce (✉ *1010 Washington Ave., Golden* ☎ *303/279–3113* ⊕ *www.goldencochamber.org*).

EXPLORING
TOP ATTRACTIONS

★   Thousands of beer lovers make the pilgrimage to the venerable **Miller-Coors Brewery** each year. Founded in 1873 by Adolph Coors, a 21-year-old German stowaway, today it's the largest single-site brewery in the world and part of MillerCoors. The free self-paced tour explains the malting, brewing, and packaging processes. Informal tastings are held at the end of the tour for those 21 and over in the lounge, where you can buy souvenirs in the gift shop. A free shuttle runs from the parking lot to the brewery. ✉ *13th and Ford Sts.* ☎ *303/277–2337* ⊕ *www.coors.com* ⊠ *Free* ⊗ *Mon.–Sat. 10–4 and Sun. noon–4 in summer. After Labor Day Thurs.–Sat. 10–4 and Sun. noon–4* ☞ *Children under 18 must be accompanied by an adult.*

Even if you never intend to go climbing, you may enjoy learning about
★   lofty adventures showcased at the **American Mountaineering Museum** here. Visual exhibits display experiences climbing some of the world's highest mountains. Artifacts from famous climbs are alongside exhibits about the 10th Mountain Division—men who fought in Italy in World War II, some of whom founded several of Colorado's ski resorts. ✉ *710 10th St.,* ☎ *303/996–2755* ⊕ *www.mountaineeringmuseum.org* ⊠ *$6.50* ⊗ *Tues.–Fri. 10–5, Sat. 10–6, Sun. 11–4.*

Golden's **12th Street,** a National Historic District, has a row of handsome 1860s brick buildings. Three properties—the Astor House, the Golden History Center, and Clear Creek History Park—have combined under the name of **Golden History Museums** (✉ *822 12th St.* ☎ *303/278–3557*

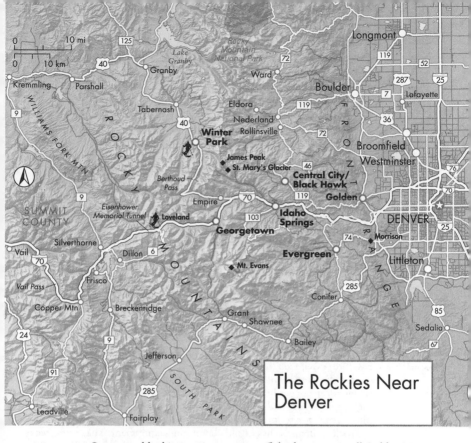

The Rockies Near Denver

⊕ *www.goldenhistorymuseums.org* ✉ *$6 for access to all Golden Museums* ☉ *Tues.–Sat. 10–4:30; June–Aug., also Sun. 11–3)*, and are all available on a $6 combination ticket. The Astor House Museum, which explores the material culture and local life of the era, is a restored late-Victorian–era Western hotel and boardinghouse.

Clear Creek History Park, interprets the Golden area circa 1843–1900 via restored structures and reproductions, including a tepee, prospector's camp, one-room schoolhouse, and cabins, and is populated with live chickens and bees. Guides in period clothing lead 45-minute tours. ✉ *11th and Arapahoe Sts.* ☎ *303/278–3557* ✉ *$6 for both museums and Clear Creek History Park* ☉ *June–Aug., Tues.–Sat. 10–4:30, Sun. 11–3; May and Sept., Sat. 10–4:30; Oct.–Apr., by appointment only; Apr.–mid-May, Sat. 10–4:30.*

★ The drive up **Lookout Mountain** to the **Buffalo Bill Museum and Grave**
↻ provides a sensational panoramic view of Denver that alone is worth the price of admission. It was this view that encouraged Bill Cody, Pony Express rider, cavalry scout, and tireless promoter of the West, to request Lookout Mountain as his burial site. Adjacent to the grave is a small museum with art and artifacts detailing Cody's life and times, as well as a souvenir shop. The grave is 100 yards past the gift shop on a paved walkway. ✉ *Rte. 5 off I–70 Exit 256, or 19th Ave. out of Golden,*

987½ Lookout Mountain Rd. ☎ *303/526–0747* ⊕ *www.buffalobill.org*
🎫 *$4* ⊙ *Museum May–Oct., daily 9–5; Nov.–Apr., Tues.–Sun. 9–4;*
grave daily until 6:30 PM.

WORTH NOTING

Ↄ Just outside Golden is a must-visit for any choo-choo lover. More than
100 vintage locomotives and cars are displayed outside the **Colorado
Railroad Museum.** Inside the replica-1880 masonry depot are historical photos and memorabilia of Puffing Billy (the nickname for steam
trains), along with an astounding model train set that steams through a
miniature-scale version of Golden. In the Roundhouse you can witness a
train's restoration in progress. ⊠ *17155 W. 44th Ave.* ☎ *303/279–4591*
⊕ *www.crrm.org* 🎫 *$8* ⊙ *Daily 9–5.*

Ↄ **Heritage Square,** a colorful re-creation of an 1880s frontier town, has
a music hall, a rip slide, an alpine slide, and some specialty shops. A
vaudeville-style review ends each evening's entertainment. ⊠ *Off the
Golden I–70 exit on Colfax/U.S. 40 north 1 mi, 18301 W. Colfax Ave.*
☎ *303/279–2789* ⊕ *www.heritagesquare.info* 🎫 *Entrance to park is
free; admission varies per ride* ⊙ *Shops: Memorial Day–Labor Day,
Mon.–Sat. 10–8, Sun. noon–8; Labor Day–Memorial Day, Tues.–Fri.
noon–5, weekends noon–6. Rides: June–Sept., daily, hrs vary.*

SPORTS AND THE OUTDOORS

GOLF

Fodor's Choice
★ **Fossil Trace Golf Club.** Created by James Engh, this spectacular 18-hole
course is set into an old quarry. You play along fairways that have been
set into deep gouges in the earth created when the quarry was mined and
hit past pillars of sandstone to reach some of the greens. Along the way,
players can stop to look at fossils of triceratops' footprints in an aeons-
old rock wall, and relics of old clay-mining equipment. The course was
ranked among the "Best Places to Play" by *Golf Digest* in 2006/2007.
⊠ *3050 Illinois St.* ☎ *303/277–8750* ⊕ *www.fossiltrace.com* 🏌 *Yards:
6,831; Green fee: $62 to walk 18 holes; $79 to ride.*

HIKING

Mount Falcon Park is a great way to explore the true foothills of the Front
Range, and the comparatively low elevation makes it a good warm-up
for higher ventures. Early in the morning mule deer can be seen grazing on the adjacent slopes. Take the **Turkey Trot Trail** from the east
parking lot in the Morrison Town Park marked with a "hikers only"
sign. The trail winds 1.7 mi up the east face of Mount Falcon through
brushy slopes before curving behind the mountain up a forested draw to
top out at around 7,000 feet. The trail loops back around and connects
to the Castle Trail for a 1.3-mi easy return to the parking lot. Allow
about 90 minutes. ⚠ **CAUTION: Stay on the path to avoid critters, including
rattlesnakes, that lie in the grass.** ⊠ *Jefferson County Open Space, start
at east parking lot* ⊕ *www.co.jefferson.co.us.*

WHERE TO EAT AND STAY

$–$$
AMERICAN
Fodor's Choice
★ ✕ **Woody's Wood Fired Pizza.** Woody's has a full menu, with pastas,
chicken, calzones, and burgers, but it's more fun to choose the $9.49
all-you-can-eat pizza, soup, and salad bar. The choices on the pizza bar
range from classic to It's Greek to Me and Margherita, and the salad is

always fresh. Woody's is so popular that the choices are always just out of the oven. Don't be surprised if you have to join the throng of families and college students waiting outside for a table on a busy night. ✉ *1305 Washington Ave.80401* ☎ *303/277–0443* ⊕ *www.woodysgolden.com* ⊟ *AE, D, MC, V* ☽ *Daily 11 AM–midnight.*

$$$ ⛄ **Golden Hotel.** Right in the heart of Golden, this hotel was renovated in early 2009, and is now a comfortable place to stay midway between downtown Denver and the mountains. The rooms now have beds covered by chocolate-colored ulta-suede duvets and quality bedding with triple sheeting, backed by a faux-leather chocolate headboard. Expect flat-screen TVs, CD players, free local calls, Wi-Fi, and bottled water in the rooms. Request a room overlooking Clear Creek. If you're traveling alone, have a drink at the community table at the inside bar, or choose the outdoor bar, with heaters for cold days. The restaurant, remodeled in muted greys and browns, has a contemporary feel. **Pros:** downtown and riverside setting. **Cons:** this hotel caters to businesspeople, so you may see many suits. ✉ *800 11th St.,* ☎ *800/233–7214 or 303/279–0100* ⊕ *www.TheGoldenHotel.com* ⇦ *62 room* ⚷ *In-room: a/c, refrigerator (some), Wi-Fi. In-hotel: restaurant, room service, bar, gym, Wi-Fi, parking (free), some pets allowed* ⊟ *AE, D, MC, V.*

EVERGREEN

20 mi west of Golden via U.S. 6 east, C–470, I–70 west, and CO Hwy. 74 (Evergreen Pkwy.); 28 mi west of Denver.

Once a quiet mountain town, today Evergreen is a tony community filled with upscale to extravagantly designed homes. The downtown core remains rustic in feel, however, and on warm-weather weekends it's filled with tourists and Denverites escaping the city heat. Visitors browse the eclectic mix of shops and mingle with locals walking their dogs on the path, which circles Lake Evergreen.

GETTING HERE AND AROUND
Where Colorado Highway 74 and County Highway 73 meet, 45 minutes from downtown Denver. Once you're in the heart of town, it's easy to find parking and explore on foot.

WHEN TO GO
The annual multiday **Evergreen Jazz Fest** (⊕ *www.evergreenjazz.org*) in July features musicians from around the country.

EXPLORING
The **Hiwan Homestead Museum** is a restored log cabin built between 1890 and 1930 that shows a popular and relaxed mountain summertime lifestyle. The museum, which includes three other buildings, has an exceptional collection of Southwestern Indian artifacts. ✉ *4208 S. Timbervale Dr.* ☎ *720/497–7650* ⊕ *www.co.jefferson.co.us/openspace/openspace_T56_R10.htm* ⛱ *Free.*

WHERE TO STAY

$$–$$$ ⛄ **Highland Haven Creekside Inn.** Walking distance from downtown Evergreen, the inn has a combination of standard and luxury rooms, suites,

Fodor's Choice   and cottages ($$$$) set alongside Bear Creek, where guests can go trout

★

fishing. Look for amenities such as flat-screen TVs, gourmet breakfasts, fireplaces, and Jacuzzis in the luxury rooms and cabins, which have even more privacy. Away from downtown, this mountain inn offers more seclusion and romance than other Evergreen lodging. **Pros:** ideally located for travelers who want to stay in a mountain town but be 35 minutes from downtown Denver or Georgetown; very quiet; romantic. **Cons:** bathrooms tend to be small; you'll have to stroll into Evergreen or drive for dinner. ⊠ *4395 Independence Trail* ☎ *303/674–3577 or 800/459–2406* ⊕ *www.highlandhaven.com* ⇆ *4 standard rooms, 2 luxury rooms, 5 suites, 6 cottages* ⚷ *In-room: kitchen (some), DVD, Wi-Fi. In-hotel: some pets allowed* ⊟ *AE, D, DC, MC, V* ⦿ *BP.*

SHOPPING

★ **Evergreen Art Gallery** (⊠ *28195 Hwy. 74* ☎ *303/674–4871*) has an excellent collection of contemporary decorative and useful ceramics, art glass, photographs, and other fine craft work.

CENTRAL CITY AND BLACK HAWK

18 mi west of Golden via U.S. 6 and Rte. 119; 38 mi west of Denver.

Recent changes in the gambling laws have created a "gold rush" to Black Hawk and Central City. As of summer 2009 the casinos may stay open 24/7, offer craps and roulette, and the betting limit was raised to $100. The two former mining towns edge up against each other with more than 40 casinos, several that are topped by big hotels. Central City offers a fleeting sense of what the original mining town looked like.

GETTING HERE AND AROUND

Both towns are about a 45-minute drive from Denver. If you want to start in Black Hawk, take the narrow and winding Colorado Highway 119. If you'd rather start in Central City, head up I–70 and take the wide Central City Parkway. Bus transportation is also available from Denver and Golden through most of the casinos and the Opera House.

TIMING

You can cover Central City and Black Hawk's main attractions in a few hours on foot, although they're hard to find amidst the crowds of gamblers.

ESSENTIALS

Visitor Info Black Hawk–Central City Visitors & Convention Bureau (☎ *303/282–8800* ⊕ *www.visitbhcc.com*).

TOP EXPERIENCE: GAMBLING

There are more than 20 casinos in Black Hawk and Central City. Many of the casinos in Central City are in buildings dating from the 1860s—from jails to mansions—and their plush interiors have been lavishly decorated to re-create the Old West era—a period when this town was known as the "Richest Square Mile on Earth." Black Hawk looks like builders stuck a load of big Vegas-style hotels and casinos right in the middle of once-quiet mountainous terrain. Virtually every casino has a restaurant with the usual all-you-can-eat buffet. The biggest casinos are in newer buildings in Black Hawk. Hotel deals are common.

The largest casinos, owned by the same company and topped with hotel rooms, are **Isle Casino and Hotel and Lady Luck Hotel and Casino** (✉ *401 Main St. and 340 Main St., Black Hawk* ☎ *800/843–4753* ⊕ *black-hawk. isleofcapricasinos.com/*). **Doc Holliday Casino** (✉ *131 Main St., Central City* ☎ *303/582–1400* ⊕ *www.dochollidaycasino.net*) is set in one of the historic buildings in Central City.

EXPLORING

★ Opera has been staged at the **Central City Opera House,** the nation's fifth-oldest opera, almost every year since opening night in 1878. Lillian Gish has acted, Beverly Sills has sung, and many other greats have performed in the Opera House. Performances are held in summer only. ✉ *124 Eureka St., Central City* ☎ *303/292–6700, 800/851–8175 Denver box office* ⊕ *www.centralcityopera.org* ☉ *Late June–early Aug.*

Teller House was once one of the West's ritziest hotels. Built in 1872, the first $30,000 for this hotel and its name came from Senator Henry Teller, the first U.S. Secretary of the Interior from Colorado. Adorning the floor of the famous Face Bar within the house is a portrait of a woman. Despite rumors about her identity, she is none other than the wife of the painter, Herndon Davis. He painted the portrait in 1936. Teller House serves box lunches during the six-week summer opera season. Tours are available. ✉ *120 Eureka St.,80427 Central City* ☎ *303/582–5283* ▤ *AE, D, MC, V* ☉ *Memorial Day–Labor Day, Tues.–Sun. 10–5. Closed Mon.*

At the **Gilpin History Museum,** photos and reproductions, as well as vintage pieces from different periods of Gilpin County history, paint a richly detailed portrait of life in a typical rowdy mining community. ✉ *228 High St., Central City* ☎ *303/582–5283* ⊕ *www.gilpinhistory.org* ▤ *$5; $8 includes admission to Thomas House Museum* ☉ *Late May– early Sept., daily 11–4; mid-Sept.–late May, by appointment only.*

WHERE TO EAT AND STAY

$$–$$$
SOUTHWESTERN
✕ **White Buffalo Grille.** Inside Black Hawk's Lodge Casino, the focus here is on steaks, seafood such as honey-bourbon glazed salmon, and Colorado rack of lamb. Garlic-herb mashed potatoes, creamed corn, and rice pilaf can be ordered as sides. For something lighter, try the tenderloin salad with beef tips pan-seared in a teriyaki sauce, jasmine rice, mixed greens, and an Asian vinaigrette. The atmosphere is upscale, and the views from the all-glass enclosure on a bridge above Richmond Street are divine. ✉ *Lodge Casino, 240 Main St., Black Hawk* ☎ *303/582– 6375* ▤ *AE, D, DC, MC, V* ☉ *Closed Mon. No lunch.*

$$
▦ **Chase Creek B&B.** This small historic house was nearly a casualty of a planned casino before owners Hal and Karen Midcap had it moved to the banks of namesake Chase Creek. The Yankee and Sleepy Hollow rooms are done up in contemporary Victorian style with lace curtains and pastel walls, while the attic Polar Star room has Mission-style furniture. Pros: two rooms have private hot tubs; in a quiet area. Cons: almost all of the nearby restaurants are in big casinos; a drive to Central City; only three rooms, so book far in advance. ✉ *250 Chase St., Black Hawk* ☎ *303/582–3550* ⊕ *www.chasecreekinn.com* ➟ *3 rooms* ♿ *In-room: no a/c. In-hotel: no kids under 21* ▤ *D, MC, V* ◎*BP.*

IDAHO SPRINGS

11 mi south of Central City via Central City Pkwy. and I–70; 33 mi west of Denver via I–70.

Colorado prospectors struck their first major vein of gold here on January 7, 1859. That year local mines dispatched half of all the gold used by the U.S. Mint—ore worth a whopping $2 million. Today the quaint town recalls its mining days, especially along portions of Colorado Boulevard, where pastel Victorians will transport you back to a century giddy with all that glitters.

GETTING HERE AND AROUND

After taking one of the I–70 Idaho Springs exits, it's hard to get lost, because the central part of this small town is bordered by the highway on one side and landlocked by a steep mountainside just a few blocks away. Head to the center of town, park, and walk around.

EXPLORING

TOP ATTRACTIONS

☺ During gold-rush days the **Argo Gold Mill** processed more than $100
★ million worth of the precious metal. To transport the ore from mines in Central City, workers dug through solid rock to construct a tunnel to Central City, 4½ mi away. When completed in 1910 the Argo Tunnel was the longest in the world. During a tour of the mine and mill, guides explain how this monumental engineering feat was accomplished. Admission includes the small museum and a gold-panning lesson. This tour focuses more on the processing of gold than visiting a gold mine. ⊠ *2350 Riverside Dr.* ☎ *303/567–2421* ⊕ *www.historicargotours.com* ⊠ *$15* ⊗ *Mid-Apr.–mid-Oct., daily 9–6, weather permitting.*

At the **Phoenix Gold Mine** a seasoned miner leads tours underground, where you can wield 19th-century excavating tools or pan for gold. Whatever riches you find are yours to keep. ⊠ *Off Trail Creek Rd.* ☎ *303/567–0422* ⊕ *www.phoenixgoldmine.com* ⊠ *$10; $5 for gold panning only* ⊗ *Daily 10–6, weather permitting.*

WORTH NOTING

Idaho Springs presently prospers from the hot springs at **Indian Springs Resort.** Around the springs, known to the Ute natives as the "healing waters of the Great Spirit," are geothermal caves that were used by tribes as a neutral meeting site. The hot springs, a translucent dome–covered mineral-water swimming pool, mud baths, and geothermal caves are the primary draws for the resort. You don't need to be an overnight guest to soak in the mineral-rich waters; day rates start at $18 for the geothermal cave baths (depending on type of bath and day of week), outdoor Jacuzzi baths $21.50, and $14 for the pool. ⊠ *302 Soda Creek Rd.* ☎ *303/989–6666* ⊕ *www.indianspringsresort. com* ⊠ *Varies according to whether one uses the bath, pool* ⊗ *Daily 7:30 AM–10:30 PM.*

Within sight of Indian Springs Resort is a 600-foot waterfall, Bridal Veil Falls. The imposing **Charlie Tayler Water Wheel**—the largest in the state—was constructed in the 1890s by a miner who attributed his strong constitution to the fact that he never shaved, took baths, or kissed women. ⊠ *South of Idaho Springs on I–70.*

Fodor'sChoice
★

St. Mary's Glacier is a great place to enjoy a mountain hike and the outdoors for a few hours. From the exit, it's a beautiful 10-mi drive up to a forested hanging valley to the glacier trailhead. The glacier, technically a large snowfield compacted in a mountain saddle at the timberline, is thought to be the southernmost glacier in the United States. During drought years it all but vanishes; a wet winter creates a wonderful Ice Age playground throughout the following summer. Most visitors are content to make the steep 0.75-mi hike on a rock-strewn path up to the base of the glacier to admire the snowfield and sparkling sapphire lake. The intrepid hiker, with the right type of gear, can climb up the rocky right-hand side of the snowfield to a plateau less than a mile above for sweeping views of the Continental Divide. Because of its proximity to Denver, St. Mary's Glacier is a popular weekend getaway for summer hikers, snowboarders, and skiers. There are no facilities or parking, except for a rough pull-out area near the base of the trail, and you risk a ticket if you park on private property. Don't look for a St. Mary's Glacier sign on I–70; it's off the Fall River Road sign. ⊠ *I–70 Exit 238, west of Idaho Springs.*

Fodor'sChoice
★

The incomparable **Mount Evans Scenic and Historic Byway**—the highest paved road in the United States—leads to the summit of 14,264-foot-high Mount Evans. This is one of only two Fourteeners in the United States that you can drive up (the other is her southern sister, Pikes Peak). More than 7,000 feet are climbed in 28 mi, and the road tops out at 14,134 feet, 130 feet shy of the summit, which is a ¼-mi stroll from the parking lot. The toll road winds past placid lakes and through stands of towering Douglas firs and bristlecone pines. This is one of the best places in the state to catch a glimpse of shaggy white mountain goats and regal bighorn sheep. Small herds of the nimble creatures stroll from car to car looking for handouts. Feeding them is prohibited, however. Keep your eyes peeled for other animals, including deer, elk, and feather-footed ptarmigans. ⊠ *From Idaho Springs, State Road 103 leads south 14 mi to the entrance to Hwy 5, which is the beginning of the scenic byway. The U.S. Forest Service fee station is here on State Rd. 3* ☎ *303/567–3000* ⊕ *www.mountevans.com* ☞ *$10* ☉ *The road is open only when road conditions are safe. Generally, the last 5 mi to summit, Memorial Day–Labor Day.*

★

Although most travelers heading to Central City take the new highway from I–70, adventurous souls can take the **Oh-My-Gawd Road.** Built in the 1870s to transfer ore, this challenging drive climbs nearly 2,000 feet above Idaho Springs to Central City. After traveling along a series of hairpin curves you arrive at the summit, where you are treated to sweeping views of Mount Evans. The dusty road is often busy with mining traffic, so keep your windows up and your eyes open. From Idaho Springs (Exit 240), drive west through town on Colorado Boulevard. Turn right on 23rd Avenue, left on Virginia Street, and right at Virginia Canyon Road (279). ⊠ *Hwy. 279.*

WHERE TO EAT AND STAY

$-$$ ✕**Beau Jo's Pizza.** This always-hopping pizzeria is the area's original
PIZZA aprés-ski destination. Be prepared for a wait on winter weekends, because Denverites often stop in Idaho Springs for dinner until the traffic thins down. Topping choices for the famous olive oil–and–honey pizza crust range from traditional to exotic. ⊠ *1517 Miner St., ☎ 303/567–4376 ⊕ www.beaujos.com* ▤ *AE, D, MC, V.*

$-$$ ✕**Buffalo Bar & Restaurant.** No surprise as to the specialties here: burg-
AMERICAN ers, fajitas, chili, and steak sandwiches, all made with heart-healthy bison meat. American Buffalo, or bison, is raised at local ranches, and the light red meat is popular because of it's low fat content. A Western theme dominates the dining room, where the walls are jam-packed with frontier memorabilia. The ornate bar dates from 1886. ⊠ *1617 Miner St., ☎ 303/567–2729 ⊕ www.buffalorestaurant.com* ▤ *AE, D, DC, MC, V.*

$-$$ ✕**Tommyknocker Brewery & Pub.** Harking back to gold-rush days, this
AMERICAN casual bar and restaurant is usually filled with skiers in winter and travelers or Denverites year-round who want to meet High Country friends halfway. The suds have a distinctly local flavor and sporty names like Alpine Glacier Lager and Black Powder Stout. In addition to fare such as buffalo burritos, the brewery has plenty of vegetarian options. ⊠ *1401 Miner St., ☎ 303/567–2688 ⊕ www.tommyknocker.com* ▤ *AE, D, MC, V.*

$$$ ▦**Peck House.** About a 10-minute drive from either Georgetown or Idaho Springs via I–70, this red-roof inn in Empire is Colorado's oldest continually operating hostelry. The dining room ($$$–$$$$) is crammed with period antiques, including tinted lithographs and etched-glass shades for the gas lamps that once hung in the state capitol. Game is the house specialty: expertly prepared quail and venison (perfect with the hearty cabernet sauce) are among the standouts. Individually decorated rooms are awash in Victorian splendor. **Pros:** classic lodging experience with nice restaurant; a few fun shops nearby. **Cons:** remote location: Winter Park is still 35 minutes away in good weather; Idaho Springs and Georgetown are 10 to 20 minutes away in opposite directions on I–70. ⌂ *Box 428, Empire 80438 ☎ 303/569–9870 ⊕ www. thepeckhouse.com ⇆ 11 rooms, 10 with bath ⚬ In-room: no a/c, no phone, no TV. In-hotel: restaurant* ▤ *AE, D, DC, MC, V* ⍾ *CP.*

SHOPPING

Ramblin' Rose Ranch (⊠ *1430 Miner St.* ☎ *303/567–1582*) sells all things Western, from attractive clothing and jewelry to housewares.

Wild Grape (⊠ *1435 Miner St.* ☎ *303/567–4670*) is filled with an eclectic collection of gift items and souvenirs and an outstanding collection of greeting cards.

CONTINENTAL DIVIDE AREA

As I–70 climbs higher into the Rockies, the population and air begin to thin. Georgetown is a former mining town; Winter Park is a mountain resort town with a more recent history. Nearby Loveland is smaller, but one of the locals favorite ski areas because of its proximity to Denver.

WINTER PARK

36 mi west of Idaho Springs; 67 mi west of Denver via I–70 and U.S. 40.

Winter Park Resort has made some dramatic changes recently, and now there's a small village at the base anchored by Zephyr Mountain Lodge and the Fraser Crossing and Founders Pointe condominiums. The Village Cabriolet—an open gondola—takes day skiers from a big parking lot to one end of the village, and they must walk past most of the shops, restaurants, and bars before reaching the lifts at the base of the resort.

GETTING HERE AND AROUND

During the winter you can catch a ride on shuttle buses that move between the resort and the town of Winter Park, a few miles away. But in the summer you'll need a car to vacation here. Valley Taxi is the local taxi service. Home James provides shuttle service between Denver Airport and the resort. Amtrak stops at nearby Fraser and Granby.

WHEN TO GO

From late November to mid-April good snow attracts winter sports lovers. Winter Park is equally popular in summer with hikers, bicyclists, and golfers, but has few tourist attractions besides its natural beauty. Mountain bikers flock here because of the diversity of the trails and the growing emphasis on downhill mountain biking.

ESSENTIALS

Visitor Info Winter Park/Fraser Valley Chamber of Commerce (⌂ *Box 3236, Winter Park 80482* ☎ *970/726–4118 or 800/903–7275* ⊕ *www.playwinterpark.com*). **Winter Park Resort** (☎ *800/729–5813 or 970/726–1564* ⊕ *www.winterparkresort.com*).

DOWNHILL SKIING AND SNOWBOARDING

★ **Winter Park** is really two interconnected ski areas: Winter Park and Mary Jane, both open to skiers and snowboarders. Between the two peaks there are four distinct skiable sections: Winter Park; the "Jane"; Vasquez Ridge, which is primarily intermediate cruising; and Vasquez Cirque, which has seriously steep inbounds off-piste terrain. Pick a meeting place for lunch in case you and your friends get separated.

The skiing on the Winter Park and Vasquez Ridge trails is generally family-friendly, and there are segregated areas for beginners. Winter Park's runs promise lots of learning terrain for beginners and easy cruising for intermediates. On busy weekends Vasquez Ridge is a good place for escaping crowds, partly because this area is a bit more difficult to find, but the run-outs can be long.

Mary Jane is famous for her bumps and chutes, delivering 2,610 vertical feet of unrelenting moguls on a variety of trails, although there are a couple of groomed intermediate runs. Experts gravitate toward the far end of the Jane to runs like Trestle and Derailer, or to Hole-in-the-Wall, Awe, and other chutes. Expert skiers and riders seeking inbound off piste–style terrain hike over to the Vasquez Cirque.

The resort's Eagle Wind terrain has advanced steeps and deeps tucked among the trees. Panoramic Express, the highest six-person lift in North America, provides access to above-the-tree-line skiing at Parsenn Bowl, Perry's Peak, and Forever Eva, as well as terrain and gladed sections. The pitch in many areas of Parsenn's is moderate, making the bowl a terrific place for intermediate skiers to try powder and crud-snow skiing.

The resort's Rail Yard, with its superpipe and terrain parks, is specially designed for freestylers. A progressive park system allows skiers and snowboarders to start small and work their way up to the bigger and more difficult features. There is also a limited access park, the Dark Territory, which is for experts only and requires an additional fee. ☎ *800/729–5813 or 970/726–5587* ⊕ *www.skiwinterpark.com.*

FACILITIES   3,060-foot vertical drop; 3,070 skiable acres; 142 trails; 8% beginner, 17% intermediate, 19% advanced, 56% expert; 24 lifts; 2 high-speed six-person chairs, 7 high-speed quad chairs, 4 triple chairs, 6 double chairs, 5 surface lifts.

LESSONS   For adult skiers and snowboarders, the **Winter Park Ski and Ride School**
AND   (⊠ *Balcony House* ☎ *800/729–7907*) has half-day lessons starting at
PROGRAMS $59. Daylong children's programs, which include lunch, start at $105. Winter Park is home to the **National Sports Center for the Disabled** (⌂ *Box 1290, Winter Park 80482* ☎ *303/726–1540*), one of the country's largest and best programs for skiers with disabilities.

LIFT TICKETS   The walk-up rate is $92, but you can save on multiday tickets, and many lodging packages include discounted tickets.

RENTALS   **Winter Park Resort Rentals** (⊠ *Zephyr Mountain Lodge*) rents skiing and snowboarding gear from Village location (☎ *970/726–1664*) and west Portal location (☎ *970/726–1662*) and includes free overnight storage. Rental equipment is also available from shops downtown.

NORDIC SKIING
TRACK SKIING

About 8 mi northwest of Winter Park, **Devil's Thumb Ranch** grooms about 65 mi of cross-country trails. Some skiing is along fairly level tree-lined trails; some is with more ups and downs and wide-open views. The ranch has rentals, lessons, and backcountry tours. ⊠ *3530 County Rd. 83, Tabernash* ☎ *970/726–5632 or 800/933–4339* ⊕ *www. devilsthumbranch.com* 🎿 *Trail fee $15.*

Snow Mountain Ranch, 12 mi northwest of Winter Park, has a 62-mi track system that includes almost 3 mi of trails lighted for night skiing. The ranch is a YMCA facility (with discounts for members) and has added bonuses such as a sauna and an indoor pool. Lessons, rentals, and on-site lodging are available. ⊠ *1101 County Rd. 53, Granby* ☎ *970/887–2152 or 800/777–9622* ⊕ *www.ymcarockies.org* 🎿 *Trail fee $15.*

BACKCOUNTRY SKIING

South of Winter Park, **Berthoud Pass** (✉ *Hwy. 40* ⊕ *www.berthoudpass. com*) is a hard place to define. At the top of the pass there is a former downhill skiing area—its lifts have been removed—which is popular with some backcountry skiers. There's no regular avalanche control on these former runs. Skiers and snowboarders venturing in must have their own rescue equipment, including beacons, shovels, and probes. Backcountry skiing on the slopes from the former ski area or anywhere else on Berthoud Pass is only for very experienced, well-conditioned, and properly prepared skiers and riders. You must check current avalanche conditions before starting out, although that's no guarantee. In addition to skiing the slopes of the former ski areas, many people pull into parking areas elsewhere alongside the highway over Berthoud Pass and go crosscountry or backcountry skiing. At many spots along the highway you'll see signs warning of avalanche blasting at any time with longe-range weaponry. (This blasting is done to help prevent avalanches from covering the highway.)

OTHER SPORTS AND THE OUTDOORS

GOLF

Pole Creek Golf Club. Designed by Denis Griffiths, Pole Creek has three 9-hole, par-36 courses and fantastic views of the mountains. You can play any combination of 18 holes, but try to get on the Ridge 9, which has particularly challenging holes with slippery greens. ✉ *5827 County Rd. 51* ☎ *970/887–9195* ⊕ *www.polecreekgolf.com* ⚑ *Meadow: Yards: 3,497/2,476. Ranch: Yards: 3,609/2,532. Ridge: Yards: 3,603/2,526. Green fee: $73/$93 for 18 holes.*

Headwaters is an 18-hole course laid out through a natural landscape passing very few buildings. The original course by Micheal Asmundson is being redesigned by the Nicklaus Design firm to turn it into a more walkable course. The back nine is fraught with interesting challenges and fast greens. ✉ *1000 Village Rd., Granby* ☎ *970/887–2709* ⊕ *www. granbyranch.com/golf* ⚑ *7,210 from the golds. Green fee: $70/$90 for 18 holes plus $15 for cart.*

HIKING

At 12,804 feet, **Byers Peak** is one of the tallest mountains overlooking Fraser, and the highest point in the Byers Peak Wilderness Area. The trail climbs the northern ridge of Byers through lodgepole pine and Engelmann spruce forests before entering the spaciousness of the alpine tundra at around 11,200 feet. Climbers are rewarded with views of the Indian Peaks Wilderness, the Gore Range, and Middle Park. The trail is only 1.5 mi, but it climbs 2,400 feet. ■ TIP→ **If you aren't used to it, high altitude can catch you off guard.** Take plenty of water with you and slather on the sunscreen. In summer an early morning start is best. Afternoon thunderstorms are frequent, and you should never be above the tree line during a storm with lightning. Plan on three hours for the round-trip hike. ✉ *Sulphur Ranger District, Arapaho-Roosevelt National Forest* ☎ *970/887–4100* ⊕ *www.fs.fed.us/r2/arnf.*

HORSEBACK RIDING

For leisurely horseback-riding tours of the Fraser Valley, your best bet is **Cabin Creek Stables at Devil's Thumb Ranch** (✉ *3530 County Rd. 83, Tabernash* ☎ *800/933–4339* ⊕ *www.devilsthumbranch.com*).

MOUNTAIN BIKING

★ Winter Park is one of the leading mountain-biking destinations in the Rockies, with some 30 mi of trails crisscrossing the main part of the resort and 600 more mi off the beaten path. **Vazquez Creek** (✉ *Trailhead: parking garage next to the visitor center at the junction of U.S. 40 and Vazquez Rd.*) is an easy but fun 4.5-mi trail that runs along a forest of blue spruce, fir, and aspen. The trail sticks to dirt roads with easy grades; the elevation gain is barely 600 feet. For more serious bikers the side trails have challenging climbs and rewarding vistas.

SNOWMOBILING

Rentals and guided tours are available from **Grand Adventures** (✉ *81699 U.S. Highway 40 S* ☎ *970/726–9247 or 800/726–9247*). Rates range from $65 per hour to $200 for a full-day tour.

SNOW TUBING

Slide downhill on an oversize inner tube; hold onto the tow-lift for a ride up to the top to do it all over again and again. When you get cold, head into the warming hut at **Fraser Snow Tubing Hill** (✉ *County Rd. 72 and Fraser Valley Pkwy.* ☎ *970/726–5954*). The hill is lighted at night, and the rate is $17 per hour.

WHERE TO EAT

$$ ✕**Carver's.** Long a local and Denverite favorite for breakfast, this casual
AMERICAN joint makes Belgian waffles that are as delicious as the variety of Bene-
★ dicts and scrambles with fresh orange or grapefruit juice. Lunch is also served. ✉ *93 Cooper Creek Way, behind Cooper Creek Sq.* ☎ *970/726–8202* ⊕ *www.carvewrsbakery.com* ▭ *AE, D, MC, V.*

$$ ✕**Deno's Mountain Bistro.** A sizable selection of beers from around the
AMERICAN world helps make this casual establishment the liveliest spot in town. But what sets it apart is a wine list that's comprehensive and fairly priced—a rarity in low-key Winter Park. The cellar full of fine vintages is a labor of love for Deno and his son, the powerhouse duo behind the restaurant. The menu ranges from sesame-crusted seared ahi tuna to Kobe "wagyu" cap of rib eye, all expertly prepared and served by friendly staffers who know their stuff. ✉ *78911 U.S. 40* ☎ *970/726–5332* ⊕ *www.denosmountainbistro.com* ▭ *AE, D, MC, V.*

$$$$ ✕**Dining Room at Sunspot.** Reached via chairlift during the day and gon-
Fodor'sChoice dola at night, this massive log-and-stone structure set at 10,700 feet above
★ sea level is a real stunner. Douglas-fir beams, Southwestern rugs on the
AMERICAN walls, and a huge stone fireplace in the bar add to the rustic charm. The real draw is the view of the surrounding mountains, including the peaks marching along the Continental Divide. A prix-fixe menu includes game and fish paired with side dishes such as wild rice and potatoes roasted in olive oil and herbs. Elk Tournedos, elk tenderloin with a sun-dried cherry demi-glace and red roasted potatoes, is one example of the signature dishes. Wines can be chosen to complement your meal. ✉ *Top of Zephyr*

Express Lift ☎ *970/726–1446* ⊕ *www.skiwinterpark.com* △ *Reservations essential* ⊟ *AE, D, DC, MC, V* ⊙ *Hrs vary with the season.*

$$ ✕**Hernando's Pizza Pub.** Bring along a dollar bill that you're willing to

PIZZA leave on the wall. It will joins hundreds of others that have been drawn on, written on, and tacked up in rows around and above the bar. Nothing fancy here, just good pasta and pizzas that keep locals and regular resort visitors coming back. If you're in a creative mood, build your own pie, with a combination of the ordinary toppings, from pepperoni to sausage, then add more unusual extras like almonds or jalapeños. ✉ 78199 U.S. 40, ☎ *970/726–5409* ⊕ *www.hernandospizzapub.com* ⊟ *AE, D, MC, V.*

$$ ✕**Smokin' Moe's Ribhouse & Saloon.** You'll fill up on delicious spicy smoky

♨ ribs, smoked BBQ chicken, or Southern-fried catfish served in huge

SOUTHERN portions, plus a choice of sides including creamy coleslaw, mashers and gravy, or smoky beans. Diners are served at long tables covered with checkered tablecloths, and there's a salad bar for a lighter option. Check out "Moe," a lifelike mannequin slouched down on a bar stool hiding behind sunglasses. ✉ 78930 U.S. 40, ☎ 970/726–4600 ⊕ *www. smokinmoes.com* ⊟ *AE, D, MC, V.*

WHERE TO STAY

GUEST RANCH ⊞**Devil's Thumb Ranch.** Many visitors come to this 5,000-acre ranch

$$$$ outside Winter Park for the unrivaled cross-country skiing, with 100

Fodor'sChoice km of groomed trails, but they wind up staying for the resort's com-

★ fort and privacy. Choose from a room or suite in the the 2008-built lodge or a cabin in the woods. The cabins range in size from 675 to 2,200 square feet, but all have wood-burning fireplaces and furnishings that reflect the resort's ranching history. In the loft cabins the beds are upstairs and bathrooms downstairs. In the lodge, upscale, Western-style rooms have some paneled walls (from lumber harvested at the ranch), pine furniture, and beds covered with colorful quilts. Some rooms have stone fireplaces. From tapping the power of geothermal springs to using trees cleared on-site to build part of the new lodge, to the on-site Ranch House restaurant ($$$) that uses sustainable and organic ingredients, this resort lives green. Take in a yoga class at the full-service spa or work with cattle on a horseback ride, fly-fish, mountain-bike, and hike in the surrounding area. **Pros:** terrific cross-country skiing and horseback riding; top-notch restaurant. **Cons:** in winter getting there can be rough; one of the pricier properties in the state; must drive to eat in any other restaurant or cook your own meals. ✉ *3530 County Rd. 83, Tabernash,* ☎ *800/933–4339* ⊕ *www.devilsthumbranch.com* ⌨ *52 lodge rooms, 16 cabins* ♿ *In-room cabins: no a/c, no TV. In-hotel: restaurant, bar, pool, spa, public Internet, parking (free), some pets allowed* ⊟ *AE, D, MC, V.*

$$–$$$ ⊞**Gasthaus Eichler.** Antler chandeliers cast a cheery glow as Strauss waltzes lilt softly in the background at this little guesthouse. The cozy guest rooms charm you with their lace curtains, wooden armoires, and beds piled high with down comforters. Here you'll find two of Winter Park's most romantic dining spots ($$–$$$): the Fondue Stube, where dinner and dessert fondues bubble, and Dezeley's, where veal and other meats are grilled to perfection. **Pros:** dreamy setting; great dining options. **Cons:** you're right in the middle of town, and on busy

weekends the streets in front of the hotel can be busy. ⊠ *78786 U.S. 40,*
☎ *970/726–5133 or 800/543–3899 ⊕ www.gasthauseichler.com* ⇆ *15
rooms ₺ In-hotel: 2 restaurants* ▤ *AE, MC, V* ⎸⊙⎹ *BP, MAP.*

$$$–$$$$ ⚏ **Iron Horse Resort.** On the banks of the Fraser River, this condo-style
hotel is ski-in ski-out, but it's removed from the resort's base village.
Simple wood and stone details fill studios for couples and the one-
and two-bedroom apartments for families. Most apartments have
full kitchens and balconies with views of a grove of aspen. **Pros:** truly
ski-in ski-out; set in a quiet location. **Cons:** isolated area, so you must
drive to the base village or to town for all the restaurants and shops;
must create your own nightlife. ⊠ *101 Iron Horse Way, Winter Park*
☎ *970/726–8851 or 800/621–8190 ⊕ www.ironhorse-resort.com* ⇆ *85
rooms ₺ In-room: kitchen, Wi-Fi. In-hotel: restaurant, bar, pool, gym*
▤ *AE, D, DC, MC, V.*

$$$ ⚏ **Vintage Hotel.** Right next to the Village Cabriolet lift, the Vintage
is the best value if you want to be close to the resort base. Most of
the comfortable rooms look out onto the mountains. The hotel has
nine room configurations, from standard rooms to lofted studios; some
have gas or wood-burning fireplaces. **Pros:** from door to base village
in five minutes on the cabriolet; pet-friendly property. **Cons:** its popularity means it might get a bit noisy at times; you'll need to drive or
take a shuttle to the town of Winter Park. ⊠ *100 Winter Park Dr.,*
☎ *970/726–8801 or 800/472–7017 ⊕ www.vintagehotel.com* ⇆ *118
rooms ₺ In-room: kitchen (some), Internet. In-hotel: no a/c, restaurant,
bar, pool, gym, laundry facilities, concierge, some pets allowed* ▤ *AE,
D, DC, MC, V.*

$$$–$$$$ ⚏ **Wild Horse Inn.** Tucked into the woods on the way to Devil's Thumb
★   Ranch, this mountain retreat is a bit off the beaten path. Your reward,
however, is complete relaxation. The lodge rooms, many with beamed
ceilings and four-poster beds, have private balconies overlooking the
forest; breakfast—perhaps peach-and-pecan pancakes or an apple,
bacon, and Brie frittata—is served in the handsome lodge or in bed.
The secluded cabins—stylish, not rustic—have a fireplace and small
kitchenette. **Pros:** very quiet at night; after an exhausting day of ski-
ing you can book an hour with the on-site massage therapist. **Cons:**
it's a 10- to 15-minute drive to get into Winter Park; must create your
own nightlife; the largest, loveliest room is on the first floor near the
entrance area. ⊠ *1536 County Rd. 83,* ☎ *970/726–0456 ⊕ www.
wildhorseinncolorado.com* ⇆ *7 rooms, 3 cabins ₺ In-room: no a/c,
Wi-Fi. In-hotel: no kids under 12* ▤ *AE, D, DC, MC, V* ⎸⊙⎹ *BP.*

$$$$ ⚏ **Zephyr Mountain Lodge, Frasier Crossing, and Founders Pointe.** These are
all condo complexes, some with individual hotel rooms, too, that are in
the village at the base a short walk from the base lifts, The one-, two-,
and three-bedroom units in the Zephyr are compact but comfortable,
and nicely equipped. The condos in the other two buildings appear
larger and brighter. **Pros:** all of these are nice places to stay in the win-
tertime, because they are so close to the lifts, and there are fireplaces in
most units; walk out the door and there are a few restaurants and bars.
Cons: choose other lodging in the summertime, because there is no air-
conditioning and only limited circulation in the units. If you want to

head into the town of Winter Park in the winter for nightlife or restaurants, you'll need to take a shuttle or have a car. ✉ *201 Zephyr Way,* ☎ *866/433–3908* ⊕ *www.zmlwp. com* ⤵ *175 rooms* ⚭ *In-room: no a/c, kitchen, Wi-Fi. In-hotel: restaurant, gym, laundry facilities* ⊟ *AE, D, DC, MC, V.*

NIGHTLIFE

For a bit of local color, head down the road a few miles to Fraser and the **Crooked Creek Saloon** (✉ *401 Zerex St.* ☎ *970/726–9250*). The motto here is "Eat till it hurts, drink till it feels better." Locals show up for the cheap beer during happy hour.

One of the hot spots in the base village is the colorful **Cheeky Monk** (✉ *Base of lifts, Winter Park Village,* ☎ *970/726–6871* ⊕ *www.thecheeky-monk.com*), which bills itself as a Belgian beer café.

The under-30 crowd hangs out at the **Pub** (✉ *78260 U.S. 40* ☎ *970/726–4929*), grooving to local bands. If you've never done your laundry while sipping a brew, don't miss **Buckets** (✉ *78415 U.S. 40* ☎ *970/726–3026*), a combination bar and coin laundry in the basement of the Winter Park Movie Theater. This friendly place seems to attract as many tourists as locals.

SHOPPING

Cooper Creek Square (✉ *47 Cooper Creek Way* ☎ *970/726–8891*) is filled with inexpensive souvenir shops and fine jewelers, upscale eateries and local cafés, plus live entertainment all summer in the courtyard.

GEORGETOWN

32 mi southwest of Winter Park via U.S. 40 and I–70; 50 mi west of Denver via I–70.

Georgetown rode the crest of the silver boom during the second half of the 19th century. Most of the impeccably maintained brick buildings that make up the town's historic district date from that period. Georgetown hasn't been tarted up, so it provides a true sense of what living was like in those rough-and-tumble times. It's a popular tourist stop in the summertime. Be sure to keep an eye out for the state's largest herd of rare bighorn sheep that often grazes alongside I–70 in this region.

GETTING HERE AND AROUND

Just west of where I–70 and U.S. 40 intersect, the downtown historic area is just a few blocks long and a few blocks wide, so park and start walking.

WINTER PARK LODGING ALTERNATIVES

Fodor's Choice ★ **Destinations West** is the premier source for luxury condos, town homes, and multi-bedroom, million-dollar homes on the fairways at Pole Creek, at the base of Winter Park, and in Granby by the lake. Price-wise, if you're bringing a family or a group of friends, it's worth comparing these luxury homes against regular condos. Concierge services are available. ✉ *Box 3478, Winter Park 80482* ☎ *800/545–9378* ⊕ *www.toski.com/destinations.*

CLOSE UP

Eisenhower Memorial Tunnel

As you travel west along I-70 you'll reach one of the world's engineering marvels, the 8,941-foot-long Eisenhower Memorial Tunnel. Most people who drive through take its presence for granted, but until the first lanes were opened in 1973 the only route west through the mountains was the perilous Loveland Pass, a heart-pounding roller-coaster ride. In truly inclement weather the eastern and western slopes were completely cut off from each other. Authorities first proposed the tunnel in 1937. Geologists warned about unstable rock, and through more than three decades of construction, their direst predictions came true as rock walls crumbled, steel girders buckled, and gas pockets caused mysterious explosions. When the project was finally completed, more than 500,000 cubic yards of solid granite had been removed from Mount Trelease. The original cost estimate was $1 million. By the time the second bore was completed in 1979 the tunnel's cost had skyrocketed to $340 million. Today there can be a long wait during busy weekends because so many travelers use I-70.

TIMING

Georgetown is close enough to attract day-trippers from Denver, but much of the summer the town is filled with vacationers who have come here to ride the Georgetown Loop Railroad. Weekdays are quieter than weekends.

ESSENTIALS

Visitor Info Georgetown (☎ 303/69–2405 ⊕ town.georgetown.co.us/).
Loveland Snow Report (☎ 800/736–3754 Ext. 221 ⊕ www.skiloveland.com).

EXPLORING

Fodor'sChoice   Hop on the **Georgetown Loop Railroad,** a 1920s narrow-gauge train that
★   connects Georgetown with the equally historic community of Silver
☾   Plume. The 6-mi round-trip excursion takes about 70 minutes, and
winds through vast stands of pine and fir before crossing the 95-foot-high Devil's Gate Bridge, where the track actually loops back over itself as it gains elevation. You can add on a tour of the **Lebanon Silver Mill and Mine,** which is a separate stop between the two towns. ⊠ *100 Loop Dr.80444* ☎ *888/456–6777* ⊕ *www.georgetownlooprr. com* ≤ *$22.50 for train; $29.50 for train ride and mine tour* ☉ *May–Oct., daily 10:25–2:55.*

South of Georgetown, the **Guanella Pass Scenic Byway** treats you to marvelous views of the Mount Evans Wilderness Area. Along the way—while negotiating some tight curves, especially as you head down to Grant—you'll get close views of Mount Evans as well as Grays and Torrey's peaks—two Fourteeners. It takes about 40 minutes to cross the 22-mi dirt and asphalt road. ⊠ *Rte. 381.*

Dating from 1869, **Hamill House** once was the home of silver magnate William Arthur Hamill. The Gothic Revival beauty displays most of its original wall coverings and furnishings. Don't miss the gleaming white structure's unique curved-glass conservatory. ⊠ *3rd and Argentine Sts.*

☏ *303/569–2840* ⊕ *www.historic-georgetown.org* ✉ *$4* ⊙ *Memorial Day–Labor Day, daily 10–4; Sept.–mid-Dec., weekends noon–4; Jan.–May, by appointment.*

The elaborate **Hotel de Paris,** built almost single-handedly by Frenchman Louis Dupuy in 1878, was one of the Old West's preeminent hostelries. Now a museum, the hotel depicts how luxuriously the rich were accommodated: Tiffany fixtures, lace curtains, and hand-carved furniture re-create an era of opulence. ✉ *409 6th St.* ☏ *303/569–2311* ⊕ *www.hoteldeparismuseum. org* ✉ *$4* ⊙ *June–Aug., daily 10–4:30; May and Sept.–Dec., weekends noon–4.*

DOWNHILL SKIING AND SNOWBOARDING

Because of its proximity to Denver (an hour's drive), lack of resort facilities and hotels, and few high-speed lifts, **Loveland Ski Area** is often overlooked by out-of-staters, but that's just the way locals like it. Loveland has some of the highest runs in Colorado spread across a respectable 1,365 acres serviced by 12 lifts. It's split between Loveland Valley, a good place for beginners, and Loveland Basin, a good bet for everyone else. Loveland Basin has excellent glade and open-bowl skiing and snowboarding, especially on the 2,410-foot vertical drop. Best of all, it opens early and usually stays open later than any other ski area except Arapahoe Basin. ✉ *I–70 Exit 216, 12 mi west of Georgetown* ☏ *303/571–5580 or 800/736–3754* ⊕ *www. skiloveland.com* ⊙ *Mid-Oct.–May, weekdays 9–4, weekends 8:30–4.*

FACILITIES 2,410-foot vertical drop; 1,365 skiable acres; 80 runs; 13% beginner, 41% intermediate, 46% advanced; 10 lifts; 3 doubles, 2 triples, 3 quads, 1 surface, and 1 magic carpet (ski school only).

LESSONS AND PROGRAMS **Loveland Ski School** (☏ *303/571–5580*) offers 2½-hour group "Newcomer Packages" beginning at 10 AM and 1 PM for $72 including all rental gear and an all-day lift ticket; advanced half-day lessons (a maximum of four people per group) are $55 or $85 with rental gear.

LIFT TICKETS In the early season, from opening to December 14, tickets are $45, but $56 is the regular season price. Discount tickets are on sale at local Safeway and King Soopers stores.

RENTALS **Loveland Rentals** (☏ *303/569–3203*) has two on-mountain locations. Sport packages are are $29, and performance packages are $39. Snowboard packages are $34; helmets run $10.

HIKING THE CONTINENTAL DIVIDE

The Continental Divide, that mythical geographic division that sends raindrops to either the Atlantic or Pacific ocean, makes a worthy pilgrimage for day hikers and backpackers alike in summer. Although it doesn't look dangerous to the untrained eye, the slopes off the Divide are avalanche prone, so it is an extremely dangerous place to ski in winter. The easiest way to reach the divide is to drive up U.S. Highway 6 over Loveland Pass at the Eisenhower Tunnel on I–70 and park on top of the divide. Hiking trails lead both east and west along the divide.

WHERE TO EAT AND STAY

$–$$ ✕**Red Ram.** This Georgetown landmark has been serving up some of the region's tastiest meals since the 1950s, right in the middle of the town's historic section. The secret is keeping the menu simple: burgers, ribs, and south-of-the-border favorites such as fajitas. Black-and-white photos of the town's heyday bedeck the walls, and wagon wheels decorate the balcony-railings. During the day you'll find families eating here; at night the saloon heritage is more obvious. Stop by on weekends when there's live entertainment. ⊠ *606 6th St. 80444* ☎ *303/569–2300* ⊕ *www.redramrestaurantandsaloon.com* ⊟ *AE, D, MC, V.*

$ ⊡**Georgetown Mountain Inn.** The Georgetown Mountain Inn, next door to the Old Georgetown Railroad, provides a quiet haven in the bustling town. Rooms are a step up from a basic motel, decorated with Western-style wood furniture and Southwestern blankets. A stone fireplace crowned with an elk rack greets you in the lobby, and a small indoor pool is a great place to soak after a day of skiing or exploring the High Country. **Pros:** right by the station for the Georgetown Loop railroad; Colorado rooms enhanced with pine-paneled walls and hand-hewn log headboards and bedside tables are particularly nice. **Cons:** several blocks away from the historic downtown; some guests have complained about noise. ⊠ *1100 Rose St.,* ☎ *303/569–3201 or 800/884–3201* ⊕ *www.georgetownmountaininn.com* ⇌ *33 rooms* ⚘ *In-room: Wi-Fi. In-hotel: pool, some pets allowed* ⊟ *AE, D, MC, V.*

$$ ⊡**Hotel Chateau Chamonix.** This hotel, with its blue exterior and green ★ roof doesn't look exceptional for the region outside, but inside it's a lovely property put together by local owners. An upscale feel is complete with king beds covered with duvets, flat-screen TVs, a steam shower in some rooms, and eclectic choices of furniture and art including pieces collected during the owners' European travels. **Pros:** some rooms overlook a stream and have a two-person hot tub on a porch; extras like espresso-cappuchino machines in the rooms. **Cons:** on one of the town's busy main streets; not quite within easy walking distance of the historic downtown area. ⊠ *1414 Argentine St.,* ☎ *303/569–1109 or 888/569–1109* ⊕ *www.HotelChateauChamonix.com* ⇌ *10 rooms* ⚘ *In-room: a/c, Wi-Fi. In-hotel: no-smoking rooms* ⊟ *AE, D, MC, V* ⎟⊙⎟ *CP.*

SHOPPING

The **Grizzley Creek Gallery** (⊠ *510 6th St.* ☎ *303/569–0433*) has wonderful scenic large-scale photographs of the Rockies and wildlife.

★ For a break from the I–70 weekend traffic or just a bit of local flavor, stop by **Canyon Wind** (⊠ *1500 Argentine St.,* ☎ *303/569–3152* ⊕ *www.canyonwindcellars.com*), just off the Georgetown exit. You can sample Colorado wines from the family-owned Canyon Wind Cellars, which owns the shop, order a cheese plate, and sit by the fireplace for a bit.

Summit County

WORD OF MOUTH

"Keystone is a hotel/ski resort. Keystone for dinner is nice—take the gondola to the top. Breckenridge is an old mining town—tons of character, small shops, great restaurants. And real people live there, not just tourists."

—DavidRW

"What Leadville lacks in trendy boutiques, touristy creature comforts, and upscale dining, it makes up for in rugged salt-of-the-earth authenticity . . . If you want a "real" Colorado mountain town (not a New York City stylized version of a Colorado mountain town), go to Leadville."

—furledleader

Updated by
Jad Davenport

Summit County, a mere hour's drive from the Denver Metro Area on a straight shot up Interstate 70, is Denver's playground. The wide-open mountain park ringed by 13,000-foot peaks greets westbound travelers minutes after they pop out the west portal of the Eisenhower Tunnel. The sharp-toothed Gore Range rises to the northwest and the Tenmile Range gathers up behind Breckenridge. Resting in the center of this bowl are the sapphire waters of Dillon Reservoir, an artificial lake fed by Blue River.

In winter Summit County is packed with tourists and Front Range day-trippers skiing the steeps at Arapahoe Basin, Breckenridge, Keystone, or Copper Mountain. The high density of first-rate ski resorts generally keeps lift lines low, particularly on weekdays. In summer the steady westbound traffic is mostly four-wheel drives stacked high with lake kayaks and mountain bikes.

Summit County, as its name implies, is relatively high. The town of Breckenridge sits at 9,603 feet (Aspen by comparison is at 7,908 feet), and the resort's newest ski lift tops out just shy of 13,000 feet. Visitors from sea level should take their time getting acclimated. Even Denverites find themselves breathless in the thin air. Drink lots of water and rest your first few days. There will be plenty of time to play.

ORIENTATION AND PLANNING

GETTING ORIENTED

The great east–west Colorado corridor I–70 cleaves through the heart of Summit County, punching west from Denver past Idaho Springs and Georgetown. The traffic here can be heavy and fast; everyone is in a hurry to make it through the Eisenhower Tunnel, the traditional gateway to Summit County. Those with an extra half hour and a yearning for hairpin turns, shaggy mountain goats, and hundred-mile views opt for Highway 6 over Loveland Pass and the Continental Divide. As it drops into the Summit County Basin on the west side of the divide, Highway 6 passes Arapahoe Basin and Keystone Ski Resort before merging with I–70. Both roads skirt Dillon Reservoir with its shoreline communities of Dillon and Frisco. The highway quickly disappears back into a narrow mountain valley and climbs to Copper Mountain and then up and over Vail Pass.

Keystone and Arapahoe Basin. Tucked up a western valley off the Continental Divide, Keystone and Arapahoe Basin tend to attract more of a

TOP REASONS TO GO

Skiing Choices: You won't find more choices to ski and ride within snowball-throw's distance of one another than in Summit County, many a mere hour's drive from the Denver Metro Area.

Mining Heritage: It was gold that built Colorado in the 1800s, and this legacy is alive and well in the rejuvenated mining town of Leadville.

Mountain Waters: Nothing beats a day of lake kayaking or fishing among the many wooded islets on Lake Dillon, the reservoir that is the heart of Summit County.

Festival Fun: Breckenridge hosts numerous festivals, including the aptly named Spring Massive Festival in April, and the weeklong Ullr Festival in January.

Trail Biking: Sure, there are plenty of single-track rides, but the real draw is the glorious paved bike trail that runs from Dillon up and over the mountains to Vail.

local—and hardier—ski crowd; and hikers in the summer. Keystone is an intimate resort town but "A-Basin" is little more than a ski area.

Lake Dillon and Breckenridge. Dillon and Frisco are twin towns hugging the shores of Dillon Reservoir, a sparkling man-made lake. Skiers will bypass both for Breckenridge, the largest ski area in Summit County. "Breck" has a blend of authentic Colorado character with a flashy dose of upscale lodges and high-end condos.

Copper Mountain and Leadville. Farther west on I–70, Copper Mountain makes up for a lack of mountain charm with its near-perfect ski mountain. The high-altitude mountain town of Leadville will leave you breathless, both from the thin air and from the gorgeous views of Colorado's highest peak, 14,440-foot Mount Elbert.

PLANNING

WHEN TO GO

Summit County is a haven for winter enthusiasts: the resorts of Arapahoe Basin and Breckenridge—and nearby Loveland in Clear Creek County—are so high that the ski season often dawns here weeks before it does in the rest of the state, with Arapahoe Basin and Loveland competing to see who has the longest season, which can begin as early as October and end as late as July. The altitude also means that it can snow on any day of the year, so be prepared. Traffic, particularly on the I–70 approaches to the Eisenhower Tunnel and the Georgetown-to–Idaho Springs stretch, moves at a snail's pace around weekend rush hours— 3 to 10 PM on Friday and all day Sunday.

GETTING HERE AND AROUND
AIR TRAVEL
Denver International Airport (DEN) is the gateway to the attractions and ski resorts in Summit County. The airport is an hour's drive from the Continental Divide along I–70.

TRANSFERS   To and from Summit County (Breckenridge, Copper Mountain, Dillon, Frisco, and Keystone), use Colorado Mountain Express and 453 Taxi, which have regular service to and from the Denver airport.

Airport Denver International Airport (DEN) (☎ *800/247–2336* ⊕ *www.flydenver.com*).

Airport Transfer Colorado Mountain Express (☎ *970/926–9800 or 800/525– 6363*). **453-Taxi** (☎ *970/453–8294*).

BUS OR SHUTTLE TRAVEL

All the resorts run free or inexpensive shuttles between the ski villages and the slopes. Summit Stage provides free public transportation to town and ski areas, in and between ski areas in Summit County.

Shuttles Summit Stage (☎ *970/668–0999*).

CAR TRAVEL

The hardest part about driving in the High Rockies is keeping your eyes on the road. A glacier-carved canyon off to your left, a soaring mountain ridge to your right, and there, standing on the shoulder, a bull elk. Some of the most scenic routes aren't necessarily the most direct. The Eisenhower Tunnel sweeps thousands of cars daily beneath the mantle of the Continental Divide, whereas only several hundred drivers choose the slower, but spectacular, Loveland Pass. Some of the most beautiful byways, like the Mount Evans Scenic and Historic Drive, are one-way roads.

Although it is severely overcrowded, I–70 is still the quickest and most direct route from Denver to Summit County. The interstate slices through the state, separating it into northern and southern halves. Breckenridge is south of I–70 on Route 9; Leadville and Ski Cooper are south of I–70 along U.S. 24 and Route 91.

The most convenient place for visitors to rent a car is at the Denver International Airport. Gasoline is readily available along I–70 and its arteries, but when venturing into more remote areas be sure you have enough fuel to get there and back. Blinding snowstorms can appear out of nowhere on the high passes at any time of the year. Chains aren't normally required for passenger vehicles on highways, but it's a good idea to carry them. A shovel isn't a bad idea, either. The highway shuts down during severe snowstorms and blizzards. Keep your eyes peeled for mule deer and for bighorn sheep, especially along the stretch of I–70 from Idaho Springs to the Eisenhower Tunnel.

PARKS AND RECREATION AREAS

Summit County is perched in a 9,000-foot-high park (a wide valley surrounded by peaks) with Lake Dillon at its recreational heart. The wild Gore Range northwest of Lake Dillon is protected within the Eagles Nest Wilderness Area, administered by the **Arapaho National Forest** (☎ *970/295–6600* ⊕ *www.fs.fed.us*) and the **White River National Forest** (☎ *970/945–2521* ⊕ *www.fs.fed.us*). As in all wilderness areas in Colorado, motorized or mechanized vehicles (forestry-speak for mountain bikes) are prohibited. You can tackle the backcountry peaks on your own two feet or on horseback. The Blue River, which bisects the county south to north and is the lifeblood of Lake Dillon, has gold-medal fishing beginning below Lake Dillon to the Green Mountain Reservoir.

RESTAURANTS

Whereas the restaurants in the celeb resorts of Aspen and Vail mimic the sophistication and style of New York and Los Angeles, Summit County eateries specialize in pub food and Mexican cuisine for calorie-hungry hikers, skiers, and boaters. You won't find much sushi here, but you will find fish tacos, shepherd's pies, and burgers with every imaginable topping. Hearty, reasonably priced pub fare is served at a number of cozy brewpubs along with handcrafted local suds like Dam Straight Lager, Avalanche Amber, and Ptarmigan Pilsner.

HOTELS

Summit County is a great place for history buffs looking for redone Victorian mining mansions–cum–bed-and-breakfasts and budget hunters who want affordable rooms close to the slopes. The county probably has the highest density of condominium units in the state. The competition tends to keep prices lower than in other resort towns. Note that staff at hotels in the region are sometimes young and inexperienced, which may result in less-than-desirable service at some otherwise excellent properties. Also note that many accommodations do not have air-conditioning. Summer nights are often cool enough in the mountains that opening the windows will do the trick.

WHAT IT COSTS					
	¢	$	$$	$$$	$$$$
Restaurants	under $8	$8–$12	$13–$18	$19–$25	over $25
Hotels	under $80	$80–$120	$121–$170	$171–$230	over $230

Restaurant prices are for a main course at dinner, excluding 7.75%–12.7% tax. Hotel prices are for two people in a standard double room in high season, excluding service charges and 8.8%–12.1% tax.

KEYSTONE AND ARAPAHOE BASIN

Just 90 mi west of Denver over Loveland Pass or through the Eisenhower Tunnel, Keystone and Arapahoe Basin are among the closest ski resorts to the Front Range. Given their location hugging the Continental Divide's western flank—both are surrounded by high-altitude peaks topping 12,000 feet—they are also among the highest resorts in the state. Both resorts can be reached by taking I–70 across the Divide to Dillon and then following U.S. 6 south and east up the narrow mountain valley.

KEYSTONE

8 mi southeast of Dillon via U.S. 6.

Fodor's Choice One of the region's most laid-back destinations, Keystone is under-
★ standably popular with families, and as the state's only large resort to offer seasonal night skiing (with lifts running until 9 PM), has long

been a local favorite. Its trails are spread across three adjoining peaks: Dercum Mountain, North Peak, and the Outback. Through the years, as the resort added more runs, it morphed from a beginner's paradise on Keystone Mountain to an early-season training stop for the national ski teams that practice on the tougher and bumpier terrain on North Peak. Keystone now also has full-day guided snowcat tours ($225; backcountry ski gear like avalanche beacons, shovels, and probes are provided). Today it's a resort for all types of skiers and riders, whether they prefer gentle slopes, cruising, or high-adrenaline challenges on the Outback's steep bowls.

The planners were sensitive to the environment, favoring colors and materials that blend inconspicuously with the natural surroundings. Lodging, shops, and restaurants are in Lakeside Village, the older part of the resort, and in River Run, a newer area at the base of the gondola that has become the heart of Keystone. Everything at the resort is operated by Keystone, which makes planning a vacation here one-stop shopping.

GETTING HERE AND AROUND
The easiest way to travel to and around Summit County is to rent a car at Denver International Airport. Catching one of the numerous shuttles up to the ski areas and then taking advantage of the free transportation by Summit Stage (taxi service is also available) is a more economical route, but requires patience and a good timetable. You'll want a car to reach both resorts, but once there both Keystone and A-Basin are easily navigated on foot.

WHEN TO GO
From late October to late April winter sports rule. But Keystone is quickly becoming a magnet in summer, with a small lake for water sports, mountain biking and hiking trails, two highly respected golf courses, and outdoor concerts and special events.

ESSENTIALS
Transportation Summit Stage (☎ 970/668–0999). **Rainbow Taxi** (☎ 970/453–8294).

Visitor Info Keystone Snow Report (☎ 970/496–4111 or 800/934–2485). **Keystone Resort** (✉ Box 38, Keystone 80435 ☎ 970/496–2316 or 877/625–1556 ⊕ www.keystone.snow.com).

DOWNHILL SKIING AND SNOWBOARDING
☾ What you see from the base of the mountain is only a fraction of the terrain you can enjoy when you ski or snowboard at **Keystone**. There's plenty more to Keystone Mountain, and much of it is geared to novice and intermediate skiers. The Schoolmarm Trail has 3.5 mi of runs where you can practice turns. Dercum Mountain is easily reached from the base via high-speed chairs or the River Run gondola. You can ski or ride down the back side of Dercum Mountain to reach North Peak, a mix of groomed cruising trails and ungroomed bump runs.

If you prefer to bypass North Peak, the River Run gondola is a short walk from the Outpost gondola, which takes you to the Outpost Lodge (home to the Alpenglow Stube, which at 11,444 feet above sea level is

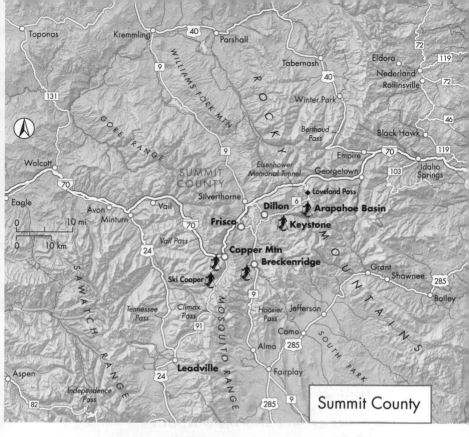

Summit County

advertised as the "highest gourmet restaurant in the country"). From here it's an easy downhill run to the third mountain, appropriately named the Outback because of its wilderness setting. Some glades have trees thinned just enough for skiers and riders who are learning to explore gladed terrain; other sections are reserved for advanced skiers. Weather permitting, the resort also has snowcat tours that whisk you up to powder skiing on some of the state's steepest terrain.

One of the most popular nonskiing or boarding sports at Keystone is **tubing.** Both Adventure Point at the summit of Dercum Mountain (Wednesday–Sunday noon–4 PM and noon–8 PM on night-skiing days) and the Keystone Nordic Center have tube rentals and runs, but reserve a day or two ahead of time. Personal sleds and tubes are not allowed. ⊠ *Hwy. 6* ☎ *970/468–2316 or 800/239–1639* ⊕ *www.keystone.snow. com* ♥ *Skiing: late Oct.–late Apr.; call for hrs.*

FACILITIES   3,128-foot vertical drop; 3,148 skiable acres; 19% beginner, 32% intermediate, 49% advanced; 20 lifts; 2 gondolas, 1 super six lift, 5 high-speed quad chairs, 1 quad chair, 1 triple chair, 3 double chairs, 1 surface lift, and 6 carpets.

LESSONS AND
PROGRAMS

Keystone has a variety of instructional programs, from half-day group lessons to specialty clinics, including mogul classes and women's seminars.

LIFT TICKETS

With prices at $96 for a lift ticket, few skiers pay the walk-up rate. Season passes, which range from 10 days of skiing to unlimited access, are available through Vail Resorts, which owns Keystone, Breckenridge,

---

BIGHORN SHEEP

Keep your eyes peeled on the northern slopes of I-70 as you drive up to Summit County from Denver (your right side). Herds of bighorn sheep congregate around Georgetown, often right off the highway.

Vail, and Beaver Creek. Most vacationers purchase lift-and-lodging packages or multiday lift passes at discounted rates online and at local Safeway and King Soopers grocery stores.

RENTALS

Rental packages (skis, boots, and poles, or snowboards and boots) start at around $35 per day for a basic package but increase quickly for high-performance gear. Cheaper ski and snowboard stores are in Breckenridge, Dillon, and Frisco.

CHILD CARE

Keystone has children's centers at the base of River Run and at the Mountain House for children three months to six years. The resort also has private classes for families.

NORDIC SKIING

The **Keystone Nordic Center** (⊠ *155 River Course Clubhouse* ☎ *970/496–4275*) has 9 mi of groomed trails and access to 35 mi of trails available for skiing and snowshoeing. Lessons and rentals of cross-country skis and snowshoes are available.

OTHER SPORTS AND THE OUTDOORS

FISHING

Summit Flyfish (⊠ *Lakeside Village at Keystone* ☎ *970/468–8945* ⊕ *www. summitflyfishllc.com*) has a shop and full- and half-day fishing trips throughout Summit, Grand, and Eagle counties. This company also leads fly-fishing float trips on several rivers.

GOLF

Keystone Golf. With 36 challenging holes, Keystone lures golfers as soon as the snow melts. **Keystone Ranch,** designed by Robert Trent Jones Jr., has a links-style front nine; the back nine has a traditional mountain-valley layout. Holes play past lodgepole pines, meander around sage meadows, and include some carries across water. **The River Course** is a par-71 stunner designed by Michael Hurdzan and Dana Fry. The front nine runs around the Snake River, whereas the back nine threads through a stand of lodgepole pines. Dramatic elevation changes, bunkers, and water hazards combine to test golfers of all levels. Add magnificent views of the Continental Divide and Lake Dillon and it's easy to see why this course is so popular. ⊠ *1239 Keystone Ranch Rd.* ☎ *800/464–3494* ⊕ *www.keystone.snow.com* ⌕ *Reservations essential* ⌕ *Keystone Ranch: 18 holes. Yards: 7,090. Par: 72. Green fee: $140. The River Course: 18 holes. Yards: 6,886. Par: 71. Green fee: $170.*

ICE-SKATING

☺ In winter 5-acre Keystone Lake freezes to become the country's largest outdoor **ice-skating rink** (✉ *Lakeside Village 800/354–4386*). You can rent skates, sleds, or even hockey sticks for an impromptu game. Lessons in figure skating and hockey are available. Weather permitting, skating runs from late November to early March.

WHERE TO EAT

$$$$ ✕**Alpenglow Stube.** The competition has heated up in recent years, but
AMERICAN   Alpenglow Stube remains among the finest mountaintop restaurants in
★   Colorado. The exposed wood beams, a stone fireplace, and floral upholstery make it elegant and cozy. At night the gondola ride you take to get here alone is worth the cost of the meal. Dinner is a six-course extravaganza, starting with the signature pinecone pâté, followed perhaps by white truffle honey-glazed elk chop. Lunch is equally delectable, with excellent pasta specials. Remove your ski boots and put on the plush slippers reserved for diners. ✉ *North Peak, 21996 U.S. 6* ☎ *970/496–4386* ⊕ *www.keystoneresort.com* ⌕ *Reservations essential* ⊟ *AE, D, DC, MC, V* ⊗ *Closed late Apr.–early June and mid-Sept.–late Nov.*

¢   ✕**Cala Inn.** A street sign noting the distance to Galway is the first clue that
IRISH   you've entered an Irish pub. It's a scruffy but entertaining place where diners and drinkers sit around wood tables inhaling pub fries, bangers and mash, and steak-and-kidney pie. If you're brave enough, down a "Nessie" shot—layered Midori and Bailey's with a floater of Jägermeister. ✉ *40 Cove Blvd.* ☎ *970/468–1899* ⊕ *www.calainn.com* ⊟ *MC, V.*

$$$$ ✕**Keystone Ranch.** This 1930s homestead was once part of a working
AMERICAN   cattle ranch, and cowboy memorabilia is strewn throughout, nicely blending with stylish throw rugs and Western crafts. The gorgeous and massive stone fireplace is a cozy backdrop for sipping an aperitif or after-dinner coffee. The seasonal six-course menu emphasizes local ingredients, including farm-raised game and fresh fish. You're in luck if the menu includes elk with wild mushrooms in juniper sauce with quince relish, or Gorgonzola flan. ✉ *Keystone Ranch Golf Course, 1239 Keystone Ranch Rd.* ☎ *970/496–4386* ⊕ *www.keystoneresort.com* ⌕ *Reservations essential* ⊟ *AE, D, DC, MC, V* ⊗ *No lunch Oct.–May.*

$$ ✕**Kickapoo Tavern.** This rustic bar and grill in Jackpine Lodge has local
AMERICAN   microbrews on tap and big portions of home-style dishes such as Cajun pasta, hearty two-mile-high meatloaf, and burritos said to be "as big as a barn." The central location, pleasant outdoor patio, and TVs tuned to sporting events keep the place hopping both après ski and après night ski. ✉ *129 River Run Rd., River Run Village* ☎ *970/496–4386 or 800/354–4386* ⊕ *www.kickapootavern.com* ⊟ *AE, MC, V.*

$$$$ ✕**Ski Tip Lodge.** In this ski lodge dating from the 1880s almost everything
NEW AMERICAN   on the menu will melt in your mouth. A four-course, prix-fixe dinner
Fodor's Choice   is a favorite in the area for its American cuisine with a Colorado twist.
★   The main course may be wood-grilled pork tenderloin, a roast pheasant with game sausage, or seafood fricassee with coconut and lime. The delicious homemade bread and soup are a meal in themselves. Adjourn to the cozy lounge for the decadent desserts and specialty coffees. The restaurant is open only during ski season. ✉ *764 Montezuma Rd., 1 mi off U.S. 6* ☎ *970/496–4386 or 800/354–4386* ⊟ *AE, D, DC, MC, V*

⊘ *Closed Tues. and Wed. Closed mid-Apr.–Oct. No lunch.*

WHERE TO STAY

$$$$ 🏨 **Keystone Lodge & Spa, a Rock Resort.** The cinder-block structure gives no hint of the gracious, pampered living just inside the door. Rooms with king-size beds are on the small side, whereas rooms with two queen-size beds tend to be more generously proportioned. Many rooms have terraces overlooking the trees. The lodge is next to the tiny lake in Keystone Village, and close to several restaurants and shops. Perhaps best of all, a short shuttle ride delivers

> ### KEYSTONE LODGING ALTERNATIVES
>
> **Keystone Resort Corporation** (🕿 877/753–9786 ⊕ *www.keystoneresort.com*) operates most of the lodgings at the resort, which range from hotel-style rooms at Keystone Lodge and the Inn at Keystone to a wide range of apartments. The condos are in Lakeside Village, River Run, and Ski Tip. Free shuttles ferry visitors to other parts of the resort.

you directly to the slopes. After skiing, the resort spa provides a welcome respite. Choose from traditional massages, or opt for a more exotic treatment like the arctic algae facial. **Pros:** one of the larger properties in the resort; spa; ski valet. **Cons:** iffy service; rooms are small; hot tubs get crowded. ⌖ *Keystone Resort, 22101 U.S. Highway 6, Keystone 80435* 🕿 *877/753–9786 ⊕ www.keystoneresort.com* ⇄ *152 rooms* △ *In-room: no a/c, Internet. In-hotel: 3 restaurants, room service, bar, tennis courts, pool, gym, spa, concierge, children's programs (ages 6 mos–6 yrs), laundry facilities, laundry service, public Internet, public Wi-Fi, airport shuttle, parking (paid)* 🖃 *AE, D, DC, MC, V.*

$ 🏨 **Ski Tip Lodge.** Opened as a stop along the stagecoach route back in the 1880s, this property was turned into the state's first ski lodge in the 1940s by skiing pioneers Max and Edna Dercum. The rooms in this charming log cabin have been given quaint names like "Edna's Eyrie." Homespun furnishings and such accessories as quilts and hand-knitted throw rugs, make each unit distinct. Some rooms have dramatic four-poster beds. In winter you can relax in the sitting room in front of a wood-burning fireplace. In summer, retreat to the patio for a view of the surrounding mountains. A delicious breakfast is included in the room rate. **Pros:** good location for the price; rustic. **Cons:** small rooms; outdated bathrooms; hit-or-miss service. ⌖ *Keystone Resort, 758 Montezuma Road, Keystone 80435* 🕿 *970/496–4500 or 877/753–9786* ⊕ *www.keystoneresort.com* ⇄ *8 rooms, 3 suites* △ *In-room: no a/c, no phone, no TV, Wi-Fi. In-hotel: restaurant, bar, concierge, airport shuttle, parking (free)* 🖃 *AE, D, DC, MC, V* ⏁◉⏁*BP.*

NIGHTLIFE

Across from Mountain View Plaza, the **Goat Soup and Whiskey** (✉ *22954 U.S. 6* 🕿 *970/513–9344*) has two bars filled with twenty- and thirty-somethings drinking whiskey and beer. There's live music during ski season. Live music with rockabilly leanings makes the **Snake River Saloon** (✉ *23074 U.S. 6* 🕿 *970/468–2788*) a good spot to stop for a beer. The fun-loving crowd is mostly under 35.

ARAPAHOE BASIN

6 mi northeast of Keystone via U.S. 6.

Arapahoe Basin was the first ski area to be built in Summit County. It has changed—but not too much—since its construction in the 1940s, and most of A-Basin's dedicated skiers like it that way. It's America's highest ski area, with a base elevation of 10,780 feet and a summit of 13,050 feet. Many of the runs start above the timberline, ensuring breathtaking views (and the need for some extra breaths). Aficionados love the seemingly endless intermediate and expert terrain and the wide-open bowls that stay open into June (sometimes July). "Beachin' at the Basin" has long been one of the area's most popular summer activities. If you've got your heart set on slope-side accommodations or fine dining, look elsewhere: A-Basin has no rooms and serves only the most basic cafeteria food. You'll have to set up your base camp in nearby Keystone, Breckenridge, Frisco, or Dillon, and shuttle in for the day.

GETTING HERE AND AROUND

Given the remoteness of Arapahoe Basin, a car is the best way to go.

WHEN TO GO

This is truly a winter destination, skiing being the only attraction. That said, winter in this high-country spot can begin in early October and last into June.

ESSENTIALS

Visitor Info Arapahoe Basin Snow Report (☎ *970/468–0718*). **Arapahoe Basin Ski Area** (✉ *Box 5808, Dillon 80435* ☎ *970/468–0718 or 888/272–7246* ⊕ *www.arapahoebasin.com*).

DOWNHILL SKIING AND SNOWBOARDING

What makes **Arapahoe Basin** delightful is also what makes it dreadful in bad weather: its elevation. Much of Arapahoe's skiing is above the tree line, and when a storm moves in, you can't tell up from down.

If that sounds unpleasant, consider the other side of the coin: on sunny spring days Arapahoe is a wonderful place, because the tundra surrounded by craggy peaks is reminiscent of the Alps. Intermediate-level skiers can have a great time here on the easier trails. But A-Basin is best known for its expert challenges: the East Wall, a steep face with great powder-skiing possibilities; Pallavicini, a wide tree-lined run; and the West Wall, from which skiers of varying degrees of bravado like to launch themselves. After a long battle with the U.S. Forest Service, A-Basin won permission to install a snowmaking machine for certain trails. In 2009 the resort opened October 9, the earliest opening ever. ✉ *Box 5808, 80435* ☎ *970/468–0718 or 888/272–7246* ⊕ *www.arapahoebasin.com* ☉ *Late Oct.–mid-June or early July.*

FACILITIES   2,270-foot vertical drop; 900 skiable acres; 10% beginner, 40% intermediate, 25% advanced, 25% expert; 1 quad, 2 triple chairs, 3 double chairs, 1 carpet.

LESSONS AND PROGRAMS   Contact **Arapahoe Basin Central Reservations** (☎ *970/468–0718*) for information on regular classes and ski clinics.

LIFT TICKETS $65, depending on the season. Multiday tickets can save you as much as 20%.

RENTALS   Daily ski-rental packages (skis, boots, and poles) start at $29, and snowboard packages at $35. Ski stores in Breckenridge, Dillon, and Frisco are even cheaper.

LAKE DILLON AND BRECKENRIDGE

Lake Dillon, a 2,300-acre artificial reservoir with four narrow arms and 25 mi of shoreline, sits at the very heart of Summit County. The Lake is guarded on the northwest by the steep Gore Range and on the southwest by the Ten Mile Range (a part of the Mosquito Range), and to the east by the Continental Divide. Along the northern shore sit Dillon and her sister town Silverthorne, while Frisco hugs a southwest arm of the lake. Breckenridge is roughly 5 mi south of Lake Dillon, backed up against the Ten Mile Range.

DILLON

73 mi west of Denver via I-70.

Dillon can't seem to sit still. Founded in 1883 as a stagecoach stop and trading post for men working in the mines, Dillon has had to pack up and move three times since. It was first relocated to be closer to the Utah and Northern Railroad, and then to take advantage of the nearby rivers. Finally, in 1955, bigwigs in Denver drew up plans to dam the Blue River so they could quench the capital's growing thirst. The reservoir would submerge Dillon under more than 150 feet of water. Once again the town was dismantled and moved, this time to pine-blanketed hills mirrored in sapphire water. Residents agreed that no building in the new location would be taller than 30 feet, so as not to obstruct the view of the reservoir, which is appropriately called Lake Dillon.

Dillon now blends with neighboring Silverthorne, where dozens of factory outlets are frequented by locals and travelers vying for bargains. Combined, the two towns have hotels, restaurants, and stores galore.

GETTING HERE AND AROUND
Private car is the best way to explore Dillon, although during the summer a network of bicycle trails around the reservoir makes pedaling an attractive option.

WHEN TO GO
Dillon is a hub for all seasons. In the winter, during ski season, Dillon is the place to get gas, groceries and directions before heading on to Keystone, A-Basin, Breck, or Copper. Beginning with the snowmelt in May, Dillon unfolds as a center for hiking, biking, and water sports.

ESSENTIALS
Visitor Info Summit Information Center (⌂ *246 Rainbow Dr., Silverthorne 80498* ☎ *970/668–2051 or 800/530–3099* ⊕ *www.summitchamber.org*).

EXPLORING

Fodor's Choice
★

Resting in the heart of Summit County at 9,017 feet is the Front Range's answer to a day at the beach—beautiful **Lake Dillon** and her two ports, Dillon, just off I–70 on the south, and Frisco, off I–70 and Highway 9 on the west. The lake is actually backed up by a 231-foot earth-filled dam that fills the valley where Dillon once sat. During the frequent Western droughts, when water levels can drop dramatically, collectors wander along the exposed shores hunting for artifacts from this Rocky Mountain Atlantis.

It was these droughts that inspired the Denver Water Board to construct the reservoir and divert the water through the Harold D. Roberts Tunnel, beneath the Continental Divide. Below the mile-long dam the Blue River babbles past the outlet shopping haven and turns into miles of gold-medal fly-fishing waters on its journey north.

The lake has been an aquatic boon to both the Front Range and the exploding Summit County population. There are more than 27 mi of gravel beaches, marshes, peninsulas, and wooded islets for picnickers to enjoy, many accessible from a 7.5-mi paved trail along the northern shores, or from the informal dirt paths elsewhere. Gaze out at the deep blue waters from Sapphire Point Lookout (a short ½-mi hike on the south side of the lake) any nice day, and you'll see a flotilla of motorboats, sailboats, canoes, kayaks, and sailboarders dancing in the waves. In winter the frozen waters are enjoyed by ice anglers and cross-country skiers.

Because the lake is considered a drinking-water source, swimming is not permitted, and the lake is patrolled vigorously by Summit County sheriffs. Just because you don't see a patrol boat doesn't mean they can't see you; their surveillance is done with binoculars.

SPORTS AND THE OUTDOORS

BIKING

Fodor's Choice
★
☺

Summit County attracts cyclists with its 40 mi of paved bike paths and extensive network of backcountry trails. There are dozens of trailheads from which you can travel through gentle rolling terrain, up the sides of mountains, and along ridges for spectacular views. Starting in Dillon, you could bike around the reservoir to Frisco. From there you could ride the Blue River Pathway, largely along the river, to Breckenridge. Or you could ride through beautiful Tenmile Canyon all the way to Copper Mountain. If you're really fit, you could even continue your ride over Vail Pass and down into Vail Village. The **Summit County Chamber of Commerce Information Center** (✉ *246 Rainbow Dr., Silverthorne* ☎ *800/530–3099* ⊕ *www.summitchamber.org*) has detailed information about bike trails in the area. Ask for a free Summit County Bike Trail Guide that outlines, with great detail, your options. Listings include distance, difficulty, and elevation changes.

BOATING

☺ The **Frisco Bay Marina** (✉ *902 E. Main St., Frisco* ☎ *970/668–4334* ⊕ *www.friscobaymarina.com*) is less crowded than Dillon and has quick access to the numerous pine-cloaked islands along the western shores. Here you can rent powerboats, canoes, and kayaks. Take I–70

Exit 203 to Highway 9 to Main Street, and follow signs to the marina. At **Dillon Marina** (⊠ *Lake Dillon* ☎ *970/468–5100* ⊕ *www.townofdillon. com*) you can rent a rowboat, sailboat, or just about anything else that floats. Reserve ahead in high season. Take I–70 Exit 205 to U.S. 6, and follow the signs to the marina.

Boats rented from the Frisco Bay and Dillon marinas are not permitted to beach; the aluminum pontoons are easily damaged on the rock and gravel shores.

FISHING

A favorite with locals, **Cutthroat Anglers** (⊠ *400 Blue River Pkwy., Silverthorne* ☎ *970/262–2878* or *888/876–8818* ⊕ *www.fishcolorado.com*) has a pro shop chock-full of gear for avid fly fishermen. Their wade trips are best for beginners; float-trip adventures are for those with a bit more experience. Both come in half-day and full-day versions.

GOLF

Raven Golf Club at Three Peaks. *Colorado Avid Golfer* magazine named this 18-hole beauty the best mountain course and the best golf experience in Colorado, both for its technically challenging layout and for its rich, natural beauty including stands of pine and aspen trees and visiting elk and deer herds. Each hole on the par-72 course has dramatic views of the Gore Mountain range. ⊠ *2929 N. Golden Eagle Rd., Silverthorne* ☎ *970/262–3636* ⊕ *www.ravengolf.com* ⚲ *Reservations essential* ⚑ *18 holes. Yards: 7,413/5,235. Par: 72. Green fee: $180.*

WHERE TO EAT

$$ ✕ **Dillon Dam Brewery.** Belly up to the horseshoe-shaped bar and sample
AMERICAN   the ales and lagers while you munch on burgers, sandwiches, or pub grub. The menu is steps above average bar food. Try the pan-seared salmon encrusted with sesame seeds or the Pilsner chicken with portobello mushrooms deglazed with beer. Carnivores and vegetarians alike have a big selection, including the Ptarmigan Portobello, a char-grilled mushroom-stuffed wrap on a whole-wheat bun topped with melted pepper jack. ⊠ *100 Little Dam St., Dillon* ☎ *970/262–7777* ⊕ *www. dambrewery.com* ▤ *AE, D, DC, MC, V.*

$$ ✕ **Historic Mint.** Built in 1862, this raucous eatery originally served as
STEAK   a bar and brothel. The olden days are still evident in the bar's brass handles and hand-carved wood, as well as in the antiques and vintage photographs covering the walls of the dining area. Red meat reigns supreme, although you'll also find chicken and fish on the menu. Either way, you cook your own meal on lava rocks sizzling at 1,100°F. If you prefer to leave the cooking to the chef, there's a prime rib special. A well-stocked salad bar complements your entrée. ⊠ *347 Blue River Pkwy., Silverthorne* ☎ *970/468–5247* ⊕ *www.mintsteakhouse.com* ▤ *MC, V* ⊘ *No lunch.*

NIGHTLIFE

The bars and clubs in Dillon rock well after midnight, especially on winter nights when the towns are packed with skiers and snowboarders.

Across from the post office, **Pug Ryan's Steak House & Brewery** (⊠ *104 Village Pl. 80435* ☎ *970/468–2145* ⊕ *www.pugryans.com*) is a popular brewpub that attracts villagers and vacationers. The **Tiki Bar** (⊠ *Dillon*

Colorado Golf

It isn't easy to define "golf" in Colorado, because the topography varies so dramatically, from the rolling plains near the Kansas state line to the flat-top buttes and mesas at the western end of the state. In the Rockies, the state's central spine, the courses climb up and down mountainsides; in the foothills the fairways roll over more gentle terrain and over canyons; and down in the cities many layouts march back and forth in confined spaces.

ROCKY MOUNTAIN COURSES
Mountain golf has unique challenges, but vacationers flock to the high-country golf courses because of their dramatic scenery. "Aim for that peak" is an oft-repeated phrase. It doesn't matter whether you are playing the Jack Nicklaus–designed 27-hole municipal course in Breckenridge, the Club at Crested Butte, or the golf course at the Snowmass Club, there's bound to be a hole where that description fits.

Resort courses, often available only to guests, are spread around mountain towns from Snowmass and Steamboat to Vail and Telluride. For example, if you stay at certain properties in Vail and Beaver Creek, you get access to the Tom Fazio course (woven through sagebrush-covered hills) and the Greg Norman course (spread around a broad valley with shots across ravines) at the posh, private Red Sky Golf Club in Edwards, 15 minutes west of Beaver Creek. Even if you're not staying in a hotel that has preferred tee times at specific resort courses, a good concierge (or your own Web search) will obtain tee times at many entertaining courses, such as the Raven

at Three Peaks in Summit County and Sheraton Steamboat Golf Club in Steamboat.

When playing high-altitude golf, you do have to deal with mountain lies and illusions. The thrill of a clean hit and watching the ball fly 300 yards downhill may be deflected by the agony of seeing a putt topple off the back edge of a green because you "knew" that the green tilted left, although it actually sloped right. Lowland golfers who come to the mountains to play golf quickly learn they may have to change club lengths and lofts, because balls fly 10%–15% farther in the thinner air and land on never-level terrain. Greens are especially difficult to read, because the ball will try to roll from the highest mountain peak to the nearest valley—unless the course architect foxes players by building up the green's lower end to counterbalance that pull. Ask the pro in the golf shop for tips before setting out.

CITY COURSES
If you aren't heading up to the mountains, there are plenty of public and semiprivate courses in and around the bigger cities. Some city-owned courses in Denver proper tend to be unimaginative layouts in confined spaces, but there's a variety of challenging and award-winning courses in the surrounding burbs, especially in Lakewood, Littleton, and Parker. On the western slopes, a big standout is the Golf Club at Redland Mesa in Grand Junction. This Jim Engh public course is woven among mesas and sand-color flat-top buttes.

—Lois Friedland

Marina ☎ *970/262–6309*) has the best sunset views in Summit County. Enjoy them from the deck overlooking Lake Dillon while you sip your rumrunner and munch on peel-and-eat shrimp. **Bootleggers** (✉ *119 La Bonte* ☎ *970/468–2006*) serves pizzas, gyros, and some of the area's best calzones.

SHOPPING
Outlets at Silverthorne (✉ *246-V Rainbow Dr., I–70 Exit 205* ☎ *970/468–9440* ⊕ *www.outletsatsilverthorne.com*) is a sprawling complex with more than 50 discount factory outlets.

FRISCO

9 mi north of Breckenridge via Rte. 9.

Keep going past the hodgepodge of strip malls near the interstate and you'll find that low-key Frisco has a downtown district trimmed with restored B&Bs. The town is a low-cost lodging alternative to pricier resorts in the surrounding communities.

GETTING HERE AND AROUND
Private car is the best way to arrive in Frisco, but the town is compact enough for walking or biking.

EXPLORING
☾ **Historic Park & Museum** re-creates the boom days. Stroll through 11 buildings dating from the 1880s, including a fully outfitted one-room schoolhouse, a trapper's cabin with snowshoes and pelts, the town's original log chapel, and a jail with exhibits on mining and skiing. ✉ *120 Main St.* ☎ *970/668–3428* 🗫 *Free* ☉ *Tues.–Sun. 10–5.*

SPORTS AND THE OUTDOORS
FISHING
Blue River Anglers (✉ *281 N. Main St.* ☎ *888/453–9171* ⊕ *www.blueriveranglers.com*) runs fly-fishing tours on the Blue, South Platte, and Williams Fork rivers, as well as various lakes and streams in the area. You can expect to catch 18- to 20-inch rainbow and brown trout.

WHERE TO EAT
$$$ ✗ **Silverheels at the Ore House.** At this longtime favorite you can join the
MEXICAN   locals who gather around the bar for margaritas and appetizers from 11 AM to 11 PM. The selection of tapas varies with the season, but may include such *bocadillos* (sandwiches) as seared ahi tuna with ginger, and Brie with sweet chili relish. Entrées range from a south-of-the-border combo that includes enchiladas and chiles rellenos to paella made with hot sausage. ✉ *603 Main St.* ☎ *970/668–0345* ⊕ *www. silverheelsrestaurant.com* ⊟ *AE, MC, V.*

WHERE TO STAY
$$ 🏨 **Frisco Lodge.** This 1885 stagecoach stop has morphed into a European-style boutique hotel complete with a chalet facade and a garden courtyard. The rooms are cozy, dressed with Victorian wallpaper and trimmed in dark woods. Antique lamps cast a warm glow on the wrought-iron beds draped with beautiful quilts. A delicious buffet breakfast of eggs, sausage, fruit, fresh breads, and Belgian waffles is included. **Pros:** great location on Main Street; outdoor hot tub and fireplace; courtyard garden.

Cons: street noise audible; thin walls. ⊠ *321 Main St.,* ☎ *800/279–6000* ⊕ *www.friscolodge.com* ⇔ *19 rooms, 13 with bath* ♿ *In-room: no a/c. In-hotel: some pets allowed* ⊟ *AE, MC, V* ⅰⅇ⊡ *BP.*

$$$$ ★ ⌕ **Hotel Frisco.** This Main Street hostelry is a great home base for skiers wanting to hit Breckenridge, Copper, Keystone, and Arapahoe Basin. After a long day of skiing you can relax in front of the two-story river-stone fireplace complete

FRISCO LODGING ALTERNATIVES
Summit Mountain Rentals (⌕ *308 Main St., 80443* ☎ *970/453-7370 or 800/383-7382* ⊕ *www.summitmountainrentals. com*), run by the owners of the Hotel Frisco, has a collection of medium and high-end condos throughout Summit County.

4

with trophy bull moose mount, or warm up in the outdoor hot tub. Owners Mark and Mary Waldman are gracious with advice about the best hiking trails and least-crowded ski runs. The hotel mascot, a yellow lab named Hannah, is equally friendly. You can rent her out for a walking fee of one dog biscuit per hour. The rooms are done in pastel colors with wood accents, and the bedding is plush—down comforters and 300-thread-count sheets. One room has a private hot tub, another has a fireplace. During high season the free parking lot behind the hotel is a godsend. **Pros:** centrally located; friendly owners; rent-a-dog service. **Cons:** small bathrooms. ⊠ *308 Main St.,* ☎ *970/668–5009 or 800/262–1002* ⊕ *www.hotelfrisco.com* ⇔ *11 rooms, 2 suites* ♿ *In-room: no a/c, kitchen (some), refrigerator (some), DVD (some), Wi-Fi. In-hotel: public Wi-Fi, parking (free), some pets allowed* ⊟ *AE, MC, V.*

$$$ ⌕ **Woods Inn.** The rooms are as distinctive as their names in this cedar-frame house one block from Frisco's Main Street. The Columbine is a nod to romance, with a canopied queen bed and private kitchenette, while the Arboretum, within earshot of a nearby waterfall, is lush with potted and hanging plants. Alpine fans will enjoy the Winterhausen Room with its queen-size four-poster bed and electric fireplace. Best of all, the outdoor hot tub bubbles 24 hours a day. The breakfast buffet is hearty and inexpensive. **Pros:** natural setting; outdoor hot tub; dog-friendly. **Cons:** can get noisy if teenage ski clubs are staying there; a bit worn around the edges. ⊠ *205 S. 2nd Ave.,* ☎ *970/668–2255 or 877/664 3777* ⊕ *www.woodsinn.biz* ⇔ *12 rooms* ♿ *In-room: no a/c, no phone, kitchen (some), refrigerator (some), DVD (some) Wi-Fi. In-hotel: laundry facilities, parking (free), some pets allowed* ⊟ *AE, MC, V.*

NIGHTLIFE

Boisterous **Backcountry Brewery** (⊠ *720 Main St.* ☎ *970/668–2337* ⊕ *www.backcountrybrewery.com*) is home to Great American Beer Festival gold medal–winner Telemark IPA and other homemade brews. The **Moose Jaw** (⊠ *208 Main St.* ☎ *970/668–3931*) is a locals' hangout. Pool tables beckon, and a plethora of old-time photographs, trophies, and newspaper articles makes the barn-wood walls all but invisible.

BRECKENRIDGE

22 mi southwest of Keystone via U.S. 6, I–70, and Rte. 9.

Breckenridge was founded in 1859, when gold was discovered in the surrounding hills. For the next several decades the town's fortunes rose and fell as its lodes of gold and silver were discovered and exhausted. Throughout the latter half of the 19th century and the early 20th century, Breckenridge was famous as a mining camp that "turned out more gold with less work than any camp in Colorado," according to the *Denver Post*. Dredging gold out of the rivers continued until World War II. Visitors today can still see evidence of the gold-dredging operations in the surrounding streams.

At 9,603 feet above sea level and surrounded by higher peaks, Breckenridge is the oldest continuously occupied town on the western slope. The town was originally dubbed Breckinridge, but the spelling was changed after its namesake, a former U.S. vice president, became a Confederate brigadier general in the Civil War. Due to an error by a cartographer, Breckenridge wasn't included on the official U.S. map until 1936, when the error was discovered by a member of the Breckenridge Women's Club.

Much of the town's architectural legacy from the mining era remains, so you'll find stores occupying authentic Victorian storefronts, restaurants, and bed-and-breakfasts in Victorian homes. Surrounding the town's historic core, condos and hotels are packed into the woods and along the roads threading the mountainsides toward the base of the Peak 8.

GETTING HERE AND AROUND

Most people arrive by car or a shuttle from Denver International Airport. Getting around is easiest by car, but can also be done by local shuttles and taxis.

TOURS ★ The **Breckenridge Heritage Alliance** leads lively tours of downtown Breckenridge, Colorado's largest National Historic District; the schedule varies seasonally.

WHEN TO GO

The ski season runs from November to April, but festivals and warm-weather activities attract visitors year-round.

FESTIVALS Festivals run rampant here, and it's rare to show up when locals aren't celebrating. Among the best festivals are the annual U.S. Snowboard Grand Prix (⊕ *www.ussnowboarding.com*) and the International Snow Sculpture championships in winter, the Spring Massive Festival (⊕ *www.springmassive.com*) in April, and Genuine Jazz (⊕ *www.genuinejazz.com*) in June. Summer events include the Toast of Breckenridge food and wine festival and the National Repertory Orchestra (⊕ *www.nationalrepertoryorchestra.com*) performances at the Riverwalk Center near the center of town.

ESSENTIALS

Transportation Contacts Breckenridge Free Shuttle (☎ *970/547–3140*).

Vistor and Tour Info Breckenridge Heritage Alliance (✉ *309 N. Main St.* ☎ *800/980–1859* ⊕ *www.breckheritage.com* ✆ *$5* ⊘ *Year-round by appointment).* **Breckenridge Snow Report** (☎ *970/496–4111 or 800/934–2485).* **Breckenridge Resort Chamber** (✉ *203 S. Main St., Breckenridge* ☎ *970/453–2918 or 888/251–2417* ⊕ *www.gobreck.com).*

EXPLORING

Downtown Breckenridge's **Historic District** is one of Colorado's largest, with about 250 buildings on the National Register of Historic Places. The district is roughly a compact 12 square blocks, bounded by Main, High, and Washington streets and Wellington Road. There are some 171 buildings with points of historical interest, from simple log cabins to Victorians with lacy gingerbread trim.

Dating from 1875, the **Edwin Carter Museum** is dedicated to the "log cabin naturalist" who helped to create Denver's Museum of Nature and Science. Look for realistic stuffed animals, including a large buffalo and a burro carrying a miner's pack. ✉ *111 N. Ridge St.* ☎ *800/980–1859* ⊕ *www.breckheritage.com* ✆ *Free* ⊘ *Tues.–Sun. 11–4.*

Ever since gold was discovered here in 1887, the **Country Boy Mine** has been one of the region's top producers. During tours of the facility you can belly up to the stove in the restored blacksmith shop. The mine has hayrides in summer and romantic dinner sleigh rides in winter. ✉ *0542 French Gulch Rd.* ☎ *970/453–4405* ⊕ *www.countryboymine.com* ✆ *$18.95 for mine tours, $55 for hot-chocolate sleigh rides* ⊘ *Days and hrs vary seasonally; call ahead.*

DOWNHILL SKIING AND SNOWBOARDING

With plenty of facilities for snowboarders, **Breckenridge** is popular with young people. There are several terrain parks and an area where you can learn to freeride. The resort's slopes are spread across four interconnected mountains in the Tenmile Range, named Peaks 7, 8, 9, and 10. The highest chairlift in North America—a high-speed quad lift on Peak 8—tops out at an air-gulping 12,840 feet. Peak 7 and Peak 8 have above-the-timberline bowls and chutes. The lower reaches of Peak 7 have some of the country's prettiest intermediate-level terrain accessible by a lift. Peak 8 and Peak 9 have trails for all skill levels. Peak 10 has long trails with roller-coaster runs.

In line with the town's proud heritage, some runs are named for the old mines, including Bonanza, Cashier, Gold King, and Wellington. During one week each January the town declares itself an "independent kingdom" during the wild revel called Ullr Fest, which honors the Norse god of snow. ☎ *970/453–5000* ⊕ *www.breckenridge.com* ⊘ *Nov.–Apr., daily 8:30–4.*

FACILITIES 4,337-foot vertical drop; 2,358 skiable acres; 14% beginner, 50% intermediate, 36% advanced; 29 lifts; 1 gondola, 2 high-speed six-person lifts, 7 high-speed quad chairs, 1 triple chair, 6 double chairs, 12 surface lifts.

LESSONS AND PROGRAMS Contact the **Breckenridge Ski & Ride School** (☎ *888/576–2754*) for information about lessons and specialty clinics. The Children's Ski and Ride School at Peak 8 has its own lift.

LIFT TICKETS   Few skiers and riders pay the mid-season walk-up rate of $86 for a one-day lift ticket. Breckenridge skiers use a variety of season passes sold by Vail Resorts, which owns Breckenridge, Beaver Creek, Keystone, and Vail. Most vacationers purchase lift and lodging packages, or buy advance multiday lift passes at discounted rates online.

> **EPIC AND SUMMIT PASSES**
>
> For unlimited skiing at Keystone, Breckenridge, and Arapahoe Basin, consider the Summit Pass ($399), all for the cost of about four daily lift tickets. The Epic Pass ($599) also includes Vail and Heavenly in California.

RENTALS   Rental packages (skis, boots, and poles; snowboards and boots) start at $30 per day. Prices vary, but not dramatically. If you can't find your brand of high-performance equipment in the first store you try, you're sure to find it elsewhere.

CHILD CARE   Breckenridge has a number of child-care programs. All-day classes or half-day classes for kids are available. Early drop-off is an option if you want to get to the slopes before everyone else. Classes meet at the Kids' Castle at Peak 8, and Beaver Run and the Village on Peak 9.

NORDIC SKIING
BACKCOUNTRY SKIING
They don't call this place Summit County for nothing—mountain passes above 10,000 feet allow for relatively easy access to high-country terrain and some of the area's best snow. But remember this word of caution: avalanche-related deaths are all too common in Summit County (more often involving snowmobilers than skiers). Don't judge an area solely on appearances, as slopes that look gentle may slide. Never head into the backcountry without checking weather conditions, wearing appropriate clothing, and carrying survival gear. For information on snow conditions and avalanche dangers, contact the **Dillon Ranger District Office of the White River National Forest** (☎ 970/468–5400).

One popular touring route is the trip to Boreas Pass, just south of Breckenridge. The 12-mi-long trail follows the route of a former railroad, with good views of distant peaks along the way. The **Summit County Huts Association** (✉ Box 2830, Breckenridge 80424 ☎ 970/453–8583 ⊕ www.summithuts.org) has four backcountry cabins where skiers can spend the night (two are open for summer hikers). If you're traveling farther afield, there are also cabins available through the **10th Mountain Division Hut Association** (☎ 970/925–5775 ⊕ www.huts.org).

TRACK SKIING
The **Breckenridge Nordic Center** (☎ 970/453–6855 ⊕ www.breckenridgenordic.com) has 18.5 mi of groomed tracks for classic and skate skiing, as well as ungroomed trails in the Golden Horseshoe. There are also 6 mi of marked snowshoe trails.

OTHER SPORTS AND THE OUTDOORS
Alpine Events (✉ 1516 Blue Ridge Rd. ☎ 970/262–0374) has a full range of summer and winter activities. In warm weather there are tours of the backcountry in all-terrain vehicles, cattle drives, and "saddle and pad-

dle" days (combining horseback riding and rafting). In winter there's snowmobiling, dogsledding, and sleigh rides.

FISHING

Mountain Angler (☏ 970/453–4665 or 800/453–4669 ⊕ *www.mountainangler.com*) organizes fishing trips, including float trips on the Colorado River, half-day trips on streams near Breckenridge, and all-day trips on rivers farther away.

FITNESS

Breckenridge Recreation Center (✉ *880 Airport Rd.* ☏ *970/453–1734*) is a 62,000-square-foot facility with a fully equipped health club, two swimming pools, climbing walls, and indoor tennis and racquetball courts. Outdoor facilities include clay tennis courts, basketball courts, a skateboard park, and bike paths.

GOLF

Breckenridge Golf Club. This is the world's only municipally owned course designed by Jack Nicklaus. You may play any combination of the three 9-hole sets: the Bear, the Beaver (with beaver ponds lining many of the fairways), or the Elk. The course resembles a nature reserve as it flows through mountainous terrain and fields full of wildflowers. ✉ *200 Clubhouse Dr.* ☏ *970/453–9104* ⊕ *www.breckenridgegolfclub.com* ⅃ *27 holes. Yards: 7,276. Par: 72. Green fee: $107.*

RAFTING

Breckenridge Whitewater Rafting (✉ *842 N. Summit Blvd., Frisco* ☏ *800/ 370–0581 or 970/423–7031* ⊕ *www.breckenridgewhitewater.com*) runs stretches of the Colorado, Arkansas, and Eagle rivers. The company also has guided fishing trips on the Colorado River and whitewater rafting through Gore Canyon.

Performance Tours (☏ *800/328–7238* ⊕ *www.performancetours.com*) leads expeditions on the Arkansas, Blue, and the upper Colorado rivers for newcomers looking for some action and experienced rafters ready for extremes. The company is based in Buena Vista, but will pick up groups in Breckenridge for all-day trips.

☙ **Whitewater Kayak Park** (✉ *880 Airport Rd.* ☏ *970/453–1734*) is a playground for kayakers, with splash rocks, eddy pools, and S-curves. This public park on the Blue River behind the Breckenridge Recreation Department is free and open from April through August.

SNOWMOBILING

Good Times Adventures (✉ *6061 Tiger Rd.* ☏ *970/453–7604 or 800/477– 0144* ⊕ *www.snowmobilecolorado.com*) runs snowmobile trips on more than 40 mi of groomed trails, through open meadows and along the Continental Divide to 11,585-foot-high Georgia Pass.

WHERE TO EAT

$ ✗ **Downstairs at Eric's.** Loud, dark, and lots of fun for young partiers,
AMERICAN this place is video-game central. Kids hang out in the arcade while their
☙ folks watch sports on the big-screen TVs. Pizzas are popular here—try them topped with veggies, seafood, or "garbage" (the management's colorful term for everything). The sandwiches are just as good. The Avalanche Burger is smothered with pizza sauce and mozzarella cheese,

and the Philly Burger is topped with sautéed green peppers, onions, and melted Swiss cheese. ⊠ *111 S. Main St.* ☎ *970/453–1401* ⊕ *www. downstairsaterics.com* ⊟ *DC, MC, V.*

$ ✗ **Giampietro Pasta & Pizzeria.** The smell of freshly baked pizza will draw
AMERICAN families to the door of this Italian eatery. Peek through the window and
ⓒ you'll see families gathered around tables covered with the ubiquitous red-checked tablecloths. There are lots of pastas on the menu, from classic baked ziti to tasty spaghetti with shrimp and pesto. Hungry diners gravitate toward the New York–style pizza with the works and the Sicilian-style deep-dish pizza. You can also build your own calzone or pizza from the huge list of ingredients. A take-out menu is available. ⊠ *100 N. Main St.* ☎ *970/453–3838* ⊕ *www.giampietropizza.com* ⊟ *MC, V.*

WHERE TO STAY

$$ ▦ **Allaire Timbers Inn.** Nestled in a wooded area, this stone-and-timber log cabin has a living room dominated by a stone fireplace, as well as a reading loft and a sunroom with a green-slate floor and handcrafted log furniture. The main deck has a hot tub and spectacular views of the Tenmile Range. The cozy rooms look rustic, with wood furniture and beds piled with handmade duvets. Two larger rooms (not quite accurately called suites) have king-size four-poster beds, two-person hot tubs, and river-rock fireplaces. A hearty breakfast is included, as are afternoon sweets and hot drinks. It's a 10-minute walk from Main Street. **Pros:** great mountain views; friendly owners; tasty homemade breakfast. **Cons:** downstairs rooms can be noisy; no elevator. ⊠ *9511 S. Main St.,* ☎ *970/453–7530 or 800/624–4904* ⊕ *www.allairetimbers. com* ⟿ *8 rooms, 2 suites* ⚷ *In-room: no a/c, Wi-Fi. In-hotel: public Wi-Fi, parking (free)* ⊟ *AE, D, MC, V* ⦿ *BP.*

$$ ▦ **Barn on the River Bed and Breakfast.** Innkeepers Fred Kinat and Diane
★ Jaynes run this timber-frame B&B. The five country-style bedrooms have fireplaces and private decks or patios overlooking the willow-lined river and the mountains. Rooms are loaded with antiques, and one has a king bed. You can't beat the central location, sandwiched into the historic Main Street shopping district right near the river, and in winter skiers can walk right around the corner to "The Breck Connect" gondola. The Continental breakfast includes homemade treats like yogurt and raspberry muffins and moist banana and apple bread. The riverside hot tub is a favorite après-ski hangout. **Pros:** all rooms are within earshot of the river; gas fireplaces; friendly owners. **Cons:** rooms fill fast; reservations are essential. ⊠ *303B N. Main St.,* ☎ *970/453–2975 or 800/795–2975* ⊕ *www.breckenridge-inn.com* ⟿ *5 rooms* ⚷ *In-room: no a/c, Wi-Fi. In-hotel: parking (free)* ⊟ *AE, D, DC, MC, V* ⦿ *BP.*

$ ▦ **Great Divide Lodge.** Close to the ski areas and dozens of shops and restaurants, this lodge is in the middle of it all. Planned as a condominium, the complex has enormous studio and one-bedroom apartments, all of which have sophisticated Southwestern style. There are thoughtful touches, such as plush robes in the baths and Starbucks coffee for the coffeemakers. The one surprising omission is air-conditioning but it's rare that you would want it. **Pros:** close to Peak 9 lift; one block off main street; free Wi-Fi. **Cons:** disinterested service; needs refurbishing. ⊠ *550 Village Rd.,* ☎ *970/547–5550 or 888/906–5698* ⊕ *www.*

breckresorts.com ⬩ *208 rooms* ⬩ *In-room: no a/c, refrigerator (some), Wi-Fi. In-hotel: restaurant, room service, bar, pool, gym, spa, concierge, laundry service, public Internet, public Wi-Fi, airport shuttle, parking (fee and no fee), some pets allowed* ⬩ *AE, D, DC, MC, V.*

$$ 🏨 **Lodge & Spa at Breckenridge.** This lodge more than compensates for its
Fodor's Choice location on a mountainside beyond the downtown area with breathtak-
★ ing views of the Tenmile Range from nearly every angle. There's regu-
lar shuttle service to the town and the ski area. The place resembles a
cozy chalet. Well-lighted, spacious rooms are comfortable, with feather
duvets and pillows. Upgrade to a suite, and you'll also have a fireplace
and a kitchenette. The full-service spa and health club is a great place
to relax after a morning of skiing. **Pros:** great mountain views; fresh
cookies and brownies in the lobby; Aveda bathroom products. **Cons:** a
bit outdated; no room service. ⬩ *112 Overlook Dr.,* ☎ *970/453–9300
or 800/736–1607* ⬩ *www.thelodgeatbreck.com* ⬩ *45 rooms, 1 house*
⬩ *In-room: no a/c, kitchen (some), refrigerator (some), Wi-Fi. In-hotel:
restaurant, bar, pool, gym, spa, parking (free), some pets allowed* ⬩ *AE,
D, DC, MC, V* ⧉ *CP.*

$$$$ 🏨 **Mountain Thunder Lodge.** Rising above the trees, this lodge constructed
from rough-hewn timber brings to mind old-fashioned ski lodges. The
property has modern amenities such as Internet access and a state-of-
the-art gym. The studio and one-, two-, and three-bedroom condos
all have fully furnished kitchens, fireplaces, balconies, and snug living
rooms where chairs are pulled up to rock fireplaces. The property is
tucked into the woods on the road leading up to Peak 8, but it's less than
a five-minute walk from Main Street. The lodge has shuttle service to
the slopes. **Pros:** family-sized suites; close to ski lifts. **Cons:** short walk
to main street; no Wi-Fi. ⬩ *50 Mountain Thunder Dr.,* ☎ *888/989–
1269* ⬩ *www.breckresorts.com* ⬩ *88 rooms* ⬩ *In-room: no a/c, kitchen
(some), refrigerator (some), DVD (some), Internet. In-hotel: pool, gym,
spa, concierge, laundry facilities, laundry service, public Internet, air-
port shuttle, parking (fee and no fee)* ⬩ *AE, D, DC, MC, V.*

$ 🏨 **Village at Breckenridge.** The word "village" puts it mildly, as this
sprawling resort is spread over 14 acres of mountainous terrain along-
side the beautiful river and right across from the historic Main Street.
Each of the units is privately owned and rented out, so accommoda-
tions range from lodge-style rooms to three-bedroom condos, and from
Southwestern chic to gleaming chrome-and-glass units, depending on
the decorating tastes of the owners. All rooms are ski-in ski-out. Stu-
dios and efficiencies all have kitchenettes. The main center for après
ski is at the Liftside Inn, where there's an indoor–outdoor pool and a
hot tub. **Pros:** great concierge; ski-in ski-out. **Cons:** some rooms have
better style than others; no on-site restaurant. ⬩ *535 S. Park Ave.,*
☎ *970/453–5192 or 888/400–9590* ⬩ *www.breckresorts.com* ⬩ *295
rooms* ⬩ *In-room: no a/c, kitchen (some), refrigerator (some), DVD
(some), Wi-Fi. In-hotel: bar, pool, gym, spa, concierge, laundry facili-
ties, laundry service, public Wi-Fi, airport shuttle, parking (fee and no
fee), some pets allowed* ⬩ *AE, D, DC, MC, V.*

NIGHTLIFE
BARS AND LOUNGES

Breckenridge Brewery (✉ 600 S. Main St. ☎ 970/453–1550 ⊕ www. breckbrew.com) serves eight microbrews, from Avalanche Amber Ale to Oatmeal Stout. It's a great après-ski spot. On the lower level of La Cima Mall, **Cecilia's** (✉ 320 S. Main St. ☎ 970/453–2243 ⊕ www. cecilias.tv) is a lounge with mouthwatering martinis. Smokers head to the cigar patio. **Downstairs at Eric's** (✉ 111 S. Main St. ☎ 970/453–1401 ⊕ www.downstairsaterics. com) is standing-room only when there's a game. There are four big-screen TVs and 34 smaller ones scattered around the bar, so you don't have to worry about missing a touchdown. More than 120 brands of bottled beers and another 21 on tap make this a favorite of aficionados. With maroon velour wallpaper and lacy curtains, **Hearthstone** (✉ 130 S. Ridge St. ☎ 970/453–1148 ⊕ www.hearthstonerestaurant.biz) hints at its roots as a bordello. Skiers and locals scarf down the happy-hour specials, including jalapeño-stuffed shrimp.

> ### BRECKENRIDGE LODGING ALTERNATIVES
>
> Several companies handle condominiums in the area. **Breckenridge Central Lodging** (☎ 970/453–2160 or 800/858–5885 ⊕ www.skibcl.com) has more than 60 condo complexes in and around Breckenridge. **Resort Quest** (☎ 970/453–4000 or 800/661–7604 ⊕ www.resortquest. com) manages Main Street Station and other complexes.

MUSIC CLUBS
Base 9 Bar (✉ 620 Village Rd. ☎ 970/453–6000 Ext. 8754) is a lively après-ski destination with two pool tables, three high-definition TVs, and a martini bar.

SHOPPING
Main Street, stretching the entire length of Breckenridge, has an abundance of shopping, with T-shirt shacks, high-end boutiques, and art galleries. It's a good idea to spend an evening window-shopping before breaking out your wallet.

In a quaint Victorian house, the **Bay Street Company** (✉ 232 S. Main St. ☎ 970/453–6303) carries colorful hand-painted furniture and collectibles. At **Images of Nature** (✉ 108 S. Main St. ☎ 970/547–2711 ⊕ www. imagesofnaturestock.com) the walls are covered with outstanding photographs by Thomas D. Mangelsen, who documents the great outdoors.

COPPER MOUNTAIN AND LEADVILLE

Skiers head to Copper Mountain because the runs make sense—you can start easy and progress to harder slopes without having to criss-cross the mountain. It also offers the largest expanse of skiing in Summit County. Although nearby Leadville has a small ski resort (Ski Cooper) and plenty of snowmobiling trails, this rustic mining town is more popular as a summer base for hiking forays to nearby Mount Elbert, the highest peak in Colorado.

COPPER MOUNTAIN

7 mi south of Frisco via I–70.

Once little more than a series of strip malls strung along the highway, Copper Mountain is now a thriving resort with a bustling base. The resort's heart is a pedestrian-only village anchored by Burning Stones Plaza, which is prime people-watching turf. High-speed ski lifts march up the mountain on one side of the plaza, and the other three sides are flanked by condominiums with retail shops and restaurants on the ground floors. Lodgings extend westward toward Union Creek and eastward to Copper Station, where a six-pack high-speed lift ferries skiers uphill.

In winter Burning Stones is filled with skiers on their way to and from the slopes and shoppers browsing for gifts to give to those left at home. In summer people relax on condo balconies or restaurant patios as they listen to free concerts on the plaza or watch athletes inch up the 37-foot-high climbing wall. Kids can also learn to kayak or float in paddleboats.

GETTING HERE AND AROUND

The easiest way to reach Copper Mountain is by car. The resort is foot-friendly, and there is also a free resort shuttle service around town.

WHEN TO GO

Skiing is from November to mid-April. During the summer the resort tends to be quieter, as most visitors gravitate to the Lake Dillon area for hiking and biking.

ESSENTIALS

Visitor Info Copper Mountain Snow Report (☎ *970/968–2100*). **Copper Mountain Resort** (✉ *Box 3001, Copper Mountain 80443* ☎ *970/968–2882 or 800/458–8386* ⊕ *www.coppercolorado.com*).

DOWNHILL SKIING AND SNOWBOARDING

Copper Mountain is popular with locals because the resort's 2,450 acres are spread across several peaks where the terrain is naturally separated into areas for beginners, intermediates, and expert skiers and snowboarders, making it easy to pick your slope. The Union Creek area contains gentle, tree-lined trails for novices. The slopes above the Village at Copper and Copper Station are an invigorating blend of intermediate and advanced trails. Several steep mogul runs are clustered on the eastern side of the area, and have their own lift. At the top of the resort and in the vast Copper Bowl there's challenging above-tree-line skiing. Freeriders gravitate to the super pipe and the Catalyst Terrain Park. Weather permitting, on several days each week beginning in mid-February expert skiers can grab a free first-come, first-served snowcat ride up Tucker Mountain for an ungroomed, wilderness-style ski experience. ☎ *970/968–2882 or 800/458–8386* ⊕ *www.coppercolorado.com* ☉ *Nov.–mid-Apr., daily 9–4.*

FACILITIES 2,601-foot vertical drop; 2,450 skiable acres; 21% beginner, 25% intermediate, 36% advanced, 18% expert; 1 high-speed six-person chair, 4 high-speed quad chairs, 5 triple chairs, 5 double chairs, 4 surface lifts, 3 conveyor lifts.

Colorado's Fragile Wilderness

More than 1,500 peaks pierce the Colorado skyline, creating one of the most extensive and pristine alpine landscapes in the United States. It is a treeless landscape that has changed little in thousands of years; summer storms bury prehistoric glaciers, colorful wildflowers push up through snowy meadows, and ice-covered mountains fill 100-mi views.

GROWING THREATS

But time is catching up with this ice-age wilderness. The very characteristics that once preserved the panoramic heights from human impact—rugged peaks, polar weather, barren vistas—are the same ones that today threaten it. Growing environmental pressures from recreational use, industrial pollution, and changing land-use patterns are taking a toll on this surprisingly fragile ecosystem.

Colorado's burgeoning population is increasing at an annual rate of 3%, a rate not seen since the gold-rush days of 1859. Many who move to the Mile High State enjoy an outdoor lifestyle that includes hiking. A popular pastime for many has been tackling the Fourteeners, the state's 54 peaks that top 14,000 feet. As more and more hikers trample up these mountains, they gouge new trails, compact thin soil, and crush root systems. This damage can take a surprisingly long time to heal. Trails across the tundra near Rocky Mountain National Park that were carved out by Ute and Arapaho scouts hundreds of years ago are still visible today.

Less subtle than erosion, and equally devastating, is the harm caused by industrial pollution. Western Slope power plants in Craig and Hayden burn low-sulfur coal. Scientists believe the resulting sulfur and nitrogen emissions may be creating acid snow in the alpine watersheds, the same watersheds that pour forth several of the great American rivers, including the Colorado, Rio Grande, and Arkansas.

Ironically, one of the greatest threats to the alpine tundra comes from attempts at preserving native wildlife. With wolves and grizzlies extinct in Colorado and hunting banned in Rocky Mountain National Park, the elk population has exploded from a handful of over-hunted animals to more than 2,500. Their sharp hooves trample summer pastures above the timberline and destroy many of the arctic willow stands that provide food and shelter for other wildlife, including the white-tailed ptarmigan.

PINE BEETLES

Had you emerged from the west portal of Eisenhower Tunnel a dozen years ago you would have been greeted by a sweeping view of green lodgepole pine forests dressing the flanks of Summit County's peaks. But today that view is tinted an ugly rust-red. That's because a pine beetle infestation is killing Colorado's lodgepole pines larger than five inches in diameter. The infestation, which began in 1996, is the result of a perfect storm. Forest-fire suppression and a regional drought created dense forests susceptible to attack, while mellow winters allowed the beetles to expand their range. Experts believe that by 2013 almost 90 percent of Summit County's pines will be dead. Spraying, selective cutting, and natural remedies are all being tried, so far in vain and the fire danger is increasing.

<table>
<tr>
<td>LESSONS AND
PROGRAMS
☼</td>
<td>Copper Mountain's **Ski and Ride School** (☎ *970/968–2318*) has classes for skiers and snowboarders, private lessons, men- and women-only groups, and special sessions such as Level Busters (to help you make a quantum leap in skills). Copper's Kids Sessions, divided into groups based on age and skill level, are designed to both teach and entertain. There's also Kids' Night Out, popular among parents who want an evening without the children.</td>
</tr>
<tr>
<td>LIFT TICKETS</td>
<td>Early-season window tickets (through mid-December) are $51 and then jump to $86 in high season. Few people pay the walk-up rate, however. Vacationers usually purchase lift-and-lodging packages, which include discounted lift rates. Copper Mountain has last-minute deals online at ⊕ *www.coppersavers.com.* Passes can save skiers and riders 20% or more. The best deal is Copper's four-pass program for $99 (with some blackout dates). If you want to short-circuit lift lines during busy times (like Christmas week and spring break, try the Bee Line Advantage—for $20 a day you can get on the lifts 15 minutes earlier in the morning and use a dedicated (and shorter) lift line. Ask about it when you book your hotel or condo; many properties have this as a free bonus.</td>
</tr>
<tr>
<td>RENTALS</td>
<td>Rental packages (skis, boots, and poles) start at $30 per day for sport ski packages and go as high as $45 per day for high-performance equipment. Snowboard rental packages (snowboard and boots) start at $42 for adults. Helmet rentals begin at $10.</td>
</tr>
<tr>
<td>CHILD CARE</td>
<td>Copper Mountain Resort has ski-school options for older kids and child care for youngsters. The smell of chocolate-chip cookies wafts from the Belly Button Bakery, day care for tots two to four years old. Belly Button Babies accepts kids six weeks to two years old. Children's programs are based in the Mountain Plaza at Center Village.</td>
</tr>
</table>

OTHER SPORTS AND THE OUTDOORS

BIKING

Hundreds of miles of bike paths weave around the resort, leading up and down mountainsides and through high-country communities. In summer there are weekly group rides for early risers. **Gravitee** (✉ *0164 Copper Rd., Tucker Mountain Lodge* ☎ *970/968–0171* ⊕ *www.gravitee. com*) has all the gear you need for cycling in the area.

For serious cyclists, Olympic medalists Connie Carpenter and Davis Phinney of the **Carpenter/Phinney Bike Camps** (☎ *303/442–2371* ⊕ *www. bikecamp.com*) conduct private camps in Summit County. Camps focus on riding technique, training methods, and bicycle maintenance.

GOLF

Copper Mountain has reasonably priced golf and lodging packages. You can also take a shuttle from the resort to the Raven Golf Club at Three Peaks, about 15 minutes away in Dillon.

Copper Creek Golf Club. Right at the resort is a par-70, 6,057-yard course designed by Pete and Perry Dye. The highest-elevation 18-hole golf course in North America, it flows up and down some of the ski trails at the base of the mountain and between condos and town homes in the resort's East Village. ✉ *104 Wheeler Pl.* ☎ *866/286–1663* ⊕ *www.*

coppercolorado.com ♿ *Reservations recommended* 🏌 *18 holes. Yards: 6,057 and down (depending on selected tees). Par: 70. Green fee: $69.*

WHERE TO EAT AND STAY

$ ✕ **Endo's Adrenaline Café.** Just a few ski-boot steps from the American
AMERICAN Eagle Lift, Endo's Adrenaline Café is one of the more hopping sports bar/restaurants. Enjoy rock music as you climb atop one of the high bar stools and catch a game on one of the TVs, or pick a table for a more intimate lunch or dinner at this high-energy establishment. Try a buffalo Reuben melt on swirled rye or a mountainous plate of Endo's MondoNachos a plateful of chips slathered in melted cheddar, jalapeño peppers, and guacamole. ⊠ *The Village at Copper* ☎ *970/968–3070* ⊕ *www.endoscafe.com* ☰ *AE, MC, V.*

$ ✕ **JJ's Rocky Mountain Tavern.** You have to love a tavern right at the base
AMERICAN of a ski lift (the Super Bee) with a 52-foot-long bar and 10 draft beers on tap. And people do, which is why this loud little pub on the first floor of Copper Station always seems like it's shoulder-to-shoulder. Many hungry skiers have stopped in for a quick lunch of buffalo quesadillas with chipotle sauce only to find themselves lingering over a dinner of homemade tomato fennel soup and wasabi pea–encrusted salmon. ⊠ *102 Wheeler Circle* ☎ *970/968–3062* ⊕ *www.jjstavern.com* ☰ *AE, D, DC, MC, V.*

$$$ ⊡ **Copper Mountain Resort.** The resort runs the majority of lodging in
🐾 the area, ranging from standard hotel rooms to spacious condos and town homes. No matter where you stay, you have use of the beautiful Copper Mountain Racquet & Athletic Club. The Village at Copper is the center of activity, as it's close to most of the shops and restaurants. Unlike Vail with it's Tyrolean feel and Breckenridge with its mining-town roots, Copper Mountain Resort was built from scratch, and has a more modern and function-over-form feel, with concrete towers showing just a hint of alpine architecture. The complex has studios and one- to four-bedroom units, many with fireplaces and balconies. East Village is not as centrally located, but provides easier access to the mountain's more challenging terrain. **Pros:** centrally located; wide range of accommodations. **Cons:** village can be noisy; quality of rooms varies greatly. ⊠ *209 Tenmile Circle,* ☎ *970/968–2882 or 800/458–8386* ⊕ *www.coppercolorado.com* ⬳ *800 rooms* ♿ *In-room: no a/c, safe (some), kitchen (some), refrigerator (some), DVD (some), Internet (some), Wi-Fi (some). In-hotel: 16 restaurants, bars, golf course, tennis courts, pool, gym, children's programs (ages 2–4), airport shuttle, parking (free), some pets allowed* ☰ *AE, D, DC, MC, V.*

NIGHTLIFE

Whether it's a warm afternoon in winter or a cool evening in summer, one of the best places to kick back is at one of the tables spreading across Burning Stones Plaza. At the base of the American Eagle lift, **Endo's Adrenaline Café** (⊠ *The Village at Copper* ☎ *970/968–3070* ⊕ *www.endoscafe.com*) is the place to be for après-ski cocktails. In the evenings there's live music and a raucous crowd. The East Village is home to **JJ's Rocky Mountain Tavern** (⊠ *102 Wheeler Circle* ☎ *970/968–3062 www.jjstavern.com*), the best place for a beer after a long day on the bumps. Musician Moe Dixon, a favorite with the locals, has people dancing on the tables when he covers everyone from John Denver to Jimmy Buffett Wednesday through Sunday during ski season.

SHOPPING

Retail shops fill the ground floors of the Village at Copper, a pedestrian-only plaza.

Visit the **Copper Clothing Company** (⊠ *The Village at Copper* ☎ *970/968–2318*) for a fleece pullover to keep you warm on the slopes, a baseball cap to shade your face, and beer mugs and other remembrances of your trip—all with Copper Mountain logos. Shop for ski and snowboard gear, book your ski lessons, and reserve rental equipment at **Mountain Adventure Center** (⊠ *The Village at Copper* ☎ *970/968–2318*).

LEADVILLE

24 mi south of Copper Mountain via Rte. 91.

Sitting in the mountains at 10,430 feet, Leadville is America's highest incorporated city. The 70 square blocks of Victorian architecture and adjacent mining district hint at its past as a rich silver-mining boomtown. In the history of Colorado mining, perhaps no town looms larger. Two of the state's most fascinating figures lived here: mining magnate Horace Tabor and his second wife, Elizabeth Doe McCourt (nicknamed Baby Doe), the central figures in John LaTouche's Pulitzer prize–winning opera *The Ballad of Baby Doe*.

The larger-than-life Tabor amassed a fortune of $12 million, much of which he spent building monuments to himself and his ambitious mistress "Baby Doe." His power peaked when his money helped him secure a U.S. Senate seat in 1883. He married Baby Doe after divorcing his first wife, the faithful Augusta. The Tabors incurred the scorn of high society by throwing their money around in what was considered a vulgar fashion. After the price of silver plummeted, Tabot died a pauper in 1899 and Baby Doe became a recluse, rarely venturing forth from her tiny unheated cabin beside the mine entrance. She froze to death in 1935.

GETTING HERE AND AROUND

A car is the only reasonable mode of transportation into Leadville. Once in town, the main street, lined with shops and restaurants, and the cozy surrounding neighborhoods make for pleasant walks in summer.

WHEN TO GO

It's not that summer never comes to Leadville, it's just that winter never really leaves. This high-altitude town can see snow almost any month, though really only a brief flurry in the summer months. In winter Leadville hibernates (except for the nearby Ski Cooper and snowmobile trails), but in summer the town is a popular and cool respite from the heat.

FESTIVALS Eccentricity is still a Leadville trait, as witnessed by the **International Pack Burro Race** over Mosquito Pass. The annual event is part of **Leadville Boom Town Days** (⊕ *www.leadville.com/boomdays*), held the first weekend of August. The event is immortalized with thousands of T-shirts and bumper stickers that read, "Get Your Ass Over the Pass."

ESSENTIALS

Visitor Info Leadville Chamber of Commerce (✉ *809 Harrison St., Leadville* ☎ *719/486–3900* ⊕ *www.leadvilleusa.com*).

EXPLORING

TOP ATTRACTIONS

The three-story **Tabor Opera House** opened in 1879, when it was proclaimed the "largest and best west of the Mississippi." It hosted luminaries such as Harry Houdini, John Philip Sousa, and Oscar Wilde. Shows on the current schedule, like *Million Dollar Baby* and *A Portrait of Molly Brown,* revisit the rags-to-riches characters of the Colorado golden days. ✉ *308 Harrison St.* ☎ *719/486–8409* ⊕ *www. taboroperahouse.net* ⊠ *$5* ⊙ *June–Aug., Mon.–Sat. 10–5.*

☾ The **National Mining Hall of Fame and Museum** covers virtually every aspect
★ of mining, from the discovery of precious ore to fashioning it into coins and other items. Dioramas in the beautiful brick building explain extraction processes. ✉ *120 W. 9th St.* ☎ *719/486–1229* ⊕ *www.mininghalloffame.org* ⊠ *$7* ⊙ *Nov.–Apr., daily 11–4; May–Oct., daily 9–5.*

☾ Still chugging along is the **Leadville, Colorado & Southern Railroad Company,** which can take you on a breathtaking trip to the Continental Divide. The train leaves from Leadville's century-old depot and travels beside the Arkansas River to its headwaters at Freemont Pass. The return trip takes you down to French Gulch for views of Mount Elbert, Colorado's highest peak. ✉ *326 E. 7th St.* ☎ *719/486–3936* ⊕ *www.leadville-train. com* ⊠ *$32.50* ⊙ *June–early Oct., daily; call for hrs.*

★ The massive, snowcapped peak watching over Leadville is **Mount Elbert.** At 14,433 feet it's the highest mountain in Colorado and the tallest peak in the entire Rocky Mountain Range, second in height in the contiguous 48 states only to California's 14,495-foot Mount Whitney.

WORTH NOTING

On a tree-lined street in downtown Leadville you'll find the **Healy House and Dexter Cabin,** an 1878 Greek Revival house and an 1879 log cabin— two of Leadville's earliest residences. The lavishly decorated rooms of the clapboard house provide as sense of how the town's upper crust, such as the Tabors, lived and played. ✉ *912 Harrison St.* ☎ *719/486– 0487* ⊠ *$5* ⊙ *June–Aug., daily 10–4:30.*

The **Matchless Mine** and Baby Doe's cabin are 1 mi east of downtown. Peer into the dark shaft, then pay a visit to the small museum with its tribute to the tragic love story of Horace and Baby Doe Tabor. ✉ *E. 7th St.* ☎ *719/486–1229* ⊕ *www.matchlessmine.com* ⊠ *$7* ⊙ *Daily 9–5.*

The **Heritage Museum** paints a vivid portrait of life in Leadville at the turn of the last century, with dioramas depicting life in the mines. There's also furniture, clothing, and toys from the Victorian era. ✉ *120 E. 9th St.* ☎ *719/486–1878* ⊠ *$4* ⊙ *June–late Oct., daily 10–4.*

DOWNHILL SKIING AND SNOWBOARDING

☾ Nine miles west of Leadville, **Ski Cooper** is one of those undiscovered boutique ski areas in the Rockies. It has 400 acres skiable via lift and another 2,400 acres of backcountry powder accessible by snowcat. The 26 groomed runs are perfect for beginning or intermediate skiers.

⊠232 County Road 29/Highway 24 ☎*719/486–3684 or 800/707–6114* ⊕ *www.skicooper.com* ⊙ *Late Nov.–early Apr., daily 9–4.*

FACILITIES   1,200-foot vertical drop; 400 skiable acres; 30% beginner, 40% more difficult, 30% advanced; 5 lifts; 1 triple chair, 1 double chair, 3 surface lifts.

LESSONS AND PROGRAMS   The **Ski Cooper Ski School** (☎*719/486–2277*) covers the gamut for skiers and snowboarders. A "Never Ever" two-hour lesson with full lift ticket and rental gear is $60, or you can join a two-hour group lesson for $45. You can also book private lessons, race and telemark clinics, and lessons for your children, which can be extended as part of the all-day child-care programs. Lessons for handicapped skiers are available by appointment.

Ski Cooper has a number of options for children, including their popular Panda Patrol for children ages 5 to 11. A full-day package (from 10 AM to 3 PM) includes a group ski lesson, equipment rental, lunch, and full mountain lift ticket for $75. The Panda Cub program caters to four-year-olds and provides a two-hour lesson, lift ticket, and rental package for $47.

Chicago Ridge Snowcat Tours (☎*719/486–2277*) are for expert backcountry skiers who want the off-piste adventure of scripting their signature across acres of untracked powder. Tickets are $275, call for prices in Nov or use last year's prices but you'll get your fill of phat snow. The terrain has tree glades and open bowls. You must be over 18 (or be accompanied by an adult) and fit; the runs are up to 10,000 feet long, and some vertical drops top 1,400 feet. Wide powder skis are available for rent for those who really want to float.

LIFT TICKETS   At $42 for a full-day lift ticket, you'll be hard-pressed to find cheaper powder. Vacationers should still shop around for discounted rates at King Soopers and Safeway stores.

RENTALS   Rental packages (skis, boots, and poles) start at $15 per day, among the cheapest in the state. Snowboarding packages start at $25. Performance packages and backcountry ski gear rentals are also available and start at $25.

OTHER SPORTS AND THE OUTDOORS
CANOEING AND KAYAKING
There's no better way to see the high country than by exploring its lakes and streams. **Twin Lakes Canoe & Kayak** (⊠*6451 State Hwy. 82, about 20 mi south of Leadville* ☎*719/251–9961*) supplies equipment to beginners who just want to stay cool and to experts wanting to run the rapids.

GOLF
Mt. Massive Golf Course. Play North America's highest 9-hole green at ★ 9,680 feet—and watch your distance increase in the thin mountain air. Just west of Leadville in the Arkansas River valley, this public golf course was opened in the 1930s to the delight of the mining community. True green fairways replaced sagebrush flats after a $50,000 grant in the 1970s heralded an automated irrigation system. ⊠*259 County Rd. 5* ☎*719/486–2176* ⊕ *www.mtmassivegolf.com* ⚐ *Reservations essential* 🏌*9 holes. Yards: 6,170. Par: 36. Green fee: $20/$36.*

HORSEBACK RIDING

If you're feeling like it's time to hit the trail, **Mega Mountain Magic** (⊠ *1100 County Rd. 18* ☎ *719/486–4570*) has a stable of horses ready for you.

SNOWMOBILING

Skiing extreme slopes isn't the only way to feel the blast of powder on your face. Fire up your own mechanical beast with **Alpine Snowmobiles** (⊠ *4037 Hwy. 91* ☎ *719/486–9899* ⊕ *www.alpinesnowmobiles. com*). Snowmobiling fans often head to **2 Mile Hi Ski-Doo** (⊠ *1719 Poplar* ☎ *719/486–1183*).

WHERE TO EAT AND STAY

$ ✕ **The Grill.** Run by the Martinez family since 1965, this locals' favorite
MEXICAN draws a standing-room-only crowd. The service is sometimes slow, but
☺ that leaves time for another of the marvelous margaritas. Tex-Mex is the specialty here, including dishes with hand-roasted green chiles. In summer you can retreat to the patio to toss horseshoes. The restaurant is open Wednesday through Monday at 4 PM for dinner. ⊠ *715 Elm St.* ☎ *719/486–9930* ⊕ *www.grillbarcafe.com* ⚹ *Reservations essential* ⊟ *AE, MC, V* ⊘ *No lunch except June–Aug. weekends.*

$$ ⬚ **Delaware Hotel.** This artfully restored 1886 hotel is one of the best
★ examples of high Victorian architecture in the area, so it's no surprise that it's listed on the National Register of Historic Places. The columned lobby has brass fixtures, crystal chandeliers, and rich oak paneling, although much of the beauty is hidden behind a rambling antique and knick-knack store. The comfortable rooms have graceful touches like lace curtains and antique heirloom quilts. **Pros:** loaded with gold-rush character; great mountain views; very friendly staff. **Cons:** lobby is one large store; the altitude in Leadville can be tough if you're arriving from sea level. ⊠ *700 Harrison Ave.,* ☎ *719/486–1418 or 800/748–2004* ⊕ *www.delawarehotel.com* ⇨ *32 rooms, 4 suites* ⚹ *In-room: no a/c. In-hotel: restaurant, bar, public Wi-Fi, parking (free)* ⊟ *AE, D, DC, MC, V* ⑩ *CP.*

$ ⬚ **Ice Palace Inn Bed & Breakfast.** Rooms in this restored Victorian—
★ some with jetted tubs for two—have period antiques and luxurious featherbeds. Innkeepers Sherry Randall and Marcie Stassi are just as inviting. A full breakfast is included in the room rate. Don't forget your slippers; no shoes are allowed on the inn's plush carpets. **Pros:** easy access to trailheads; gracious owners; romantic. **Cons:** short walk to the main street; adults only. ⊠ *813 Spruce St.,* ☎ *719/486–8272 or 800/754–2840* ⊕ *www.icepalaceinn.com* ⇨ *5 rooms* ⚹ *In-hotel: public Wi-Fi, no kids* ⊟ *AE, D, DC, MC, V* ⑩ *BP.*

Vail Valley

WORD OF MOUTH

"Vail local responding here: You could ski Vail all week and never ski the same run twice. Why go anywhere else?"

—localgal

"We were in Vail last July and loved it . . . the Sunday Farmer's Market was great. We also had a wonderful time riding the gondola up Vail Mountain and riding mountain bikes back down the trails. The younger kids in our group rode the gondola up and down the mountain all day long! There is a (sports bar type) restaurant at the base of the mountain near where you catch the gondola and we had a great time sitting on their patio watching others come down the mountain on bikes."

—Outinkerbelle

Updated by
Jad Davenport

If Aspen is Colorado's Hollywood East, then her rival Vail is Wall Street West. So popular is this ski resort with the monied East Coast crowd that locals sometimes refer to particularly crowded weeks as "212" weeks, in reference to the area code of their visitors. The attraction for vacationers from all over is the thin, aspen-cloaked Vail Valley, a narrow corridor slit by Interstate 70 and bounded by the rugged Gore Range to the north and east and the tabled Sawatch escarpments to the south. Through it all runs the sparkling Eagle River.

The resorts begin just west of Vail Pass, a saddle well below tree line, and stretch 20 mi through the communities of Vail, Eagle-Vail, Minturn, Avon, Beaver Creek, Arrowhead, and Edwards. The vibe in these places varies dramatically, from Beaver Creek, a gated community of second (and probably third) megahomes, to Edwards, a rapidly growing worker town, to Vail, filled with styles of lodging, dining, and shopping appealing to many tastes.

In winter this region is famous for the glittering resorts of Vail and Beaver Creek. Between these two areas skiers and snowboarders have almost 7,000 acres at their disposal, including the unforgettable Back Bowls far beyond the noise of I–70 traffic.

In summer these resorts are great bases from which you can explore the high country on foot, horseback, raft, or bike. But take heed: all trails go up—though you can cheat and catch the Eagle Bahn Gondola up and hike or ride down. Some trails are designated for bikers, others for hikers, and many for both. Always remember that bikers should yield to hikers, though in practice it's considered courteous to let them blow by. In addition, there are hundreds of miles of trails weaving through the White River National Forest. Warm-weather weekends are filled with an exciting range of cultural events, including performances by such groups as the New York Philharmonic and the Bolshoi Ballet.

ORIENTATION AND PLANNING

GETTING ORIENTED

Finding your way around the Vail Valley is relatively easy; the valley runs east and west, and everything you need is less than a mile or two off the I–70 corridor (and the constant drone of traffic), which parallels the Eagle River. The Gore Range to the north and east is one of the most rugged wilderness areas in Colorado—the peaks are jagged and broken, and any hiking here immediately involves a steep and

TOP REASONS TO GO

The Slopes: Vail is as real and challenging a ski mountain as you'll find anywhere in the western United States, with the steeps and back bowls to prove it.

Romantic Meals: A number of intimate restaurants are hidden away among the peaks, reachable by ski, on horseback, and even by horse-drawn sleighs.

Rugged Scenery: The Gore Range presents some of the most sharp-spined backcountry in the state, with ice-cold tarns, sheer cliffs, and shaggy white mountain goats.

High Altitude Golf: The thin air at this elevation lets your Titleist fly much farther—enjoy those hero swings at more than a dozen venues.

Summer Festivals: Check out some of Vail's many cultural activities—summer is full of music, culinary, and dance festivals.

5

sustained climb. To the south, the tabled heights of the Sawatch Mountain Range are gentler, and give Vail her superb skiing, particularly in the famed Back Bowls. Beaver Creek feels more isolated, being set off the highway behind a series of gates that control access to the posh communities within.

Vail. European-style cafés and beautifully cobbled streets lined with boutiques are more than just window dressing—Vail is no longer just known for its serious skiing. The nearby town of Minturn is a much more modest burg.

Beaver Creek. As the entrance gates will remind you, Beaver Creek is the most exclusive skiing community in Colorado. This is resort-to-resort skiing set among gorgeous glades of aspens; it never seems to get crowded.

PLANNING

WHEN TO GO

Winter is by far the most crowded time in Vail Valley, with early spring seeing the highest number of visitors hoping to catch that blissful blend of thick powder and china-blue skies. Naturally, prices are highest then as well, though you can sometimes get pre- and post-season deals. Although summer is quickly gaining in popularity, the real deals can be had in the shoulder seasons—late autumn and late spring when the ski slopes are closed. Restaurants will often have two-for-one entrées with a bottle of wine, and hotels run deeply cut rates. Traffic through the I–70 corridor moves at a good clip unless snows have stacked up truckers putting on chains on either side of Vail Pass. The pass itself is low, and stays below tree line, affording it some protection from drifting and blowing snow.

GETTING HERE AND AROUND

AIR TRAVEL

Denver International Airport (DEN), the gateway to the High Rockies, is 119 mi east of Vail. It's a 90-minute drive from Vail, but if you get caught in ski traffic it could take two hours (and much longer if a blizzard hits). The Vail Valley is served by Eagle County Airport (EGE), 34 mi west of Vail. During ski season, American, Continental, Delta, and United have nonstop flights to Eagle County from several gateways. United and American fly here year-round.

If possible, try snagging a direct flight straight into the Eagle County Airport from your hometown. But if your trip involves a connection through Denver or another hub, it is often faster to rent a car and make the scenic 90-minute drive through the mountains or catch one of the many shuttle services. Although winter mountain weather can be fickle and delay flights, the two high passes on I–70 between Denver–Loveland and Summit County–Vail are rarely closed, though traffic might slow to a creep.

Airports Denver International Airport (DEN) (☎ 800/247–2336 ⊕ www.flydenver.com). **Eagle County Airport (EGE)** (☎ 970/328–8600 ⊕ www.eaglecounty.us/airport).

Airport Transfers Colorado Mountain Express (☎ 970/926–9800 or 800/525–6363). **453-Taxi** (☎ 970/453–8294).

BUS AND SHUTTLE TRAVEL

All the resorts run free or inexpensive shuttles between the ski villages and the slopes. Locals and visitors alike hop the free Town of Vail buses up and down from East Vail to West Vail (a distance of nearly 6 mi, with Lionshead at the center). For trips to Beaver Creek, catch the ECO Transit bus from the Vail Transportation Center in Vail Village, beside the Vail Information Center.

Contacts ECO Transit (☎ 970/328–3520 ⊕ www.eaglecounty.us/eco_transit). **Avon/Beaver Creek Transit** (☎ 970/748–4120 ⊕ www.avon.org). **Colorado Mountain Express** (☎ 800/525–6363 or 970/468–7600 ⊕ www.ridecme.com). **Town of Vail** (☎ 970/479–2100 ⊕ www.vailgov.com).

CAR TRAVEL

The most convenient place for visitors to rent a car is at Denver International Airport. Alamo, Avis, Budget, Dollar, Enterprise, Hertz, and National have offices in Eagle County Airport as well.

Although it is often severely overcrowded, I–70 is still the quickest and most direct route from Denver to Vail. For the first 45 minutes it climbs gradually through the dry Front Range mountains before ducking into the Eisenhower Tunnel. The last 45 minutes are through the high Summit County Basin and up and over the mellow grade of Vail Pass.

PARKS AND RECREATION AREAS

The Vail Valley has two wilderness areas in close proximity—the truly untrampled Eagle's Nest Wilderness Area to the northeast in the Gore Range, and the more-popular Holy Cross Wilderness to the southwest. The land in between, including much of the ski resorts' slopes, is part of the **White River National Forest** (☎ 970/945–2521 ⊕ www.fs.fed.us/r2/

whiteriver). The Eagle River, whose headwaters are on the north side of Tennessee Pass, is an excellent fishing stream, mostly for brook and brown trout in the 6- to 12-inch range. Public access is easiest upriver of Red Cliff on Forest Service land. There's some superb rafting in Gore Canyon on the Colorado River west of Vail, particularly in spring when the river is boiling with snow runoff.

RESTAURANTS

Unlike the nearby Summit County ski resorts, which pride themselves on standard "mining fare" like surf and turf, Vail has a distinctly European dining experience. This is the town in which to sample creamed pheasant soup or bite into a good cut of venison. For the most romantic options, look into a slope-side restaurant like Beano's, where the fixed-course menus and unique transportation (horses in summer and sleighs in winter) make the experience more than just a meal. The farther down-valley you move, the more the prices drop.

HOTELS

Vail and Beaver Creek are purpose-built resorts, so you won't find any quaint historic Victorians converted into bed-and-breakfasts here as you will in Breckenridge and Aspen. Instead, Vail lodgings come in three flavors—European chalets that blend with the Bavarian architecture, posh chain resorts up side canyons, and loads of small but serviceable condominiums perfect for families. Down-valley in Edwards and Minturn you'll find that accommodation prices drop, but so does the accessibility to the slopes.

WHAT IT COSTS					
	¢	$	$$	$$$	$$$$
Restaurants	under $8	$8–$12	$13–$18	$19–$25	over $25
Hotels	under $80	$80–$120	$121–$170	$171–$230	over $230

Restaurant prices are for a main course at dinner, excluding 4.4%–8.4% tax. Hotel prices are for two people in a standard double room in high season, excluding service charges and 5.4%–9.8% tax.

VAIL

100 mi west of Denver via I–70.

Consistently ranked as one of North America's leading ski destinations, Vail has a reputation few can match. The four-letter word means Valhalla for skiers of all skill levels. Vail has plenty of open areas where novices can learn the ropes. It can also be an ego-building mountain for intermediate and advanced skiers who hit the slopes only a week or two a season. Some areas, like Blue Sky Basin, make you feel like a pro.

Although Vail is a long, thin town spread for several miles along the Eagle River and composed of East Vail, Vail Village, Lionshead in the center, and West Vail, the hub of activity in winter and summer revolves around Vail Village, and the newly redone Lionshead. The newly redone Lionshead has shops, restaurants, a heated gondola, and

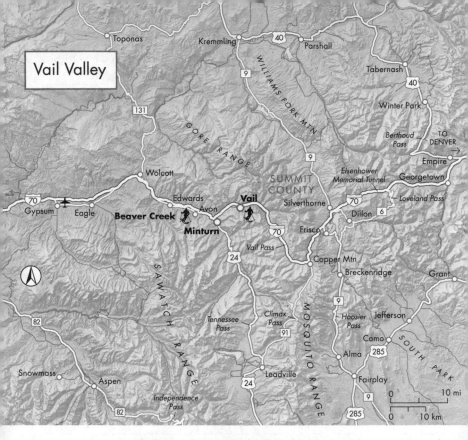

even a glockenspiel tower. Vail Village has shops and restaurants and direct lift access to the mountain.

Vail, along with most savvy ski resorts, actively courts families through special packages, classes for youngsters, and activities geared to people of all ages. At Vail kids can play in specially designed ski parks like Chaos Canyon and Fort Whippersnapper. After a day on the slopes, the whole family can get in on the action at Adventure Ridge, where activities range from kids' snowmobile rides to tubing and biking at night by headlamp.

In terms of size, Vail overwhelms nearly every other ski area in North America. There are 5,289 acres popular with skiers and riders of all skill levels. Areas are clearly linked by a well-placed network of lifts and trails. The Front Side is draped with long trails; the infamous Back Bowls beckon powder skiers. A few hours of adventure skiing in Blue Sky Basin is a must for intermediate to advanced skiers and riders.

When the snows melt and two-for-one dinners are advertised in restaurant windows, you can be sure of two things—Vail is in the heart of the mud season, and the tranquillity won't last long. With the blooming of summer columbines come the culture crowds for music and culinary festivals and self-enrichment in writing workshops and health-food seminars. While the valley teems with visitors, hikers and mountain bikers stream up the steep slopes on foot and via the Eagle Bahn Gondola to head into the network of trails that web the seemingly endless backcountry.

GETTING HERE AND AROUND

The best way to get to the Vail Valley is with a rental car. Once in the valley, a free shuttle makes it's easy to get around town.

TOURS Vail's Nova Guides runs jeep and all-terrain-vehicle tours, as well as rafting, fishing, snowmobiling, and hiking expeditions.

WHEN TO GO

Vail has grown into a year-round resort, skiing being the main attraction from December through March, and outdoor pursuits like hiking, biking, and fishing the rest of the year. While May and June have pleasant temperatures, many of the hiking and biking trails are still buried beneath snowdrifts. For those interested in seeing wildflowers, mid-July is the time to hit the peaks. The colorful aspen trees generally change to a golden red sometime in September.

FESTIVALS Vail hosts a wide variety of festivals, starting with the Teva Mountain Games (⊕ *www.tevamountaingames.com*), showcasing such sports as kayaking, rafting, and mountain biking. Then there are the Taste of Vail (⊕ *www.tasteofvail.com*), Gourmet on Gore, Spring Back to Vail (⊕ *www.springbacktovail.com*), Snow Daze, CarniVail, Bravo!, and the Vail International Dance Festival, to name just a few. There are also free outdoor concerts by up-and-coming musicians, as well as concerts both on and off the mountain by some of the biggest names in the business.

Fodor'sChoice Stretching from late June through early August, the annual **Bravo! Vail**
★ **Valley Music Festival** (☎ *877/812–5700* ⊕ *www.vailmusicfestival.org*) is a month-and-a-half-long celebration of music. Among the performers in residence for a few days or more than a week are the New York Philharmonic and the Dallas Symphony Orchestra. Chamber-music concerts, many performed by the ensemble-in-residence, are popular events. There's also music from an American composer-in-residence.

★ Held early in August, the annual **Vail International Dance Festival** (☎ *970/949–1999* ⊕ *www.vvf.org*) hosts an unparalleled collection of ballet and modern dance groups from around the globe. The performers vary from year to year, but frequently include guest artists from the American Ballet Theatre, the Pacific Northwest Ballet, and other world-class companies. In recent years visitors enjoyed Savion Glover of the Tony Award–winning *Bring in Da Noise, Bring in Da Funk*. Most performances are at the Vilar Center for the Arts and the Gerald R. Ford Amphitheater, an outdoor venue where some people sit in the seats, but many more recline on blankets on the surrounding lawn.

ESSENTIALS

Tour Contacts Nova Guides (✉ *Red Cliff* ☎ *719/486–2656*). **Timberline Tours** (✉ *Vail* ☎ *970/831–1414*).

Vistor Info Vail Snow Report (☎ *970/754–4888*). **Vail Resorts, Inc.** (✉ *Box 7, Vail* ☎ *800/404–3535* ⊕ *vail.com*). **Vail Valley Partnership** (✉ *101 Fawcett Rd., Ste. 240, Avon* ☎ *970/476–1000 or 800/653–4523* ⊕ *www.visitvailvalley.com*).

5

EXPLORING

★   The **Betty Ford Alpine Gardens,** open daily from snowmelt (around Memorial Day) to snowfall (Labor Day or a bit later), are an oasis of forsythia, heather, and wild roses. These are the highest public botanical gardens in North America. ⊠ *Ford Park* ☎ *970/476–0103* ⊕ *www. bettyfordalpinegardens.org* ⌦ *Free* ⊙ *May–Sept., daily dawn–dusk.*

The **Colorado Ski & Snowboard Museum and Hall of Fame** traces the development of the sport throughout the world, with an emphasis on Colorado's contributions. On display are century-old skis and tows, early ski fashions, and an entire room devoted to the 10th Mountain Division, an Army division that trained nearby. Snowboard enthusiasts will get a kick out of two original "snurfers"—prehistoric boards from 1966 and 1967, along with some vintage Burton boards. ⊠ *231 S. Frontage Rd.* ☎ *970/476–1876* ⊕ *www.skimuseum.net* ⌦ *Free* ⊙ *Daily 10–6.*

DOWNHILL SKIING AND SNOWBOARDING

Year after year, **Vail** logs more than a million "skier days" (the ski industry's measure of ticket sales), perpetuating its ranking as one of the top two or three most-popular resorts in North America. From the top of China Bowl to the base of the Eagle Bahn Gondola at Lionshead, the resort is more than 7 mi across. The vast acreage is roughly divided into three sections: the Front Side, the Back Bowls, and Blue Sky Basin. Snowboarders will find plenty of steeps on the Front Side, and technical challenges at the Golden Peak or Bwana terrain parks, but they should avoid the Back Bowls, where long catwalks can get slow in the afternoon sun.

Vail is perhaps best known for its legendary **Back Bowls,** more than 3,000 acres of wide-open spaces that are sensational on sunny days. Standing in any one of them, it's difficult to get a visual perspective, as skiers on the far side resemble Lilliputians. These bowls stretch from the original Sun Up and Sun Down to Game Creek on one side and Teacup, China, Siberia, and Outer Mongolia bowls on the far side. The terrain ranges from wide, groomed swatches for intermediate skiers to seemingly endless bump fields to glades so tight that only an expert boarder can slither between the trees. When there's fresh powder, these bowls beckon to skiers intermediate and above. But after the fresh snow has been tracked up by skiers and pummeled by wind and sun, it may be wise for less-than-expert skiers to stay in the groomed sections of the bowls.

The **Front Side** of Vail Mountain delivers a markedly different experience. Here there's lots of wide-trail skiing, heavily skewed toward groomed intermediate runs, especially off the Northwood Express, Mountaintop Express, and Avanti Express lifts, as well as the slopes reachable via the Eagle Bahn Gondola. Pockets of advanced and expert terrain are tucked in and around the blue-marked slopes. The upper parts of Riva Ridge (the Glade) and the top of Prima (the Cornice) are just a few of the places you'll find skilled skiers. The best show in town is on Highline (you can see it while riding Chair 10), where the experts groove through the moguls and those with a bit less experience careen around the bumps. The other two extremely difficult double-black-diamond trails off this slow lift are the best cruisers on the mountain for skilled skiers.

It takes time (as long as 45 minutes) to reach **Blue Sky Basin,** made up of three more bowls, but it's worth the effort. Tucked away in a secluded corner of Vail, this 645-acre area has been left in a wilder state, and the majority of the terrain is never groomed. Intermediate skiers will find a few open trails with spectacular views of rugged mountain peaks. For advanced and expert skiers, the real fun is playing in glades and terrain with names such as Heavy Metal, Skree Field, the Divide, and Champagne Glade. ☎ 970/476–5601 ⊕ www.vail.com ☉ Late Nov.–mid-Apr., daily 9–3:30.

FACILITIES 3,450-foot vertical drop; 5,289 skiable acres; 18% beginner, 29% intermediate, 53% expert (the majority of this terrain is in the Back Bowls); 1 gondola, 16 high-speed quads, 1 fixed grip quad, 3 triples, 1 double, 3 surface lifts and 6 conveyors.

LESSONS AND PROGRAMS The **Vail and Beaver Creek Ski and Snowboard School** (☎ 970/479–4330) runs classes for skiers of all levels. The school at Vail has almost 1,000 instructors who teach in 30 languages. Afternoon-only group lessons are $80 to $90, depending on the season. All-day lessons are $120. Special workshops and clinics are offered throughout the year. Beginners take three-day courses that include equipment rental and lift passes. Workshops for women, teen sessions, and telemark courses are among the programs targeting specific groups.

LIFT TICKETS Few skiers pay the walk-up rate of $97 for a one-day lift ticket. Colorado's Front Range skiers purchase a variety of season passes. Most vacationers purchase lift-and-lodging packages, or go online to buy multiday lift passes at discounted rates. A lift ticket purchased at either Vail or Beaver Creek may also be used at Breckenridge, Keystone, and Arapahoe Basin.

RENTALS **Vail Sports** (✉ 600 Lionshead Pl. ☎ 970/479–0600 ⊕ www.vailsports.com) is within steps of the lifts. The shop rents a wide range of ski gear, including high-end equipment. Prices for skis range from $35 to $55 a day. Book online and save up to 10% on daily rentals and up to 20% for rentals of five days or more. At Lionshead, at **One Track Mind Snowboard Shop** (✉ 492 E. Lionshead Circle ☎ 970/476–1397) you can rent everything you need for snowboarding.

NORDIC SKIING

BACKCOUNTRY SKIING

Fodor'sChoice ★ The **10th Mountain Division Hut and Trail System** is one of Colorado's outdoor gems. This network of 29 huts is in the mountains near Camp Hale, where the decorated namesake World War II division trained. Skiers and snowshoers in winter (snowmobiles are not permitted to approach the huts) and hikers and mountain bikers in summer tackle sections of the more than 350 mi of trails linking new and rustic cabins on day trips or weeklong expeditions. Apart from the joy of a self-reliant adventure among rugged mountains, travelers enjoy the camaraderie of communal living (there are very few private rooms in the huts), and evenings spent swapping stories by the glow of a wood-burning stove or the twinkle of summer stars. Maps and other information are available through the **10th Mountain Division Hut Association** (✉ *1280 Ute Ave., Aspen* ☎ *970/925–5775* ⊕ *www.huts.org*). Hut reservations should be made at least a month in advance.

> ### KNOW YOUR SNOW
>
> Vail is known for its "powder": slopes puffed with light, fluffy flakes that make you feel like you are gliding on silk. Ungroomed runs, however, can quickly turn to "crud" as they get "tracked out" (scarred with deep tracks). That's when it's time to hunt up the "corduroy"—freshly groomed runs.

If you aren't familiar with the area's backcountry trails, hiring a guide is a good idea. In Vail, contact **Paragon Guides** (✉ *Box 130, Vail* ☎ *970/926–5299* ⊕ *www.paragonguides.com*).

TRACK SKIING
The cross-country skiing at the **Vail Nordic Center** (✉ *1778 Vail Valley Dr.* ☎ *970/476–8366* ⊕ *www.vailnordiccenter.com*) is on a golf course. It's not the most beautiful route, but it's free.

OTHER SPORTS AND THE OUTDOORS

Mountain Information Center (☎ *800/503–8748*) has the lowdown on events in the area. In summer, **Adventure Ridge** (✉ *600 Lionshead Circle* ☎ *970/476–9090*), at Eagle's Nest high above Lionshead, is the hub of Vail Mountain activities. It's cool and high, and it has the views. It also has tons of activities like Friday Afternoon Club live bands, beer, sunset watching, the Dino Dig (a large sandbox with buried plastic dinosaur bones for kids), a gravity trampoline, horseshoe pits, volleyball nets, Frisbee golf, horaeback riding, a climbing wall, and free guided nature hikes through the Gore Range Natural Science School's Discovery Center. In winter you can go tubing, play laser tag, ice-skate, or try a ski bike.

BIKING
A popular summer destination for both road bikers and mountain bikers, Vail has a variety of paved bike paths (including one that leads up to Vail Pass), plus dozens of miles of dirt mountain-bike trails. You can take bikes on lifts heading uphill, then head downhill on an array of routes. **Vail Ski Tech** (✉ *555 E. Lionshead Circle* ☎ *800/525–5995* ⊕ *www.vailskitech. com*) rents and repairs bikes. Best of all, they are only steps from the Eagle Bahn Gondola, a summer gateway to the ski slope trails.

Each summer riders from around the region participate in races sponsored by the **Vail Recreation District** (✉ *700 S. Frontage Rd. E* ☎ *970/479–2279* ⊕ *www.vailrec.com*).

FITNESS AND SPAS
Deciding to get a massage or spa treatment is the easy part—deciding where to get it is a bigger problem, because there are many outstanding spas and health clubs in the area. The **Aria Spa & Club** (✉ *1300 Westhaven Dr.* ☎ *970/476–7111* ⊕ *www.vailcascade.com*) is one of the best places to be pampered. If you're up for a full-spa experience, ask about

the Symphony for the Senses packages. This 78,000-square-foot facility in the Vail Cascade Resort & Spa also has racquetball, basketball, and tennis courts. In the Sonnenalp Resort the lovely **Sonnenalp Spa** (✉ *20 Vail Rd.* ☎ *970/479–5404* ⊕ *www.sonnenalp.com*) is a European-style facility where you can relax on one of the lounge chairs around a big fireplace as you sip juice from the nearby bar.

GOLF

Golfers who love to play mountain courses know that some of the best are in Vail Valley. These courses meander through the valleys dividing the area's soaring peaks. The region is home to more than a dozen courses, and there are another half-dozen within easy driving distance. It's all just a matter of where you're staying and how much you want to spend. Some courses are only open to members and to guests at certain lodges.

Sonnenalp Golf Course. This Robert Cupp–Jay Morrish design threads through an upscale neighborhood 13 mi west of Vail. There are some serious elevation changes. Guests at the Sonnenalp Resort get preferred tee times. ✉ *1265 Berry Creek Dr., Edwards* ☎ *907/477–5372* ⊕ *www. sonnenalp.com* ⚲ *Reservations essential* ⚑ *18 holes. Yards: 7,100. Par: 71. Green fee: $125.*

Vail Golf Club. The area's municipal course rolls along between homes and condominiums in East Vail. ✉ *1778 Vail Valley Dr.* ☎ *970/479– 2260* ⊕ *www.vailgolf.com* ⚲ *Reservations essential* ⚑ *18 holes. Yards: 7,024. Par: 71. Green fee: $70.*

HIKING

If you aren't used to it, high altitude can catch you off guard. Drink plenty of water to help stave off the effects of altitude sickness—dizziness, shortness of breath, headache, and nausea. Slather on the sunscreen—it's easy to get sunburned up here. And in summer an early morning start is best, as afternoon thunderstorms are frequent and a danger above the tree line.

Eagle's Loop starts at 10,350 feet, but it's a mellow, 1-mi stroll along the mountaintop ridge with panoramic views of the Mount of the Holy Cross. Allow about half an hour. ✉ *Trailhead: Top of Eagle Bahn Gondola*).

Fodor'sChoice ★ **Booth Lake** is one of Vail's most popular hikes, so get on the trail early or pick a weekday during the summer high season. This is a sustained 6-mi one-way climb from 8,400 feet to Booth Lake at 11,500 feet, right above the tree line. Fit hikers can do this in about seven hours. En route, hikers can cool off at the 60-foot Booth Creek Falls; at only 2 mi in, this is also a great spot to turn around if you're feeling winded (this should take about two to three hours round-trip, and is a great option for an easier hike). The reward for pushing on is a nice view of Booth Lake cradled among the alpine tundra. ✉ *Trailhead: Take Exit 180 from I–70 to end of Booth Falls Rd.*

OUTFITTERS AND EXPEDITIONS **Paragon Guides** (✉ *Box 130, Vail* ☎ *970/926–5299* ⊕ *www.paragonguides.com*) runs backcountry adventures. In summer there's rock climbing, mountain biking, and day and overnight llama treks in and around Vail Valley. In winter the company runs daylong ski trips through the backcountry, and three- to six-day trips along the 10th Mountain Division Hut System.

HORSEBACK RIDING

One of the best ways to see Vail Valley is from the back of a horse. On scenic Sweetwater Lake **A.J. Brink Outfitters** (⊠ *3406 Sweetwater Rd., Sweetwater* ☎ *970/524–9301* ⊕ *www.brinkoutfitters.com*) has day and overnight horseback excursions high in the Flat Tops Wilderness.

About 12 mi north of Vail, **Piney River Ranch** (⊠ *Piney Lake* ☎ *970/477– 1171* ⊕ *www.pineyriveradventures.com*) has pony rides for kids and guided one-hour horseback rides for adults.

NATURE CENTERS

The **Vail Nature Center** (⊠ *Adjacent to Ford Park* ☎ *970/479–2291* ⊕ *www.vailrec.com*) occupies an old homestead just across from the Betty Ford Alpine Gardens. You can sign up for half-day and full-day backcountry hikes, wildflower walks, morning birding expeditions, and evening beaver-pond tours. In winter backcountry snowshoe excursions ★ and photography classes are available at the **Vail Nordic Center** (⊠ *1778 Vail Valley Dr.* ☎ *970/476–8366*).

SNOWMOBILING

Adventure Ridge (⊠ *600 Lionshead Circle* ☎ *970/476–9090*), at the top of Lionshead, leads twilight snowmobile excursions, as well as snowshoe, snow inner-tubing, and ice-skating trips. **Nova Guides** (⊠ *7088 U.S. Hwy. 24, Red Cliff* ☎ *970/719/486–2656* ⊕ *www.novaguides.com*) has snowmobile rentals and guided tours.

WHERE TO EAT

$$$$
NEW AMERICAN
★

✕ **Atwater on Gore Creek.** This tavern in the Vail Cascade Resort has beautiful floor-to-ceiling windows, hardwood furniture, cream-colored walls, and a nice gas fireplace. The Atwater stakes its repuation on organic and farm-fresh foods, including Kobe meatloaf with roast mushrooms and whipped potatoes and Black Hills buffalo carpaccio with arugula and violet mustard. Or go hearty from the tavern with the Nachos Primo, corn tortillas decorated with jalapeño jack and cheddar cheese and buried in guacamole. ⊠ *Vail Cascade Resort, 1300 Westhaven Dr., Cascade Village* ☎ *970/479–7014* ⊕ *www.vailcascade.com* ⊟ *AE, D, DC, MC, V.*

$
AMERICAN

✕ **Bart & Yeti's.** Grilled portobello-mushroom sandwiches, spicy Southwestern green chile, and Irish stew are among the choices at this laidback restaurant. Pictures of cowboys on horseback, wagon wheels, and other odds and ends line the rough log walls. If you want a full meal, entrées include favorites like barbecued baby back ribs and crispy fried chicken. The deck is a popular gathering spot in warm weather. The place is in Lionshead, just north of the Eagle Bahn Gondola. ⊠ *553 E. Lionshead Cir., Lionshead* ☎ *970/476–2754* ⊟ *AE, D, MC, V.*

¢
AMERICAN

✕ **Big Bear Bistro.** Locals kick off their mornings with a pit stop at this joint near the Vista Bahn lift to grab an $8 combo cup of java and a breakfast burrito—scrambled eggs, roast potatoes, cheddar cheese, and applewood smoked ham (you can get them wrapped to go). The service is quick and there's a simple but decent range of baked goods, fresh fruit, and organic options. The cobbled patio with a picnic table is a great place to enjoy a sandwich for lunch and during winter the inside is decorated with evergreen trimmings like a Tyrolean bistro. ⊠ *304 Hanson Ranch Rd., Lionshead* ☎ *970/300–1394* ⊟ *AE, D, MC, V.*

$$$$
AMERICAN
Fodor'sChoice
★
✕ **Game Creek Restaurant.** Getting to this restaurant is certainly half the fun, as you must catch a gondola up the mountain, then hop on a snowcat to get across Game Creek Bowl during the winter. During the summer you can travel by shuttle or take a horseback ride one-way. The Bavarian-style lodge is members-only for lunch, but open to the public for dinner all year and for an outstanding Sunday brunch in summer. Be prepared to linger over a multicourse prix-fixe meal as you enjoy spectacular views of the slopes and the mountains beyond. You might start with butter-poached prawns with fried vermicelli followed by duo of dry-aged Black Angus beef. ⊠ *278 Hanson Ranch Rd.* ☎ *970/479–4275* ⊕ *www.gamecreekclub.com* ⌕ *Reservations essential* ⊟ *AE, D, DC, MC, V* ☾ *No lunch.*

$$$$
ITALIAN
✕ **La Bottega.** This casual, small restaurant has a loyal following that appreciates the creative northern Italian fare in a romantic setting with brick alcoves and blonde wood tables. Customers especially love the lunch specials, which include creative pizzas from the stone ovens and delicious pastas. Some people turn out for a glass of vino in the wine bar, which takes up one side of the establishment. The cellar is one of the best in town. ⊠ *100 E. Meadow Dr., Vail Village* ☎ *970/476–0280* ⊕ *www.labottegavail.com* ⊟ *D, MC, V.*

$$$$
NEW AMERICAN
✕ **Larkspur Restaurant.** An open kitchen bustling with activity is the backdrop at Larkspur, popular with a parka-clad crowd at lunch and well-dressed diners in the evening. Owner and chef Thomas Salamunovich has a talent for blending cuisines, so the menu is filled with creative entrées such as house-made ricotta ravioli with Parmesan emulsion and certified organic chicken with "smashed" potatoes. Leave room for decadent desserts such as warm chocolate spice cake and petite doughnuts with chocolate and espresso sabayon. ⊠ *Golden Peak Lodge, 458 Vail Valley Dr., Vail Village* ☎ *970/754–8050* ⊕ *www.larkspurvail.com* ⌕ *Reservations essential* ⊟ *AE, MC, V.*

$
PIZZA
☾
✕ **Pazzo's Pizzeria.** This hole-in-the-wall is right in the heart of Vail Village. It serves some of the best pizzas in the area, ready to eat in the dining room or to take to one of the tables outside. Create your own masterpiece from a list of more than 20 ingredients, or opt for the cheesy lasagna, the chicken parmigiana, or one of the chubby calzones. Ask about the happy-hour specials. There are also locations in Avon and Eagle. ⊠ *122 E. Meadow Dr., Vail Village* ☎ *970/476–9026* ⊕ *www. itsblank.com/pazzos* ⊟ *D, MC, V.*

$$$$
NEW AMERICAN
✕ **Sweet Basil.** The decor may be understated—blond-wood chairs and buff-color walls—but the contemporary cuisine is anything but. The freshest seasonal ingredients available are used, so the menu changes about once a month. You might find cardamom-spiced duck breast with duck confit and champagne-vanilla pickled cherries or 28-day dry-aged Heritage pork chop with grilled Colorado peaches. Pair these entrées with one of the hundreds of wines from the restaurant's expansive cellar. Leave room for luscious desserts such as caramel corn beignets with

sweet-corn ice cream. ⊠ *193 E. Gore Creek Dr., Vail Village* ☎ *970/476–0125* ⊕ *www.sweetbasil-vail.com* ☐ *AE, MC, V.*

$$$$
NEW AMERICAN
★

✕ **Terra Bistro.** With spacious glass windows and track lighting, this sleek, sophisticated space in the Vail Mountain Lodge & Spa looks as if it belongs in a big city. Only the fireplace reminds you that this is Vail. The menu focuses on contemporary American cuisine that throws in a few Asian, Mediterranean, and Southwestern influences. Grilled Amish beef tenderloin with Yukon mashed potatoes and cornmeal-crusted Rocky Mountain trout with sweet-potato hash are headliners; organic produce and free-range meat and poultry are used whenever possible. ⊠ *Vail Mountain Lodge & Spa, 352 E. Meadow Dr., Vail Village* ☎ *970/476–6836* ⊕ *www.vailmountainlodge.com* ☐ *AE, D, MC, V.*

WHERE TO STAY

$$$$
▦ **The Arrabelle at Vail Square, A Rock Resort.** Arrabelle, which opened in January 2008, is the latest addition to Vail's collection of ski-in ski-out luxury lodges. It is centrally located in Vail Square, surrounded by shops, restaurants, and galleries, and is just steps away from the Eagle Bahn Gondola (which runs right to the top of Vail Mountain). The decor of the 62-room hotel looks like a sophisticated, cozy, European-style chalet. Rooms at the hotel are spacious (averaging 550 square feet) and romantic, featuring fireplaces and a lavish floor-to-ceiling drapery canopy over the bed. French brasserie Centre V serves delicious steak frites, duck confit, and incredible cheese plates, while the Great Room is a relaxing space for après-ski. Besides the rooftop pool and two hot tubs, the resort has a 10,000-square-foot wellness center with 11 treatment rooms, whirlpools, steam rooms, saunas, and a state-of-the-art fitness center. **Pros:** ski and boot butler service and storage; new room amenities; great location; fabulous on-site spa and restaurant. **Cons:** the valet parking entrance is hard to find. ⊠ *675 Lionshead Pl., Vail* ☎ *970/754–7777 or 866/662–7625* ⊕ *www.arabelle.rockresorts.com* ⇄ *62 rooms* ⚬ *In-room: safe, refrigerator, DVD, Wi-Fi, kitchen (some). In-hotel facilities: restaurant, room service, bar, gym, pool, spa, laundry service, public Wi-Fi, parking (paid)* ☐ *AE, D, MC, V.*

$$$$
▦ **Galatyn Lodge.** This luxury lodge in a quiet part of Vail Village maintains a low profile, which is just the approach its hard-core skiing regulars prefer. There are a handful of large condos that can be partitioned off into smaller spaces. All of these apartments are spacious, luxuriously decorated, and have kitchens with all the latest gadgets. **Pros:** indoor-outdoor heated pool; high percentage of return guests; apartment style. **Cons:** no children's programs; no restaurant or bar. ⊠ *365 Vail Valley Dr., Vail Village</neighb>* ☎ *970/479–2418 or 800/943–7322* ⊕ *www.thegalatynlodge.com* ⇄ *4 4-bedroom condos* ⚬ *In-room: safe (some), kitchen (some), refrigerator (some), DVD, Wi-Fi. In-hotel: pool, concierge, laundry facilities, laundry service, public Internet, public Wi-Fi, airport shuttle, parking (free)* ☐ *AE, MC, V.*

$$$$
▦ **Gasthof Gramshammer.** Pepi Gramshammer, a former Austrian Olympic ski racer who runs some of the country's best intensive ski programs, operates this guesthouse. Rooms are done up in pastels, filled with original oil paintings and fluffy down comforters. In keeping with the theme,

the waitresses are done up in dirndls. **Pros:** European flavor; village location. **Cons:** no room service; fewer amenities than larger properties. ⊠ *231 E. Gore Creek Dr., Vail Village* ☎ *970/476–5626 or 800/610–7374* ⊕ *www.pepis.com* ⇨ *30 rooms, 9 suites and apartments* ⅙ *In-room: no a/c, safe (some), kitchen (some), refrigerator, DVD (some), Wi-Fi (some). In-hotel: restaurant, bar, pool, laundry facilities, laundry service, public Wi-Fi, airport shuttle, parking (free)* ☱ *AE, D, MC, V.*

$$$$ 🛎 **Lodge at Vail.** The first facility to open in Vail, in 1962, the sprawling lodge—modeled after the Lodge at Sun Valley—is popular with skiers and families because of its fabulous location only 150 feet from the village's main lift, the Vista Bahn. Ski valets ready your skis every morning (after the complimentary wax) and collect your gear for drying in the evening. The quality and size of the rooms varies tremendously. The older wing has smaller, individually decorated rooms with a homey feel, while the newer wing has larger suites with modern touches like heated marble floors in the bathrooms and gas fireplaces. Mickey's piano bar is a favored après-ski spot. **Pros:** on-mountain ski storage; located near main ski lift. **Cons:** can get noisy with partiers; quality of rooms varies. ⊠ *174 E. Gore Creek Dr., Vail Village* ☎ *970/476–5011 or 877/528–7625* ⊕ *www.lodgeatvail. rockresorts.com* ⇨ *79 rooms, 46 suites, 44 1-, 2-, and 3-bedroom condos* ⅙ *In-room: no a/c (some), safe (some), kitchen (some), refrigerator (some), DVD (some), Wi-Fi. In-hotel: 2 restaurants, room service, bar, golf course, pool, gym, spa, concierge, laundry facilities, laundry service, public Internet, public Wi-Fi, airport shuttle, parking (paid), some pets allowed* ☱ *AE, D, DC, MC, V.*

$$$$ 🛎 **Sitzmark Lodge.** This cozy lodge buzzes with a dozen languages, thanks to the international guests who return year after year. Rooms, which range from moderate to large, have balconies that look out onto Vail Mountain or Gore Creek. Some have gas-burning fireplaces to keep things comfortable. The decor is a blend of light woods and cheerful floral fabrics. The staff is extremely friendly, encouraging you to congregate in the sunny, split-level living room on winter afternoons for complimentary mulled wine. The lodge is only 75 yards from the lifts, and a Continental breakfast is served in winter. **Pros:** easy access to ski lifts; international ambience; great views. **Cons:** breakfasts are standard in winter; customer service varies. ⊠ *183 Gore Creek Dr., Vail Village* ☎ *970/476–5001 or 888/476–5001* ⊕ *www.sitzmarklodge.com* ⇨ *35 rooms* ⅙ *In-room: no a/c, safe (some), kitchen (some), refrigerator (some), DVD (some), Wi-Fi (some). In-hotel: restaurant, bar, pool, concierge, laundry facilities, laundry service, public Internet, public Wi-Fi, parking (free)* ☱ *AE, MC, V.*

$$$$ 🛎 **Sonnenalp Resort.** It's the sense of family tradition and European elegance that makes the Sonnenalp Resort the most romantic of all hotels in Fodor's Choice the faux-Tyrolean village of Vail. Four generations of the Fassler family ★ have worked in the hotel business, and the Sonnenalp showcases their expertise not only in the Bavarian architecture and style (stucco walls hatched with wood beams and balconies with flower boxes) but also in the impeccable manners of everyone from front-desk receptionists to the waiters at Ludwig's. Room configurations vary from two-story suites to cozy rooms barely bigger than the overstuffed beds. The first-floor spa is

5

set around an alcove fireplace, but the indoor heated pool flows outdoors and fronts a beautiful garden beside Gore Creek. **Pros:** classic alpine ambience; incredible buffet breakfasts; spa. **Cons:** removed from lifts; tough to regulate room temperature in winter. ⊠ *20 Vail Rd., Vail Village,* ☎ *970/476–5656 or 800/654–8312* ⊕ *www.sonnenalp.com* ⇄ *12 rooms, 115 suites* ₺ *In-room: safe (some), kitchen (some), refrigerator (some), DVD (some), Wi-Fi. In-hotel: 3 restaurants, room service, bar, golf course, pool, gym, spa, concierge, children's programs (ages 5–12), laundry service, public Internet, public Wi-Fi, airport shuttle, parking (paid), some pets allowed* ⊟ *AE, D, DC, MC, V* ⍩◯⍝ *BP.*

$$$$ ⌗ **Vail Cascade Resort & Spa.** Down-to-earth yet luxurious is the best way to describe this family-oriented ski-in ski-out hotel. Despite its size, it manages to remain intimate. Rooms reflect a "mountain eclectic" style, with rich plaid and floral fabrics, wicker furniture, and wrought-iron lamps. The restaurant has garnered acclaim for its outstanding grilled foods and fine selection of wines. You'll have access to the adjoining Aria Spa & Club and the full-service health club with racquetball, squash, and basketball courts. The best deals at any time of year are the packages, which might include lift tickets in winter or sports massages in summer. **Pros:** right on the slope; spa and health club; nice views of creek. **Cons:** staff can be hard to find; concrete exterior; expensive parking. ⊠ *1300 Westhaven Dr., Cascade Village</neighb>* ☎ *970/476–7111 or 800/420–2424* ⊕ *www.vailcascade.com* ⇄ *292 rooms, 27 suites, 80 condominiums* ₺ *In-room: no a/c, safe (some), kitchen (some), refrigerator (some), DVD (some), Internet, Wi-Fi. In-hotel: restaurant, room service, bars, tennis courts, pool, gym, spa, concierge, children's programs (ages 3 mo–12), laundry facilities (some), laundry service, public Internet, public Wi-Fi, airport shuttle, parking (paid)* ⊟ *AE, D, DC, MC, V.*

NIGHTLIFE

Near the gondola in Lionshead, **Garfinkel's** (⊠ *333 E. Lionshead Circle* ☎ *970/476–3789* ⊕ *www.garfsvail.com*) has plenty of televisions where you can catch the game. It's open late, especially on weekends. In the Lodge at Vail, **Mickey's** (⊠ *174 E. Gore Creek Dr.* ☎ *970/476–5011*) attracts the après-ski crowd. A pianist plays soothing standards. The **Red Lion** (⊠ *304 Bridge St.* ☎ *970/476–7676* ⊕ *www.theredlion.com*) is a tradition in Vail. It's standing-room only in the afternoon, and a bit mellower in the evening. Most nights there's guitar or piano music. **Sarah's** (⊠ *356 E. Hanson Ranch Rd.* ☎ *970/476–5641*) showcases Helmut Fricker, a Vail institution who plays accordion while yodeling up a storm on Fridays in the winter. You can catch him during the ski season Tuesday and Friday evenings. A young crowd scarfs down excellent late-night pizzas at **Vendetta's** (⊠ *291 Bridge St.* ☎ *970/476–5070* ⊕ *www.vendettasvail.com*).

SHOPPING

BOUTIQUES

Across from the Children's Fountain, **Axel's** (✉ *201 Gore Creek Dr.* ☎ *970/476–7625* ⊕ *www.axelsltd. com*) carries high-end European fashions including Italian suede pants, riding boots, and shearling coats. For years, a golden bear (papa-, mama-, or baby-size) on a chain has been a popular souvenir from this ski resort. The **Golden Bear** (✉ *286 Bridge St.* ☎ *970/476– 4082* ✉ *Village Hall, Beaver Creek* ☎ *970/845–7881* ⊕ *thegoldenbear. com*) makes many versions of its namesake, as well as other popular items such as hammered-gold necklaces and bracelets. You can also purchase fashionable clothes and accessories. Stocking buffalo-hide coats and bowls filled with potpourri, **Gorsuch** (✉ *263 E. Gore Creek Dr.* ☎ *970/476–2294* ✉ *70 Promenade, Beaver Creek* ☎ *970/949–7115* ⊕ *www.gorsuch.com*) is an odd combination of an upscale boutique and a sporting-goods store. **Pepi's Sports** (✉ *231 Bridge St.* ☎ *970/476–5202* ⊕ *pepisports.com*) sells chic ski clothing and accessories from designers such as Bogner, Skea, Descente, and Spyder.

VAIL AND BEAVER CREEK LODGING ALTERNATIVES

Vail/Beaver Creek Reservations (☎ *800/525–2257*) is the place for one-stop shopping. You can buy lift tickets, arrange ski and snowboard lessons, get updates on events and activities, and book lodging at many of the hotels and condominium properties in the Vail Valley. **Vail Valley Partnership** (☎ *800/653–4523*) operates a central reservations service for properties in Vail, Avon, and Beaver Creek. It also gives out information on events and activities and reports on snow conditions.

ART GALLERIES

The **Claggett/Rey Gallery** (✉ *100 E. Meadow Dr.* ☎ *800/252–4438* ⊕ *www.claggettrey.com*) is the place to purchase canvases and sculptures by well-known Western artists. You'll be dazzled by handblown creations at the **Pismo Gallery** (✉ *122 E. Meadow Dr.* ☎ *970/476–2400* ⊕ *www.pismoglass.com*). The outstanding collection of handblown glass ranges from perfume bottles to paperweights.

MINTURN

5 mi west of Vail; 105 mi west of Denver via I–70.

The Vail Valley stretches far beyond the town of Vail. Minturn began to thrive in 1987, when the Rio Grande Railway extended a narrow-gauge line into town to carry away the zinc, copper, silver, and lead extracted from nearby mines. The main street has an eclectic collection of antiques, curio, and other shops, plus popular restaurants housed in the old buildings. It's a good place to take a break from skiing and grab a bite.

GETTING HERE AND AROUND

As you travel west along Interstate 70, Exit 171 leads to this quiet community.

EXPLORING

Minturn Cellars Winery (✉ *107 Williams St.* ☎ *970/827–4065*) is a wine-tasting room featuring some of the finest local wines.

WHERE TO EAT AND STAY

$$$
STEAK

✗ **Minturn Country Club.** This homey hangout is one of those "you've gotta go" places people talk about after returning home as much for the concept—you are your own chef—as the prime and choice cuts of aged steak. Choose from steaks, poultry, and fish and head to one of several lava rock grills—heated to 1,100-degrees—and sear your meat (ask if you need some pointers). Sounds like too much work? Order some slow-cooked baby back ribs or the one-pound Alaskan king crab legs and let the chefs cook it for you. Favorite sides like sweet potato fries and shrimp kabobs are ordered from the kitchen. And don't miss the Minturn Tater for dessert—a cookie and ice cream loaf drizzled with chocolate. ✉ *131 Main St.* ☎ *970/827–4114* ⊕ *www.minturncountryclub.com* ≜ *Reservations not accepted* ⊟ *MC, V* ⊘ *No lunch.*

$$
MEXICAN
☯

✗ **Minturn Saloon.** After a day on the slopes, reward yourself with margaritas made with real lime juice and baskets of tortilla chips served with homemade salsa. No wonder the place is always packed with locals. In a dining room that calls to mind the Old West, you can feast on such specialties as *chiles rellenos* (stuffed peppers) and a steak-and-quail plate. There's even a children's menu. ✉ *146 N. Main St.* ☎ *970/827–5954* ⊕ *www.minturnsaloon.com* ≜ *Reservations not accepted* ⊟ *AE, MC, V* ⊘ *No lunch.*

$

🏨 **Minturn Inn.** This three-story 1915 log home, one of the town's oldest residences, was converted into an inn with hewn-log beds and antler chandeliers. When business became brisk, the owners added the neighboring Eagle Street Bed & Breakfast and the Grouse Creek Inn. These properties have two-person hot tubs, river-rock fireplaces, and private decks or patios overlooking the Eagle River. Hearty breakfasts are included. **Pros:** historic lodgings; view of the river; fireplaces. **Cons:** removed from the ski resort; few room and hotel amenities. ✉ *442 Main St.,* ☎ *970/827–9647 or 800/646–8876* ⊕ *www.minturninn.com* ⇆ *18 rooms, 1 cabin* ♿ *In-room: no a/c, Wi-Fi. In-hotel: parking (free)* ⊟ *AE, D, MC, V* ⧀⧀ *BP.*

10TH MOUNTAIN DIVISION

A pair of red-crossed swords on a blue shield is the familiar insignia of the famed 10th Mountain Division, created to train soldiers in mountain and winter warfare during World War II. One of their first training centers, Camp Hale, was opened in 1942 in a small park between Red Cliff and Leadville. The high valley must have borne at least a passing resemblance to the Himalayas, because before it closed in 1966 the CIA also secretly trained Tibetan guerrillas there to wage a war of independence in their Chinese-occupied homeland.

BEAVER CREEK

12 mi west of Vail; 110 mi west of Denver via I–70.

As with the majority of the area's resorts, the heart of Beaver Creek is a mountainside village. What sets Beaver Creek apart is that it's a series of cascading plazas connected by escalators. In this ultraposh enclave even boot-wearing skiers and snowboard-hauling riders ride the escalators from the hotels and shuttle stops on the lower levels. Opened in 1980 as a smaller version of Vail, Beaver Creek has overshadowed its older sibling. In fact, its nearest rival in the luxury market is Utah's Deer Valley.

Locals know that Beaver Creek is the best place to ski on weekends, when Vail is too crowded, or anytime there's fresh powder. Beaver Creek is just far enough from Denver that it doesn't get the flood of day-trippers who flock to Vail and the other Front Range resorts. The slopes of Beaver Creek Mountain are connected to those of even ritzier Bachelor Gulch. These are close to Arrowhead, creating a village-to-village ski experience like those found in Europe.

Savvy travelers have learned that Beaver Creek is even lovelier in summer, when diners can enjoy a meal on a spacious patio, mountain bikers can hitch a ride uphill on the chairlift, and golfers can play on the beautiful Beaver Creek Course or on one of the dozen others in the Vail Valley. On special evenings you can attend concerts, get tickets to the theater, or head to a performance at the Beaver Creek Vilar Center for the Arts. In Beaver Creek you have easy access to all of the activities in Vail Valley.

Beaver Creek speaks loudly and clearly to a settled and affluent crowd, but visitors on a budget can also enjoy the resort's many attractions. Just drive past the pricier lodgings in the village and opt instead for a room in nearby Avon, Edwards, or even Vail.

GETTING HERE AND AROUND

Driving is the most convenient way to get around Beaver Creek, but there are private shuttles and public buses.

WHEN TO GO

Beaver Creek's seasons are the same as Vail; winter is great for snow sports and summer also attracts outdoor enthusiasts.

ESSENTIALS

Transportation Contacts Avon/Beaver Creek Transit (☎ 970/748–4120 ⊕ www.avon.org). **Colorado Mountain Express** (☎ 800/525–6363 or 970/468–7600 ⊕ www.ridecme.com).

DOWNHILL SKIING AND SNOWBOARDING

Beaver Creek is a piece of nirvana, partly because of its system of trails and partly because of its enviable location two hours from Denver. Although only a third the size of Vail, Beaver Creek is seldom crowded. The skiable terrain extends from the runs down Beaver Creek to the slopes around Bachelor Gulch to the network of trails at Arrowhead. You can easily ski from one village to another. The omnipresent and helpful ambassadors are always willing to point you in the right direction, and even give you a lift back to your lodge if you forgot your goggles.

Skiing and Snowboarding Tips

Although downhill skiing has long been the classic winter activity, snowboarding—once the bastion of teenage "riders" in baggy pants—is fast catching up as a mainstream sport. Telemarking and cross-country skiing still have loyal followings, though these skiers tend to prefer the wide-open backcountry to the more-populated resorts.

Although it snows somewhere in the Colorado high country every month—and resorts can open their lifts as early as October and close as late as the fourth of July—the traditional ski season usually runs from December until early April. Christmas through New Year's Day and the month of March (when spring-breakers arrive) tend to be the busiest periods for most ski areas. The slower months of January and February often yield good package deals, as do the early and late ends of the season.

EQUIPMENT RENTAL

Rental equipment is available at all ski areas and at ski shops around resorts or in nearby towns. It's often more expensive to rent at the resort where you'll be skiing, but then it's easier to go back to the shop if something doesn't fit. Experienced skiers can "demo" (try out) premium equipment to get a feel for new technology before upgrading.

LESSONS

In the United States the Professional Ski Instructors of America (PSIA) has devised a progressive teaching system that is used at most ski schools. This allows skiers to take lessons at different ski areas. Classes range in length from hour-long skill clinics to half- or full-day workshops. Deals can be had for first-time and beginner skiers and snowboarders who attend morning clinics and then try out their new skills on beginner and intermediate slopes for the remainder of the day.

Most ski schools follow the PSIA teaching approach for children, and many also incorporate SKIwee, another standardized teaching technique. Classes for children are arranged by ability and age group; often the ski instructor chaperones a meal during the teaching session. Children's ski instruction has come a long way in the last 10 years; instructors specially trained in teaching children, and equipment designed for little bodies, mean that most children can now begin to ski successfully as young as three or four. Helmets are often de rigueur.

LIFT TICKETS

With some lift ticket prices increasing every year, the best advice is to shop around. Single-day, adult, holiday-weekend passes cost the most, but better bargains can be had through off-site purchase locations (check newspaper Sunday sections and local supermarkets, such as King Soopers and Safeway), online discounts, multiple-day passes, and season passes. You can always call a particular resort's central reservations line to ask where discount lift tickets can be purchased. With a little legwork you should never have to pay full price.

TRAIL RATING

Ski areas mark and rate trails and slopes—Easy (green circle), Intermediate (blue square), Advanced (black diamond), and Expert (double black diamond).

Beaver Creek has a little of everything, from smoother slopes for beginners to difficult trails used for international competitions. Grouse Mountain, in particular, is famed for its thigh-burning bump runs. Beginners have an entire peak, at the summit of Beaver Creek Mountain, where they can learn to ski or practice on novice trails. And newcomers can return to the village on one of the lifts if they are too tired to take the long trail all the way to the bottom. Intermediate-level skiers have several long cruising trails on the lower half of Beaver Creek Mountain and in Larkspur Bowl. Both locations also have black-diamond trails, so groups of skiers and snowboarders of varying abilities can ride uphill together. The Birds of Prey runs, like Peregrine and Redtail, are aptly named, because the steepness of the trails can be a surprise for skiers who mistakenly think they are skilled enough to take on this challenging terrain. The days of snowboarders getting snubbed in Beaver Creek are long gone, and shredders can tackle a series of terrain parks with increasing difficulty from Park 101 to the Zoom Room and on to the Moonshine half-pipe.

The slopes of neighboring **Bachelor Gulch** are a mix of beginner and intermediate trails. Here you can often find fresh powder hours after it's gone elsewhere. Many of the open slopes weave past multimillion-dollar homes; cost of real estate is even higher than in Beaver Creek. The Ritz-Carlton Bachelor Gulch, which sits at the base of the lift, is one of the region's most beautiful hotels. A stop here is a must for any architecture buff. Many skiers plan to arrive in time for a hearty lunch at Remington's or an après-ski cocktail in the Buffalo Bar or the Fly Fishing Library. There are shuttles handy to take you back to Beaver Creek.

The third village in the area, **Arrowhead,** has the best and usually the least crowded intermediate terrain. Locals take advantage of sunny days by sitting on the spacious deck at the Broken Arrow Café. It's not much more than a shack, but the burgers can't be beat. The European concept of skiing from village to village was introduced here in 1996, when the new owners, Vail Associates, decided to connect Arrowhead, Beaver Creek, and Bachelor Gulch via lifts and ski trails. ☎ *800/404–3535* ⊕ *www.beavercreek.com* ☾ *Late Nov.–mid-Apr., daily 9–4.*

FACILITIES 4,040-foot vertical drop; 1,805 skiable acres; 19% beginner, 43% intermediate, 38% advanced; 2 gondolas, 10 high-speed quads, 2 triples, 2 doubles, 1 surface lift.

LESSONS AND PROGRAMS The **Vail and Beaver Creek Ski and Snowboard School** (☎ *970/754–8245*) runs classes at both resorts. At Beaver Creek there are about 600 instructors; lessons are available in more than 20 languages. Afternoon-only group lessons are $80 to $90, depending upon the season. All-day lessons are $120. Special clinics run throughout the year, like workshops for women, teen sessions, and telemark courses. Beginners take three-day courses that include equipment rental and lift passes.

LIFT TICKETS Few skiers pay the walk-up rate of approximately $97 for a one-day lift ticket. Most vacationers purchase lift-and-lodging packages for Beaver Creek, or go online to ⊕ *www.snow.com* and purchase multiday lift passes at discounted rates. A lift ticket purchased at Beaver Creek may also be used at Vail, Breckenridge, Keystone, and Arapahoe Basin.

RENTALS   **Beaver Creek Sports** (✉ *Beaver Creek Village* ☎ *970/754–5400*) rents ski equipment for $45 to $60, depending upon whether you choose regular or high-performance gear.

NORDIC SKIING

TRACK SKIING

★ The prettiest place for cross-country skiing is **McCoy Park,** with more than 19 mi of trails groomed for traditional cross-country skiing, skate skiing, and snowshoeing, all laid out around a mountain peak. To reach McCoy Park, take the Strawberry Park chairlift—a plus because it gets you far enough from the village that you're in a pristine environment. The groomed tracks have a fair amount of ups and downs (or perhaps because the elevation rises to 9,840 feet, it just seems that way) (☎ *970/754–5313* ⊕ *www.beavercreek.com*).

Lessons, equipment rentals, and guided tours are available through **Beaver Creek Nordic Sports Center** (✉ *Strawberry Park Condo Bldg., at the bottom of Chair 12* ☎ *970/745–5313* ⊙ *Daily 9–4*).

OTHER SPORTS AND THE OUTDOORS

The **Activities Desk of Vail** (☎ *970/476–9090*) gives you the lowdown on many of the activities in the region, summer or winter.

BIKING

Colorado Bike Services (✉ *41149 U.S. Hwy. 6 and 24* ☎ *970/949–4641* ⊕ *www.coloradobikeservice.com*) is a great bike shop where you can get more information about the trails around Beaver Creek.

Each summer, riders from around the region participate in races sponsored by the **Vail Recreation District** (✉ *700 S. Frontage Rd. E, Vail* ☎ *970/479–2279* ⊕ *www.vailrec.com*).

FITNESS AND SPAS

It's easy to find a full-body massage in Beaver Creek, as many hotels have full-service spas included. In the Park Hyatt Beaver Creek, the **Allegria Spa** (✉ *136 E. Thomas Pl.* ☎ *970/748–7500* ⊕ *www.allegriaspa.com*) has a full range of services, including a wonderful "barefoot" massage.

GOLF

The Club at Cordillera. The Lodge & Spa at Cordillera has three 18-hole courses and a 10-hole course. Hotel guests can play the Jack Nicklaus–designed Summit Course, which surrounds a peak like a string of pearls. The Hale Irwin Mountain Course runs through aspen groves, past lakes, and through meadows surrounded by luxury homes. The Dave Pelz–designed 10-hole course lets you show off (or makes you practice) your short-game skills. ✉ *2205 Cordillera Way, Edwards* ☎ *970/569–6480* ⊕ *www.cordillera-vail.com* ⌦ *Reservations essential* 𝕏 *Mountain: 18 holes. Yards: 7,413. Par: 72/72. Green fee: $10.*

★ **Eagle Ranch Golf Club.** This 6,600-foot-high course was landscaped in the lush wetlands of the Brush Creek valley. Caddies like to joke that the perfect club might actually be a fly rod. Arnold Palmer, who designed the 18-hole course, said, "The fairways are very playable and the roughs are not extremely rough." ⊠ *50 Lime Park Dr., Eagle* ☎ *970/328–2882 or 866/328–3232* ⊕ *www.eagleranchgolf.com* ⚑ *Reservations essential* ⚑ *18 holes. Yards: 7,500. Par: 72. Green fee: $99.*

Red Sky Golf Club. At this tony private course a few miles west of Beaver Creek members alternate with guests on two courses designed by Tom Fazio and Greg Norman. The Tom Fazio Course's front nine are laid out on sagebrush-covered hills, but the back nine flows up and down a mountainside covered with groves of junipers and aspens. The Greg Norman Course sprawls through a broad valley. Some shots require carries across jagged ravines. Norman's signature bunkers abound, guarding slippery greens. In order to play at Red Sky Golf Club you must be staying in the Lodge at Vail, the Pines Lodge in Beaver Creek, the Ritz-Carlton Bachelor Gulch, other hotels owned by Vail Resorts, or other partner properties. ⊠ *376 Red Sky Rd., Wolcott* ☎ *970/754–8425* ⊕ *www.redskygolfclub.com* ⚑ *Reservations essential* ⚑ *Greg Norman: 18 holes. Yards: 7,580. Par: 72. Green fee: $250. Tom Fazio: 18 holes. Yards: 7,113. Par: 72. Green fee: $250.*

HIKING

The **Holy Cross Wilderness Area** is southwest of Beaver Creek. **Eagle Lake** is a great trail for hikers who want to test their bodies at altitude without overdoing it. The trail starts at 9,100 feet (just slightly higher than Beaver Creek's base at 7,400 feet) and contours through a glacial valley for almost 2.5 mi around Woods Lake to Eagle Lake at 10,000 feet. Plan on a five-hour round-trip journey. You can continue up the valley to explore more lakes if you're feeling fit. ⊠ *Holy Cross Ranger District, White River National Forest* ☎ *970/827–5715* ⊕ *www.fs.fed. us/r2/whiteriver/recreation/wilderness/holycross.*

The **Beaver Creek Hiking Center** (⊠ *Beaver Creek Village* ☎ *970/754– 5373*) arranges everything from easy walks to difficult hikes. If you're traveling with kids, ask about educational programs.

HORSEBACK RIDING

Beaver Creek Stable (⊠ *Box 2050, Eagle* ☎ *970/845–7770*) arranges outings ranging from one-hour rides to all-day excursions. Many trips include a tasty picnic lunch. In the evening there are hayrides and sunset rides.

WHERE TO EAT

$$$$
FRENCH
✗ **8100 Mountainside Bar & Grill.** In 2008, this bistro in the Park Hyatt opened with its name based on the altitude and slopeside locale. An open kitchen with a 66-inch wood burning grill and an outdoor firepit make this a favorite for après-ski diners. Chef Reese Hay favors a seasonal menu that includes favorites like trout with lemon capers and marinated elk loin. The bar—with a full range of organic wines and the best of Colorado microbrews—seats 20 along a polished stone counter. ⊠ *Park Hyatt Beaver Creek Resort & Spa, 50 W. Thomas Pl.* ☎ *970/827–6600* ⊕ *www.8100barandgrill.com* ⚑ *Reservations essential* ▭ *AE, MC, V.*

$$$$ ✕**Beano's Cabin.** One of the memorable experiences during a trip to
NEW AMERICAN Beaver Creek is traveling in a sleigh to this former hunting lodge. In
summer you can get here on horseback or by shuttle van. During the
journey, your driver will undoubtedly fill you in on some local history.
The pine-log cabin, warmed by a crackling fire, is an unbeatable location for a romantic meal. Choose from among the entrées that change
with the seasons. Pair pan-seared halibut with duo of venison then top it
all off with a bourbon pecan torte. ✉ *Larkspur Bowl* ☎ *970/754–3463
or 866/395–3185* ⚲ *Reservations essential* ▤ *AE, MC, V* ⊘ *Closed
May, June, Oct., Nov.*

$ ✕**Fiesta's.** The Marquez sisters, Debbie and Susan, use old family recipes
SOUTHWESTERN brought to Colorado by their great-grandparents to create great Southwestern cuisine. Among the favorites are chicken enchiladas in a white
jalapeño sauce and blue-corn enchiladas served Santa Fe style with an
egg on top. Handmade corn tamales are stuffed with pork and smothered in a classic New Mexican–chile sauce. The eatery in Edwards Plaza
is brightly decorated with New Mexican folk art and paintings. More
than 20 tequilas keep the bar—and patrons—hopping. ✉ *57 Edwards
Access Rd., Edwards* ☎ *970/926–2121* ▤ *AE, D, MC, V.*

$$$ ✕**The Gashouse.** This longtime hangout set inside a 1930s-era log cabin
AMERICAN has walls covered with hunting trophies. (If stuffed animal heads aren't
your thing, think twice about eating here.) Locals swear by the buf-
falo, prime rib, and elk. Stop in for a brew and some buffalo wings and
watch how some of the Vail Valley residents kick back. ✉ *34185 U.S.
Hwy. 6, 4 mi west of Beaver Creek, Edwards* ☎ *970/926–3613* ⊕ *www.
gashouse-restaurant* ▤ *AE, MC, V.*

$$ ✕**Gore Range Brewery.** After a morning on the slopes or an afternoon
AMERICAN playing a few rounds of golf, locals gravitate here for a burger or spicy
ribs and a locally brewed beer. In the Edwards Village Center, the
brewery blends high-tech styling with a laid-back aura on its spacious
outdoor patio and in comfortable indoor booths. ✉ *0105 Edwards
Village Blvd., Edwards* ☎ *970/926–2739* ⊕ *www.gorerangebrewery.
com* ▤ *AE, MC, V.*

$$$$ ✕**Mirabelle.** In a restored farmhouse at the entrance to Beaver Creek,
CONTINENTAL Mirabelle is one of the area's loveliest restaurants. Owner and chef
Daniel Joly serves superb Belgian–French cuisine. His preparations
are a perfect blend of colors, flavors, and textures. The menu changes
regularly, but if it's available, try hot foie gras with caramelized golden
apples, and roasted elk fillet with rhubarb jam. Depending on your
point of view, the elaborate desserts are either heavenly or sinful. The
wine list is roughly two-thirds European—to match the menu—and
a third domestic. ✉ *55 Village Rd., Avon* ☎ *970/949–7728* ⊕ *www.
mirabelle1.com* ▤ *AE, D, MC, V* ⊘ *Closed Sun. No lunch.*

$$$$ ✕**Spago.** At the Ritz Carlton, Wolfgang Puck's restaurant, is housed in
NEW AMERICAN an expansive, dining room whose vegetable-dyed wood paneling and
enlarged black-and-white photographs achieves a sleekly modern look
without contradicting the resort's rustic mountain sensibility. Puck's
seasonal menu often favors Asian accents and regional ingredients. In
late autumn the menu's pumpkin soup is deliciously intensified with car-
damom cream, and Colorado lamb chops spiced with Hunan eggplant

and cilantro-mint vinaigrette. The pumpkin and mascarpone *agnolotti* with sage butter is not to be missed, and for dessert the *kaiserschmarren*, a soufléd crème fraîche pancake with strawberry sauce, is otherwordly. Service is impeccable, if a touch formal; those who prefer a low-key (or less bank-breaking) meal might consider dining in the bar area. ⌧ *0130 Daybreak Ridge, at the Ritz Carlton, Bachelor Gulch Avon,* ☎ *970/343–1555* ⊕ *www.wolfgangpuck.com* ⌧ *Reservations essential* ▭ *AE, D, DC, MC, V.*

$$$$
NEW AMERICAN

✕ **Splendido.** With elegant marble columns and custom-made Italian linens, this posh eatery is the height of opulence. Owner and chef David Walford is a master of New American cuisine, and he borrows freely from many traditions. He is equally adept at turning out rack of lamb with rosemary as he is grilling up an elk loin with braised elk osso buco. Retire for a nightcap to the classically elegant piano bar, where Peter Vavra entertains. ⌧ *17 Chateau La., Beaver Creek Village* ☎ *970/845–8808* ⊕ *www.splendidobeavercreek.com* ▭ *AE, D, DC, MC, V* ☉ *No lunch.*

$$$$
ITALIAN

✕ **Toscanini.** You have a ringside seat at the ice rink in the heart of Beaver Creek when you dine at this casual eatery. The menu is authentic Italian, starting with a variety of dipping oils for the fresh bread, then beef tenderloin carpaccio with Kalamata olives and shaved Parmesan. Entrées include pan-seared diver scallops with roasted fennel mashed potatoes. Don't pass up the rosemary and garlic–marinated lamb chops with basil risotto. ⌧ *60 Avondale Rd., Beaver Creek (technically in the town of Avon, but the village of Beaver Creek, same zip) Village* ☎ *970/754–5590* ▭ *AE, D, DC, MC, V* ☉ *Closed May, June, Oct., Nov.*

WHERE TO STAY

$$$$
★

🏨 **Beaver Creek Lodge.** A central atrium grabs all the attention at this European-style lodge a few hundred yards from the lifts. Rooms are generously proportioned—you'll probably get more space for your money here than at most other properties in the heart of the village, which makes it great for families. The style is mountain chic—polished leather furniture, original art, sleek cabinets, flat-screen TV in the bedroom, and beds plumped with pillow-top mattresses. **Pros:** right next to the lifts; large rooms; good value. **Cons:** fee for parking; no spa. ⌧ *26 Avondale La., Beaver Creek Village* ☎ *970/845–9800* ⊕ *www. beavercreeklodge.net* ⇨ *72 suites* ⌧ *In-room: safe, kitchen (some), refrigerator (some), DVD, Wi-Fi. In-hotel: 2 restaurants, room service, bar, pool, gym, concierge, children's programs (ages 3–12), laundry facilities, laundry service, public Internet, public Wi-Fi, airport shuttle, parking (paid)* ▭ *AE, D, DC, MC, V.*

$$$

🏨 **Charter at Beaver Creek.** With its elegantly angled blue-slate roof, this sprawling property is one of the area's handsomest accommodations. Wisps of smoke from the fireplaces in many rooms rise above, giving the place a homey feel perfect for families. There are plenty of choices for rooms, including one- to five-bedroom condominiums catering to families, many with balconies that let you gaze over the tops of the trees. The location is perfect—the ski-in ski-out hotel is a short walk from the main plaza at Beaver Creek. **Pros:** attractive architecture; ski-in ski-out.

5

Cons: mediocre breakfasts; pools can be noisy with children. ✉ *120 Offerson Rd., Beaver Creek Village* ☎ *970/949–6660 or 800/525–2139* ⊕ *www.thecharter.com* ⟿ *73 rooms, 138 condominiums* ⚲ *In-room: no a/c, safe (some), kitchen (some), refrigerator (some), DVD (some), Wi-Fi. In-hotel: 2 restaurants, room service, bar, pools, gym, spa, concierge, laundry facilities, laundry service, public Internet, public Wi-Fi, airport shuttle, parking (free)* ⊟ *AE, MC, V.*

$$$$ 🏨 **Lodge & Spa at Cordillera.** An aura of quiet luxury prevails at this mountaintop lodge with a style that calls to mind the finest alpine hotels, and is popular with return guests. The rooms vary quite a bit in size; those in the newer wing tend to be larger. There are wood-burning fireplaces in some of the older rooms, whereas the newer rooms have gas fireplaces. The indoor pool has a view of the mountains through the wall of windows. The lodge is in the gated community of Cordillera, 15 minutes from Beaver Creek. The lodge operates a shuttle to the lifts. **Pros:** spa; fireplaces in rooms. **Cons:** must take shuttle or drive to lifts or town; rooms are a bit outdated. ✉ *2205 Cordillera Way,* ✒ *Box 1110, Edwards* ☎ *970/926–2200 or 800/877–3529* ⊕ *www. cordilleralodge. com* ⟿ *56 rooms* ⚲ *In-room: refrigerators (some), DVD (some), Wi-Fi. In-hotel: 4 restaurants, room service, bars, golf courses, pool, gym, spa, concierge, laundry service, public Internet, public Wi-Fi, airport shuttle, parking (free)* ⊟ *AE, D, DC, MC, V.*

$$$$ 🏨 **The Osprey at Beaver Creek, A Rock Resort.** You can't get any closer to
FodorsChoice   a ski run in the U.S. than the Osprey, unless you sleep on the lift. Rein-
★   carnated in 2009 from the rather Victorian Inn at Beaver Creek, this sleek, chic new slope-side hotel is literally steps from the Strawberry Park Express high-speed quad lift. The rooms in this truly boutique property (there are a mere 41 of them including a two-bedroom penthouse suite) are refreshingly spacious and airy, illuminated with large lamps and a cozy gas fireplace. Among the amenities you'll find in the "minibar" are nail polish and bottled oxygen. Couples can enjoy tapas at the 18-seat bar next to the "living room" lounge or compete at the nearby Wiigaming station. **Pros:** best location at any ski resort; rooms are fresh and light; intimate feel. **Cons:** often sold out well in advance; geared mostly toward couples. ✉ *10 Elk Track La.,* ☎ *970/754–7400 or 866/621–7625* ⊕ *www. ospreyatbeavercreek.rockresorts.com* ⟿ *40 rooms* ⚲ *In-room: Wi-Fi. In-hotel: restaurant, bar, pools, spa, parking (free/paid)* ⊟ *AE, D, DC, MC, V* ⎆ *BP.*

$$$$ 🏨 **Park Hyatt Beaver Creek Resort & Spa.** With a magnificent antler chandelier and towering windows opening out onto the mountain, the lobby of this ski-in ski-out hotel manages to be both cozy and grand. Rooms are designed with skiers in mind, so they have nice touches like heated towel racks. Perhaps the ultimate in pampering is stepping into your warmed and waiting ski boots. Once the boots are off, enjoy a hot toddy by the outdoor fire pit. The on-site Allegria Spa and the nearby Beaver Creek Golf Club (with preferred tee times for guests) make this hotel popular with nonskiers. **Pros:** cozy Colorado mountain vibe; ski-in ski-out. **Cons:** fee for parking; views vary; uninterested staff. ✉ *136 E. Thomas Pl., Beaver Creek Village* ☎ *970/949–1234 or 800/233–1234* ⊕ *www.beavercreek.hyatt.com* ⟿ *190 rooms, 15 suites* ⚲ *In-room:*

safe, kitchen (some), refrigerator, DVD (some), Wi-Fi. In-hotel: 2 res-taurants, room service, bars, golf course privileges, tennis courts, pool, gym, spa, concierge, children's programs (ages 3–12), laundry facilities, laundry service, public Internet, public Wi-Fi, airport shuttle, parking (paid) ☰ *AE, D, DC, MC, V.*

$$$$ 🏨 **Pines Lodge.** This ski-in ski-out lodge is a winner for skiers, combining upscale accommodations with an unpretentious attitude. The aura of laid-back luxury comes from little extras such as afternoon tea by the fireplace in the lobby and a ski concierge who can arrange a complimentary guided tour. Rooms vary in size, so ask for one at the end facing the mountain; these have an extra sofa for contemplating the views from the large windows. Some rooms have balconies overlooking the ski area. **Pros:** slope-side; ski concierge. **Cons:** valet parking only; staff sometimes difficult to locate; gym needs updating. ⊠ *141 Scott Hill Rd., Beaver Creek Village* ☎ *970/754–7200 or 866/859–8242* ⊕ *www. pineslodge.rockresorts.com* ↪ *60 rooms, 12 condos* ⚹ *In-room: no a/c, safe, kitchen (some), refrigerator (some), DVD (some), Wi-Fi. In-hotel: restaurant, room service, bar, golf course, pool, gym, spa, concierge, laundry facilities, laundry service, public Internet, public Wi-Fi, airport shuttle, parking (paid)* ☰ *AE, D, MC, V.*

$$$$ 🏨 **Ritz-Carlton, Bachelor Gulch in Beaver Creek.** The stone-and-timber resort
★ crowns Beaver Creek Mountain above the bustle of Vail Valley like one of King Ludwig's Bavarian castles. Inside this imposing hotel are all the amenities any royal might desire—panoramic views from most rooms, stone fireplaces in more than a third, and high, plush beds in all. You can borrow Bachelor, the resident yellow Lab, for company on hikes (Bachelor's tips go to the Eagle Valley Humane Society). When you're finished hiking or skiing (or grow tired of gazing out at your kingdom from a balcony), head to the 21,000-square-foot spa and fitness center for a dose of bottled oxygen at the fresh-air salon or a dip in the cascading grotto hot tub. Remington's, Buffalo Bar, and Fly Fishing Library are restaurant and bar destinations in their own right. **Pros:** the most luxurious property on the mountain; excellent guest service; ski-in ski-out. **Cons:** high altitude (9,000 feet); removed from the Village. ⊠ *0130 Daybreak Ridge, Bachelor Gulch Village* ☎ *970/748–6200, 800/241–3333* ⊕ *www.ritzcarlton.com* ↪ *140 rooms, 40 suites* ⚹ *In-room: safe, kitchen (some), refrigerator (some), DVD, Wi-Fi. In-hotel: 4 restaurants, room service, bars, golf course, tennis courts, pool, gym, spa, bicycles, concierge, children's programs (ages 5–12), laundry service, public Internet, public Wi-Fi, airport shuttle, parking (paid), some pets allowed* ☰ *AE, D, DC, MC, V.*

NIGHTLIFE AND THE ARTS

THE ARTS

★ **Vilar Performing Arts Center** (⊠ *68 Avondale La.* ☎ *970/845–8497 or 888/920–2787* ⊕ *www.vilarpac.org*) is an artwork in itself, with gold-color wood paneling and an etched-glass mural re-creating with bold strokes the mountains outside. Seating more than 500, the horseshoe-shaped auditorium has great views from just about every seat. Throughout the year there's a stellar lineup of events, including concerts by orchestras and pop stars, great theater, and even a circus. In the surrounding plazas you'll find many art galleries. Just walking around Beaver Creek is a feast for the eyes, because sculptures are set almost everywhere you look.

NIGHTLIFE

The boisterous **Coyote Café** (✉ *210 The Plaza* ☎ *970/949–5001* ⊕ *www. coyotecafe.net*) is a kick-back-and-relax sort of place, where locals hang out in the afternoon and evening. If you're into local brews or giant margaritas, head to the **Dusty Boot Saloon** (✉ *210 Offerson Rd.* ☎ *970/748–1146* ⊕ *www.dustyboot.com*). At the base of the mountain, **McCoy's Café** (✉ *136 East Thomas Pl.,Village Hall* ☎ *970/949–1234*) draws crowds most afternoons in the winter months with live music.

SHOPPING

Christopher & Co. (✉ *105 Edwards Village Blvd., Edwards* ☎ *970/926– 8191* ⊕ *www.christopherco.com*) has vintage poster art dating from the 1890s to the 1950s. Depictions of American and European ski resorts are among the more than 3,000 posters on display. Walk carefully around the **Pismo Gallery** (✉ *45 W. Thomas Pl. Village Hall* ☎ *970/949– 0908* ⊕ *www.pismoglass.com*), as there's an outstanding collection of handblown glass. Look for the fragile, colorful creations by Dale Chihuly. Although the **Shaggy Ram** (✉ *210 Edwards Village Blvd., Edwards Village Center, Edwards* ☎ *970/926–7377* ⊕ *www.theshaggyram.com/*) sounds like it would stock mostly Western items, this shop is filled with French and English antiques. Items range from fringed lamps to crystal decanters to elegant old desks.

Aspen and the Roaring Fork Valley

WORD OF MOUTH

"The past two summers we have visited Aspen during our annual August vacation. We love being within walking distance of everything—rarely did we use our rental car. We love the varied outdoor activities (hiking, fishing, outdoor concerts, mountain activities, swimming, golf) and we also love the town with its galleries, dining, shopping, etc."
—ljf1958

Updated by
Jad Davenport

Forever honored in the lyrics of John Denver, the Roaring Fork Valley—and Aspen, its crown jewel—is the quintessential Colorado Rocky Mountain High. A rampart of the state's famed Fourteeners (peaks over 14,000 feet) guards this valley. There are only two ways in or out: over the precipitous Independence Pass in summer or up the four-lane highway through the booming Roaring Fork Valley that stretches nearly 50 mi from Glenwood Springs to Aspen.

Outside Aspen, Colorado natives regard the city and its eclectic populace of longtime locals, newly arrived ski bums, hard-core mountaineers, laser-sculpted millionaires, and tanned celebs with a mixture of bemusement and envy. The "real Aspenites," who came for the snow and stayed for summers, have been squeezed out by seven-digit housing prices. Most have migrated down-valley to the bedroom communities of Basalt and Carbondale. In the words of one refugee, "the Aspen millionaires are making room for the billionaires."

The quest for wealth in the valley dates back to the mid-1800s, when the original inhabitants, the Ute people, were supplanted by gold prospectors and silver miners, who came to reap the region's mineral bounty. The demonetization of silver in 1893 brought the quiet years, as the population dwindled and ranching became a way of life. Nearly half a century later the tides turned again as downhill skiing gave new life to Aspen. Today the Roaring Fork Valley weaves together its past and present into a unique blend of small-town charm and luxurious amenities, all surrounded by the majestic beauty of central Colorado's 2-million-acre White River National Forest.

ORIENTATION AND PLANNING

GETTING ORIENTED

Wedged in a valley between the Elk Mountain palisades to the southwest and the high-altitude massifs of the Sawatch Range in the east, the Roaring Fork Valley is a Rocky Mountain Shangri-la with Aspen at the headwaters. The charm and beauty of this isolation can make reaching Aspen both a scenic and frustrating journey.

The only way in or out of Aspen is Highway 82—either up the Roaring Fork Valley from Glenwood Springs or over Independence Pass in summer from the eastern side of the mountains (the pass begins at the junction of U.S. 24 and Highway 82). Aspen's explosive growth hasn't come without some headaches. Despite expanded lanes, Highway 82 quickly clogs with skiers and day commuters.

TOP REASONS TO GO

The Scene: You'll see it all in Aspen—Hollywood celebs in cowboy boots, glamorous wives of Saudi royalty shopping, tanned European ski instructors, and fascinating and friendly locals.

Historic Hotels: Thanks to moneyed preservationists, the Victorian Hotel Jerome in Aspen and the Medici-inspired Hotel Colorado in Glenwood Springs still stand.

The Mountains: You'll find postcard Colorado in the 14,000-foot Maroon

Bell peaks, especially when the the steep-faced pyramid peaks reflect a dusting of snow in Maroon Lake.

Fine Fare: From Matsuhisa sushi to lobster strudel, Aspen, Carbondale, and Glenwood Springs have just about any dish you can imagine.

Hot Springs: At Glenwood Springs the 90°F mineral-water pool has been a therapeutic retreat since the Ute Indians knew it as *Yampah* or "healing waters."

Aspen. Head here for a dose of the high life in an almost too-pretty town, where Hollywood celebrities and couch-surfing ski bums cross paths on the slopes and in the hot tubs. The twin Fourteener peaks and aspens of the Maroon Bells constitute one of the state's iconic images.

The Roaring Fork Valley. Snowmass is a year-round family resort destination rather than a true town. The historic towns of Glenwood Springs, Redstone, and Marble offer a pleasant—and less expensive—alternative experience, and have great fly-fishing and rafting in summer.

PLANNING

WHEN TO GO

Aspen and the Roaring Fork Valley are a year-round destination. If it's skiing you're after, February and March have the best snow and warmest winter weather (and prices are lower than the peak Thanksgiving-to-Christmas season). Aspen summers are legendary for their food, art, and music festivals. Although only 6,000 locals call Aspen home, the population more than quadruples to 27,000 in summer and winter high seasons. June is best for rafting (snowmelt spawns high-octane rapids), but many high-country hiking and mountain-biking trails are buried under snowdrifts until July, when the wildflowers peak. Mid-September brings hotel-room deals, cooler days, photogenic snow dustings in the Maroon Bells, and flame-orange aspen groves.

GETTING HERE AND AROUND

AIR TRAVEL

Aspen-Pitkin County Airport (ASE) is 3 mi from Aspen and 7 mi from Snowmass. It is served daily by United Express, Delta (from Salt Lake City and Atlanta), Frontier Airlines (from Denver), and has nonstop United service to Los Angeles. During ski season United also offers nonstop service from Chicago and San Francisco.

TRANSFERS Your best bet for traveling to and from Aspen and Snowmass Village is Roaring Fork Transit Agency, which provides bus service from Aspen-

Pitkin County Airport to the Rubey Park bus station right at the base of the ski mountain. Colorado Mountain Express and Colorado Grayline connect Aspen with Denver, Grand Junction, and the Eagle County/Vail airport. High Mountain Taxi will also provide charter service outside the Roaring Fork Valley.

Airports Aspen-Pitkin County Airport (ASE) (☎ 970/920–5384 ⊕ www.aspenairport.com). **Denver International Airport (DEN)** (☎ 800/247–2336 ⊕ www.flydenver.com).

Airport Transfers Colorado Mountain Express (☎ 970/926–9800 or 800/525–6363). **High Mountain Taxi** (☎ 970/925–8294). **Colorado Grayline** (☎ 970/544–2057 or 877/277–3690).

SHUTTLE TRAVEL

The Roaring Fork Transit Agency provides bus service up and down the valley; many resorts have free private shuttles.

Shuttles Roaring Fork Transit Agency (☎ 970/925–8484 ⊕ www.rfta.com).

CAR TRAVEL

If you are flying into Aspen, you can rent a car from Alamo or National at the airport.

In summer the 160-mi, three-hour drive from Denver to Aspen is a delightful journey up the I–70 corridor and across the Continental Divide through the Eisenhower Tunnel (or by way of the slower, but more-spectacular, Loveland Pass), down along the eastern ramparts of the Collegiate Peaks along State Highway 91 and U.S. Highway 24, with a final push on serpentine State Highway 82 up and over 12,095-foot Independence Pass.

The scenery, particularly south of Leadville on U.S. 24, is among the best in Colorado, with western views of 14,433-foot Mount Elbert, the highest mountain in the state. Independence Pass is closed in winter (timing depends on snowfall, typically late October–late May), but motorists should always drive cautiously. Blinding snowstorms—even in July—can erase visibility and make the pass treacherously icy. Be especially careful on the western side, where the road narrows and vertigo-inducing drop-offs plunge thousands of feet from hairpin curves. Both Route 82 and I–70, like all Colorado roads, should be driven with caution, especially at night when elk, bighorn sheep, and mule deer cross without warning.

Generally speaking, driving to Aspen from Denver in winter is more trouble than it's worth, unless you plan to stop along the way. The drive west on I–70 and east on Route 82 takes more than three hours at best, depending on weather conditions and, increasingly, ski traffic. On the other hand, the 3-mi drive from the Aspen-Pitkin County Airport is a breeze along the flat valley floor. The 70-mi drive from the Eagle County Airport-Vail—which doesn't cross any mountain passes—is another option. Traffic and parking during both winter and summer high seasons can try your patience.

TRAIN TRAVEL

Glenwood Springs is on Amtrak's *California Zephyr* route, which runs from Emeryville California to Chicago.

Train Contacts Amtrak (⊕ *www.amtrak.com*).

PARKS AND RECREATION AREAS

The Roaring Fork Valley is ringed by recreational land, checkerboarded between wilderness areas and national forests. To the southeast in the Collegiate Peaks Wilderness area more 14,000-foot summits beckon peak baggers and day hikers than anywhere else in the Lower 48.

The often-overlooked Hunter-Fryingpan Wilderness Area is one of Colorado's hidden secrets—a thin-air spine of unnamed peaks and excellent trout rivers in the Williams Mountains just east of Aspen. On the other side of the Continental Divide, the Hunter-Fryingpan becomes the Mount Massive Wilderness Area, named for Colorado's second-highest peak, which stands 14,421 feet tall. Most of these wilderness areas are encompassed within the much larger—and more fragmented—White River National Forest.

RESTAURANTS

Sushi? Coconut curry? Bison and lobster? Colorado's culinary repertoire reaches its zenith in Aspen. With all the Hummers and designer handbags comes a certain sophistication that eclipses the rest of the state. Plates can be pricey, particularly in Aspen, but many eateries have several moderately priced entrées (usually pastas) as a nod to the budget-conscious. For those who want a break from Aspen, there are good dining options down-valley in Basalt and Carbondale as well.

HOTELS

There's no shortage of lodging in Aspen and the Roaring Fork; however, you'll pay the highest rates in the state. Downriver alternatives like Carbondale and Glenwood Springs are attractive for budget hunters—but you'll face a surprising amount of traffic when commuting to Aspen. Before booking down-valley, however, look for special deals in town that might include lift tickets and parking. If you're staying for more than a weekend or are traveling with a large group, condominiums are an affordable option and have the added bonus of a kitchen.

WHAT IT COSTS					
	¢	$	$$	$$$	$$$$
Restaurants	under $8	$8–$12	$13–$18	$19–$25	over $25
Hotels	under $80	$80–$120	$121–$170	$171–$230	over $230

Restaurant prices are for a main course at dinner, excluding 8.2%–8.6% tax. Hotel prices are for two people in a standard double room in high season, excluding service charges and 8.6%–10.7% tax.

Independence Pass

From Memorial Day to Labor Day the most beautiful route to Aspen is over Independence Pass. From the Vail–Leadville–Buena Vista corridor on the east side of the Sawatch Mountains Highway 82 climbs up and over 12,080-foot Independence Pass and switchbacks down to Aspen, along the way passing above tree line and making some spectacular white-knuckle hairpin turns (drive slowly to appreciate the scenery, and also because you might have to yield to oncoming traffic in narrow, one-lane sections). The pass divides the Mount Massive Wilderness to the north from the Collegiate Peaks to the south, and is not for the fainthearted, given the long exposed drops and the possibility for snow at any time of the year. Elk and mule deer herds can sometimes be seen at dawn and dusk grazing in the willow thickets beside Lake Creek as it cascades down the eastern flank of the pass. As soon as the autumn snow flies, however, the pass closes and Aspen becomes a cul-de-sac town accessible only via Glenwood Springs.

WORD OF MOUTH
"You are mostly on the inside lane going to Aspen from Vail [on Independence Pass], and it is a spectacular drive not to be missed—the windy road a little narrow with very steep drop-offs at times (mostly experienced going the opposite: Aspen to Vail) but totally worth it." —Stephie

ASPEN

220 mi west of Denver via I–70 and Hwy. 82.

One of the world's fabled resorts, Aspen practically defines glitz, glamour, and glorious skiing. To the uninitiated, Aspen and Vail are synonymous. To residents, a rivalry exists, with locals of each claiming to have the state's most epic skiing, finest restaurants, and hottest nightlife. The most obvious distinction is the look: Vail is a faux-Bavarian development, whereas Aspen is an overgrown mining town. Vail is full of politicians—it's where Gerald Ford, Dan Quayle, and John Sununu fled to escape the cares of state—whereas Aspen is popular with singers and movie stars like Melanie Griffith, Antonio Banderas, and Jack Nicholson. One of the valley's newest—and fittest—citizens is Lance Armstrong. Aspen is also where Barbra Streisand took a stand against state legislation that discriminated against gay people.

Between the galleries, museums, music festivals, and other glittering social events, there's so much going on in Aspen that even in winter many people come simply to "do the scene," and never make it to the slopes. High-end boutiques have been known to serve free Campari-and-sodas après-ski, a practice so over the top that there's a certain charm to it. At the same time, Aspen is a place where people live fairly average lives, sending their children to school and working at jobs that may or may not have to do with skiing. It is, arguably, America's original ski-bum destination, a fact that continues to give the town's character an underlying layer of humor and texture. You can come to Aspen and have a reasonably straightforward, enjoyable ski vacation, because once you've stripped away the veneer, Aspen is simply a great place to ski.

Aspen has always been a magnet for cultural and countercultural types. The late bad-boy gonzo journalist Hunter S. Thompson was one of the more visible citizens of the nearby community of Woody Creek. One of Aspen's most amusing figures is Jon Barnes, who tools around in his "Ultimate Taxi" (it's plastered with 3-D glasses, crystal disco balls, and neon necklaces, and is redolent of dry ice and incense). You'll find everyone from socialites with *Vogue* exteriors and vague interiors to longhaired musicians in combat boots and fatigues. Ultimately, it doesn't matter what you wear here, as long as you wear it with conviction.

GETTING HERE AND AROUND

The rich arrive by private planes, but almost everyone else arrives in Aspen by car or shuttle bus. Parking is a pricey pain, and traffic, especially on weekends, slows the streets. The Roaring Fork Transit Agency has bus service connecting the resort with the rest of the valley. The easiest way to get around Aspen is on foot or by bike. For longer trips hop aboard the free Aspen Skiing Company Shuttle which connects Aspen, Aspen Highlands, Buttermilk, and Snowmass base areas.

TOURS A romantic way to orient yourself to the backcountry is by taking a private sleigh ride with Aspen Carriage Company. They also have carriage tours around downtown and the historic West End.

WHEN TO GO

The summer season in the Roaring Fork Valley runs from June to August, and winter season starts in November and lasts through March.

FESTIVALS The **Aspen Music Festival and School** (☎ 970/925–3254 ⊕ *www.aspen-*
Fodor's Choice *musicfestival.com*), focusing on chamber music to jazz, runs from late
★ June to mid-August. Musicians like Joshua Bell and Sarah Chang make pilgrimages here to perform at more than 350 events held at the 2,050-seat Benedict Music Tent, the Victorian Wheeler Opera House, and the Harris Concert Hall. Tickets are readily available online. A quarter of the performances are free, and one of the great pleasures of the festival is showing up on the free-seating lawn outside the Benedict Music Tent with some friends, a blanket, and a bottle of shiraz.

ESSENTIALS

Tour Info Aspen Carriage Co. (☎ 970/925–3394 ⊕ www.aspencarriages.com). **Maroon Bells bus tour** (⊠ Aspen ☎ 970/925–8484 ⊕ www.rfta.com).

Visitor Info Aspen Snow Report (☎ 907/925–1220 ⊕ www.aspensnowmass. com). **Aspen Chamber Resort Association** (⊠ 425 Rio Grande Pl. ☎ 970/925–1940 or 800/670–0792 ⊕ aspenchamber.org).

EXPLORING

TOP ATTRACTIONS

Many of Aspen's beautiful buildings were constructed in the 1880s, when the surrounding mines were overflowing with silver. Jerome Wheeler, one of the town's most prominent citizens, constructed the

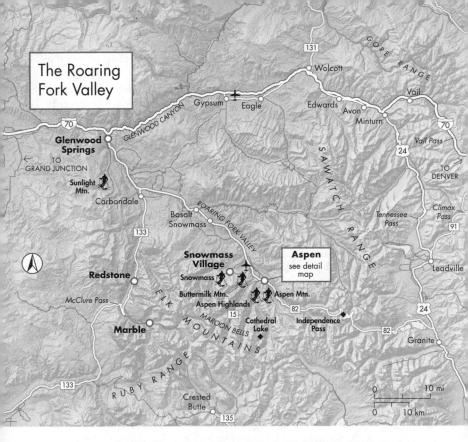

The Roaring Fork Valley

1889 **Hotel Jerome** (⊠ *330 E. Main St.* ☎ *970/920–1000*). Peek into the ornate lobby to get a sense of turn-of-the-20th-century living.

QUICK BITES

Follow the locals to **Ink! Coffee** (⊠ *520 E. Durant Ave.* ☎ *970/544–0588* ⊕ *www.inkcoffee.com*), where you can sample hot and cold coffee, tea, and other drinks, including their signature Blended Black and White—iced espresso mixed with black and white chocolate. The café also serves pastries and snacks. In summer the patio is a nice place to relax.

Works by top regional and national artists are exhibited at the **Aspen Art Museum.** An endowment from John and Amy Phelan keeps admission to the museum free. ⊠ *590 N. Mill St.* ☎ *970/925–8050* ⊕ *www. aspenartmuseum.org* ⊡ *Free* ⊙ *Tues., Wed., Fri., and Sat. 10–6; Thurs. 10–7; Sun. noon–6.*

Fodor'sChoice
★
☯
The majestic **Maroon Bells** (⊠ *White River National Forest, Maroon Creek Rd., 10 mi west of Aspen*) are twin peaks more than 14,000 feet high. The colorful peaks, thanks to mineral streaking, are so vivid you'd swear they were blanketed with primrose and Indian paintbrush. It's one of the most-photographed spots in the state. Before 9 AM and after 5 PM cars can drive all the way up to the lake (and vehicles with children in car seats are permitted anytime). Otherwise, cars are allowed only partway, but the Roaring Fork Transportation Authority

provides shuttle buses that leave regularly in summer months from the Aspen Highlands. A convenient pass, available for $28, includes one trip to the Maroon Bells and one ride up Aspen Mountain's Silver Queen Gondola, where concerts, nature walks, amazing hiking, and other activities await you.

WORTH NOTING

You can get a taste of Victorian high life at the Queen Anne–style **Wheeler/Stallard House Museum,** which displays memorabilia collected by the Aspen Historical Society. While you're there, ask about the organization's newest endeavor, the Holden–Marolt Ranching and Mining Museum, a hands-on exploration of Aspen's past housed in an old barn on the western edge of town. ⊠ *620 W. Bleeker St.* ☎ *970/925–3721* ⊕ *www.aspenhistorysociety.com* ✉ *$6* ⊗ *Tues.–Sat. 1–5.*

With a trail that winds through gravestones dating to the 1800s, **Ute Cemetery** (⊠ *Next to Ute Park off Ute Ave.*) is a reminder of Aspen's roots.

Built in 1889, the elegant **Wheeler Opera House** (⊠ *320 E. Hyman Ave.* ☎ *970/920–5770*) still serves as a concert venue.

DOWNHILL SKIING AND SNOWBOARDING

6

Aspen is really four ski areas rolled into one resort. Aspen Highlands, Aspen (or Ajax) Mountain, Buttermilk, and Snowmass can all be skied with the same ticket. Most are clustered close to downtown Aspen, but Snowmass is down the valley near Snowmass Village. A free shuttle system connects the four.

Locals' favorite **Aspen Highlands** is essentially one long ridge with trails dropping off either side. Over the past few years the antiquated lift system has been replaced by three high-speed quads, and a massive base-area village has risen, turning the maverick ski hill into a destination in and of itself. Aspen Highlands has thrilling descents at Golden Horn, Olympic Bowl, and now, Highland Bowl, a hike-in experience unlike any in Colorado. The steep and often bumpy cluster of trails around Steeplechase and Highland Bowl makes this mountain one of the best places to be on a good-powder day. Aspen Highlands has a wide-open bowl called Thunder that's popular with intermediate skiers, as well as plenty of lower-mountain blue runs. The best overall downhill run is Highland Bowl. Besides the comparatively short lift lines and some heart-pounding runs, a highlight of Aspen Highlands is your first trip to the 12,500-foot summit. The view, which includes the Maroon Bells and Pyramid Peak, is the most dramatic in the area, and one of the best in the country. ⊠ *Maroon Creek Rd.* ☎ *970/925–1220 or 800/525–6200* ⊕ *www.aspensnowmass.com* ⊗ *Early Dec.–early Apr., daily 9–4.*

Open since 1947, **Aspen Mountain** is a dream destination for mogul and steep skiers. Nearby Bell Mountain provides some of the best bump skiing anywhere, followed by Walsh's (also a favorite for snowboarders), Hyrup's, and Kristi's. Those wanting long cruisers head to the ridges or valleys: Ruthie's Run, Ridge of the Bell, and International are the classics. Newcomers should note that there are no novice-level runs here. This is a resort where nearly half the trails are rated advanced or expert, and a black-diamond trail here might rank as a double-black diamond elsewhere. The narrow ski area is laid out on a series of steep, unforgiving ridges with little room for error. Most skiers spend much of the morning on intermediate trails off the upper-mountain quad. Then they head for lunch on the deck of Bonnie's, the mid-mountain restaurant that on sunny days is one of the great people-watching scenes in the skiing world. After a big storm there's snowcat skiing on the back side of the mountain. The biggest

> **WHEN DO THE WILDFLOWERS PEAK?**
>
> The Maroon Bells Snowmass Wilderness Area southwest of Aspen is famed for dramatic escarpments and alpine meadows. The bloom will start first in the valleys and eventually climb above the 11,200-foot tree line. Most Colorado wildflowers will reach their peak from just before the summer solstice until mid-July.

drawback to skiing at Aspen Mountain is that too many trails funnel into Spar Gulch, making the end-of-day rush to the bottom chaotic and often dangerous—a situation that has become increasingly tense because snowboarders are now part of the mix. ⊠ *Durant St.* ☎ *970/925–1220 or 800/525–6200* ⊕ *www.aspensnowmass.com* ☼ *Late Nov.–mid-Apr., daily 9–4.*

If you're looking for an escape from the hustle and bustle of Aspen, spend a day at **Buttermilk**—a family-friendly place where it's virtually impossible to get into trouble. Buttermilk is terrific for novices, intermediates, and, thanks to its half-pipe and 2-mi-long Crazy T'rain Park, snowboarders. It's a low-key, lighthearted sort of place, and an antidote to the kind of hotdogging you might encounter at Aspen Mountain. Sterner Run is a favorite for its length and curves, while Racer's Edge appeals to speed demons. Among the featured attractions is a hangout for children named Fort Frog. The Tiehack section to the east, with sweeping views of Maroon Creek valley, has several advanced runs (though nothing truly expert). It also has superb powder, and the deep snow sticks around longer because many serious skiers overlook this mountain. Buttermilk's allure hasn't been lost on pros, however; it now hosts the Winter X Games. ⊠ *W. Buttermilk Rd.* ☎ *970/925–1220 or 800/525–6200* ⊕ *www.aspensnowmass.com* ☼ *Early Dec.–mid-Apr., daily 9–4.*

FACILITIES   **Aspen Highlands:** 3,635-foot vertical drop; 790 skiable acres; 131 trails; 18% beginner, 30% intermediate, 16% advanced, 36% expert; 3 high-speed quad chairs, 2 triple chairs.

Aspen Mountain: 3,267-foot vertical drop; 673 skiable acres; 76 trails; 48% intermediate, 26% advanced, 26% expert; 1 6-passenger gondola, 1 high-speed quad chair, 2 quad chairs, 1 high-speed double chair, 3 double chairs.

Buttermilk: 2,030-foot vertical drop; 435 skiable acres; 44 trails; 35% beginner, 39% intermediate, 26% advanced; 2 high-speed quad chairs, 3 double chairs, 4 surface lifts.

LESSONS AND   **Aspen Skiing Company** (☎ *970/925–1220 or 800/525–6200*) gives lessons
PROGRAMS   sons at all four mountains. Half-day group lessons start at $93, and a private half-day lesson for up to six people will cost you $449. A

noteworthy deal is the three-day guaranteed learn-to-ski or learn-to-snowboard package at Snowmass or Buttermilk, which includes lessons, rental gear, and lift tickets for $96. The company also runs snowcat trips on Aspen Mountain.

Aspen Mountain Powder Tours (☎ 970/925–1220) provides access to 1,500 acres on the back side of Aspen Mountain via snowcats. Most of the terrain is negotiable by confident intermediates, with about 10,000 vertical feet constituting a typical day's skiing. Reservations are required at least a day in advance, but you should book as early as possible. Full-day trips—including a hot lunch, two guides and all the skiing you can do—cost $390.

LIFT TICKETS   Lift tickets are $96, but almost nobody pays full price, thanks to multi-day savings, early- and late-season specials, and other discounts.

RENTALS   Numerous ski shops in Aspen rent equipment. Rental packages (skis, boots, and poles) start at around $45 per day and rise to $75 or more for the latest and greatest equipment. Snowboard packages (boots and boards) run about $50. Bargain shopping at stores around town may turn up better deals. **Aspen Sports** (✉ 408 E. Cooper Ave. ☎ 970/925–6331 ⊕ www.aspensports.com) has plenty of gear to choose from. **Durrance Sports** (✉ 414 E. Cooper Ave. ☎ 970/429–0101 ⊕ www.durrancesports. com), in Aspen Highlands Village, has equipment from many companies. **Pomeroy Sports** (✉ 614 E. Durant Ave. ☎ 970/925–7875 ⊕ www. pomeroysports.com), at the base of Aspen Mountain gondola, has good deals on equipment.

NORDIC SKIING

BACKCOUNTRY SKIING

The **Alfred A. Braun Hut System** is one of Aspen's major backcountry networks. The trailhead leads from the Ashcroft Ski Touring Center into the Maroon Bells–Snowmass Wilderness. Take the usual precautions, because the trails cover terrain prone to avalanche. Huts sleep 7 to 14 people. They're open in winter only, and reservations can be made beginning May 1. ⌂ Box 7937, Aspen ☎ 970/925–5775 ⊕ www.huts. org ✉ $25 per person per night, 4-person minimum.

★   The **10th Mountain Hut & Trail System,** named in honor of the U.S. Army's 10th Mountain Division, includes 10 huts along the trail connecting Aspen and Vail. The main trail follows a generally avalanche-safe route in altitudes from 8,000 feet to 12,000 feet. This translates to a fair amount of skiing along tree-lined trails and a good bit of high-alpine ups and downs. You must be in good shape, and some backcountry skiing experience is extremely helpful. Accommodations along the trail vary, but this system does include the Ritz-Carltons of backcountry huts, supplied with mattresses and pillows, precut logs for wood-burning stoves, and utensils for cooking. Huts sleep from 6 to 16 people (more if you're willing to cuddle). For a $25 membership fee you can enter a reservation lottery in March. Otherwise, reservations are accepted beginning in April; weekends in peak ski season fill up quickly. ✉ 1280 Ute Ave. ☎ 970/925–5775 ⊕ www.huts.org ✉ $30 and up per person per night.

If you're either unfamiliar with the hut system or inexperienced in backcountry travel, you should hire a guide. One reliable company is **Aspen Alpine Guides** (⌂ *Box 659, Aspen* ☎ *970/925–6618* ⊕ *www.aspenalpine.com*). In Aspen the best place for backcountry-gear rentals, including ski equipment, climbing skins, packs, sleeping bags, and mountaineering paraphernalia is the **Ute Mountaineer** (✉ *308 S. Mill St.* ☎ *970/925–2849* ⊕ *www.utemountaineer.com*).

> **LIFT LINE TIP**
>
> Lift lines dragging? Pull the local skip and hop in the singles line with your significant other. You might get lucky and ride together, or you might get even luckier and meet some new friends.

TRACK SKIING

There is something to be said for maintaining a wealthy tax base. Subsidized by local taxes, the **Aspen/Snowmass Nordic Council** (⌂ *Box 10815, Aspen* ☎ *970/429–2039* ⊕ *www.aspennordic.com*) charges no fee for the 48 mi of maintained trails in the Roaring Fork Valley, making it the largest free groomed Nordic-trail system in North America. For a longer ski, try the Owl Creek Trail, connecting the Aspen Cross-Country Center trails with the Snowmass Club trail system. More than 10 mi long, the trail leads through some lovely scenery.

Lessons and rentals are available at the **Aspen Cross-Country Center** (✉ *39551 Hwy. 82* ☎ *970/925–2145*). Diagonal, skating, racing, and light-touring setups are available.

About 12 mi from Aspen, the **Ashcroft Ski Touring Center** (✉ *11399 Castle Creek Rd.* ☎ *970/925–1971* ⊕ *www.pinecreekcookhouse.com/ashcroft. html*) is sequestered in a high-alpine basin up Castle Creek, which runs between Aspen Mountain and Aspen Highlands. The 25 mi of groomed trails are surrounded by the high peaks of the Maroon Bells–Snowmass Wilderness, and crisscross the ghost town of Ashcroft. This is one of the most dramatic cross-country sites in the High Rockies.

OTHER SPORTS AND THE OUTDOORS

★ **Aspen Center for Environmental Studies** (✉ *100 Puppy Smith St.* ☎ *970/925–*
☺ *5756* ⊕ *www.aspennature.org*) is a research center and wildlife sanctuary where children and adults alike can take refuge. The facility sponsors snowshoe walks with naturalist guides in winter, and wildlife workshops that teach everything from how to create a small wildlife sanctuary in your own backyard to what animals you might find on local trails. In summer there are bird-watching hikes and "special little naturalist" programs for four- to seven-year-olds, which include nature walks and arts and crafts.

FISHING

The **Roaring Fork River,** fast, deep, and uninterrupted by dams from its
★ headwaters to its junction with the Colorado, is one of the last freeflowing rivers in the state. The healthy populations of rainbow and brown trout—of the hefty 12- to 18-inch variety—make the Roaring Fork a favorite with anglers. From the headwaters at Independence Pass to within 3 mi of Aspen most of the river access is on public lands, and

is best fished in summer and early fall. Downstream from Aspen the river crosses through a checkerboard pattern of private and public land; it's fishable year-round. The river's rounded stones make felt soles or studs a good idea for waders. See ⊕ *www.wildlife.state.co.us/fishing*for more information.

Aspen Trout Guides (✉ *520 E. Durant Ave.* ☎*970/379–7963* ⊕ *aspentroutguides.com*) runs fly-fishing tours of local waterways. The company is in the Hamilton Sports Pro Shop. **Taylor Creek Fly Shop** (✉ *408 E. Cooper Ave.* ☎*970/920–1128* ⊕ *www.taylorcreek.com*) has the town's best selection of flies and other supplies.

FITNESS

The upscale **Aspen Club & Spa** (✉ *1450 Crystal Lake Rd.* ☎*970/925–8900* ⊕ *aspenclub.com*) has plenty of weight-training and cardiovascular equipment, as well as indoor courts for squash, basketball, and other sports. It's also home to John Clendenin's Ski Doctor indoor ski simulator. When you're finished getting all sweaty, relax in the luxurious full-service spa.

HIKING

If you aren't used to it, high altitude can catch you off guard. Drink plenty of water to help stave off the effects of altitude sickness—dizziness, shortness of breath, headache, and nausea. Slather on the sunscreen—it's easy to get sunburned at altitude. And in summer an early morning start is best, as afternoon thunderstorms are frequent and can be dangerous above the tree line.

Fodor'sChoice Aspen excels at high-altitude scenery (seven of the state's 54 Fourteeners
★ are in the Elk Mountain range), and nowhere is the iconic image of the Colorado Rockies more breathtaking than in the **Maroon Bells–Snowmass Wilderness Area.** In summer, shuttle buses take visitors up Maroon Creek Road to Maroon Lake at the base of the peaks from 9 AM until 5 PM. Private cars are allowed at all other times (there is a $10 recreational fee). More ambitious sightseers can select from a number of trails. ✉ *Sopris Ranger District, White River National Forest, Maroon Creek Rd., 10 mi west of Aspen* ☎*970/963–2266* ⊕ *www.fs.fed.us/r2/whiteriver.*

★ You'll get a taste of several ecozones as you tackle **Cathedral Lake,** a 5.6-mi round-trip trail. The trail starts gently in aspen and pine groves but earns sweat quickly in a long, steep climb into a high valley. Another series of steep, short switchbacks ascend a headwall. From there it's a short stroll to a shallow alpine lake cupped by a wall of granite cliffs. When the high-country snows melt off in mid-July the meadows and willow thickets surrounding the lake are colored with blooming wildflowers. ✉ *Sopris Ranger District, White River National Forest* ☎*970/963–2266* ⊕ *www.fs.fed.us/r2/whiteriver.*

HORSEBACK RIDING

For day or overnight horseback tours into the spectacular Maroon Bells–Snowmass Wilderness, try **Maroon Bell Outfitters** (✉ *3129 Maroon Creek Rd.* ☎*970/920–4677* ⊕ *maroonbellsaspen.com*).

ICE SKATING

The **Aspen Recreation Center** (✉ *0861 Maroon Creek Rd.* ☎ *970/544–4100* ⊕ *www.aspenrecreation.com*) is home to an indoor ice rink big enough for National Hockey League games. There's also an Olympic-size swimming pool. If you prefer outdoor skating, try the **Silver Circle** (✉ *433 E. Durant Ave.* ☎ *970/925–1710*).

MOUNTAIN BIKING

Crystal and Lead King Basin is a scenic 16-mi loop on four-wheel-drive roads surrounded by the Maroon Bells–Snowmass Wilderness. The first
★ 6 moderate mi get you to the ghost mine of Crystal. You can turn back here, or tackle the rugged, remaining 2 mi and enjoy views from the 10,800-foot summit. Keep your eyes out for bouncing jeeps behind you. ✉ *Trailhead: From north side of Beaver Lake in Marble, continue driving up Forest Service Rd. 314 (Daniel's Hill). The ride begins wherever you park.*

Aspen Sports (✉ *408 E. Cooper Ave.* ☎ *970/925–6331* ⊕ *www.aspensports.com*) has the area's widest selection of rental bikes and all types of carriers for kids. **Blazing Adventures** (✉ *555 E. Durant Ave.* ☎ *970/923–4544 or 800/282–7238* ⊕ *www.blazingadventures.com*) leads downhill bicycle tours through Aspen and the surrounding valleys. **Hub of Aspen** (✉ *315 E. Hyman Ave.* ☎ *970/925–7970* ⊕ *www.hubofaspen.com*) has high-performance mountain and road bikes.

PARAGLIDING

It seems a pity to enjoy Aspen only from a horizontal viewpoint when so much of its scenery is vertical. If you've ever considered **paragliding,** Aspen—with its shining river and black-diamond ski slopes—is the place to do it. Though they look like rectangular parachutes, paragliders are actually classed as aircraft, and can fly high on warm thermals. After a short safety briefing, you'll be harnessed to an instructor for a mad dash down one of the steep ski slopes until the wind fills the "wing" and you are airborne. The ride along the ridges and over the valley can last anywhere from 10 minutes to over an hour, depending on the weather. **Aspen Paragliding** (✉ *414 E Cooper.* ☎ *970/925–6975 or 970/379–6975* ⊕ *www.aspenparagliding.com*) provides everything you'll need for a safe and memorable flight.

RAFTING

For the truly adventurous, **Blazing Adventures** (✉ *48 Upper Village Mall Snowmass Village* ☎ *970/923–4544 or 800/282–7238* ⊕ *www.blazingadventures.com*) runs mild to wild excursions on the Shoshone, Upper Roaring Fork, Colorado, and Arkansas rivers.

Long-time Aspen paddler Charlie MacArthur has set up the **Aspen Kayak Academy** (✉ *Box 5283 Snowmass* ☎ *970/925–4433* ⊕ *www.aspenkayakacademy.com*), where you can learn to roll, drop in on a wave, and even try the new sport of stand-up kayaking, like surfboarding with a paddle.

For the real adrenaline junkies, water sledging—kind of like cruising through rapids on a large kickboard—has arrived from New Zealand. **Aspen Seals** ☎ *970/618–4569* ⊕ *www.aspenseals.com*) provides the instruction, wet suits, helmets, and PFDs, and takes you out on the Roaring Fork and Arkansas rivers.

WHERE TO EAT

Use the coordinate (B2) at the end of each listing to locate a site on the corresponding map.

$$$$ ✗ **Ajax Tavern.** So close to the gondola you can keep your boots on, this
AMERICAN pub-style restaurant is mountainside in the Little Nell. Most of the tavern
★ has big glass windows, and there's also a nice patio with slopeside views. Wide plank floors and brick walls with dark wood paneling define this spot popular both for its location and hearty surf-n-turf dishes (they even have a raw bar). A popular dish to kick off with some brews is the Grand Plate: 18 oysters, 9 clams, 9 shrimp, and half a crab. Filling entrées include Colorado lamb Bolognese and grilled yellowfin tuna with heirloom beans. ✉ *675 E. Durant St.* ☎ *970/920–4600* ⊕ *www. thelittlenell.com* ☙ *Reservations essential* ☐ *AE, DC, MC, V* ✛ *C5.*

$ ✗ **Boogie's Diner.** This cheerful spot filled with diner memorabilia
AMERICAN resounds with rock-and-roll faves from the 1950s and '60s. The menu has true diner range—from vegetarian specialties to grilled cheese and half-pound beef or turkey burgers. Other items are excellent soups, a monster chef salad, meat loaf and mashed potatoes, and a hot turkey sandwich. There's even a potato bar with 1-pound taters and many toppings. Save room for a gigantic milk shake, malted, or float. ✉ *534 E. Cooper Ave.* ☎ *970/925–6610* ☐ *AE, MC, V* ✛ *C5.*

$$$–$$$$ ✗ **Cache Cache.** The sunny flavors of Provence explode on the palate
MEDITERRANEAN thanks to chef Chris Lanter's savvy use of garlic, tomato, eggplant, fennel, and rosemary. The Brandt Farms filet mignon served with whipped potatoes and a Dijon-peppercorn sauce is a perfect reward for a day on the slopes; salads and rotisserie items are sensational; desserts are worth leaving room for. The bar menu offers a budget-conscious way to sample this outstanding cuisine. ✉ *205 S. Mill St.* ☎ *970/925–3835 or 888/511–3835* ⊕ *www.cachecache.com* ☐ *AE, DC, MC, V* ◷ *No lunch* ✛ *B4.*

$ ✗ **Hickory House Ribs.** Tie on your bib and dig in. No one will mind if your
SOUTHERN hands and face are covered in the secret sauce that tops the slow-cooked meats and chicken at this log cabin–style joint. These hickory-smoked baby back ribs have won more than 40 national competitions. Feeling brave? Try "The Beast," a massive smoked pork or beef sandwich on garlic bread ($12). The rustic Hickory House is also home to Aspen's only Southern-style breakfast, grits and all. And after a late night on the town, nothing beats a breakfast of ribs and eggs. ✉ *730 W. Main St.* ☎ *970/925–2313* ⊕ *www.hickoryhouseribs.com* ☐ *D, MC, V* ✛ *C2.*

$$$ ✗ **L'Hostaria.** This subterranean hot spot is sophisticated yet rustic, with
NEW AMERICAN an open-beam farmhouse ceiling, sleek blond-wood chairs, contemporary art, and a floor-to-ceiling glass wine cooler in the center of the room. The menu relies on simple, subtle flavors in specialties such as grilled beef tenderloin with homemade grain-mustard sauce and polenta, and traditional dishes like penne with fresh-chopped tomato and black olives. For a change of pace, check out the carpaccio bar,

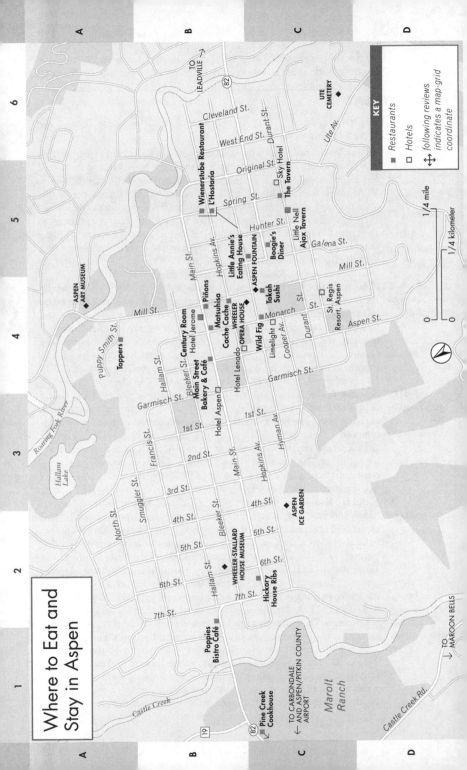

Where to Eat and Stay in Aspen

KEY

■ Restaurants
□ Hotels

✢ following reviews indicates a map-grid coordinate

Roaring Fork River
Hallam Lake

TO LEADVILLE →
82
Cleveland St.
West End St.
Original St.
Spring St.
Hunter St.
Durant St.
Ute Av.

ASPEN ART MUSEUM

Wienerstube Restaurant
l'Hostaria

Sky Hotel
The Tavern

Little Nell
Ajax Tavern
Galena St.

Boogie's Diner

ASPEN FOUNTAIN
Little Annie's Eating House

Pinons
Matsuhisa
Cache Cache
WHEELER OPERA HOUSE
Takah Sushi

Mill St.
Monarch St.
Durant St.
Aspen St.

St. Regis Resort, Aspen

Wild Fig
Limelight
Cooper Av.

Toppers

Puppy Smith St.
Mill St.
Hallam St.
Bleeker St.
Century Room
Hotel Jerome
Main Street Bakery & Café
Hotel Lenado
Hotel Aspen

Garmisch St.
Garmisch St.
1st St.
1st St.
2nd St.
Main St.
Hopkins Av.
Hyman Av.

Francis St.
Smuggler St.
North St.
3rd St.
4th St.
5th St.
6th St.

Bleeker St.
Hallam St.
WHEELER-STALLARD HOUSE MUSEUM

4th St.
5th St.
6th St.
7th St.

ASPEN ICE GARDEN

Hickory House Ribs

Poppies Bistro Café

Pine Creek Cookhouse
82
19

TO CARBONDALE AND ASPEN/PITKIN COUNTY AIRPORT ←

Castle Creek
Marolt Ranch
Castle Creek Rd.

TO MAROON BELLS →

UTE CEMETERY

0   ¼ mile
0   ¼ kilometer

which features wonderful cured meats and fish. ✉ *620 E. Hyman Ave.* ☎ *970/925–9022* ⊕ *www.hostaria.com* ▤ *AE, MC, V* ✛ *B5.*

$$
AMERICAN
✗ **Little Annie's Eating House.** Everything at this casual charmer is simple, from the wood paneling and red-and-white-checked tablecloths to the fresh fish, barbecued ribs and chicken, and Colorado lamb. Annie's is a big favorite with locals, who like the relaxed atmosphere, dependable food, and reasonable prices, not to mention the Bundt cake and "shot and a beer" special at the noisy bar. ✉ *517 E. Hyman Ave.* ☎ *970/925–1098* ⊕ *www.littleannies.com* ▤ *AE, DC, MC, V* ✛ *B5.*

$
CAFE
✗ **Main Street Bakery & Café.** Perfectly brewed coffee and hot breakfast buns and pastries are served at this café, along with a full breakfast menu that includes homemade granola. On sunny days, head out back to the deck for the mountain views. This is also a good spot for lunch and dinner (it's a quiet respite during the heart of the season). Try the chicken potpie and homemade soups. ✉ *201 E. Main St.* ☎ *970/925–6446* ▤ *AE, MC, V* ✛ *B4.*

$$$$
JAPANESE
★
✗ **Matsuhisa.** Renowned in Los Angeles, New York, London, and Tokyo, Nobu Matsuhisa has brought his Nouveau Japanese cuisine to Aspen. Although you shouldn't expect to see Nobu in the kitchen, his recipes and techniques are unmistakable. His shrimp with wasabi pepper sauce is scrumptious, his *king crab tempura* is delicious, his new-style sashimi marvelous, and his prices astronomical. Check out Matsuhisa Lounge upstairs (or outdoors in warm weather) for cocktails and a limited but still superb menu. ✉ *303 E. Main St.* ☎ *970/544–6628* ⊕ *www.matsuhisaaspen.com* ⌔ *Reservations essential* ▤ *AE, MC, V* ☽ *No lunch* ✛ *B4.*

$$$$
NEW AMERICAN
✗ **Pine Creek Cookhouse.** You can drive here, but it's more fun to strap on cross-country skis or board a horse-drawn sleigh (or hike in summer) to get to this homey log cabin. The emphasis is on game specialties, including bison, elk, and wild boar. Lunch offerings include hot smoked-salmon salad, spinach crepes, and Hungarian goulash. In winter or summer, shoot for a seat on the deck for breathtaking views of the Elk Mountains. ✉ *11399 Castle Creek Rd.* ☎ *970/925–1044* ⊕ *www.pinecreekcookhouse.com* ⌔ *Reservations essential* ▤ *AE, MC, V* ✛ *C1.*

$$$$
NEW AMERICAN
✗ **Piñons.** The Southwestern ranch–style dining room has leather-wrapped railings, a teal-green ceiling, and upholstered walls. The contemporary American menu scores high on creativity. Try the duck quesadilla appetizer, a Southwestern surprise from chef-owner Rob Mobilian, or the seared loin of New Zealand elk entrée. The service and wine list are impeccable. ✉ *105 S. Mill St.* ☎ *970/920–2021* ⊕ *www.pinons.net* ⌔ *Reservations essential* ▤ *AE, MC, V* ☽ *No lunch* ✛ *B4.*

$$$–$$$$
JAPANESE
★
✗ **Takah Sushi.** In a town with several sushi haunts, locals will tell you that Takah Sushi has the best plates and prices (a bento box with miso soup and hot sake runs $36). It has an outdoor patio right off the pedestrian mall for the see-and-be-seen crowd, and a rowdy basement for larger parties. The large and tasty appetizers include *gyoza* (pork and vegetable pot stickers) and Takah's terrific egg roll. Those who are sushied-out might like straight seafood plates such as blackened tuna steak in Cajun spices and baked black cod fillets. ✉ *320 S. Mill St.* ☎ *970/925–8588 or 877/925–8588* ⊕ *www.takahsushi.com* ▤ *AE, MC, V* ✛ *C4.*

$$ ✕ **Toppers.** Cheerful chef-owner Greg Topper runs a fuss-free café and
AMERICAN   take-out shop with first-rate American food. He serves fresh salads,
soups, and fancy pizzas (think truffle oil), and the best sandwiches in
town. Locals love the Aspen Bowls: You mix and match main items,
such as fennel-spiced pork stew, chicken cacciatore, and tofu and veg-
etable ragu with various sides. If you come for dinner, try the pro-
sciutto pizza or pappardelle with slow-roasted Colorado lamb. ⊠ *211A
Puppy Smith St.* ☎ *970/920–0069* ⊕ *www.toppersaspen.com* ⊟ *MC,
V* ✛ *A4.*

$ ✕ **Wienerstube Restaurant.** When he took over in 2008, chef-owner
AUSTRIAN   Harald Neuweg breathed new life into this always popular European
breakfast nook that was founded in 1965 by expanding the menu to
include lunch and dinner. Breakfast is still a popular meal and served
until 3 pm. A favorite is Harald's Wake Up Call, a European medley
of two eggs any style, Black Forest ham, Swiss cheese, and a kaiser roll
with apricot jam. For lunch, try the spicy Serbian white-bean soup. The
standard schnitzel and bratwurst dinners are favorites on snowy nights.
Ski patrollers still claim that the Wienerstube has the best Bloody Marys
in town. ⊠ *633 E. Hyman Ave.* ☎ *970/925–3357* ⊕ *www.weinerstube.
com* ⊟ *AE, MC, V* ✛ *B5.*

$$$$ ✕ **Wild Fig.** For a sunny taste of the Mediterranean-meets-the-Middle
MEDITERRANEAN   East, head to the Wild Fig, a friendly brasierre with an unbeatable loca-
Fodor's Choice   tion right off the pedestrian mall. The restaurant is small but cozy with
★   cheerful yellow walls trimmed in dark wood and a marble bar. Favorites
include chicken Milanese in roasted tomato sauce to Middle Eastern
staples including falafel with hummus and Tagine steak swarma. The
restaurant also has one of Aspen's more unusual plates: "fish in the
bag" (fish of the night is cooked and served in a brown paper bag).
For dessert, try the warm figs, of course, and a cup of amante cof-
fee, custom-roasted in the northern Italian tradition. ⊠ *315 E. Hyman
Ave.* ☎ *970/925–5160* ⊕ *www.thewildfig.com* ⚄ *Reservations essential*
⊟ *AE, MC, V* ✛ *C4.*

WHERE TO STAY

$$$ ⊞ **Hotel Aspen.** Just a few minutes from the mall and the mountain, this
hotel on the town's main drag is a good, if sometimes noisy, find. The
modern exterior opens up with huge windows that take full advantage
of the spectacular view; the lobby has a sleek Southwestern influence.
Rooms are comfortable, if not luxurious, with plenty of down pillows
and comforters. Most have balconies or terraces, and a few have hot
tubs. A Continental breakfast is included in the room rate, as is après-
ski wine and cheese. **Pros:** affordable; great location; free parking. **Cons:**
traffic can be noisy; no restaurant. ⊠ *110 W. Main St.* ☎ *970/920–1379
or 800/527–7369* ⊕ *www.hotelaspen.com* ⤴ *37 rooms, 8 suites* ⚄ *In-
room: kitchen (some), refrigerator, DVD, Wi-Fi. In-hotel: pool, laundry
service, public Internet, public Wi-Fi, airport shuttle, some pets allowed*
⊟ *AE, D, DC, MC, V* ⏣I *CP* ✛ *B4.*

$$$$ ⊞ **Hotel Jerome.** One of the state's truly grand hotels since it opened in
1889, Hotel Jerome is filled with romantic Victoriana. The sumptuous
public rooms have five kinds of wallpaper, antler sconces, and rose

damask curtains, as well as crystal chandeliers, intricate woodwork, and gold-laced floor tiling. Guest rooms are generously sized, with high ceilings, sprawling beds, and huge bathtubs. The restaurants are held in high regard, and the J-Bar is legendary. Ask about "ski free" packages. **Pros:** historic property with modern amenities; great location; great bar; summer music in the gardens. **Cons:** street-facing rooms can be noisy; only valet parking. ⊠ *330 E. Main St.* ☎ *970/920–1000 or 800/331–7213* ⊕ *www.hoteljerome.rockresorts.com* ⇌ *92 rooms, 8 suites* ⚅ *In-room: safe, refrigerator (some), DVD, Internet. In-hotel: 2 restaurants, room service, bar, pool, gym, concierge, laundry service, public Internet, public Wi-Fi, airport shuttle, parking (paid), some pets allowed* ⊟ *AE, DC, MC, V* ✥ *B4.*

$$$$ 🏨 **Hotel Lenado.** The focal point of this dramatic inn, a favorite with
★ couples, is a modern, 28-foot-tall stone-and-concrete fireplace. The smallish rooms contain either intricate carved apple-wood or hickory beds (*lenado* is Spanish for wood, and much of it appears throughout the hotel). You'll also find antique armoires and wood-burning stoves, in addition to modern amenities such as cable TV. Rates include a full breakfast, served in the urbane bar area, which is also a great place to enjoy an evening aperitif. **Pros:** romantic; great breakfast cooked to order. **Cons:** no restaurant; rooms facing street can be noisy. ⊠ *200 S. Aspen St.* ☎ *970/925–6246 or 800/321–3457* ⊕ *www.hotellenado. com* ⇌ *19 rooms* ⚅ *In-room: refrigerator (some), Wi-Fi. In-hotel: bar, concierge, laundry service, public Internet, public Wi-Fi, parking (paid), some pets allowed* ⊟ *AE, DC, MC, V* ⊗ *BP* ✥ *B4.*

$$$ **Limelight Lodge.** This family-owned 1950s classic has been completely leveled and reborn as a spacious, modern mountain lodge complete with bison and elk heads on the wall. It's a great choice for families and skiers because of its prime location, just two blocks from the mall and three blocks from Lift 1A on Aspen Mountain. This isn't a plush, pampered, tip-demanding place—there's no concierge and no ski butler—but it has a breakfast bar space and an outdoor grill near the hot tubs. The large rooms are furnished with simple but comfortable beds and dressers. **Pros:** new building but classic location; underground parking for a fee. **Cons:** busy; difficult to get a room in high season. ⊠ *55 S. Monarch St.* ☎ *970/925–3025 or 800/433–0832* ⊕ *www.limelightlodge.com* ⇌ *126 rooms* ⚅ *In-room: refrigerators, wireless Internet. In-hotel: pools, parking (paid), laundry, some pets allowed* ⊟ *AE, D, DC, MC, V* ⊗ *CP* ✥ *C4.*

$$$$ 🏨 **Little Nell.** With the best location in Aspen—right at the base of the
Fodor's Choice gondola—this hotel is the only true ski-in ski-out property in town.
★ Belgian wool carpets and overstuffed couches distinguish the lobby. The luxurious rooms have fireplaces, beds piled with down comforters, and large marble baths. Equally superior is the professional staff, whose training differentiates them from the seasonal workers at other hotels. This is the first all no-smoking hotel in Aspen. The Montagna restaurant ($$$$) serves delicious farmhouse fare, and Ajax Tavern has classy pub food. In summer the most sought-after tables are on the patio, with views of Aspen Mountain; even your dog can enjoy a fine meal from the doggie menu. The bar hosts the town's most fashionable

6

après-ski scenes. **Pros:** ski-in ski-out; great people-watching; luxurious. **Cons:** expensive; difficult to get a room in high season. ⊠ *675 E. Durant Ave.* ☎ *970/920–4600 or 888/843–6355* ⊕ *www.thelittlenell.com* ⏎ *78 rooms, 14 suites* ♿ *In-room: safe (some), DVD (some), Wi-Fi. In-hotel: 2 restaurants, room service, bars, pool, gym, concierge, laundry service, public Internet, public Wi-Fi, airport shuttle, parking (paid), some pets allowed* ⊟ *AE, D, DC, MC, V* ♻ *C5.*

$$$$ 📺 **Sky Hotel.** Aspen's trendiest hotel attracts a young, peacocking crowd. The Sky has a sleek style and slope-side locale (just across the street) that make it ideal for those in search of something a bit different. The lobby, with its black walls and oversize white leather chairs—think *Alice in Wonderland*—leads to the ultracool and ultracrowded 39 Degrees bar and the daily "altitude adjustment" happy hour with complimentary wine. The rooms, with yellow walls, white headboards, and black accents, are small but unforgettable. Signature touches like high-definition TVs, L'Occitane bath products, and your own small bottle of oxygen make this hotel stand out from the rest. **Pros:** dramatic style; great location for skiers. **Cons:** can be noisy; valet parking only. ⊠ *709 E. Durant Ave.* ☎ *970/925–6760 or 800/882–2582* ⊕ *www.theskyhotel. com* ⏎ *90 rooms* ♿ *In-room: safe, refrigerator, DVD (some), Wi-Fi. In-hotel: restaurant, room service, bar, pool, gym, concierge, laundry service, public Internet, public Wi-Fi, airport shuttle, parking (paid), some pets allowed* ⊟ *AE, D, DC, MC, V* ♻ *C5.*

$$$$ 📺 **St. Regis Resort, Aspen.** This hotel is a memorable one, even by Aspen's
Fodor'sChoice exacting standards. The posh reception area is comfortably furnished
★ with overstuffed chairs, soft suede pillows, leather-top tables, and rawhide lamp shades. The rooms follow suit, with dark-wood furniture, muted colors, and signature touches like bowls of fresh fruit. Luxurious baths are stocked with Remde toiletries. The Remde Spa has 15 treatment rooms and a reclining oxygen bar. **Pros:** one of Aspen's most luxurious properties; close to the slopes; ultra-posh spa. **Cons:** expensive; rooms are small; only valet parking. ⊠ *315 E. Dean St.* ☎ *970/920–3300 or 888/454–9005* ⊕ *www.stregisaspen.com* ⏎ *155 rooms, 24 suites* ♿ *In-room: safe, DVD, Wi-Fi. In-hotel: restaurant, room service, bars, pool, gym, spa, concierge, laundry service, public Internet, public Wi-Fi, airport shuttle, parking (paid), some pets allowed* ⊟ *AE, D, DC, MC, V* ♻ *C4.*

NIGHTLIFE AND THE ARTS

THE ARTS

The **Aspen Writers' Foundation** (☎ *970/925–3122* ⊕ *aspenwritersfoundation.org*) has a weekly writers' group that visitors are welcome to attend and a summer literary festival. **Jazz Aspen Snowmass** (☎ *970/920–4996*
⊕ *www.jazzaspen.com*) has festivals in June and September, and also
★ sponsors free Thursday-night concerts in summer. **Wheeler Opera House** (⊠ *320 E. Hyman Ave.* ☎ *970/920–5770* ⊕ *www.wheeleroperahouse. com*) presents big-name classical, jazz, pop, and opera performers, especially in summer.

ASPEN LODGING ALTERNATIVES

Aspen Alps (✉ 700 Ute Ave. ☎ 970/925–7820 or 877/711–0526 ⊕ www.aspenalps.com), right behind the Little Nell, has nicely appointed ski-in ski-out condos. **Coates, Reid & Waldron** (✉ 720 E. Hyman Ave. ☎ 970/925–1400 or 800/222–7736 ⊕ www.resortquest. com) rents everything from studios to large homes. **Frias Properties** (✉ 730 E. Durant Ave. ☎ 970/920–2010 or 800/633–0336 ⊕ www. friasproperties.com) has lavish homes and condos in the mountains. **The Gant** (✉ 610 W. End St. ☎ 970/925–5000 or 800/345–1471 ⊕ www.gantaspen.com) has impressive accommodations with an excellent pool and meeting space. **Gems of Aspen** (⌖ Box 408, ☎ 866/770–8358 ⊕ www. gemsofaspen.com) is a collection of a dozen affordable family-owned inns. All accommodations are within walking distance of downtown and most include breakfast.

NIGHTLIFE

BARS AND LOUNGES

East Hyman Avenue is the best place for bar-hopping—a cluster of nightspots share the same address and phone number. **Aspen Billiards** (✉ 315 E. Hyman Ave. ☎ 970/920–6707) is the town's most upscale pool hall. Challenge the locals to a game of eight ball. The smoky **Cigar Bar** (✉ 315 E. Hyman Ave. ☎ 970/920–6707) is a dimly lighted joint straight from Humphrey Bogart movies. Overstuffed chairs and sofas and velvet curtains set the mood. Whiskey—and lots of it—is the claim to fame of **Eric's Bar** (✉ 315 E. Hyman Ave. ☎ 970/920–6707), a hip little watering hole that attracts a rowdy crowd. There's a varied lineup of imported beers on tap. Inside Hotel Jerome, the **J-Bar** (✉ 330 E. Main St. ☎ 970/920–1000) is a fun, lively spot. You can't say you've seen Aspen until you've set foot in this place. **Su Casa** (✉ 315 E. Hyman Ave. ☎ 970/920–6707) is the place to get your fill of margaritas or sangria. **Woody Creek Tavern** (✉ 2 Woody Creek Plaza Woody Creek ☎ 970/923–4585) is a great place to grab a beer and play some games; Hunter S. Thompson was a regular. Join the party by riding your bike here in summer via the Rio Grande Trail.

CABARET

Once a country-and-western saloon and now a swanky dance club with grooved, wavy walls and a warm wooden bar, **The Regal Watering Hole** (✉ 220 S. Galena St. ☎ 970/925–4567) is the only place in town to shake it up on the dance floor.

MUSIC AND DANCE CLUBS

Jazz is all that's needed to draw crowds to the cozy but crowded bar at **Little Nell** (✉ 675 E. Durant Ave. ☎ 970/920–4600). For late-night jazz of truly astounding quality, head to **Syzygy** (✉ 520 E. Hyman Ave. ☎ 970/925–3700).

6

SHOPPING

Downtown Aspen is an eye-popping display of conspicuous consumption. For an eclectic mix of glitz and glamour, T-shirts, and trinkets, stroll past the shops lining Cooper Street.

★ Show up on Hunter and Hopkins streets any Saturday from mid-June to late October and you can enjoy the **Aspen Saturday Market,** a sort of farmers' market–meets–arts fair. You can buy ceramic plates, mugs, and serving dishes from a number of local potters—be sure to take a look at Alleghany Meadows—some of whom also supply flatware to local restaurants. For beautiful rings and dangling earrings, try Cathleen Crenshaw or Harmony Scott. There's even a blacksmith, Stephen Bershenyi, who crafts delicate flowers out of iron. Hungry? Don't forget the food vendors, including Jack Rabbit Hill Winery, Cloud Nine Brownie, and the Haystack Goat Dairy.

For chic boutiques, check out the **Brand Building** (⊠ *Hopkins Ave. between Mill and Galena Sts.*). This edifice is home to Gucci, Louis Vuitton, and Christian Dior, as well as local lions like Cashmere Aspen. For something silly for the folks back home, your best bet is the **Hyman Avenue Mall** (⊠ *Hyman Ave. between Mill and Galena Sts.*).

SPECIALTY SHOPS

ART GALLERIES

Baldwin Gallery (⊠ *209 S. Galena St.* ☎ *970/920–9797* ⊕ *www.baldwingallery.com*) is the place to see and be seen at receptions for nationally known artists. **David Floria Gallery** (⊠ *525 E. Cooper Ave.* ☎ *970/544–5705* ⊕ *www.floriagallery.com*) exhibits the hottest new artists. **Galerie Maximillian** (⊠ *602 E. Cooper Ave.* ☎ *970/925–6100* ⊕ *www.galeriemax. com*) is the place to find high-quality paintings and sculpture. **Magidson Fine Art** (⊠ *525 E. Cooper Ave.* ☎ *970/920–1001* ⊕ *www.magidson. com*) is known for its well-rounded collection of contemporary art. **Soroka Gallery** (⊠ *400 E. Hyman Ave.* ☎ *970/920–3152*) specializes in rare photos. For offbeat exhibits, including works by such notables as Hunter S. Thompson and Andy Warhol, drive to the **Woody Creek Store** (⊠ *6 Woody Creek Plaza Woody Creek* ☎ *970/922–0990*).

BOOKS

Escape is an independent bookstore in a Victorian house. The store stocks more than 100,000 books, and is particularly noted for its political, travel, and literature sections. The upstairs bistro is a perfect place for a light meal or snack. ⊠ *221 E. Main St.* ☎ *970/925–5336 bookstore, 970/925–5338 bistro* ⊕ *www.explorebooksellers.com* ⊗ *Bookstore, daily 10–10; bistro, early Sept.–Nov., daily 11:30–9; Dec.–Aug., daily 11:30–10.*

BOUTIQUES

In downtown Aspen, **Boogie's** (⊠ *534 E. Cooper Ave.* ☎ *970/925–6111*) sells clothing and accessories from jeans to jewelry. **Chepita's** (⊠ *525 E. Cooper Ave.* ☎ *970/925–2871*) calls itself a "toy store for adults," which means it sells kinetic clothing and designer watches and jewelry. **Pitkin County Dry Goods** (⊠ *520 E. Cooper Ave.* ☎ *970/925–1861* ⊕ *www. pitkincountydrygoods.com*) has a good selection of men's and women's apparel. **Scandinavian Designs** (⊠ 675 E. Cooper Ave. ☎ 970/925–7299) features some of Aspen's finest hand-knit sweaters, as well as everything Scandinavian, like Swedish clogs and Norwegian trolls.

SPORTING GOODS

Aspen Sports (⊠ 408 E. Cooper Ave. ☎ 970/925–6331 ⊕ www.aspensports.com) is the biggest sporting-goods store in town. It stocks a full line of apparel and equipment for all sports. **Ute Mountaineer** (⊠ 308 S. Mill St. ☎ 970/925–2849 ⊕ www.utemountaineer.com) has mountaineering clothes and equipment.

THE ROARING FORK VALLEY

Moving down-valley from Aspen along the Roaring Fork River, down past the family resort of Snowmass, is a journey to a humbler Colorado. Even the landscape changes, going from lush, alpine aspen groves into the drier typical Western Slope steppe.

SNOWMASS

10 mi northwest of Aspen via Hwy. 82.

Snowmass is one of four ski mountains owned by Aspen Skiing Company. The town at the mountain's base, also called Snowmass, has a handful of chic boutiques and eateries, but it's less self-absorbed and more family-oriented and outdoorsy than Aspen.

Snowmass was built in 1967 as Aspen's answer to Vail—a ski-specific resort—and although it has never quite matched the panache or popularity of Vail, it has gained stature with age, finding its identity as a resort destination rather than the village it once called itself.

Still, an effort has been made to breathe new life into Snowmass to the tune of $25.5 million in improvements including the Treehouse Kid's Adventure Center (full of fun activities for children ages eight weeks and up) and new restaurants and shops. In general, Snowmass is the preferred alternative for families with young children, leaving the town of Aspen to a more up-at-the-crack-of-noon crowd. Snowmass, one of the best intermediate hills in the country, has more ski-in ski-out lodgings and a slower pace than Aspen.

GETTING HERE AND AROUND

Heading east along Highway 82 toward Aspen, you'll spot the turn-offs (Brush Creek and Owl Creek roads) to the Snowmass Ski Area. Snowmass is best navigated with your own car or the free Aspen Skiing Company Shuttle Bus which runs roughly every 15 minutes. All parking in Snowmass is free during the summer, but there's usually a fee in the winter season.

WHEN TO GO

Snowmass Village is a year-round resort, though the peak times are summers for hiking—June through September, and winter for skiing, November through April.

OFF THE
BEATEN
PATH

Basalt. As you drive down Highway 82 through the bedroom communities of Carbondale and El Jebel on the way to Aspen and Snowmass, a detour through this old railroad town is well worth the trouble. Basalt, at the confluence of the Fryingpan and Roaring Fork rivers, has the feeling of a ski town without the lift. Walking down its main drag, Midland Avenue, you get a hint of what Aspen must have been like years ago. Browse the town's small shops and surprisingly upscale galleries, then dine at one of several newer and impressive restaurants.

DOWNHILL SKIING AND SNOWBOARDING

Snowmass is a sprawling ski area, the biggest of the four Aspen–area mountains. Aspen Highlands, Aspen Mountain, Buttermilk, and Snowmass can all be skied with the same ticket. A free shuttle system connects all four. Snowmass now includes 64,000 square feet of shops and restaurants, the Elk Camp Gondola, and Elk Camp Meadows Activity Center. There are six distinct sectors: Elk Camp, High Alpine–Alpine Springs, Big Burn, Sam's Knob, Two Creeks, and Campground. Except for the last two, all these sectors funnel into the pedestrian mall at the base. Snowmass is probably best known for Big Burn, itself a great sprawl of wide-open, intermediate skiing. Experts head to such areas as Hanging Valley and the Cirque for the best turns.

At Snowmass 50% of the 3,128 skiable acres are designated for intermediate-level skiers. The route variations down Big Burn are essentially inexhaustible, and there are many other places on the mountain for intermediates to find entertainment. The novice and beginning-intermediate terrain on the lower part of the mountain makes Snowmass a terrific place for younger children.

But don't overlook the fact that Snowmass is four times the size of Aspen Mountain, and has triple the black- and double-black-diamond terrain of its famed sister, including several fearsomely precipitous gullies at Hanging Valley. Although only 32% of the terrain is rated advanced or expert, this huge mountain has enough difficult runs, including the consistently challenging Powderhorn and the more-relaxed Sneaky's Run, to satisfy all but the most demanding skiers.

Snowboarders take note: This mountain has one of the most comprehensive snowboarding programs in the country, with the heart of the action in the Headwall Cirque. A special terrain map points out the numerous snowboard-friendly trails and terrain parks while steering riders away from flat spots. You'll want to visit Trenchtown in the Coney Glade area, which has two lift-accessed pipes, video evaluation, piped-in music, and a yurt hangout complete with couches and snacks. ⊠ *West of Aspen via Brush Creek Rd. or Owl Creek Rd.* ☎ *970/925–1220 or 800/525–6200* ⊕ *www.aspensnowmass.com* ♥ *Late Nov.–mid-Apr., daily 9–4.*

FACILITIES   4,406-foot vertical drop; 3,100 skiable acres; 88 trails; 6% beginner, 50% intermediate, 12% advanced, 32% expert; 24 lifts, 1 8-passenger gondola, 1 high-speed 6-passenger chair, 1 6-passenger gondola, 6 high-speed quad chairs, 2 quads, 4 double lifts, 5 magic carpets, 2 school lifts, 2 platter pulls.

LESSONS AND PROGRAMS **Aspen Skiing Company** (⊠ *97 Lower Mall, Snowmass Village Mall* ☎ *970/925–1220 or 800/525–6200*) gives lessons at Snowmass and Aspen's other mountains.

LIFT TICKETS Lift tickets are $96, but almost nobody pays full price, thanks to multi-day savings, early- and late-season specials, and other discounts.

RENTALS Snowmass has numerous ski shops offering rental packages (skis, boots, and poles). **Aspen Sports** (⊠ *70 Snowmass Village Mall* ☎ *970/923–6111* ⊕ *www.aspensports.com*) is one of the best-known outfitters in Snowmass. **Incline Ski Shop** (⊠ *1 Snowmass Village Mall* ☎ *970/923–4726* ⊕ *www.inclineski.com*) is just steps from the shuttle-bus stop.

NORDIC SKIING

TRACK SKIING

Aspen/Snowmass Nordic Council (☎ *970/429–2039* ⊕ *www.aspennordic.com*) has 48 mi of maintained trails in the Roaring Fork Valley. Probably the most varied, in terms of scenery and terrain, is the 18-mi Snowmass Club trail network. For a longer ski, try the Owl Creek Trail, connecting the Snowmass Club trail system and the Aspen Cross-Country Center trails. More than 10 mi long, the trail provides both a good workout and a heavy dose of woodsy beauty, with many ups and downs across meadows and aspen-gladed hillsides. Best of all, you can take the bus back to Snowmass Village when you're finished.

OTHER SPORTS AND THE OUTDOORS

BALLOONING

Unicorn Balloon Company (☎ *970/925–5752*) flies you over the slopes of Aspen, and gives you a personal flight video as a keepsake.

DOGSLEDDING

★ With about 200 dogs ready to go, **Krabloonik** (⊠ *4250 Divide Rd.* ☎ *970/923–3953* ⊕ *krablonikrestaurant.com*) can always put together a half-day ride. These trips, beginning at 8:30 AM and 12:30 PM, include lunch or dinner at the Krabloonik restaurant, one of the best in the area. In summer, meet the dogs during daily kennel tours.

FISHING

Aspen Skiing Company (⊠ *97 Lower Mall, Snowmass Village Mall* ☎ *970/923–8647*) can hook you up with outfitters that lead trips on the Colorado, Roaring Fork, and Fryingpan rivers.

MOUNTAIN BIKING

Aspen Skiing Company (⊠ *97 Lower Mall, Snowmass Village Mall* ☎ *970/925–1220*) can give you a map of area trails, including the terrain park accessed by the Burlingame Lift. The company can also sell you a lift ticket so you won't have to ride uphill. **Aspen Sports** (⊠ *70 Snowmass Village Mall* ☎ *970/923–6111* ⊕ *www.aspensports.com*) has the widest selection of rental bikes in town, plus carriers for the kids.

6

WHERE TO EAT

$$$ ✕**Butch's Lobster Bar.** Once a lobsterman off Cape Cod, Butch Darden
SEAFOOD knows his lobster, and serves it up countless ways. The menu includes
plenty of other seafood favorites, including crab legs, shrimp, and
steamers. There are also the obligatory steak and chicken dishes.
Although it isn't fancy and the service isn't doting, this is the best place
in town to get your seafood fix. ✉ *Timberline Condominiums, 2nd fl.,
264 Snowmelt Rd.* ☎ *970/923–7311* ⚖ *Reservations essential* ☰ *AE,
MC, V* ☉ *No lunch.*

$$$$ ✕**Il Poggio.** In the cutthroat competition between resort-town restau-
ITALIAN rants, this unassuming Italian place is smart enough to let the big boys
duke it out. It wins in the end; it's quite possibly the best casual restau-
rant in the village. The classic Italian food is well received by the après-
ski crowd. Try one of the hearth-baked pizzas, a hearty pasta dish, or
any beef or chicken entrée. ✉ *73 Elbert La.* ☎ *970/923–4292* ⊕ *www.
snowmassvillage.com* ☰ *AE, DC, MC, V* ☉ *No lunch.*

$$$$ ✕**Krabloonik.** Owner Dan MacEachen has a penchant for dogsled
AMERICAN racing, and Krabloonik (Eskimo for "big eyebrows," and the name
of his first lead dog) helps subsidize his expensive hobby. This rustic
yet elegant log cabin is on the slopes, which means you'll be treated
to wonderful views on your way there. Although you can drive to
the restaurant, the best—and most memorable—way to arrive is by
dogsled. You'll dine sumptuously on some of the best game in Colo-
rado, like caribou, elk, and wild boar, as well as house-smoked trout
and signature wild-mushroom soup. Wash it all down with a selec-
tion from Snowmass's most extensive wine list. ✉ *4250 Divide Rd.*
☎ *970/923–3953* ⊕ *www.krabloonikrestaurant.com* ⚖ *Reservations
essential* ☰ *AE, MC, V.*

WHERE TO STAY

$$$–$$$$ ▦ **Silvertree Hotel.** This ski-in ski-out property, under the same manage-
ment as the Wildwood Lodge next door, is built into Snowmass Moun-
tain. It's a sprawling complex—virtually everything you need is under
one roof. After a morning on the slopes, warm up in one of the hot
tubs or in the steam room. Rooms and suites are small but done in sub-
dued colors, with all the expected amenities. Condos are also available,
with full use of hotel facilities. **Pros:** ski-in ski-out; steam room. **Cons:**
self-parking is removed from hotel; rooms get hot in summer. ✉ *100
Elbert La.* ☎ *970/923–3520 or 800/525–9402* ⊕ *www.silvertreehotel.
com* ➳ *262 rooms, 15 suites, 200 condos* ⚴ *In-room: safe (some),
refrigerator (some), no a/c, DVD, Wi-Fi. In-hotel: 2 restaurants, room
service, bars, pools, gym, spa, concierge, laundry facilities, laundry ser-
vice, public Internet, airport shuttle, parking (paid), some pets allowed*
☰ *AE, D, DC, MC, V.*

$$ ▦ **Snowmass Inn.** This family-owned lodge is one of Snowmass's original digs; it commands a prime location in the middle of the Snowmass
Village Mall. It's also a short stroll from the slopes. Rooms are spacious and comfortable, although some are showing signs of wear. Still,
this is the perfect place for those on a budget or looking to be in the
middle of the action. **Pros:** good location for skiers; big rooms; moderately priced for Snowmass. **Cons:** poor customer service; few room

or hotel amenities. ⊠ *67 Daily La.* ☎ *970/923–4204 or 800/635–3758* ⊕ *www.snowmassinn.com* ⤵ *39 rooms* ⚄ *In-room: no a/c, refrigerator (some). In-hotel: laundry facilities, laundry service, public Internet, airport shuttle, parking (fee in winter)* ⊟ *AE, D, DC, MC, V* ⎆⎗ *CP.*

$$$$
★ ▦ **Stonebridge Inn.** Slightly removed from the hustle and bustle of the Village Mall, this inn is the nicest lodging option in Snowmass. The lobby and bar are streamlined and elegant, with mood lighting and contemporary furniture. The cozy, window-ringed Artisan restaurant serves simple, hearty preparations of the freshest regional ingredi-

SNOWMASS LODGING ALTERNATIVES

Snowmass Lodging Company (⌂ *425 Wood Rd.* ☎ *970/923–3232 or 800/365–0410*) rents a wide variety of condominiums. **Stay Aspen Snowmass** (☎ *888/649–5982* ⊕ *www.stayaspensnowmass.com*) is the central lodging service for the area. **Village Property Management** (⌂ *100 Elbert La.* ☎ *970/923–3520 or 800/837–4255*) has everything from studio apartments to fully stocked homes.

ents. There's also an inexpensive bar menu. A Continental breakfast is included. Rooms, all with Adirondack-style beds, have rough paneling and soft wood and stone colors for a contemporary mountain style. **Pros:** recently remodeled; quiet location; good on-site restaurant. **Cons:** must catch a shuttle to lifts. ⊠ *300 Carriage Way* ☎ *866/939–2471* ⊕ *www.stonebridgeinn.com* ⤵ *90 rooms 5 suites, 28 condos* ⚄ *In-room: DVD. In-hotel: restaurant, bar, pool, gym, concierge, laundry facilities, laundry service, public Internet, public Wi-Fi, airport shuttle, parking (paid)* ⊟ *AE, D, DC, MC, V* ⎆⎗ *CP.*

NIGHTLIFE

The **Office at the Cirque** (⊠ *105 Snowmass Village Mall* ☎ *970/923–8686*) has the most happening après-ski scene, with live music most evenings. The sun-soaked deck is a popular place in summer. For a mellow experience, try the **Conservatory** (⊠ *100 Elbert La.* ☎ *970/923–3520*). It has a heated deck and occasional live music. **Zane's Tavern** (⊠ *10 Snowmass Village Sq.* ☎ *970/923–3515* ⊕ *www.zanestavern.com*) is your classic mountain-town bar with pool tables, $1.25 drafts, and an Internet jukebox. **Sneaky's Tavern** (⊠ *0239 Snowmass Club Circle* ☎ *970/923–8787* ⊕ *www.sneakystavern.com*) is a popular spot with an indoor-outdoor bar.

SHOPPING

Anderson Ranch Arts Center (⊠ *5263 Owl Creek Rd.* ☎ *970/923–3181* ⊕ *www.andersonranch.org*) exhibits the work of resident artists. It also hosts lectures, workshops, and other special events. **Aspen Sports** (⊠ *70 Snowmass Village Mall* ☎ *970/923–6111* ⊕ *www.aspensports.com*) is the biggest store around, with a full line of apparel and equipment for all sports.

GLENWOOD SPRINGS

27 mi northwest of Aspen via Hwy. 82; 159 mi west of Denver via I–70.

Once upon a time, Glenwood Springs, the famed spa town that forms the western apex of a triangle with Vail and Aspen, was every bit as tony as those chic resorts are today, attracting a faithful legion of the pampered and privileged who came to enjoy the waters of the world's largest natural hot springs, said to cure everything from acne to rheumatism.

GETTING HERE AND AROUND

The easiest way to arrive is by car on I–70, the main east–west highway in Colorado. Public transport is more limited than in neighboring Aspen, so you'll need a vehicle to explore much beyond the main street.

WHEN TO GO

Glenwood Springs comes into its own in the early summer, when rafters, fishermen, and spa goers arrive to sample the gifts of the Colorado River and its underground mineral springs.

ESSENTIALS

Visitor Info Glenwood Springs Chamber Resort Association (✉ *1102 Grand Ave.* ☎ *970/945–6589* ⊕ *glenwoodchamber.com*).

EXPLORING

Today the town feels more like a bedroom community for Aspen workers; it's marred by the proliferation of strip malls, chain motels, and fast-food outlets. Remnants of her glory days can still be seen in the grand old **Hotel Colorado** (✉ *526 Pine St.*), regally commanding the vaporous pools from a patrician distance. Modeled after the Villa de Medici in Italy, the property opened its doors in 1893. Teddy Roosevelt even made it his unofficial "Little White House" in 1905.

★ **Hot Springs Pool,** formerly called Yampah Hot Springs, was discovered
☾ by the Utes (yampah is Ute for "big medicine"). Even before the heyday of the hotel, Western notables from Annie Oakley to Doc Holliday came to take the curative waters. In Doc's case, however, the cure didn't work, and six months after his arrival in 1887 he died—broke, broken down, and tubercular. (He lies in Linwood Cemetery, 0.5 mi east of town.) The smaller pool is 100 feet long and maintained at 104°F. The larger is more than two city blocks long (405 feet), and contains more than a million gallons of constantly filtered water that is completely refilled every six hours and maintained at a soothing 90°F. ✉ *401 N. River St.* ☎ *970/947–2955 or 800/537–7946* ⊕ *www.hotspringspool. com* 🎫 *$18.25* ⊗ *Late May–early Sept., daily 7:30* AM*–10* PM*; mid-Sept.–mid-May, daily 9* AM*–10* PM.

The **Yampah Spa & Salon** is a series of three natural underground steam baths. The same 120°F-plus springs that supply the pool flow under the floors of the only known natural vapor caves in North America. Each chamber is successively hotter than the last, and with 15 minerals in the waters, you can purify your body (and soul, according to Ute legend) in a matter of minutes. A variety of spa treatment are also available, whether you prefer a massage or a body wrap. ✉ *709 E. 6th St.*

Doc Holliday

John Henry "Doc" Holliday was a gunslinger with an attitude. Part scholar, part rebel, he was often only one step ahead of the law. Born on August 14, 1851, in Griffin, Georgia, Holliday went to dental school. Shortly after opening his practice, he was diagnosed with tuberculosis. On the advice of his doctor, Holliday moved west in 1873 in search of a drier climate.

While living in Texas, Holliday took up gambling, which became his sole means of support. His violent temper turned him into a killer. After shooting a prominent citizen and leaving him for dead, Holliday had to flee Texas. Carrying one gun in a shoulder holster, another on his hip, and a long-bladed knife (just in case), he blazed a trail of death across the Southwest. It's not known just how many men died at his hands, but some have

estimated the number to be as high as 25 or more. However, historians generally believe the true number is considerably less. Holliday's reasons for killing run the gamut from fights over cards to self-defense—or so he claimed. He will forever be known for his role in one of the most famous gunfights in the history of the Wild West: a 30-second gunfight at the O.K. Corral in Tombstone, Arizona.

In May 1887 Holliday moved to Glenwood Springs, hoping that the sulfur vapors of the hot springs there would help his failing lungs. He lived out his dying days at the Hotel Glenwood. On the last day of his life Holliday knocked back a glass of whiskey and remarked, "This is funny." A few minutes later he was dead. Holliday was 36 years old.

6

☎ 970/945–0667 ⊕ *www.yampahspa.com* ✉ *$12 for caves, additional cost for treatments* ⊗ *Daily 9–9.*

☾ Glenwood is home to many caves, including **Fairy Caves and Glenwood Caverns,** whose subterranean caverns, grottoes, and labyrinths are truly a marvel of nature (the area was touted as the "Eighth Wonder of the World" upon its public opening in 1887). Now part of the Glenwood Caverns Adventure Park (think tourist trap), the still-amazing caves are easily accessible via the Iron Mountain Tramway, a seven-minute gondola ride with a bird's-eye view of Glenwood Springs and the surrounding landscape. You can take one of two cavern tours: a two-hour, family-friendly walk; or a more extensive, crawl-on-your-belly spelunking adventure. For a second helping of adrenaline, try the gravity-powered alpine coaster that drops 3,400-feet, ride the 50-MPH zip line, or sail out over 1,300 feet above the Colorado River cliffs on a giant swing. ⊠ *51000 Two Rivers Plaza Rd.* ☎ *800/530–1635* ⊕ *www.glenwoodcaverns.com* ✉ *$12 and up* ⊗ *Times vary, so call ahead.*

Along I–70 east of town is the 15-mi-long **Glenwood Canyon.** Nature began the work as the Colorado River carved deep granite, limestone, and quartzite gullies—buff-tint walls brilliantly streaked with lavender, rose, and ivory. This process took a half-billion years. Then man stepped in, seeking a more direct route west. In 1992 the work on I–70 through the canyon was completed, at a cost of almost $500 million. Much of the expense was attributable to the effort to preserve the natural landscape as much as possible. When contractors blasted cliff faces, for example, they stained the exposed rock to simulate nature's weathering. Biking trails were also created, providing easy access to the hauntingly beautiful **Hanging Lake Recreation Area.** Here Dead Horse Creek sprays ethereal flumes from curling limestone tendrils into a startlingly turquoise pool, as jet-black swifts dart to and fro. It's perhaps the most transcendent of several idyllic spots in the canyon reachable by bike or on foot. The intrepid can scale the delicate limestone cliffs pocked with caverns and embroidered with pastel-hue gardens.

DOWNHILL SKIING AND SNOWBOARDING

Sunlight Mountain Resort, 20 minutes south of Glenwood Springs, is affordable Colorado skiing at its best. Overshadowed by world-class neighbors, the resort sees far less traffic than typical Colorado slopes. Fresh powder, typically skied off at Aspen within an hour, can last as long as two days here on classic downhill runs like Sun King and steeps like Beaujolais; you won't stand in any lines at the four lifts. The resort has 67 trails, including the super-steep glades of Extreme Sunlight, with a drop of 2,010 vertical feet. The varied terrain, sensational views, and lack of pretension make this a local favorite. The lift tickets are also 50% cheaper than nearby Aspen. Snowboarders even have a dedicated feature—the Peace Pipe. Families will appreciate that every child under 12 skis free with an adult and every slope meets at the bottom. For winter sports enthusiasts who don't want to ride a chairlift, there's a 20-mi network of cross-country ski and snowshoe trails just off the slopes. The cafeteria has cold sandwiches, burgers, and pizzas. ✉ *10901 County Rd. 117* ☎ *970/945–7491 or 800/445–7931* ⊕ *www. sunlightmtn.com* ⊙ *Late Nov.–early Apr., daily 9–4.*

FACILITIES   2,010-foot vertical drop; 470 skiable acres; 67 trails; 20% beginner, 55% intermediate, 20% advanced, 5% expert; 4 lifts, 1 triple chair, 2 double chairs, 1 surface lift.

LESSONS AND   Two-hour ski lessons (including gear rental and lift ticket) cost $90;
PROGRAMS   snowboarding is $95. Four-hour ski lessons are $140, $145 for snowboarding.

The resort, in conjunction with Glenwood Springs, also has a ski-stay-swim package. It includes one night's lodging, a big breakfast, a full-day ski pass, and a full day at the Glenwood Hot Springs Pool.

LIFT TICKETS   Lift tickets are the second-cheapest in the state, only $50 at the window. But, as at all Colorado ski resorts, no one ever needs to pay full price. Purchase a discounted pass at the Safeway or King Soopers grocery store in Glenwood Springs.

RENTALS   **Sunlight Mountain Ski Resort** (✉ *10901 County Rd. 117* ☎ *970/945–7491 or 800/445–7931*) has complete rental gear setups on shaped skis. Rentals of the latest snowboards are available for as little as $20. The resort's retail outlet, **Sunlight Ski and Bike Shop** (✉ *309 9th St.* ☎ *970/945–9425*), is in Glenwood Springs.

OTHER SPORTS AND THE OUTDOORS

BIKING

Though it's a shame that I–70 heads through the spectacular depths of Glenwood Canyon, the busy corridor has opened up this gorge to biking. The **Glenwood Canyon Bike Path,** a concrete path sandwiched between the Colorado River and the freeway traffic, runs 34.6 mi from Dotsero east to Glenwood Springs. Fortunately, the path generally runs below, and out of sight of, the interstate, and the roar of the river drowns out the sound of traffic. Because of the mild climate on Colorado's Western Slope, the trail can be ridden almost year-round. The concrete path also has several dirt spurs that head up into White River National Forest for hikers and mountain bikers. A choice ride is the 18-mi round-trip from Glenwood Springs east up to Hanging Lake, where you can leave your bike and hike a steep mile (climbing 900 feet) to the beautiful lake. Horseshoe Bend, 2 mi from the Vapor Caves, is a perfect picnic spot, since the highway ducks out of sight into a series of tunnels. ⊠ *Trailhead: enter path from either Yampah Hot Springs Vapor Caves in Glenwood Springs or farther west on I–70 at the Grizzly Creek rest area.*

OUTFITTER **Sunlight Ski and Bike Shop** (⊠ *309 9th St.* ☎ *970/945–9425*) rents mountain
★ and comfort bikes; $5 per hour, $18 for four hours, or $22 for the day.

FISHING

Roaring Fork Anglers (⊠ *2205 Grand Ave.* ☎ *970/945–0180* ⊕ *www. roaringforkanglers.com*) leads wade and float trips throughout the area. **Roaring Fork Outfitters** (⊠ *2022 Grand Ave.* ☎ *970/945–5800* ⊕ *www. rfoutfitters.com*) has a huge selection of flies, and guides who'll make sure you find the right ones.

GOLF

River Valley Ranch Golf Club. Jay Moorish designed this course on the banks of the Crystal River. There is lots of water, a constant breeze, and superb—if not distracting—views of Mount Sopris. The course is in Carbondale, 15 mi from Glenwood Springs. ⊠ *303 River Valley Ranch Dr. Carbondale* ☎ *970/963–3625* ⊕ *www.rvrgolf.com* ⅃. *18 holes. Yards: 7,348/5,168. Par: 72/72. Green fee: $80.*

RAFTING

When the ski season is over and Colorado's white gold starts to melt, many ski instructors swap their sticks for paddles and hit the mighty **Colorado River** for the spring and summer rafting seasons. Stomach-churning holes, chutes, and waves beckon adrenaline junkies, while calmer souls will revel in the shade of Glenwood Canyon's towering walls. All the outfitters below run a basic half-day raft trip on the Colorado.

OUTFITTER **Blue Sky Adventures** (⊠ *319 Hwy. 6* ☎ *970/945–6605 or 877/945–6605*
AND ⊕ *www.blueskyadventure.com*) offers a unique "pedal and paddle"
EXPEDITIONS deal that includes a half-day raft trip followed by a half-day bike tour.
★ If you're the independent type, lead your own white-water rafting
☾ adventure by putting in at the boat ramp operated by the **Colorado Division of Wildlife** (⊠ *County Rd. 106* ☎ *970/947–2920*). It's on the Roaring Fork River, just east of town. **Colorado Whitewater Rafting** (⊠ *I–70 at*

CLOSE UP

Rafting the Roaring Fork Valley

The key to understanding white-water rafting is the rating system. Rivers are rated from Class I, with small waves where you really don't need to paddle to avoid anything, to Class VI, which is almost impossible to run and a mistake can be fatal. To confuse matters, rivers change classes depending on how fast they are flowing (measured in cubic feet of water per second). May and June are peak rafting seasons for those who want the adrenaline rush of fighting spring runoff. By mid-August many rivers are little more than lazy float trips.

The Roaring Fork, a free-flowing river (no dams), is regularly considered a Class III. Because it runs away from major highways through the heart of ranch country, you're liable to see more wildlife than on the Colorado; in June your guides may point out a nest full of croaking bald eaglets. Cemetery Rapids, a half-mile churning stretch of white water, is the most exciting run.

The stretch of the mighty Colorado that runs through the steep, spectacular walls of Glenwood Canyon alongside I–70 is divided into two sections: the rough and tumble Shoshone below the dam, and the wider, mellower regions beyond. During the peak runoff season, the Shoshone is considered a Class IV river, with aptly named rapids like Maneater and Baptism. The lower Colorado still has some exciting stretches, including Maintenance Shack, a Class III rapid that can flip a large raft. By July and August you can hit the same rapid sideways or backward and barely get wet. The lower stretches of the Colorado pass by several hidden, and not-so-hidden shallow hot springs. If you'd like to warm up in them, ask your guides.

Exit 114 ☎ *970/945–8477 or 800/993–7238*) is home of the "Double Shoshone," a round-trip through the area's most hair-raising rapids. **Rock Gardens Rafting** (✉ *1308 County Rd. 129* ☎ *970/945–6737 or 800/958–6737* ⊕ *www.rockgardens.com*) runs trips down the Colorado and Roaring Fork rivers, and operates a full-service campground on the banks of the Colorado.

WHERE TO EAT

$ ✗ **The Bayou.** "Food so good you'll slap yo' mama," trumpets the menu

SOUTHERN   at this casual Cajun eatery, whose most distinctive attribute is its frog awning—two bulbous eyes beckon you in. Choose from "pre-stuff, wabbit stuff, udder stuff," such as lip-smacking gumbo that looks like mud (and is supposed to), étouffée and blackened fish, or lethal Cajun martinis. And when the menu labels an item "hurt me" hot, it's no joke. There's karaoke and a DJ on weekends. ✉ *919 Grand Ave.* ☎ *970/945–1047* ▤ *AE, MC, V.*

$$ ✗ **Florinda's.** The peach walls of this handsome space are graced by con-

ITALIAN   stantly changing art exhibits. The chef has a deft hand with northern and southern Italian dishes. Try the double-cut veal chops served with a shiitake mushroom sauce or the nightly specials, which are always extensive and superb. And don't miss homemade Italian desserts like tiramisu, zabaglione, and cannoli. ⊠ *721 Grand Ave.* ☏ *970/945–1245* 🖃 *MC, V* ⊘ *Closed Sun. No lunch.*

$ ✕ **Narayan's Nepal Restaurant.** In a cow town like Glenwood Springs,
ASIAN finding good foreign fare is no easy feat, but this little eatery, tucked into a strip mall beside the highway, has tasty Nepalese food. The chef, a former Sherpa who now owns this restaurant and its twin in Aspen, serves dishes so authentic that you'll swear you're in the high Himalayas. Try fish *kawab* (marinated overnight and then baked in a tandoor) with a side of garlicky *naan* (spongy flat bread) if you're skeptical. ⊠ *6824 Hwy. 82* ☏ *970/945–8803* 🖃 *AE, MC, V* ⊘ *No lunch Sun.*

WHERE TO STAY

$$$ 🏨 **Hot Springs Lodge.** This lodge is perfectly located, just steps from the Hot Springs Pool (which is used to heat the property). The attractive rooms, decorated in jade, teal, buff, and rose, have a Southwestern flavor. Deluxe rooms have small fridges and tiny balconies, in addition to standard conveniences such as cable TV. Breakfast and free passes to the pool are included. **Pros:** right next to the hot springs; comfortable rooms. **Cons:** no bar; small rooms; disinterested management. ⊠ *415 E. 6th St. Glenwood Springs* ☏ *970/945–6571 or 800/537–7946* ⊕ *www. hotspringspool.com* ⤳ *107 rooms* ⌂ *In-room: refrigerator (some), safe (some), Wi-Fi. In-hotel: restaurant, pool, gym, laundry facilities, public Internet, public Wi-Fi, airport shuttle, parking (free)* 🖃 *AE, D, DC, MC, V* ⦿| *CP.*

$$$ 🏨 **Hotel Colorado.** When you catch sight of the graceful sandstone colonnades and Italianate campaniles of this exquisite building, you won't be surprised that it's listed in the National Register of Historic Places. The impression of luxury continues in the imposing yet gracious marble lobby and public rooms. The sunny rooms and suites—most with high ceilings, fireplaces, gorgeous period wainscoting, marble bathrooms, and balconies affording gorgeous vistas—are designed to match. The notable (Teddy Roosevelt) and notorious (Al Capone) stayed here in the hotel's halcyon days. The on-site bike shop and white-water rafting outfitter can get you geared up for adventures outside the hotel. **Pros:** one of the most historic properties in the valley; large rooms; great views. **Cons:** no air-conditioning; some rooms need refurbishing. ⊠ *526 Pine St.* ☏ *970/945–6511 or 800/544–3998* ⊕ *www.hotelcolorado.com* ⤳ *130 rooms, 30 suites* ⌂ *In-room: no a/c, kitchen (some), refrigerator (some), DVD, Wi-Fi. In-hotel: restaurant, room service, bar, gym, spa, concierge, laundry service, public Wi-Fi, parking (free), some pets allowed* 🖃 *AE, D, DC, MC, V.*

$$ 🏨 **Hotel Denver.** Although this hotel was built in 1914, its most striking features are the numerous Art Deco touches throughout. Most rooms open onto a view of the nearby springs or a three-story New Orleans–style atrium bedecked with colorful canopies. The accommodations are a bit dated, but comfortable, and so quiet it's hard to believe you're only footsteps from the train station. Glenwood's only microbrewery—the Glenwood Canyon Brewing Company—is the hotel restaurant. **Pros:** right downtown; romantic; on-site brewpub. **Cons:** no concierge; no room service. ⊠ *402 7th St.* ☏ *970/945–6565 or 800/826–8820* ⊕ *www.*

6

thehoteldenver.com ↳ *72 rooms* ♿ *In-room: kitchen (some), refrigerator (some), DVD (some), Wi-Fi. In-hotel: restaurant, bar, gym, laundry facilities, laundry service, public Wi-Fi, parking (free), some pets allowed* ⊟ *AE, D, DC, MC, V.*

$$ 🏨 **Sunlight Mountain Inn.** This traditional ski lodge, perfect for couples and families, is a few hundred feet from the Sunlight Mountain Resort lifts. It brims with country ambience, from the delightful lounge (with a carved fireplace and wrought-iron chandeliers) and Western-flair restaurant to the cozily rustic rooms, all with pine-board walls and rough-hewn armoires. The restaurant, open in winter only, specializes in apple dishes made with local fruit; the bar is a perfect place to end your day. This is a true get-away-from-it-all place, so there are no TVs to distract you. A full breakfast is included year-round. **Pros:** a wonderfully remote getaway; delicious meals; no distractions. **Cons:** no cell-phone service; limited room and hotel amenities; restaurant open seasonally. ✉ *10252 County Rd. 117* ☎ *970/945–5225 or 800/733–4757* ⊕ *www. sunlightinn.com* ↳ *20 rooms* ♿ *In-room: no a/c, refrigerator (some), no TV. In-hotel: restaurant, bar, parking (free), some pets allowed* ⊟ *AE, D, MC, V* ⏸ *BP.*

REDSTONE AND MARBLE

29 mi south of Glenwood Springs via Hwy. 82 and Hwy. 133.

Redstone is a attractive artists' colony whose streets are lined with galleries and boutiques, and whose boundaries are ringed by the impressive sandstone cliffs from which the town draws its name.

Summer sees streams of visitors strolling the main drag, Redstone Boulevard; in winter, horse-drawn carriages carry people along the snow-covered road.

GETTING HERE AND AROUND

The best way to reach Redstone and Marble is by car, both because the scenery demands plenty of appreciative stops and also because there is no public transportation available.

WHEN TO GO

Redstone and Marble are popular June through August destinations for hiking in the nearby Elk Mountains and fly fishing. From September to October there is usually a brief autumn which peaks with the blazing turning of the aspen trees. From October to May, the area—less than an hour from Aspen and—offers downhill and cross-country skiing and ice climbing.

EXPLORING

Redstone's history dates to the late 19th century, when J. C. Osgood, director of the Colorado Fuel and Iron Company, built Cleveholm Manor, now known as **Redstone Castle** (✉ *58 Redstone Blvd.* ☎ *970/963–9656*). Here he entertained other titans of his day, such as John D. Rockefeller, J. P. Morgan, and Teddy Roosevelt. Among the home's embellishments are gold-leaf ceilings, maroon velvet walls, silk brocade upholstery, marble and mahogany fireplaces, Persian rugs, and Tiffany chandeliers. Although the Castle has been closed as a public lodge for several years, Redstone Historical Society is overseeing operations, so that you can still catch a glimpse of the baronial splendor during sporadic tours.

A few miles up Highway 133 is **Marble**, a sleepy town that's undergoing a small renaissance as seekers of rural solitude are making it their summer residence and winter retreat. Incorporated in 1899 to serve workers of the Colorado Yule Marble Quarry, the tiny hamlet includes many historic sites, including the old quarry (marble from this spot graces the Lincoln Memorial and Tomb of the Unknowns in Washington, D.C.), a one-room schoolhouse that houses the Marble Historical Society Museum, and the Marble Community Church. Marble is also the gateway to one of Colorado's most-photographed places: the **Crystal Mill**. Set on a craggy cliff overlooking the river, the 1917 mill harkens back to the area's mining past; it's also the perfect place to enjoy a picnic lunch in the solitude of the Colorado Rockies. A four-wheel-drive vehicle is needed to get you here in good weather (your feet will have to do on rainy days when the road isn't passable).

SPORTS AND THE OUTDOORS

FISHING

6

Often overlooked by anglers anxious to cast their lines in the Roaring Fork, the Crystal River runs for more than 35 mi from its headwaters near the town of Marble to its junction with the Roaring Fork in Carbondale. In spring and fall this junction has excellent fishing for brown and rainbow trout as they attempt a run up the Crystal to spawn. Mountain whitefish can also be hooked. The upper reaches of the river traverse public land in the White River National Forest, but the last 6 mi are mostly private property. Be sure to check signage. Near the confluence, public fishing is possible at the Days Inn in Carbondale, Satank Road, and the Division of Wildlife Fish Hatchery on Highway 133, 1 mi south of Carbondale. Redstone Lodge offers fishing for a fee.

The riverscape ranges from deep boulder pools and white-water rapids to slow, flat sections. Because of the steep shore terrain, storm runoff can sometimes cloud the river, making sight-casting difficult.

OUTFITTER **Roaring Fork Anglers** (⌂ 2205 Grand Ave. Glenwood Springs ☎ 970/945–0180 ⊕ www.roaringforkanglers.com) has everything you need to get started. See ⊕ www.wildlife.state.co.us/fishing for more fishing information.

WHERE TO EAT AND STAY

$$$ ╳ **SIX89.** Locals might argue that the best food in the valley is not
ECLECTIC served in the posh eateries of Aspen but in this Carbondale favorite.
Fodor's Choice The irreverent menu and whimsical lexicon (a glossary is provided for
★ your reference), superb service, and inventive preparations of excellent local produce, game, and fish create a downright delightful dining experience. Try the peach and bourbon barbecued Berkshire pork or the grilled Tasmanian salmon with lobster succotash. There's an extensive wine list (and a knowledgeable sommelier) to complement your meal. If you're feeling adventurous, put yourself in chef Mark Fischer's capable hands with "Random Acts of Cooking," a family-style tasting menu.

✉ *689 Main St. Carbondale* ☎ *970/963–6890* ⚱ *Reservations essential* ⊟ *AE, D, MC, V* ⊘ *No lunch.*

$$ ⊞ **Crystal Dreams Bed & Breakfast and Spa.** Built in 1994 in the Redstone National Historic District, this three-story Victorian has all the charm of its character with the benefits of modern construction. Innkeeper Lisa Wagner, originally from Oahu does up a gourmet Polynesian breakfast complete with stuffed guava pancakes and Hawaiian coffee and fresh fruit. She also doubles as an aesthetician for in-room facials; local massage therapists can provide in-room treatments. The Bighorn and Casa Mountain rooms are accented with antiques and have views of the rugged Elk Mountain Range—you can see bighorn sheep out the windows in spring and autumn. The Moon River Room has a deep, two-person claw-foot tub and views of the Crystal River (there's flyfishing off the back lawn). **Pros:** beautiful views; romantic spot for couples; gourmet breakfast. **Cons:** no credit cards accepted; no children under 12. ✉ *0475 Redstone Blvd. Redstone* ☎ *970/963–8240* ⊕ *www.crystaldreamsgetaway.com* ⌨ *3 rooms* ⚲ *In-room: Wi-Fi. In-hotel: parking (free)* ⊟ *No credit cards* ⦿ *BP.*

THE ARTS

The studio gallery and sculpture garden at the **Redstone Arts Center** (✉ *173 Redstone Blvd.* ☎ *970/963–3790* ⊕ *www.redstoneart.com*) display such art and crafts as sculpture, painting, jewelry, and pottery.

Boulder and North Central Colorado

WITH ESTES PARK AND GRAND COUNTY

WORD OF MOUTH

"Boulder is well worth seeing and exploring . . . you could go hiking in the Flatirons, the hills above the city, spend time on the Pearl St. Mall, a pedestrian shopping area, visit a very cool restaurant, the Dushanbe Teahouse, stroll around the Colorado University campus . . ."

—tekwriter

Updated
by Martha
Connors

Lured by spectacular scenery and an equally appealing climate, visitors (and transplanted residents) in north central Colorado find a string of sophisticated yet laid-back cities and the endless opportunities for outdoor adventure in Colorado's Front Range. It's all here: restaurants serving cuisines from around the world, universities, eclectic shopping, high-tech industries, ranching, breweries, bustling nightlife, and concerts are mere minutes from the idyll of the wilderness, with hiking, rock climbing, cycling, skiing, and kayaking.

North central Colorado encompasses three counties—Boulder, Grand, and Larimer—each with its own unique appeal. But despite their differences, these areas share a few common traits: natural beauty, rich history, and an eclectic cultural scene.

This part of Colorado also encompasses the Front Range, the easternmost edge of the Rocky Mountains—where the Rockies meet the Great Plains. Just west of what's known as the I–25 Corridor (a strip that includes the cities of Ft. Collins, Denver, Colorado Springs, and Pueblo, which line up almost perfectly along the north–south interstate highway), the Front Range is Colorado's most populous area, known for its blend of historic cities and towns, verdant landscapes, and wealth of outdoor recreational opportunities.

North central Colorado became part of the United States in 1803 through the Louisiana Purchase—hence towns with names like La Porte, Platteville, and La Salle, as well as the river named Cache la Poudre. Coal and silver mines attracted settlers in the late 1800s and early 1900s, but the region grew mostly on agriculture and ranching. Out-of-state leisure travelers first came in the early 20th century to benefit from both the dry air and the curative waters of spas like Eldorado Springs and Hot Sulphur Springs. Reminders of a grand style of touring survive in resort towns such as Estes Park and Grand Lake, the gateways to Rocky Mountain National Park.

ORIENTATION AND PLANNING

GETTING ORIENTED

Outside of Denver, Boulder and Fort Collins are the two biggest and most prominent cities of the region. Between these two energetic university towns you'll find the sprawling cities of Loveland and Longmont and a few former coal-mining towns with homey, small-town character (like Marshall, Louisville, Lafayette, and Erie). To the west are the proud, independent mountain hamlets of Lyons, Nederland, Ward,

TOP REASONS TO GO

The local breweries: A vacation could be filled with sampling myriad ales, stouts, and lagers. In late June the state's small brewers congregrate in Fort Collins for the Colorado Brewers' Festival.

Hiking near Boulder and in the Indian Peaks Wilderness: On weekends year-round you'll find the trails packed. The views are spectacular, especially in midsummer when the wildflowers bloom.

Boulder Dushanbe Teahouse: This traditional Central Asian teahouse was carved and painted by master artisans and given to Boulder by the city of Dushanbe, Tajikistan.

Chautauqua Park: You can still attend a lecture, a silent film, or a classical concert here much like visitors did 100 years ago. Enjoy a picnic on the green or dine in the hall before the event.

The Arts: Theater buffs have enjoyed the Colorado Shakespeare Festival for 50 summers and the Grammy-Award winning Takács Quartet is beloved for its stunning performances.

and Jamestown. Beyond the high peaks are broad valleys dotted with unpretentious ranching communities like Granby and Kremmling, and right in the middle of it all is the area's crown jewel, Rocky Mountain National Park with its two gateways, Grand Lake and Estes Park.

Boulder. Boulder is the region in a nutshell. Every conceivable trend in food, alternative health care, education, and personal style has come through town, and yet the place still feels wild. Boulder is also very much a college town—the University of Colorado at Boulder is here.

Boulder Side Trips. Nederland, Niwot, and Lyons are easy to explore from Boulder—all can be reached in under an hour. Each is known for its natural beauty, historic character, and funky atmosphere.

Estes Park. The Eastern gateway to Rocky Mountain National Park, resort town Estes Park is nestled against Roosevelt National Forest on its other three sides.

Grand County. West of the Rocky Mountain National Park, guest ranches and golf courses dot the land. In Grand Lake, waterskiing, sailing, canoeing, ice fishing, and snowmobiling dominate the scene.

Fort Collins. Famous for its own college, as well as its open spaces and its beer—Fort Collins also has a rich history and vibrant cultural scene.

PLANNING

WHEN TO GO

Visiting the Front Range is pleasurable in any season. Wintertime in the urban corridor is generally mild, but the mountainous regions can be cold and snowy. Snowfall along the Front Range is highest in spring, particularly March, making for excellent skiing but unpredictable driving and potentially lengthy delays. Spring is capricious—75°F one day and a blizzard the next—and June can be hot or cool (or both). July typically ushers in high summer, which can last through September, although most 90-plus–degree days occur in July and early August and at lower elevations. In the higher mountains summer temperatures are generally 15–20 degrees cooler than in the urban corridor. Afternoon spring and summer thunderstorms can last 30 minutes or a few hours. Fall has crisp sunny days and cool nights, some cold enough for frost in the mountains.

Art and music festivals start up in May and continue through September. With them comes an increase in visitor traffic. Spring and summer are typically the best times to fish or watch for wildlife.

GETTING HERE AND AROUND
AIR TRAVEL
Denver International Airport, known to locals as DIA (although the airport code is DEN), 23 mi northeast of downtown Denver, is the primary commercial passenger airport serving north central Colorado. Allegiant Air connects Fort Collins and Las Vegas with scheduled service to the Fort Collins/Loveland Airport (FNL). Boulder and Granby have municipal airports but no commercial service.

TRANSFERS   The Denver Airport's Ground Transportation Information Center assists visitors with car rentals, door-to-door shuttles, public transportation, wheelchair services, charter buses, and limousine services. Boulder is approximately 45 mi (45 minutes–1 hour) from DIA; Granby approximately 110 mi (a little more than 2 hours); Fort Collins approximately 80 mi (1¼–1½ hours); and Estes Park approximately 80 mi (about two hours).

Estes Park Shuttle (reservations essential) serves Estes Park and Rocky Mountain National Park from Denver, Denver International Airport, and Boulder. Super Shuttle serves Denver and Boulder, and Shamrock Airport Shuttle serves Fort Collins. Home James serves Granby, Grand Lake, and the guest ranches of Grand County.

Airports Denver International Airport (DEN) (⊠ 8500 Peña Blvd., Denver ☎ 800/247–2336 or 303/342–2000 ⊕ www.flydenver.com). **Fort Collins-Loveland Municipal Airport (FNL)** (⊠ 4900 Earhart Rd., Loveland ☎ 970/962–2852 ⊕ www.fortloveair.com).

Airport Shuttles Estes Park Shuttle (☎ 970/586–5151 ⊕ www.estesparkshuttle.com). **Ground Transportation Information Center** (☎ 303/342–4059 ⊕ www.flydenver.com/gt/index.axp). **Home James** (☎ 970/726–5060 or 800/359–7536 ⊕ www.homejamestransportation.com). **Super Shuttle** (☎ 970/482–0505 ⊕ www.rideshamrock.com).

BUS TRAVEL
The expansive network of the Regional Transportation District (RTD) includes service from Denver and Denver International Airport to and within Boulder, Lyons, Niwot, Nederland, and the Eldora Ski Resort. The Hop bus (part of the RTD network) is a circulator that makes for easy carless travel within Boulder between the university, the Hill, the Twenty-Ninth Street shopping area, and downtown. Transfort serves Fort Collins's main thoroughfares.

Bus Contacts Regional Transportation District (RTD) (☎ 303/299–6000 or 800/366–7433 ⊕ www.rtd-denver.com). **Transfort** (☎ 970/221–6620 ⊕ fcgov.com/transfort).

CAR TRAVEL

Interstate 25, the most direct route from Denver to Fort Collins, is the north–south artery that connects the cities in the urban corridor along the Front Range. From Denver, U.S. 36 runs through Boulder, Lyons, and Estes Park to Rocky Mountain National Park. The direct route from Denver to Grand County is I–70 west to U.S. 40 (Empire exit) and to U.S. 34. If you're driving directly to Fort Collins or Estes Park and Rocky Mountain National Park from DIA, take the E–470 tollway to Interstate 25. U.S. 36 between Boulder and Estes Park is heavily traveled, but Highways 119, 72, and 7 have much less traffic.

Gasoline and service are available in all larger towns and cities in the region. Bicyclists are common except on arteries; state law gives them the same rights and holds them to the same obligations as any other vehicle. Expect extensive road construction along the northern Front Range; arterial routes, state highways, and city streets are being rebuilt to accommodate increasing traffic in the urban corridor. Although the state plows roads regularly, a winter snowstorm can slow traffic and create wet, slushy, or icy conditions. A cell phone is recommended, since some mountain roads have long, uninhabited stretches, although you can't always count on getting service in sparsely populated—or very mountainous—areas.

Car Travel Contacts AAA Colorado (☎ *303/753–8800*). **Colorado Department of Transportation CDOT Road Information** (☎ *303/639–1111 or 877/315–7623* ⊕ *www.dot.state.co.us*). **Colorado State Patrol** (☎ *303/239–4501, *277 from cell phone*). **Rocky Mountain National Park Road Information** (☎ *970/586–1333*).

TRAIN TRAVEL

Amtrak provides passenger rail service to and within north central Colorado. The Chicago–San Francisco *California Zephyr* stops in downtown Denver, in Winter Park/Fraser, and in Granby, once each day in both directions.

Train Contact Amtrak (☎ *800/872–7245 or 303/534–2812* ⊕ *www.amtrak.com*).

PARKS AND RECREATION AREAS

Rocky Mountain National Park is known for its scenery, hiking, wildlife-watching, camping, and snowshoeing. *See the Rocky Mountain National Park section in this book.*

Spanning the Continental Divide between Grand Lake and Nederland just south of Rocky Mountain National Park is the **Indian Peaks Wilderness,** a 76,586-acre area that lies within the Arapaho and Roosevelt national forests and is a favorite destination for hiking and backcountry camping (☎ *303/541–2500* ⊕ *www.fs.fed.us/r2/arnf/recreation/wilderness/indianpeaks*).

The **Arapaho and Roosevelt National Forests and Pawnee National Grassland** (⊠ *USDA Forest Service Sulphur Ranger District, 9 Ten Mile Dr., Granby* ☎ *970/887–4100* ⊕ *www.fs.fed.us/r2/arnf*), an enormous area that encompasses 1.5 million acres, has fishing, sailing, canoeing, and waterskiing, as well as hiking, mountain biking, birding, and camping. Contained within the Arapaho National Forest is the **Arapaho**

7

National Recreation Area (ANRA), a 36,000-acre expanse that contains Lake Granby, Shadow Mountain Lake, Monarch Lake, and Willow Creek and Meadow Creek reservoirs, collectively known as Colorado's Great Lakes.

North central Colorado also has six state parks—Eldorado Canyon, Barr Lake, and St. Vrain, which are close to Boulder, plus Boyd Lake, State Forest, and Lory, which are close to Fort Collins—each popular for different activities. In Boulder and Fort Collins you can literally walk out your door, up the street, and into the mountains or foothills on a hiking trail. There are also plenty of riparian trails and open-space paths within the city limits that can take you for miles and have plenty of access points.

The northern Front Range is home to a small downhill ski areas. Eldora Mountain Resort is 21 mi west of Boulder.

RESTAURANTS
Thanks to the influx of people from around the world, you have plenty of options here. Restaurants in north central Colorado run the gamut—you'll find simple diners with tasty, homey basics and elegant establishments with wine lists featuring hundreds of vintages. Increasingly, eateries are featuring organic and sustainable ingredients, and several serve exclusively organic meals and locally produced foods. Some restaurants take reservations, but many, particularly those in the middle price range, seat on a first-come, first-served basis.

HOTELS
Bed-and-breakfasts and small inns in north central Colorado include old-fashioned cottages, rustic lodges, and modern, sleek establishments. Ever-popular guest ranches and spas are places to escape and be pampered after having fun outdoors. In the high-country resorts of Estes Park and Grand Lake and in towns nearby, the elevation keeps the climate cool, which means that there are very few air-conditioned accommodations. The region is also full of chain motels and hotels, often at the access points to cities.

WHAT IT COSTS					
	¢	$	$$	$$$	$$$$
Restaurants	under $8	$8–$12	$13–$18	$19–$25	over $25
Hotels	under $80	$80–$120	$121–$170	$171–$230	over $230

Restaurant prices are for a main course at dinner, excluding 5.75%–8.46% tax. Hotel prices are for two people in a standard double room in high season, excluding service charges and 5.75%–10.25% tax.

BOULDER

No place in Colorado better epitomizes the state's outdoor mania than Boulder, where sunny weather keeps locals busy through all seasons. There are nearly as many bicycles as cars in this uncommonly beautiful and beautifully uncommon city, and Boulder has more than 1,500 mi of trails for hiking, walking, jogging, and bicycling. One of Boulder's most uncommon features is its setting. In 1960 its citizens voted to buy the land surrounding the city to protect it from urban sprawl and preserve its historic and ecological resources. Boulder started taxing itself in 1967 in order to buy these greenbelts, and now can boast more than 43,000 acres of city-owned open space—more than 120,000 acres if you add lands owned by Boulder County—which means there's three times as much protected land surrounding the city as developed land. Even in winter, residents cycle to work and jog on the open-space paths. It's nearly a matter of civic pride to spend a lunch hour playing Frisbee, in-line skating, hiking with the family dog, and even rock climbing on the Flatirons.

Boulder is also a brainy place. The University of Colorado at Boulder and Naropa University are located here. In addition, Boulder is home to more than a dozen national laboratories, including the National Center for Atmospheric Research (NCAR) and the National Oceanic and Atmospheric Administration (NOAA).

GETTING ORIENTED

In town, the red-tile roofs of the University of Colorado at Boulder dominate the landscape in the southern end of the city, where Boulder Creek courses along the south side of the downtown area at the bottom of University Hill (called "the Hill" by locals), on which both the university and its surrounding offbeat neighborhood are located. At the northern end of town you'll find Boulder Reservoir, a 700-acre park that hosts every water sport imaginable (including swimming, rowing, kayaking, sailing, windsurfing, and waterskiing).

GETTING HERE AND AROUND

Although 10 minutes of walking separate downtown and the Hill, the milieus seem miles and ages apart: downtown—particularly the Pearl Street pedestrian mall—bustles with families, street performers, upscale boutiques, and eateries, while the Hill pulsates with trendy shops, packed coffeehouses, bars, and restaurants geared more to students. Parking and driving in these sections of Boulder can be frustrating and time-consuming. Leave your car at the hotel and try the Hop, a bus that circulates in both directions through downtown, the Hill, and the university for about the cost of an hour at a parking meter. Buses run in both directions every 6–10 minutes weekdays and 15–20 minutes on weekends.

TOURS **Banjo Billy's Bus Tours** offers a 90-minute tour of downtown Boulder, part of the University of Colorado, Chautauqua Park, and the Hill, aboard a bus that has been built to look like a log cabin. Everyone on the bus gets to vote on the topic of the tour: ghost stories, history, folklore, or crime stories. Your seat may be a saddle or a recliner, or you can opt to sit on the couch.

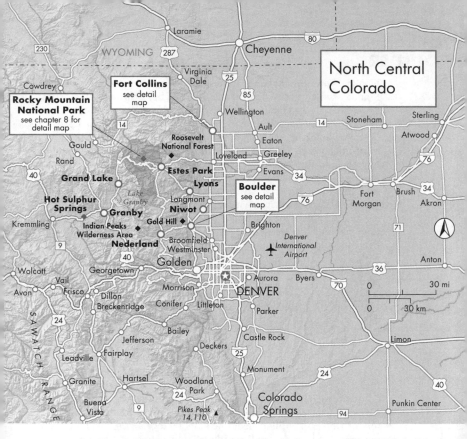

Historic Boulder provides free brochures for seven self-guided walking tours, including the University of Colorado at Boulder, the Hill, Chautauqua Park, the Mapleton Historic District, and the Downtown Boulder Historic District.

WHEN TO GO

Boulder is a great place to visit in any season—like the rest of the Front Range, it boasts beautiful weather year-round. The city definitely feels livelier when school is in session, especially on big football weekends, and summer weekends often bring big crowds of tourists (including day-trippers from Denver).

FESTIVALS The **Boulder Creek Festival** lasts all Memorial Day weekend: you can feast at the pancake breakfast, browse the bazaar, learn about alternative healing, and see regional artistic talent at the art show and the artists' marketplace. Children have fun with dance, theater, and hands-on activities at the Kids' Place. Live music runs the gamut: Irish, Senegalese, John Philip Sousa, and jazz. Don't miss the **Great Rubber Duck Race** on Memorial Day afternoon. Get a rubber duck and compete against hundreds of others in Boulder Creek.

ESSENTIALS

Transportation Contacts Yellow Cab (☎ 303/777–7777
⊕ www.boulderyellowcab.com). **Boulder Custom Rides** (☎ 303/442–4477
⊕ www.bouldercustomrides.com).

Visitor and Tour Info Banjo Billy's Bus Tours (⊠ Tour starts from Hotel
Boulderado, 2115 13th St. ☎ 720/938–8885 ⊕ www.banjobilly.com ⚏ Reservations essential ⚏ $20 ⊙ Closed Mon.). **Boulder Convention & Visitors
Bureau** (⊠ 2440 Pearl St., ☎ 303/442–2911 or 800/444–0447 ⊕ www.
bouldercoloradousa.com). **Boulder Creek Festival** (☎ 303/652–4942 ⊕ www.
bouldercreekevents.com). **Historic Boulder** (⊠ 1123 Spruce St. ☎ 303/444–
5192 ⊕ www.historicboulder.org).

EXPLORING BOULDER

TOP ATTRACTIONS

Pearl Street, between 8th and 20th streets in the downtown area, is the
city's hub, an eclectic collection of boutiques, consignment shops, bookstores, art galleries, cafés, bars, and restaurants. A four-block pedestrian
mall was set aside in 1976, between 11th and 15th streets.

The late-19th- and early-20th-century commercial structures of the
Downtown Boulder Historic District once housed mercantile stores and
saloons. The period architecture—including Queen Anne, Italianate,
and Romanesque styles in stone or brick—has been preserved, but stores
inside cater to modern tastes, with fair-trade coffees and Tibetan prayer
flags. The area is bounded by the south side of Spruce Street between
10th and 16th streets, Pearl Street between 9th and 16th streets, and the
north side of Walnut Street between Broadway and 9th Street.

South of downtown is the **University of Colorado at Boulder.** Red sandstone
buildings with tile roofs (built in the "Rural Italian" architectural style
that Charles Z. Klauder created in the early 1920s) complement the
campus's green lawns and small ponds.

A favorite student hangout is the funky neighborhood known as **the Hill,**
just across Broadway from the CU campus (⊠ 13th St. between Pennsylvania St. and College Ave.), which is home to eateries, music and dance
venues, record shops, bars, coffeehouses, and hip boutiques.

The **Boulder Museum of Contemporary Art** hosts local and national contemporary art exhibits, performance art, dance, experimental film, and
poetry readings. From May to September, when the farmers' market
takes place in front of the museum, hours are extended: Wednesday 11–8
and Saturday 9–4. ⊠ 1750 13th St. ☎ 303/443–2122 ⊕ bmoca.org ⚏ $5
⊙ Tues., Thurs., and Fri. 11–5, Weds. 11–8, Sat. 9–4, Sun. noon–3.

WORTH NOTING

Star shows and laser shows set to classic compositions like Peter and
the Wolf or the music of well-known rock bands entertain at the university's **Fiske Planetarium and Science Center.** During the academic year
shows begin Friday at 9:30 and 10:45 PM. "Star Talks" are at 7:30 PM on
Thursday and Friday during the school year and 8 during the summer.
Matinees take place in summer on Tuesday, Wednesday, and Thursday
at 2 PM and 3 PM. ⊠ Regent Dr. ☎ 303/492–5002 ⊕ fiske.colorado.edu

📷 *Laser shows and matinees $5; Star Talks $6; observatory free* ☉ *Planetarium, year-round, days vary. Observatory, Fri. 9 PM–11 PM. Closed on university holidays.*

Three blocks north of Pearl Street and west of Broadway is the **Mapleton Historic District.** This neighborhood of turn-of-the-20th-century homes shaded by old maple and cottonwood trees is bounded roughly by Broadway, the alley between Pearl and Spruce streets, 4th Street, and the alley between Dewey Street and Concord Avenue.

The **CU campus** began in 1875 with the construction of Old Main, which borders the **Norlin Quadrangle,** now on the National Register of Historic Places, a broad lawn where students sun themselves or play a quick round of Frisbee between classes. The **CU Heritage Center** (✉ *Old Main Bldg. on Norlin Quadrangle* ☎ *303/492–6329* ⊕ *cuheritage.org* 📷 *Free* ☉ *Weekdays 10–6*) preserves the history of the university—including notable alumni accomplishments and a lunar sample on long-term loan from NASA. Also displayed are the personal memorabilia of alumni such as Robert Redford and Glenn Miller. One room is devoted to CU's 20 astronauts, including Ellison Onizuka, who was killed aboard the *Challenger* space shuttle in 1986, and Kalpana Chawla, who died on the *Columbia* in 2003. The natural history collection at the **University of Colorado Museum** (✉ *Henderson Bldg. 80309* ☎ *303/492–6892* ⊕ *cumuseum.colorado.edu* 📷 *$3Free* ☉ *Weekdays 9–5, Sat. 9–4, Sun. 10–4*) includes dinosaur relics and has permanent and changing exhibits. You can take a walking tour of the campus year-round. ✉ *University Memorial Center* ☎ *303/492–1411, 303/492–6301 to reserve tour* ⊕ *www.colorado.edu* 📷 *Free* ☉ *Campus tours year-round weekdays 9:30 and 2:30, most Saturdays at 10:30* ☞ *Reservations essential.*

QUICK BITES

The actor Robert Redford worked at **The Sink** (✉ **1165 13th St.** ☎ **303/444–7465** ⊕ *thesink.com*) during his years as a student at the University of Colorado at Boulder. The restaurant has served great pizza, burgers, beer, and other student dietary staples since 1958.

Housed in the 1889 Harbeck-Bergheim mansion, the **Boulder History Museum** documents the story of Boulder and the surrounding region from 1858 to the present. If you're interested in the sartorial styles of the 19th century—whether rugged cowboy and miner duds or high-society finery—this museum will delight. It's home to one of Colorado's largest clothing collections, with pieces dating as far back as 1820. ✉ *1206 Euclid Ave.* ☎ *303/449–3464* ⊕ *www.boulderhistorymuseum.org* 📷 *$6* ☉ *Tues.–Fri. 10–5, weekends noon–4, closed Mon.*

The scent of hops fills the air during free one-hour tours and ale tastings at the **Boulder Beer Company,** Colorado's first microbrewery. The brew house's own pub is open weekdays 11 AM–9 PM. ✉ *2880 Wilderness Pl.* ☎ *303/444–8448* ⊕ *www.boulderbeer.com* 📷 *Free* ☉ *Tours weekdays 2 PM.*

☺ Talking about the weather is *not* boring at the **National Center for Atmospheric Research,** where the hands-on exhibits, video presentation, and one-hour tour fires up kids' enthusiasm for what falls out of the sky. I.M. Pei's famous buildings stand majestically on a mesa at the base of the mountains, where you can see mule deer and other wildlife. After browsing the field guides and science kits, follow the interpretive Walter Orr Roberts Nature and Weather Trail to learn about the mesa's weather, climate, plants, and wildlife. The 4-mi loop is wheelchair accessible. If you can't make the guided tour, self-guided and audio tours are available during regular hours. ⊠ *1850 Table Mesa Dr., from southbound Broadway, turn right onto Table Mesa Dr.* ☎ *303/497–1174* ⊕ *www.ncar.ucar. edu* ☞ *Free* ☺ *Weekdays 8–5, weekends 9–4. Tour daily at noon.*

PARKS AND GREENBELTS

★ For the prettiest views of town, follow Baseline Rd. west from Broadway to **Chautauqua Park** (⊠ *900 Baseline Rd.*), site of the Colorado Music Festival and a favorite picnic spot for locals on weekends. Continue farther up Flagstaff Mountain to Panorama and Realization points, where people jog, bike, and climb.

★ **Eldorado Canyon State Park,** with its steep walls and pine forests, offers outdoor activities for thrill-seekers and observers. Kayakers get adrenaline rushes on the rapids of South Boulder Creek, while rock climbers scale the canyon's granite walls. Picnickers can choose from 42 spots, and anglers' catches average 8 inches. Bird-watchers and artists find plenty of inspiration, and hikers have 12 mi of trails to wander. The **Streamside Trail** is a mostly level, 1-mi round-trip that parallels South Boulder Creek 0.5 mi to West Ridge; 300 feet of the trail is wheelchair accessible. Half of 1.5-mi round-trip **Fowler Trail** is wheelchair accessible. The trail has interpretive signs about the wildlife. For the best views of the canyon and the Front Range plains, head up **Rattlesnake Gulch Trail.** The round-trip 3-mi switchback trail ends at an overlook 800 feet higher in elevation than the trailhead, where you can see the high Rockies of the Continental Divide. Snowshoeing is popular here in winter. Mountain bikers crank on Rattlesnake Gulch Trail and Fowler Trail. **Eldorado Canyon Trail** is open to horseback riding. ⊠ *9 Kneale Rd. Drive south on Broadway (Hwy. 93) 3 mi to Eldorado Canyon Dr. (Rte. 170). The paved road ends at the village of Eldorado Springs. Drive through town to park entrance Eldorado Springs* ☎ *303/494–3943* ⊕ *www.parks.state. co.us/Parks/eldoradocanyon* ☞ *$7 per vehicle.*

SPORTS AND THE OUTDOORS

RACES

Early May finds locals at the Boulder Reservoir for the annual **Kinetic Challenge** (⊕ *www.kbco.com/kinetics [works seasonally]*). The competition requires each team to build a craft that can race over the land, slog through the mud, and not sink in the water. Teams are allowed to provide their own judges and bribe other judges. Speed is not necessarily the determining factor—creativity and onboard sculpture count, too.

Fodor's Choice ★ Memorial Day brings the annual 10-km **Bolder Boulder** (☎ *303/444–7223* ⊕ *www.bolderboulder.com*), when more than 54,000 runners, including top international competitors, run the country's largest race and the fifth-largest in the world. About 100,000 spectators line the route and fill CU's Folsom Stadium to cheer on the participants. Along the racecourse rock bands, jazz musicians, African drumming groups,

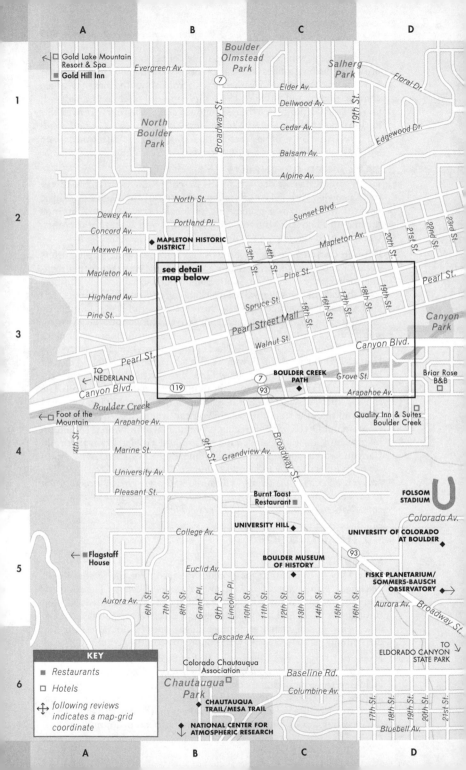

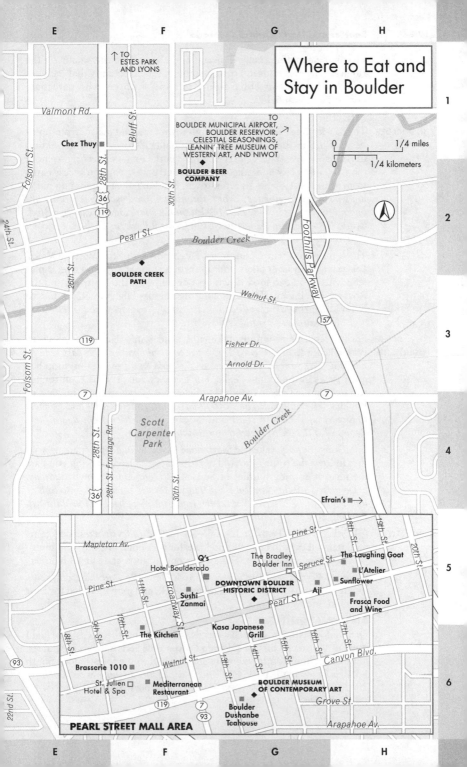

Elvis impersonators, belly dancers, and classical quartets spur on the runners. The race ends in Folsom Stadium for a ceremony that includes a flyover by U.S. Air Force fighter jets and skydivers who parachute onto the stadium field.

BIKING

IN BOULDER The **Boulder Creek Path** winds through town for about 5.5 mi from Boulder Canyon in the west to the Stazio Ballfields (near the intersection of Arapahoe Ave. and Cherryvale Rd.) in the east, connecting to more than 100 mi of city and greenbelt trails and paths. You can access paths from nearly every cross street in town, but don't always count on parking nearby. ⊠ *Trailheads: From downtown, the best access points are behind the public library parking lot on the south side of Canyon Blvd. between 9th St. and Broadway or in Central Park on 13th St. between Canyon Blvd. and Arapahoe Ave.*

The 8-mi round-trip Community Ditch portion of the **Marshall Mesa/Community Ditch Trails** takes you up through pine stands and over a plateau where you can look down on Boulder, with the Flatirons and the Rockies in full view. The trail continues across Highway 93 almost to Eldorado Springs. ⊠ *Trailhead: Just east of the intersection of Hwy. 93 and Marshall Rd. Parking is on right.*

IN THE MOUNTAINS For a strenuous mountain bike ride, head 8 mi west out of town to **Walker Ranch** (⊠ *Trailhead: Look for the trailhead on the east side of Flagstaff Rd., about 7.5 mi west of Baseline Rd.*) ; the 7.5-mi loop has great views of the Indian Peaks. For scenic cycling, try the 6-mi round-trip trek on the **Canyon Loop Trail** in Betasso Preserve, about 6 mi west of Boulder. (⊠ *Trailhead: Take Broadway south to Hwy. 119 and go west to Sugarloaf Rd.; turn right onto Sugarloaf and then right again onto Betasso Rd. Look for the turnout on the left.*)

For a long journey, take the **Switzerland Trail**, a 9- to 13-mi ride one-way that follows the route of an old narrow-gauge railroad, taking you past the historic mining hamlet of Sunset. ⊠ *Trailhead: From Broadway, drive west 5 mi on Canyon Blvd./Hwy. 119 and turn right onto Sugarloaf Rd./Hwy. 72. After 5 mi, turn right onto Sugarloaf Mountain Rd. Parking area is 1 mi farther.*

OUTFITTERS **Full Cycle** (⊠ *1795 Pearl St.* ☎ *303/440–1002* ∰ *fullcyclebikes.com*) rents mountain bikes with helmets and locks for four-hour, one-day, and multiple-day biking adventures. There's a second location at 1211 13th Street.

University Bicycles (⊠ *839 Pearl St.* ☎ *303/444–4196* ∰ *ubikes.com*) rents mountain and town bikes with helmet, lock, and map included for four hours to one week.

BIRD-WATCHING
Ornithologists have spotted kestrels, falcons, and the occasional bald eagle in the steep cliffs of **Eldorado Canyon State Park.** Owls, chickadees, nuthatches, and woodpeckers are at home in the pine forests along South Boulder Creek in the park. ⊠ *9 Kneale Rd. Eldorado Springs* ☎ *303/494–3943* ∰ *www.parks.state.co.us/Parks/eldoradocanyon* ✑ *$7 per vehicle ($6 Oct.–Apr.).*

Walden Ponds Wildlife Habitat/Sawhill Ponds, formerly a gravel quarry, are now home to songbirds, waterfowl, and raptors. Nearly 3 mi of groomed paths encircle and connect the area's ponds and lead into wooded areas along Boulder Creek, where owls roost. April to May is when most birds migrate through the Front Range, although the ponds have plenty of year-round residents. ⊠ *Jay Rd. and N. 75th St. Drive north on 28th St. (U.S. 36) and turn right at Valmont Rd. Drive east 4 mi and turn left at 75th St. The sign marking the ponds is about ½ mi farther* ☉ *Dawn–dusk.*

FISHING

Eldorado Canyon State Park offers excellent fly-fishing. Fish generally measure between 8 and 14 inches long, although anglers bring in a few specimens up to 24 inches long each year. See ⊕ *www.wildlife.state. co.us/fishing* for more information.

OUTFITTERS **Kinsley Outfitters** (⊠ *2070 Broadway* ☎ *303/442–6204 or 800/442–7420* ⊕ *www.kinsleyoutfitters.com*) provides Orvis-endorsed guides for the world-class waters of the Colorado and South Platte rivers. You can arrange a personalized half- or full-day guided fishing trip that includes transportation, lunch, and equipment.

Rocky Mountain Anglers (⊠ *1904 Arapahoe Ave.* ☎ *303/447–2400* ⊕ *www. rockymtanglers.com*) can sell you a few flies or set up a guided tour. The guides have access to private ranches and know where to find secluded fishing holes on public lands. Fees include transportation, gear including flies, and lunch.

GOLF

Indian Peaks Golf Course. This local favorite has views of the Continental Divide, plus some "Fourteeners" (mountain peaks over 14,000 feet) not visible from Boulder. The well-tended course boasts low scores and has tee boxes for all skill levels. ⊠ *2300 Indian Peaks Trail, Baseline Rd. to Indian Peaks Trail, 10 mi east of Boulder Lafayette* ☎ *303/666–4706* ⚑ *18 holes. Yards: 7,083/5,468. Par: 72/72. Green fee: $39/$47.*

HIKING

The **City of Boulder Open Space & Mountain Parks** administers most of the 150 mi of trails in and close to Boulder. Most trails are open to dogs, provided they are leashed or under voice control and registered with the city's Voice and Sight Dog Tag Program. There are 34 trailheads in and around Boulder. Most are free, but a few require a $3 parking permit for all non-resident vehicles. You can purchase a daily pass either at self-serve kiosks in the mountain parks or at the OSMP office. ⊠ *66 S. Cherryvale Rd.* ☎ *303/441–3440* ⊕ *www.osmp.org* ☉ *Weekdays 8–5.*

IN BOULDER For a relaxing amble, take the **Boulder Creek Path** (*see Bicycling, above*), which winds from west of Boulder through downtown and past the university to the eastern part of the city—there are multiple places to access the trail. Within the eastern city limits are ponds, gaggles of Canada geese, and prairie-dog colonies. People-watching is also great fun: you'll see cyclists, joggers, and rollerblading dads and moms with their babies in jogging strollers. You'll have great views of the mountains as you walk back toward downtown. Walk west along the path from Broadway to Boulder Canyon, and you'll see kayakers negotiating the boulders and inner-tubers cooling off in the summer heat.

Even a short walk up the grassy slope between **Chautauqua Park** and the base of the mountains brings out hikers and their dogs to take in some sun. On sunny summer mornings the dining hall at Chautauqua Park fills with hungry people ready to tuck into a hearty breakfast. Afternoon walkers relax on the park's gently sloping lawn with a picnic and gaze up at the foothills stretching along the Front Range. To reach the parking lot, take Baseline Road west from Broadway. The park is on the left just past the intersection with 9th Street.

★ Locals love the **Chautauqua Trail** (⊠ *Trailhead: 900 Baseline Rd., Main parking lot*), a 1.6-mi round-trip loop, for its great views of the city and occasional peeks at the rock climbers on the Flatirons. From the trailhead, go up the Chautauqua Trail 0.6 mi to the Bluebell/Baird trail. Go left 0.4 mi and then left again onto the Mesa Trail, which takes you the 0.6 mi back to the parking area. The trail is a long slope at the beginning, but once you're in the trees you won't gain much more elevation. Allow a couple of hours for a leisurely walk on this easy hike. The 4-mi round-trip **Royal Arch Trail** (⊠ *Trailhead: 900 Baseline Rd., Main parking lot*) leads to Boulder's own rock arch. The Royal Arch is definitely worth the steep hike, as are the views of the foothills and cities of the Front Range. The trail spurs off the Chautauqua Trail loop and follows along the base of the Flatirons. You'll climb 1,270 feet in 2 mi. Go under the arch to the precipice for the views. If you turn around, the arch frames a couple of Flatirons for a good photo.

IN THE MOUNTAINS Two popular trails on the edge of town get you into the mountains quickly. The parking areas are across the street from each other and fill fast, so it's best to go early in the morning or later in the afternoon. Carry a picnic on the **Red Rocks Loop** (⊠ *Trailhead: Mapleton Ave., 1 mi west of Broadway on left 80302*) and enjoy the mountain and city views. The Red Rocks Trail goes to the right from the parking lot and takes you through wildflowers and grassy meadows on the way up to the rock outcropping. The 0.5-mi round-trip trek takes about 20 minutes and gains 340 feet. If you have time for the full 2.3-mi loop, allow about an hour. You'll gain most of the 600 feet in elevation change on the way back. The **Sanitas Valley Loop** (⊠ *Trailhead: Mapleton Ave., 1 mi west of Broadway on left 80302*), known locally as Mount Sanitas, is an easy 3.5-mi hike that provides constant mountain scenery in Sunshine Canyon as you climb 540 feet going up the west flank of Mount Sanitas. From the trailhead, head left onto the Mount Sanitas Trail, which becomes the East Ridge Trail as it wraps around the north side of the mountain. From here you can descend to the right on either the Sanitas Valley Trail back to the parking area or along the Dakota Ridge Trail if you want more city views. Be sure not to take the sharp left at the Dakota Ridge intersection, which leads straight downhill to town. Boulder will be on your left all the way back to the trailhead. Allow two hours.

★ **Flagstaff Mountain Open Space** offers hikers several different hikes. An easy walk along the **Boy Scout Trail** to May's Point offers glorious views of the city and Boulder Valley along the way and exceptional views of the Indian Peaks once you reach May's Point. The 1.5-mi round-trip trail starts at Sunrise Amphitheater, where it goes to the left into the spruce forest. After about 0.75 mi and only 140 feet elevation gain, head to the right at the fork in the trail. It's a short distance to May's Point. ⊠ *Trailhead: Drive west on Baseline Rd. to sharp curve to right that is Flagstaff Rd., then turn right at Summit Rd. The trail starts from parking area about 0.5 mi in.*

Green Mountain Loop, which begins in Boulder Mountain Park, rewards ambitious hikers with beautiful vistas of the Front Range and the Indian Peaks. The Gregory Canyon, Ranger, E. M. Greenman, and Saddle Rock trails create a 5.5-mi loop that takes three to four hours to hike. It's a 2,344 foot gain in elevation to Green Mountain's summit at 8,144 feet. Follow the Gregory Canyon Trail to the Ranger Trail, and go left. Stay to the right at the E. M. Greenman Trail. At the intersection with Green Mountain West Ridge Trail, turn left. Go on to the summit and descend along the E. M. Greenman and Saddle Rock trails after taking in the view. ⊠ *Trailhead (Gregory Canyon Trail): Drive west on Baseline Rd. to Flagstaff Rd., and then turn left immediately after curve. Parking area is at end of short road where trail starts.*

INNER-TUBING
In July and August, when the daytime temperatures can reach the 90s, Boulderites take to tubing in **Boulder Creek**—especially near Eben G. Fine Park, at the mouth of Boulder Canyon near the junction of Arapahoe Avenue and Canyon Boulevard on the western end of town. Need a tube? Closer to the center of town, the **Conoco** gas station (⊠ *1201 Arapahoe Ave., at Broadway* ☎ *303/442–6293*), which is about a block away from the creek, sells inner tubes ($13). The station is open from 7 AM until 9 PM weekdays and Saturday, and 8 AM–8 PM Sunday.

KAYAKING AND CANOEING
Serious kayakers run the slaloms in Clear Creek, Lefthand Canyon, and the South Platte, but Boulder Creek—from within Boulder Canyon midway into the city—is one of the locals' favorites. Water in the creek can create Class II–III rapids when summer conditions are right. If calmer waters better suit your style, you can rent a canoe at the **Boulder Reservoir.** ⊠ *6 mi northeast of downtown. Drive northeast on Hwy. 119 and turn left at Jay Rd. Turn right immediately onto 51st St. and follow it to sign that marks entrance station, 5100 N. 51st St.* ☎ *303/441–3468* ⊕ *www.bouldercolorado.com* 🎫 *$8.*

OUTFITTERS **Alpine Sports** (⊠ *2510 47th St.* ☎ *303/325–3231 or 877/325–3231*) rents touring and sit-on-top kayaks, canoes, and rafts for $25–$35 per day. Gear packages, which include helmets, paddles, and life preservers, rent for $25 a day. Multiday discounts apply. **Boulder Outdoor Center** (⊠ *2525 Arapahoe Ave., Suite E4–228* ☎ *303/444–8420 or 800/364–9376* ⊕ *www.boc123.com*) organizes group rafting trips to rivers on the Front Range and also offers canoeing and kayaking instruction.

SNOWSHOEING
Winter sports in Colorado are not limited to skiing. You can strap on a pair of snowshoes and tramp along many trails you would walk in summer, taking in stunning views and getting a bit of exercise, too.

Don't forget the sunscreen—at this altitude, you can sunburn quickly, even in winter. Dressing in layers is also imperative, as temperatures and weather conditions can fluctuate dramatically throughout the day.

The Brainard Lake Recreation Area, in the Roosevelt National Forest, has well-marked trails and gorgeous views of the snow-covered Indian Peaks and the Continental Divide. There's a $9 fee for a five-day pass. ⊠ *5 mi west of Rte. 72 on Brainard Lake Rd. (Rte. 102) at Ward. Drive west on Hwy. 119 to Nederland and turn north at Rte. 72* ⊕ *www.fs.fed.us/r2/arnf/recreation/brainard/* ☎ *303/541–2500.*

You can also head to **Peaceful Valley Campground** for crisp pine–scented air and plenty of terrain to explore—it's closed to campers during the winter. ⊠ *Drive 15 mi west from Boulder on Hwy. 199 to Nederland (about 15 mi). Go north on Hwy. 72 for 17.6 mi, then take a left onto Peaceful Valley Rd. (near mile marker 50), then a quick right onto County Rd. 92. The campground is on your right. Allenspark 80540* ☎ *303/541–2500.*

OUTFITTER   For $15 per day you can rent snowshoes from **Alpine Sports** (⊠ *2510 47th St.* ☎ *303/325–3231 or 877/325–3231* ⊕ *www.alpinesportsoutlet. com*). Multiday discounts apply.

WHERE TO EAT

Use the coordinate (✛ B2) at the end of each listing to locate a site on the corresponding map.

$$–$$$ ✕ **Aji.** Enjoy a South American cocktail like a *caipirinha, mojito,* or *pisco*
LATIN AMERICAN   *sour* before dinner in this busy restaurant. The storefront windows let in plenty of light, the seating is spacious, and the service is great. Try *ceviche* (shrimp or fish marinated in lime juice and served with fun accompaniments like banana, pickled peppers, or mango) or empanadas (savory pastries) to start. The presentation of entrées such as pumpkin seed–crusted trout, grilled duck breast, or steak stuffed with caramelized onions and garlic, is innovative and stunning. A chocolate *empanada* and a cup of French-press coffee round out a meal here wonderfully. ⊠ *1601 Pearl St.* ☎ *303/442–3464* ⊕ *www.ajirestaurant.com* ▭ *AE, D, MC, V* ✛ *G5.*

$–$$ ✕ **Boulder Dushanbe Teahouse.** Unique to Colorado, this teahouse was
Fodor's Choice   a gift from Boulder's sister city Dushanbe, Tajikistan, and opened in
★   1998. Tajik artisans decorated the building in a traditional style that
CAFÉ   includes ceramic Islamic art and a carved, painted ceiling. The menu presents a culinary cross section of the world; your meal could include such dishes as Basque-style steak, Tajik shish kebab, or Tabrizi *kufteh* (Persian meatballs with dried fruits, nuts, and herbs in a tomato sauce). Relax during high tea at 3 PM (reservations required) with one of more than 80 varieties of tea. Creekside patio tables have views of Central Park. Brunch is served on weekends. ⊠ *1770 13th St.* ☎ *303/442–4993* ⊕ *www.boulderteahouse.com* ▭ *AE, D, MC, V* ✛ *G6.*

$$$ ✕ **Brasserie 1010.** Locals head here for great food and a casual and
FRENCH   spirited atmosphere, which starts at happy hour (from 3 to 6 every day). The extensive menu includes the classic French offerings, plus several imaginative salads and *petit plats* featuring burgers, crepes, and sliders. The bar serves 23 different beers, 20 martinis (including

Quick Bites in Boulder

Not every meal requires a lengthy restaurant visit. Boulder has plenty of healthy, inexpensive, and prepared-to-order food, as well.

For breakfast, try a crisp, light brioche or buttery croissant at **Breadworks Cafe** (✉ 2644 Broadway ☎ 303/444–5667 ⊕ www.breadworks.net). Lunch is casseroles or mac and cheese, meat or vegetarian panini—made with one of their artisan breads—or pizza, a savory soup, and a saucer-size cookie. **Illegal Pete's** (✉ 1447 Pearl St. ☎ 303/440–3955 ⊕ www.illegalpetes.com ☎ 303/444–3055) serves hefty burritos made to order with fresh ingredients and a choice of three salsas. If you're hankering for a delicious Philly-style steak-and-cheese sandwich or a New York–style

deli sandwich, **Salvaggio's Italian Delicatessen** (✉ 2609 Pearl St. ☎ 303/938–1981) will make one to order with your choice of deli meats and cheeses. **Falafel King** (✉ 1314 Pearl St. ☎ 303/449–9321 ⊕ www.falafelkingboulder.com) has excellent pita pockets of hot and crispy falafel, spicy gyros, and marinated grilled chicken breast. Get an order of tabouli, hummus, or dolmas to round out lunch. The thin and crispy pizzas at **Abo's** (✉ 1110 13th St. ☎ 303/443–3199 ⊕ www.abospizza.com) will not disappoint. **Whole Foods** (✉ 2905 Pearl St. ☎ 303/545–6611 ⊕ www.wholefoodsmarket.com/stores/boulder) has a sushi bar, a self-serve salad bar, a coffee bar, and a deli with ready-made sandwiches, panini, and pizza.

7

the TenTenTini, made with blue cheese-stuffed olives) and eight varieties of single-malt scotch. Don't miss the grilled-cheese sandwich made with fresh buffalo mozzarella and figs. ✉ 1011 Walnut St. ☎ 303/998–1010 ⊕ www.brasserietenten.com ⚒ Reservations essential ▤ AE, D, MC, V ✛ F6.

$ ✕ **Burnt Toast Restaurant.** The hearty breakfasts served until 3 PM each
CAFE day are just one reason to visit this homey café in a 100-year-old house on the Hill in downtown Boulder. Omelets are hot and fluffy, potatoes savory and crisp, the buttery coffee cake is laced with spices and nuts, and the cappuccinos have perfectly frothy caps. Have a light breakfast of home-baked pastries at the coffee bar or eat in the sunny dining room, which houses an eclectic collection of antique wooden tables. An ever-changing dinner menu incorporates fresh local foods. Reservations are only necessary for a four-course Sunday dinner served family style. ✉ 1235 Pennsylvania Ave. ☎ 303/440–5200 ⊕ www.burnttoastrestaurant.com ▤ AE, D, DC, MC, V ⊘ No dinner Mon. or Tues. ✛ C4.

$$ ✕ **Chez Thuy.** This restaurant is popular among Boulder's vegetarians,
VIETNAMESE who line up for the flavorful, inexpensive fare. Any of the various Viet-
★ namese soups make a wonderful starter before an entrée of seafood or tofu pad thai, or a traditional hotpot made with seafood or pork. The well-lighted dining room fills up every night with families and students, though the ambience is a little lacking. Everything is made fresh to order, portions are ample, and the service is fast and friendly.

✉ *2655 28th St.* ☎ *303/442–1700* ⊕ *www.chezthuy.com* ⊟ *AE, D, MC, V* ⊹ *E1.*

$ ✕ **Efrain's Mexican Restaurant & Cantina.** It's worth the drive to Lafayette

MEXICAN for the savory *chile verde* (green chile) that Efrain cooks every day. His family's homey café has simple, green-painted arbors and hand-painted tables. The porch is a great place to relax before dinner with a margarita served in a pint-size mason jar. Efrain prepares low-fat, authentic entrées with fresh beef and succulent pulled chicken. The large-grain rice is light, and refried beans are creamy but not greasy. Finish your meal with a crisp, hot *sopapilla* (a light, fried pastry served hot with honey). Expect to wait for a table on a weekend night. ✉ *101 E. Cleveland St., Lafayette Drive 11 mi east on Baseline Rd. to Lafayette and turn right onto Public Rd., then left onto Cleveland St.* ☎ *303/666–7544* ⊟ *AE, D, MC, V* ☺ *Closed Tues.* ⊹ *F4.*

$$$$ ✕ **Flagstaff House Restaurant.** Sit on the patio at one of Colorado's finest

AMERICAN restaurants and drink in the sublime views of Boulder from the side of

★ Flagstaff Mountain, about 5 minutes from downtown. Executive Chef Mark Monette has fresh fish flown in daily, grows some of his own herbs, and is noted for his exquisite combinations of ingredients—some organic—and fanciful, playful presentations. The menu changes daily, but sample entrées include ruby red trout with salmon and scallops in caviar butter and watercress sauce; buffalo filet mignon and foie gras. The wine list is remarkably comprehensive. ✉ *1138 Flagstaff Rd. Drive west on Baseline Rd. and turn right onto Flagstaff Rd. Follow it up the hill for about ¾ mi, then look for the restaurant on your right.* ☎ *303/442–4640* ⊕ *www.flagstaffhouse.com* ⌖ *Reservations essential* ⊟ *AE, D, DC, MC, V* ☺ *No lunch* ⊹ *A5.*

$$$–$$$$ ✕ **Frasca Food and Wine.** In the Friuli region of Italy the *frasca* (tree

ITALIAN branch) is a historic marker for a neighborhood eatery where you'll

★ be warmly welcomed and well fed. At this Frasca, you can start with *salumi*, a platter of northern Italian cured meats such as *prosciutto daniele, speck,* and *salumeria biellese coppa,* then dig into sliced Quebec veal loin salad, house-made *tagliatelle,* or butter-roasted Atlantic halibut. The menu is based on locally and naturally raised foods, while the extensive wine list focuses on Italian regional wines. ✉ *1738 Pearl St.* ☎ *303/442–6966* ⊕ *www.frascafoodandwine.com* ⌖ *Reservations essential* ⊟ *AE, D, MC, V* ☺ *Closed Sun. No lunch* ⊹ *H5.*

$$$$ ✕ **Gold Hill Inn.** About 10 mi from downtown Boulder, this humble log

AMERICAN cabin, on the dirt road going through the former mining town of Gold Hill, hardly looks like a bastion of *haute cuisine,* but the six-course, $33 prix-fixe dinner is something to rave about. Entrées stick to a Western theme, and may include roast duck with raspberry sauce or leg of lamb marinated in buttermilk, juniper berries, and cloves. Portions are generous, but try to save room for dessert. Service is friendly, and the inn also hosts regular "murder mystery" nights with professional actors in the adjacent Bluebird Lodge. ✉ *401 Main St., Gold Hill, Take Mapleton Ave. west from Broadway. It becomes Sunshine Canyon Dr., then Main St.* ☎ *303/443–6461* ⊕ *www.goldhillinn.com* ⌖ *Reservations essential* ⊟ *MC, V* ☺ *Closed Tues. June–Sept., and Mon. and Tues. in May and Oct. No lunch* ⊹ *A1.*

$$–$$$ ✕**Kasa Japanese Grill and Bar.** Architect Edward Suzuki designed this
JAPANESE elegant and understated restaurant that features black-granite tables,
★ wooden flooring, imported Japanese tiles, and inverted white umbrellas
hanging from the ceiling (*kasa* means "umbrellas" in Japanese)—and a
menu filled with authentic Japanese *yakitori* (meat and vegetable skew-
ers), sushi, and sashimi. Don't miss the yogurt ice cream for dessert.
✉ *1468 Pearl St.* ☎ *303/938–8888* ⊕ *www.kasainboulder.com* ▭ *AE,
D, MC, V* ⊗ *Closed Mon.* ✛ *G5.*

$$$ ✕**The Kitchen.** This unique "community bistro" offers an elegant yet
AMERICAN relaxed dinner with great service, and includes a casual wine and beer
Fodor'sChoice lounge on its second floor. Locals come in for "shared plates" during
★ Community Hour (3 to 5:30 weekdays), a boardinghouse-like experi-
ence that provides the same great food and drinks at reduced prices.
Exceptional entrées like the lamb sausage ravioli and the beef flank
steak spotlight free-range meats and organic and seasonal local produce.
Don't forget dessert: lemon tart with mascarpone and a glass of mus-
catel or the sticky toffee pudding with vanilla ice cream and a cup of
robust coffee are heavenly. The combination of chic bistro and big-city
hot spot can be a bit loud. ✉ *1039 Pearl St.* ☎ *303/544–5973* ⊕ *www.
thekitchencafe.com* ⌂ *Reservations essential* ▭ *AE, D, MC, V* ✛ *F6.*

$$$–$$$$ ✕**L'Atelier.** Chef Radek Cerny, a native of Prague and master of *nouvelle*
FRENCH *cuisine*, creates delicious French meals with artistic flourish (and a slight
★ Spanish accent). Seafood is his forte, and the tuna tartare salad with
oranges is a wonderful starter before an entrée of lobster ravioli with
beurre blanc or Maine lobster meunière. Be sure to save a crust of bread
to use as a sippet in the savory sauces before ending with a chocolate
raspberry miroir, made with chocolate mousse and almond meringue.
The extraordinary wine list covers all price ranges and vintages. ✉ *1739
Pearl St.* ☎ *303/442–7233* ⊕ *www.latelierboulder.com* ▭ *AE, D, MC,
V* ⊗ *No lunch; closed on Sundays* ✛ *H5.*

¢ ✕**The Laughing Goat Coffeehouse.** This bohemian-style café two blocks west
CAFE of the pedestrian mall serves bagels, muffins, cinnamon rolls, and granola
for breakfast, and sandwiches and soups for lunch. The excellent lattes
made with cow, goat, or soy milk have an artistic pattern drawn in the
crema. Students like to take up table space with laptops and textbooks,
but they'll happily make room for you. You can hear live music and
poetry by locals Tuesday through Sunday. ✉ *1709 Pearl St.* ☎ *303/440–
4628* ⊕ *www.thelaughinggoat.com* ▭ *AE, D, MC, V* ✛ *H5.*

$$$ ✕**Mediterranean Restaurant.** After work, when all of Boulder shows up to
MEDITERRANEAN enjoy tapas, "the Med" becomes a real scene. If the crowd gets to be too
much, try a table on the patio. The decor is Portofino meets Santa Fe,
with abstract art, terra-cotta floors, and brightly colored tile. The open
kitchen turns out Italian, Spanish, French, and Greek fare, including
daily specials such as pork saltimbocca, halibut puttanesca, and horse-
radish-crusted tuna—all complemented by an extensive, well-priced
wine list. ✉ *1002 Walnut St.* ☎ *303/444–5335* ⊕ *www.themedboulder.
com* ▭ *AE, D, DC, MC, V* ✛ *F6.*

$$$–$$$$ ✕**Q's.** Coffered ceilings, stained-glass windows, and mosaic tile floors
AMERICAN create a classy feel at this quiet restaurant housed in the 100-year-
old Hotel Boulderado. The menu features dishes using local, seasonal,

7

organic, and sustainably produced ingredients, and the excellent international wine list features a few local vintages, as well. Regional sweet-corn soup or roast beef and arugula salad are delightful starters before entrées like roast Colorado rack of lamb. If you're in the mood to be surprised, try the five-course chef's tasting menu ($55). End on a sweet note with a dish of homemade ice cream or a seasonal fruit tart. ⊠ *2115 13th St., in Hotel Boulderado* ☎ *303/442–4880* ⊕ *www.qsboulder.com* ⊟ *AE, D, DC, MC, V* ✛ *F5.*

$$–$$$
AMERICAN

✕ **Sunflower Organic Dining.** Storefront-size windows allow plenty of light into the colorfully painted dining room, where you'll find savory meals based on fresh, organic ingredients—and plenty of vegetarian options, such as tempeh korma. Meat-based entrées include buffalo au poivre, Colorado bass, and duck confit. End your lunch or dinner with a seasonal Colorado peach crisp or the decadent molten chocolate cake. Brunch is served on weekends. ⊠ *1701 Pearl St.* ☎ *303/440–0220* ⊕ *www.sunflowerboulder.com* ⊟ *AE, D, DC, MC, V* ✛ *H5.*

$$–$$$
JAPANESE

✕ **Sushi Zanmai.** The delicious seafood is prepared fresh, and the wasabi is zesty at Boulder's perennial favorite sushi restaurant, a bright, open place that fills early. Enjoy dinner at a table or sit at the sushi bar and watch the chefs' intricate artwork with food. The miso soup is salty and tangy, and the mochi-ice dessert (a truffle-size bite of ice cream wrapped in a fruit or chocolate-flavored rice paste) is not to be missed. Happy hour for sushi and drinks is Monday–Saturday from 5 to 6:30 and all night on Sunday. The official karaoke night is Saturday (10 to midnight). ⊠ *1221 Spruce St.* ☎ *303/440–0733* ⊕ *www.sushizanmai. com* ⊟ *AE, MC, V* ☺ *No lunch weekends* ✛ *F5.*

WHERE TO STAY

$$$–$$$$
★

🏨 **The Bradley Boulder Inn.** Elegant and contemporary, this downtown inn has a spacious great room with warm tones and an inviting stone fireplace. Local artwork is on display throughout. Each room is individually decorated, and all have flat-screen TVs and DVD players, 400-thread-count cotton duvets and bed linens, and Aveda bath products. Some rooms have Jacuzzi tubs, fireplaces, and balconies. Breakfast, included in the room rate, features fresh fruit parfaits, French toast casserole, quiche, made-to-order eggs, and excellent coffee. You've also got access to a local fitness center—and bottled water, organic coffee and tea, soda, and snacks in the lobby. **Pros:** quiet inn one block from Pearl Street shopping and dining; daily wine-and-cheese hour; privileges at nearby gym. **Cons:** books early; no young children. ⊠ *2040 16th St.,* ☎ *303/545–5200 or 800/858–5811* ⊕ *www.thebradleyboulder.com* ➘ *12 rooms* ♨ *In-room: a/c, DVD, Internet, Wi-Fi. In-hotel: Wi-Fi, business center, parking (free), no kids under 12* ⊟ *AE, MC, V* ❡⊘❘ *BP* ✛ *G5.*

$$–$$$

🏨 **Briar Rose B&B.** Innkeeper Gary Hardin, a Zen monk, warmly welcomes guests to his ecologically sound B&B. The inn has received accolades for its commitment to zero waste. The full breakfast is exclusively organic, and you can eat your homemade granola in the dining area or in your own room. Tea trays with homemade shortbread cookies are available anytime during the day. There are eight rooms in the sturdy, 1890s brick main house and two in the adjacent carriage house. The individually decorated rooms have down comforters, organic-cotton sheets, and flowers stenciled above the headboards; some have wood-burning fireplaces. **Pros:** green commitment; the only B&B in central Boulder; close to downtown shopping and dining; delicious (and healthy) breakfast. **Cons:** on a busy and noisy street; small inn that books early. ⊠ *2151 Arapahoe Ave.,* ☎ *303/442–3007* ⊕ *www. briarrosebb.com* ⇆ *10 rooms* ⚘ *In-room: no TV (some), Wi-Fi. In-hotel: parking (free)* ⊟ *AE, MC, V* ⊚❙ *BP* ✚ *D3.*

$$–$$$ ⊡ **Colorado Chautauqua Association.** The association was founded in 1898 as part of the Chautauqua movement and still fulfills its charge to provide a venue for recreation and cultural and educational enrichment. The upgraded, fully furnished lodge rooms and cottages retain their unique historic charm and include linens and cooking utensils (but not daily housekeeping). The lawn is a terrific spot for a picnic on a sunny afternoon. The property is in Chautauqua Park at the foot of the Flatirons; myriad hiking trails take you into the mountains right from your front door. **Pros:** unique lodging; arts, dining, and recreation on property; well-kept cabins; amazing views of town and mountains. **Cons:** no maid service; park tends to fill with nonresidents there for various events and dining. ⊠ *900 Baseline Rd.,* ☎ *303/442–3282* ⊕ *www. chautauqua.com* ⇆ *22 rooms, 60 cottages* ⚘ *In-room: kitchen, no a/c, no phone, no TV, Wi-Fi. In-hotel: restaurant, tennis courts, some pets allowed* ⊟ *AE, MC, V* ✚ *B6.*

$ ⊡ **Foot of the Mountain Motel.** With its distinctive knotty-pine siding, bright red doors, and colorful flower boxes, this motel is near the mouth of Boulder Canyon and the Boulder Creek Path. It seems far from Boulder's bustle, yet it's only a few minutes' walk from downtown. The cabin-style rooms are simple but cozy (and quiet). Pets can board, too, for an extra $5 per night (there are no pets allowed in the suites). **Pros:** excellent value for the area; quiet neighborhood; close to recreation. **Cons:** no-frills accommodations; no on-site restaurant. ⊠ *200 Arapahoe Ave.,* ☎ *303/442–5688 or 866/773–5489* ⊕ *www.footofthemountainmotel. com* ⇆ *18 rooms, 2 suites* ⚘ *In-room: no a/c, refrigerator. In-hotel: parking (free), some pets allowed* ⊟ *D, MC, V* ✚ *A4.*

$$$$ ⊡ **Gold Lake Mountain Resort & Spa.** At this casual resort you can dip into
★   one of four lakeside hot pools, canoe, fly-fish, snowshoe, horseback ride, hike, and partake in luxurious spa treatments while still staying near Eldora Mountain Resort and Estes Park. You'll slumber peacefully on luxurious linens in a rustic, 1920s lakeside cabin with a stylish mix of contemporary and antique furnishings. The chef at Alice's Restaurant ($$$$) has a gift for drawing savory and indulgent three- or seven-course meals out of whole, organic ingredients, and bakes all pastries and breads on the premises. The rustic, mountain-style dining room has a large stone fireplace and leather chairs for relaxing after dinner. **Pros:** well situated for hiking; professional and attentive staff. **Cons:** remote location 32 mi northwest of Boulder (about 45 mins); few amenities nearby. ⊠ *3771 Gold Lake Rd., Ward* ☎ *303/459–3544 or 800/450–3544* ⊕ *www.goldlake.com* ⇆ *19 cabins* ⚘ *In-room: no a/c, no TV. In-hotel: restaurant, bar, spa, parking (free)* ⊟ *AE, D, MC, V* ✚ *A1.*

7

$$$
Fodor's Choice
★

Hotel Boulderado. The gracious lobby of this elegant 1909 beauty has a soaring stained-glass ceiling, and the mezzanine beckons with romantic nooks galore. When choosing a room, opt for the old building, with spacious quarters filled with period antiques and reproductions. The new wing is plush and comfortable but has less Victorian character. Rooms with mountain views are available on request. The hotel has two restaurants: Q's ($$$$) offers upscale dining, while the Corner Bar ($–$$) serves less formal lunch and dinner. Downstairs, the Catacombs Blues Bar is always hopping, and has live music three nights a week. Guests have access to the nearby health club, One Boulder Fitness. **Pros:** well-maintained historic building; downtown location; excellent restaurants. **Cons:** on busy and noisy streets; large, busy hotel. ⊠ *2115 13th St.,* ☎ *303/442–4344 or 800/433–4344* ⊕ *www.boulderado.com* ↩ *160 rooms* ⚹ *In-room: Wi-Fi. In-hotel: 3 restaurants, bars, public Wi-Fi* ⊟ *AE, D, DC, MC, V* ⊙| *EP* ✛ *F5.*

$$
Quality Inn & Suites Boulder Creek. Just a 10-minute walk from the Pearl Street Mall and 5 minutes from the University of Colorado, this hotel provides the personal attention and services of a B&B, including a free hot-breakfast buffet. The caring staff has been known to scrape ice off guests' car windshields. The well-lighted, spacious rooms, with 32" flat-panel TVs, custom iron lamps, and wood and leather furniture in rich earth tones, create a sophisticated yet comfortable feel. **Pros:** friendly and personable staff; free off-street parking; close to sights and activities. **Cons:** on busy street; chain hotel has less personality than some local options. ⊠ *2020 Arapahoe Ave.,* ☎ *303/449–7550* ⊕ *www. qualityinnboulder.com* ↩ *40 rooms, 6 suites* ⚹ *In-room: TV, a/c, refrigerator, microwave, Wi-Fi. In-hotel: pool, gym, laundry service, public Internet, parking (free)* ⊟ *AE, D, MC, V* ⊙| *BP* ✛ *D4.*

$$$$
St. Julien Hotel & Spa. Unwind in the indulgent luxury of this classy yet casual hotel. The Colorado red-sandstone structure has walnut floors, marble staircases, and a golden onyx bar. Most rooms have stunning mountain views, and all have custom-made beds with European pillow tops and duvets, photography by local artists, and oversize slate bathrooms with soaking tubs and seamless walk-in showers. The hotel is downtown, minutes on foot from the Boulder Creek Path. **Pros:** convenient downtown location; close to outdoor activities and mountains. **Cons:** large hotel; quite busy. ⊠ *900 Walnut St.,* ☎ *720/406–9696 or 877/303–0900* ⊕ *www.stjulien.com* ↩ *201 rooms, 11 suites* ⚹ *In-room: a/c, safe, Wi-Fi. In-hotel: restaurant, room service, bar, pool, gym, spa, parking (paid)* ⊟ *AE, D, DC, MC, V* ✛ *F6.*

NIGHTLIFE AND THE ARTS

THE ARTS

ARTS FESTIVALS

Between late June and early August, the **Colorado Music Festival** (⊠ *Chautauqua Park, 900 Baseline Rd.,* ☎ *303/440–7666 or 303/449–1397* ⊕ *www. coloradomusicfest.org*), 33 years old in 2010, brings classical music to Chautauqua Auditorium. Visiting artists have included the Santa Fe Guitar Quartet and the Takács Quartet, as well as plenty of international talent such as William Barton, a didgeridoo performer from Australia, and Lynn Harrell, who plays a 1673 Stradivarius. Evening meals are available in the dining hall, or you can pack a picnic and settle in on the Green to take in views of the mountains before the concert.

Fodor's Choice ★ CU's Mary Rippon Outdoor Theater is the venue for the annual **Colorado Shakespeare Festival** (☎ *303/492–0554* ⊕ *www.coloradoshakes.org*), presenting the bard's comedies and tragedies from early July to mid-August.

THEATER, MUSIC, AND DANCE
The Boulder Philharmonic (⌂ *2590 Walnut St,* ⊠ *University of Colorado, Macky Auditorium* ☎ *303/449–1343* ⊕ *www.boulderphil.org*) presents its own concert season, as well as chamber music concerts, the Boulder Ballet Ensemble, and performances by visiting divas such as Kathleen Battle.

> ### CHAUTAUQUA MOVEMENT
>
> The Colorado Chautauqua National Historic Landmark is on 26 acres in Boulder at the base of the foothills. It opened on July 4, 1898, and is the only remaining Chautauqua west of the Mississippi River in continuous operation with its original buildings. One of only three remaining in the United States today, it was once one of 12,000 venues on the national circuit where educational speeches and artistic performances took place. You can still have dinner and attend seasonal concerts, lectures, and a silent film series here.

At the University of Colorado the superb **College of Music** (☎ *303/492–8008* ⊕ *www.cuconcerts.org*) presents concerts year-round, including chamber music by the internationally renowned Takács String Quartet.

The **Department of Theater and Dance** (☎ *303/492–8181* ⊕ *www.colorado.edu/theatredance*) stages excellent student productions year-round.

The **Dairy Center for the Arts** (☎ *303/440–7826* ⊕ *www.thedairy.org*) hosts art shows in the gallery featuring local painters. The center is also a venue for locally produced plays; music, ballet, and dance performances; and film.

★ Concerts take place throughout summer at Boulder's peaceful **Chautauqua Community Hall** (⊠ *900 Baseline Rd.* ☎ *303/442–3282* ⊕ *www.chautauqua.com*). Performers have included Branford Marsalis, Lucinda Williams, Indigo Girls, and the Afro Celt Sound System.

The Art Deco **Boulder Theater** (⊠ *2032 14th St.* ☎ *303/786–7030* ⊕ *www.bouldertheater.com*) is a venue for top touring bands and movies, as well as for most installments of the weekly radio show *E-Town* (⊕ *www.etown.org*), broadcast on NPR. E-Town emcees Helen and Nick Forster host musical talent and discuss environmental and community issues.

Dine while you catch a popular musical at **Boulder's Dinner Theatre** (⊠ *5501 Arapahoe Ave.* ☎ *303/449–6000* ⊕ *www.theatreinboulder.com*).

NIGHTLIFE
BARS AND LOUNGES
Business lunches and after-work gatherings take place at the **Corner Bar** (⊠ *2115 13th St.* ☎ *303/442–4344* ⊕ *www.boulderado.com/thecornerbar.html*) in the Hotel Boulderado. It's a contemporary American pub with both indoor and outdoor seating. **The New Foundry** (⊠ *1109 Walnut*

St. ☎ *303/447–1803* ⊕ *www.thenewfoundry.com*) is where the hip of all ages hang out; upstairs, there's a rooftop deck with its own bar. The main bar has 10 pool tables and a mezzanine overlooking all the action. The cozy **Pearl Street Pub and Cellar** (✉ *1108 Pearl St.* ☎ *303/939–9900*), with its laid-back atmosphere and impressive beer list, is a great place to chat over a quiet drink. There's pool and darts downstairs if you're in the mood for a game. Bartenders at **Rio Grande Mexican Restaurant** (✉ *1101 Walnut St.* ☎ *303/444–3690* ⊕ *www.riograndemexican.com*) make Boulder's best margaritas—so good, in fact, that there's a 3-per-person limit. There's also a great rooftop patio here. The **West End Tavern** (✉ *926 Pearl St.* ☎ *303/444–3535* ⊕ *www.thewestendtavern.com*), with its rooftop deck, is a popular after-work hangout serving beers, cocktails, and good pub grub.

BREWPUBS AND BREWERIES

The **Mountain Sun Pub & Brewery** (✉ *1535 Pearl St.* ☎ *303/546–0886* ⊕ *www.mountainsunpub.com*) crafts more than 50 beers throughout the year, and there are always about 18 on tap. A favorite of Boulderites is the Colorado Kind, a nicely hopped amber. Tours are available upon request. Stay to have a burger or for the live music Sunday nights. The **Walnut Brewery** (✉ *1123 Walnut St.* ☎ *303/447–1345* ⊕ *www.walnutbrewery.com*) keeps several brews and cask-conditioned ales on tap. A new seasonal is tapped each month, and every season also has a new wheat beer. Try the Buffalo Gold ale or the malty St. James Irish Red Ale. The excellent beer goes well with the upscale pub fare, which includes mahi tacos, smoked salmon fish-and-chips, and buffalo fajitas. Tours are available anytime.

MUSIC AND DANCE CLUBS

The **Fox Theatre** (✉ *1135 13th St.* ☎ *303/443–3399* ⊕ *www.foxtheatre.com*) movie palace hosts touring music and comedic talent. Whether DJs are spinning for '80s or hip-hop night, there's dancing every night Tuesday through Saturday at **Round Midnight** (✉ *1005 Pearl St.* ☎ *303/442–2176* ⊕ *www.roundmidnight.tv* ☾ *Daily 5 PM–2 AM*). There's live music in the backroom and a rotating roster of DJs out front every Thursday, Friday, and Saturday at **The B.Side Lounge** (✉ *2017 13th St.* ☎ *303/473–9463* ⊕ *www.thebsidelounge.com* ☾ *Daily 4 PM–2 AM*). **Rock 'n Soul Cafe** (✉ *5290 Arapahoe Ave.* ☎ *303/443–5108* ⊕ *www.rocknsoulcafe.com* ☾ *Mon.–Sat. 9 AM–11 PM*) serves up live music most nights, accompanied by espresso drinks and wine by the glass. The café also serves food: soups, teriyaki, and pastries.

SHOPPING

SHOPPING NEIGHBORHOODS

Boulder's **Pearl Street Mall** (✉ *Pearl St. between 11th and 15th Sts.*) is a shopping extravaganza, with upscale boutiques, art galleries, bookstores, shoe shops, and stores with home and garden furnishings. Street musicians and magicians, caricaturists, and buskers with lovebirds entertain locals and visitors alike. Stroll along **Twenty-Ninth Street** (✉ *29th St. between Arapahoe Ave. and Pearl St.* ⊕ *www.twentyninthstreet.com*), Boulder's newest area to shop, and pick up a pair of shoes, some outdoor gear, a funny greeting card, or a new yoga outfit. The outdoor mall has plenty of nationally known clothiers, a bookstore, a stationer, coffee shops, and eateries. **University Hill** (the Hill) (✉ *13th St. between College Ave. and Pennsylvania St.*) is a great place for hip duds, new and used CDs, and CU apparel. One of the metropolitan area's most popular shopping centers is **Flatiron Crossing** (✉ *U.S. 36 between Boulder and Denver, Broomfield 80021* ☎ *720/887–9900* ⊕ *www.flatironcrossing. com*) about 10 mi southwest of Boulder. Shoppers can hit stores such as Nordstrom, Coach, Borders, and Sharper Image; browse at a few locally owned jewelers and galleries; and take a break in the food court or in one of the full-service restaurants.

SPECIALTY SHOPS

ANTIQUES

Serendipitous discoveries and glorious antique furniture, jewelry, and silver services move fast at the **Amazing Garage Sale** (✉ *4919 N. Broadway* ☎ *303/447–0417*), so it's worth a visit while you're in Boulder.

BOOKSTORES

Boulder has one of the largest concentrations of used-book sellers in the United States. Most shops are on Pearl Street between 8th and 20th streets.

★ **Boulder Bookstore** (✉ *1107 Pearl St.* ☎ *303/447–2074* ⊕ *www.boulder-bookstore.com*) has thousands of new and used books in all genres, including a great selection of photography, history, and art books about Colorado. It also carries a few out-of-town and foreign newspapers and periodicals. Sip a robust latte at **Trident Booksellers and Cafe** (✉ *940 Pearl St.* ☎ *303/443–3133*) while browsing the eclectic collection of mostly used books—including foreign-language, but also many new books at marked-down prices.

CHILDREN'S ITEMS

Boulder kids' favorite store is **Grandrabbit's Toy Shoppe** (✉ *2525 Arapahoe Ave.* ☎ *303/443–0780* ⊕ *www.grtoys.com*). The coolest kites can be found at **Into the Wind** (✉ *1408 Pearl St.* ☎ *303/449–5356* ⊕ *www.intothewind. com*), which sells traditional and out-of-the-ordinary kites, plus imaginative wind decorations, flags, and boomerangs. **Little Mountain Outfitters** (✉ *1136 Spruce St.* ☎ *303/443–1757* ⊕ *www.littlemountainoutfitters. com*) carries outdoor clothing and camping goods for children. They also and rent child-carrier backpacks and all-terrain strollers. **PlayFair Toys** (✉ *1690 28th St.* ☎ *303/444–7502* ⊕ *www.playfairtoys.com*), owned and operated by one Professor Playfair, sells all kinds of educational toys, including Lego and Brio brands, as well as books for kids of all ages, puzzles, and fun items like robotic tarantulas and "brain kits."

CLOTHING BOUTIQUES

Alpaca Connection (✉ *1326 Pearl St.* ☎ *303/447–2047* ⊕ *www.theal-pacaconnection.com*) sells gorgeous alpaca garments, mostly made in Peru, for men and women. **Fresh Produce** (✉ *1218 Pearl St.* ☎ *303/442– 7507* ⊕ *www.freshproducesportswear.com*) is a Boulder-based company that makes brightly colored and whimsically designed cotton clothing for women and children. **Jacque Michelle** (✉ *2670 Broadway*

7

☏ *303/786–7628*) has fashionably casual and unique women's clothing and accessories. The store also sells cutting-edge gifts.

CRAFTS AND ART GALLERIES
Art Source International (✉ *1237 Pearl St.* ☏ *303/444–4079* ⊕ *www.raremaps.com*) is Colorado's largest antique print and map dealer. **Boulder Arts & Crafts Gallery** (✉ *1421 Pearl St.* ☏ *303/443–3683* ⊕ *www.boulderartsandcrafts.com*), owned and operated by 42 artists, is a popular place to find unique gifts and decorative items. The 150-odd Colorado artists represented create everything from photographs and pottery to hand-painted silk scarves and leather handbags to furniture and glass objets d'art. The aptly named **Hangouts** (✉ *1328 Pearl St.* ☏ *303/442–2533* ⊕ *www.hangouts.com*) carries handmade Mayan- and Brazilian hammocks and hanging chairs. **The Middle Fish** (✉ *1500 Pearl St.* ☏ *303/443–0835*) sells all kinds of home and garden decorations, including quirky one-of-a-kind clocks crafted from a combination of metals, locally made jewelry, mosaic mirrors, and unusual furniture. **SmithKlein Gallery** (✉ *1116 Pearl St.* ☏ *303/444–7200* ⊕ *www.smithklein.com*) showcases classic modern art—glass and bronze sculpture, jewelry, and paintings.

GIFT STORES
Belvedere Belgian Chocolate Shop (✉ *1936 14th St.* ☏ *303/447–0336* ⊕ *www.belvedereboulder.com*) makes and sells amazing chocolates. Pick up "three hearts in a heart" for your own sweetheart (three heart-shaped chocolates inside a larger chocolate heart). **Paper Doll** (✉ *1141 Pearl St.* ☏ *303/449–1661*) is an eclectic and original gift shop with something for everyone, from classy stationery and wrapping paper to jewelry and porcelain teapots shaped like cats. **Two Hands Paperie** (✉ *803 Pearl St.* ☏ *303/444–0124* ⊕ *www.twohandspaperie.com*) carries elegant European stationery, handmade paper, and handcrafted, leather-bound journals. **Where the Buffalo Roam** (✉ *1320 Pearl St.* ☏ *303/938–1424*) sells quirky T-shirts, CU and Colorado souvenirs, and tacky trinkets.

HOME AND GARDEN
The store to visit for the finest selection in crockery, cookware, table linen, and kitchen utensils, as well as epicurean food items and cookbooks, is **Peppercorn** (✉ *1235 Pearl St.* ☏ *303/449–5847 or 800/447–6905* ⊕ *www.peppercorn.com*). Gardeners will find treasures at the **West End Gardener** (✉ *777 Pearl St.* ☏ *303/938–0607*), purveyors of vintage and new garden tools and accessories.

SPORTING GOODS
Boulder Army Store (✉ *1545 Pearl St.* ☏ *303/442–7616* ⊕ *www.boulderarmystore.com*) packs the racks and shelves tightly with name-brand outdoor clothing and camping gear from manufacturers like Columbia, Under Armour, and Carhartt marked a few dollars less than regular retail. **McGuckin Hardware** (✉ *Village Shopping Center, 2525 Arapahoe Ave.* ☏ *303/443–1822* ⊕ *www.mcguckin.com*) is a Boulder institution that stocks home appliances and gadgets, hardware, and a mind-boggling array of outdoor merchandise. The omniscient salespeople know where everything is. The Boulder branch of **REI** (✉ *1789 28th St.* ☏ *303/583–9970* ⊕ *www.rei.com*) carries outdoor equipment for all sports and has some rental camping gear.

SIDE TRIPS FROM BOULDER

Boulder has a few neighboring towns that are interesting destinations in their own right, well worth a drive and a short stop if not a longer layover. Nederland, Niwot, and Lyons all have quirky, interesting (albeit small) downtown areas, rich histories, and awesome surroundings filled with mountains, forests, and streams.

NEDERLAND

16 mi west of Boulder

A former mining and mill town at the top of Boulder Canyon and on the scenic Peak-to-Peak Highway, "Ned" embodies that small, mountain-town spirit in look and attitude: laid-back, independent, and friendly.

Nederland started out as a mill town, processing the silver mined in the now-deserted nearby town of Caribou. The town got its name from a Dutch company that owned several mines in the area: "Nederland" is Dutch for "Netherlands," or low lands, and Nederland was "below" Caribou. Nederland was also well known for its tungsten mining during World War I. Around town you'll see references to "wolf's tongue," a word play on wolframite, the ore from which tungsten is extracted. The downtown retains the character of its silver-milling days, and has several good bars, cafés, and restaurants. Shops sell used books, antiques, organic groceries, fabrics, and gemstones. Nederland is the gateway to skiing at Eldora Mountain Resort and high-altitude hiking in the Indian Peaks Wilderness.

GETTING HERE AND AROUND

Nederland is an easy drive from Boulder. Take Highway 119 west (Canyon Blvd.).

WHEN TO GO

FESTIVALS **Frozen Dead Guy Days.** Every March, Nederland celebrates an annual event that's true to its oddball spirit. The three-day event includes a slow-motion parade, coffin races, and a charity polar plunge into (usually frozen) Chipeta Park Pond. ⊠ *Chipeta Park and Town Square* ☎ *303/258–3936* ⊕ *www.nederlandchamber.org* ⊠ *Free* ⊗ *First weekend in Mar.*

The Nederland Music & Arts Festival, a weekend of bluegrass, world beat, and jazz music known as the **NedFest** (⊕ *www.nedfest.com*), takes place in late August on the west shore of Barker Reservoir. A few thousand people come to relax in the sun, dance, or stroll by the art stands. Admission is steep ($30–$55 for a single day, $115–$135 for all three days), but children under 12 get in for free.

ESSENTIALS

Visitor Info Nederland Area Chamber of Commerce (✉ *Box 85, Nederland* ☎ *303/258–3936* ⊕ *www.nederlandchamber.org*).

EXPLORING

★ The **Peak-to-Peak Scenic and Historic Byway** (CO Hwys. 119, 72, and 7), a 55-mi stretch that winds from Central City through Nederland to Estes Park, is not the quickest route to the eastern gateway to Rocky Mountain National Park, but is certainly the most scenic. You'll pass through the old mining towns of Ward and Allenspark and enjoy spectacular mountain vistas. Mount Meeker and Longs Peak rise magnificently behind every bend in the road. The descent into Estes Park provides grand vistas of snow-covered mountains and green valleys.

An afternoon drive along this route is a rite of autumn, when the sky is deeper blue and stands of aspens distinguish themselves from the evergreen pine forests with their golden leaves. ⊠ *From Nederland, drive north on Hwy. 72. Turn left at intersection with Hwy. 7 and continue to Estes Park.*

SPORTS AND THE OUTDOORS

HIKING

If you aren't used to it, high altitude can catch you off guard. Drink plenty of water to help stave off the effects of altitude sickness—dizziness, shortness of breath, headache, and nausea. You also should slather on the sunscreen, as it's easy to get sunburned up here. And in summer an early morning start is best, as afternoon thunderstorms are frequent and potentially dangerous above the tree line.

★ The **Indian Peaks Wilderness** has some of the most popular hiking in the area, and you'll always have company in summer. The area encompasses more than 50 lakes, 133 mi of trails, and six mountain passes crossing the Continental Divide. Wildflowers are prolific, and peak in late July and early August. Cinquefoil, harebell, stonecrop, flax, wild geranium, yarrow, larkspur, lupine, and columbine (the state flower) all mix in a mosaic of colors on the slopes and in the meadows. Parking at trailheads in the wilderness area is limited, so plan to start out early in the day. "No Parking" signs are posted, and, if the designated parking lot is full, the etiquette is to park your car on the outbound side of the road at a spot where there's still room for vehicles to pass. There's no central access point to the area; contact the U.S. Forest Service or check its Web site for trail information and driving directions. Permits are not required for day visitors. ⊠ *Boulder Ranger District Office, Arapaho National Forest, 2140 Yarmouth Ave.* ☎ *303/541–2500* ⊕ *www.fs.fed.us/arnf/recreation/wilderness/ indianpeaks/index.shtml.*

The easy, 2.8-mi (round-trip) hike to **Lost Lake** has enough altitude to give you views of the high peaks under the brilliant blue sky. You'll gain a mere 800 feet on this two-hour walk. ⊠ *Trailhead: From Nederland, drive south on Hwy. 119 to County Rd. 130. About 1 mi after the pavement ends, look for a road on the left that goes sharply downhill (marked Hessie Trail). Park there and hike ½ mi to the trailhead.*

The well-traveled trail to **Diamond Lake** starts out as the Arapaho Pass Trail at the Fourth of July trailhead. It's steep as you climb through the pines, but the elevation gain between the trailhead and the lake is only 800 feet. The trail delivers terrific views of Jasper Peak and the Arapaho Peaks. In late July, when the snowfields are gone, the wildflowers cover the slopes and meadows with bursts of color. At the junction with the Diamond Lake trailhead to the left, the trail passes a waterfall and crosses a stream (with a bridge) before it descends to Diamond Lake. Relax at the lake and enjoy the views before returning. Allow three hours to hike the 5-mi round-trip. ⊠ *Trailhead: From Nederland, drive south on Hwy. 119 to County Rd. 130. About 5 mi after the pavement ends, look for signs for the Fourth of July trailhead.*

The **DeLonde Trail/Blue Bird Loop** at the Caribou Ranch Open Space is an easy 4.5-mi walk through forests and wildflower-filled meadows. An elk herd resides on the open space, so listen for the bulls bugling in fall. The 1.2-mi DeLonde Trail starts to the left of the trailhead information kiosk and connects to the Blue Bird Loop just above the former DeLonde homestead site. You can take a break at the picnic table overlooking the pond near the ranch house before continuing on the loop to the former Blue Bird Mine complex. Allow about one to two hours to complete the hike. ⊠ *Trailhead: From Nederland, drive north on Hwy. 72 to County Rd. 126, turn left, and go 1 mi* ☏ *303/678–6200.*

Indian Peaks Ace Hardware (⊠ *74 Hwy. 119* ☏ *303/258–3132*) is a good place to get information, maps, and gear. You can get water and food for your hike plus deli sandwiches and other groceries at the **B&F Mountain Market** (⊠ *60 Lakeview Dr.* ☏ *303/258–9470*).

SKIING AND SNOWBOARDING

With a 1,600-foot vertical drop (the longest run is 3 mi), **Eldora Mountain Resort** has 53 trails, 12 lifts, and 680 acres; 25 mi (40 km) of groomed Nordic track; and four terrain parks accommodating different ability levels for snowboarders and skiers. Tucked away in the mountains at 9,200 feet (summit elevation is 10,800 feet), Eldora's annual snowfall is more than 300 inches. Daily lift tickets are $65. The Indian Peaks Lodge rents skis, runs a ski school, and has a cafeteria-style restaurant. ⊠ *2861 Eldora Ski Rd., 5 mi west of Nederland off Hwy. 119 and Eldora Rd., Nederland* ☏ *303/440–8700* ⊕ *www. eldora.com* ⊠ *$62* ⊙ *Mid-Nov.–mid-Apr., weekdays 9–4; weekends and holidays 8:30–4.*

WHERE TO EAT AND STAY

$$
CAFE

✕ **Sundance Café and Lodge.** Locals love this place for its low-key atmosphere and great food—they serve a diner-style breakfast, lunch, and dinner. Try the Robbie Burger, which is topped with bacon and Brie. From both the deck and the inside, enjoy the great views of the Indian Peaks to the west, Boulder to the east, and Roosevelt National Forest on all sides. ⊠ *23492 Hwy. 119,* ☏ *303/258–0804* ⊕ *www.sundance-lodge.com* ⊟ *AE, D, MC, V* ⊙ *Daily 8 AM–9 PM (they close at 2:30 on Tues., early Nov.–early Apr.).*

$$
AMERICAN

✕ **Wild Mountain Smokehouse and Brewery.** This brewpub has it all: hand-crafted beer, delicious food, and a truly spectacular deck. Stop in for some seriously smoky BBQ (like the Ned-E-Que Platter) or a salad topped with maple-glazed salmon. Add a pint of their home brew and soak in the atmosphere, whether you're sitting out on the deck or inside the lodge style dining room with its fireplace and cathedral ceilings. ⊠ *70 E. 1st St.,* ☏ *303/258–9453* ⊕ *www.wildmountainsb.com* ⊟ *AE, D, MC, V* ⊙ *Sun.–Thurs. 11 AM–10 PM (kitchen closes at 8:30), Fri. and Sat. 11 AM–MIDNIGHT (kitchen closes at 9:30).*

$ ⌂ **Best Western Lodge at Nederland.** Built in 1994 with rough-hewn timber, this lodge is all modern inside. Upstairs rooms have cathedral ceilings, and those downstairs have gas fireplaces; all are spacious, and have coffeemakers and hair dryers. The enthusiastic staff will help to arrange any outdoor activity you desire—and the possibilities are just about endless. An excellent choice for those who want to be central, the property is within a half-hour's drive of Boulder, the Eldora ski area, and Central City. **Pros:** property has mountain style, in spite of being a franchise; quiet; good value for location. **Cons:** Nederland can feel remote unless you're spending a lot of time hiking and skiing; hotel is on a heavily traveled road. ⊠ *55 Lakeview Dr., Nederland* ☎ *303/258–9463 or 800/279–9463* ⊕ *www.bestwesterncolorado.com* ⇩ *23 rooms, 1 suite* ⌂ *In-room: no a/c, refrigerator, Wi-Fi. In-hotel: parking (free)* ⊟ *AE, D, DC, MC, V* �⌷ *CP.*

NIWOT

10 mi northeast of downtown Boulder via CO Hwy. 119.

Niwot is the Arapaho Indian word for "left hand," and this is where Chief Niwot (born circa 1820) and his tribe lived along the banks of Left Hand Creek until the early 1860s. European settlers arrived in the latter half of the 1800s to take up farming, after gold mining in the mountains became less lucrative. The town's importance grew once the railroad came in the 1870s, and its most famous business now is probably Crocs footwear, which was started in Niwot in 2004. Antiques aficionados have made Niwot their mecca in Boulder County. The historic district, full of brick buildings decorated with flower boxes, runs along 2nd Avenue and the cross streets Franklin and Murray.

GETTING HERE AND AROUND

If you're driving to or from Boulder on Highway 119, consider stopping at the Celestial Seasonings factory and Leanin' Tree Museum of Western Art along the way.

EN
ROUTE

On the way to Niwot from Boulder you pass by the Celestial Seasonings tea factory and the Leanin' Tree Museum of Western Art. Both are worth a visit, so plan an extra hour or two if you stop.

Celestial Seasonings, North America's largest herbal-tea producer (sealing 8 million tea bags every 24 hours), offers free tours of its factory. Before the tour you can sample from more than 60 varieties of tea. The famous "Mint Room" will clear your sinuses. You can also grab a bite to eat at the on-site Celestial Café. ⊠ *4600 Sleepytime Dr., Boulder* ⊠ *8 mi northeast of downtown Boulder. Take Hwy. 119 to Jay Rd., turn right and follow for about 1 mi., then turn left onto Spine Rd. After about ½ mi, turn left onto Sleepytime Dr.* ☎ *303/530–5300* ⊕ *www. celestialseasonings.com* ▦ *Free* ☉ *Tours hourly; Mon.–Fri. 10–4, Sat. 10–3, Sun. 11–3.*

The **Leanin' Tree Museum of Western Art** is one of the country's largest privately owned collections of post-1950 cowboy and Western art. More than 200 paintings of Western landscapes, wildlife, and the pioneers' ranch life, and 85 bronze sculptures by renowned, contemporary artists including Bill Hughes and Frank McCarthy recall an era in the

Boulder Valley before lattes. ⊠ *6055 Longbow Dr. About 8 mi northeast of Boulder. From Hwy. 119, take 63rd St. south, then Longbow Dr. west, Boulder* ☎ *303/530–1442* ⊕ *www.leanintreemuseum.com* 🖅 *Free* ⊙ *Weekdays 8–5, weekends 10–5; closed on major holidays.*

QUICK
BITES

The Eye Opener Coffee House (⊠ *136 2nd Ave.* ☎ *303/652–8137* ⊕ *www. eyeopenercoffee.com*) serves delicious coffee drinks, breakfast burritos, and bagels, plus gourmet sandwiches and fresh pastries, muffins, and Danishes.

WHERE TO EAT AND STAY

$$
ITALIAN

✕ **Treppeda's Italian Restaurant.** For lunch, try one of the tasty panini made from authentic ingredients and fresh focaccia at this casual and elegant Italian café with shaded outdoor seating. Enjoy a crunchy housemade cannoli and an espresso for dessert at the bar. Dinner in the cozy terra-cotta–painted dining room with classy paintings features traditional dishes like primavera gnocchi, lemon and garlic shrimp bucatini, and lamb Siciliana, along with some delicious daily specials like roasted white sea bass. Desserts include *tres leches* cake, berry napoleon, and chocolate truffles with fresh strawberries. ⊠ *300 2nd Ave.* ☎ *303/652–1607* ⊕ *www.treppedas.com* ▭ *AE, MC, V* ⊙ *Closed Sun.*

$$

▦ **Niwot Inn and Spa.** Now redecorated from the baseboards up, this small inn has a cozy, Southwestern feel, right down to the hardwood floors and handwoven wool rugs. Spacious, handsome rooms, all named for Colorado "Fourteener" peaks, are done in rustic reds and blues and outfitted with handmade aspen-wood furniture. Some rooms have gas fireplaces and comfy chairs. **Pros:** great Continental breakfast buffet; close to excellent restaurants. **Cons:** somewhat noisy neighborhood; drive to Boulder can be horribly congested. ⊠ *342 2nd Ave.* ⌂ *Box 1044, Niwot* ☎ *303/652–8452* ⊕ *www.niwotinn.com* ⏳ *14 rooms* ⚘ *In-room: Wi-Fi, flat-screen TV, a/c. In-hotel: public Wi-Fi, parking (free)* ▭ *AE, D, DC, MC, V* ⦿| *CP.*

SHOPPING

Antiques dealers and a few notable shops selling vintage women's clothing and quilts are in the Niwot historic district along 2nd Avenue. Just 0.25 mi east of old-town Niwot is Cottonwood Square, with a grocer, a gas station, a handful of gift shops, and a few eateries.

Niwot Antiques (⊠ *135 2nd Ave.* ☎ *303/652–2587*) is the area's biggest antiques dealer, with a large selection of antique furniture and other items. **Elysian Fields** (⊠ *6924 79th St.* ☎ *303/652–2587*) is an antiques auction house that holds a country estate auction the second Sunday of most months. **Wise Buys Antiques** (⊠ *190 2nd Ave.* ☎ *303/652–2888*) sells and repairs antique furniture, including fireplace mantels—some with mirrors—and usually has more than a hundred in stock.

7

LYONS

14 mi north of Boulder.

Lyons is a peaceful, down-to-earth community just inside the red-sandstone foothills at the confluence of the North St. Vrain and South St. Vrain creeks. Founded in 1881, it's crammed with historic buildings—there are 15 structures listed in the National Register of Historic Places—and the whole downtown area has the feel of a turn-of-the-century frontier outpost. The cafés, restaurants, art galleries, and antiques stores serve more than just the small population of 1,600. Visitors also come for the recreation opportunities and top-notch music festivals.

GETTING HERE AND AROUND
To drive to Lyons from Boulder, travel north on U.S. 36.

WHEN TO GO
FESTIVALS   The summer outdoor music season kicks off with **Lyons Good Old Days** at the end of June, and goes into September with midweek concerts in Sandstone Park (at 4th and Railroad avenues). Cafés and restaurants host bands regularly. Check the Chamber of Commerce Web site for event schedules.

Planet Bluegrass (☎ *303/823–0848 or 800/624–2422* ⊕ *www.bluegrass. com*) presents artists such as Susan Tedeschi, Indigo Girls, Patty Griffin, and Warren Haynes at the three bluegrass festivals it holds in Lyons: RockyGrass, at the end of July, the Folks Festival in August, and the Festival of the Mabon (autumn Equinox) in September.

ESSENTIALS
Visitor Info Lyons Chamber of Commerce (✉ *Box 426, Lyons* ☎ *303/823–5215 or 877/596–6726* ⊕ *www.lyons-colorado.com*).

SPORTS AND THE OUTDOORS
BIRD-WATCHING
Ornithologists gather at **Bohn Park** at sunrise and sunset to spot some of the many species of songbirds that reside along St. Vrain Creek. Golden eagles have been sighted in the red cliffs on the southwest side of town. Lazuli buntings inhabit the foliage along both the **Old St. Vrain Road** southwest of town and **Apple Valley Road** northwest of town. ✉ *From northbound U.S. 36, turn left onto Park St. and then left onto 2nd St.*

HIKING AND MOUNTAIN BIKING
★   More than 12 mi of trails at **Hall Ranch** are open to hikers, mountain bikers, and equestrians. The **Bitterbrush Trail/Nelson Loop** follows the Bitterbrush Trail for 3.7 mi and has a 680-foot elevation gain, crossing meadows and ascending and descending through stands of pine trees and rock outcroppings. It connects to the 2.2-mi Nelson Loop, which leads to the original Nelson Ranch House. The slight 400-foot elevation gain of the Nelson Loop brings you up onto a plateau that provides great views of the mountains to the north. Allow five to six hours to hike the trail, less for biking it. ✉ *0.75 mi west of Lyons on Hwy. 7* ⊕ *www.co.boulder.co.us/openspace.*

Rabbit Mountain has several lengthy but easy trails that afford views of the High Rockies and the plains. Be sure to pick up the interpretive pamphlet at the trailhead that explains the history of the area, including the dramatic metamorphosis of Rabbit Mountain from a lush, tropical swamp inhabited by dinosaurs to the present-day, mile-high desert that's home to raptors, prairie dogs, coyotes, and the occasional rattlesnake. The 2-mi round-trip **Little Thompson Overlook Trail** forks off to the left before you come to the gravel road and climbs a mere 500 feet to the point where you can see Longs Peak, the plains to the east, and Boulder Valley to the south. The 5-mi **Eagle Wind Trail** loop has short spurs to viewpoints. From the parking area, head out on the trail to the gravel road and then right onto the single-track loop. ⊠ *2 mi east of Lyons* ⊕ *www.co.boulder.co.us/openspace.*

WHERE TO EAT

$–$$ ✕ **Oskar Blues Cajun Grill & Brewery.** The first U.S. microbrewery to put
AMERICAN   its beer into cans, and now the largest-producing brewpub in America, Oskar Blues has become Lyons's hot spot for beer as well as music and pub grub. Try Dale's Pale Ale—it's not as hoppy as most American ales—or any of the other robust beers brewed in small (20-barrel) batches. The burgers are consistently awesome, and come in interesting varieties, including a spicy Creole number, plus three named in honor of music legends—Elvis, B.B. King, and Satchmo. Blues instruments and covers of blues CDs decorate the restaurant. In the basement, a "juke joint" frequently hosts live music, and there's a bluegrass jam every Tuesday night. ⊠ *303 Main St.* ☎ *303/823–6685* ⊕ *www.oskarblues. com* ▭ *AE, D, MC, V.*

ESTES PARK

40 mi northwest of Boulder via U.S. 36 (28th St. in Boulder).

The scenery on the U.S. 36 approach to Estes Park gives little hint of the grandeur to come, but if ever there was a classic picture-postcard Rockies view, Estes Park has it. The town sits at an altitude of more than 7,500 feet, in front of a stunning backdrop of 14,255-foot Longs Peak and surrounding mountains. The town itself is very family-oriented, albeit somewhat kitschy, with lots of stores selling Western-themed trinkets. Many of the small businesses and hotels lining the roads are mom-and-pop outfits that have been passed down through several generations. Estes Park is also the most popular gateway to Rocky Mountain National Park (RMNP), which is just a few miles down the road.

GETTING HERE AND AROUND

To get to Estes Park from Boulder, take U.S. 36 north through Lyons and the town of Pinewood Springs (about 38 mi). You also can reach Estes Park via the incredibly scenic Peak-to-Peak Scenic and Historic Byway. To reach the byway from Boulder, take Highway 119 west to Nederland and turn right (north) onto Highway 72, or follow Sunshine Canyon Drive/Gold Hill Road into Ward, and pick up Highway 72 there.

Estes Park's main downtown area is walkable, which is good news on summer weekends, when traffic can be heavy (and parking can be challenging).

The National Park Service operates a free bus service in and around Estes Park and between Estes Park and Rocky Mountain National Park. Buses operate daily from early June to Labor Day, then on weekends only until the end of September.

ESSENTIALS

Transportation Contacts NPS Shuttle Buses (☎ 970/586–1206 ⊕ www.nps. gov/room/planyourvisit/shuttle_bus_route.htm).

Visitor Info Estes Park Convention and Visitors Bureau (⊠ 500 Big Thompson Ave. ⬧ Box 1200 ☎ 970/577–9900 or 800/443–7837 ⊕ www.estesparkcvb.com).

EXPLORING

As a resort town, Estes attracted the attention of genius entrepreneur F. O. Stanley, inventor of the Stanley Steamer automobile and several photographic processes. In 1905, having been told by his doctors he would soon die of tuberculosis, he constructed the regal **Stanley Hotel** on a promontory overlooking the town. Stanley went on to live another 30-odd years, an extension that he attributed to the area's fresh air. The hotel soon became one of the most glamorous resorts in the Rockies, a reputation it holds to this day. The hotel was the inspiration for Stephen King's horror novel *The Shining*, part of which he wrote while staying here.

Archaeological evidence displayed at the **Estes Park Area Historical Museum** makes an eloquent case that Native Americans used the area as a summer resort. The museum also has an assortment of pioneer artifacts, displays on the founding of Rocky Mountain National Park, and changing exhibits. The museum publishes a self-guided walking tour of historic sites, mostly along Elkhorn Avenue downtown. ⊠ 200 4th St. ☎ 970/586–6256 ⊕ www.estesnet.com/Museum 🖾 Free ⊙ May–Oct., Mon.–Sat. 10–5, Sun. 1–5; Nov.–Apr., Fri. and Sat. 10–5, Sun. 1–5.

The **MacGregor Ranch Museum,** on the National Register of Historic Places and a working ranch, offers views of the Twin Owls and Longs Peak (towering more than 14,000 feet). Although the ranch was homesteaded in 1873, the present house was built in 1896; it provides a well-preserved record of typical ranch life. ⊠ MacGregor Ave. off U.S. 34 ☎ 970/586–3749 ⊕ www.macgregorranch.com 🖾 $3 ⊙ June–Aug., Tues.–Fri. 10–4.

SPORTS AND THE OUTDOORS

Rocky Mountain National Park, 4 mi from Estes Park, is ideal for hiking, fishing, wildlife-viewing, rock climbing, snowshoeing, and cross-country skiing. *See the Rocky Mountain National Park section in this book.*

FISHING

The Big Thompson River, which runs east of Estes Park along U.S. 34, is popular for its good stock of rainbow and brown trout. See ⊕ www.wildlife.state.co.us/fishing for more information on fishing licenses. **Rocky Mountain Adventures** (⊠ 358 E. Elkhorn Ave., ☎ 970/586–6191 or 800/858–6808 ⊕ www.shoprma.com) offers guided fly- and float-fishing trips on the Big Thompson and in Rocky Mountain National Park from its Estes Park office.

HORSEBACK RIDING

Sombrero Ranches (☎ 970/586–4577 ⊕ www.sombrero.com) has several stables in the Estes Park region, including Rocky Mountain National Park. They offer both guided and unguided trail rides (from one to eight hours long), plus overnight camping trips, breakfast rides, and steak dinner rides.

RAFTING AND KAYAKING

White-water rafting trips fill up fast, so it's a good idea to book with an outfitter a couple of weeks in advance.

OUTFITTERS **Rapid Transit Rafting** (☎ 970/577–7238 or 800/367–8523 ⊕ www. rapidtransitrafting.com) arranges guided rafting trips on the Colorado and Cache la Poudre rivers. **Rocky Mountain Adventures** (☎ 970/493–4005 or 800/858–6808 ⊕ www.shoprma.com) provides half- and full-day kayaking-instruction trips for all levels. All gear is included.

WHERE TO EAT

$–$$ ✕ **Bighorn Restaurant.** An Estes Park staple since 1972, this family-run AMERICAN   outfit is where the locals go for breakfast. Since it opens as early as ★   6 AM, you can get a double-cheese omelet, huevos rancheros, or grits before heading into the park. Owners Laura and Sid Brown are happy to pack up a lunch for you—just place your order with breakfast, and your sandwich, chips, homemade cookie, and drink will be ready to go when you leave. This homey spot also serves lunch and dinner. ✉ 401 W. Elkhorn Ave. ☎ 970/586–2792 ⊕ www.estesparkbighorn. com ⊟ D, MC, V.

$–$$ ✕ **Ed's Cantina and Grill.** The fajitas and well-stocked bar make this lively MEXICAN   Mexican restaurant popular with locals and visitors alike. The decor is bright, with light woods and large windows. Try to get patio seating by the river. If you're hungry, try one of the enchilada platters—including mahimahi, chicken *mole*, and vegetarian—the authentic pork tamales, smothered in green or red chile sauce, or the *carne asada*. Breakfast is also good here (served until 11 AM on weekends), with both Mexican and all-American options. ✉ 390 E. Elkhorn Ave. ☎ 970/586–2919 ⊕ www.edscantina.com ⊟ AE, D, MC, V.

$$ ✕ **Estes Park Brewery.** If you're not sure which beer suits you or would AMERICAN   go with your meal, head downstairs to the tasting area to sample a couple of brews. There are eight beers and four seasonals on tap. The Staggering Elk, a crisp lager, and the Estes Park Gold ale come highly recommended. The food is no-frills (beer chili is the specialty here), and the menu includes pizza, burgers, sandwiches, and chicken or steak dinners. ✉ 470 Prospect Village Dr. ☎ 970/586–5421 ⊕ www.epbrewery. com ⊟ AE, D, MC, V.

$$$ ✕ **Hunter's Chophouse.** This popular steak house fills quickly in the eve-STEAK   ning, and for good reason. The locals head here for the savory and spicy barbecue: steaks, venison, buffalo, chicken, and seafood. If you're not hungry enough for 12 ounces of beef (or buffalo), Hunter's has special burgers, like the avocado bacon burger, and a long list of sandwiches,

including a traditional French dip and a grilled salmon fillet on focaccia. There's a good kids' menu, too, with fish-and-chips, a junior sirloin, and a mini burger. ⊠ *1690 Big Thompson Ave.* ☎ *970/586–6962* ⊕ *www. hunterschophouse.net* ⌕ *Reservations essential* ☐ *AE, D, MC, V.*

$$–$$$ ✗ **Mama Rose's.** An Estes institution, Mama Rose's serves consistently
ITALIAN   good family-style Italian meals. The lasagna with sliced meatballs and sausage and the tricolor baked pasta are popular entrées, and the wine cellar has a good selection. The spacious Victorian dining room with plenty of fine art harks back to earlier eras in Estes Park, minus the formal dress code. In warm weather there's a patio along the Big Thompson River. ⊠ *338 E. Elkhorn Ave.* ☎ *970/586–3330* ⊕ *www. mamarosesrestaurant.com* ☐ *AE, D, DC, MC, V* ☺ *No lunch.*

$ ✗ **Poppy's Pizza & Grill.** This casual riverside eatery serves the classics,
PIZZA   plus creative signature pizzas. Try the spinach, artichoke, and feta pie made with sun-dried tomato pesto or one made with smoked trout, capers, and cream cheese. You can also create your own pie from the five sauces and 40 toppings on the menu. They also sell sandwiches, wraps, salads, and burgers. Poppy's has patio seating at the river and an extensive selection of wine and beer. ⊠ *342 E. Elkhorn Ave.* ☎ *970/586– 8282* ⊕ *www.poppyspizzaandgrill.com* ☐ *AE, D, DC, MC, V* ☺ *Closed Jan., plus Thanksgiving, Christmas, and Easter.*

WHERE TO STAY

$$$ ▦ **Boulder Brook.** Luxury suites at this secluded spot on the river are tucked into the pines, yet close to town and 1½ mi from Rocky Mountain National Park. Sleep regally on linens with at least 300-thread count. All the suites have private entrances and are furnished and appointed individually—stylishly and elegantly. Suites have either a full kitchen or kitchenette, a private deck, and a gas fireplace, and all but two have a jetted tub. **Pros:** scenic location; quiet area; attractive grounds. **Cons:** not within walking distance of attractions; no nearby dining. ⊠ *1900 Fall River Rd.,* ☎ *970/586–0910 or 800/238–0910* ⊕ *www.boulderbrook.com* ➾ *19 suites* ⌂ *In-room: no a/c, kitchen (some), DVD. In-hotel: parking (free)* ☐ *AE, D, MC, V.*

¢–$ ▦ **Estes Park Center/YMCA of the Rockies.** This 890-acre family-friendly
☺   property has a wealth of attractive and clean lodging options among its five lodges and 11 cabins. Sign up for a class and learn a skill like calligraphy, fly-fishing, or compass reading. Accommodations range from lodge rooms (with either queen beds or bunks) and simple cabins for two to four people up to larger cabins that can take as many as 40 people. A meal plan is available for the all-you-can-eat buffet. There's a Frisbee-golf course, and a climbing wall to hone your rock-climbing skills. **Pros:** good value for large groups and for longer stays; lots of family-oriented activities and amenities; stunningly scenic setting. **Cons:** very large, busy, and crowded property; fills fast; location requires vehicle to visit town or the national park. ⊠ *2515 Tunnel Rd.,* ☎ *970/586–3341, 303/448–1616, or 800/777–9622* ⊕ *www. ymcarockies.org* ➾ *688 rooms, 220 cabins* ⌂ *In-room: no a/c, no TV. In-hotel: restaurant, tennis court, pool, children's programs (ages 3–18), parking (free)* ☐ *MC, V* ⦿ *MAP.*

$-$$ ⬚ **Glacier Lodge.** Families are the specialty at this secluded, 19-acre guest
♻   resort on the banks of the Big Thompson River. The kids will take home
plenty of fun memories from the twice-weekly "soda saloons," nature
walks, arts-and-crafts workshops, and campfires. The whole family will
enjoy the once-weekly "mountain breakfast" with omelets and flap-
jacks before a guided trail ride, some into the national park. You can
stay in former Colorado governor (in office 1902–04) James Peabody's
summer residence. There's a minimum stay of four nights. All linens
and kitchen utensils and dinnerware are provided. **Pros:** great place for
families; attractive grounds on the river; on free bus route. **Cons:** not
within walking distance of attractions; along rather busy road. ✉ *2166
Hwy. 66* ⬚ *Box 2656,* ☎ *970/586–4401 or 800/523–3920* ⊕ *www.
glacierlodge.com* ⇝ *24 single-family cabins, 4 cabins for 12–30* ⬚ *In-
room: no a/c, kitchen (some), TV, DVD. In-hotel: pool, children's programs (ages 4–10), parking (free)* ⊟ *AE, D, MC, V.*

$$-$$$ ⬚ **Mary's Lake Lodge and Resort.** This 1913 chalet-style lodge overlooks
peaceful Mary's Lake, a couple of miles south of town. Original woodwork and antiques adorn the rooms; look for the Victorian floral lamps
in the hallways. Some rooms still have claw-foot tubs, and others have
Jacuzzi tubs. The elegant in-house restaurant, the Chalet Room ($$$–
$$$$), serves such entrées as cioppino, bouillabaisse, and Provimi veal
chops, and has an excellent wine list. Reservations are essential. The
Tavern ($$$) is more casual, and has seating on the porch with expan-
sive views. Popular dishes are the shepherd's pie and the lamb shank.
There's live music every night: an ever-changing roster of musicians in
the Tavern, plus a classical guitarist in the Chalet Room on Fridays
and Saturdays. The lodge also rents fully modern luxury condominiums that can accommodate up to 6 people. **Pros:** two excellent on-
site restaurants; beautiful views. **Cons:** not within walking distance
of attractions or other dining; large, older hotel. ✉ *2625 Mary's Lake
Rd.,* ☎ *970/586–5958 or 877/442–6279* ⊕ *www.maryslakelodge.com*
⇝ *16 rooms, 54 condos* ⬚ *In-room: Wi–Fi, TV, DVD player, kitch-
enette (some), a/c. In-hotel: 2 restaurants, pool, hot tub, spa, parking
(free)* ⊟ *AE, D, MC, V* ⊓⊙⊏ *CP.*

$-$$$ ⬚ **Riverview Pines.** Do some fishing or just sit and read on the expansive
lawn at this peaceful hotel, the least expensive along the beautiful Fall
River Road between Estes and Rocky Mountain National Park. You
can stay in a lodge room (with a fireplace or kitchenette) or a cabin
with full kitchen, fireplace, and deck (with a gas grill) facing the river. A
two-night stay is required. **Pros:** friendly and helpful owner-managers;
quiet and scenic location on river; low rates for the area. **Cons:** very
basic rooms without much decoration; on a busy road. ✉ *1150 W. Elk-
horn Ave.* ⬚ *Box 690, Estes Park* ☎ *970/586–3627 or 800/340–5764*
⊕ *www.riverviewpines.com* ⇝ *18 rooms, 8 cabins* ⬚ *In-room: no a/c,
kitchen (some), refrigerator. In-hotel: hot tub, laundry facilities, parking
(free)* ⊟ *D, MC, V* ⊙ *Closed mid-Oct.–May.*

$-$$ ⬚ **Saddle & Surrey Motel.** Friendly owners manage this comfortable and
quiet 1950s-style motel that is close to town and outdoor activities.
The pristine rooms are all at ground level, and have all been updated
with new bathrooms, plumbing, and carpet. Some have fireplaces or

7

kitchenettes. Note that there is no smoking on-site. **Pros:** good value; on shuttle-bus route; quiet area at night. **Cons:** not within walking distance of attractions or downtown dining. ⊠ *1341 S. St. Vrain Ave.* ☐ *Box 591, Estes Park* ☎ *970/586–3326 or 800/204–6226* ⊕ *www. saddleandsurrey.com* ➲ *26 rooms* ⚲ *In-room: Wi-Fi. In-hotel: pool, hot tub, parking (free)* ▤ *D, MC, V* ⅋ *CP.*

$$$–$$$$ ⊡ **Stanley Hotel.** Perched regally on a hill, with a commanding view of the
★ the town, the Stanley is one of Colorado's great old hotels, impeccably maintained in its historic state, yet with all the modern conveniences. Inventor and entrepreneur F.O. Stanley began construction in 1907, and when the hotel opened in 1909 it was the first in the world with electricity and the first in the United States with in-room telephones. The hotel that inspired Stephen King's novel *The Shining* conducts historical and "ghost" tours daily, and the hotel is a popular location for weddings (they're booked back-to-back most weekends). Many of the sunny rooms have mountain views and are decorated with antiques and period reproductions. **Pros:** historic hotel; many rooms have been updated recently; good restaurant. **Cons:** some rooms are small and tight, building is old; no air-conditioning. ⊠ *333 Wonderview Ave.,* ☎ *970/586–4000 or 800/976–1377* ⊕ *www.stanleyhotel.com* ➲ *138 rooms* ⚲ *In-room: no a/c, TV (some), Wi-Fi. In-hotel: restaurant, bar, pool, spa, public Wi-Fi, parking (free)* ▤ *AE, D, DC, MC, V.*

$$$ ⊡ **Taharaa Mountain Lodge.** Every room at this luxury B&B accesses the wraparound deck and its views of the High Rockies and Estes Valley. Rooms are decorated with individual themes, like indigenous cultures (the Ute Indian), floral (the Columbine), and fishing (the Big Thompson), and all have a gas fireplace. Enjoy happy hour in the Great Room. The full breakfast hints at the owners' Southern heritage. Note that there is no smoking on the property. **Pros:** beautiful mountain views; friendly hosts. **Cons:** not within walking distance of attractions; not on bus route; no young children allowed; two-day minimum stay (three-day minimum for summer and holidays). ⊠ *3110 S. St. Vrain Ave.* ☐ *Box 2586, 4 mi south of downtown Estes Park* ☎ *970/577–0098 or 800/597–0098* ⊕ *www.taharaa.com* ➲ *9 rooms, 9 suites* ⚲ *In-room: a/c, DVD, TV, Wi-Fi. In-hotel: spa, gym, sauna, parking (free), no kids under 13* ▤ *AE, D, MC, V* ⅋ *BP.*

NIGHTLIFE AND THE ARTS

THE ARTS

Visit up to 20 galleries and artists' studios on the self-guided **Summer Art Walk** daily from mid-June through Labor Day—or take the same route in the **Autumn Art Walk**, which goes from mid-September to late November. Maps and information are available at **Cultural Arts Council of Estes Park** (⊠ *304 E. Elkhorn Ave.* ☐ *Box 4135,* ☎ *970/586–9203* ⊕ *www.estesarts.com*). The Council also operates a fine art gallery and hosts other art walks, studio tours, art shows, concerts, and film events throughout the year.

The **Estes Park Music Festival** (☎ *970/586–9519* ⊕ *www.estesparkmusicalfestival.org*) stages concerts at 2 PM on Sunday afternoons from

November through April at the Stanley Hotel.

Relax with some chamber music while taking in views of the mountains at the **Rocky Ridge Music Center** (✉ *465 Longs Peak Rd., 9 mi south of Estes Park off Hwy. 7 at the turnoff to Longs Peak Campground* ☎ *970/586–4031* ⊕ *www.rockyridge.org*). The faculty hold their own classical chamber music concerts June through August.

ESTES PARK LODGING ALTERNATIVES

Range Property Management (✉ *342 W. Riverside Dr.* ✆ *Box 316,* ☎ *970/586–7626 or 888/433–5211* ⊕ *www.rangeprop.com* ▭ *No credit cards*) rents fully equipped houses, condos, and cabins in the Estes Park area. Pets are not allowed.

NIGHTLIFE

Blues and rock bands play regularly at **Lonigans Saloon** (✉ *110 W. Elkhorn Ave.* ☎ *970/586–4346* ⊕ *www.lonigans.com*), and there are open mike nights on Tuesdays and karaoke on Wednesdays and Fridays. **The Tavern** (✉ *Mary's Lake Lodge, 2625 Mary's Lake Rd.* ☎ *970/586–5958* ⊕ *www.maryslakelodge.com*) has live music, ranging from bluegrass to funk, every night. The venerable **Wheel Bar** (✉ *132 E. Elkhorn Ave.* ☎ *970/586–9381* ⊕ *www.thewheelbar.com*) is among the choice watering holes in town.

SHOPPING

Shopping in Estes Park includes a few run-of-the-mill trinket, T-shirt, and souvenir shops, plus a number of upscale shops and galleries.

CRAFTS AND ART GALLERIES

The cooperative **Earthwood Artisans** (✉ *145 E. Elkhorn Ave.* ☎ *970/586–2151*) features the work of jewelers, sculptors, wood-carvers, and potters. **Earthwood Collections** (✉ *141 E. Elkhorn Ave.* ☎ *970/577–8100* ⊕ *www.earthwoodartisans.com*) is a cooperative that sells a wide assortment of art, including ceramics and photography. **Estes ParkGlassworks** (✉ *323 Elkhorn Ave.* ☎ *970/586–8619* ⊕ *www.epglassworks.com*) offers glassblowing demonstrations and sells a rainbow of glass creations. **Images of Rocky Mountain National Park** (✉ *205A Park La.* ☎ *970/372–5212* ⊕ *www.imagesofrmnp.com*) showcases photographer Erik Stensland's stunning images of the park. **Spectrum** (✉ *116 E. Elkhorn Ave.,* ☎ *970/586–2497*) sells fine arts and crafts exclusively by Colorado studio artists, including spectacular nature photography, hand-thrown and signed pottery, and hand-turned woodcrafts made from mesquite, aspen, and cedar. **Wild Spirits Gallery, Ltd.** (✉ *148 W. Elkhorn Ave.* ☎ *970/586–4392* ⊕ *www.wildspiritsgallery.com*) carries open and limited-edition prints, both photographs and paintings or drawings, of the Southwest and Rocky Mountain National Park.

GIFTS

Head to **Thirty Below Leather** (✉ *356 E. Elkhorn Ave.* ☎ *970/586–2211* ☉ *Closed Sun.*) for high-quality leather travel gear, handbags, wallets, and accessories, all priced at less than $30. **Rocky Mountain Chocolate Factory and Malt Shop** (✉ *125 Moraine Ave.* ☎ *970/586–5652* ⊕ *www.*

rmcfestespark.com) sells fudge, truffles, and fantastic caramel apples, plus traditional malts and shakes.

WESTERN PARAPHERNALIA
Rustic Mountain Charm (⊠ *135 E. Elkhorn Ave.* ☎ *970/586–4344* ⊕ *www. rusticmountaincharm.net*) sells clothing, local foodstuffs, and home accessories with the lodge look, including furniture, quilts, baskets, and throws. **The Twisted Pine Fur and Leather Company** (⊠ *450 Moraine Ave.* ☎ *970/586–4539 or 800/896–8086* ⊕ *www.thetwistedpine.com*) carries certified Native American–made weavings and traditional leather or fur Western clothing, as well as housewares, rugs, and jewelry.

GRAND COUNTY

Grand County is the high country and rolling ranchlands at once. Vistas of the Rockies to the east and south and of the Gore Range to the west frame these grasslands, which the early French explorers named Middle Park. By the time the Moffat Railroad came to Grand County in 1905, ranchers were already living on the flat, open meadows.

Although Grand County is ranching country, the word "range" today evokes more the excellent golf courses instead of the plains where cowboys herd cattle. The town of Granby has two golf courses, and Grand County hosts several annual tournaments. Golfers aren't the only sportsmen in town: summer brings droves of anglers and cyclists, and large-game hunters replace them in the late fall. The area west of Granby along U.S. 40 is marked by a number of small towns with resorts and guest ranches.

GRAND LAKE

1.5 mi west of Rocky Mountain National Park via U.S. 34.

The tiny town of Grand Lake, known to locals as Grand Lake Village, is doubly blessed by its surroundings. It's the western gateway to Rocky Mountain National Park and also sits on the shores of its namesake, the state's largest natural lake and the highest-altitude yacht anchorage in America. With views of snowy peaks and verdant mountains from any vantage point, Grand Lake Village is favored by Coloradans for sailing, canoeing, waterskiing, and fishing. In winter it's *the* snowmobiling and ice-fishing destination. Even with its wooden boardwalks, Old West–style storefronts, and usual assortment of souvenir shops and motels, the town seems less spoiled than many other resort communities.

GETTING HERE AND AROUND
Grand Lake is about 60 mi from Boulder or 96 mi from Denver, as the crow flies, but to get there by car you've got to circle around the mountains and travel more than 100 mi from Boulder and 171 mi from Denver. You've got two options: Take the highway the whole way (U.S. 36, CO Hwy. 93, I–70, U.S. 40, and U.S. 34) or take the scenic route (U.S 36 north to Estes Park, then U.S. 34 across Rocky Mountain National Park). The section of U.S. 34 that passes through RMNP, known as Trail

Base Camp: Estes Park or Grand Lake?

Many more people stay in **Estes Park** rather than Grand Lake because it's closer to the cities of the Front Range—but the traffic, particularly on summer weekends, reflects that. Expect parking in downtown Estes Park to be difficult, and count on delays while driving through town. There are also more options for lodging and meals here than in Grand Lake. A hotel room averages $150 per night, and a burger will run you about $8. The Safeway in Stanley Village at the intersection of U.S. 34 (Big Thompson Ave.) and U.S. 36 (St. Vrain Ave.) is the best place to pick up insect repellent, sunscreen, and water and snacks (including deli sandwiches) for hiking.

Grand Lake is a smaller resort than Estes Park. Getting around in a car is easier, and parking is rarely a problem. It's also a bit closer—only 2 mi—from Grand Lake village to the RMNP entrance. The outdoor activities here are more diverse than in Estes Park; the list includes water sports on Grand Lake, mountain biking, and snowmobiling. Grand Lake village is also close to skiing and ice-fishing, and hiking in the Indian Peaks Wilderness and the Arapaho National Recreation Area. A hotel room averages about $110 per night, and a burger costs around $8. The Mountain Food Market at 400 Grand Avenue sells insect repellent, water, and snacks for hiking.

Ridge Road, is the highest paved road in America. Trail Ridge Road closes every winter, typically between mid-October and late May.

When you get there, you can explore most of the town on foot, including the historic boardwalk on Grand Avenue, with more than 60 shops and restaurants. Happily, Grand Lake doesn't get the hordes of tourists that can descend on Estes Park, meaning traffic and parking aren't a problem.

ESSENTIALS

Visitor Info Grand Lake Chamber of Commerce Visitor Center (⊠ *West Portal Rd. and U.S. 34, at the western entrance of Rocky Mountain National Park* ☎ *970/627–3402 or 800/531–1019* ⊕ *www.grandlakechamber.com*).

EXPLORING

★ According to Ute legend, the fine mists that shroud **Grand Lake** at dawn are the risen spirits of women and children whose raft capsized as they were fleeing a marauding party of Cheyennes and Arapahoes. Grand Lake feeds into two much larger man-made reservoirs, Lake Granby and Shadow Mountain Lake, which together form the "Great Lakes of Colorado."

SPORTS AND THE OUTDOORS

Rocky Mountain National Park, 2 mi from Grand Lake Village, is ideal for hiking, fishing, wildlife-viewing, rock climbing, snowshoeing, and cross-country skiing. *See the Rocky Mountain National Park section in this book.*

Grand Lake Sports (⊠ *900 Grand Ave.* ☎ *970/627–8124*) is an all-purpose outfitter that rents and sells snowshoes, kayaks, canoes, and pet gear. When they're not at work, staff members are out hiking and bicycling the region, and therefore give excellent advice about fun outdoor experiences for thrill-seeking adventurers as well as for families.

BIKING

One of the best bike rides in the state starts just down the road from Grand Lake, in Granby. The **Willow Creek Pass** route covers about 25 mi (round-trip) of rolling terrain and climbs 1,770 feet to the summit of one of the gentler passes on the Continental Divide. This ride takes you through quiet aspen and pine forests where you'll encounter little traffic (but perhaps some moose and deer, which are often spotted just off the road). ⊠ *The route starts on U.S. 40 in Granby and goes north to Hwy. 125 to County Rd. 21, then turns around and goes back the same way.*

BIRD-WATCHING

The islands in Shadow Mountain Reservoir and Lake Granby are wildlife refuges home to osprey and many other migrating birds. The best way to get close to them is by canoe or foot trail. Be sure to take binoculars, because you're not permitted to land on the islands. **East Shore Trail** and **Knight Ridge Trail** will take you along the shores of Shadow Mountain Reservoir and Lake Granby for good bird-spotting opportunities. Shadow Mountain Lake lies within the Arapaho National Recreation Area, and is maintained through the Sulphur Ranger District in Granby; contact them for more information: 970/887–4100. ⊠ *Access trails either from Grand Lake Village between Grand Lake and Shadow Mountain Reservoir, or from Green Ridge Campground at south end of Shadow Mountain Reservoir.*

BOATING AND FISHING

There's plenty of water to share here. Anglers enjoy plentiful catches of rainbow trout, mackinaw (lake trout), and kokanee salmon; recreational sailors and water-skiers ply acres of water; and paddlers still get to canoe in peace. Ice fishers will not want to miss the big contest held the first weekend in January on Lake Granby. Contestants must catch five different species of fish, and winners collect from the booty of $20,000 in cash and prizes. See ⊕ *www.wildlife.state.co.us/fishing* for more information on fishing licenses.

OUTFITTERS **Beacon Landing Marina** rents 20-, 24-, and 29-foot pontoon boats and fishing equipment, including ice augers and ice rods. ⊠ *1026 County Rd 64, drive south 5 mi on U.S. 34 to County Rd. 64, turn left and go 1 mi* ☎ *970/627–3671* ⊕ *www.beaconlanding.us.*

Visit the **Trail Ridge Marina** (⊠ *12634 U.S. 34, 2 mi south of Grand Lake on U.S. 34* ☎ *970/627–3586* ⊕ *www.trailridgemarina.com*) on the western shore of Shadow Mountain Lake to rent a Sea-Doo or motor boat for two to six hours.

HIKING

A hike here can be a destination in itself: generally speaking, the trails on this side of the Continental Divide are longer than those on the Western Slope, meaning you'll trek farther and higher than you might have expected to your destination. Many trails take you 5 mi one-way before you reach a lake or peak. If you hike in the backcountry, be sure you're outfitted for adverse weather. The *National Geographic Trails Illustrated Map No. 503* (Winter Park/Grand Lake) has excellent coverage of hiking and biking trails in the area, with information about regulations.

For those who'd rather not venture quite so far, there are many shorter hikes in and around Grand Lake, all of which offer gorgeous scenery and wonderful relaxation, as the trails here tend to have fewer hikers on them than those near Estes Park.

At the southeast end of Lake Granby, the **Indian Peaks Wilderness Area,** located within the Arapaho National Recreation Area, is great for hiking. The area around Monarch Lake is popular with families for the selection of trails and the views of the Indian Peaks and the Continental Divide. Trails range in distance from 1.5 to 10.8 mi one-way. The easy **Monarch Lake Loop** is 3.8 mi and a mere 110 feet in elevation gain. You can get a day pass ($5) from the staff or at the self-serve pay station. ⊠ *Take U.S. 34 south to County Rd. 6. Follow the lakeshore road about 10 mi* ☎ *970/887–4100* ⊕ *www.fs.fed.us/r2/arnf/recreation/trails/srd/monarchlake/shtml.*

HORSEBACK RIDING

Sombrero Ranches. Sombrero's Grand Lake stables offers guided rides into the wilderness and national park, including scenic and relaxing early-morning breakfast rides, evening rides (including cowboy-style steak and beans for dinner), and "drop camps," in which they'll bring you and your gear into the backcountry via horseback, then bring the horses back and get you a day or two later. Guided horseback-riding trips last two hours, four hours, or all day. ⊠ *304 W. Portal Rd.* ☎ *970/627–3514* ⊕ *www.sombrero.com* ⊠ *$50–$120 for guided rides, $200 per horse for drop camps* ☉ *Mid-May–mid-Sept.*

NORDIC SKIING AND SNOWSHOEING

When crystalline snow glitters under the clear blue sky, it's time to strap on skis or snowshoes and hit the trails in Rocky Mountain National Park, the Arapaho National Recreation Area, and the Indian Peaks Wilderness Area. You also can stay in town: the **Grand Lake Metropolitan Recreation District** (⊠ *1415 County Rd. 58* ⟟ *Box 590,* ☎ *970/627–8872* ⊕ *www.grandlakerecreation.com*) has nearly 22 mi (35 km) of cross-country ski trails with views of the Never Summer Range and the Continental Divide. Come springtime, they open another 15 mi of hiking and biking trails. **Never Summer Mountain Products** (⊠ *919 Grand Ave.* ☎ *970/627–3642* ⊕ *www.neversummermtn.com*) rents cross-country skis, backcountry skis and snowshoes, plus packs and camping equipment.

SNOWMOBILING

Many consider Grand Lake to be Colorado's snowmobiling capital, with more than 300 mi of trails (150 mi groomed), many winding through virgin forest. There are several rental and guide companies in the area. If you're visiting during the winter holidays, it's wise to make reservations about three weeks ahead. **Grand Adventures LLC** (⊠ *304 W. Portal Rd.* ☎ *970/726-9247 or 800/726–9247* ⊕ *www.grandadventures.com*) offers guided tours and arranges unguided rentals. **On The Trail Rentals** (⊠ *1447 County Rd. 491* ☎ *970/627–0171 or 888/627–2429* ⊕ *www.onthetrailrentals.com*) rents snowmobiles and organizes unguided trips into Arapaho National Forest.

WHERE TO EAT

$
CAFES
Fodor's Choice
★

✕ **Fat Cat Cafe.** Located right on the boardwalk, this small one-room breakfast and lunch spot offers delicious food at very reasonable prices. Their $12 weekend breakfast buffet is downright amazing, with close to 50 items at a time—everything from biscuits and gravy to scones and Scotch eggs to Mexican-style omelets with beans and green chile. If you have to wait for a table (which you might on a summer Sunday), they offer coffee and cinnamon rolls to tide you over. ⊠ *916 Grand Ave.,* ☎ *970/627–0900* ☰ *MC, V* ⊗ *Open Mon. and Wed.–Fri. 7–2, Sat.–Sun. 7–1, closed Tues.*

¢
AMERICAN

✕ **Grand Lake Brewing Company.** A handcrafted beer and a bratwurst with the works or a pulled chicken sandwich will hit the spot at this rustic brewpub outfitted with a tin ceiling and wooden bar with brass rails. Eat at the bar or at a table in the small but sunny dining area; the food is standard pub fare, inexpensive if uninspired. The beer's the real draw here. For example, the crisp and light White Cap Wheat is an unfiltered brew that tastes best with a slice of orange or lemon, while the Plaid Bastard, a rich Scotch ale served in a brandy snifter to highlight its deep aromas and flavors, really packs a punch at 8% alcohol. Can't decide? Try a flight—4 oz of each of the 9 available beers—then take home a 64-oz growler as a memento of your visit. ⊠ *915 Grand Ave.,* ☎ *970/627–1711* ⊕ *www.grandlakebrewing.com* ☰ *AE, D, MC, V.*

$$
SOUTHERN

✕ **Sagebrush BBQ & Grill.** Falling-off-the-bone, melt-in-your-mouth barbecue pork, chicken, and beef draw local and out-of-town attention to this homey café, where you can munch on old-fashioned peanuts (and toss the shells on the floor) while waiting for your table. Comforting sides such as baked beans, corn bread, coleslaw, and potatoes top off the large plates. The breakfast menu includes omelets, pancakes, and biscuits as well as chicken-fried steak and *huevos rancheros* platters for heartier appetites. ⊠ *1101 Grand Ave.* ☎ *970/627–1404 or 866/900–1404* ⊕ *www.sagebrushbbq.com* ☰ *AE, D, DC, MC, V.*

WHERE TO STAY

$–$$
Fodor's Choice
★

▦ **Historic Rapids Lodge & Restaurant.** This handsome lodgepole-pine structure on the Tonahutu River dates to 1915. The seven lodge rooms—each with ceiling fan—are done in the Rocky Mountain rustic style with a mix of antique furnishings such as claw-foot tubs and carved-hardwood beds. The innkeepers also rent condos for large groups or families. The delightful Rapids Restaurant ($$$–$$$$) is Grand Lake's most romantic for fine dining, with stained glass and timber beams. Select a cocktail from the excellent wine list and enjoy it creekside before dinner. The specialty is Rapids' tournedo—an 8-ounce filet mignon with artichokes and béarnaise sauce. **Pros:** in-house restaurant; condos are great for longer stays; quiet area of town. **Cons:** unpaved parking area; lodge rooms are above restaurant; all lodge rooms are on second floor and there's no elevator. ⊠ *209 Rapids La.,* ⬚ *Box 1400* ☎ *970/627–3707* ⊕ *www.rapidslodge.com* ⇔ *6 rooms, 8 suites, 5 cabins, 10 condos* ⬚ *In-room: no a/c, kitchen (some). In-hotel: restaurant, bar, parking (free), some pets allowed* ☰ *AE, MC, V* ⊗ *Closed Apr. and Nov.*

$–$$

▦ **Mountain Lakes Lodge.** The scent of the pine forest welcomes you to these charming and comfortable log cabins whimsically decorated with animal and sports themes—down to the curtains and drawer pulls. The Little Log House has three bedrooms and can house nine people. Some cabins have private decks and gas stoves. Dogs are enthusiastically welcomed with treats in the cabins and their own private fenced yards. Cabins accommodate two to six humans. **Pros:** dog-friendly; close to fishing; good value. **Cons:** 4 mi from town (and services); two-day

> ### GRAND LAKE LODGING ALTERNATIVES
>
> **Grand Mountain Rentals** (✉ 1028 Grand Ave. ☎ Box 808, ☎ 970/627–1131 or 877/982–2155 ⊕ www.grandmountainrentals. com) arranges rentals—some pet-friendly—around Grand Lake for from three days to six months.

minimum stay (three-day minimum for holidays and special events). ✉ 10480 U.S. 34, ☎ Box 2062, ☎ 970/627–8448 or 877/627–3220 ⊕ www.mountainlakeslodge.com ⟁ 10 cabins, 1 house ⚹ In-room: no a/c, no phone, kitchen, Wi-Fi. In-hotel: parking (free), some pets allowed ⊟ MC, V.

$$ ▦ **Western Riviera Motel and Cabins.** All rooms in this friendly motel face the lake. It books up far in advance thanks to its relatively low prices, affable owners, and comfortable accommodations. Even the cheapest units—although small—are pleasant, done in mauve and earth tones. The motel also rents cabins with fully equipped kitchens in Grand Lake, some lakeside, for up to six persons. **Pros:** helpful and friendly staff; views of the lake; clean rooms. **Cons:** rooms and bathrooms can be a little cramped; lobby is a bit small. ✉ 419 Garfield Ave., ☎ 970/627–3580 ⊕ www.westernriv.com ⟁ 16 rooms, 22 cabins ⚹ In-room: no a/c, Wi-Fi. In-hotel: no-smoking rooms ⊟ MC, V.

NIGHTLIFE AND THE ARTS

THE ARTS

The professional **Rocky Mountain Repertory Theatre** (✉ Community Centre, 1025 Grand Ave. ☎ Box 1682, ☎ 970/627–3421 ⊕ www.rockymountainrep.com) stages performances of popular Broadway shows like Brigadoon and musicals such as Footloose and Seussical in a cabin-style theater.

NIGHTLIFE

The popular **Lariat Saloon** (✉ 1121 Grand Ave., on Boardwalk 80447 ☎ 970/627–9965) is the local hot spot, with live rock music almost every night. Look for the talking buffalo amid the eclectic Western decor. The bar also has pinball, pool, and darts.

SHOPPING

Shopping in Grand Lake tends toward the usual resort-town souvenir shops, although a handful of stores stand out.

Grand Lake Art Gallery (✉ 1117 Grand Ave. ☎ 970/627–3104 ⊕ www. grandlakeartgallery.com) purveys superlative photography, original oil paintings, wood carvings, weavings, pottery, stained glass, and paintings done by more than 180 Colorado artists.

Humphrey's Cabin Fever (✉ 1100 Grand Ave. ☎ 970/627–8939), housed in a 130-year-old log building, sells upscale cabin collectibles, rustic home furnishings, clothes, bedding, and ceramics—and lots of moose-themed stuff—in all price ranges.

For outdoor gear and clothing, head for **Never Summer Mountain Products** (⊠ *919 Grand Ave.* ☎ *970/627–3642* ⊕ *www.neversummermtn.com*).

GRANBY

20 mi south of Grand Lake via U.S. 34.

The small, utilitarian town of Granby (elevation 7,935 feet) serves the working ranches in Grand County, and you'll see plenty of cowboys, especially if you go to one of the weekly rodeos in summer. What the town lacks in attractions it makes up for with its views of Middle Park and the surrounding mountains of the Front and Gore ranges and with its proximity to outdoor activities, particularly its top-class golf courses just south of town.

GETTING HERE AND AROUND

Granby is 20 minutes from Rocky Mountain National Park and 15 minutes from the ski resorts Winter Park and Mary Jane and the mountain-biking trails of the Fraser Valley.

To get here from Grand Lake, take U.S. 34 south for 20 mi. From Boulder, you'll drive about 18 mi south on CO 93, 28 mi west on I–70, then take U.S. 40 north about 46 mi. From Denver, take U.S. 40 south (about 46 mi) to I–70, then drive east about 30 mi. You can also take the train: Amtrak's Zephyr train, which runs between Chicago and Emeryville, California, stops here twice a day. The town is pretty small, and you can easily find a parking spot and walk from one end to the other.

ESSENTIALS

Visitor Info Greater Granby Area Chamber of Commerce (⊠ *365 E. Agate, Suite B* ⊡ *Box 35,* ☎ *970/887–2311 or 800/325–1661* ⊕ *www.granbychamber.com*).

EXPLORING

Watch cowboys demonstrate their rodeo skills at the **Flying Heels Rodeo Arena** (⊠ *63032 U.S. 40, 1½ mi east of Granby* ☎ *970/887–2311* ⊕ *www.granbyrodeo.com*) every weekend beginning Memorial Day weekend. The rodeo finale and fireworks show is on the Saturday nearest the July 4 holiday.

SPORTS AND THE OUTDOORS

The **Greater Granby Area Chamber of Commerce** (☎ *970/887–2311* ⊕ *www.granbychamber.com*) has a free *Grand County Trail Map* that shows trails for hiking, biking, horseback riding, snowmobiling, and snowshoeing as well as information about regulations. You can also find the map at local sporting goods and outdoor stores.

BIRD-WATCHING

The reservoir at **Windy Gap Wildlife Viewing Area** is on the waterfowl migration route for geese, pelicans, swans, eagles, and osprey. The park has information kiosks, viewing scopes, viewing blinds, a picnic area, and a nature trail that's also wheelchair accessible. ⊠ *2 mi west of Granby on U.S. 40 where it meets Rte. 125* ☎ *970/725–6200* ◷ *May–Sept., daily dawn–dusk.*

FISHING

Serious fly fishers head to the rivers and streams of Grand County for relaxing solitude with excellent fishing in riparian areas. Angling on the **Fraser River** begins downstream from Tabernash, and is not appropriate for families or dogs. At **Willow Creek** you'll bag plenty of rainbow trout and brookies. The **Colorado River** between Shadow Mountain Dam and Lake Granby and downstream from Hot Sulphur Springs is also popular with anglers. See ⊕ *www.wildlife.state.co.us/fishing* for more information on fishing licenses.

GOLF

The scenery and wildlife-viewing opportunities at Grand County's four golf courses make good excuses for being distracted during a critical putt or drive. You can expect secluded greens, expansive vistas, and an occasional interruption from deer, foxes, elk, or even a moose.

★ **Grand Elk Ranch & Club.** Designed by PGA great Craig Stadler, the challenging course is reminiscent of traditional heathland greens in Britain. ✉ *1300 Tenmile Dr.* ☎ *970/887–9122 or 877/389–9333* ⊕ *www.grandelk.com* ⌂ *Reservations essential* ☖ *18 holes. Yards: 7,144/5,095. Par: 71/71. Green fee: $60/$125.*

Headwaters Golf Course at Granby Ranch. Tucked back in a valley at the end of a gravel road, entirely within the mountains and meadows, this club has roomy practice facilities as well as a large deck at the clubhouse. ✉ *2579 County Rd. 894 Drive 2 mi south on U.S. 40 from Granby to the Inn at Silver Creek. Turn left and drive past the lodge to the gravel road marked by the sign. Follow the road about 3 mi into the valley* ☎ *970/887–2709 or 888/850–4615* ⊕ *www.granbyranch.com* ⌂ *Reservations essential* ☖ *18 holes. Yards: 7,206/5,095. Par: 72/72. Green fee: $70–$90.*

MOUNTAIN BIKING

Indian Peaks Wilderness Area is not open to mountain biking, but there are moderate and difficult trails in the **Arapaho National Forest** (☎ *970/887–4100* ⊕ *www.fs.fed.us/r2/arnf*). In addition, Grand County has several hundred miles of easy to expert-level bike trails, many of which are former railroad rights-of-way and logging roads. The 3.2-mi one-way **Doe Creek Trail** is a good workout of uphill climbs (and descents) with plenty of forest scenery. ✉ *From Granby, take U.S. 34 to County Rd. 6 (Arapaho Bay Rd.) and follow it for about 3 mi. The trailhead is on your right.*

DOWNHILL SKIING

You can get in some skiing at **SolVista Basin at Granby Ranch,** a small but family-friendly ski area 2 mi south of Granby. ✉ *1000 Village Rd.* ☎ *888/850–4615* ⊕ *www.solvista.com* ✉ *$54.*

WHERE TO EAT AND STAY

$$ ✕ **Longbranch Restaurant and Schatzi's Pizza & Pasta.** This smoke-free West-
ECLECTIC ern-style family restaurant has a warming fireplace, rustic wood interior, and wagon-wheel chandeliers and is popular for its delicious German food (bratwurst, goulash, schnitzel, sauerbraten, and heavenly homemade spaetzle)—plus some decidedly non-German food (pizza and spaghetti). The traditional German desserts are authentic, and the strudel

7

gets particularly high marks. The bar serves many domestic and foreign beers as well as a few microbrews. ⊠ *185 E. Agate Ave. (U.S. 40)* ☎ *970/887–2209* ☐ *D, MC, V* ⊘ *Closed Sun. No lunch Oct.–May.*

GUEST RANCH
$$$$
⟳

▥ **C Lazy U Guest Ranch.** Secluded in a broad, verdant valley, this deluxe guest ranch attracts an international clientele, including both Hollywood royalty and the real thing. You enjoy your own personal horse, luxurious Western-style accommodations (with humidifiers), fine meals, live entertainment, and any outdoor activity you can dream up—it's the ultimate in hedonism without ostentation. The instructors are top-notch, the ratio of guests to staff is nearly one to one, and the children's programs are unbeatable. They'll take you up nearby Baldy Mountain in a snow cat during ski season, and are also a top-notch fly-fishing operation. The minimum stay is seven days in summer and five days during the December holiday season, but the ranch has a few summer weeks set aside with a shorter three-day minimum. All meals are included. **Pros:** kid- and family-friendly; helpful staff. **Cons:** rather distant from other area attractions; no pets. ⌂ *Box 379, Granby 3½ mi north on Hwy. 125 from U.S. 40 junction* ☎ *970/887–3344* ⊕ *www. clazyu.com* ⇆ *19 rooms, 20 cabins* ⚬ *In-room: no a/c, no phone, no TV. In-hotel: restaurant, bar, tennis courts, pool, gym, children's programs (ages 3–17), parking (free)* ☐ *AE, MC, V* ⊘ *Closed mid-Sept.–mid-Dec. and mid-Jan.–mid-May* ⊠ *AI.*

HOT SULPHUR SPRINGS

10 mi west of Granby via U.S. 40.

The county seat, Hot Sulphur Springs (population 512), is a faded resort town whose hot springs were once the destination for trains packed with people, including plenty of Hollywood types in the 1950s.

GETTING HERE AND AROUND

From Boulder, take U.S. 36 about 43 mi north to Estes Park. Take U.S. 34 west to Granby (53½ mi), then take U.S. 40 west for another 9 mi. From Fort Collins, take U.S. 287 south to Loveland (about 10 mi), then head west on U.S. 34 into Estes Park and then across Rocky Mountain National Park and into Granby (abut 54 mi). Turn onto U.S. 40 and drive about 9 mi west.

You'll need a car to explore this area, as attractions, dining, and lodging are spread out.

EXPLORING

Soak or pamper yourself with a massage, wrap, facial, or salt glow at the newly renovated **Hot Sulphur Springs Resort & Spa.** Temperatures range from 85° to 112°F in 20 open-air pools and four private, indoor pools. For views at 102°F, head for the slate pools uphill from the others. The seasonal swimming pool is just right for recreation at a comparatively frigid 80°F. ⊠ *5609 County Rd. 20, From U.S. 40, head north onto Park St., then go left onto Spring Rd./County Rd. 20. The resort is 0.7 mi ahead, on your right* ☎ *970/725–3306 or 800/510–6235* ⊕ *www. hotsulphursprings.com* ⊠ *$17.50* ⊘ *Daily 8 AM–10 PM.*

The old Hot Sulphur School is now the **Grand County Museum.** Artifacts depict Grand County history, including the original settlers 9,000 years ago, the role of pioneer women, and the archaeology of Windy Gap. Photographs show life in the early European settlements, and the original county courthouse and jail are on the site. ⊠ *110 E. Byers Ave.* ☏ *970/725–3939* ⊕ *www.grandcountymuseum.com* ⊠ *$4* ⊙ *Oct.–May, Wed.–Sat. 10–4; May–Oct., Tues.–Sat. 10–5.*

WHERE TO STAY

$ ⊞ **Hot Sulphur Springs Resort & Spa.** The 1940s rooms are newly refurnished and have comfortable lodgepole beds, desks, and en-suite showers, although the trains passing nearby can be noisy. Room rates include unlimited use of the pools during your stay. You can soak or pamper yourself with a massage, wrap, facial, or salt glow. The premises have no restaurant, but a diner in town serves breakfast and the Riverside Hotel occasionally serves dinner. Restaurants in Granby and Grand Lake are about 15 minutes and 30 minutes away, respectively. **Pros:** quick access to hot pools and spa; close enough that a visit can be tacked onto an outdoor activity. **Cons:** trains passing through during the night are noisy; most dining establishments are 30 minutes away. ⊠ *5609 County Rd. 20,* ☏ *970/725–3306 or 800/510–6235* ⊕ *www.hotsulphursprings. com* ⊲ *17 rooms, 1 cabin* ⊙ *In-room: no a/c, no phone, no TV, no pets. In-hotel: pool, parking (free)* ⊟ *MC, V.*

GUEST RANCH
$$$$
⟳

⊞ **Latigo Ranch.** Considerably more down-to-earth than other Colorado guest ranches, Latigo has a caring staff that helps create an authentic ranch experience. You can test your skills as a cowboy on a cattle drive or an overnight pack trip. The all-inclusive ranch also organizes white-water rafting excursions. Children's programs are tailored by age group, and the "Ute Scouts" overnight camping trip is a popular outing geared specifically to 6- to 10-year-olds. Accommodations are in comfortable, carpeted, one- to three-bedroom contemporary log cabins fitted with wood-burning stoves. Although providing fewer amenities than comparable properties, the ranch offers views of the Indian Peaks range, complete seclusion, and superb cross-country trails. Remember to bring your own beer. **Pros:** stunning scenery; quiet and secluded area. **Cons:** no nearby restaurants or other attractions. ⊠ *County Rd. 1911* ⌂ *Box 237, Kremmling* ☏ *970/724–9008 or 800/227–9655* ⊕ *www. latigotrails.com* ⊲ *10 cabins* ⊙ *In-room: no a/c, no phone, no TV. In-hotel: restaurant, pool, children's programs (ages 3–13), laundry facilities, public Wi-Fi, parking (free)* ⊟ *MC, V* ⊙ *Closed Apr., May, and mid-Oct.–mid-Dec.* ⊠ *AI.*

FORT COLLINS

The city sits on the cusp of the high plains of eastern Colorado, but is sheltered on the west by the lower foothills of the Rockies, giving residents plenty of nearby hiking and mountain-biking opportunities. By plugging a couple of gaps in the foothills with dams, the city created Horsetooth Reservoir, which you won't be able to see from town. To view the high mountains, you'll need to head up into Lory State Park or Horsetooth Mountain Park, which are just west of town. A walk through Old Town Square and the neighborhoods to its south and west demonstrates Fort Collins's focus on historic preservation.

The city was established in 1868 to protect traders from the natives, while the former negotiated the treacherous Overland Trail. After the flood of 1864 swept away Camp Collins—a cavalry post near today's town of LaPorte—Colonel Will Collins established a new camp on 6,000 acres where Fort Collins stands today. The town grew on two industries: education (CSU was founded here in 1879) and agriculture (rich crops of alfalfa and sugar beets). Today there are plenty of shops and art galleries worth visiting in this relaxed university city. With the Budweiser brewery and six microbreweries—the most microbreweries per capita in the state—crafting ales, lagers, and stouts, it's the perfect location for the two-day Colorado Brewers' Festival every June.

GETTING HERE AND AROUND

From Boulder, take U.S. 36 east to Interloken Loop/Storage Tek Drive, follow for about 0.3 mi, then get onto Northwest Highway for about 8.5 mi. Take Interstate 25 North for about 41 mi, get off at the Prospect Road exit. Head west on East Prospect Road for about 4 mi.

You can also get to Ft. Collins via Allegiant Air, which flies into Ft. Collins/Loveland Airport (FNL), about 15 mi south of town. They offer a direct flight to and from Las Vegas. There is a local taxi service, and the city's bus system, Transfort, operates more than a dozen routes throughout the city, which run primarily Monday to Saturday.

Downtown is very walkable, but you can also borrow wheels—for free—from the city's unique Bike Library for as little as an hour or as long as a week. There are two locations: the Café Bicyclette, at the corner of Walnut and Linden streets in Old Town Square, and at the Lory Student Center on the CSU campus.

WHEN TO GO

For Collins's outdoor recreation and cultural pursuits attract visitors year-round, but it is is definitely a college town, so you can expect a decidedly different atmosphere depending on whether or not CSU is in session.

FESTIVALS Colorado is ranked third in the United States in the number of brew-pubs and small breweries, and during the last full weekend of June more than 40 Colorado brewers show off their finest with 300 kegs of beer in Old Town Fort Collins at the **Colorado Brewers' Festival** (✉ *Old Town Sq.* ☎ *970/484–6500* ⊕ *www.downtownfortcollins.com*). There's live music by regional talent for the two-day, Colorado-brews-only festival that Fort Collins brewers started in 1989.

ESSENTIALS

Transportation Contacts Allegiant Air (☎ *702/508–8888* or *970/663–7307* ⊕ *www.allegiantair.com*). **Bike Lilbrary** (☎ *970/419–1050* or *970/491–6444* ⊕ *www.fcbikelibrary.org*). **Ft. Collins/Loveland Airport (FNL)** (✉ *4824 Earhart Rd.about 3½ mi west of I-25, off Mulberry St., Loveland* ☎ *970/962–2850* ⊕ *www.fortloveair.com*). **Ft. Collins Yellow Cab** (☎ *970/224–2222*). **Transfort** (⊕ *www.fcgov.com/transfort*).

Visitor Info Fort Collins Convention & Visitors Bureau (✉ *19 Old Town Square, Suite 137,* ☎ *970/232–3840* or *800/274–3678* ⊕ *www.ftcollins.com*).

EXPLORING

Numbers in the margin correspond to numbers on the Fort Collins map.

TOP ATTRACTIONS

❶ The Fort Collins Convention & Visitors Bureau has designated a historic walking tour of more than 20 buildings, including the original university structures and the stately sandstone **Avery House,** named for Franklin Avery, who planned the old town's broad streets when he surveyed the city in 1873. ✉ *328 W. Mountain Ave.* ☎ *970/221–0533* 🌐 *www.poudrelandmarks.com* 🎫 *Free* ⏲ *Wed. and Sun. 1–3.*

❷ **Old Town Square** (✉ *Mountain and College Aves.* ☎ *970/484–6500* 🌐 *www.downtownftcollins.com*), a National Historic District, is a pedestrian zone with sculptures, fountains, and 24 historic buildings, which now house shops, galleries, jewelers, boutiques, and bars. The square's several restaurants and cafés have plenty of shaded outdoor seating. In summer, musicians and theater groups entertain Thursday and Friday evenings and Sunday afternoon at 3 PM.

❸ The **Fort Collins Museum and Discovery Science Center** has historical and scientific exhibits designed to draw visitors of all ages. An 1860s-era cabin from the town's original military camp and a 1905 vintage schoolhouse are right on the museum grounds, and there are interactive exhibits geared to younger kids at the science center. ✉ *200 Matthews St.* ☎ *970/221–6738* 🌐 *www.fcmdsc.com* 🎫 *$4* ⏲ *Tues.–Sat. 10–5, Sun. noon–5. Closed Mon.*

❻ ★ Famous for its Fat Tire brand, the **New Belgium Brewing Company** also crafts a few brews available only on-site at the "mother ship" (the employees' term of endearment for their brewery). Tours of the first 100% wind-powered brewery in the United States are first-come, first-served, or can be reserved online. The brewery is north of Old Town, near Heritage Center Park. ✉ *500 Linden St.* ☎ *970/221–0524* 🌐 *www.newbelgium.com* 🎫 *Free* ⏲ *Tours Tues.–Sat. 10–6.*

WORTH NOTING

❹ CSU's Warner College of Natural Resources' **Environmental Learning Center** conducts educational tours for families and other groups on a 1.2-mi trail loop within a 200-acre nature preserve. The raptor cages and the walk-through wetland animal habitat are an excellent educational family activity, and fun for anyone curious about animal habitats. Staff conduct special walks like the full-moon hike. ✉ *Colorado Welcome Center, 3745 E. Prospect Rd.* ☎ *970/491–1661* 🌐 *www.cnr.colostate.edu/elc* 🎫 *$3.50* ✍ *Reservations essential* ⏲ *Information center mid-May–Aug., daily 10–5; Sept.–Apr., weekends 10–5. Learning Center year-round, daily dawn–dusk.*

❺ **Swetsville Zoo** is the unique creation of an insomniac dairy farmer who stayed up nights fashioning more than 150 dinosaurs, birds, insects, and other fantastic creatures from scrap metal, car parts, and old farm equipment. ✉ *4801 E. Harmony Rd., ¼ mi east of I–25* ☎ *970/484–9509* 🎫 *Free* ⏲ *Daily dawn–dusk (call for details).*

❼ Take in the brewing process up close and personally in a tour at the **Odell Brewing Company,** one of the first microbreweries to open shop in town in 1989—out of a pickup-truck bed. Eternally favorite 90 Shilling, Easy Street Wheat, and 5 Barrel Pale Ale are not to be missed. In winter, try the seasonal Isolation Ale. ⊠ *800 E. Lincoln Ave.* ☎ *970/498–9070 or 888/887–2797* ⊕ *www.odellbrewing.com* ⊠ *Free* ⊙ *Tap Room Mon.– Sat. 11–6; tours Mon.–Sat. 1, 2, and 3.*

❽ Learn lots of facts about the large-scale brewing process at **Anheuser- Busch** during a free tour. Free tours start every 30 minutes and last one hour and 15 minutes. If you're really interested in the goings on, sign up for a lengthier Brewmaster Tour ($25 per person, reservations essential), which will take you through the starting cellar, packaging facility, quality assurance department, and the Clydesdales stables. ⊠ *2351 Busch Dr.* ☎ *970/490–4691* ⊕ *www.budweisertours.com* ⊠ *Free* ⊙ *June– Sept., daily 10–4; Oct.–May, Thurs.–Mon. 10–4.*

OFF THE
BEATEN
PATH

State Forest State Park. Rugged peaks, thick forests, and burbling streams make up this 70,768-acre park. Here you can fish for trout, boat the azure alpine lakes, ride horseback, hike or mountain bike, and explore a few four-wheel-drive roads with views of the 12,000-foot Medicine Bow and Never Summer mountain ranges. Yurts and camping are available in winter, so you can explore the 70 mi of groomed snowmobiling trails or the 50 mi of groomed and signed cross-country skiing and snowshoeing trails. **Red Feather Guides and Outfitters** in Walden, a few mi west of the park, arrange guided fly-fishing and horseback-riding trips (⊠ *49794 Hwy. 14, Walden* ☎ *970/723–4204 or 970/524–5054* ⊕ *www.redfeatherguides.com*). **Never Summer Nordic** (⊠ *247 County Rd. 41* ☎ *970/723–4070* ⊕ *www.neversummernordic.com*) rents the yurts in the state park to hikers and mountain bikers (as well as snowshoers and backcountry or cross-country skiers) for hut-to-hut trips year-round. They also offer half-day, full-day, and overnight guided trips into the park. ⊠ *56750 Hwy. 14, Walden. From Ft. Collins, drive 75 mi west on Rte. 14 to County Rd. 41. From Granby, take U.S. 125 north to Walden (about 53 mi), then Hwy. 14 south for about 32 mi to County Rd. 41* ☎ *970/723–8366* ⊕ *www.parks.state.co.us/Parks/ StateForest* ⊠ *$6 a day per vehicle.*

SPORTS AND THE OUTDOORS

BIKING

Both paved-trail cycling and single-track mountain biking are within easy access of town.

The **Poudre River Trail** (about 20 mi round-trip) is an easy riparian jaunt within Fort Collins. ⊠ *Trailheads: Lions Park on North Overland Trail or Environmental Learning Center on East Drake Rd.*

For short, single-track rides, Pineridge and Maxwell trails do not disappoint, and connect to other trails for longer adventures. Head west on Drake Road to where it bends right and becomes South Overland Trail; turn left on County Road 42C and drive almost 1 mi to the posted fence opening. Serious gearheads crank at **Horsetooth Mountain Park** on the southwest side of Horsetooth Reservoir. Several single-tracks and jeep trails provide any level of challenge (⊕ *www.co.larimer.co.us/parks/ htmp.htm*).

OUTFITTER **Recycled Cycles** (✉ *4031 S. Mason St.* ☎ *970/223–1969 or 877/214–1811* ⊕ *www.recycled-cycles.com*) rents city bikes, mountain bikes, road bikes, kid trailers, and tandems for $25–$40 per day.

FISHING

The North Platte, Laramie, and Cache la Poudre rivers are renowned for excellent fishing. See ⊕ *www. wildlife.state.co.us/fishing* for more information on fishing licenses.

OUTFITTER The knowledgeable chaps at **St.**
★ **Peter's Fly Shop** (✉ *202 Remington St.* ☎ *970/498–8968* ⊕ *www. stpetes.com*) arrange half-day to full-day guided or instructional wade and float trips in northern Colorado and southern Wyoming that can include permits for waters not open to the public. The store also sells gear, and the staff gladly provides information on conditions to independent fishermen.

> ### NORTHERN FRONT RANGE BREWERIES
>
> The Front Range boasts several brewing firsts. In 1959 Coors of Golden introduced the first beer in an aluminum can. Boulder Beer is Colorado's first microbrewery, founded in 1979. The Great American Beer Festival, which started in 1981 in Boulder (now held in Denver), was the nation's first beer festival. A tour of northern Front Range breweries could take you through Boulder, Nederland, Lyons, Longmont, Loveland, Greeley, and finally Fort Collins, where you can visit the legendary Clydesdales at Anheuser-Busch.

GOLF

Mariana Butte Golf Course. This hilly course in Loveland has 30-mi views of the mountains. The course, designed by Dick Phelps, along the Big Thompson River skirts rock outcroppings and plenty of ponds. Don't forget your camera. ✉ *701 Clubhouse Dr., Loveland Go west on 1st St., take a right onto Rossum Dr. and another quick right onto Clubhouse Dr.* ☎ *970/667–8308* ⊕ *www.golfloveland.com* ⚲ *Reservations essential* ⛳ *18 holes. Yards: 6,572/5,420. Par: 36/72. Green fees: $40/$55.*

HIKING

Twenty-nine miles of trails in **Horsetooth Mountain Park** offer easy to difficult hikes, some with views of the mountains to the west and the plains to the east. An easy 2.25-mi round-trip walk to **Horsetooth Falls** is a good hike that takes you into the foothills for a couple of hours. From the parking area, head up the Horsetooth Falls Trail and keep right at the junction with the Soderberg Trail. Go left at the next junction to get to the falls. ✉ *Drive west on Harmony Rd., which becomes County Rd. 38E. Follow for about 5 mi to park entrance* ☎ *970/679–4570* ⊕ *www. larimer.org/parks/htmp.htm* ✉ *$6 per vehicle.*

Wildlife, songbirds, and springtime wildflowers abound along the trails in **Lory State Park**, about 15 minutes west of downtown. For unbelievable views of the Front Range and the city from 7,000-foot Arthur's Rock, take **Arthur's Rock Trail** (✉ *Trailhead: Parking area at end of service road*). You climb fast on the switchbacks in the sparse woods before the trail levels off to cross the meadow, a breather before the final steep approach to the summit. Allow about two to three hours to

7

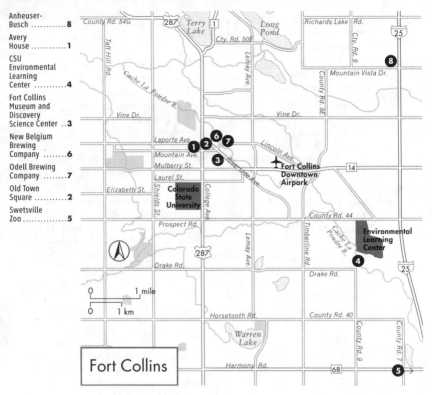

Fort Collins

hike the trail (3.4 mi round-trip and about 1,300 feet gain in elevation). Watch for poison ivy and be mindful of the occasional rattlesnake. ⊠ *708 Lodgepole Dr., Bellvue. Drive north on Overland Trail and turn left on Bingham Hill Rd. Turn left at County Rd. 23 north and go 1.3 mi to County. Rd. 25G and turn right. It's 1½ mi to park entrance* ☎ *970/493–1623* ⊕ *parks.state.co/Parks/lory* ⌦ *$6 per vehicle.*

RAFTING AND KAYAKING

The Cache la Poudre River is famous for its rapids, and river trips fill fast. It's wise to book with an outfitter at least two weeks in advance. The state-certified guides of **A-1 Wildwater Rafting** (⊠ *2801 N. Shields St.,* ☎ *970/224–3379 or 800/369–4165* ⊕ *www.a1wildwater.com*) arrange guided tours as well as daylong and half-day trips for groups. A-1 also rents inflatable rafts for one to two people called "duckies."

WHERE TO EAT

$$
ITALIAN
★

✗ **Canino's.** Hearty Italian specialties are served in this historic four-square house that still has a few stained-glass windows. Tables are set in wood-trim rooms that have hardwood floors with carpets. Appetizers like bruschetta and entrées such as *pollo alla cacciatora* and veal marsala are made in classic Italian style. Homemade cheesecake, tiramisu, or gelato—paired with a robust espresso—finish dinner on a sweet note. ✉ *613 S. College Ave.* ☎ *970/493–7205* ⊕ *www.caninositalian-restaurant.com* ▭ *AE, D, MC, V.*

$–$$ ✗ **Cozzola's.** Base your pizza on thin "New York"–style crust or a thick
PIZZA herb or whole-wheat and poppy-seed crust, and then select a sauce: basil-tomato, fresh garlic, pesto, or spinach ricotta. Finally, select from the seemingly endless list of toppings that includes everything from artichoke hearts to feta cheese to applewood-smoked bacon. The roomy restaurant is done in rough-hewn wood and is bright and airy. You can get a couple of slices as a snack—made to order with your choices of toppings. There's a second location at 1112 Oakridge Drive. ✉ *241 Linden St.* ☎ *970/482–3557* ⊕ *www.cozzolaspizza.com* ▭ *AE, MC, V.*

$–$$ ✗ **Rio Grande Mexican Restaurant.** Like its other Front Range brethren,
MEXICAN the Fort Collins branch of this seven-location chain always satisfies, with old favorites such as tacos, quesadillas, burritos, flame-broiled Yucatan shrimp, and fajita steak dishes, as well as fierier Tex-Mex fare such as *camarones diabla* (shrimp in chilé de árbol). This spacious restaurant with old storefront windows draws mostly casual diners out for a wonderful, relaxed dinner. ✉ *143 W. Mountain Ave.* ☎ *970/224–5428* ⊕ *www.riograndemexican.com* ▭ *AE, D, MC, V.*

$ ✗ **Silver Grill Cafe.** This cool spot, sleek with hardwood floors, red soda-
AMERICAN fountain stools, and boxy booths, is the oldest café in northern Colorado, operating since 1933. The cinnamon rolls are legendary, and the cinnamon-roll French toast is also popular. The café's coffee is custom roasted, and the Café Royal, a house special that mixes cappuccino with brown sugar, vanilla, and a twist of lemon, is particularly tasty. The breakfast menu includes omelets, biscuits and gravy, hotcakes, breakfast burritos, and trout 'n eggs, plus a few vegetarian options. Lunch is sandwiches or salads, burgers, or platters of chicken-fried steak and a few other traditional, homey comfort foods. Doors open at 6:30 for breakfast, and lunch is served until 2 PM. ✉ *218 Walnut St.* ☎ *970/484–4656* ⊕ *www.silvergrill.com* ▭ *D, MC, V* ⊘ *No dinner.*

¢ ✗ **Starry Night Coffee Company.** Espresso drinkers sip their sustenance,
CAFE including espresso smoothies, on leather couches or at tables under the night-blue ceiling while reading, chatting, or mulling over the sunflowers and the mural *Starry Night over Fort Collins* (inspired by van Gogh's original). Beyond breakfast, there are soups, salads, and sandwiches at lunch and dinnertime. The café serves wine and sangria by the glass. For dessert, there are pastries, scones, and tiramisu. ✉ *112 S. College Ave.* ☎ *970/493–3039* ▭ *D, MC, V.*

$–$$ ✗ **Suehiro.** Sit at the high bar overlooking Linden Street in this light and
JAPANESE open restaurant or, for more intimacy, ask for a table in the tearoom. The well-priced sushi is made fresh at the bar, and seafood entrées like salmon teriyaki or tempura always satisfy. Choose from more than 10 hot and cold sakes and specialty drinks. The green-tea ice cream will refresh your palate at dessert. ✉ *223 Linden St., Suite 103* ☎ *970/482–3734* ⊕ *www.suehirofc.com* ▭ *AE, D, MC, V*

7

WHERE TO STAY

$ ⛏ **Armstrong Hotel.** Walk into this refurbished 1923 downtown hotel's lobby with the original terrazzo floor and pressed-tin ceiling, and go back in time to the Art Deco 1920s. Take the sweeping staircase to a vintage room with hardwood floors and antique or reproduction furnishings and a claw-foot tub. Even the modern rooms have a retro look and feel at the Armstrong, which is on the National Register of Historic Places. The beds are made up with cotton sheets and feather duvets and pillows, and each room has a writing desk and coffeemaker. For a longer stay, there are two studio rooms and two apartment suites, all with full kitchens. Note that this is a no-smoking hotel. **Pros:** helpful staff; downtown location; low rates for a classy, historic lodging. **Cons:** on a rather noisy street, particularly on weekend nights. ✉ *259 S. College Ave.,* ☎ *970/484–3883 or 866/384–3883* ⇗ *24 rooms, 2 apartment suites, 2 studios, 15 suites* ♿ *In-room: kitchen (some), Wi-Fi. In-hotel: parking (free), no smoking rooms* ⊕ *www.thearmstronghotel. com* ⊟ *AE, D, MC, V.*

$$$$ ⛏ **Colorado Cattle Company & Guest Ranch.** A real-deal working ranch, the adults-only cattle company has 750 head of cattle and 10,000 acres of land in the canyons and plains of northeast Colorado. Saddle up with the ranch hands and help with the daily chores, drive cattle, eat ranch-style meals and hang out around the campfire while learning the basics of roping, tying, branding, and cutting. You'll stay in rustic cabins with private baths and porches. Prices include lodging, meals, and activities. **Pros:** truly authentic experience; ability to mix cattle work with relaxation. **Cons:** no kids allowed; authentic experience includes chores. ✉ *70008 Weld County Rd. 132, New Raymer* ☎ *970/437–5345* ⊕ *www.coloradocattlecompany.com* ⇗ *14 cabins* ♿ *In-hotel: bar, pool, gym, laundry service, parking (free), some pets allowed, no kids under 21* ⊟ *AE, D, MC, V* ☺ *Closed Nov.–mid-Apr.* ⫯◎⫯ *AI.*

$$ ⛏ **Edwards House B&B.** This quiet Victorian inn with hardwood floors
★ and light birchwood trim is four blocks from downtown. Guests enjoy gourmet breakfasts, with dishes such as gingerbread pancakes or eggs Florentine. A movie library is well stocked for those who forego relaxing on the large front porch or reading in the parlor. Unfussy, old-fashioned rooms are elegantly arranged with sleigh or canopy beds, gas stoves, Jacuzzis or claw-foot tubs, writing desks, and slate fireplaces. **Pros:** on a busy but quiet street near downtown; helpful and professional staff; pleasant grounds. **Cons:** small inn; fills up quickly. ✉ *402 W. Mountain Ave.,* ☎ *970/493–9191 or 800/281–9190* ⊕ *www.edwardshouse.com* ⇗ *8 rooms* ♿ *In-room: Wi-Fi. In-hotel: gym, sauna, public Wi-Fi, parking (free), no kids under 10* ⊟ *AE, D, MC, V* ⫯◎⫯ *BP.*

NIGHTLIFE

BARS AND CLUBS

College students line the bar at **Lucky Joe's Sidewalk Saloon** (✉ *25 Old Town Sq.* ☎ *970/493–2213*) for live music Wednesday to Sunday nights.

Mishawaka Amphitheater ($\boxtimes$ *13714 Poudre Canyon Hwy., Bellvue 80512, 25 mi north of Fort Collins on Rte. 14* ☎ *970/482–4420* ⊕ *www.mishawakaconcerts.com*), an outdoor venue on the banks of the Poudre River, corrals an eclectic mix of bands on weekends, including national acts like the Subdudes to reggae stars Steel Pulse. Most shows are evenings, and some are afternoons.

BREWPUBS AND MICROBREWERIES

The sports bar **C.B. & Potts Restaurant and Brewery** ($\boxtimes$ *1415 W. Elizabeth St.* ☎ *970/221–1139* ⊕ *www.cbpotts.com*) is known for its burgers, barbecue, and international selection of beers. The establishment has a game room and a pool hall with a full bar. The brewery always has six house beers and two seasonals on tap. All brews are crafted and bottled on-site in a 15-barrel, direct-fire brewing system. Tours are available by appointment. After taking a tour of the brewery at **Coopersmith's Pub & Brewery** ($\boxtimes$ *5 Old Town Sq.* ☎ *970/498–0483* ⊕ *www.coopersmithspub.com*), you can enjoy lunch on the patio with a crisp Punjabi Pale Ale or one of the other seven house-made beers on tap. The brewery always has three to five seasonal specialties to offer. Coopersmith's own pool hall, just outside the front door at 7 Old Town Square, has 12 tournament-style tables and serves pizza.

SHOPPING

Old Town Square ($\boxtimes$ *College and Mountain Aves. and Jefferson St.*) and adjacent Linden Street have historic buildings that house galleries, bookshops, cafés, brewpubs, and shops. Fifteen Old Town art galleries host the **First Friday Gallery Walk** on the first Friday of each month—no matter the weather—with appetizers and music from 6 PM to 9 PM. **Alpine Arts** ($\boxtimes$ *112 N. College Ave.* ☎ *970/493–1941*) has some real standouts, particularly the photography and watercolors, among the more usual pottery, carved wooden boxes, and jewelry. Everything is made by Colorado artists. The shopkeepers at the **Clothes Pony and Dandelion Toys** ($\boxtimes$ *111 N. College Ave.* ☎ *970/224–2866* ⊕ *www.clothespony.com*) enjoy playing with the toys as much as the young customers do. The shop carries books, CDs, imported toys like Lego and Rokenbok, and classics like marbles, dolls, and stuffed animals. **Green Logic** ($\boxtimes$ *261 Linden St.* ☎ *970/484–1740* ⊕ *www.green-logic.net*) purveys boxes made from books, notepads with old floppy disks as covers, clocks made from 45-rpm vinyl records, and dishes made from recycled glass. There are also biodegradable bags for leaves, and clothing made from organic cotton. **Trimble Court Artisans** ($\boxtimes$ *118 Trimble Ct.* ☎ *970/221–0051* ⊕ *www.trimblecourt.com*), a co-op with more than 40 members, sells paintings, jewelry, clothing, weavings, stained glass, and pottery.

7

Rocky Mountain National Park

WORD OF MOUTH

"If you're in RMNP for 9 days, I'd spend one day driving over Trail Ridge Road to Grand Lake. It would make a very nice, scenic day trip. Grand Lake is beautiful and there are lots of nice restraurants in the little town. Our kids used to like to play miniature golf there, too, which is also in town. And Trail Ridge Road is spectacular."

—MaureenB

WELCOME TO ROCKY MOUNTAIN NATIONAL PARK

TOP REASONS TO GO

★ **Gorgeous scenery:** Peer out over dozens of lakes, gaze up at majestic mountain peaks, and look around at pine-scented woods that are perfect for whiling away an afternoon.

★ **Over 355 mi of trails:** Hike to your heart's content on mostly moderate trails crisscrossing the park.

★ **Continental Divide:** Straddle this great divide, which cuts through the western part of the park, separating water's flow to either the Pacific or Atlantic Ocean.

★ **Awesome ascents:** Trek to the summit of Longs Peak or go rock climbing on Lumpy Ridge. In winter, you can even ice climb.

★ **Wildlife viewing:** Spot elk and bighorn sheep; there are more than 2,000 and 800 of them, respectively.

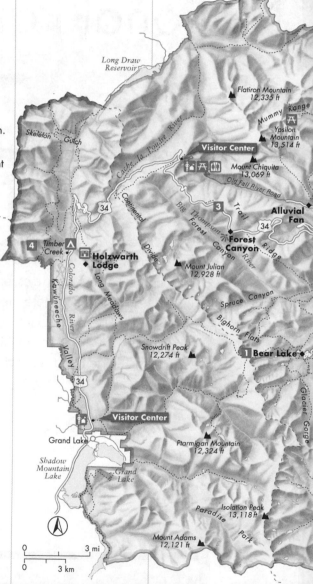

Long Draw Reservoir

Skeleton Gulch

Flatiron Mountain 12,335 ft

Mummy Range

Ypsilon Mountain 13,514 ft

Cache la Poudre River

Visitor Center

Mount Chiquita 13,069 ft

Old Fall River Road

34

Continental Divide

Big Thompson Forest

Trail Ridge

3

Alluvial Fan

34

Forest Canyon

Timber Creek

4

Holzwarth Lodge

Mount Julian 12,928 ft

Colorado River

Long Meadows

Spruce Canyon

Kawuneeche Valley

Bighorn Flats

Snowdrift Peak 12,274 ft

1 Bear Lake

34

Glacier Gorge

Visitor Center

Grand Lake

Ptarmigan Mountain 12,324 ft

Shadow Mountain Lake

Grand Lake

Isolation Peak 13,118 ft

Paradise Park

Mount Adams 12,121 ft

0   3 mi

0   3 km

1 **Bear Lake.** One of the most photographed places in the park, Bear Lake is the hub for many trailheads. It gets crowded in summer.

2 **Longs Peak.** The highest peak in the park and the toughest to climb, this Fourteener pops up in many park vistas. If you want to reach the summit on a daylong trek, it's recommended you begin at 3 AM.

3 **Trail Ridge Road.** The alpine tundra of the park is the highlight here as the road climbs beyond the timberline.

4 **Timber Creek.** The park's western area is much less crowded, though it has its share of amenities and attractions, including a campground, historic sites, and a visitor center.

5 **Wild Basin Area.** Far from the crowds, the park's southeast quadrant consists of lovely expanses of subalpine forest punctuated by streams and lakes.

COLORADO

GETTING ORIENTED

Rocky Mountain National Park's 416-square-mi wilderness of meadows, mountains, and mirror-like lakes lie just 65 mi from Denver. The park is nine times smaller than Yellowstone, yet it receives almost as many visitors—3 million a year.

8

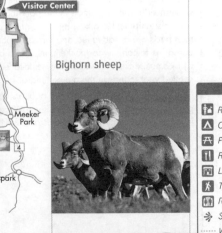

Bighorn sheep

Bighorn Mountain
11,463 ft

Black Canyon

Visitor Center

34

Estes Park

36

36

Moraine Park

Visitor Center

66

4

Sprague Lake

Glacier Basin

Boulder Brook

Visitor Center

Longs Peak

2

Longs Peak
14,255 ft

Meeker Park

4

North St. Vrain Creek

5

Allenspark

KEY	
🏠	Ranger Station
△	Campground
⛱	Picnic Area
🍴	Restaurant
🏠	Lodge
🚶	Trailhead
🚻	Restrooms
⇘	Scenic Viewpoint
⋯⋯	Walking/Hiking Trails
⋯⋯	Bicycle Path

ROCKY MOUNTAIN NATIONAL PARK PLANNER

When to Go

More than two-thirds of the park's annual 3 million visitors come in summer and fall. **For thinner high-season crowds, come in early June or September.** But there is a good reason to put up with summer crowds: only from Memorial Day to mid-October can you make the unforgettable drive over Trail Ridge Road (weather-permitting).

Spring is capricious—75°F one day and a blizzard the next (March sees the most snow). June can range from hot to cool and rainy. July typically ushers in high summer, which can last through September. Up on Trail Ridge Road, it can be 15°–20° cooler. Spring and summer are the best times for wildlife viewing and fishing. In early fall, the trees blaze with brilliant foliage. Winter, when backcountry snow can be 4 feet deep and the wind brutal, is the time for skiing, snowshoeing, and ice fishing.

AVG. HIGH/LOW TEMPS

Flora and Fauna

Volcanic uplifts and the savage clawing of receding glaciers have brought about Rocky Mountain's majestic landscape. You'll find three distinct ecosystems here—verdant mountain valleys towering with proud ponderosa pines and Douglas firs; higher and colder subalpine mountains with wind-whipped trees (krummholz) that grow at right angles; and harsh, unforgiving alpine tundra with dollhouse-size versions of familiar plants and wildflowers. The high, wind-whipped ecosystem of alpine tundra is seldom found outside the Arctic, yet it makes up one-third of the park's terrain. Few plants can survive at the tundra's elevation, but many beautiful wildflowers—including alpine forget-me-nots—bloom briefly in late June or early July.

The park has so much wildlife that you can often enjoy prime viewing from the seat of your car. Fall, when many animals begin moving down from higher elevations, is an excellent time to spot the park's animal residents. This is also when you'll hear the male elk bugle mating calls (popular "listening" spots are Horseshoe Park, Moraine Park, and Upper Beaver Meadows).

May through mid-October is the best time to see the bighorn sheep that congregate in the Horseshoe Park–Sheep Lakes area, just past the Fall River entrance. If you want to glimpse a moose, try Kawuneeche Valley, on the park's western side. Other animals in the park include mule deer, squirrels, chipmunks, pikas, beavers, and marmot. Common birds are broad-tailed and rufous hummingbirds, peregrine falcons, woodpeckers, mountain bluebirds, and Clark's nutcracker, as well as the white-tailed ptarmigan, spotted year-round on the alpine tundra.

Mountain lions, black bears, and bobcats also inhabit the park but are rarely spotted by visitors. Altogether, the park is home to 63 species of mammals and 280 bird species.

Getting Here and Around

Estes Park and Grand Lake are the Rocky Mountain's gateway communities; from these you can enter the park via U.S. 34 or 36. The closest commercial airport is **Denver International Airport** (DEN). Its **Ground Transportation Information Center** (☎ 800/247–2336 or 303/342–4059) assists visitors with car rentals, door-to-door shuttles, and limousine services. From the airport, the eastern entrance of the park is 80 mi (about two hours). **Estes Park Shuttle** (☎ 970/586–5151; reservations essential) serves Estes Park and Rocky Mountain from Denver, the airport, and Boulder. Greyhound Lines serve Denver, Boulder, and Fort Collins, and Amtrak's California Zephyr stops in downtown Denver, Winter Park/Fraser, and Granby.

U.S. 36 runs from Denver through Boulder, Lyons, and Estes Park to the park; the portion between Boulder and Estes Park is heavily traveled—especially on summer weekends. Colorado Routes 119, 72, and 7 have much less traffic. If you're driving directly to Rocky Mountain from the airport, the E–470 tollway connects Peña Boulevard to Interstate 25.

The **Colorado Department of Transportation** (for road conditions, call ☎ 303/639–1111) plows roads efficiently, but winter snowstorms can slow traffic and create wet or icy conditions.

The main thoroughfare in the park is Trail Ridge Road; in winter, it's plowed up to Many Parks Curve on the east side and the Colorado River trailhead on the west side. Gravel-surfaced, extremely curvy Old Fall River Road is open from July to September. Pulled trailers and vehicles longer than 25 feet are prohibited.

Two free park shuttle-bus routes operate along the park's popular Bear Lake Road from mid-June to mid-October. Unless you arrive early enough to get one of the few parking spaces beyond the park-and-ride, you must take the shuttle. One bus line runs every 30 minutes between 7:30 AM and 7:30 PM from near the Fern Lake Trailhead to the Moraine Park Museum and on to Glacier Basin Campground. The other runs every 15 minutes between 7 AM and 7 PM from the campground to the Bear Lake Trailhead. There's also a hiker shuttle bus running from the **Estes Park Visitor Center** to the park during the peak summer season (call ☎ 970/586–1206 for times); it passes most lodging and shopping areas, and many visitors like to use it as a free sightseeing tour bus. You must have a park pass if you transfer to the buses that enter the national park.

Festivals and Events

MID-MAY Jazz Fest. Pack a picnic and bring the kids for a weekend afternoon of free jazz performances and an art walk at the outdoor amphitheater downtown. ✉ Estes Park ☎ 800/443–7837 ⊕ www.estesnet.com/events/.

JUNE The Wool Market. Watch shearing, spinning, and herding contests, and view animal shows where angora goats, sheep, llamas, and alpacas are judged for their wool. ✉ Estes Park ☎ 800/443–7837.

JULY Rooftop Rodeo. A tradition for more than 80 years, this six-day event features a parade and nightly rodeos. Admission runs $10–$15. ✉ Fairgrounds, Estes Park ☎ 800/443–7837 ⊕ www.estesnet.com/events/.

SEPT. ★ Longs Peak Scottish/Irish Highland Festival. A traditional tattoo kicks off this four-day fair of athletic competitions, Celtic music, dancing, a parade, and seminars on topics such as heraldry and Scotch whisky. ✉ Fairgrounds, Estes Park ☎ 970/586–6308 or 800/903–7837 ⊕ www.scotfest.com.

NOV.–APR. The **Estes Park Music Festival** stages concerts at 2 PM on Sunday afternoons from November through April at the Stanley Hotel (333 E. Wonderview Ave.). ✉ 333 E. Wonderview Ave., Estes Park ☎ 970/586–9519 or 800/443–7837 ⊕ www.estesparkmusicalfestival.org.

8

Updated
by Barbara
Colligan

Anyone who delights in alpine lakes, mountain peaks, and an abundance of wildlife—not to mention dizzying heights—should consider Rocky Mountain National Park. Here, a single hour's drive leads from a 7,800-foot elevation at park headquarters to the 12,183-foot apex of the twisting and turning Trail Ridge Road. More than 355 mi of hiking trails take you to the park's many treasures: meadows flushed with wildflowers, cool dense forests of lodgepole pine and Engelmann spruce, and the noticeable presence of wildlife, including elk and bighorn sheep.

PARK ESSENTIALS

ACCESSIBILITY

All visitor centers are fully accessible to mobility-impaired people. The Sprague Lake, Bear Lake, Coyote Valley, and Lily Lake trails are hard-packed gravel, ½- to 1-mi, accessible loops. A backcountry campsite at Sprague Lake accommodates up to 12 campers, including six in wheelchairs. Bear Lake shuttles are wheelchair accessible.

ADMISSION FEES AND PERMITS

Entrance fees are $20 for a weekly pass, or $10 if you enter on bicycle, motorcycle, or foot. An annual pass costs $40.

From May through October, the backcountry camping cost is $20 per party (it's free the rest of the year, but you still need a permit). Pick up the permit at the backcountry office, east of Beaver Meadows Visitor Center, or at Kawuneeche Visitor Center. Phone reservations for backcountry campsites can be made between March 1 and May 15 and after October 1 by calling the backcountry office at 970/586–1242.

ADMISSION HOURS

The park is open 24/7, year-round; some roads close in winter. It is in the mountain time zone.

ATMS/BANKS

There are no ATMs within the park. The nearest ATMs and banks are in Estes Park.

CELL-PHONE RECEPTION

Cell phones work in much of the park. Pay phones may be found at the Beaver Meadows, Kawuneeche, and Fall River visitor centers.

PARK CONTACT INFORMATION

Rocky Mountain National Park (✉ *1000 U.S. 36, Estes Park, CO* ☎ *970/586–1206* ⊕ *www.nps.gov/romo*).

ROCKY MOUNTAIN IN ONE DAY

Begin your adventure with a hearty breakfast at the **Bighorn Restaurant** in Estes Park. While you're enjoying your short stack with apple-cinnamon-raisin topping, you can put in an order for a packed lunch.

Drive west on U.S. 34 into the park, and stop at the **Fall River Visitor Center** to watch the orientation film and pick up a park map. Also inquire about road conditions on Trail Ridge Road, which you should plan to drive either in the morning or afternoon, depending on the weather. If possible, save the drive for the afternoon, and use the morning to get out on the trails before any afternoon lightning threatens your safety.

For a beautiful and invigorating hike, follow the route that takes you from the trailhead at **Bear Lake** to **Nymph Lake** (an easy ½-mi hike),

then onto **Dream Lake** (an additional 0.6 mi with a steeper ascent), and finally to **Emerald Lake** (an additional 0.7 mi of moderate to challenging terrain). You can stop at several places along the way. The trek down is much easier, and quicker, than the climb up. ■TIP→ **If you prefer a shorter, simpler, yet still scenic walk, consider the Bear Lake Nature Trail, a 0.6-mi loop that is partially wheelchair and stroller accessible.**

You'll need the better part of your afternoon to drive the scenic **Trail Ridge Road.** If you're heading to Grand Lake and destinations west, take Trail Ridge Road west, over the Continental Divide; otherwise, after you reach the top, take it back east and end your day with a ranger-led talk or evening campfire program.

SCENIC DRIVES

8

Bear Lake Road. This 9-mi drive offers superlative views of Longs Peak (14,255-foot summit) and the glaciers surrounding Bear Lake, winding past shimmering waterfalls perpetually shrouded with rainbows. ⊠ *Runs from the Beaver Meadow Entrance Station to Bear Lake.*

Old Fall River Road. A one-way 11-mi loop up to the Alpine Visitor Center and back down along Trail Ridge Road is a scenic alternative to driving Trail Ridge Road twice. Start at West Horseshoe Park, which has the park's largest concentrations of sheep and elk, and head up the paved and gravel Old Fall River Road, passing Chasm Falls. Early visitors to the park traveled Old Fall River Road before Trail Ridge Road was built. ⊙ *July–Sept.*

Fodor's Choice **Trail Ridge Road.** This is the park's star attraction and the world's highest
★ continuous paved highway, topping out at 12,183 feet. The 48-mi road connects the park's gateways of Estes Park and Grand Lake. The views around each bend—of moraines and glaciers, and craggy hills framing emerald meadows carpeted with columbine and Indian paintbrush—are truly awesome. As it passes through three ecosystems—montane, subalpine, and arctic tundra—the road climbs 4,300 feet in elevation. As you drive the road, take your time at the numerous turnouts to gaze over verdant valleys, brushed with yellowing aspen in fall, that slope between the glacier-etched granite peaks. **Many Parks Curve** affords views of the crest of the Continental Divide and of the **Alluvial Fan,** a

huge gash a vicious flood created after an earthen dam broke in 1982. ■ TIP→ Pick up a copy of the *Trail Ridge Road Guide*, available at visitor centers, for an overview of what you will be seeing as you drive the road. In normal traffic, it's a two-hour drive across the park, but it's best to give yourself three to four hours to allow for leisurely breaks at the overlooks. Note that the middle part of the road closes down again by mid-October, though you can still drive up about 10 mi from the west and 8 mi from the east. ⊠ *Trail Ridge Rd. (U.S. 34)* ⊙ *June–mid-Oct.*

WHAT TO SEE

HISTORIC SITES

Rocky Mountain has more than 100 sites of historic significance. In order to be nominated for the National Register of Historic Places, a park building must tie in strongly to the park's history in terms of architecture, archaeology, engineering, or culture. Most buildings at Rocky Mountain are done in the rustic style, a design preferred by the National Park Service's first director, Stephen Mather. The rustic style is a way to incorporate nature within man-made structures.

ℭ **Holzwarth Historic Site.** A scenic ½-mi interpretive trail leads you over the Colorado River to the original "dude ranch" that the Holzwarth family ran between the 1920s and 1950s. Allow about an hour to explore the buildings and chat with a ranger. It's a great place for families to learn about homesteading. ⊠ *Trail Ridge Rd., about 13 mi west of the Alpine Visitor Center* ⊠ *Free* ⊙ *Daily 10:30–4:30.*

Lulu City. A few remnants of cabins and mining equipment are all that's left of this onetime silver mining town, established in 1880. Reach it by hiking the 3.6-mi Colorado River Trail. Look for wagon ruts from the old Stewart Toll Road and the ruins of cabins in Shipler Park. The Colorado River is a mere stream at this point, flowing south from its headwaters at nearby La Poudre Pass. ⊠ *Off Trail Ridge Rd., 10½ mi north of Grand Lake.*

Moraine Park Museum. Lectures, slide shows, and displays explain the park's geology, botany, and history. ⊠ *Bear Lake Rd., off U.S. 36* ⊠ *Free* ⊙ *May–Sept., daily 9–5.*

SCENIC STOPS

Alluvial Fan. On July 15, 1982, the 79-year-old dam at Lawn Lake burst, and water roared into Estes Park, killing three people and causing major flooding. The flood created the alluvial fan, a pile of glacial and stream-bed debris up to 44 feet deep on the north side of Horseshoe Park. A ½-mi trail allows you to explore it up close. You also can view it from the Rainbow Curve lookout on Trail Ridge Road. ⊠ *Fall River Rd., 3 mi from the Fall River entrance station.*

★ **Bear Lake.** Thanks to its picturesque location, easy accessibility, and the good hiking trails nearby, this small alpine lake below Flattop Mountain and Hallett Peak is one of the most popular destinations in the park. Free park shuttle buses can take you here. ⊠ *Bear Lake Rd., 10 mi southwest of Beaver Meadows Visitor Center, off Highway 36.*

Forest Canyon Overlook. Beyond the classic U-shaped glacial valley lies a high-alpine circle of ice-blue pools (the Gorge Lakes) framed by ragged peaks. ☒ *Trail Ridge Rd., 14 mi east of Alpine Visitor Center, on Highway 34.*

VISITOR CENTERS

Alpine Visitor Center. At the top of Trail Ridge Road, this visitor center is open only when that road is navigable. There's a snack bar inside. ☒ *Trail Ridge Rd., at Fall River Pass 22 mi from the Beaver Meadows entrance, on Highway 34* ☎ *970/586–1206* ⊙ *June–mid-Oct., daily 9–5.*

★ **Beaver Meadows Visitor Center.** Housing park headquarters, this visitor center was designed by students of the Frank Lloyd Wright School of Architecture at Taliesen West using the park's popular rustic style, which integrates buildings into their natural surroundings. Completed in 1966, it was named a National Historic Landmark in 2001. The surrounding utility buildings are also on the National Register and are noteworthy examples of the rustic-style buildings that the Civilian Conservation Corps constructed during the Depression. The visitor center has a terrific orientation film and a large relief map of the park. ☒ *U.S. 36, before the Beaver Meadows entrance* ☎ *970/586–1206* ⊙ *Mid-June–Labor Day, Mon.–Wed. 8–8 and Thurs.–Sat. 8–9; early Sept.–mid-June, daily 8–4:30.*

Fall River Visitor Center. The Discovery Room, which houses everything from old ranger outfits to elk antlers, coyote pelts, and bighorn sheep skulls for hands-on exploration, is a favorite with kids (and adults) at this northeast center. ☒ *U.S. 34 at the Fall River entrance station* ☎ *970/586–1206* ⊙ *Mid-June–Labor Day, daily 9–5; winter hrs vary.*

Kawuneeche Visitor Center. The park's only west-side source of visitor information has exhibits on the plant and animal life of the area, as well as a large three-dimensional map of the park and an orientation film. ☒ *U.S. 34, before the Grand Lake entrance station* ☎ *970/586–1206* ⊙ *Mid-June–mid-Aug., daily 8–6; mid-Aug.–mid-June, daily 8–4:30.*

SPORTS AND THE OUTDOORS

BIRD-WATCHING

Spring and summer, early in the morning, are the best times for bird-watching in the park. **Lumpy Ridge** is a nesting ground for raptors such as golden eagles, red-tailed hawks, and peregrine falcons. Migratory songbirds from South America have summer breeding grounds near the **Endovalley Picnic Area.** The **alpine tundra** is habitat for white-tailed ptarmigan. The **alluvial fan** is the place for viewing broad-tailed hummingbirds, hairy woodpeckers, ouzels, and the occasional raptor.

FISHING

Rocky Mountain is a wonderful place to fish, especially for trout—German brown, brook, rainbow, cutthroat, and greenback cutthroat—but check at a visitor center about regulations and information on specific closures, catch-and-release areas, and limits on size and possession. No fishing is allowed at Bear Lake. Rangers recommend the more-remote backcountry lakes, since they are less crowded. To fish in the park,

8

ROCKY MOUNTAIN WILDLIFE

If you see a group of cars pulled over at a seemingly random section of road, with passengers staring intently at something in the distance, it's a good bet that an animal is within sight. May through mid-October is the best time to see the bighorn sheep that congregate in the Horseshoe Park–Sheep Lakes area, just past the Fall River entrance. Elk can be seen year-round in the park and the surrounding area. Kawuneeche Valley, on the park's western side, is the most likely location to glimpse a moose. At night, listen for the eerie vocalizing of coyotes.

Fall is an excellent time to spot wildlife, when many animals begin moving down from the higher elevations, is an excellent time to spot wildlife. This is also when you'll hear the male elk bugle mating calls to their female counterparts, which draws large crowds to popular "listening" spots in the early evening: Horseshoe Park, Moraine Park, and Upper Beaver Meadows—in the early evening.

Spring and summer are the best times for bird-watching. Go early in the morning, before the crowds arrive. Lumpy Ridge is the nesting ground of raptors such as golden eagles, red-tailed hawks, and peregrine. You can see migratory songbirds from South America in their summer breeding grounds near the Endovalley Picnic Area. The alpine tundra is habitat for white-tailed ptarmigan. The alluvial fan, along the Roaring River, is an excellent place for viewing broad-tailed hummingbirds, hairy woodpeckers, robins, ouzels, and the occasional raptor.

Keep a telephoto lens handy for those close-ups of animals. Approaching, chasing, or feeding any wildlife in the park not only is forbidden, but unduly stresses the animals and diminishes the enjoyment of others watching the wildlife.

anyone 16 and older must have a valid Colorado fishing license, which you can obtain at local sporting-goods stores. See ⊕ *www.wildlife.state. co.us/fishing* for details.

OUTFITTERS AND EXPEDITIONS　**Estes Angler** (⊠ *338 W. Riverside Dr., Estes Park* ☎ *970/586–2110 or 800/586–2110* ⊕ *www.estesangler.com*) arranges four-, six-, and eight-hour fly-fishing trips—including on horseback—into the park's quieter regions. **Scot's Sporting Goods** (⊠ *2325 Spruce Ave.* ⊠ *870 Moraine Ave., Estes Park* ☎ *970/586–2877* ⊕ *www.scotssportinggoods.com* ✉ *$80–$190* ⊙ *May–Sept., daily 8–8*) rents and sells gear, and provides four-, six-, and eight-hour fishing instruction trips daily from May through September. Clinics, geared toward first-timers, focus on casting, reading the water, identifying insects for flies, and properly presenting natural and artificial flies to the fish. Half-day excursions into the park are available for three or more people. **Kirk's Fly Shop** (⊠ *230 E. Elkhorn Ave., Estes Park* ☎ *970/577–0790* ⊕ *www.kirksflyshop.com*) has various guided fly-fishing trips, as well as backpacking, horseback riding, showshoeing, and llama trips. The store also carries fishing and backpacking gear.

HIKING

Fodor's Choice
★

Rocky Mountain National Park contains more than 355 mi of hiking trails, so you could theoretically wander the park for weeks. Most visitors explore just a small portion of these trails, so some of the park's most accessible and scenic paths can resemble a backcountry highway on busy summer days. The high-alpine terrain around Bear Lake is the park's most popular hiking area, and it's well worth exploring. However, for a truly remote experience, hike one of the trails in the far northern end of the park or in the Wild Basin area to the south. Keep in mind that trails at higher elevations may have some snow on them even in July. And because of afternoon thunderstorms on most summer afternoons, an early morning start is highly recommended; the last place you want to be when a storm approaches is on a peak or anywhere above the tree line. All trails are round-trip unless stated otherwise.

EASY

★ **Bear Lake.** The virtually flat nature trail around Bear Lake is an easy, 1-mi walk that's wheelchair accessible. Sharing the route with you will likely be plenty of other hikers as well as songbirds and chipmunks. ⊠ *Trailhead at Bear Lake, Bear Lake Rd.*

☺ **Copeland Falls.** The 0.6-mi hike to these Wild Basin Area falls is a good option for families, as the terrain is relatively flat (only a 15-foot elevation gain). ⊠ *Trailhead at Wild Basin.*

Cub Lake. This 4.6-mi, three-hour hike takes you through meadows and stands of aspen trees and up 540 feet in elevation to a lake with water lilies. ⊠ *Trailhead at Cub Lake. Take Bear Lake Road to Moraine Park Campground, turn right, then left at road to trailhead.*

East Inlet Trail. You can get to **Adams Falls** in about 15 minutes on this 0.3-mi route with an 80-foot climb in elevation. The trail to the falls will likely be packed with visitors, so if you have time, continue east on the trail past the falls to enjoy more solitude, see wildlife, and catch views of Mount Craig from near the East Meadow campground. Note, however, that beyond the falls the elevation climbs between 1,500 and 1,900 feet, making it a challenging hike. ⊠ *Trailhead at East Inlet, end of W. Portal Road; W. Portal Road spurs off Trail Ridge Road by entrance to Grand Lake Village. Stay left at junction with Grand Ave.*

Glacier Gorge Trail. The 5-mi hike to **Mills Lake** can be crowded, but the reward is one the park's prettiest lakes, set against the breathtaking backdrop of Longs Peak, Pagoda Mountain, and the Keyboard of the Winds. There's a modest elevation gain of 700 feet. About 1 mi in, you pass **Alberta Falls,** a popular destination in and of itself. The hike travels along Glacier Creek, under the shade of a subalpine forest. Give yourself at least four hours for hiking and lingering time. ⊠ *Trailhead at off Bear Lake Rd., 9 mi south of the Beaver Meadows entrance station.*

★ **Sprague Lake.** With virtually no elevation gain, this 1-mi, pine-lined path is wheelchair accessible and provides views of Hallet Peak and Flattop Mountain. ⊠ *Trailhead at Sprague Lake, Bear Lake Rd.*

8

MODERATE

Fodor'sChoice ★ **Bear Lake to Emerald Lake.** This scenic, caloric-burning hike begins at Bear Lake and takes you first on a moderately level, ½ mi journey to **Nymph Lake.** From here, the trail gets steeper, with a 425-foot elevation gain, as it winds around for 0.6 mi to **Dream Lake.** The last stretch is the most arduous part of the hike, an almost all-uphill 0.7-mi trek to lovely **Emerald Lake,** where you can perch on a boulder and enjoy the view. Round-trip, the hike is 3.6 mi, with an elevation gain of 605 feet. Allow two hours or more, depending on stops. ⊠ *Trailhead at Bear Lake, off Bear Lake Rd.*

Colorado River Trail. This walk to the ghost town of Lulu City on the west side of the park is excellent for looking for the bighorn sheep, elk,

> **HIKERS SHUTTLE**
>
> The many trails in the Bear Lake area of the park are so popular that parking areas at the trailheads usually cannot accommodate all of the hikers' cars. Shuttle buses connect a large park-and-ride facility at the Glacier Basin Campground with the Cub Lake, Fern Lake, Glacier Gorge Junction, Sprague Lake, and Bear Lake trailheads. Buses run daily between mid-June and mid-September. The Bear Lake shuttle runs approximately every 15 minutes between 7 AM and 7 PM; the Moraine Park shuttle runs approximately every 30 minutes between 7:30 AM and 7:30 PM.

and moose that reside in the area. Part of the former stagecoach route that went from Granby to Walden, the 7.4-mi trail parallels the infant Colorado River to the meadow where Lulu City once stood. Elevation gain is 350 feet. ⊠ *Trailhead at Colorado River, off Trail Ridge Rd.*

Fern Lake Trail. Heading to Odessa Lake from the north involves a steep hike, but usually you'll encounter fewer fellow hikers than if you begin at Bear Lake. Along the way, you'll come to the Arch Rocks; The Pool, an eroded formation in the Big Thompson River; two waterfalls; and Fern Lake (4 mi from your starting point). Odessa Lake itself lies at the foot of Tourmaline Gorge, below the craggy summits of Gabletop Mountain, Little Matterhorn, Knobtop Mountain, and Notchtop Mountain. For a full day of spectacular scenery, continue past Odessa to Bear Lake (8½ mi total), where you can pick up the shuttle back to the Fern Lake Trailhead. Total elevation gain is 1,375 feet. ⊠ *Trailhead off Bear Lake Road, about 1½ mi south of the Beaver Meadows entrance station.*

DIFFICULT

Chasm Lake Trail. Nestled in the shadow of Longs Peak and Mount Meeker, Chasm Lake offers one of Colorado's most impressive backdrops, so en route to it, expect to encounter plenty of other hikers. The 4.2-mi Chasm Lake trail, reached via the Longs Peak Trail, has a 2,360-foot elevation gain. Just before the lake, you'll need to climb a small rock ledge, which can be a bit of a challenge for the less surefooted; follow the cairns for the most straightforward route. Once atop the ledge, you'll catch your first memorable view of the lake. ⊠ *Trailhead at Rte. 7, 9 mi south of Estes Park.*

★ **Longs Peak Trail.** Climbing this 14,255-foot mountain (one of 54 Fourteeners in Colorado) is an ambitious goal for many people—but only those who are very fit and acclimated to the altitude should attempt it.

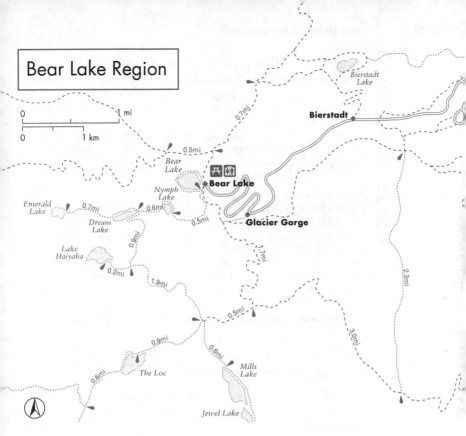

Bear Lake Region

The 16-mi round-trip hike up Longs requires a predawn start (3 AM is ideal), so that you're off the summit before the typical summer afternoon thunderstorm hits. Also, the last 2 mi or so of the trail are very exposed—you have to traverse narrow ledges with vertigo-inducing drop-offs. That said, summiting Longs can be one of the most rewarding hikes you'll ever attempt. The Keyhole route is the traditional means of ascent, and the number of people going up it on a summer day can be astounding given the rigors of the hike. Though just as scenic, the Loft route, between Longs and Mount Meeker from Chasm Lake, is not clearly marked and is therefore difficult to navigate. ⊠ *Trailhead: off Rte. 7, 9 mi south of Estes Park.*

HORSEBACK RIDING

Horses and riders can access 260 mi of trails in Rocky Mountain.

OUTFITTERS AND EXPEDITIONS

National Park Gateway Stables and Cowpoke Corner Corrals. Guided trips into the national park range from two-hour rides to Little Horseshoe Park to full-day rides along the Roaring River to Lawn or Ypsilon Lake. ⊠ *46000 Fall River Rd., Estes Park* ☎ *970/586–5269 or 970/586–5890* ⊕ *www.nationalparkgatewaystables.com* ⊠ *$45–$125* ⊟ *D, MC, V* ☉ *Mid-May–early Oct.*

Sombrero Ranches, Inc. Sombrero offers guided rides into the wilderness and national park, including scenic and relaxing early-morning breakfast

CLOSE UP

Longs Peak: The Northernmost Fourteener

At 14,255 feet above sea level, **Longs Peak** has long fascinated explorers to the region. Isabella L. Bird wrote of it, "It is one of the noblest of mountains, but in one's imagination it grows to be much more than a mountain. It becomes invested with a personality."

It was named after Major Stephen H. Long, who led an expedition in 1820 up the Platte River to the base of the Rockies. Long never ascended the mountain—in fact, he didn't even get within 40 mi of it—but a few decades later, in 1868, the one-armed Civil War veteran John Wesley Powell climbed to its summit.

In the park's southeast quadrant, Longs Peak is northernmost of the 54 mountains in Colorado that reach above the 14,000-foot mark, and one of more than 114 named mountains in the park higher than 10,000 feet. You can see its distinctive flat-top, rectangular summit from many spots on the park's east side and Trail Ridge Road.

If you want to make the ambitious climb to Longs summit—it's only recommended for those who are strong climbers and well acclimated to the altitude—begin by 3 AM so you're down from the summit when the typical afternoon thunderstorm hits.

rides and pack trips. The Boulder-based company also arranges private camping trips. Guided horseback riding trips last two to five hours. ⊠ *Grand Lake Stables, 304 W. Portal Rd., Grand Lake* ☎ *970/627–3514* ⊕ *www.sombrero.com* ✉ *$30–$80* ۞ *Mid-May–mid-Sept.* ⊠ *Glacier Creek Stables, Off Bear Lake Rd., near Sprague Lake* ☎ *970/586–3244* ⊠ *Moraine Park Stables, Off Bear Lake Rd.* ☎ *970/586–2327.*

ROCK CLIMBING

Expert rock climbers as well as novices can try hundreds of classic climbs here. The burgeoning sport of ice climbing also thrives in the park. The Diamond, Lumpy Ridge, and Petit Grepons are the places for rock climbing, while well-known ice-climbing spots include Hidden Falls, Loch Vale, and Emerald and Black lakes.

OUTFITTER   **Colorado Mountain School** is the oldest continuously operating U.S. guide
★   service and an invaluable resource. You can take introductory half-day and one- to seven-day courses on climbing and rappelling technique, or sign up for guided introductory trips, full-day climbs, and longer expeditions. Make reservations as far as six weeks in advance for summer climbs. The school also runs a 16-bed hostel. ⊠ *341 Moraine Ave., Estes Park* ☎ *800/836–4008 Ext. 3* ⊕ *www.totalclimbing.com* ✉ *$75–$395.*

WINTER SPORTS

Each winter, the popularity of snowshoeing in the park increases. It's a wonderful way to experience Rocky Mountain's majestic winter side, when the jagged peaks are softened with a blanket of snow and the summer hordes are nonexistent. You can snowshoe any of the summer hiking trails that are accessible by road; many of them also become well-traveled cross-country ski trails.

Backcountry skiing within the park ranges from gentle cross-country outings to full-on telemarking down steep chutes and glaciers. Come spring, when avalanche danger decreases, the park has some classic ski descents for those on telemark or alpine touring equipment. Ask a ranger about conditions and gear up as if you were spending the night. If you plan on venturing off trail, take a shovel, probe pole, and avalanche transceiver. Two trails to try are Tonahutu Creek Trail (near Kawuneeche Visitor Center) and the Colorado River Trail to Lulu City (start at the Timber Creek Campground).

Only on the west side of the park are you permitted to snowmobile, but you must register at Kawuneeche Visitor Center before traveling up the unplowed section of Trail Ridge Road up to Milner Pass. Check the park newspaper, *High Country Headlines,* for ranger-guided tours.

OUTFITTERS
AND
EXPEDITIONS
Estes Park Mountain Shop. Rent snowshoes and skis here, as well as fishing, hiking, and climbing equipment. The store gives half- and full-day guided fly-fishing trips into the park year-round for all levels as well as four- and eight-hour climbing trips to areas near Rocky Mountain National Park. ⊠ *2050 Big Thompson Ave., Estes Park* ☎ *970/586–6548 or 866/303–6548* ⊕ *www.estesparkmountainshop.com.*

Never Summer Mountain Sports (⊠ *919 Grand Ave., Grand Lake* ☎ *970/627–3642*) rents cross-country skis, boots, and poles, and sells hiking and some climbing gear.

EDUCATIONAL OFFERINGS

ART PROGRAM

Artist-in-Residence. Professional writers, sculptors, composers, and visual and performing artists can stay in a rustic cabin for two weeks in summer while working on their art. During their stay, they must do two park presentations, and donate a piece of original work to Rocky Mountain that relates to their stay. Applications must be received by December for requests for the following summer. ☎ *970/586–1206.*

CLASSES AND SEMINARS

★ **Rocky Mountain Field Seminars.** The Rocky Mountain Nature Association sponsors some 100 hands-on seminars for adults and children on such topics as natural history, geology, bird-watching, wildflower identification, wildlife biology, photography, and sketching. Children's classes run three hours, and adult classes last one to five days. All are taught by expert instructors. College students often receive academic credit, and teachers can receive recertification credit. ⊠ *1895 Fall River Rd., Estes Park* ☎ *970/586–3262* ⊕ *www.rmna.org* ⊠ *$20–$75 per day* ☉ *Jan.–Oct.*

RANGER PROGRAMS

☽ **Junior Ranger Program.** Pick up a Junior Ranger activity book (in English or Spanish) at any visitor center. Program content has been developed for children ages 12 and under; the material focuses on environmental education, identifying birds and wildlife, and outdoor safety skills. Once a child has completed all of the activities, a ranger will look over the book and award a Junior Ranger badge. ☎ *970/586–1206* ⊠ *Free.*

8

☺ **Ranger-Led Programs.** With more than 150 programs each summer, there
★ are many opportunities to join in on free hikes, talks, and activities
conducted by those who know the park best. Topics may include the
wildlife, geology, vegetation, or park history. At night, storytelling, slide
shows, and talks may be part of the evening campfire program, held in
summer at park campgrounds and at Beaver Meadows Visitor Center.
There are also evening hikes and stargazing sessions. On Friday, stories,
songs, and marshmallow roasts take place at Holzwarth Historic Site.
In winter, rangers lead snowshoeing and cross-country ski tours. Special programs for kids include "Ranger for a Day," "Skins and Skulls,"
and "Tales for Tots" (for preschool-age kids with an accompanying
adult). Look for the extensive program schedule in the park's newspaper. ☎ *970/586–1206* ✉ *Free.*

NEARBY TOWNS

Estes Park, 5 mi east of Rocky Mountain, is the park's most popular
gateway. The town sits at an altitude of more than 7,500 feet, with
14,255-feet Longs Peak and a chorus of surrounding mountains as its
stunning backdrop. Many of the small hotels lining the roads are mom-
and-pop outfits that have been passed down through several generations. Estes Park's quieter cousin, **Grand Lake,** 1½ mi outside the park's
west entrance, gets busy in summer, but overall has a low-key, Western
graciousness. In winter, it's *the* snowmobiling capital and ice-fishing
destination for Coloradans. At the park's southwestern entrance are
Arapaho National/Roosevelt Forest, Arapaho National Recreational
Area, and the small town of **Granby,** the place to go for big-game hunting, mountain biking, and skiing at nearby SolVista resort, Winter Park,
and Mary Jane. *For more information on Estes Park, Grand Lake, and
Granby, see the Boulder and North Central Colorado section.*

WHAT IT COSTS				
	¢	$	$$	$$$	$$$$
Restaurants	under $8	$8–$12	$13–$20	$21–$30	over $30
Hotels	under $70	$70–$100	$101–$150	$151–$200	over $200
Camping	under $10	$10–$17	$18–$35	$36–$50	over $50

Restaurant prices are per person for a main course at dinner. Hotel prices are per
night for two people in a standard double room in high season, excluding taxes
and services charges. Camping prices are for a standard (no hookups, pit toilets,
fire grates, picnic tables) campsite per night.

WHERE TO EAT AND STAY

ABOUT THE RESTAURANTS
In the park itself, there are no real dining establishments, though you
can get snacks and light fare at the top of the Trail Ridge Road. The
park also has a handful of scenic picnic areas, all with tables and pit
or flush toilets.

ABOUT THE HOTELS

In Estes Park, Grand Lake, and nearby towns, the elevation keeps the climate cool, and you'll have a tough time finding air-conditioned lodging. For a historic spot, try the Stanley Hotel in Estes Park—with its stately structure, it would fit right in on Mackinac Island in Michigan. The park has no hotels or lodges.

ABOUT THE CAMPGROUNDS

Five top-notch campgrounds in the park meet the needs of campers, whether you're staying in a tent, trailer, or RV (only two campgrounds accept reservations; the others fill up on a first-come, first-served basis). Backcountry camping requires advance reservations or a day-of-trip permit, contact **Backcountry Permits, Rocky Mountain National Park** (⊠ *Beaver Meadows Visitor Center, U.S. 36 southwest of Estes Park* ☎ *970/586–1242* ☉ *May–Sept., daily 7–7; Oct.–Apr., daily 8–4:30*) before starting out.

WHERE TO EAT

¢ ✕**Trail Ridge Store Snack Bar.** Pick up snacks and sandwiches, burgers, AMERICAN and soups at the Alpine Visitor Center. ⊠ *Trail Ridge Rd.* ☎ *970/586–3097* ▤ *AE, D, MC, V* ☉ *Closed mid-Oct.–May.*

PICNIC AREAS **Endovalley.** With 32 tables and 30 fire grates, this is the largest picnic area in the park. The views here are of aspen groves, Fall River Pass, and a beautiful lake. ⊠ *U.S. 34, at the beginning of Old Fall River Rd.*

Hollowell Park. In a meadow near Mill Creek, this lovely spot for a picnic has nine tables. The Mill Creek Basin trailhead is nearby. There is no running water and no fire grates. ⊠ *Off Bear Lake Rd., between the Moraine Park Museum and Glacier Basin campground.*

☉ **Sprague Lake.** With 23 tables, there's plenty of room for the whole gang at this dining al fresco spot. The wheelchair-accessible picnic area has restrooms, too. ⊠ *0.6 mi from the intersection of Bear Lake Road and U.S. 36.*

WHERE TO STAY

IN THE PARK

CAMPING 🏕**Aspenglen Campground.** This quiet, east-side spot near the north
$$ entrance is set in open pine woodland along Fall River. It doesn't have the views of Moraine Park or Glacier Basin, but it is small and peaceful. There are a few excellent walk-in sites for those who want to pitch a tent away from the crowds but still close to the car. All sites accommodate RVs, tents, trailers, or campers. Firewood and ice are for sale. Reservations are not accepted. **Pros:** good paved road; very peaceful; sites with trees; close to town but still very private. **Cons:** no great mountain views. ⊠ *Drive past Fall River Visitor Center on U.S. 34 and turn left at the campground road* ☎ *No phone* 🏕 *54 tent/RV sites* ⌂ *Flush toilets, drinking water, fire grates, public telephone* ⌧ *Reservations not accepted* ▤ *AE, D, MC, V* ☉ *Closed mid-Sept.–late May.*

$$ 🏕 **Longs Peak Campground.** Hikers going up Longs Peak can stay at this year-round campground. Sites, which are first-come, first-served,

8

are limited to eight people; ice and firewood are sold in summer. **Pros:** good camp site for Longs Peak hikers. **Cons:** tents only; drinking water isn't available off season. ⊠ *9 mi south of Estes Park on Rte. 7* ☎ *No phone* ⚠ *26 tent sites* ⚲ *Flush toilets, pit toilets, drinking water (mid-May–mid-Sept.), fire grates, ranger station* ⚲ *Reservations not accepted* ⊟ *AE, D, MC, V.*

$$ ⚠ **Moraine Park Campground.** This popular campground hosts ranger-led
★ campfire programs and is near hiking trails. Sites accommodate RVs, tents, trailers, and campers. Reservations are essential from mid-May to late September. **Pros:** abundant shady trees; near many hiking trails; nice pine scent. **Cons:** no drinking water outside summer months. ⊠ *Drive south on Bear Lake Rd. from U.S. 36, 0.75 mi to campground entrance* ☎ *877/444–6777* ⚠ *245 tent/RV sites* ⚲ *Flush toilets, pit toilets, dump station, drinking water (mid-May–mid-Sept.), fire grates, public telephone* ⊟ *AE, D, MC, V.*

$$ ⚠ **Timber Creek Campground.** Anglers love this spot on the Colorado River, 10 mi from Grand Lake village. In the evening you can sit in on ranger-led campfire programs. All sites accommodate RVs, tents, trailers, or campers, and are limited to eight people. Firewood is sold here. Reservations are not accepted. **Pros:** great fishing spot by the Colorado River. **Cons:** mountain pine beetle has necessitated cutting of many mature Lodgepole Pines (but new growth is evident); no drinking water in the off season. ⊠ *Trail Ridge Rd. 1, 2 mi west of Alpine Visitor Center* ☎ *No phone* ⚠ *98 tent/RV sites* ⚲ *Flush toilets, pit toilets, dump station, drinking water (mid-May to mid-Sept.), fire grates, public telephone* ⚲ *Reservations not accepted* ⊟ *AE, D, MC, V.*

Northwest Colorado and Steamboat Springs

WORD OF MOUTH

"When I booked my very first trip to Steamboat two years ago, I had every intention of trying a new Western ski resort each year. However, after my first visit, I was hooked and just keep going back to Steamboat. It simply has everything I'm looking for—no crowds, relaxed atmosphere, nice scenery."

—Miramar

Updated by
Kyle Wagner

Varied terrain attracts bold outdoors enthusiasts, and genteel towns are tucked among the craggy cliffs for those seeking quieter pursuits. Whatever your choice, the northwest
region's more remote location and mountain-dominated
landscape give it a largely undiscovered feel, and many of
the activities lack the crowds and frenzy attached to those
in more heavily populated areas.

Adventures in these far-western and northern regions of the state might
range from a bone-jarring mountain-bike ride on the Kokopelli Trail—
a 142-mi route through remote desert sandstone and shale canyon from
Grand Junction to Moab—to a heart-pounding raft trip down the Green
River, where Major John Wesley Powell made his epic exploration of
this continent's last uncharted wilderness in 1869. Colorado National
Monument and Dinosaur National Monument have endless opportunities for hiking. For the less adventurous, a visit to the wine country
makes for a relaxing afternoon, or try your hand at excavating prehistoric bones from a dinosaur quarry. Rich in more recent history as well,
the area is home to the Museum of Western Colorado and Escalante
Canyon, named after Spanish missionary explorer Francisco Silvestre
Velez de Escalante, who with father Francisco Atanasio Dominguez led
an expedition through the area in 1776.

Farther east, flanked by mountains with some of the softest snow in the
world, even the cowboys don skis. Steamboat Springs is Colorado at its
most authentic, where hay bales and cattle crowd pastures, McMan-
sions are regarded with disdain, high-schoolers compete in local rodeos,
deer hang from front porches during hunting season, and high fashion
means clean jeans. Steamboat Ski Resort has none of the pretensions
of the glitzier Colorado resorts.

Even the less-visited corners of the region have plenty of cultural opportunities for those willing to seek them out. Dotting the area are art galleries, antiques shops, and many small eateries with alfresco seating.
People are friendly and share plenty of tourist tips just for the asking.
As for quirky festivals, you might have a hard time choosing between
the Olathe Sweet Corn Festival, Country Jam, or the Mike the Headless
Chicken Festival. The laid-back lifestyle here is the perfect example to
follow—chill out and explore the region at your own pace.

ORIENTATION AND PLANNING

GETTING ORIENTED

A little planning goes a long way when visiting this region. Grand Junction, the largest city between Denver and Salt Lake City, makes an ideal
hub for exploring. Many of the sights, except for Steamboat Springs, are

TOP REASONS TO GO

Colorado National Monument:
Gaze out over Grand Junction toward the Bookcliffs along the 23-mi Rim Rock Drive or hike one of the many trails through sandstone canyons.

Grand Junction and Palisade Wine tasting: More than two-dozen local wineries have garnered attention for their grapes grown in the unique high-altitude soil.

Strawberry Park Hot Springs:
Though it takes some work to get here, it's well worth the effort to soak away what ails you in the rustic, rock-lined setting.

Steamboat Springs Horseback riding: Choose from an authentic dude ranch experience, a pack trip into the wilderness, or a gentle alpine trail ride.

Dinosaur National Monument:
Wander among thousands of skeletons that remain embedded in the rugged hillsides or take a raft trip down the Green or Yampa rivers.

less than two hours from Grand Junction. You can make the loop from Delta to Cedaredge and Grand Mesa to Palisade easily in a day. If you want to break up the trip, stop in Cedaredge. The loop in the opposite direction—including Meeker, Craig, Dinosaur National Monument, and Rangely—is longer, but there's decent lodging along the way, with the exception of Dinosaur National Monument (camping only).

If you're headed to Steamboat Springs from Denver in winter, exercise caution on Highway 40. It sees less traffic than I–70, but it can be treacherous in the Berthoud Pass stretch during snowstorms.

Grand Junction and Around. This narrow city is a quiet, gracious locale that easily balances raucous outdoor adventures and a thriving cultural scene. The Colorado National Monument and Bookcliffs dominate the landscape, but Palisade, with its peaches and wines, and Fruita, a burgeoning mountain-biking mecca, command ever-increasing attention.

Steamboat Springs. Unlike some of the other ski towns, Steamboat has always been a "real" town. With its undercurrent of Old West Lite and plenty of cowboys still hanging around, visitors are usually torn—hot springs, horseback riding, or skiing?

Northwest Corner. The world's largest flat-topped mountain, the Grand Mesa, has a 55-mile Scenic Byway that feels a little like "Land of the Lost." Meanwhile, Dinosaur National Monument offers thousands of fossils and hiking trails galore. Stop in nearby Craig or Rangely to refuel yourself and your vehicle.

PLANNING

WHEN TO GO

The region has four distinct seasons. The heaviest concentration of tourists is in summer, when school is out and families hit the road for a little together time. Temperatures in summer frequently reach into the high 80s and 90s, although the mercury has been known to top triple digits on occasion. You might have a hard time finding a hotel room during late May and late June thanks to the National Junior College World Series (baseball) and Country Jam music festival, both in Grand Junction. Hotels fill quickly in fall, which brings an explosion of colors. Days are warm, but nights are crisp and cool. There's still time to enjoy activities like fishing, hiking, and backpacking before the snow flies. Grand Mesa is a winter favorite among locals looking for a quick fix for cabin fever. Powder hounds can't wait to strap on their newly waxed skis and hit the slopes at Steamboat and Powderhorn ski resorts.

GETTING HERE AND AROUND

AIR TRAVEL

Walker Field Airport (GJT) is in Grand Junction. It's served by America West Express, Sky West, Great Lakes (Frontier), and United Express.

Yampa Valley Regional Airport (HDN) is in Hayden, 22 mi from Steamboat Springs. American, Continental, Delta, Northwest, and United fly nonstop from various gateways during ski season.

Taxis and shuttle services are available in Grand Junction and Steamboat Springs.

Airport Contacts Walker Field Airport (GJT) (✉ *Grand Junction* ☎ *970/244–9100* ⊕ *www.walkerfield.com*).**Yampa Valley Regional Airport (HDN)** (✉ *Hayden* ☎ *970/276–3669*).

CAR TRAVEL

In northwestern Colorado I–70 (U.S. 6) is the major thoroughfare, accessing Grand Junction and Grand Mesa (via Route 65, which runs to Delta). Meeker is reached via Route 13 and Rangely and Dinosaur via Route 64. U.S. 40 east from Utah is the best way to reach Dinosaur National Monument and Craig.

From Denver, Steamboat Springs is about a three-hour drive northwest via I–70 and U.S. 40. The route traverses some high-mountain passes, so it's a good idea to check road conditions before you travel.

Grand Junction has gas stations that are open 24 hours. Most gas stations in the smaller towns are open until 10 PM in summer, and even some automated credit-card pumps shut down at that hour.

Most roads are paved and in fairly good condition. Summer is peak road-construction season, so expect some delays. Be prepared for winter driving conditions at all times. Enterprise is in downtown Grand Junction, with free pickup. Avis and Hertz are in the Walker Field Airport terminal. Depending on where you're traveling, you might want a four-wheel drive. Avis has car rentals in Steamboat Springs.

Car Travel Contacts AAA Colorado (☎ *970/245–2236* ⊕ *www.aaa.com*). **Colorado State Patrol** (☎ *970/249–4392* ⊕ *www.csp.state.co.us*). **Road Report** (☎ *877/315–7623* ⊕ *www.cotrip.org*).

TRAIN TRAVEL

Amtrak provides daily service to the East and West coasts through downtown Grand Junction.

Train Contacts Amtrak (☎ *800/872–7245* ⊕ *www.amtrak.com*).

PARKS AND RECREATION AREAS

The blushing red-rock cliffs of the **Colorado National Monument** are easily accessible by winding roads that open to miles of hiking trails. **Dinosaur National Monument** holds a stunning cache of fossils as well as spectacular scenery aboveground for family-friendly hiking.

Grand Mesa National Forest (⊕ *www.fs.fed.us/r2/gmug*) shimmers with peaceful alpine lakes and great fishing and hiking in summer, along with trails for snowmobiling in winter. A bird-watcher's paradise with species from ducks to bald eagles, the remote **Browns Park Wildlife Refuge** (⊕ *www.fws.gov/brownspark*) northwest of Maybell can be navigated by car or horseback, or on foot. The **Flat Tops Wilderness** (⊕ *www.fs.fed. us/r2/whiteriver*) is an alpine mesa with good stream and lake fishing and excellent deer and elk hunting. It's southwest of Steamboat Springs. Steamboat Springs is surrounded by the **Medicine Bow/Routt National Forests** (⊕ *www.fs.fed.us/r2/mbr*), which stretch across northern Colorado and into southern Wyoming, embracing more than half a dozen mountain ranges, including the Gore, Flat Tops, Park, Medicine Bow, Sierra Madre, and Laramie.

RESTAURANTS

Once restricted to chicken-fried steak and burgers, the region's dining scene has expanded far past the Old West. The usual chain restaurants ring Grand Junction, but they're joined by eclectic gourmet pizza joints and authentic Mexican restaurants. Look for made-from-scratch delicacies at mom-and-pop bakeries—especially worth seeking out during summer fruit harvests. In season, Palisade peaches, Olathe sweet corn, and Cedaredge apples find their way onto menus, paired with the multitude of increasingly mature local wines. Still, there's nothing wrong with a great hand-battered chicken-fried steak smothered in creamy gravy—which you can still find in just about any town in the area.

The town of Steamboat Springs, in the heart of cattle country, has far more carnivorous delights—including elk, deer, and bison—than you're likely to find in the trendier resorts of Aspen, Telluride, and Vail. The Steamboat ski resort, separated geographically from town, works toward a more-cosmopolitan mix, with small sushi bars and Mediterranean cafés hidden among the boutiques.

9

HOTELS

The region is growing, and that means more lodging choices. In Grand Junction Horizon Drive has the largest concentration of hotels and motels, conveniently near Walker Field Airport and within walking distance of a handful of restaurants. For the budget conscious, there are many clean, no-frills motels as well as most of the well-known chains. History buffs might enjoy a stay at a dude ranch, one of the many rustic cabin rentals, or the famed Meeker Hotel, once frequented by Teddy Roosevelt. For those looking for the comforts of home, the area has a nice selection of bed-and-breakfasts, including one that has a llama herd and others set in fruit orchards and vineyards. Be sure to ask for off-season lodging rates, which could save you a bundle.

Steamboat Springs is unique in the state because it has high-end dude ranches and ranch resorts, which are absent in resort areas like Aspen, Summit County, and Vail.

WHAT IT COSTS				
	¢	$	$$	$$$	$$$$
Restaurants	under $8	$8–$12	$13–$18	$19–$25	over $25
Hotels	under $80	$80–$120	$121–$170	$171–$230	over $230

Restaurant prices are for a main course at dinner, excluding 6.5%–8.4% tax. Hotel prices are for two people in a standard double room in high season, excluding service charges and 9.4%–10.65% tax.

GRAND JUNCTION AND AROUND

With its mild climate and healthy economy, Grand Junction and the surrounding area make northwestern Colorado an inviting destination. A thriving retirement community and mountain-biking headquarters, the Grand Valley also counts superior soil and top-notch ranching among its assets. The contrast between the sandstone of the Bookcliffs and the canyons of the Colorado National Monument with the greenery of the lush orchards below, particularly in nearby Palisade, makes for a pleasant road trip.

GRAND JUNCTION

255 mi west of Denver via I–70.

Grand Junction is where the mountains and desert meet at the confluence of the mighty Colorado and Gunnison rivers—a grand junction indeed. No matter which direction you look, there's an adventure waiting to happen. The city, with a population of approximately 42,000, is nestled between the picturesque Grand Mesa to the south and the towering Bookcliffs to the north. Surprisingly sophisticated, with a small-town flair, this city is a great base camp for a vacation—whether you're into art galleries, boutiques, hiking, horseback riding, rafting, mountain biking, or winery tours.

The Art on the Corner exhibit showcases leading regional sculptors, whose latest works are installed on the Main Street Mall. Passersby may find their faces reflected in an enormous chrome buffalo (titled *Chrome on the Range*) or, a few streets down, encounter an enormous cactus made entirely of rusted (but still prickly) chainsaw chains.

GETTING HERE AND AROUND

A Touch With Class has regular limo service into Grand Junction and outlying communities. Sunshine Taxi serves Grand Junction. Amtrak runs the California Zephyr round-trip from San Francisco to Chicago, which stops in Grand Junction, Glenwood Springs, Winter Park, and Denver. Grand Valley Transit operates 11 public bus routes that are geared to commuters between Grand Junction, Palisade, Clifton, Orchard Mesa, and Fruita.

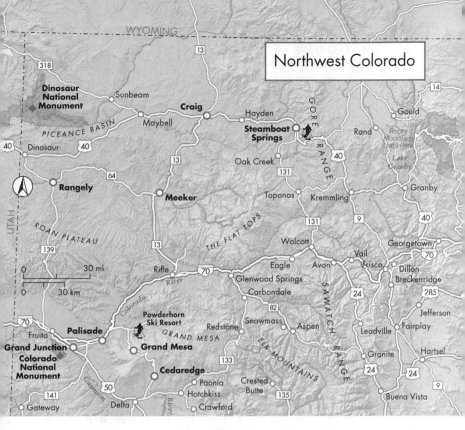

Eagle Tree Tours runs tours of Colorado National Monument and the Grand Junction area, including some with four-wheel-drive vehicles, hiking, or biking. Dinosaur Journey leads one- and three-day paleontological treks that include work in a dinosaur quarry.

WHEN TO GO

FESTIVALS **Country Jam** is held every June and draws the biggest names in country music, such as Faith Hill and Toby Keith, while **Rock Jam** is held in September with headliners such as Def Leppard.

ESSENTIALS

Festivals Country Jam and Rock Jam (✉ Country Jam USA Ranch, Mack ☎ 800/530–3020 ⊕ countryjam.com).

Transportation Contacts A Touch With Class (☎ 970/245–5466).**Sunshine Taxi** (☎ 970/245–8294). **Amtrak** (☎ 800/872–7245 ⊕ www.amtrak.com). **Grand Valley Transit** (☎ 970/256–7433 ⊕ www.gvt.mesacounty.us). **Sunshine Taxi** (✉ Grand Junction ☎ 970/245–8294.

Tour Info Eagle Tree Tours (✉ 538 Teller, Grand Junction ☎ 970/241–4792). **Dinosaur Journey** (✉ 550 Jurassic Ct., Fruita ☎ 970/858–7282 ⊕ www. dinosaurjourney.org).

Visitor Info Grand Junction Visitor & Convention Bureau (✉ 740 Horizon Dr. ☎ 800/962–2547 ⊕ www.visitgrandjunction.com).

EXPLORING

The **Art Center** rotates a fine permanent collection of Native American tapestries and Western contemporary art, including the only complete series of lithographs by noted printmaker Paul Pletka. The fantastically carved doors—done by a WPA artist in the 1930s—alone are worth the visit. Take time to view the elegant historic homes along North 7th Street afterward. Admission is free on Tuesdays and always for children under 12. ⊠ *1803 N. 7th St.* ☎ *970/243–7337* ⊕ *www.gjartcenter.org* ≦ *$3* ⊙ *Tues.–Sat. 9–4.*

The **Cross Orchards Historic Site** recreates a historic agricultural community of the early 20th century on its 24½-acre site, listed on the National Register of Historic Places. A workers' bunkhouse, blacksmith shop, country store, and an extensive collection of vintage farming and road-building equipment are among the exhibits. Tours lasting 1½–2 hours, or tailored to visitors' interests, are available upon request. ⊠ *3073 F Rd.* ☎ *970/434–9814* ⊕ *www.museumofwesternco.com* ≦ *$4* ⊙ *Apr.–Oct., Tues.–Sat. 9–4.*

The **Museum of Western Colorado/Museum of the West** relates the history of the area since the 1880s, with a time line, a firearms display, and a Southwest pottery collection. The area's rich mining heritage is perfectly captured in the uranium mine that educates with interactive sound and exhibit stations. The museum also runs the Cross Orchards Living History Farm and the Dinosaur Journey Museum, and oversees paleontological excavations. ⊠ *462 Ute Ave.* ☎ *970/242–0971* ⊕ *www. museumofwesternco.com* ≦ *$5.50* ⊙ *May–Sept., Mon.–Sat. 9–5, Sun. noon–4; Oct.–Apr., Tues.–Sat. 10–3.*

EXPERIENCE A DINOSAUR DIG Ever wonder what it's like to be on a dinosaur expedition? Here's your chance. The Museum of Western Colorado sponsors one- to five-day **Dino Digs** (☎ 888/488–3466 ⊕ www. dinodigs.org) all over northwestern Colorado, and folks find fresh fossils all the time. The area includes some rich Late Jurassic soil, Morrison Formation sites, and other well-preserved zones that make for impressive discoveries, and you never know what might be unearthed.

OFF THE BEATEN PATH

Little Bookcliffs Wild Horse Range. One of just three ranges in the United States set aside for wild horses, it encompasses 30,261 acres of rugged canyons and plateaus in the Bookcliffs. Eighty to 120 wild horses roam the sagebrush-covered hills. Most years new foals can be spotted with their mothers in spring and early summer on the hillsides just off the main trails. Local favorites for riding include the Coal Canyon Trail and Main Canyon Trail, where the herd often goes in winter. Vehicles are permitted on designated trails. ⊠ *2815 H Rd., about 8 mi northeast of Grand Junction* ☎ *970/244–3000* ⊕ *www.co.blm.gov* ≦ *Free* ⊙ *Daily dawn–dusk.*

SPORTS AND OUTDOOR ACTIVITIES

For information about hiking, horseback riding, and rafting, see Colorado National Monument.

★ **The Golf Club at Redlands Mesa.** The 18-hole championship course is set at an elevation of 4,600 feet in the shadows of the Colorado National Monument, just minutes from downtown. ⊠ 2299 *W. Ridges Blvd.* ☎ *970/263–9270* ⊕ *www.redlandsgolf.com* ⚘ *Reservations essential* ⟐ *18 holes. Yards: 7,007/4,916. Par: 72/72. Green fee: $61/$89.*

MOUNTAIN BIKING

Several routes through Grand Junction are well suited to bicycle use. The city also has designated bike lanes in some areas. You can bike along the Colorado Riverfront Trails, a network that winds along the Colorado River, stretching from the Redlands Parkway to Palisade.

Kokopelli Trail links Grand Junction with the famed Slickrock Trail outside Moab, Utah. The 142-mi stretch winds through high desert and the Colorado River valley before climbing the La Sal Mountains. Those interested in bike tours should contact the **Colorado Plateau Mountain Bike Trail Association** (☎ *970/244–8877* ⊕ *www.copmoba.org*).

OUTFITTERS **Brown Cycles** (⊠ *Grand Junction* ☎ *970/245–7939* ⊕ *www.browncycles. com*) has reasonable day rates for road, mountain, and hybrid bikes starting around $35 a day, sells and fixes bikes, and offers a full line of tandems for families with expanded kid options for rent and sale, as well. Aficionados should allow some extra time to check out the interesting bike museum, with models from as early as the 1860s. **Over the Edge Sports** (⊠ *202 E. Aspen Ave., Fruita* ☎ *970/858–7220* ⊕ *www. otesports.com*) offers mountain-biking lessons and half- or full-day customized bike tours. **Ruby Canyon Cycles** (⊠ *Grand Junction* ☎ *970/241–0141* ⊕ *www.rubycanyoncycles.com*) rents high-end, full-suspension mountain bikes for $50 the first day, $40 consecutive days. The cycle shop also sponsors weekly evening rides around the area.

WHERE TO EAT

$ ✕ **Dos Hombres.** Casual and colorful, Dos Hombres serves the usual
MEXICAN variety of combination platters and Mexican specialties, and loads up
ⓒ the plates for low prices. The fajitas and enchiladas are particularly well made, with quality meats and a noticeable lack of grease, and they have an unusually large menu of interesting salads (check out the Cancun version, with pineapple and fried tortilla strips). Service is snappy and friendly, and the staff is accommodating to kids. The margaritas and cervezas are inexpensive, too—and half-price during the weekday 3-hour happy hour. ⊠ *421 Brach Dr.* ☎ *970/242–8861* ⊕ *www.go2dos. com* ⊟ *MC, V.*

$$–$$$ ✕ **Il Bistro Italiano.** With a chef hailing from the birthplace of Parmi-
ITALIAN giano-Reggiano, this restaurant's authenticity is assured, down to that
★ perfectly delivered final shredded topping. Diners are greeted by a case of pasta made fresh daily and pampered by a staff that knows the origins of each home-style dish. Entrées include seafood lasagna and wood-fired pizzas along with veal, pork, and chicken dishes finished with innovative sauces such as artichokes and capers in a white-wine cream sauce and deep-fried sage with Gorgonzola butter. ⊠ *400 Main St.* ☎ *970/243–8622* ⊕ *www.ilbistroitaliano.com* ⊟ *AE, D, MC, V.*

9

¢–$ ✕ **Pablo's Pizza.** Drawing inspiration from Pablo Picasso's artwork, the
PIZZA pizzas at this funky joint make for a diverse palette of flavors and fun.
Ⓒ Specialties include creations such as Popeye's Passion (featuring spinach
and "olive oyl") or Dracula's Nemesis (studded with roasted garlic). For
kids, they even serve (we're not making this up) a peanut-butter-and-
jelly pizza. With brick walls covered only by eclectic local paintings,
Pablo's can get loud when busy. They pour local wines by the glass
and Palisade Brewery beer and root beer by the bottle. ⊠ *319 Main St.*
☎ *970/255–8879* ⊕ *www.pablospizza.com* ▤ *AE, D, MC, V.*

$$$$ ✕ **The Winery.** This is *the* place for the big night out and special occa-
AMERICAN sions. It's awash in stained glass, wood beams, exposed brick, and
hanging plants, with dark nooks and crannies and ends of aging barrels
as art, all of which combines for an intimate atmosphere. The menu
isn't terribly adventuresome, but the kitchen does turn out fresh-fish
specials and top-notch steak, chicken, prime rib, and shrimp in simple,
flavorful sauces. The real draw is for wine fans who want to try a
more obscure bottle from the extensive, domestic-heavy roster. ⊠ *642
Main St.* ☎ *970/242–4100* ⊕ *www.winery-restaurant.com* ▤ *AE, D,
DC, MC, V* ☺ *No lunch.*

WHERE TO STAY

$ 🏨 **Grand Vista Hotel.** Plush high-back chairs invite visitors to relax in
Ⓒ the spacious lobby of this hotel that lives up to its name. A private-
club look dominates the hotel's main restaurant, and an old-fashioned
charm characterizes the rooms, though artwork and re-tiled bathrooms,
as well as some of the newer furniture, have a fresh, more modern feel.
Pros: you can't beat the views; they will store your bike for you; the
price is right. **Cons:** the breakfast buffet is mediocre; service is hit or
miss; children are allowed to run rampant. ⊠ *2790 Crossroads Blvd.,*
☎ *970/241–8411* ⊕ *www.grandvistahotel.com* ⇌ *158 rooms* ⬧ *In-
room: Wi-Fi. In-hotel: restaurant, bar, pool, gym, public Wi-Fi, airport
shuttle, some pets allowed* ▤ *AE, D, DC, MC, V.*

$–$$ 🏨 **Hawthorn Suites L.T.D. Hotel.** With a sofa and two oversize chairs, the
plush suites here have plenty of room to sit back and relax. The many
amenities include coffeemakers, and then there's the complimentary full
breakfast. Business travelers appreciate the Internet access and those
suites with full kitchens; all rooms have cushy Swedish Tempur-Pedic
beds. The hotel is in the heart of downtown, within walking distance
of restaurants and boutiques. **Pros:** business travelers' dream in terms
of amenities; indoor and outdoor pools; decent buffet breakfast. **Cons:**
airport shuttle can be crowded at peak times; rooms are showing wear
and tear; small fitness center. ⊠ *225 Main St.,* ☎ *970/242–2525 or
800/527–1133* ⊕ *www.hawthorn.com* ⇌ *70 suites* ⬧ *In-room: Wi-Fi,
kitchen (some), refrigerator, VCR, Internet. In-hotel: pool, gym, airport shuttle, some pets allowed, guest laundry, Internet* ▤ *AE, D, DC,
MC, V* ❙◯❙ *BP.*

$$ 🏨 **Los Altos Bed & Breakfast.** This luxurious, panoramic hilltop is a peace-
ful, centralized home base for exploring the area. Only a few minutes
from downtown Grand Junction, the modern-yet-cozy home opens to
views stretching from Colorado National Monument to the Bookcliffs
and Grand Mesa. Set on 3½ acres perched above a quiet residential

neighborhood, the B&B has seven large rooms (including one sprawling executive suite) furnished with elegant hardwood beds. Breakfast includes cream cheese–filled French toast and fresh fruit. Call for directions; it's easy to get lost in the nearby neighborhood. **Pros:** close to downtown but quiet; stunning views; private baths. **Cons:** thin walls mean that sometimes you can hear your neighbors. ⊠ *375 Hillview Dr.,* ☎ *970/256–0964 or 888/774–0982 ⊕ www.losaltosgrandjunction.com* ⇨ *4 rooms, 3 suites ৬ In-hotel: public Wi-Fi* ▤ *MC, V* ⏀*l BP.*

$–$$ 🔳 **Two Rivers Winery & Chateau.** Open a bottle of wine inside the vine-
★   yard where it was created at this country French–styled inn set among acres of vines. Roses and lavender bloom at the entrance, and there are views of the Colorado National Monument as well as an expansive balcony. Large, elegant rooms are furnished with beautiful hardwood beds and heavy, comfortable couches. The inn adjoins the Two Rivers Winery, which has tastings and tours throughout the day and bottles for purchase in every room. **Pros:** idyllic locale for weddings or other special occasions; tasty wines always at hand, expansive Continental breakfast. **Cons:** winery and functions mean noisier than the usual B&B; rooms are chilly in winter; kitchen is inconsistent. ⊠ *2087 Broadway,* ☎ *970/241–3155 or 866/312–9463 ⊕ www.tworiverswinery.com* ⇨ *10 rooms ৬ In-room: Wi-Fi. In-hotel: some pets allowed* ▤ *AE, D, DC, MC, V* ⏀*l CP.*

NIGHTLIFE AND THE ARTS
THE ARTS
The **Avalon Theatre** (⊠ *645 Main St.* ☎ *970/263–5700 ⊕ www.tworiversconvention.com*) is one of the largest performing arts complexes in western Colorado, offering traveling lectures, dance, theater, and other cultural performances. The popular monthly "Dinner and a Movie" nights bring classic and popular old blockbusters to the big screen, with receipts from a meal in town garnering free admission.

The 65-piece **Grand Junction Symphony** (☎ *970/243–6787 ⊕ www.gjsymphony.org*) is highly regarded and performs in venues throughout the city.

NIGHTLIFE
Bistro 743 Lounge (⊠ *743 Horizon Dr.* ☎ *970/241–8888 Ext. 121*) inside the Doubletree Hotel serves beverages, appetizers, and light snacks. Occasionally entertainers perform outside on the beer-garden stage. The **Blue Moon** (⊠ *120 N. 7th St.* ☎ *970/242–4506*) is a favorite Cheers-like neighborhood bar where patrons nurse their favorite brew while catching up with colleagues or friends. The **Rockslide Brewery** (⊠ *401 Main St.* ☎ *970/245–2111*) has won awards for its ales, porters, and stouts. The patio is open in summer.

SHOPPING
The best place in the area for Tony Lama boots and Minnetonka moccasins is **Champion Boots & Saddlery** (⊠ *545 Main St.* ☎ *970/242–2465*), in business since 1936. The sweetest deal in town, **Enstrom's** (⊠ *200 S. 7th St.* ☎ *970/242–1655*) is known for its scrumptious candy and world-renowned toffee. The Main Street boutique **Girlfriends** (⊠ *316 Main St.* ☎ *970/242–3234*) sells a line of comfy clothes, pottery, benches,

9

candles, and one-of-a-kind gifts. The cute but upscale boutique **Heirlooms for Hospice** (⊠ *635 Main St.* ☎ *970/254–8556*) has great secondhand designer clothing and shabby-chic furniture. **Working Artists Studio and Gallery** (⊠ *520 Main St.* ☎ *970/256–9952*) carries prints, pottery, stained glass, and unique gifts.

PALISADE

12 mi east of Grand Junction via I–70.

Palisade is Colorado's version of Napa Valley, with the highest concentration of wineries in the state. It's an easy day trip from Grand Junction; meander through the vineyards and stop for lunch in the tiny, slow-paced town framed by stately Victorian homes and sweetened by homespun festivals. The orchards also are a big draw; the long, frost-free growing season intensifies the fruit sugars, resulting in intensely flavorful peaches, cherries, apricots, and nectarines. At harvest time the area sees a steady flow of visitors stopping by the orchards themselves, many of which have on-site sales, as well as the roadside stands that pop up seasonally to sell preserves, salsas, pies, and other fruit-based products.

GETTING HERE AND AROUND

A car is the best way to get to and around Palisade. Public transportation options are limited.

WHEN TO GO

A variety of produce is available through the summer months, but the peaches and other fruits famous in the Palisade area are at the height of their season from late June to early October.

FESTIVALS In summer **Grande River Vineyards** (⊠ *787 Elberta Ave.* ☎ *970/464–5867* ⊕ *www.granderiverwines.com*) hosts a concert series featuring classical, country, blues, and rock music. The natural landscape contributes to the good acoustics, not to mention the spectacular sunsets. Concertgoers lounge in lawn chairs, enjoying picnics and dancing barefoot on the grass, and sometimes the concerts are held in the cellars.

Palisade celebrates the harvest for four days every August during the **Palisade Peach Festival** (☎ *970/464–7458* ⊕ *www.palisadepeachfest.com*). September brings the annual **Colorado Mountain Winefest** (☎ *800/704–3667* ⊕ *www.coloradowinefest.com*).

ESSENTIALS

Visitor Info Palisade Chamber of Commerce (⊠ *319 Main St.,* ☎ *970/464–7458* ⊕ *www.palisadecoc.com*).

EXPLORING

Fodor'sChoice One of Colorado's best-kept secrets is its **winery tours.** It's a great way to
★ see how your favorite wine goes from vineyard to glass. You can learn about the grape-growing process and what varieties of grapes grow best in western Colorado's mild climate. Depending on the time of the year, you may also see the grape harvesting and crushing process. For a self-guided tour, visit ⊕ *www.visitgrandjunction.com* and print out its maps and directions to the wineries. If you're taking the self-guided route, call to reserve tours that take you beyond the tasting room and

into the winemaking process. Of course the best part of the tour is sampling the wines.

QUICK BITES

Changing artwork decorates the light and airy Palisade Café (⊠ 113 W. 3rd St. ☎ 970/464–0657). It offers a nice selection of breakfast, lunch, and dinner choices, including soups, salads, burgers, French dips, Reuben sandwiches, and vegetarian dishes.

American Spirit Shuttle operates scheduled tours in 14-passenger vans on Saturdays. The tours visit at least four wineries and last approximately four hours. Wine lovers get to sample a variety of Colorado wines in the tasting rooms, with the added benefit of having someone else do the driving. ⊠ 204 4th St., Clifton ☎ 970/523–7662 ⊕ www.americanspiritshuttle. net ⊠ $30 ☉ May–Oct., Sat. 1–5.

FARM STAND PICNIC

Considering the plethora of produce in the Grand Junction and Palisade area, you would think that great restaurants would be easy to come by, but not so. Better to eat the ingredients in their most unadulterated form straight from the source; spend some time stopping by the dozens of farm stands that dot the landscape. A favorite is Talbott Farms and its store, the Mountain Gold Market, where two-dozen kinds of peaches can be had, as well as other local products. Look for local jams, honey, fruits and vegetables, cider, and freshly baked items, all perfect for an impromptu picnic.

WHERE TO EAT AND STAY

¢
CAFE
Fodor's Choice
★

✕ **Slice O' Life Bakery.** Aromatic goodies are baked with whole grains and fresh local fruits at this down-home–style bakery known around the region for its melt-in-your-mouth pastries, sweet rolls, Jamocha brownies, and fresh-fruit cobblers. Owners Tim and Mary Lincoln have even made the lowly fruitcake into a craveable commodity, studding them with fresh Palisade peaches and mailing them around the country (in fact, they do some of the best things with peaches in town, including pie). Cold sandwiches and fresh-baked bread are also available. ⊠ 105 W. 3rd St. ☎ 970/464–0577 ▤ No credit cards ☉ Closed Sun. and Mon. No dinner.

$

🏠 **Orchard House Bed & Breakfast.** Set in a peaceful peach orchard a few miles from downtown, this home lives up to its name. During harvest season in August it's possible to pick your own sweet snack from the grove. A large porch spanning two sides of the house beckons you to sit a spell and enjoy views of Grand Mesa and the Bookcliffs. **Pros:** homey; elaborate breakfasts with fresh peaches in season; lovingly cared for property. **Cons:** pet policy is not popular with everyone. ⊠ 3573 E½ Rd., ☎ 970/464–0529 ⊕ www.theorchardhouse.com ⇆ 4 rooms, 3 with bath ♿ In-room: no a/c (some), no TV. In-hotel: some pets allowed ▤ AE, D, MC, V ⊠ BP.

SHOPPING

Harold and Nola Voorhees (⊠ 3702 G ⁷⁄₁₀ Rd. ☎ 970/464–7220) sell a range of dried fruits, including cherries, pears, apricots, and peaches. **Talbott Farms Mountain Gold Market** (⊠ 3782 F ½ Rd. ☎ 877/834–6686) puts out nearly two-dozen kinds of peaches, as well as apples and pears and the juices of all three. The huge, fourth generation–run operation sells local products and will take you on a tour of the place if you ask.

9

COLORADO NATIONAL MONUMENT

23 mi west of Grand Junction via Rte. 340.

GETTING HERE AND AROUND

From I–70 westbound, take Exit 31 (Horizon Drive) and follow signs through Grand Junction; eastbound take Exit 19 (Fruita) and drive south 3 mi on Highway 340 to the west entrance.

TOURS   American Spirit Shuttle offers scheduled and customized tours of Colorado National Monument.

WHEN TO GO

FESTIVALS   Fruita celebrates **Mike the Headless Chicken Days** (☎ 970/858–3894 ⊕ *www. miketheheadlesschicken.org*) every May with the Chicken Dance and the Run Like A Headless Chicken 5K Race. The town's **Fat Tire Festival** brings mountain bikers from all over together to take on the area's trails every April. (☎ 970/858–7220 ⊕ *www.fruitamountainbike.com*).

ESSENTIALS

Tour Contacts American Spirit Shuttle (⊠ 204 4th St., Clifton ☎ 970/523–7662 ⊕ www.americanspiritshuttle.net).

EXPLORING

Sheer red-rock cliffs open to 23 mi of steep canyons and thin monoliths that sprout as high as 450 feet from the floor of **Colorado National Monument.** This vast tract of rugged, ragged terrain was declared a national monument in 1911 at the urging of an eccentric visionary named John Otto. Cold Shivers Point is just one of the many dramatic overlooks along **Rim Rock Drive**, a 23-mi scenic route with breathtaking views. The town of Fruita, at the base of Colorado National Monument, is a haven for mountain bikers and hikers. It makes a great center for exploring the area's canyons—whether from the seat of a bike or the middle of a raft, heading for a leisurely float trip.

Scheduled programs, such as guided walks and campfire talks, are posted at the **Visitor Center** (☎ 970/858–3617 ☉ *June–Aug., daily 8–6; Sept.–May, daily 9–5*). Maps and trail information are also available. Rock climbing is popular at the monument, as are horseback riding, cross-country skiing, biking, and camping. ⊠ *Fruita* ☎ 970/858–3617 ⊕ *www.nps.gov/colm* ⊠ *$7 per wk per vehicle. Visitors entering on bicycle, motorcycle, or foot pay $4 for weekly pass* ☉ *Daily.*

★ ☉ Roaring robotic stegosaurs and meat-shredding animatronic Allosaurs prowl **Dinosaur Journey,** a fun, informative attraction just off I–70 a few minutes from the western entrance to Colorado National Monument. Unlike many museums, this one encourages kids to touch everything— friendly paleontologists may even allow kids to hold a chunk of fossilized dino dung. In addition to the amazing lifelike replicas, there are more than 20 interactive displays. Children can stand in an earthquake simulator; dig up "fossils" in a mock quarry; or make dino prints in dirt, along with reptile and bird tracks for comparison. The museum also sponsors daily digs nearby, where many of the fossils were found. Local volunteers are at work cleaning and preparing fossils for study. ⊠ *550 Jurassic Ct., Fruita* ☎ 970/858–7282 or 888/488–3466 ⊕ *www. dinosaurjourney.com* ⊠ *$7* ☉ *Daily 9–5.*

Fodor's Choice Ten miles west of Grand Junction, stretching from Fruita to just across
★ the Utah border, the **McInnis Canyons National Conservation Area** (formerly
Colorado Canyons National Conservation Area) is rife with natural
arches, along with numerous rock canyons, caves, coves, and spires.
Rattlesnake Canyon has nine arches, making it the second-largest concentration of natural arches in the country. The canyon can be reached
in summer from the upper end of Rim Rock Drive with four-wheel-drive
vehicles or via a 7-mi hike by the intrepid.

Though much of the territory complements the red-dirt canyons of Colorado National Monument, McInnis Canyons is more accessible to horseback riding, mountain biking, all-terrain vehicle and motorcycle trails,
and for trips with dogs (most of these activities aren't allowed at the monument). Designated in 2000 by act of Congress, the conservation area
was created from a desire of nearby communities to preserve the area's
unique scenery while allowing multiple-use recreation. Be prepared for
biting gnats from late May to late July. Contact the Bureau of Land Management for a map before venturing out. ⊠ *2815 H Rd.* ☎ *970/244–3000*
⊕ *www.blm.gov/co/st/en/fo/mcnca.html* 🖃 *Free* ☉ *Year-round.*

SPORTS AND THE OUTDOORS
HIKING
A good way to explore **Colorado National Monument** is by trail. There are
more than a dozen short and backcountry trails ranging from 0.25 mi
to 8.5 mi. An easy 30-minute stroll with sweeping canyon views, **Otto's
Trail** (⊠ *Trailhead: Rim Rock Dr., 1 mi from western gate visitor center*) greets hikers with breezes scented by sagebrush and juniper, which
stand out from the dull red rock and sand. The trail leads to stunning
sheer drop-offs and endless views. At the end of the half-mile trail at
Otto's Overlook you can hear the wind in the feathers of birds as they
soar out of the canyon. **Serpents Trail** (⊠ *Trailhead: Serpents Trail parking lot, 0.25 mi from east gate*) has been called the "Crookedest Road
in the World" because of its more than 50 switchbacks. The fairly
steep but rewarding trail, which ascends several hundred feet, takes
about two hours to complete, depending on your ability (and the heat).
☎ *970/858–3617* ⊕ *www.nps.gov/colm.*

HORSEBACK RIDING
Rimrock Adventures (⊠ *927 Hwy. 340, Fruita* ☎ *970/858–9555 or 888/
712–9555* ⊕ *www.rradventures.com*) runs horseback rides near Colorado National Monument as well as through Little Bookcliffs Wild
Horse Preserve.

RAFTING
Adventure Bound River Expeditions (⊠ *2392 H Rd.* ☎ *970/245–5428 or
800/423–4668* ⊕ *www.raft-colorado.com*) runs trips on the Colorado,
Green, and Yampa rivers—the latter through the canyons of Dinosaur National Monument. **Rimrock Adventures** (⊠ *927 Hwy. 340, Fruita*
☎ *970/858–9555 or 888/712–9555* ⊕ *www.rradventures.com*) has a
variety of rafting excursions and easygoing float trips.

9

CLOSE UP

The Legacy of Mike the Headless Chicken

Mike the Headless Chicken was a freak bound for fame. It all started with a run-in with a Fruita farmer who had bad aim, or so the tale goes. The year was 1945. Mike, a young Wyandotte rooster, was minding his own business in the barnyard when farmer Lloyd Olsen snatched him from the chicken coop. It seems that Clara, the farmer's wife, wanted chicken for dinner that night. Mike was put on death row. Well, faster than you can say pinfeathers, farmer Olsen stretched Mike's neck across the chopping block and whacked off his head. Apparently undaunted by the ordeal, Mike promptly got up, dusted off his feathers and went about his daily business pecking for food, fluffing his feathers, and crowing, except Mike's crow was now reduced to a gurgle. Scientists

surmised that Mike's brain stem was largely untouched, leaving his reflex actions intact. A blood clot prevented him from bleeding to death. The headless chicken dubbed "Miracle Mike" toured the freak-show circuit, where the morbidly curious could sneak a peek at his nogginless nub for a quarter. Mike's incredible story of survival (he lived for 18 months without a head!) soon hit the pages of two national magazines, *Time* and *Life*. The headless wonder, who was fed with an eyedropper, eventually met his demise in an Arizona motel room, where he choked to death. His legacy lives on in Fruita, where the tiny town throws a gigantic party every May to celebrate Mike's life. Even in death, Mike is still making headlines.

ROCK CLIMBING

The stunning stark sandstone and shale formations of Colorado National Monument are a rock climber's paradise. Independence Monument is a favorite climb. Experienced desert-rock guide Kris Hjelle owns and operates **Desert Crags & Cracks** (✉ *Box 2803, Fruita* ☎ *970/245–8513* ⊕ *www.desertcrags.com*), specializing in guiding and instruction on the desert rocks of western Colorado and eastern Utah.

WHERE TO EAT

$ ✕**The End Zone Sports Pub.** A quintessential sports bar with plenty of
MEXICAN TVs and pool tables for playing your own games when there's nothing
� to watch. The menu is pub grub done well and for a fair price: burgers, hefty sandwiches, fish-and-chips, and steaks, as well as huge wedges of cake for dessert and a kids' menu priced according to age—$4.75 for 10 and under, $6.95 11 and over. The "holy moley" Buffalo-style wings will blow your ears off, but locals swear by them. The atmosphere is noisy but never overly raucous, and it's popular with mountain bikers, who stop in for a post-ride beer. ✉ *152 S. Mesa St., Fruita* ☎ *970/858–0701* ☉ *Closed Mon.* ▱ *AE, D, MC, V.*

$–$$ ✕**Fiesta Guadalajara Restaurant.** Authentic and family-friendly, this
MEXICAN Mexican restaurant serves up good food. Try the chiles rellenos, super
� nachos, and especially the chili Colorado: fork-tender beef simmered in a savory red-pepper sauce. The appetizer combo plate is a meal in itself, and to feed an army, order Fiesta Fajitas. ✉ *103 Hwy. 6 and 50, Fruita* ☎ *970/858–1228* ▱ *AE, D, MC, V.*

GRAND MESA

47 mi southeast of Grand Junction via I–70 and Hwy. 65.

Small, quiet towns along the 63-mi Grand Mesa Scenic and Historic Byway (Highway 65) provide just enough support for the plethora of outdoor opportunities available in the diverse range of ecosystems on the world's largest flat-topped mountain.

GETTING HERE AND AROUND

A car is needed to explore Grand Mesa. In northwestern Colorado I–70 (U.S. 6) is the major thoroughfare, accessing Grand Junction and Grand Mesa (via Route 65, which runs to Delta).

ESSENTIALS

Transportation Contacts Walker Field Airport (GJT) (⊠ *Grand Junction* ☎ *970/244–9100* ⊕ *www.walkerfield.com*). **Amtrak** (☎ *800/872–7245* ⊕ *www. amtrak.com*).

Visitor Info Battlement Mesa Chamber of Commerce (⌂ *Box 93, Parachute* ☎ *970/285–7934* ⊕ *www.parachutechamber.org*).

EXPLORING

The world's largest flattop mountain towers nearly 11,000 feet above the surrounding terrain and sprawls an astounding 53 square mi. **Grand Mesa National Forest** attracts the outdoor enthusiast who craves the simple life: fresh air, biting fish, spectacular sunsets, a roaring campfire under the stars, and a little elbow room to take it all in. The landscape is filled with more than 300 sparkling lakes—a fisherman's paradise in summer. The mesa, as it's referred to by locals, offers excellent hiking and camping (try Island Lake Campground) opportunities. There are also a handful of lodges that rent modern cabins. You can also downhill ski at Powderhorn Resort, cross-country ski, snowshoe, snowmobile, or ice fish. ⊠ *2250 Hwy. 50, Delta* ☎ *970/874–6600* ⊕ *www. fs.fed.us/r2/gmug.*

SPORTS AND THE OUTDOORS

DOWNHILL SKIING

Powderhorn Resort has 42 trails, 4 lifts, 1,600 acres, and a 1,650-foot vertical drop. The slopes intriguingly follow the fall line of the mesa, carving out natural bowls. Those bowls on the western side are steeper than they first appear. Lift tickets are reasonable—kids under 6 ski for $15—and the skiing is surprisingly good. Powderhorn averages 250 inches of snowfall per year. ⊠ *Rte. 65, Mesa* ☎ *970/268–5700* ⊕ *www. powderhorn.com* ⧆ *Lift ticket $43–$53* ⊙ *Dec.–Apr., daily 9–4.*

FISHING

The lakes and reservoirs provide some of the best angling opportunities in Colorado for rainbow, cutthroat, and brook trout.

⟳ **Battlement Mesa Outfitters** (⊠ *20781 Kimball Creek Rd.* ☎ *970/487–9918* ⊕ *www.bmoutfitters.com*) sits about 40 minutes north of Grand Mesa in Collbran, and will take you fishing in just about any of its 200 lakes, custom-fitting the trip to your interests.

9

HIKING

Ⓒ **Grand Mesa Discovery Trail** (✉ *Trailhead: Grand Mesa visitor center, near intersection of Hwy. 65 and Trickel Park Rd.*) is a great beginning hike for kids and adults attempting to acclimate themselves to the altitude—and the slow-paced attitude—of the mesa. Pick up a brochure at the visitor center for information on the landscape. The gently sloping 20-minute trail gives a fascinating glimpse of what to expect on longer hikes.

WHERE TO STAY

$$ 🛏 **Alexander Lake Cabins.** The mirror-calm Alexander Lake reflects towering pine trees that also overlook the vast majority of this resort's cozy cabins, which are designed for tranquillity. Still, there's plenty of room for fishing, horseback riding, boating, or snowmobiling. Updated cabins—which hold as many as seven people—have modern, comfortable beds and kitchens of varying sizes. **Pros:** pay cash and save $20–$35; fishing and snowmobiling right on the property; quiet and peaceful. **Cons:** rather remote; no restaurant. ✉ *21221 Baron Lake Dr., 17 mi north of Cedaredge, 2 mi from Grand Mesa visitor center on Forest Rd. 121, 81413* ☎ *970/856–2539 or 800/850–7221* ⊕ *www.alexanderlakelodge.com* �`7 cabins ♿ In-room: no phone, kitchen, no TV ⊟ AE, D, MC, V.

$$ 🛏 **Spruce Lodge Resort.** French doors in each of the spacious cabins open
★ onto pure, thin air perfumed by the pine forest of the mesa. The decor inside the lodge, built in 1956, changes with the season, but remains comfy. The restaurant ($$–$$$) has a diverse menu. The modern cabins, heated by propane fireplaces, have kitchenettes, microwaves, coffeemakers, and hair dryers. Each cabin's deck has a table, chairs, and an umbrella, as well as an outside grill with picnic table and fire pit. **Pros:** pay cash and save $20–$35; cabins have a secluded feel; hot tubs are delightful in cooler temps. **Cons:** might be too remote for some. ✉ *20658 Baron Lake Dr., 16 mi north of Cedaredge; 1 mi from Grand Mesa visitor center on Hwy. 65 and Forest Rd. 121,* ☎ *970/856–6240 or 877/470–6548* ⊕ *www.sprucelodgecolorado.com* ➚ *11 cabins ♿ In-room: no a/c, no phone, kitchen, no TV (some). In-hotel: restaurant, bar ⊟ AE, D, DC, MC, V.

EN
ROUTE
    The **Grand Mesa Scenic Byway** (☎ 970/856–3100) is 63 mi long and winds its way along Highway 65 through meadows sprinkled with wildflowers, shimmering aspen groves, aromatic pine forests, and endless lakes. Scenic overlooks (Land-O-Lakes is a standout), rest areas, and picnic areas are clearly marked. There are two visitor centers on the Byway, which has endpoints at I–70 near Palisade and in Cedaredge.

CEDAREDGE

15 mi south of Grand Mesa via Hwy. 65.

Cedaredge is called the gateway to the Grand Mesa, the world's largest flat-topped mountain. An elevation of 6,100 feet makes for a mild climate that is perfect for ranching, as well as for growing apples, peaches, and cherries. The town is charming with its abundance of galleries, gift shops, antiques stores, and wineries.

GETTING HERE AND AROUND
Driving is the best way to get around the area; this small town is best explored on foot.

ESSENTIALS
Visitor Info Cedaredge Chamber of Commerce (⌂ *Box 278, Cedaredge* ☎ *970/856–6961* ⊕ *www.cedaredgecolorado.com*).

EXPLORING
The town site was originally the headquarters of a cattle spread, the Bar-I Ranch. **Pioneer Town,** a cluster of 23 authentic buildings that re-create turn of-the-20th-century life, includes a country chapel, the Lizard Head Saloon, original silos from the Bar-I Ranch, and a working blacksmith shop. ⊠ *315 S. W. 3rd Ave.* ☎ *970/856–7554* ☒ *$3* ☼ *June–late Sept., Mon.–Sat. 10–4, Sun. 1–4.*

WHERE TO EAT AND STAY
$$ ✕ **Grill at Deer Creek Village.** With dishes ranging from crab-and-artichoke

ECLECTIC dip to Thai chicken satay, this casual but elegant restaurant satisfies golfers from the adjoining Deer Creek Golf Club, as well as tourists looking to fill up after a long day on the mesa or antiques shopping. Steaks and seafood dishes are the mainstays, accompanied by an extensive local wine list. Call for directions. ⊠ *500 S. E. Jay Ave.* ☎ *970/856–7782* ⊕ *deercreekvillage-golf.com* ▭ *D, MC, V.*

¢ ✕ **Pizza to the Limit.** This locals' pizza joint has many tables jammed into

AMERICAN a tiny space. The old-fashioned letterboard menu is hard to read behind

☖ the counter, but whatever pie you order—maybe the Taco, with its beef, onions, lettuce tomato and tortilla chips, or the Cheezzy that lives up to its name—it's sure to be a crunchy-crusted pie with plenty of sauce and toppings. Cash only. ⊠ *105 S.E. Frontier Ave.* ☎ *970/856–7229* ▭ *No credit cards.*

$ ▦ **Cedars' Edge Llamas B&B.** A herd of curious—and hungry—llamas

☖ greets you at this modern cedar house and guest cottage and its four neatly furnished rooms, each with its own theme, overlooking 100-mi views of the Grand Valley. The innkeepers, Ray and Gail Record, are more than happy to share their encyclopedic knowledge of llamas; after you start your day in the breakfast room or on your own private deck, you are welcome to help feed hay or apples from the orchard to the herd. **Pros:** breakfast on your private deck is a nice option; close proximity to national forest; who doesn't love a llama? **Cons:** dated decor; maybe everyone doesn't love a llama; some of the rooms require stairs or walking a graded gravel path to the back of the property. ⊠ *2169 Hwy. 65,* ☎ *970/856–6836* ⊕ *www.llamabandb.com* ⇥ *4 rooms, 1 cottage* ☖ *In-room: no phone, refrigerator (some), no TV* ▭ *AE, MC, V* ⏩ *BP.*

SHOPPING
Once an apple-packing shed, the **Apple Shed** (⊠ *250 S. Grand Mesa Dr.* ☎ *970/856–7007*) has been restored and remodeled into a series of unusual gift shops and arts and crafts galleries. The attached deli ($) serves fresh peach milk shakes in season and top-notch sandwiches, sure to fuel your drive up the next pass.

9

STEAMBOAT SPRINGS

42 mi east of Craig via U.S. 40; 160 mi west of Denver via I–70, Rte. 9, and U.S. 40.

Steamboat got its name from French trappers who, after hearing the bubbling and churning hot springs, mistakenly thought a steamboat was chugging up the Yampa River. Here Stetson hats are sold for shade and not for souvenirs, and the Victorian-era buildings, most of them fronting the main drag of Lincoln Avenue, were built to be functional, not ornamental.

Steamboat Springs is aptly nicknamed Ski Town, U.S.A., because it has sent more athletes to the Winter Olympics than any other ski town in the nation. When sizing up the mountain, keep in mind that the part that's visible from below is only the tip of the iceberg—much more terrain lies concealed in back. Steamboat is famed for its eiderdown-soft snow; in fact, the term "champagne powder" was coined (and amusingly enough registered as a trademark) here to describe the area's unique feathery drifts, the result of Steamboat's fortuitous position between the arid desert to the west and the moisture-magnet of the Continental Divide to the east, where storm fronts duke it out.

The mountain village, with its maze of upscale condos, boutiques, and nightclubs, is certainly attractive, but spread out and a little lacking in character. To its credit, though, this increasingly trendy destination has retained much of its down-home friendliness.

GETTING HERE AND AROUND

Yampa Valley Regional Airport (HDN) is in Hayden, 22 mi from Steamboat Springs. American, Continental, Delta, Northwest, and United fly nonstop from various gateways during ski season. Alpine Taxi and Storm Mountain Express provide door-to-door service to Steamboat Springs from Yampa Valley Regional Airport. A one-way trip with either costs $33.

Steamboat Springs Transit (SST) provides free shuttle service between the ski area and downtown Steamboat year-round. Most of the major properties also provide shuttles between the two areas for their guests.

From Denver, Steamboat Springs is about a three-hour drive northwest via I–70 and U.S. 40. The route traverses some high-mountain passes, so it's a good idea to check road conditions before you travel.

Steamboat's Sweet Pea Tours visits nearby hot springs.

WHEN TO GO

A popular year-round destination, Steamboat becomes most dramatic in mid-September, when the leaves turn brilliant gold in the forests along the highways and the air cools considerably. By the first week of November, the ski season has begun, and it doesn't end until mid-April.

FESTIVALS **Strings in the Mountains Music Festival.** The focus is on chamber music and chamber-orchestra music presented by more than 150 musicians, including Grammy winners and other internationally renowned talents, throughout summer, primarily in the tent on the weekends. But Strings also offers big names in jazz, country, big band, bluegrass, and world music, as well as free concerts during its "Music on the Green" lunchtime series at Yampa River Botanic Park on Thursday in summer. ✉ *Steamboat Springs Music Festival Tent at the corner of Mt. Werner and Pine Grove Rds.,* ☎ *970/879–5056* ⊕ *www. stringsinthemountains.com.*

Hot Air Balloon Rodeo and Annual Art in the Park. For three decades, mid-July in Steamboat has meant hot-air balloons and fine art, a free combination that draws folks from miles around to watch more than 40 balloons float out over the valley from Bald Eagle Lake each morning of the event. The rest of weekend is devoted to the display and sale of hundreds of works of art from all over the world at West Lincoln Park. ✉ *35565 S. U.S. 40,* ☎ *877/754– 2269* ⊕ *www.steamboat-chamber.com.*

> ## WHERE IS STEAMBOAT SPRING?
>
> Don't waste time looking for Steamboat Spring, the one for which the town was named— it is dry now. It sits next to the Yampa River along the 13th Street Bridge, and once was so feisty people miles away thought the 15-foot-high spewer sounded like a steamboat churning down the river. When the railroad came to Steamboat in 1909, the spring mysteriously became nothing but a burble; some believe the railroad company somehow had something to do with that.

ESSENTIALS

Transportation Contacts Yampa Valley Regional Airport (HDN) (✉ *Hayden* ☎ *970/276–3669*). **Alpine Taxi** (✉ *Steamboat Springs* ☎ *800/343–7433* ⊕ *www.alpinetaxi.com*). **Sunshine Taxi** (✉ *Grand Junction* ☎ *970/245–8294*). **Storm Mountain Express** (✉ *Steamboat Springs* ☎ *877/844–8787* ⊕ *www. stormmountainexpress.com*). **Steamboat Springs Transit** (☎ *970/879–3717*).

Tour Contacts Sweet Pea Tours (✉ *Steamboat Springs* ☎ *970/879–5820* ⊕ *www.sweetpeatours.com*).

Visitor Info Steamboat Springs Snow Report (☎ *970/879–7300*). **Steamboat Ski & Resort Corporation** (✉ *2305 Mount Werner Circle, Steamboat Springs* ☎ *970/879–6111* ⊕ *steamboat.com*). **Steamboat Springs Chamber Resort Association** (✉ *1255 S. Lincoln Ave.,* ☎ *970/879–0880 or 800/922–2722* ⊕ *steamboatchamber.com*).

EXPLORING

The **Tread of Pioneers Museum,** in a restored Queen Anne Victorian home, is an excellent spot to bone up on local history. It includes ski memorabilia dating to the turn of the 20th century, when Carl Howelsen opened Howelsen Hill, still the country's preeminent ski-jumping facility. ✉ *8th and Oak Sts.* ☎ *970/879–2214* ⊕ *www.treadofpioneers.org* ✉ *$5* ⊙ *Tues.–Sat. 10–5.*

There are more than 150 mineral springs of varying temperatures in the Steamboat Springs area. In the middle of town **Old Town Hot Springs** gets its waters from the all-natural Heart Spring. The modern facility has a lap pool, relaxation pool, climbing wall, and health club. Two waterslides are open noon to 6 PM in summer and 4 to 8 PM in winter and require an additional fee. ✉ *136 Lincoln Ave.* ☎ *970/879–1828*

⊕ *www.steamboathotsprings.org* ✉ *$12* ⊙ *Weekdays 5:30* AM–*9:45* PM, *Sat. 7* AM–*8:45* PM, *Sun. 8* AM–*8:45* PM.

Fodor's Choice
★
About 7 mi west of town the **Strawberry Park Hot Springs** is a bit remote and rustic. If you're not sure of the way, go with a guide. The way the pool is set up to offer semi-privacy at this extremely popular spot makes for an intimate setting and relaxation. It's family-oriented during the day, but after dark clothing is optional and no one under 18 is admitted. ⊠ *Strawberry Park Rd.* ☎ *970/879–0342* ⊕ *www.strawberryhotsprings. com* ✉ *$10* ⊙ *Sun.–Thurs. 10* AM–*10:30* PM; *Fri. and Sat. 10* AM–*midnight* ⊟ *No credit cards.*

In summer Steamboat serves as the gateway to the magnificent **Medicine Bow/Routt National Forests,** with a wealth of activities from hiking to mountain biking to fishing. Among the nearby attractions are the 283-foot **Fish Creek Falls** and the splendidly rugged **Mount Zirkel Wilderness Area.** To the north, two sparkling man-made lakes, **Steamboat** and **Pearl,** each in its own state park, are a draw for those into fishing and sailing. In winter the area is just as popular. Snowshoers and backcountry skiers are permitted to use the west side of Rabbit Ears Pass, whereas snowmobilers are confined to the east side. ⊠ *Hahns Peak-Bears Ears Ranger District Office* ☎ *970/879–1870* ⊕ *www.fs.fed.us/r2/mbr.*

DOWNHILL SKIING AND SNOWBOARDING

The **Steamboat Springs Ski Area** is perhaps best known for its tree skiing and "cruising" terrain—the latter term referring to wide, groomed runs perfect for intermediate-level skiers. The abundance of cruising terrain has made Steamboat immensely popular with those who ski once or twice a year and who aren't looking to tax their abilities. On a predominantly western exposure—most ski areas sit on north-facing exposures—the resort benefits from intense sun, which contributes to the mellow atmosphere. In addition, one of the most extensive lift systems in the region allows skiers to take many runs without having to spend much time waiting in line. The Storm Peak and Sundown high-speed quads, for example, each send you about 2,000 vertical feet in less than seven minutes. Do the math: A day of more than 60,000 vertical feet is entirely within the realm of possibility.

All this is not to suggest, however, that Steamboat is a piece of cake for more experienced skiers. Pioneer Ridge encompasses advanced and intermediate terrain. Steamboat is renowned as a breeding ground for top mogul skiers, and for good reason. There are numerous mogul runs, but most are not particularly steep. The few with a vertical challenge, such as Chute One, are not especially long. If you're looking for challenging skiing at Steamboat, take on the trees. The ski area has done an admirable job of clearing many gladed areas of such nuisances as saplings, underbrush, and fallen timber, making Steamboat tree skiing much less hazardous than at other areas. The trees are also where advanced skiers—as well as, in some places, confident intermediates—can find the best of Steamboat's much-ballyhooed powder. Statistically, Steamboat doesn't report significantly more snowfall than other Colorado resorts, but somehow snow piles up here better than at the others. Ask well-traveled Colorado skiers, and they'll confirm that when it comes to consistently good, deep snow, Steamboat is hard to beat. ✉ *2305 Mount Werner Circle* ☎ *970/879–6111* ⊕ *www.steamboat.com* ⊙ *Late-Nov.–mid-Apr., daily 8:30–3:30.*

The tiny **Howelsen Hill Ski Area**, in the heart of Steamboat Springs, is the oldest ski area still open in Colorado. Howelsen, with four lifts, 15 trails, one terrain park, and a 440-foot vertical drop, is home of the Steamboat Springs Winter Sports Club, which has more than 700 members. The ski area not only has an awesome terrain park, but has night skiing as well. It's the largest ski-jumping complex in America, and a major Olympic training ground. ✉ *845 Howelsen Pkwy.* ☎ *970/879–8499* ⊙ *Nov.– Mar., Mon. 11–6:30, Tues.–Fri. 11–8, Sat. 9–8, Sun. 9–4:30.*

FACILITIES 3,128-foot vertical drop; 3,148 skiable acres; 19% beginner, 49% intermediate, 32% advanced; 2 8-passenger gondolas, 5 high-speed quad chairs, 1 high-speed 6-person, 1 quad chair, 1 triple chair, 3 double chairs, and 7 surface lifts.

LESSONS AND PROGRAMS Half-day group lessons begin at $81; all-day lessons are $99. Clinics in moguls, powder, snowboarding, and "hyper-carving"—made possible by the design of shaped skis—are available. General information about the ski areas is available through the **Steamboat Ski and Resort Corporation** (☎ *970/879–6111*). Intensive 2- and 3-day training camps in racing and advanced skiing are scheduled through the **Billy Kidd Center for Performance Skiing** (☎ *800/299–5017*). Programs for kids from 6 months to 15 years of age are given through the **Kids' Vacation Center** (☎ *970/871–5375*). Day care is also available.

Snowcat skiing—where a vehicle delivers you to hard-to-reach slopes— has been called the poor man's version of helicopter skiing, although at $200 to $300 a day it's not exactly skiing for the lunch-pail crowd. But snowcat users don't have to worry about landing, and can get to places that would be inaccessible by helicopter. Buffalo Pass, northeast of Steamboat, is reputed to be one of the snowiest spots in Colorado, and that's why it's the base for **Steamboat Powder Cats** (☎ *970/879–5188 or 800/288–0543* ⊕ *www.steamboatpowdercats.com*). There's a maximum of 24 skiers per group, so the open-meadow skiing is never crowded.

LIFT TICKETS $91. Savings of 5% or less on multiday tickets. Children 12 and under ski free when adults purchase a five-day ski ticket.

RENTALS Equipment packages are available at the gondola base as well as at ski shops in town. Packages (skis, boots, and poles) average about $41 a day, less for multiday rentals. Call **Steamboat Central Reservations** (☎ *970/879–0740 or 800/922–2722*) for rental information.

NORDIC SKIING
BACKCOUNTRY SKIING
The most popular area for backcountry skiing around Steamboat Springs is Rabbit Ears Pass, southeast of town. It's the last pass you cross if you're driving from Denver to Steamboat. Much of the appeal is its easy access to high-country trails from U.S. 40. There are plenty of routes you can take. Arrangements for backcountry tours can be made through **Steamboat Ski Touring Center** (✉ *Box 775401, Steamboat Springs* ☎ *970/879–8180* ⊕ *www.nordicski.net/*).

A popular backcountry spot is Seedhouse Road, about 25 mi north of Steamboat near the town of Clark. A marked network of trails across the rolling hills has good views of distant peaks. For maps and information on snow conditions, contact the **Hahns Peak Ranger Office** (✉ *925 Weiss Dr.,* ☎ *970/879–1870*).

Touring and telemarking rentals are available at ski shops in the Steamboat area. One of the best is the **Ski Haus** (✉ *1457 Pine Grove Rd.* ☎ *970/879–0385* ⊕ *www.skihaussteamboat.com*).

TRACK SKIING

Laid out on and along the Sheraton Steamboat Golf Club, **Steamboat Ski Touring Center** has a relatively gentle 18.5-mi trail network. A good option for a relaxed afternoon of skiing is to pick up some vittles at the Picnic Basket in the main building and enjoy a picnic along Fish Creek Trail, a 3-mi-long loop that winds through pine and aspen groves. Rental packages (skis, boots, and poles) are available. ⬚ *Box 775401, Steamboat Springs* ☎ *970/879–8180* ⊕ *nordicski.net* ✉ *Trail fee $18.*

★ **Vista Verde Guest Ranch** (⬚ *Box 465, Steamboat Springs* ☎ *970/879–3858 or 800/526–7433* ⊕ *www.vistaverde.com*) has a well-groomed network of tracks, as well as access to the adjacent national forest.

OTHER SPORTS AND THE OUTDOORS

Dogsledding, hot-air ballooning, and snowmobiling can be arranged by calling the activities department at **Steamboat Central Reservations** (☎ *970/879–4070 or 800/922–2722*).

GOLF

Haymaker Golf Course. Three miles south of Steamboat Springs, this public-access 18-hole Keith Foster course has a pro shop and café. The challenging, rolling course has hills, streams, and native grasses, as well as exceptional views. The course is noted for being well maintained, with large greens and a 10,000-square-foot putting green. ✉ *34855 U.S. 40* ☎ *970/870–1846* ⊕ *www.haymakergolf.com* ⚐ *Reservations essential* ⚑ *18 holes. Yards: 7,308/6,728. Par: 72/72. Green fee: $58/$98.*

Rollingstone Ranch Golf Club at the Sheraton Steamboat Resort. Expect to see plenty of wildlife; bear and elk have been spotted on the 18-hole championship course designed by the legendary Robert Trent Jones Jr. A recent remodel has revitalized the greens and added new tee boxes at many of the holes. The Fish Creek Grille ($) serves lunch and a well-rounded happy hour and appetizer menu after 3 PM. ✉ *2000 Clubhouse Dr.* ☎ *970/879–1391* ⊕ *www.sheratonsteamboatgolf.com* ⚐ *Reservations essential* ⚑ *18 holes. Yards: 6,902/5,462. Par: 72/72. Green fee: $75/$140.*

HIKING

In the **Medicine Bow/Routt National Forests,** a mellow half-mile trail leads
★ to a 280-foot waterfall at **Fish Creek Falls**. You can extend your hike another 2 mi to the Upper Falls and then another 5 mi to 9,850-foot-high Long Lake. ✉ *Hahns Peak-Bears Ears Ranger District Office* ☎ *970/879–1870* ⊕ *www.fs.fed.us/r2/mbr.*

HORSEBACK RIDING

Because of the ranches surrounding the Yampa and Elk rivers, Steamboat is full of real cowboys as well as visitors trying to act the part. **Horseback riding** is one of the most popular pastimes here, with good reason: seeing the area on horseback is not only easier on the legs, but it also allows riders to get deeper into the backcountry—which is crisscrossed by a web of deer and elk trails—and sometimes closer to wildlife than is possible on foot. Riding, however, isn't for everyone. There's usually a personal weight limit of 250 pounds, and children need to be able to handle their own mount. If you've never ridden a horse before, book a short test ride first. Allergies and sore muscles can turn a dream ride into an epic journey. Riding, instruction, and extended pack trips are offered at a number of ranches in the area, although some may require a minimum stay of a week.

OUTFITTERS
★

One facility that has the full gamut of activities, from hour-long tours to journeys lasting several days, is **Del's Triangle 3 Ranch** (⌂ *Box 893, Clark* ☎ *970/879–3495* ⊕ *www.steamboathorses.com*). It's about 20 mi north of Steamboat via Highway 129. **Sombrero Ranch** (⌂ *835 River Rd.* ☎ *970/879–2306* ⊕ *www.sombrero.com/steamboatsprings*) is right in town and has one-hour guided tours perfect for novices. Every Friday and Saturday evening in summer, rodeos are held at the **Howelsen Rodeo Grounds** (⌂ *5th St. and Howelsen Pkwy.* ☎ *970/879–1818*).

MOUNTAIN BIKING

Fodor's Choice
★

Steamboat Springs' rolling mountains, endless aspen glades, mellow valleys, and miles and miles of jeep trails and single-track make for great **mountain biking**. In summer, when Front Range trails are baking in the harsh summer sun and cluttered with mountain bikers, horse riders, and hikers, you can pedal some of the cool backcountry trails in Steamboat without passing a single cyclist.

The 27.5-mi **Gore Pass Loop** (⌂ *Trailhead: Follow Hwy. 134 to Gore Pass Park at the junction of Hwy. 134 and Forest Rd. 185, 80483*) takes you through aspen and pine forests, with gradual hill climbs and long, sweet descents. **Orange Peel Bikes** (⌂ *71136 Yampa St., Steamboat Springs* ☎ *970/879–2957* ⊕ *www.orangepeelbikes.com*) offers a sweet line of demos that cost only $15–$20 more than the regular rental rates that start at $30—a good deal if you're in the market for a new bike.

RAFTING

High Adventures/Bucking Rainbow Outfitters (⌂ *730 Lincoln Ave.* ☎ *970/879–8747* ⊕ *www.buckingrainbow.com*) runs rafting excursions to the Yampa, Elk, and Eagle rivers. Half-day to two-day trips are available for all levels.

SNOWMOBILING

Steamboat Snowmobile Tours (☎ *970/879–6500* ⊕ *www.steamboatsnowmobile.com*) has guided tours. A shuttle serves most hotels.

WHERE TO EAT

$$$–$$$$
ECLECTIC

✕ **Antares.** The owners of this hot spot cut their culinary teeth at some of Steamboat's finest restaurants, including Harwig's/L'Apogée. With fieldstone walls, pressed-tin ceilings, and beautiful stained-glass windows, the splendid Victorian building attracts all the attention at first. Then Paul

LeBrun's exciting, eclectic dishes arrive. You might feast on elk medallions with a Bing cherry–merlot sauce, or Maine lobster over chili-pepper linguine. The four-course tasting menu is a good bet, too, and comes out quickly. ⊠ *57½ 8th St.* ☎ *970/879–9939* ⌂ *Reservations essential* ⊟ *AE, MC, V* ⊗ *Closed Sun., Mon, Tues. in summer. No lunch.*

¢–$ **WCreekside Café & Grill.** This café's hearty breakfasts and lunches are
AMERICAN crafted to get folks through a day of skiing or biking, served in a casual
☺ atmosphere that's family—and group—friendly. The most popular item on the menu, and for good reason, is the roster of a dozen eggs Benedicts, including "the Arnold," with smoked bacon, ham, and chorizo. On nice days, ask to sit on the patio next to pretty Soda Creek. In season the place is usually jam-packed. Everything on the great kids' menu is $3 to $4. ⊠ *131 11th St.* ☎ *970/879-4925* ⊕ *www.creekside-cafe.com* ⌂ *Reservations essential* ⊟ *D, MC, V* ⊗ *No dinner.*

$–$$ ✕ **Cugino's Pizzeria & Italian Restaurant.** The South Philly sensibility of this
ITALIAN pizzeria lends authenticity to its filling strombolis, stuffed pizzas that
☺ purportedly originated just outside Philadelphia. The casual dining room offers a lot of breathing room, with the wooden tables set far apart, which means plenty of space for big groups to maneuver, a spacious patio deck, and a small bar area with a TV and an attached deck. Food comes in big portions, there are two patios for people-watching and views of the Yampa River, and the staff here will take good care of you. Try the crispy New York–style pizza and the authentic-tasting spaghetti. ⊠ *41 8th St.* ☎ *970/879–5805* ⊕ *www.cuginosrestaurant.com* ⊟ *MC, V.*

$$$$ ✕ **Harwigs/L'Apogee.** Steamboat's most intimate restaurant, Harwigs/
FRENCH L'Apogee is in a building that once housed Harwig's Saddlery and West-
★ ern Wear. There are two dining rooms, one that is more formal, the other casual. The classic French cuisine, with subtle Asian influences, is well crafted. Especially fine are the half crispy duck over oven-roasted yams, the Alaskan king crab cakes, and pan-seared foie gras topped with warm chèvre. Still, the menu takes a backseat to the admirable wine list. Oenophile alert: Owner Jamie Jenny is a collector whose magnificent wine cellar contains more than 10,000 bottles; you can order more than 40 wines by the glass. From May to December they offer a popular and reasonably priced Thai menu on Monday nights. ⊠ *911 Lincoln Ave.* ☎ *970/879–1919* ⊕ *www.lapogee.com* ⌂ *Reservations essential* ⊟ *AE, DC, MC, V* ⊗ *No lunch.*

¢–$ ✕ **Johnny B. Good's Diner.** Between the appealing kids' menu and the
AMERICAN memorabilia that suggests Elvis has not left the building, Johnny's is
☺ all about fun and family. Breakfast (until 2 PM), lunch, and dinner are served daily, and they are all budget minded and large portioned. The menu is mostly what you'd expect—meat loaf and mashed potatoes, burgers, milk shakes, biscuits and gravy—but they also do an above-average rib eye and some better-than-gringo Mexican, as well as a popular list of hot "dawgs." ⊠ *738 Lincoln Ave.* ☎ *970/870–8400* ⊕ *www. johnnybgoodsdiner.com* ⊟ *D, MC, V.*

$$$–$$$$ ✕ **La Montaña.** This Tex-Mex establishment is among Steamboat's most
SOUTHWESTERN popular restaurants, and with good reason. The kitchen incorporates indigenous specialties into the traditional menu. Among the standouts are sunflower seed–crusted tuna with a margarita beurre blanc,

enchiladas layered with Monterey Jack and goat cheese and roasted peppers, and elk loin crusted with pecan nuts and bourbon cream sauce. ⊠ *2500 Village Dr., at Après Ski Way* ☏ *970/879–5800* ⊟ *AE, D, MC, V* ⊘ *Closed Sun.–Tues. June–Aug. No lunch.*

$$ ✕ **Riggio's.** In a dramatic industrial space, this Italian eatery evokes the
ITALIAN Old Country with tapestries, murals, and landscape photos. The menu includes tasty pizzas (with toppings such as goat cheese and clams) and pasta dishes (*sciocca,* with rock shrimp, eggplant, tomatoes, and basil, is superb). Standards such as manicotti, chicken cacciatore, and saltimbocca are also well prepared. Try the house salad with Gorgonzola vinaigrette. ⊠ *1106 Lincoln Ave.* ☏ *970/879–9010* ⊕ *www. riggiosfineitalian.com* ⊟ *AE, D, DC, MC, V* ⊘ *No lunch.*

WHERE TO STAY

$$ 🛏 **Alpine Rose Bed and Breakfast.** Views of Strawberry Park and an easy walk into town make the Alpine Rose a wonderful alternative to pricey hotels, especially during ski season. The owners serve simple breakfasts, such as fruit with omelets or waffles, and the rooms are homey. One room has an adjoining room with a bunk bed for kids. The efficiency apartment, with its own entrance and Jacuzzi tub, is ideal for longer stays. On weekends and some holidays a two-night minimum is in effect. **Pros:** close to town; relatively close to ski area (five-minute drive); reasonably priced. **Cons:** not right next to ski area; two-night minimum can be an issue. ⊠ *724 Grand St.,* ☏ *970/879–1528 or 888/879–1528* ⊕ *www.alpinerosesteamboat.com* ⮐ *5 rooms* ⚹ *In-room: no a/c, no phone. In-hotel: public Wi-Fi, no kids under 6* ⊟ *MC, V.*

¢ 🛏 **Bunkhouse Lodge.** River or mountain views await you at the budget-
☾ minded Bunkhouse, which counts a river-rock fireplace surrounded by cozy couches and a Jacuzzi on the deck among its charms. Continental breakfast is included, and served in the cheery great room, and the free bus leaves from the end of the driveway to take you to the mountain or downtown. Rooms are sparse but adequate. **Pros:** great views; spacious rooms; bargain prices. **Cons:** very simple decor; linens are not exactly luxury. ⊠ *3155 S. Lincoln St.,* ☏ *877/245–6343 or 970/871–9121* ⊕ *www.thebunkhouselodge.com* ⮐ *38 rooms* ⚹ *In-room: refrigerator, Wi-Fi. In-hotel: laundry facilities* ⊟ *AE, D, MC, V.*

$$$$ 🛏 **Home Ranch.** You won't be roughing it at this all-inclusive retreat, a
☾ Relais & Chateaux property nestled among towering stands of aspen north of Steamboat near Clark. With a magnificent fieldstone fireplace surrounded by plush leather armchairs and sofa, the main room couldn't be cozier. The dining room, where the chef turns out tasty Southwestern fare, has soaring ceilings and wonderful views. Accommodations are in the main lodge or in individual cabins with terraces and private hot tubs. The style leans toward Native American rugs and prints, lace curtains, terra-cotta tile or hardwood floors, and stenciled walls. A seven-night minimum stay is required; they offer adults-only weeks in the fall. **Pros:** luxury experience; excellent food, family-friendly. **Cons:** pricey, seven-day stay can be prohibitive, less authentic. ⊠ *54880 County Rd. 129, Clark* ☏ *970/879–1780* ⊕ *www.homeranch.com* ⮐ *6 rooms, 8 cabins* ⚹ *In-hotel: bar, pool* ⊟ *AE, D, MC, V* ⊘ *Closed late Mar.–May and early Oct.–late Dec.* ⦿ *FAP.*

9

$$ ⚏ **Hotel Bristol.** A delightful small hotel nestled in a 1948 building, the Bristol not only has location working for it, but also old-fashioned personalized service. Situated right downtown, it is surrounded by shops and eateries and it has an immediately inviting lobby, with a fireplace and bookshelf. The staff goes out of its way to recommend local sights and dining, and although the Western-style decor is a bit faded, the cramped but serviceable rooms are well kept and tidy. Families and groups will appreciate their special family-style rooms, which offer four people the ability to stay in two rooms connected by a bathroom for about $40–$50 more per night. **Pros:** families and groups can stay comfortably for a small extra fee; convenient location; ski lockers; computer in lobby. **Cons:** rooms may seem uncomfortably small, bathrooms even more so. ✉ *917 Lincoln Ave.,* ☎ *970/879–3083 or 800/851–0872* ⊕ *www.steamboathotelbristol.com* ⮐ *24 rooms* ⚲ *In-room: DVD (some), Wi-Fi. In-hotel: restaurant* ⊟ *AE, D, MC, V.*

$$$ ⚏ **Inn at Steamboat.** Rustic knotty pine, leather furniture, sophisticated yet comfortable linens, and panoramic views of the Yampa Valley make the inn a good choice for folks looking to stay somewhere that feels like a mountain lodge at slightly lower-than-ski-resort prices. Each room has sliding doors that let you step out into the mountain air and onto a common balcony. It's near the shuttle services to the ski area and town, and also has its own shuttle to activities in winter. Continental breakfast, including make-your-own waffles, is included. **Pros:** magnificent views; even from the heated pool and particularly in fall; reasonable rates. **Cons:** not ski-in ski-out. ✉ *3070 Columbine Dr.,* ☎ *800/872–2601 or 970/879–2600* ⊕ *www.steamboatresorts.com* ⮐ *29 rooms, 4 suites* ⚲ *In-room: Wi-Fi, refrigerator, DVD. In-hotel: pool, laundry facilities, public Internet, public Wi-Fi* ⊟ *AE, D, MC, V* ⦿ *CP.*

$$ $$$ ⚏ **Ptarmigan Inn.** Situated on the slopes, this laid-back lodging, once part of the Best Western chain but now independently owned, couldn't have a more convenient location. The modest rooms, which still feel a little dated but are clean and comfortable, are decorated in pastels and have balconies with views of the surrounding mountains. The staff is very helpful and friendly—there's a ski valet and a decent pool. **Pros:** great location; ski-in ski-out; mountain views. **Cons:** chain hotel feel. ✉ *2304 Après Ski Way* ⬚ *Box 773240, Steamboat Springs* ☎ *970/879–1730 or 800/538–7519* ⊕ *www.steamboat-lodging.com* ⮐ *77 rooms* ⚲ *In-room: refrigerator, Internet, Wi-Fi. In-hotel: restaurant, bar, pool* ⊟ *AE, D, DC, MC, V.*

$–$$ ⚏ **Rabbit Ears Motel.** The playful, pink-neon bunny sign outside this motel has been a local landmark since 1952, making it an unofficial gateway to Steamboat Springs. The location is ideal if you're visiting the springs (across the street); the ski area (the bus stops outside); and the downtown shops, bars, and restaurants. All rooms are standard motel style, and most have balconies with views of the Yampa River. Continental breakfast is included. **Pros:** great location, family- and pet-friendly. **Cons:** kitschy, nothing fancy. ✉ *201 Lincoln Ave.,* ☎ *970/879–1150 or 800/828–7702* ⊕ *www.rabbitearsmotel.com* ⮐ *65 rooms* ⚲ *In-room: refrigerator, Wi-Fi. In-hotel: laundry facilities, some pets allowed* ⊟ *AE, D, DC, MC, V* ⦿ *CP.*

$$$$ ⛷ **Sheraton Steamboat Resort & Conference Center.** This bustling high-rise is Steamboat's only true ski-in ski-out property, and it finished a huge remodel in 2009 to bring the place out of the 1970s. The amenities are classic resort-town, with a ski shop, golf course, and four rooftop hot tubs with sweeping views of the surrounding ski slopes. The public areas were revamped to offer you cozy hangout "pods," including a comfortable segregated area for Wi-Fi users. Updated rooms have green accents and hip furnishings. **Pros:** convenient location, with the slopes, restaurants, and town right there; large size means lots of amenities. **Cons:** rooms somewhat cramped; lobby areas noisy; prices now on par with major ski areas. ⊠ *2200 Village End Ct.,* ☎ *970/879–2220 or 800/848–8877* ⊕ *www.starwoodhotels. com* ⇨ *315 rooms* ⚬ *In-room: safe, refrigerator. In-hotel: 2 restaurants, room service, bar, golf course, pool, gym, concierge, laundry service* ⊟ *AE, D, DC, MC, V.*

> **STEAMBOAT SPRINGS LODGING ALTERNATIVES**
>
> **Mountain Resorts** (⊠ *2145 Resort Dr., Suite 100,* ☎ *800/525–2622* ⊕ *www.mtn-resorts.com*) manages condominiums at more than 15 locations. Torian Plum, one of the properties managed by **Resort Quest Steamboat** (⊠ *1855 Ski Time Sq.,* ☎ *970/879–8811 or 800/228–2458* ⊕ *www. resortqueststeamboat.com*), has elegant one- to five-bedroom units in a ski-in ski-out location. Hot tubs are available. **Steamboat Resorts** (⌖ *Box 772995, Steamboat Springs* ☎ *800/276–6719* ⊕ *www.steamboatresorts. com*) rents plenty of properties near the slopes.

$$$$ ⛷ **Vista Verde Guest Ranch.** On a working ranch, the luxurious Vista
Fodor'sChoice Verde provides city slickers with an authentic Western experience.
★ Lodge rooms are huge and beautifully appointed, with lace curtains, Western art, and lodgepole furniture. Cabins are more rustic, with pine paneling and old-fashioned wood-burning stoves, plus refrigerators, coffeemakers, and porches. Three-, five-, and seven-night packages are available. Two weeks a year you can participate in a cattle drive; there are also weeks for adults only. **Pros:** authentic experience; variable stays; family-friendly. **Cons:** pricey. ⊠ *3100 County Rd. 64, Clark* ☎ *970/879–3858 or 800/526–7433* ⊕ *www.vistaverde.com* ⇨ *3 rooms, 9 cabins* ⚬ *In-room: no a/c, no TV. In-hotel: gym* ⊟ *MC, V* ⊗ *Closed mid-Mar.–early June and Oct.–mid-Dec.* ❉ *FAP.*

NIGHTLIFE
Mahogany Ridge Brewery & Grill (⊠ *435 Lincoln Ave.* ☎ *970/879–3773*) serves superior pub grub and pours an assortment of homemade ales, lagers, porters, and stouts. Live music is a nice bonus on weekends. The **Old Town Pub** (⊠ *600 Lincoln Ave.* ☎ *970/879–2101*) has juicy burgers and music from some great bands. On the mountain, the **Tugboat** (⊠ *1860 Ski Time Sq.* ☎ *970/879–7070*) is the place for loud rock and roll. You can also challenge locals to a game of pool.

SHOPPING
At the base of the ski area are three expansive shopping centers—Ski Time Square, Torian Plum Plaza, and Gondola Square.

Downtown Steamboat's **Old Town Square** (⊠ *7th St. and Lincoln Ave.*) is a collection of upscale boutiques and retailers. There are also plenty of places to get a good cup of coffee.

BOOKSTORES

Off the Beaten Path (⊠ *68 9th St.* ☎ *970/879–6830* ⊕ *www.steamboatbooks.com*) is a throwback to the Beat Generation, with poetry readings, lectures, and concerts. It has an excellent selection of New Age works, in addition to the usual best sellers and travel guides.

BOUTIQUES AND GALLERIES

In Torian Plum Plaza the **Silver Lining** (⊠ *1855 Ski Time Sq. Dr.* ☎ *970/879–7474*) displays art, crafts, and clothing from around the world, including Balinese cradle watchers, carved wooden figures believed to keep evil spirits away from sleeping children. You can make your own earrings at the bead counter. **White Hart Gallery** (⊠ *843 Lincoln Ave.* ☎ *970/879–1015*) is a magnificent clutter of Western-theme paintings and objets d'art. Native American images adorn the walls of the **Wild Horse Gallery** (⊠ *2200 Village End Ct.* ☎ *970/879–7660* ⊕ *www.wildhorsegallery.com*). This shop inside the Sheraton Steamboat is the place to buy artwork, jewelry, and blown glass.

SPORTING GOODS

Ski Haus (⊠ *1457 Pine Grove Rd.* ☎ *970/879–0385* ⊕ *www.skihaussteamboat.com*) can outfit you for the slopes. **Straightline Sports** (⊠ *744 Lincoln Ave.* ☎ *970/879–7568* ⊕ *www.straightlinesports.com*) is a good bet for downhill necessities.

WESTERN PARAPHERNALIA

Owned by the same family for four generations, **F.M. Light and Sons** (⊠ *830 Lincoln Ave.* ☎ *970/879–1822* ⊕ *fmlight.com*) caters to the Marlboro man in all of us. If you're lucky you'll find a bargain—how about cowboy hats for $4.98? **Into the West** (⊠ *807 Lincoln Ave.* ☎ *970/879–8377*) is owned by Jace Romick, a former member of the U.S. Ski Team and a veteran of the rodeo circuit. He crafts splendid textured lodgepole furniture. There are also antiques (even ornate potbellied stoves), cowhide mirrors, and handicrafts such as Native American–drum tables and fanciful candleholders fashioned from branding irons. **Soda Creek Western Outfitters** (⊠ *224 Arthur Ave., Oak Creek* ☎ *800/824–8426* ⊕ *www.soda-creek.com*) is about 30 mi west of Steamboat and worth the drive if authentic attire, including boots and hats, is on your shopping list. They also sell all manner of cowboy collectibles, home-decor items, gear, kitschy stuff for your dog, horse, and truck, and locally crafted jewelry.

NORTHWEST CORNER

Between the Flat Tops Scenic Byway and Dinosaur National Monument, the northwest corner of the state, which feels remote and desolate in parts but is improving in terms of amenities and development, is overflowing with history. Dinosaur fans will delight in exploring the monument, and folks looking for evidence of early Indian habitation will delight in the petroglyphs and pictographs. The towns are small and sleepy, but their inhabitants, many devoted to fishing, hunting, and other area outdoor pursuits, could not be more welcoming.

MEEKER

43 mi north of Rifle via Rte. 13.

Once an outpost of the U.S. Army, Meeker is still a place where anyone in camouflage dress always remains in fashion. Famous for its annual sheepdog championships—a sheepdog statue keeps watch over the sleepy town—it remains a favorite spot for hunting, fishing, and snowmobiling. Interesting historical buildings include the Meeker Hotel on Main Street, where Teddy Roosevelt stayed.

GETTING HERE AND AROUND
Meeker is fairly isolated, and nearly equidistant between Grand Junction and Steamboat Springs. There are no transportation services in town and a car is needed.

WHEN TO GO
FESTIVALS   You can watch professional sheepdogs in action at the annual **Meeker Classic Sheepdog Trials,** a prestigious five-day international competition and one of the town's biggest draws. Sheepdogs and their handlers perform sheepherding maneuvers on a closed course while competing for a $10,000 purse. The event takes place the weekend after Labor Day. ☎ *970/878–5510 or 970/878–0080* ⊕ *www.meekersheepdog.com* ☜ *$10.*

ESSENTIALS
Visitor Info Meeker Chamber of Commerce (✆ *Box 869, Meeker* ☎ *970/878–5510* ⊕ *www.meekerchamber.com*).

EXPLORING
The **White River Museum** is housed in a long building that served as a barracks for U.S. Army officers. Inside are exhibits such as a collection of guns dating to the Civil War and the plow used by Nathan Meeker to dig up the Ute's pony racetrack. ✉ *565 Park Ave.* ☎ *970/878–9982* ⊕ *www.meekercolorado.com/museum.htm* ☜ *Free* ☉ *May–Oct., weekdays 9–5, weekends 10–5; mid-Nov.–Apr., Fri. and Sat. 11–4.*

SPORTS AND THE OUTDOORS
FISHING
The White River valley is home to some of the best fishing holes in Colorado, including Meeker Town Park, Sleepy Cat Access, and Trappers Lake. Some of the best fishing is on private land, so you need to ask permission and you might have to pay. Your best bet—if you don't want to go it alone—is to hire a guide familiar with the area, such as **JML Outfitters** (✉ *300 Country Rd. 75* ☎ *970/878–4749* ⊕ *www.jmloutfitters.com*), which has been in the outfitting business for three generations, offering photography and wildlife-viewing trips, kids' camps, and trail rides.

SNOWMOBILING
One of Meeker's best-kept secrets is the fantastic snowmobiling through pristine powder in the backcountry, which some say rivals Yellowstone—without the crowds. Trail maps for self-guided rides are available

through the Chamber of Commerce or the U.S. Forest Service, or from **Welder Outfitting Services** (☎ *970/878–9869* ⊕ *www.flattops.com*), which guides snowmobiling in the White River National Forest and Flat Tops Wilderness.

WHERE TO STAY

$ 📷 **Meeker Hotel and Cafe.** At this Old West–style restaurant ($$–$$$)

AMERICAN   you'll feel like you're being watched—dozens of massive trophy elk and deer peer down from every wall. Peruse the menu with lively stories of Meeker's past, then try the homemade soup, chicken-fried steak, and mashed potatoes with cream gravy. The hotel, listed on the National Register of Historic Places, is filled with a veritable forest of rustic furniture. The lobby is lined with framed broadsheet biographies of famous figures—such as Teddy Roosevelt and, more recently, Dick Cheney—who stayed here. Rooms have claw-foot tubs and heavy beds; the bargain-price bunk wing has rooms with shared baths. **Pros:** delightful decor; delicious food in the café; bargain-hunters can go the communal-bathroom route. **Cons:** the café can get crowded and noisy; the walls are paper-thin. ⊠ *560 Main St.,* ☎ *970/878–5062 or 970/878–5255* ⊕ *www.themeekerhotel.com* 📠 *24 rooms* ♿ *In-room: no phone. In-hotel: restaurant, bar* ▤ *AE, D, MC, V.*

SHOPPING

Featuring original watercolor paintings and limited-edition prints by Colorado artist John T. Myers, **Fawn Creek Gallery** (⊠ *315 6th St.* ☎ *970/878–0955* ⊕ *www.fawncreek.com*) also sells Fremont and Ute rock-art replicas and duck carvings made from 100-year-old cedar fence posts.

An old-fashioned mercantile building with original display cases, tin ceilings, and wood floors, **Wendll's Wondrous Things** (⊠ *594 Main St.* ☎ *970/878–3688*) sells an eclectic mix of clothing, housewares, body-care products, greeting cards, Brighton jewelry, and Native American turquoise and sterling silver from Arizona.

CRAIG

48 mi north of Meeker via Rte. 13, 42 mi west of Steamboat Springs via U.S. 40.

Craig is home to some of the best fishing in the area. Guided trips to some of the hottest fishing spots are available, as are horseback pack trips into the wilderness. Depending on the season, you might spot bighorn sheep, antelope, or nesting waterfowl, including the Great Basin Canada goose.

GETTING HERE AND AROUND

U.S. 40 west from Denver or east from Utah is the best way to reach Craig. All Around Taxi provides service in town.

ESSENTIALS

Transportation Contacts All Around Taxi (⊠ *Craig* ☎ *970/824–1177*).

Visitor Info Greater Craig Chamber of Commerce (⊠ *360 E. Victory Way,* ☎ *970/824–5689* ⊕ *www.colorado-go-west.com*).

EXPLORING

One of Craig's most prized historical possessions, the **Marcia Car** in City Park was the private Pullman car of Colorado magnate David Moffat, who at one time was full or partial owner of more than 100 gold and silver mines. Moffat was also instrumental in bringing railroad transportation to northwest Colorado. He used his private car to inspect construction work on the Moffat Railroad line. Named after his only child, the car has been restored and makes for an interesting tour. ⊠ *U.S. 40 81625* ☎ *970/824–5689* ⌦ *Free* ☉ *Late May–mid-Oct., weekdays 8–5.*

The **Museum of Northwest Colorado** elegantly displays an eclectic collection of everything from arrowheads to a fire truck. The upstairs of this restored county courthouse holds the largest privately owned collection of working cowboy artifacts in the world. Bill Mackin, one of the leading traders in cowboy collectibles, has spent a lifetime gathering guns, bits, saddles, bootjacks, holsters, and spurs of all descriptions. ⊠ *590 Yampa Ave.* ☎ *970/824–6360* ⊕ *www.museumnwco.org* ⌦ *Free, donations accepted* ☉ *Mon.–Fri. 9–5, Sat. 10–4.*

SPORTS AND THE OUTDOORS

FISHING

Around Craig and Meeker, the Yampa and Green rivers, Trappers Lake, Lake Avery, and Elkhead Reservoir are known for pike and trout. Contact the **Sportsman's Center at the Craig Chamber of Commerce** (⊠ *360 E. Victory Way* ☎ *970/824–3046*) for information. Get the scoop on hot fishing spots from **Craig Sports** (⊠ *124 W. Victory Way* ☎ *970/824–4044* ⊕ *craigsports.net*) while loading up on tackle and other supplies.

WHERE TO EAT

$–$$
ITALIAN
☾

✕ **Cugino's Pizzeria & Italian Restaurant.** The same South Philly sensibility found at the Steamboat Springs location found its way to Craig in 2008. Filling strombolis and stuffed pizzas are authentic Philadelphia-style. Food comes in big portions, and the staff is friendly and accommodating. The owners have reworked the space that had been Bad to the Bone BBQ and made it even more inviting, with plenty of space between tables and a great foliage-lined patio, which looks more like someone's backyard than an eatery. Try the crispy New York–style pizza and the authentic-tasting spaghetti. ⊠ *572 Breeze St.* ☎ *970/824–6323* ⊕ *www. cuginosrestaurant.com* ⊟ *MC, V.*

$$
AMERICAN

✕ **Golden Cavvy.** A cavvy is the pick of a team of horses, and this restaurant is a favorite in town for the price. Its coffee-shop atmosphere is enlivened by mirrors, hanging plants, faux-antique chandeliers, and masonry of the 1900s fireplace of the Baker Hotel, which burned down on this spot. Hearty breakfasts, homemade pies and ice cream, burgers, pork chops, and anything deep-fried—try the mesquite-fried chicken— are your best bets. They also serve decent breakfasts. ⊠ *538 Yampa Ave.* ☎ *970/824–6038* ⊟ *MC, V.*

9

DINOSAUR NATIONAL MONUMENT

90 mi west of Craig via U.S. 40.

GETTING HERE AND AROUND

U.S. 40 west from Denver or east from Utah is the best way to reach Dinosaur National Monument. You also can take Highway 139 and Route 64 from Grand Junction. The town of Dinosaur, with a few somewhat dilapidated cement dinosaur statues watching over their namesake town, merits only a brief stop on the way to the real thing: Dinosaur National Park.

EXPLORING

Fodor'sChoice
★
☾

Straddling the Colorado–Utah border, **Dinosaur National Monument** is a must for any dinosaur enthusiast. A two-story hill teeming with fossils—many still in the complete skeletal shapes of the dinosaurs—greets visitors at one of the few places in the world where you can touch a dinosaur bone still embedded in the earth. The **Dinosaur Quarry** (⊠ *Visitor center: 7 mi north of Jensen, Utah, on Rte. 139* ☎ *970/374–3000*) is closed because of damage to the structural integrity of the building. There is a temporary visitor center set up, and although the main exhibit wall of dinosaur fossils is also closed, some of them can still be seen by hiking about a half-mile from the temporary site. A shuttle bus carries visitors from the temporary visitor center to the quarry. The Colorado side of the park offers some of the best hiking in the West, along the Harpers Corner and Echo Park Drive routes and the ominous-sounding Canyon of Lodore (where the Green River rapids buffet rafts). The drive is only accessible in summer—even then, four-wheel drive is preferable—and some of the most breathtaking overlooks are well off the beaten path. ⊠ *4545 E. Hwy. 40, Dinosaur* ☎ *435/781–7700* ⊕ *www.nps.gov/dino* ☜ *$10 per vehicle* ☼ *Daily.*

SPORTS AND THE OUTDOORS

HIKING

☾

The **Desert Voices Nature Trail** (⊠ *Split Mountain area, across from boat ramp*) is near the quarry. The 1.5-mi loop is moderate in difficulty and has a series of trail signs produced for kids by kids.

RAFTING

One of the best ways to experience the rugged beauty of the park is on a white-water raft trip. **Adventure Bound River Expeditions** (⊠ *2392 H Rd., Grand Junction* ☎ *800/423–4668* ⊕ *www.raft-colorado.com*) runs two- to five-day white-water raft excursions on the Colorado, Yampa, and Green rivers.

WHERE TO EAT

¢
AMERICAN
☾
★

✕ **BedRock Depot.** Co-owners and longtime residents Leona Hemmerich and Bill Mitchem understand both the cravings of the area's visitors and the spectacular vistas they come to see. New batches of homemade ice cream show up almost every day at their roadside shop where the walls are a gallery for their photography and artwork. The shop sells fresh sandwiches—including a terrific roast beef on their house-baked rolls—and specialty coffees (with names like "Mochasaurus") and bottled root beer, cream soda, and ginger ale. The Depot's immaculate restroom makes for one of the most pleasant pit stops on the long drive ahead. Call for winter hours from November to March. ✉ *214 Brontosaurus W. Blvd., Dinosaur* ☎ *970/374–2336* ⊕ *www.bedrockdepot. com* 🍴 *AE, D, MC, V*

$$
AMERICAN

✕ **Massadona Tavern & Steakhouse.** A restaurant and bar, Massadona has an old-time eatery feel—it's small, homey, and rustic, with a smattering of Western decor items and a mixture of tables and booths. It's also a casual, inviting, and relaxing place—kind of in the middle of nowhere, even though it's about 20 minutes east of Dinosaur and a half-hour drive from the monument—to stop after a day of digging around in dinosaur dirt, and the inexpensive steaks go down well with an also reasonably priced cocktail. They also do excellent breaded shrimp, good burgers (try the bacon cheeseburger), fish-and-chips, and classic Reubens. ✉ *22927 Hwy. 40* ☎ *970/374–2324* 🍴 *MC, V* ⊗ *Closed Mon., no lunch weekdays.*

RANGELY

20 mi southeast of Dinosaur National Monument, 96 mi northwest of Grand Junction via Rte. 139 and 1–70.

The center of one of the last areas in the state to be explored by European settlers, Rangely was dubbed an "isolated empire" by early pioneers. You can search out the petroglyphs left by Native American civilizations or just stroll the farmers' market in Town Square. If you enjoy backroad mountain biking, the Raven Rims have an abundance of trails. You may even spot elk, mules, deer, coyotes, and other wildlife as you spin your wheels through the multihued sandstone rims and mesas north of town. Kenney Reservoir 5 mi north of town offers fishing and swimming, and a trip to the Cathedral Bluffs gives new definition to "isolated empire."

GETTING HERE AND AROUND

U.S. 40 west from Denver or east from Utah and then Route 64 south is the best way to get to Rangely. You can also take Highway 139 from Grand Junction. There are no transportation services in town.

ESSENTIALS

Visitor Info Rangely Chamber of Commerce (✉ *209 E. Main St.,* ☎ *970/675–5290* ⊕ *www.rangely.com*).

EXPLORING

One of Rangely's most compelling sights is the superb Fremont petroglyphs—carved between AD 600 and 1300—in Douglas Creek canyon, ★ south of town along Route 139. This stretch is known as the **Canyon Pintado National Historic District,** and the examples of rock art are among the best-preserved in the West; half the fun is clambering up the rocks to find them. A brochure listing the sights is available at the Rangely Chamber of Commerce. ✉ *209 E. Main St.* ☎ *970/675–5290* ⊕ *www. co.blm.gov* 🎟 *Free* ⊗ *Daily.*

SPORTS AND THE OUTDOORS

FISHING

Just below Taylor Draw Dam, **Kenney Reservoir** draws anglers in search of black crappie, channel catfish, and rainbow trout. The best fishing is right below the dam. If you hook one of Colorado's endangered pikeminnow,

9

you'll have to throw it back. You can also go camping, boating, water-skiing, wildlife-watching, and picnicking. Locals come to the reservoir to watch the sun's last rays color the bluffs behind the lake.

MOUNTAIN BIKING

The best mountain-biking trails north of town are in the Raven Rims, named in honor of the abundant population of the large, noisy birds that live in the area. Contact the **Town of Rangely** (✉ *209 E. Main St.* ☎ *970/675–8476*) for trail information.

WHERE TO EAT AND STAY

¢–$

ITALIAN

✕ **Giovanni's Italian Grill.** Between the thick, hearty pizzas, big-as-your-head strombolis, and overflowing plates of pasta served at this incredibly friendly, casual eatery, it's impossible to walk out of here without feeling stuffed. The sauces are homemade, and the red sauce in particular is flavorful and authentic. The decor is nothing fancy, but that makes families feel welcome—check out the reasonably priced kids' menu, with nothing over $4, and so does the staff, which is sometimes made up of the owners' family members. ✉ *855 E. Main St.* ☎ *970/675–8986* ⊕ *www.giovannisrangely.com* ▤ *AE, D, MC, V* ☉ *Closed Sun.*

¢–$

MEXICAN

✕ **Los Tres Potrillos.** This casual Mexican restaurant has the usual selection of burritos and tacos and the only patio in town. Try the fajitas, enchiladas, and carne asada. Mexican pottery, serapes, and sombreros in green, orange, and black make up the colorful backdrop. The young service staff is accommodating, and the inexpensive beers and so-so margaritas come fast. ✉ *302 W. Main St.* ☎ *970/675–8870* ▤ *AE, D, MC, V* ☉ *Closed Sun.*

$$

▥ **Blue Mountain Inn & Suites.** Rooms are very simple but spacious at this reliable hotel that conveniently opened next to the grocery store in 2008. The large bathrooms, fluffy pillows, and complimentary Continental breakfast—a variety of juices, fresh pastries, and toast options and fresh fruit—make it a welcome addition to a town that had been lacking in varied lodging options. **Pros:** inviting heated indoor pool and hot tub; welcoming lobby with soft, cozy chairs; centrally located. **Cons:** has a chain feel; rooms are sparsely decorated. ✉ *37 Park St.,* ☎ *970/675–8888* ⊕ *www.bluemountaininnrangely.com* ➷ *47 rooms, 3 suites* ⌂ *In-room: refrigerator, Wi-Fi. In-hotel: pool, public Internet, laundry facilities* ▤ *AE, D, MC, V* ⦿| *CP.*

SHOPPING

Fresh produce, baked goods, and live entertainment can be found at the **Main Street Farmers' Market** (✉ *Town Sq* ☎ *970/675–5290*), held Saturday from 8:30 to 12:30. One of the more popular items is the elk jerky. A wood-burning stove graces the front of charming **Sweetbriar** (✉ *781 W. Hwy. 64* ☎ *970/675–5353*), a little store that sells a variety of gifts and home decor.

Southwest Colorado

THE SAN JUAN MOUNTAINS AND BLACK CANYON OF THE GUNNISON

WORD OF MOUTH

"Ouray is mainly a mining area and located at the head of a canyon with pretty steep mountains on three sides. Telluride is also a mining area but has great skiing and so has attracted more high dollar development and is a more ritzy moneyed place, especially on the Mountain. There are a lot of nice lower elevation drives around Telluride that are probably open if there has been snow that shut down the higher elevation jeep roads."

—Bill_H

Updated by
Carrie Frasure

The ruddy or red-hue rocks found in much of the state, particularly in the southwest, give Colorado its name. The region's terrain varies widely—from yawning black canyons and desolate monochrome moonscapes to pastel deserts and mesas, glistening sapphire lakes, and wide expanses of those stunning red rocks. It's so rugged in the southwest that a four-wheel-drive vehicle or hiker's sturdiness is necessary to explore much of the wild and beautiful backcountry.

The region's history and people are as colorful as the landscape. Southwestern Colorado, as well as the "Four Corners" neighbors of northwestern New Mexico, northeastern Arizona, and southeastern Utah, was home to the Ancestral Puebloan peoples formerly known as Anasazi, meaning "ancient ones." They constructed impressive cliff dwellings in what are now Mesa Verde National Park, Ute Mountain Tribal Park, and other nearby sites. This wild and woolly region, dotted with rowdy mining camps and boomtowns, also witnessed the antics of such notorious outlaws as Butch Cassidy, who embarked on his storied career by robbing the Telluride Bank in 1889, and Robert "Bobby" Clark, who hid out in Creede from the James Gang after he shot Jesse in the back. Even today, the more ornery, independent locals, disgusted with the political system, periodically talk of seceding from the union. They can be as rough as the country they inhabit.

Southwest Colorado has such diversity that, depending on where you go, you can have radically different vacations. You can spiral from the towering peaks of the San Juan range to the plunging Black Canyon of the Gunnison, taking in alpine scenery along the way, as well as the eerie remains of old mining camps, before winding through striking desert landscapes, the superlative Ancestral Puebloan ruins, and the Old West railroad town of Durango. If you're not here to ski or golf in the resorts of Crested Butte, Purgatory, or Telluride, there's still much to experience in this part of the state.

ORIENTATION AND PLANNING

GETTING ORIENTED

Southwest Colorado is the land beyond the interstates. Old mining roads, legacies of the late 19th and early 20th centuries when gold and silver mining was ascendant, lead through drop-dead gorgeous mountain valleys to the rugged high country. However, much of this part of the state is designated as wilderness area which means that no roads may be built and no wheeled or motorized vehicles are permitted. This is a region where some state highways are unpaved, a federal

TOP REASONS TO GO

Hiking the Colorado Trail: Bike, hike, or photograph the more than 500 mi of volunteer-maintained trail traversing eight mountain ranges from Durango to Denver.

Mountain Biking Crested Butte: There's a reason the Mountain Biking Hall of Fame resides here—the town is one of the birthplaces of fat-tire biking and it's surrounded by up-close mountain scenery and sweet single-track.

Riding the Durango & Silverton Narrow Gauge Railroad: This nine-hour journey along the Animas River will take you back in time on a coal- and steam-powered train. The views include dramatic canyons and the sweeping panoramas of the San Juan National Forest.

Downhill Skiing and Snowboarding at Telluride: There's rarely a wait to get at the sweeping, groomed trails and seemingly endless tree runs and moguls available at this, the largest collection of 14,000-foot mountains in the country.

highway known as U.S. 550 corkscrews over a high mountain pass known for heavy snows and a lack of guardrails, and snowmobiles regularly replace other motor vehicles as winter transportation. High-clearance, four-wheel-drive vehicles in summer and snowmobiles in winter are required for backcountry exploration, but regular passenger cars can travel most roads.

Crested Butte and Gunnison. Explore this mountain paradise on single track in summer and Nordic track in the winter. The Taylor and Gunnison rivers round out the adventure with white-water rafting, kayaking, and great fly-fishing.

Black Canyon of the Gunnison National Park and Montrose. The western town of Montrose makes a great base for exploring the majestic canyon that plunges 2,000 feet down sheer vertical cliffs to the roaring Gunnison River.

Lake City and Creede. Route 149 meanders south of the Black Canyon of the Gunnison through a scattering of cozy, laid-back communities, including Lake City and Creede.

Telluride and the San Juan Mountains. Old mining camps including Silverton, Ouray, and Telluride now welcome adventurers seeking other riches—wilderness trekking, rugged four-wheeling, mountain climbing, extreme winter sports, and horseback riding.

Mesa Country. Durango makes an ideal base for exploring Mesa Country and its star attraction—Mesa Verde National Park. This college town is a hot spot known for its eclectic eateries, historic hotels, and modern boutiques.

10

PLANNING

WHEN TO GO

Southwest Colorado, like the rest of the state, is intensely seasonal. Snow begins falling in the high country in late September or early October, and by Halloween seasonal closures turn most unpaved roads into routes for snowmobiles. The San Juan Mountains are the snowiest region of the Colorado Rockies, with average annual snowfalls approaching 400 inches in some spots. Winter lingers well into the season that is called spring on the calendar—the greatest snowfalls generally occur in March and April. Skiing winds down in early to mid-April, and ski towns virtually shut down until summer. Gunnison and Durango, being college towns, keep rolling throughout the year.

In mid-April the snow in the higher elevations begins to melt. Cresting streams provide thrilling, if chilling, white-water rafting and kayaking. Hiking trails become accessible, and wildflowers begin their short, intense season of show. Summer is glorious in the mountains, with brilliant sunshine and cobalt-blue skies. Late summer brings brief and often intense showers on many an August afternoon, sometimes accompanied by dramatic thunder and lightning. Summer tourism winds down after Labor Day and shuts down completely in October, and the cycle begins again. Spring and fall are the best times to visit the harsh dry climate of the mesa-and-canyon country around the Four Corners.

GETTING HERE AND AROUND

AIR TRAVEL

The Gunnison–Crested Butte Regional Airport (GUC) serves the nearby resort area. GUC is served by American Airlines, United, and United Express.

The closest regional airport to the Black Canyon of the Gunnison National Park is Montrose Airport (MTJ). It's served by American, Continental, United, Skywest, and Delta.

Telluride is notorious for being one of the hardest ski resorts in the country to fly into, mainly because the elevation of Telluride Regional Airport (TEX) is well above 9,000 feet. A little turbulence, a few clouds, and the next thing you know you're landing at Montrose Airport, 67 mi away, and taking a shuttle to Telluride. Telluride Airport welcomes flights from America West, Frontier, Great Lakes Aviation, and United.

The Durango–La Plata Airport (DRO) is your closest option for Silverton, Durango, Pagosa Springs, Mesa Verde National Park, and the Four Corners region. It's served by America West Express, Delta, US Airways, and United Express.

Something to consider for travel to the Four Corners region, given your location and airline schedules, is to at least check into flying to Albuquerque instead of Denver. The Albuquerque International Sunport (ABQ) is host to many of the major airlines and is closer than Denver.

TRANSFERS   Several companies run transportation options between the airports and the resorts. Shuttles average $15–$30 per person. Advance reservations may be required. In Crested Butte, Gunnison, and Montrose, try

Alpine Express. Telluride Express offers service to Telluride, Durango, Montrose, Cortez, Gunnison, and Grand Junction.

In Crested Butte, Telluride, and Durango free shuttles operate between town and the ski area during the winter season.

Airports Albuquerque International Sunport (ABQ) (☎ 505/244–7700 ⊕ www.cabq.gov/airport). **Durango–La Plata Airport (DRO)** (☎ 970/247–8143 ⊕ www.durangoairport.com). **Gunnison–Crested Butte Regional Airport (GUC)** (☎ 970/641–2304). **Montrose Airport (MTJ)** (☎ 970/249–3203 ⊕ www.montroseairport.com). **Telluride Regional Airport (TEX)** (☎ 970/728–5313 ⊕ www.tellurideairport.com).

Airport Transfers Alpine Express (☎ 970/641–5074 or 800/822–4844 ⊕ alpineexpressshuttle.com). **Telluride Express** (☎ 970/728–6000 or 888/212–8294 ⊕ www.tellurideexpress.com).

CAR TRAVEL

Dollar, Thrifty, Hertz, and National car-rental agencies have counters at the Montrose Airport. Avis, Budget, Dollar, Hertz, and National all have counters at Gunnison–Crested Butte Regional Airport, Telluride Regional Airport, and Durango–La Plata Airport.

The main roads in the region are Route 135 between Crested Butte and Gunnison; U.S. 50 linking Poncha Springs, Gunnison, Montrose, and Delta; Route 149 between Gunnison, Lake City, and Creede; U.S. 550 from Montrose to Ridgway to Silverton to Durango; Route 62 and Route 145 linking Ridgway with Telluride, Dolores, and Cortez; and U.S. 160, which passes from Cortez to Durango to Pagosa Springs via the Mesa Verde National Park north entrance. With the exception of Kebler Pass, none of these roads officially closes for winter, but be prepared at any time during snowy months for portions of the roads to be closed or down to one lane for avalanche control or to clear ice or snowdrifts.

TAXI TRAVEL

In most resort towns you'll need to call for a cab. The wait is seldom more than 15 minutes.

PARKS AND RECREATION AREAS

Southwest Colorado includes a wealth of national and state parks and recreational areas. Of the 13 rivers designated as "gold medal" waters by the Colorado Wildlife Commission, the Animas, Gunnison, and Rio Grande are all here. Blue Mesa Reservoir, the state's largest lake, is a destination for boaters, kayakers, waterskiers, windsurfers, anglers, and scuba divers. Up in rustic Almont, a small community near the Gunnison headwaters, they *live* fly-fishing. Anglers love Ridgway State Park, with access to rainbow trout and other prize fish, and camping and hiking areas. ■TIP→ **Anyone older than 16 needs a Colorado fishing license, which you can obtain at local sporting-goods stores. See** ⊕ **www.wildlife.state.co.us/fishing for more information.**

The precipitous Black Canyon of the Gunnison National Park is a mysterious and powerful attraction. Some of the most intact of what remains of the ancient, little-known Puebloan culture is inside Mesa Verde National Park and Canyons of the Ancients National Monument.

For information about Mesa Verde National Park, see the Mesa Verde National Park section.

The San Juan Mountains stretch through 12,000 square mi of southwest Colorado, encompassing the Weminuche Wilderness Area, half a million acres along the Continental Divide administered by three federal agencies. The San Juan National Forest, which ranges from east of Pagosa Springs to the western border of the state, is a virtual paradise for all kinds of adventuring. The Colorado Trail, the premier backpacking experience in the state, goes north from near Durango to Denver, 500 mi away.

The Rio Grande National Forest stretches from the magisterial Sangre de Cristo Mountains across the San Luis Valley—at 7,600-feet elevation, the world's largest alpine valley—to the eastern San Juan Mountains on its western borders. It is less well known, but no less spectacular, than the rest of the area.

RESTAURANTS

With dining options ranging from creative contemporary cuisine in the posh ski resorts of Telluride and to a lesser extent Crested Butte and Durango to no-frills American fare in down-home ranching communities, no one has any excuse to visit a chain restaurant here. The leading chefs are tapping into the region's local bounty, so you can find innovative recipes for ranch-raised game, lamb, and trout. Many serve only locally raised, grass-fed meats. Olathe sweet corn is a delicacy enjoyed across the state in restaurants and grocery stores. Seasonal produce is always highlighted on the best menus.

HOTELS

No matter what you're looking for in vacation lodging—luxurious slope-side condominium, landmark inn in a historic town, riverside cabin, bed-and-breakfast inn, budget motel, or chock-full-of-RVs campground—southwest Colorado has it in abundance. In ski resorts, especially, the rates vary from season to season. Some properties close in fall once the aspens have shed their golden leaves, open in winter when the lifts begin running, close in spring after the snow melts, and open again in mid-June.

WHAT IT COSTS				
¢	$	$$	$$$	$$$$
Restaurants	under $8	$8–$12	$13–$18	$19–$25	over $25
Hotels	under $80	$80–$120	$121–$170	$171–$230	over $230

Restaurant prices are for a main course at dinner, excluding 5.9%–8.1% tax. Hotel prices are for two people in a standard double room in high season, excluding service charges and 7.6%–9.9% tax.

VISITOR INFORMATION

Contact Southwest Colorado Travel Region (☎ *800/933-4340* ⊕ *www.swcolotravel.org).*

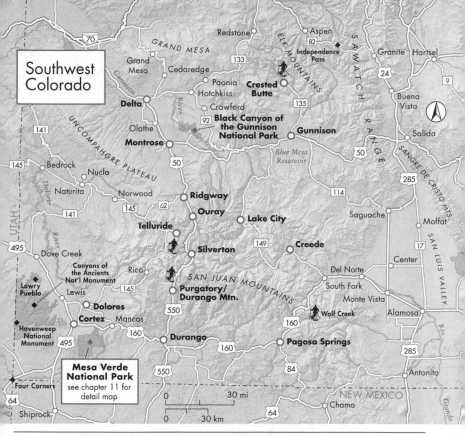

CRESTED BUTTE AND GUNNISON

The area is dominated and shaped by the Gunnison River basin, which gathers water from the Continental Divide and finally hooks up with the Colorado River near Grand Junction. Near Cimarron the river has cut the Black Canyon of the Gunnison, a forbidding, 48-mi abyss often deeper than it is wide. Farther upriver is the Blue Mesa Reservoir, the state's largest lake, with boating, sporting, and backpacking opportunities. The Elk Mountains stretch from the north edge of the Black Canyon through Crested Butte. Almont, off Highway 135 between Crested Butte and Gunnison, is a still-rustic fly-fishing hideaway.

CRESTED BUTTE

30 mi north of Gunnison via Rte. 135, 90 mi northeast of Montrose.

Like Aspen, the town of Crested Butte was once a small mining village. The Victorian gingerbread-trim houses remain—albeit painted in whimsical shades of hot pink, magenta, and chartreuse. Unlike Aspen, however, Crested Butte never became chic. A controversial ad campaign for the ski area touted it as "Aspen like it used to be, and Vail like it never was."

A lovelier setting could not be imagined. The town sits at the top of a long, broad valley that stretches 17 mi all the way south to Gunnison.

10

Mount Crested Butte, which looms over the town, is the most visible landmark in the entire valley. The Elk Mountains, north of Crested Butte, stretch to the Maroon Bells and Aspen, and the West Elk Mountains extend southwest to the Black Canyon.

Crested Butte has always been cutting-edge when it comes to embracing new ways to take advantage of the powdery snow. It was an early hotbed of telemark skiing, a graceful, free-heel way of cruising downhill; and was popular with snowboarders back when few people had heard of the sport. But it's as an extreme-skiing mecca that Crested Butte earned its reputation with some of the best skiers in the land. Although many resorts are limiting their "out-of-bounds" terrain owing to increasing insurance costs and lawsuits, Crested Butte has steadily increased its extreme-skiing terrain to 550 ungroomed acres. The Extreme Limits and the North Face should only be attempted by advanced or expert skiers, but there are plenty of cruise-worthy trails for skiers of all levels.

Crested Butte is just as popular in summer. Blanketed with columbine and Indian paintbrush, the landscape is mesmerizing. It has grown into one of the country's major mountain-biking centers. Once the snow melts, mountain bikers challenge the hundreds of miles of trails surrounding the town.

The ski resort, at the base of the lifts a couple of miles uphill from the old town, is properly called Mount Crested Butte. When people talk about Crested Butte, they might be referring to the old town, the ski resort, or both. You'll have to figure it out from the context.

GETTING HERE AND AROUND

Crested Butte is just over the mountain from Aspen, but a short drive in summer turns into a four-hour trek by car in winter, when Kebler Pass (on Rte. 135) is closed and it's necessary to drive a circuitous route. Both Aspen and Crested Butte are surrounded by designated wilderness areas, which mean that few roads pass through this region.

Alpine Express will transport you between the airports and the resorts. Mountain Express is a reliable free shuttle-bus service between the town and the resort, which are about 3 mi apart, every 15 minutes during ski season. Although a car is unnecessary and even unnerving for those not comfortable driving on snow and ice, having one makes the going much easier.

WHEN TO GO

The town more or less shuts down between mid-April and Memorial Day, and again between October and the start of ski season in mid-December. Businesses may stay shuttered for a month or more.

FESTIVALS The surrounding mountains are carpeted with such abundant growth that Crested Butte has been nicknamed the "Wildflower Capital of Colorado." For one glorious week in mid-July the town celebrates this beautiful bounty with the **Crested Butte Wildflower Festival.** (☎ 970/349–2571 ⊕ *www.crestedbuttewildflowerfestival.com*). There are guided wildflower walks, wildflower identification workshops, wildflower photography classes, hayrides, and four-wheel-drive wildflower tours.

★ From early July through early August the **Crested Butte Music Festival** (☎ 970/349–0619 ⊕ *www.crestedbuttemusicfestival.com*) presents concerts including jazz, bluegrass, opera, chamber, dance, and symphony in a variety of venues. In August you might pop up at the **Wild Mushroom Festival** (☎ 970/596–4841 ⊕ *www.crested-butte-wild-mushroom-festival.com*), with workshops, talks, seminars, cooking, and the thrill of the hunt for the finest fungi.

> **CRESTED BUTTE WILDFLOWERS**
>
> Take a four-wheel-drive tour any time in summer and picnic in a galaxy of wildflowers. Look for the blue-and-white columbine, Colorado's state flower. But remember to bring your friend to the flower, not the flower to your friend—it is illegal to pick a blue columbine within state borders.

For information about Fat Tire Bike Week, see Mountain Biking below.

ESSENTIALS

Transportation Contacts Alpine Express (☎ 970/641–5074 or 800/822–4844 ⊕ *alpineexpressshuttle.com*). **Mountain Express** (☎ 970/349–5616 ⊕ *www.crestedbutte-co.gov*).

Visitor Info Crested Butte–Mount Crested Butte Chamber of Commerce (✉ *601 Elk Ave., Crested Butte* ☎ *970/349–6438 or 800/545–4505* ⊕ *www.cbchamber.com*). **Crested Butte Snow Report** (☎ *888/442–8883*). **Crested Butte Vacations** (✉ *Box 5700, Mount Crested Butte,* ☎ *970/349–2222 or 800/810–7669* ⊕ *www.skicb.com*).

EXPLORING

Crested Butte Mountain Heritage Museum & Mountain Bike Hall of Fame. Housed in a turn-of-the-20th-century hardware store, the museum uses its front room to produce an exact replica of the essentials marketed for survival in a rugged mining town. There's an exquisite diorama of the town in the 1920s, complete with a moving train; information on the Utes who used to roam the area; skiing, sledding, Flauschink (a traditional ceremony for the welcoming of Spring); and biking exhibits; and the Mountain Bike Hall of Fame. ✉ *331 Elk Ave.* ☎ *970/349–1880* ⊕ *www.mtnbikehalloffame.com* ✉ *$3* ⊙ *June–Sept., daily 10–8; Dec.–Mar., daily noon–6.*

DOWNHILL SKIING AND SNOWBOARDING

Crested Butte skiing has a split personality, which is plain to see when you check out the skiers who come here year after year. Its traditional side is the trail network, characterized by long lower-intermediate and intermediate runs. There's a wonderful expanse of easy terrain from the Keystone lift—not just a trail network but rolling, tree-dotted meadows with plenty of opportunities to poke around off the beaten track. Families flock to Crested Butte for the excellent slope-side child-care and children's ski school facilities, as well as the resort's laid-back and friendly vibe.

The wilder side of Crested Butte's personality is the **Extreme Limits**, several hundred acres of steep bowls, gnarly chutes, and tight tree skiing. It's no surprise that Crested Butte has hosted the U.S. Extreme

10

Freeskiing Championship and the U.S. Extreme Borderfest, both nationally televised events full of thrills and spills. That's not to say you have to be a hotshot to enjoy some of Crested Butte's more challenging terrain. You do, however, need to be able to handle snow that hasn't been groomed.

The best skiing on the main trail network is on the front side of the mountain. The Silver Queen high-speed quad shoots you up 2,000 vertical feet in one quick ride. From there you have a choice of lifts and runs, roughly segmented by degree of challenge, with the steep twisters off to the right, the easier cruisers concentrated on the left, and the gnarly steeps above. The Paradise Chair Lift brings you directly to Crested Butte's half-pipe and the best intermediate terrain.

> **ICE BAR**
>
> Mount Crested Butte's cool **Ice Bar** relies on temperatures in the freezing range. Made from snow and ice, the bar is set up in November near Twister Lift, midway on Mount Crested Butte, next to what is now known as the Ice Bar Restaurant. When the sun starts to warm things up, the Ice Bar goes away, as do the fur-clad servers and bartenders who wait on the 15–20 stools set up around this chilly, but very hot, après-ski spot.

The Extreme Limits is backcountry-style skiing and riding that's not for the faint of heart. If you're lucky enough to have good snow, skiing in this steep and rocky region will be the thrilling highlight of your visit. Strong, confident skiers and riders ready to tackle this terrain should sign up for a group tour. ⊠ *12 Snowmass Rd., Mount Crested Butte,* ☎ *970/349–2222 or 800/544–8448* ⊕ *www.skicb.com* ☼ *Open mid-Nov. or mid-Dec.–mid-Apr., daily 9–4.*

FACILITIES 2,775-foot vertical drop; 1,167 skiable acres; 23% beginner, 51% intermediate, and 20% advanced; 4 detachable high-speed quad chairs, 2 fixed-grip quad chairs, 2 triple chairs, 3 double chairs, 3 surface lifts, and 2 magic carpets (beginners' lifts).

LESSONS AND PROGRAMS The Full Day Beginner Adventure with a lift ticket costs $145. The full-day lesson practically guarantees you'll be skiing or snowboarding green runs by the end of the day. For kids ages 3 through 16, Camp CB all-day lessons are $140, and jump-start lessons are $90. Intermediate, advanced, and private lessons are also available. For more information, contact **CB Mountain School** (☎ *970/349–2252, 800/444–9236, 800/600–7349 Kid's World* ⊕ *www.skicb.com*).

LIFT TICKETS The walk-up rates for lift tickets range from $87 for one day to $581 for a week; prices are lower in early and late season. Look online for discounts and some days when everybody skis free.

RENTALS Full rental packages (including skis, boots, and poles), as well as telemark, snowshoe, and snowboard equipment, are available through **Crested Butte Sports** (⊠ *35 Emmons Loop Rd.* ☎ *970/349–7516 or 800/301–9169* ⊕ *www.crestedbuttesports.com*). Rates start at $19 per day. They also have a full repair shop.

NORDIC SKIING
BACKCOUNTRY SKIING

Crested Butte abounds with backcountry possibilities. Skiing or snow-shoeing on the old mining roads that radiate from town are among the most popular pastimes. Washington Gulch, Slate River Road, and Gothic Road are among the most accessible routes. Dogs are permitted, and you'll have to contend with snowmobiles on some trails. Hardy locals hike up the slopes for above-tree-line telemarking, but this requires strong legs, strong lungs, and real avalanche awareness. You'll need the right equipment, including a functioning beacon and a shovel. Make sure you ski with a group—this is territory where going it alone is asking for trouble. Keep in mind that this is the high country (the town itself is around 9,000 feet, and things go up from there). Weather conditions can change with little or no warning.

To play it safe, arrange a tour into the backcountry with the **Crested Butte Nordic Center** (⊠ 620 2nd St. ☎ 970/349–1707 ⊕ www.cbnordic.org). Half- and full-day packages include transportation, guides, and equipment. For those wishing to extend their experience, staff can make arrangements for the rental of a ski hut in the old town site of Gothic. The center also hosts the Annual Alley Loop Nordic Marathon, held in early February. This is an American Birkebeiner qualifying race, but townsfolk, as well as visitors, join the experts in their cross-country race through the town's snow-covered streets and alleys, past snow-corniced homes, and down the scenic trails along the edge of town.

RENTALS The **Alpineer** (⊠ 419 6th St. ☎ 970/349–5210 ⊕ www.alpineer.com) rents top-notch backcountry and telemark equipment and provides information on routes and snow conditions.

TRACK SKIING

The **Crested Butte Nordic Center** (⊠ 620 2nd St. ☎ 970/349–1707 ⊕ www.cbnordic.org) maintains an extensive network of Nordic trail systems. There are 50 km (31 mi) of trails, roughly divided into the northwest, south, and east sides of Crested Butte. The trails cover flat and moderately rolling terrain across meadows and through aspen groves near the valley floor. The views of some of the distant peaks are stunning. Snowshoers are allowed on all tracks, and dogs are permitted on some. One activity of note is the Moonlight Tour—on full-moon nights participants are guided down a moon-washed trail to a cozy yurt for snacks and hot chocolate; the cost is $25 per person.

LESSONS AND PROGRAMS The **Crested Butte Nordic Center** (⊠ 620 2nd St. ☎ 970/349–1707 ⊕ www.cbnordic.org) has snowshoeing, skate skiing, and classic track skiing lessons. Learn to Ski adult packages start at $55 and include a trail pass, rentals, and a 60-minute group lesson. Private lessons start at $45 for adults and $35 for children. Learn to skate ski for free at 1 PM on the first Thursday of each month from December through March. The free clinic is limited to 12 participants, so reservations are necessary. An annual **Thanksgiving Training Camp** is held every November. Former Olympians and collegiate coaches present clinics for expert, advanced, intermediate, and beginning students. Clinic fees are $40. Waxing clinics are free.

10

TRAIL PASSES   An adult day pass costs $15. The center also has a variety of season passes, ranging from $50 for a child's season pass to $150 for one adult and $350 for a family.

RENTALS   The **Crested Butte Nordic Center** (✉ *620 2nd St.* ☎ *970/349–1707* ⊕ *www. cbnordic.org*) rents classic track skis, skate skis, backcountry touring skis, snowshoes, skates, and sleds.

OTHER SPORTS AND THE OUTDOORS

Alpine Express. Take an open-top four-wheel-drive tour on the old mining roads that crisscross the Elk Mountain range. Visit meadows of wildflowers and sit by pristine mountain lakes (four-person minimum). Jeep tours are $50 for adults. ☎ *970/641–5074 or 800/822–4844* ⊕ *www. alpineexpressshuttle.com.*

OUTFITTERS
AND
EXPEDITIONS   **Adventures to the Edge** (✉ *308 3rd St.* ☎ *970/209–3980* ⊕ *www.swissmountainguide.com*) creates customized high-country treks, cross-country skiing expeditions, and alpine ascents in the Crested Butte area.

Crested Butte Mountain Guides. This outfitter's packages are tailored to your needs in rock climbing, ice climbing, mountain biking, cross-country and backcountry skiing, backpacking, hiking, snowshoeing, and sea kayaking. They also run four-wheel-drive tours in summer. Expect a small guide-to-client ratio. ✇ *Box 1718, Crested Butte* ☎ *970/349–5430* ⊕ *www.crestedbutteguides.com.*

Three Rivers Resort & Outfitting (✉ *130 County Rd. 742, Almont* ☎ *970/641–1303 or 888/761–3474* ⊕ *www.3riversresort.com*) runs guided fly-fishing excursions, kayaking lessons, and white-water rafting trips on the Gunnison and Taylor rivers.

FISHING

At **Almont**, south of Crested Butte, the East and Taylor rivers join to form the Gunnison River, making this tiny angler-oriented hamlet one of Colorado's top fly-fishing centers. It's also one of the most crowded with tourists, however. Local fishing outfitters rent equipment, teach fly-fishing, and lead guided wading or float trips both to public and private waters.

OUTFITTERS
AND
EXPEDITIONS   **Almont Anglers** (✉ *10209 Hwy. 135, Almont* ☎ *970/641–7404* ⊕ *www. almontanglers.com*) has a solid fly and tackle shop with an enormous selection of flies. There are clinics for beginners and guided wading and float-fishing trips on the East, Taylor, and Gunnison rivers.

Dragonfly Anglers (✉ *307 Elk Ave.* ☎ *970/349–1228 or 800/491–3079* ⊕ *www.dragonflyanglers.com*) is Crested Butte's oldest year-round guide service and fly-fishing outfitter. They guide half- and full-day trips to choice fly-fishing spots, including the famed Gunnison Gorge (full-day only) in the Black Canyon. Their shop concentrates on high-tech rods, and has a selection of reels, flies, and outdoor gear.

At Three Rivers Resort & Outfitting, **Willowfly Anglers** (✉ *130 County Rd. 742, Almont* ☎ *970/641–1303 or 888/761–3474* ⊕ *www.willowflyanglers.com*) has a full-service fly shop and provides gear for anglers of all skill levels.

GOLF

The Club at Crested Butte. Golf legend Robert Trent Jones Jr. designed this ravishing 18-hole course surrounded by gorgeous mountain peaks. The first nine holes follow a traditional format, but the second nine offer a Highlands-style surprise with their Scottish-links design. Water hazards are present on 14 of the 18 holes, so be sure to bring extra balls. The semi-private course belongs to the country club, but it's open to the public. The dress code bars denim and mandates stand-up collars for all. ⊠ *385 Country Club Dr.* ☎ *970/349–6127 or 800/628–5496* ⊕ *www. theclubatcrestedbutte.com* ⚲ *Reservations essential* ⚐. *18 holes. Yards: 7,208/5,702. Par: 72/72. Green fee: $135/$95.*

HIKING

Near three designated wilderness areas (Maroon Bells–Snowmass to the north, Raggeds to the west, and Collegiate Peaks to the east), as well as other areas with equally stunning scenery, Crested Butte has an extensive system of trails. In wilderness areas you can find splendid trails far off the beaten path. ■**TIP→ Outside of these protected areas, you may have to share routes with mountain bikers and even four-wheel-drive vehicles.** One of the easiest hiking trails is a 2-mi round-trip to **Judd Falls.** The path climbs about 100 feet and slices through groves of aspen and, in spring, a crop of glacier lilies and more than 70 local wildflower varieties. At the end, look over Judd Falls from a bench named after Garwood Judd, "the man who stayed" in the mining town of Gothic. ⊠ *Gunnison Ranger District, Gunnison National Forest* ☎ *970/641–0171* ⊕ *www.fs.fed.us/r2/gmug.*

The maintenance roads at the **Crested Butte Mountain Resort** make nice hiking trails in summer for moderate to serious hikers. Start at the resort's Gothic Building and create your own path up, following well-signed roads and paths to the summit at 12,162 feet, where you can take in the entire Crested Butte valley. Those who prefer a more aerial view may buy a lift ticket to the top and walk back downhill.

HORSEBACK RIDING

One of the best ways to see Crested Butte is from atop a horse. **Fantasy Ranch** (⊠ *Gothic Rd.* ☎ *970/349–5425 or 888/688–3488* ⊕ *www. fantasyranchoutfitters.com*) gives guided horseback tours into the Elk Mountains, Maroon Bells, and Gunnison National Forest. Ninety-minute trail rides are $55, half-day trips start at $85, and full-day wilderness adventures are $120.

HOT-AIR BALLOONING

The conditions must be just right, but on a clear, windless morning this wide-open basin surrounded by mountain ranges, must surely be one of the country's best places to be aloft in a balloon. For information on these flights of fancy, contact **Big Horn Balloon Company** (☎ *970/596–1008* ⊕ *www.balloon-adventures.com*). Trips are $350 per person, with a minimum of two people; group and family discounts are available.

10

ICE-SKATING

If you're eager to practice a figure eight, the **Crested Butte Nordic Center** (⊠ 620 2nd St. ☎ 970/349–1707 or 970/349–0974 for skate times ⊕ www. cbnordic.org) operates the adjacent outdoor skating rink. The lodge rents skates for $9.

KAYAKING AND RAFTING

The rivers around Crested Butte are at their best from May through September. **Three Rivers Resort & Outfitting** (⊠ 130 Country Rd. 742, Almont ☎ 970/641–1303 or 888/761–3474 ⊕ www.3riversresort.com) takes you on rafting trips and gives kayaking lessons on the Taylor and Gunnison rivers.

MOUNTAIN BIKING

★ Crested Butte is probably the **mountain-biking** center of Colorado. This is a place where there are more bikes than cars, and probably more bikes than residents. Many people own two mountain bikes: a town bike for hacking around and a performance bike for *serious* hacking around. Mountain-bike chroniclers say that Pearl Pass is the route that got the mountain-biking craze started in the mid-1970s. After a group of Aspen motorcyclists rode the rough old road over Pearl Pass to Crested Butte, the town's mountain bikers decided to retaliate and ride to Aspen. They hopped on board their clunky two-wheelers—a far cry from the sophisticated machinery of today—and with that, a sport was born. The 40-mi trip over Pearl Pass can be done in a day, but you must be in excellent condition and acclimatized to the elevation to have a chance of finishing. Altitude is your main foe; the pass crests at 12,700 feet. The trip is daunting, and not to be undertaken lightly. One option for your return journey to Crested Butte is a scenic two-day ride along the road—better than retracing your route over the pass. Otherwise you'll need to make arrangements to travel by car or even by plane.

The **Lower Loop** (⊠ Trailhead: Near the 4-way stop at the corner of Elk Ave. and Hwy. 135) is a popular 8- to 9-mi trail that will help orient you to the area. It's a 1-hour ride mostly on pavement with a couple of miles of single-track, and it hooks up to several longer, easy rides with views of mountain peaks, the Paradise Divide, and the Slate River valley. Along the Lower Loop, watch for **Tony's Trail**, a moderate climb for the more serious biker. The trail gains 1,200 feet on a 9-mi loop, and it rewards your efforts by winding through aspen forests and alpine meadows bursting (in season) with wildflowers to a final elevation of about 10,000 feet.

OUTFITTERS The **Alpineer** (⊠ 419 6th St. ☎ 970/349–5210 ⊕ www.alpineer.com)
AND prides itself on having the latest gear and a staff knowledgeable enough
EXPEDITIONS to get you on the right bike and trail as quickly as possible. If you're going to spend time here, find local rider Holly Annala's *Crested Butte Singletrack,* a fascinating guide to the local biking landscape. Guided tours of nearby trails are available through **Crested Butte Mountain Guides** (☎ 970/349–5430 ⊕ www.crestedbutteguides.com).

FESTIVALS Each summer, mountain-biking enthusiasts roll in for the **Fat Tire Bike Week** (☎ 800/545–4505 or 970/349–6438 ⊕ www.ftbw.com), the country's longest-running mountain-bike festival. The event, held in late

June, is a solid week of racing, touring, silly competitions, and mountain-biker bonding.

RENTALS **Crested Butte Sports** (⊠ *35 Emmons Loop Rd.* ☎ *970/349–7516 or 800/301–9169* ⊕ *www.crestedbuttesports.com*) rents mountain bikes, gear, and helmets. Discounts are offered for multiday rates. They also have a full bike repair shop.

WHERE TO EAT

¢–$ ✕ **Donita's Cantina.** This down-home, adobe-washed Mexican restaurant
MEXICAN is housed in an 1880s hotel and still has the original pressed tin ceilings. The food is simply good, with solid standards such as fajitas and enchiladas served with homemade red and green chile. The specialty at the bar is predictably the margarita—concocted in all flavors and colors with 100% agave tequila. The cantina is popular with local families as well as with extreme skiers. ⊠ *330 Elk Ave.* ☎ *970/349–6674* ⊕ *www.donitascantina.com* ⌲ *Reservations not accepted* ⊟ *AE, D, MC, V* ☉ *No lunch.*

$$ ✕ **Ginger Cafe.** The small, sun-color dining room provides a cheerful
ASIAN backdrop for the superb East–West fusion and pan-Asian food. There is also a full bar and inventive cocktail menu including ginger-infused martinis and mango ginger mojitos. Try the pad thai with a delicious homemade tamarind sauce. ⊠ *313 3rd St.* ☎ *970/349–7291* ⊟ *D, MC, V.*

$$ ✕ **Slogar.** In a lovingly renovated Victorian tavern awash in handmade
AMERICAN lace and stained glass, this restaurant is just plain cozy. Slogar turns out some of the juiciest fried chicken west of the Mississippi. The fixings are sensational: flaky biscuits fresh from the oven, creamy mashed potatoes swimming in chicken gravy, and sweet-and-sour coleslaw from a Pennsylvania Dutch recipe. Served family style, dinner, including ice cream, is only $14.95 (or $28 for steak). ⊠ *517 2nd St.* ☎ *970/349–5765* ⊟ *AE, MC, V* ☉ *Closed mid-Oct.–Nov. and mid-Apr.–mid-May. No lunch.*

$$$$ ✕ **Soupçon.** "Soup's on" (get it?) occupies two intimate rooms in the
FRENCH historic Kochevar cabin and dishes up Nouveau American cuisine with
★ a strong French accent. Local produce is accented with organic herbs grown on the premises. Try the chef's signature almond-crusted rack of lamb, or the seared Hudson Valley foie gras with roasted pear, complemented by a glass of wine from the comprehensive wine cellar. Call ahead for your seating time: 6 PM or 8:15 PM. ⊠ *127 Elk Ave. (behind Kochevar's)* ☎ *970/349–5448* ⌲ *Reservations essential* ⊟ *AE, MC, V* ☉ *Closed Sun. and Apr.–May. No lunch.*

¢ ✕ **Teocalli Tamale.** A small, historic building is the venue for tasty, inex-
MEXICAN pensive Mexican takeout (or a claustrophobic eat-in experience). For breakfast, which lasts until 11-ish, order the *huevos paperos* (eggs over easy topped with chilies and salsa over potatoes instead of the usual corn tortillas) or *huevos tamaleros* (eggs with mild and spicy homemade tamales). Bacon or chorizo can be added to any dish. Locals know this place for its generous proportions of tacos, tamales, and Baja fish. ⊠ *311 Elk Ave.* ☎ *970/349–2005* ⊟ *MC, V.*

$$$$ ✕ **Timberline Restaurant.** This elegant, two-story restaurant changes its
AMERICAN menu monthly, but always has a selection of wild game. The upper floor has a formal European style to it, while the downstairs area, with its huge windows, is a great place to watch the snow falling while

10

discussing your triumphs on the slopes. Elk medallions, smoked scallops with saffron, and coriander Hawaiian ahi are among the many delicacies served on a seasonal basis. There is a handsome bar and a respectable wine list. Top off your epicurean experience by indulging in an after-dinner liqueur or the memorable Belgian chocolate soufflé. ⊠ *201 Elk Ave.* ☎ *970/349–9831* ⊕ *www.timberlinerestaurant.com* ⌂ *Reservations essential* ▤ *AE, D, MC, V* ⊘ *No lunch.*

WHERE TO STAY

$ **Cristiana Guesthaus.** This alpine-style ski lodge with a huge stone fireplace in a high-beam lobby provides a cozy, unpretentious haven. Wood-panel rooms are decorated in neutrals with traditional country pine furnishings. The hot tub sits on a redwood deck facing a breathtaking view of the mountains. Historic downtown is within walking distance, and hiking, biking, and Nordic ski trails are only minutes away. The innkeepers are avid sports people, and happily give winter and summer trail advice. Homemade muesli and pastries are included in the generous Continental breakfast. **Pros:** friendly, comfortable lodge; knowledgeable hosts; great value. **Cons:** children under 5 discouraged; TV only in common area. ⊠ *621 Maroon Ave.,* ☎ *970/349–5326 or 800/824–7899* ⊕ *www.cristianaguesthaus.com* ⇆ *21 rooms* ⌂ *In-room: no a/c, no TV, Wi-Fi. In-hotel: public Wi-Fi, no kids under 5* ▤ *AE, D, MC, V* ⊘ *Closed mid-Apr.–early May* ⫿◉⫿ *CP.*

$$ **Elk Mountain Lodge.** Step into the lobby of the Elk Mountain Lodge and encounter a slower pace of life and unsurpassed attention to detail. Originally a boardinghouse built for miners in 1919, this historic hotel has been painstakingly renovated. The rooms are full of light, and the full-service bar is a deep, rich walnut. There's a library and a mini-grand piano on which jazz is played every Friday night. An enhanced Continental breakfast is served in a cheerfully trimmed breakfast nook. **Pros:** historic building; warm, intimate; in the middle of old-town Crested Butte. **Cons:** 3 mi from ski area; stairs are a bit steep and there's no elevator. ⊠ *129 Gothic Ave.,* ☎ *970/349–7533 or 800/374–6521* ⊕ *www.elkmountainlodge.com* ⇆ *19 rooms* ⌂ *In-room: no a/c, Wi-Fi (some). In-hotel: bar, public Wi-Fi, no kids under 4* ▤ *AE, D, MC, V* ⫿◉⫿ *CP.*

$$$ **Grand Lodge Crested Butte.** This luxurious ski-in ski-out lodge is popular with upscale skiers and business travelers. A warm stone-and-log lobby with a huge fireplace welcomes you. Spacious rooms are decorated in muted earth and pastel tones with copper accents. Both bar and grill have fireplaces, and the pool is indoor-outdoor to accommodate seasonal changes. **Pros:** next to ski area; luxurious with numerous amenities; nice touches such as cookies left out for guests. **Cons:** windows don't open; 3 mi from town of Crested Butte; can feel impersonal. ⊠ *6 Emmons Loop, Mount Crested Butte,* ☎ *888/823–4446* ⊕ *www.grandlodgecrestedbutte.com* ⇆ *226 rooms, 106 suites* ⌂ *In-room: no a/c, safe, refrigerator, Internet, Wi-Fi. In-hotel: restaurant, bar, pool, gym, spa, laundry service, public Wi-Fi, some pets allowed* ▤ *AE, MC, V.*

$$ **Nordic Inn.** This slope-side inn with alpine-style trim is one of the last old-style ski lodges in a sea of cookie-cutter condominiums. Simply decorated rooms, a cozy lobby perfect for lounging, and an inviting breakfast room are reminders of the way mountain vacations used to be. An outdoor hot tub graces a modest deck with a stupendous view of the mountains. **Pros:** one block from ski lifts; small, informal setting; Continental breakfast included. **Cons:** old and starting to fray; 3 mi from the old town of Crested Butte. ⊠ *14 Treasury Rd., Mount Crested Butte,* ☎ *800/542–7669* ⊕ *www.nordicinncb. com* ⇆ *24 rooms* ⚭ *In-room: no a/c, Internet. In-hotel: public Wi-Fi* ⊟ *AE, MC, V* ⦾ *CP.*

$$ 🖼 **Pioneer Guest Cabins.** Situated on a riverside meadow in the Gunnison National Forest, this getaway is about 8 mi from town. You can hike, bike, cross-country ski, or snowshoe from trails that start right at their door. The East River, 2 mi away, is an outstanding fishing stream. Or, you can simply watch hummingbirds while lounging in Adirondack chairs. Rustic log cabins from the 1930s have been appointed with down comforters and antique furnishings. Each cabin has hardwood floors, a fully equipped kitchen, and a fireplace. Cabins are open year-round and are dog-friendly. **Pros:** beautiful, secluded setting; close to trails and fishing. **Cons:** 8 mi from town can seem very far in winter; no restaurant; two-night minimum. ⊠ *2094 Cement Creek Rd.,* ☎ *970/349–5517* ⊕ *www. pioneerguestcabins.com* ⇆ *8 cabins* ⚭ *In-room: no a/c, kitchen, no TV. In-hotel: some pets allowed* ⊟ *MC, V.*

NIGHTLIFE
NIGHTLIFE

Kochevar's (⊠ *127 Elk Ave.* ☎ *970/349–6745*), a hand-hewn 1896 log cabin, is a classic saloon where locals play pool. The popular **Wooden Nickel** (⊠ *222 Elk Ave.* ☎ *970/349–6350*) is packed for happy hour each day from 4 to 6. Stay for a fine steak dinner.

GUNNISON

60 mi east of Montrose, 28 mi south of Crested Butte via Rte. 135.

At the confluence of the Gunnison River and Tomichi Creek, Gunnison is a traditional ranching community that has been adopted by nature lovers because of the excellent fishing and hunting nearby. In fact, long before these types arrived, the Utes used the area as summer hunting grounds. Gunnison provides economical lodging and easy access to Crested Butte and Blue Mesa Reservoir. Gunnison's other claim to fame is that it has recorded some of the coldest temperatures ever reported in the continental United States.

10

GETTING HERE AND AROUND

Getting in and out of Gunnison is a breeze. U.S. 50 travels right through town, heading east to Interstate 25 in Pueblo and northwest to I–70 in Grand Junction. U.S. 50 goes by the name Tomichi Avenue as it travels 18 blocks through town. Western State College and the Pioneer Museum are on east side of town, and the rodeo grounds and airport are south of Tomichi Avenue/U.S. 50.

WHEN TO GO

FESTIVALS Get a feel for the life of the cowboy at Gunnison's **Cattlemen's Days,** held at the Fred R. Field Western Heritage Center in July (⊠ *275 S. Spruce St.0* ⊕ *www.cattlemensdays.com*). Thrill to the sight of bare bronc and bull riding, barrel racing, and calf roping, or listen to the dulcet strains of cowboy poetry. For an amazing display of marksmanship combined with horsemanship, attend **Gunsmoke-n-Gunnison** (☎ *970/641–8561*), held at the Fred R. Field Western Heritage Center during the last weekend in July.

ESSENTIALS

Visitor Information Gunnison County Chamber of Commerce (⊠ *500 E. Tomichi Ave., Gunnison* ☎ *970/641–1501 or 800/274–7580* ⊕ *www. gunnisonchamber.com*).

EXPLORING

Nine miles west of Gunnison is the **Curecanti National Recreation Area,** set amid a striking eroded volcanic landscape and stretching for more than 60 mi. Dams built along the Gunnison River during the 1960s created three reservoirs, including **Blue Mesa Reservoir,** the state's largest body of water. Here you can fish, swim, or even windsurf. The reservoirs provide a wealth of recreational opportunities, including fine camping and hiking. Rangers lead education programs, including twice-daily boat tours of the Upper Black Canyon of the Gunnison. The tour starts 232 stairs up the Pine Creek Trail and reservations are required. At the western entrance to the Curecanti National Recreation Area the **Cimarron Visitor Center** (⊠ *U.S. 50* ☎ *970/249–4074* ☉ *June–Sept., hrs vary*) displays vintage locomotives, a reconstructed stockyard, and an 1882 trestle that's listed on the National Register of Historic Places. The **Elk Creek Campground** (⊠ *102 Elk Creek, off U.S. Hwy. 50* ☎ *970/641–2337* ⊕ *www.nps.gov/cure*) has a small bookstore and information center where boat permits for the Blue Mesa Reservoir may be purchased and reservations for boat tours can be made. The center also has information about the various camping sites around the Blue Mesa and is open Memorial Day to Labor Day.

☉ Anyone interested in the region's history shouldn't miss the **Pioneer Museum.** The complex spreads out over 6 acres, and includes an extensive collection of vehicles from Model As and Ts to 1960s sedans. There's a great train complete with coal tender, caboose, and boxcar; a red barn with wagons and displays of ranch life; and an old schoolhouse. ⊠ *U.S. 50 and S. Adams St.* ☎ *970/641–4530* ▤ *$7* ☉ *June–Sept., Mon.–Sat. 9–5, Sun. 11–5.*

SPORTS AND THE OUTDOORS

FISHING

Gene Taylor's (⊠ *201 W. Tomichi Ave.* ☎ *970/641–1845*) guided lake and river fishing tours are with two different outfitters. **Gunnison Sports Outfitters** (⊕ *www.gunnisonsportsoutfitters.com*) runs lake tours on the Blue Mesa Reservoir. **High Mountain Drifters** (⊕ *www.highmtndrifters.com*) fly-fishing tours will take you to one of four sections of private water along the Gunnison or one of its tributaries. All equipment is provided.

HORSEBACK RIDING

Lazy F Bar Outfitters (✉ *2991 County Rd. 738* ☎ *970/349–1755* ⊕ *www. lazyfbarranch.com*) rents horses for rides in the high country from June to early September and sleigh rides in the valleys from December to early April.

Tenderfoot Outfitters (✉ *501 Tomichi Ave. [U.S. 50]* ☎ *970/641–0504 or 800/641–0504* ⊕ *www.tenderfoot-outfitters.com*) specializes in guided wilderness rides.

WATER SPORTS

At 26 mi long, Blue Mesa Reservoir ranks as Colorado's largest body of water. Created in the mid-1960s when the state dammed the Gunnison River in three places, the lake is some 7,500 feet above sea level. It has become a mecca for water-sports enthusiasts. Anglers are drawn by the 3 million stocked rainbow, lake, brown, and brook trout and kokanee salmon.

In addition to the Cimarron Visitor Center at Curecanti National Recreation Area, there are smaller seasonal ranger stations at Lake Fork, Cimarron, and East Portal. If you have your own boat, you can use the ramps at Ponderosa (northern end at Soap Creek Arm), Stevens Creek (eastern end of the north shore), and Lola (eastern end on the south shore). A two-day boat permit is $4, and a two-week permit is $10. Annual boat permits run $30.

Elk Creek Marina (✉ *North side of lake* ☎ *970/641–0707* ⊕ *www.bluemesares.com*), about 15 mi west of Gunnison on U.S. 50, rents pontoon boats, rowboats, and aluminum fishing boats from May through September, 7 AM to 7 PM. The marina also runs guided fishing trips to Blue Mesa and Morrow Point reservoirs. A convenient restaurant is located above the dock, where you can sit and enjoy a light repast while watching other fishermen try their luck.

WHERE TO EAT

¢

CAFÉ

✕ **The Bean.** This brightly hued coffee shop is a great place for a morning or afternoon break. The walls are decorated with revolving art exhibits, and there are plenty of papers and magazines available. Hook up your laptop to their Wi-Fi. An impressive selection of espresso drinks is served, plus smoothies, bagels, crepes, fresh-baked pastries, and sandwiches. Ask about the crepe of the day; it's always delicious. The Bean is open until 7 PM every day. ✉ *120 N. Main St.* ☎ *970/641–2408* ⊕ *www. thebeancoffeehouseandeatery.com* ▭ *MC, V.*

$$$

ITALIAN

✕ **Garlic Mike's.** The menu at this unpretentious Italian spot is surprisingly rich and complex. Don't miss the fried green tomatoes, Parmesan-dusted sweet-potato fries, homemade thin-crust pizza, and eggplant parmigiana. The marinated strip-steak carbonara wins hands down as the house favorite. The heated outdoor patio overlooking the Gunnison River is a divine place to relax in summer. Be prepared for a leisurely dinner, the service can be slow. ✉ *2674 Hwy. 135* ☎ *970/641–2493* ⊕ *www.garlicmikes.com* ▭ *AE, MC, V* ⊗ *No lunch.*

$

AMERICAN

✕ **Gunnison Brewery.** A revolving list of home-crafted brews are on tap at this busy old downtown bar. They're known for a fine Dunkel Weizen, a strong-flavored, dark, wheat beer; the menu has the usual brewery

10

fare with burgers and fried food. There is live music on Wednesday and Friday nights from 10 PM to 2 AM. ⊠ *138 N. Main St.* ☎ *970/641–2739* ⊟ *D, MC, V* ☺ *No lunch Sun.*

$$ ✕ **Ol' Miner Steakhouse.** A meat lover's dream—choose T-bone, strip,
STEAK kebab, rib eye, or prime rib cooked the way you like it in this rustic restaurant decorated with elk and deer mounts, tin ceilings, and scarred wood furniture. Rocky Mountain oysters (bull testicles) are available for culinary risk-takers. There's also an unlimited soup-and-salad bar starting at $6.99, a respectable array of sandwiches for lunch, and traditional, as well as steak-enhanced, breakfasts. ⊠ *139 N. Main St.* ☎ *970/641–5153* ⊟ *AE, D, MC, V.*

WHERE TO STAY

$$ ⊞ **Holiday Inn Express Hotel.** Chain-hotel luxury is the focus here. The lobby is high-ceilinged, with a large gray stone fireplace and leather couches. The muted earth tones of the lobby are carried over into the rooms, all of which are equipped with a flat-screen TV, refrigerator, microwave, and Wi-Fi. There's a splendid indoor pool, indoor and outdoor hot tubs, and gym. Continental breakfast is included. **Pros:** numerous amenities; business facilities; reasonably priced. **Cons:** 1 mi from town; no restaurant; large and impersonal, chain hotel. ⊠ *910 E. Tomichi Ave., Gunnison* ☎ *970/641–1288 or 888/465–4329* ⊕ *www. hiexpress.com* ⟿ *107 rooms, 23 suites* ⌂ *In-room: refrigerator, Wi-Fi. In-hotel: pool, gym, laundry facilities, laundry service, public Wi-Fi* ⊟ *AE, D, MC, V* ⟟◯⟦ *CP.*

$ ⊞ **Rockey River Resort.** A tetherball on the turf, an old Ford pickup parked in the shadow of the milk house, sheets hung on the line, and the smell of cowboy coffee perking. These are just a few of the touches that make this old homestead a uniquely pleasant place to stay. There are 15 modernized cabins with fully equipped kitchens on the Gunnison River. You can fish right outside your door or drive to the Blue Mesa Reservoir, just 18 mi away. The resort is dog-friendly, and the proprietors are knowledgeable about fishing, trails, and local history. **Pros:** close to fishing, historic setting, very pet-friendly. **Cons:** 6 mi from Gunnison; some RVs on grounds; TV only in common area, not in cabins. ⊠ *4359 CR 10, off CO 135,* ☎ *970/641–0174* ⟿ *15 cabins* ⌂ *In-room: no a/c, no phone, kitchens, no TV. In-hotel: bicycles, Internet terminal, some pets allowed* ⊟ *MC, V.*

SHOPPING

The **Rocky Mountain Chocolate Factory** (⊠ *1000 N. Main St., Ste. 2* ☎ *970/ 641–1023* ⊕ *www.rockymountainchocolatefactory.com*) chain has a tasty array of homemade cookies, fudge, and gourmet chocolates as well as malts, shakes, and sundaes. **Rocky Mountain Gear** (⊠ *718 N. Main St.* ☎ *970/641–1380*) has a nice selection of outdoor equipment and camping supplies. **Western World** (⊠ *200 W. Tomichi Ave.* ☎ *970/641– 6566*) is the place to go for all things cowboy. They have a large selection of cowboy hats, boots, belts, jeans, and shirts for adults and kids. They also sell saddles, bridles, bits, and lassos. It's fun just to go in and look around.

BLACK CANYON OF THE GUNNISON NATIONAL PARK

South Rim: 15 mi east of Montrose, via U.S. 50 and Rte. 347. North Rim: 11 mi south of Crawford, via Rte. 92 and N. Rim Rd.

Updated by Martha Connors

The Black Canyon of the Gunnison River is one of Colorado's, and indeed the West's, most awe-inspiring places. A vivid testament to the powers of erosion, the canyon is roughly 2,000 feet deep. At its narrowest point, it spans 1,000 feet at the rim and only 40 feet at the bottom. The steep angles of the cliffs make it difficult for sunlight to fully break through during much of the day, and ever-present shadows blanket the canyon walls, leaving some places in almost perpetual darkness. No wonder it's called the "Black Canyon."

The primary gateway to Black Canyon is **Montrose,** 15 mi northeast of the park. The legendary Ute chief, Ouray, and his wife, Chipeta, lived near here in the mid-19th century. Today, Montrose straddles the important agricultural and mining regions along the Uncompahgre River, and its traditional downtown is a shopping hub.

GETTING HERE AND AROUND

Located in southwest Colorado, Black Canyon of the Gunnison lies between the cities of Gunnison and Montrose. Both have small regional airports.

The park has three roads. South Rim Road, reached by Route 347, is the primary thoroughfare and winds along the canyon's South Rim. From about late November to early April, the road is not plowed past the visitor center at Gunnison Point. North Rim Road, reached by Route 92, is usually open from May through Thanksgiving; in winter, the road is unplowed. The serpentine East Portal Road descends abruptly to the Gunnison River on the park's south side. The road is usually open from the beginning of May through the end of November. Because of the grade, vehicles or vehicle-trailer combinations longer than 22 feet are not permitted. The park has no public transportation.

ORIENTATION

Black Canyon of the Gunnison is a park of extremes—great depths, narrow widths, tall cliffs, and steep descents. It is not a large park, but it offers incredible scenery and unforgettable experiences, whether you're hiking, fishing, or just taking it all in from the car.

East Portal. The only way you can get down to the river via automobile in Black Canyon is on the steep East Portal Road.

North Rim. The area's remoteness and difficult location mean the North Rim is never crowded; the road is partially unpaved and closes in the winter. There's also a small ranger station here.

South Rim. This is the main area of the park. The park's only visitor center is here, along with a campground and a few picnic areas.

WHEN TO GO

Summer is the busiest season, with July experiencing the greatest crowds. A spring or fall visit gives you two advantages: fewer people and cooler temperatures—in summer, especially in years with little rainfall, daytime

10

PARK ESSENTIALS

ACCESSIBILITY
South Rim Visitor Center is accessible to people with mobility impairments. Drive-to overlooks on the South Rim include Tomichi Point, the alternate gravel viewpoint at Pulpit Rock (the main one is not accessible), Chasm View (gravel), Sunset View, and High Point. Balanced Rock (gravel) is the only drive-to viewpoint on the North Rim.

ADMISSION FEES AND PERMITS
Entrance fees are $15 per week per vehicle. Visitors entering on bicycle, motorcycle, or on foot pay $7 for a weekly pass. To access the inner canyon, you must pick up a back-country permit (no fee).

ADMISSION HOURS
The park is open 24/7 year-round. It's in the mountain time zone.

ATMS/BANKS
The park has no ATMs. The nearest ATMs are in Montrose.

CELL-PHONE RECEPTION
Cell-phone reception in the park is unreliable and sporadic. There are public telephones at South Rim Visitor Center and South Rim Campground.

PARK CONTACT INFORMATION
Black Canyon of the Gunnison National Park ⊠ *102 Elk Creek, Gunnison, CO* ☎ *970/641–2337* ⊕ *www.nps.gov/blca.*

temperatures can reach into the 90s. A winter visit to the park brings even more solitude, as all but one section of campsites are shut down and only about 2 mi of South Rim Road, the park's main road, are plowed.

November through February is when the snow hits, with 9 to 24 inches of it monthly on average. April and May, and September through November are the rainiest, with a monthly average of 1.7 to 2.2 inches of rain. June is generally the driest month, with only about 1 inch of rain on average. Temperatures at the bottom of the canyon are about 8 degrees warmer than at the rim.

EXPLORING

SCENIC DRIVES
Two scenic rim roads offer deep and distant views into the canyon. Both also offer several lookout points and short trails along the rim. The trails that go into the canyon are steep and strenuous, not to mention relatively unmarked, and so are reserved for experienced (and very fit) hikers only.

East Portal Road. The only way to access the Gunnison River from the park by car is via this paved route, which drops approximately 2,000 feet down to the water in only 5 mi, giving it a steep, 16% grade. (Vehicles longer than 22 feet are not allowed on the road; if you're towing a trailer, you can unhitch it at a parking area near the entrance to South Rim campground.) The bottom of the road is actually in the adjacent Curecanti National Recreation Area. A tour of East Portal Road, with a brief stop at the bottom, takes about 45 minutes.

North Rim Road. Black Canyon's North Rim is much less frequented, but no less spectacular—the walls here are near vertical—than the South Rim. To reach the 15½-mi-long North Rim Road, take the signed turn-off from Route 92 about 3 mi south of Crawford. The road is paved for about the first 4 mi; the rest is gravel. After 11 mi, turn left at the intersection (the North Rim Campground and ranger station are to the right). There are six overlooks as the road snakes along the rim's edge. Kneeling Camel, 4½ mi out at road's end, provides the broadest view of the canyon. Set aside about two hours for a tour of the North Rim.

South Rim Road. This paved 7-mi stretch from Tomichi Point to High Point is the park's main road. The drive follows the canyon's level South Rim; 12 overlooks are accessible from the road, most via short gravel trails. Several short hikes along the rim also begin roadside. Allow between two and three hours round-trip.

WHAT TO SEE
SCENIC STOPS

★ **Chasm and Painted Wall Views.** At the heart-in-your-throat Chasm viewpoint, the canyon walls plummet 1,820 feet to the river, but are only 1,100 feet apart at the top. As you peer down into the depths, keep in mind that this section is where the Gunnison River descends at its steepest rate, dropping 240 feet within the span a mile. A few hundred yards farther, you'll find the best place to see Painted Wall, Colorado's tallest cliff. Pinkish swathes of pegmatite (a crystalline, granitelike rock) give the wall its colorful, marbled appearance. ⊠ *Approximately 3½ mi from the Visitor Center on South Rim Rd.*

Narrows View. Look upriver from this North Rim overlook and you'll be able to see into the canyon's narrowest section, just a slot really, with only 40 feet between the walls at the bottom. The canyon is also taller (1,725 feet) here than it is wide at the rim (1,150 feet). ⊠ *North Rim Rd., first overlook past the ranger station.*

VISITOR CENTERS AND RANGER STATIONS

North Rim ranger station. This small facility on the park's North Rim is open in the summer. Rangers here that can provide information and assistance, as well as issue permits for backcountry use and rock climbing. ⊠ *North Rim Rd., 11 mi from Rte. 92 turnoff* ☎ *970/641–2337* ⊙ *Late May–Labor Day, daily 8–6.*

South Rim Visitor Center. The park's only visitor center offers interactive exhibits as well as two orientation videos—one details the geology and history of the canyon, the other includes the history of the Gunnison Water Diversion Tunnel and flora and fauna in the park. ⊠ *1½ mi from the entrance station on South Rim Rd.* ☎ *970/249–1914 Ext. 423* ⊙ *Late May–early Sept., daily 8–6; early Sept.–late May, daily 8:30–4.*

SPORTS AND THE OUTDOORS

Recreational activities in Black Canyon run the gamut from short and easy nature trails to world-class (and experts-only) rock climbing and kayaking. The cold waters of the Gunnison River are well known to trout anglers.

10

BIRD-WATCHING

The sheer cliffs of Black Canyon, though prohibitive to human habitation, provide a great habitat for birds. Naturally, cliff dwellers such as peregrine falcons and white-throated swifts revel in the dizzying heights, while at river level the American dipper is a common sight as it forages for food in the rushing waters. Canyon wrens, which nest in the cliffs, are more often heard than seen, but their hauntingly beautiful songs are unforgettable. Great horned owls and Steller's jays frequent the canyon rims. Best times for birding: spring and early summer.

BOATING AND KAYAKING

★ The Gunnison River is one of the premier kayak challenges in North America, with Class IV and Class V rapids, and difficult portages required around bigger drops. The spectacular 14-mi stretch of the river that passes through the park is so narrow in some sections that the rim seems to be closing up above your head. Once you're downstream from the rapids (and out of the park), the canyon opens up into what is called the Gunnison Gorge. The rapids ease considerably, and the trip becomes more of a quiet float on Class I to Class III water. Kayaking the river through the park requires a wilderness use permit (and lots of expertise), and rafting is not allowed. However, several outfitters offer guided raft and kayak trips in the Gunnison Gorge and other sections of the Gunnison River.

BOAT TOURS   Running twice daily (except Tuesday) in the summer, at 10 AM and 12:30 PM, **Morrow Point Boat Tours** (✉ *Pine Creek Boat Dock* ☎ *970/641– 2337 Ext. 205*) take up to 42 passengers on a 90-minute tour via pontoon boat. The cost is $16. Reservations are required.

FISHING

★ The three dams built upriver from the park in Curecanti National Recreation Area have created prime trout fishing in the waters below. In fact, the section of Gunnison River that goes through the park is designated Gold Medal Water, with abundant rainbow and brown trout. Certain restrictions apply: Only artificial flies and lures are permitted, and a Colorado fishing license is required for people aged 16 and older. Rainbow trout are catch-and-release only, and there are size and possession limits on brown trout (check at the visitor center). Most anglers access the river from the bottom of East Portal Road; an undeveloped trail goes along the riverbank for about .75 mi.

HIKING

All trails can be hot in summer and most don't receive much shade, so bring water, a hat, and plenty of sunscreen. Dogs are permitted, on leash, on Rim Rock, Cedar Point Nature, and Chasm View Nature trails. Hiking into the inner canyon, while doable, is not for the faint of heart—or step. Six named routes lead down to the river, but they are not maintained or marked. In fact, the park staff won't even call them trails; they refer to them as "controlled slides." These super-steep, rocky routes vary in one-way distance from 1 to 2.75 mi, and the descent can be anywhere from 1,800 to 2,702 feet. Your reward, of course, is a rare look at the bottom of the canyon and the fast-flowing Gunnison. ■ TIP→ Don't attempt an inner-canyon hike without plenty of water (the park's recommendation is one gallon per person, per day). For descriptions of the routes, and the necessary permit to hike them, stop at the visitor center at the South Rim or North Rim ranger station. Dogs are not permitted in the inner canyon.

EASY **Cedar Point Nature Trail.** This 0.7-mi round-trip interpretive trail leads out from South Rim Road to two overlooks. It's an easy stroll, and signs along the way detail the surrounding plants. ⊠ *Trailhead off South Rim Rd., 4.2 mi from South Rim Visitor Center.*

Deadhorse Trail. Despite its unpleasant name, Deadhorse Trail (about 5 mi round-trip) is actually an easy-to-moderate hike, starting on an old service road from the Kneeling Camel View on the North Rim Road. The trail's farthest point provides the park's easternmost viewpoint. From this overlook, the canyon is much more open, with pinnacles and spires rising along its sides. If you want to give yourself a bit of a scare, take the mile-long loop detour, about halfway through the hike. (The detour isn't marked; just look for the only other visible trail). At the two informal overlooks, you'll be perched—without guardrails—atop the highest cliff in this part of the canyon. Make sure to keep your children by your side at all times. ⊠ *Trailhead at the southernmost end of North Rim Rd.*

MODERATE **Chasm View Nature Trail.** The park's shortest trail (0.3 mi round-trip) starts at North Rim Campground and offers an impressive 50-yard walk right along the canyon rim as well as an eye-popping view downstream of Painted Wall, 1,100 feet across on the South Rim. ⊠ *Trailhead at North Rim Campground, 11.25 mi from Rte. 92.*

North Vista Trail. The moderate round-trip hike to and from Exclamation Point is 3 mi; a more difficult foray to the top of 8,563-foot Green Mountain (a mesa, really), with about 800 feet of elevation gain, is 7 mi round-trip. You'll hike along the North Rim; keep an eye out for especially gnarled pinyon pines—the North Rim is the site of some of the oldest groves of pinyons in North America, between 400 and 700 years old. ⊠ *Trailhead at North Rim ranger station, off North Rim Rd., 11 mi from Rte. 92 turnoff.*

Fodor'sChoice **Warner Point Nature Trail.** The 1½-mi round-trip hike starts from High
★ Point. You'll enjoy fabulous vistas of the San Juan and West Elk Mountains and Uncompahgre Valley. Warner Point, at trail's end, has the steepest drop-off from rim to river: a dizzying 2,722 feet. ⊠ *Trailhead: at the end of South Rim Rd.*

DIFFICULT **Oak Flat Trail.** This 2-mi loop trail is the most demanding of the South Rim hikes, as it brings you about 300 feet below the canyon rim. In places, the trail is narrow and crosses some steep slopes, but you won't have to navigate any steep drop-offs. Oak Flat is the shadiest of all the South Rim trails; small groves of aspen and thick stands of Douglas fir along the loop offer some respite from the sun. ⊠ *Trailhead: just west of the South Rim Visitor Center.*

HORSEBACK RIDING

OUTFITTERS Run by the Montrose Recreation District, **Elk Ridge Trail Rides** (⊠ *10203*
AND *Bostwick Park Rd., Montrose* ☎ *970/240–6007* ⊕ *www.elkridgeranchinc.*
EXPEDITIONS *com* ⊗ *May–Sept., daily, weather permitting*) is the only outfitter allowed to guide rides in Black Canyon National Park. It offers a four-hour ride to the canyon rim along the Deadhorse Trail. Riders must be in good physical condition, at least 8 years old, and weigh no more than 230 pounds.

10

ROCK CLIMBING

Fodor's Choice ★ For advanced rock climbers, climbing the sheer cliffs of the Black Canyon is one of Colorado's premier big-wall challenges. Some routes can take several days to complete, with climbers sleeping on narrow ledges or "portaledges." Though there's no official guide to climbing in the park, reports from other climbers are kept on file at the South Rim Visitor Center. Nesting birds of prey may lead to wall closure at certain times of year.

Rock climbing in the park is for experts only, but if you want to get in some easier climbing, head for the Marmot Rocks bouldering area, about 100 feet south of South Rim Road between Painted Wall and Cedar Point overlooks (park at Painted Wall). Four boulder groupings offer a variety of routes rated from easy to very difficult; a pamphlet with a diagrammed map of the area is available at the South Rim Visitor Center.

OUTFITTERS AND EXPEDITIONS
In the summer months, advanced climbers can take a full-day guided tour with **Crested Butte Mountain Guides** (✉ *218 Maroon Ave.,* ⌂ *Box 1718, Crested Butte* ☎ *970/349–5430* ⊕ *www.crestedbutteguides.com*) for $300 (one person), $450 (two people), or $525 (three people). Come winter, the guides also lead day-long ice-climbing trips in the park for $270 for one to two people, $135 for each additional person. Intermediate to advanced climbers can take a one-, three-, or five-day guided tour with **Skyward Mountaineering** (⌂ *Box 323, Ridgway* ☎ *970/209–2985* ⊕ *www.skywardmountaineering.com* ☉ *Mar.–Nov.*) ; per-day rates are $350 for one person, $450 for two, and $600 for three.

WINTER SPORTS

From late November to early April, South Rim Road is not plowed past the visitor center, offering park guests a unique opportunity to cross-country ski or snowshoe on the road. It's possible to ski or snowshoe on the unplowed North Rim Road, too, but it's about 4 mi from where the road closes, through sagebrush flats, to the canyon rim.

OUTFITTERS AND EXPEDITIONS
In winter, rangers offers **Guided Snowshoe Walks** (☎ *970/249–1914 Ext. 423*), usually once a day on weekends. Tours leave from the South Rim Visitor Center and go along the rim for about 2 mi, often on Rim Rock Trail. A limited supply of snowshoe gear is available for use at no charge. Call ahead to reserve equipment and a space on a tour.

EDUCATIONAL OFFERINGS

RANGER PROGRAMS

☾ **Junior Ranger Program.** Kids ages 5 to 12 can participate in this program with an activities booklet to fill in while exploring the park.

WHERE TO STAY

There are two campgrounds in the national park. The smaller North Rim Campground is first-come, first-served, and is closed in the winter. South Rim Campground is considerably larger, and has a loop that's open year-round. Reservations are accepted in South Rim Loops A and B. Power hookups only exist in Loop B, and vehicles more than 35 feet long are discouraged from either campground. At both of the park's drive-to campgrounds there's a limit of eight people per site, and camping is limited to 14 days. Water has to be trucked up to the campgrounds, so use it in moderation; it's shut off in mid- to late September. Generators are not allowed at South Rim and are highly discouraged on the North Rim.

CAMPING
¢
Fodor'sChoice
★

South Rim Campground. Stay on the canyon rim at this main campground right inside the park entrance. Loops A and C have tent sites only. The RV hookups are in Loop B, and those sites are priced higher than those in other parts of the campground. It's possible to camp here year-round (Loop A stays open all winter), but the loops are not plowed, so you'll have to hike in with your tent. **Pros:** easy access to the canyon; never crowded. **Cons:** extra-large vehicles (more than 35 feet long) aren't recommended; because park staff must bring in all water by truck, there's no water for dishes or bathing (just drinking fountains). ⊠ *South Rim Rd., 1 mi from the visitor center* ⚐ *65 tent sites, 23 RV sites* ⚐ *Pit toilets, partial hookups (electric) in Loop B, drinking water, fire grates, picnic tables, public telephone* ▭ *No credit cards* ⊙ *Loops B and C closed Nov.–Apr.*

¢

North Rim Campground. This small campground, nestled amid pine trees, offers the basics along the quiet North Rim. **Pros:** amazing views; fragrant campsites among pinions and junipers. **Cons:** occasionally fills on summer weekends; close proximity to the rim makes it less than ideal for small children; no hookups. ⊠ *North Rim Rd., 11 mi from Rte. 92* ⚐ *13 tent/RV sites* ⚐ *Pit toilets, drinking water, fire grates, picnic tables, ranger station* ▭ *No credit cards* ⊙ *Closed Nov.–Apr.*

MONTROSE

15 mi southwest of Black Canyon of the Gunnison; 65 mi west of Gunnison via U.S. 50.

Updated by
Carrie Frasure

The self-described "Home of the Black Canyon" sits amid glorious surroundings, but it's an otherwise nondescript town with little more than a collection of truck stops, trailer parks, strip malls, and big-box stores frequented by area residents. Montrose also has a small airport that's a good gateway for skiers heading to Telluride, whose airport is often closed due to weather, and to Crested Butte. Montrose is perfectly placed for exploring the Black Canyon of the Gunnison and Curecanti National Recreation Area to the east; the San Juan Mountains to the south; the world's largest flattop mountain, Grand Mesa, to the north; and the fertile Uncompahgre Plateau to the west.

U.S. 550 enters Montrose from the south and turns into Townsend Avenue. At the intersection of Townsend Avenue and Main Street, U.S. 550 turns into U.S. 50 and continues north to Delta. Main Street doubles as the other extension of U.S. 50, which travels east to Black Canyon National Park and Gunnison.

ESSENTIALS

Visitor Info Montrose Visitors and Convention Bureau (⊠ *1519 E. Main St., Montrose* ☎ *970/252–0505 or 800/873–0244* ⊕ *www.visitmontrose.com*).

10

EXPLORING

If you're interested in the lives of the region's original residents, stop by the excellent **Ute Indian Museum**, 3 mi south of town on U.S. 550. The museum contains several dioramas and the most comprehensive collection of Ute materials and artifacts in Colorado. The museum is housed in the 1956 homestead of Ute Chief Ouray and his wife Chipeta. Today, the complex includes the Chief Ouray Memorial Park, Chipeta's Crypt, a native plants garden, picnic areas, and shaded paths linked to the city-wide walking trail. ⊠ *17253 Chipeta Rd.* ☎ *970/249–3098* ⊕ *www.coloradohistory.org* ⬚ *$3.50* ⊙ *May 15–Oct. 15, Mon.–Sat. 9–4:30, Sun. 1–4:30; Oct. 16–Dec. 31, Mon.–Sat. 8:30–5; Jan. 2–May 14, Tues.–Sat. 8:30–5.*

SPORTS AND THE OUTDOORS

BOATING

Lake Fork Marina (⊠ *West side of lake* ☎ *970/641–3048* ⊕ *www.bluemesares.com*) rents all types of boats on Blue Mesa Reservoir. If you have your own boat, there's a ramp at the marina. A two-day boat permit is $5; a two-week permit is $10.

HIKING

For information on backcountry hiking in the Uncompahgre Plateau and other nearby wilderness areas, contact the Montrose office of the **Grand Mesa, Uncompahgre, and Gunnison national forests** (⊠ *2505 S. Townsend Ave., Montrose* ☎ *970/240–5300* ⊕ *www.fs.fed.us/r2/gmug*).

WHERE TO EAT AND STAY

$$–$$$
SOUTHWESTERN

✕ **Camp Robber.** The name refers to a native Colorado bird called the Canada jay, famous for stealing food from campsites; you'll want to steal the recipes for hearty Southwestern dishes such as spicy chimayo shrimp and the signature green chile chicken potato soup. Other favorite dishes on the menu include the chile-pistachio-crusted pork medallions, the Sonoran steak pasta, and the Asian barbecue chicken salad. The rustic decor in various shades of evergreen and earthy browns warms up the restaurant. Generous portions for reasonable prices make it popular with families and groups, and the servers are friendly, accommodating, and knowledgeable. ⊠ *1515 Ogden Rd.* ☎ *970/240–1590* ⊕ *www.camprobber.com* ⊟ *AE, MC, V* ⊙ *No dinner Sun.*

¢–$
ECLECTIC

✕ **Cazwellas.** Consistently voted the best in the valley by the locals, the comfortably upscale, internationally themed eatery presents exposed-brick walls and a laid-back attitude. The menu, mostly organically and seasonally focused, contains both complicated dishes and simple preparations. Bison cocktail meatballs and seared sea scallops with roasted grapes are favorite starters, and you can't go wrong with the double-cut pork chop or any of the Angus steaks, especially the rib eye rubbed with ancho chilies. ⊠ *320 E. Main St.* ☎ *970/252–9200* ⊟ *AE, DC, MC, V* ⊙ *Closed Sun and Mon. No lunch.*

$

🏨 **Best Western Red Arrow Motor Inn.** This low-key establishment is one of the nicest lodgings in the area, mainly because of the large, prettily appointed rooms filled with handsome mahogany furnishings. The full baths include soothing whirlpool tubs. **Pros:** reasonably priced; convenient downtown location; good-size rooms. **Cons:** Main Street can be noisy. ⊠ *1702 E. Main St.,* ☎ *970/249–9641 or 800/468–9323* ⊕ *www. bestwestern.com* ⊅ *60 rooms* ᗐ *In-room: Wi-Fi. In-hotel: pool, gym, laundry service, some pets allowed* ⊟ *AE, D, DC, MC, V* ⭕ *CP.*

¢ ⬚ **Black Canyon Motel.** Spacious, well-maintained rooms with refrigerators and microwaves, friendly staff, and reasonable prices make this motel a good option for families. A small swimming pool and above-average complimentary breakfast (make-your-own waffles, bagels, muffins, and juices) add to the appeal. **Pros:** excellent value; pets allowed. **Cons:** nothing fancy; Main Street can be noisy. ⊠ *1605 E. Main St.,* ☎ *970/ 249– 3495 or 800/348–3495* ⊕ *www.blackcanyonmotel.com* ⊅ *49 rooms* ᗐ *In-room: refrigerator, Wi-Fi. In-hotel: pool, laundry facilities, Wi-Fi, some pets allowed* ⊟ *AE, D, DC, MC, V* ⭕ *CP.*

SHOPPING

Got a sweet tooth? The **Russell Stover Factory Outlet** (⊠ *2185 Stover Ave.* ☎ *970/249–5372* ⊕ *www.russellstover.com* ⊙ *Mon.–Sat. 9–6, Sun. 11–6*) sells fresh chocolates made in the factory across the street. The store is easy to find—it's south of downtown off U.S. 550. Pack a picnic lunch for the Black Canyon with local bounty at the **Montrose Farmers' Market** (⊠ *Centennial Plaza, Main and Uncompahgre Sts.* ☎ *970/209–8463* ⊕ *www.montrosefarmersmarket.com* ⊙ *Mid-May–Oct., Wed. and Sat. 8:30–1*). In late summer keep your eyes peeled for locally grown and locally beloved sweet corn.

DELTA COUNTY

46 mi south of Grand Junction via U.S. 50.; 22 mi north of Montrose via U.S. 50

Travel moves at a leisurely pace in Delta County; the area's focus is on wildlife, ranching, and agriculture. Seven murals, most of them lining Delta's Main Street, were painted by local artists in the late 1980s and celebrate various aspects of local life in *Delta County Ark*, *High Country Roundup*, *A Tribute to Agriculture*, and *Labels of Delta County*. Delta is also a good jumping-off point for visiting Black Canyon of the Gunnison National Park and the nearby farming and ranching communities of Crawford, Hotchkiss, and Paonia—the last named known for its fabulous gardens and orchards.

10

From Delta, Highway 65 heads north to Cedaredge, which is the starting point for the Grand Mesa Scenic and Historic Byway. Highway 92 loops east and south, taking a lazy tour past the farming and ranching communities of Hotchkiss and Crawford before meeting up with the North Rim of Black Canyon of the Gunnison National Park. For a side tour, a short 9-mi jaunt on Highway 133 leads to Paonia.

WHEN TO GO

The cornucopia of ripening fruits and vegetables paired with a delightful array of local wines make summer the best time to visit this remote area.

ESSENTIALS

Visitor Info Crawford Area Chamber of Commerce (✉ *Crawford* ☎ *970/921–4000* ⊕ *www.crawfordcounty.org*). **Delta Area Chamber of Commerce and Visitor Center** (✉ *301 Main St., Delta* ☎ *970/874–8616* ⊕ *www.deltacolorado.org*). **Hotchkiss Community Chamber of Commerce** (✉ *Hotchkiss* ☎ *970/872–3226* ⊕ *www.hotchkisschamber.com*). **Paonia Chamber of Commerce** (✉ *Paonia* ☎ *970/527–3886* ⊕ *www.paoniachamber.com*). **The Town of Cedaredge** (✉ *235 W. Main St., Cedaredge* ⊕ *www.cedaredgecolorado.com*).

EXPLORING

Ò A blast from the past, the **Tru-Vu Drive-in Theater** (✉ *1001 Hwy. 92, Delta* ☎ *970/874–9556*) is a designated historic landmark, and one of only 500 remaining drive-in movie theaters in the United States.

Learn about the town's rich history with a visit to **Fort Uncompahgre,** on a self-guided tour through an 1826 fur-trading post. ✉ *Confluence Park, 230 Gunnison River Dr., Delta* ☎ *970/874–1718* 🖅 *$3.50* ⊙ *Daily 9–3.*

One of the more interesting artifacts at the **Delta County Museum** is a collection of guns used in a failed bank-robbery attempt in Delta on September 7, 1893. That day, the notorious McCarty Gang rode into town to rob the Farmers & Merchants Bank. The robbery went bad from the start, when one of the robbers shot and killed the cashier. The gunfire alerted a hardware-store clerk, who grabbed his Sharps rifle and killed two of the robbers during their getaway. ✉ *251 Meeker St., Delta* ☎ *970/874–8721* 🖅 *$2* ⊙ *May–Sept., Tues.–Sat. 10–4; Oct.–Apr., Wed. and Sat. 10–4.*

In a renovated milk processing plant, the two-story **Creamery Arts Center** (✉ *165 W. Bridge St., Hotchkiss* ☎ *970/872–4848* ⊕ *www.northforkarts.org* ⊙ *Mon.–Sat. 11–6, Sun. 11–4*) houses the work of regional artists. In addition to four art galleries, the center also contains a glass studio, a clay studio, and an art classroom for workshops and classes.

OFF THE BEATEN PATH

Escalante Canyon. Named after Spanish missionary explorer Francisco Silvestre Velez de Escalante, who with father Francisco Atanasio Dominguez led an expedition through the area in 1776, Escalante Canyon shelters homesteader cabins (including the 1911 Walker Cabin), Native American rock art, and hiking trails. One of the pioneer homes was built by Captain H.A. Smith. His stone cabin, built into the side of a boulder, has a hollowed-out slab for a bed and a smaller niche carved out of the stone wall to hold a bedside pistol. Signs are visible from the main highway, and the sites are well marked. You can hike the several miles on the dirt road off the main highway or drive right up to the site. As of March 30, 2009, Escalante Canyon became protected as part of the Dominguez-Escalante National Conservation Area, which encompasses 209,610 acres of Bureau of Land Management (BLM) area in Mesa, Delta, and Montrose counties in southwestern Colorado. ✉ *10 mi north of Delta on U.S. 50,* ✉ *2505 S. Townsend Ave., Montrose* ☎ *970/240–5367* ⊕ *www.blm.gov* 🖅 *Free* ⊙ *Year-round.*

TOP EXPERIENCE: FARMS, ORCHARDS, AND WINERIES

FARMS AND
ORCHARDS

Gardens and orchards add a green sheen to this high mountain valley. For farming at its finest, check out the fresh selection of fruits and vegetables at the many roadside stands.

Delicious Orchards. This lovely orchard markets it organic apples, apricots, cherries, nectarines, peaches, pears, and plums all summer long. The gift shop also showcases local wines, produce, and body-care products. ⊠ *39126 Hwy. 133, Paonia* ☎ *970/527–1110* ⊕ *www.freshapplecider. com* ☉ *May–Dec., daily 8–6.*

Orchard Valley Farms. Family fun takes an organic approach at this friendly farm. Take a stroll through the gardens and orchards and pick your own fruits and vegetables or choose from a nice selection at the farm market. ⊠ *15836 Black Bridge Rd., Paonia* ☎ *970/527–6838* ⊕ *www. orchardvalleyfarms.com* ☉ *Call ahead for hours.*

WINERIES

At the foot of the West Elk Mountain Range, the West Elks American Viticultural Area (AVA) produces an array of Central European varietals including reisling, pinot gris, pinot noir, merlot, and chardonnay grapes. **Check out ⊕ www.coloradowine.com for a wine trail map,** or just hit a few of the highlights while enjoying the fresh mountain air and high-altitude valley scenery.

Alfred Eames Cellars. Puesta del Sol Vineyards in Paonia is a casual winery with a nice selection of top-notch red wines, including a 2006 Sangre del Sol, a blended cabernet sauvignon and merlot, and 2006 Noche, a potent blend comprised of syrah, merlot, and cabernet. For a great paring of wines and local foods, check out the annual wine festival held here in August. ⊠ *11931 4050 Rd., Paonia* ☎ *970/527–3269* ⊕ *www. alfredeamescellars.com* ☉ *Call ahead for hours.*

Black Bridge Winery. Orchard Valley Farms has been growing wine grapes since 1997, and released its own organic wines in 2005. Since then, this winery has made great strides with its nice selection of cabernet, merlot, pinot noir, and chardonnay wines. ⊠ *15836 Black Bridge Rd., Paonia* ☎ *970/527–6838* ⊕ *www.blackbridgewinery.com* ☉ *June– Oct., daily 9–6.*

Peak Spirits Distillery. Spice things up a bit with the spirited selections at this organic distillery. Fruit products from the Jack Rabbit Hill Biodynamic Farm combine to create CapRock Organic Gin, CapRock Organic Vodka, Peak Organic Eaux de Vie, and Peak Biodynamic Grappas. ⊠ *26567 North Rd., Hotchkiss* ☎ *970/872–3677* ⊕ *www. peakspirits.com* ☉ *Call ahead for hours.*

Stone Cottage Cellars. This North Fork Valley Winery specializes in chardonnay, Gewürztraminer, merlot, and syrah varietals. For summer fun, stop by for a vineyard tour and wine tasting. ⊠ *41716 Reds Rd., Paonia* ☎ *970/527–5234* ⊕ *www.stonecottagecellars.com* ☉ *June–Oct., daily 11–6.*

10

SPORTS AND THE OUTDOORS

HIKING For information on backcountry hiking in the Uncompahgre Plateau and other nearby wilderness areas, contact the district office of the **Grand Mesa, Uncompahgre, and Gunnison national forests** (⊠ *2250 U.S. 50, Delta* ☎ *970/874–6600* ⊕ *www.fs.fed.us/r2/gmug*).

WHERE TO EAT

$$$ ✕ **The Flying Fork Café and Bakery.** You might not expect classic European
ITALIAN dining in this High Country valley, that is until you've tasted Paonia chef Kelly Steinmetz's Muscovy duck. Chef Steinmetz utilizes the freshest local ingredients and creates a menu renowned for its hand-tossed pizzas, colorful salads, and delectable pastas. Specials change daily, but some of the favorite dinner items include braised Colorado lamb shank with roast garlic and truffle mashed potato, pollo marsala served over a medley of wild rice and orzo, and calamari Parmesan with pomodora sauce over linguini. Local varietals top the wine list for lunch and dinner, and the bakery serves a mouth-watering array of homemade breads for breakfast along with a local selection of jams, syrups, honey, and coffee. ⊠ *101 3rd St., at Main St., Paonia* ☎ *970/527–3203* ⊕ *www.flyingforkcafe.com* ⩘ *Reservations essential* ▤ *AE, D, MC, V* ⊙ *Closed Mon.*

$–$$ ✕ **Miller's Deitch Haus.** Braced by thick wooden beams, this well-known
AMERICAN Delta buffet diner serves a wide selection of chicken, steaks, and fish. Specialties include prime rib on weekends and *Jäger Schnitzel* (breaded veal in a hearty brown mushroom sauce). The all-you-can-eat buffet includes plates for the popular soup and salad bar. This bustling cafeteria is light on atmosphere but not on your wallet. For an extra fee you can try one of the homemade pies for dessert. ⊠ *820 Hwy. 92, Delta* ☎ *970/874–4413* ⊕ *www.millersdeitchhaus.com* ▤ *MC, V.*

WHERE TO STAY

$ 🛏 **Best Western Sundance.** Within walking distance of Delta's downtown, this motel has up-to-date rooms, a full-service restaurant and lounge, a heated seasonal pool, and a spa and fitness center. **Pros:** in-hotel Sundance Restaurant; relaxing on-site lounge; full hot breakfast. **Cons:** rooms show some wear. ⊠ *903 Main St.,* ☎ *970/874–9781 or 800/626–1994* ⊕ *www.bestwestern.com* ➪ *41 rooms* ⅙ *In-room: Wi-Fi. In-hotel: restaurant, room service, pool, gym, spa, laundry facilities, some pets allowed* ▤ *AE, D, DC, MC, V* ⅋〇⅋ *BP.*

$ 🛏 **Fresh & Wyld Farmhouse Inn and Gardens.** This rambling Paonia farmhouse turned B&B has two suites on the main floor and four smaller rooms, with shared bathrooms, on the second floor. The upstairs rooms are clean and cheery, with quilted bedcovers and sunny windows. The two suites on the main floor have sitting rooms and private bathrooms. Each morning you'll wake up to a farm-fresh, organic breakfast. ■**TIP→** **Fridays at the Farmhouse is a popular communal cooking experience featuring local ingredients, open to both guests and non-guests for $15.** The Farmhouse adds to the selection with home-grown vegetables and orchard fruit. These culinary experiences are scheduled on Friday at 6:30 year-round and on Sunday for brunch at 10 and noon from June through mid-October. Other fun options include canning and cooking workshops, on-site massage, and a boutique loaded with local goodies.

Pros: delicious local and organic food; farmhouse setting. **Cons:** the four rooms upstairs are basic and have shared bathrooms. ⊠ *1978 Harding Rd., Paonia* ☎ *970/527–4374* ⊕ *www.freshandwyldinn.com* ⇝ *6 rooms* ⌂ *In-room: no a/c, no phone* ⊟ *D, MC, V* ⎟⎠⎢ *BP.*

$$$$ ☒ **Smith Fork Ranch.** Rustic charm and Western hospitality are the keys
☻ to this historic dude ranch's success. Lodge rooms and log cabins com-
★ bine modern amenities with Western art and hand-crafted furniture. The main lodge offers a billiard room, dining room, a fully stocked bar, a game room, a fitness center, and a fly shop. All-inclusive ranch activities include archery, fly-fishing, casting clinics, horseback riding, and guided hikes. Kids especially have fun with the tree house, authentic Indian tepees, and swimming ponds. Breakfast, lunch, and dinner are served daily. Kids have a choice of dinner entrées, but adults all eat the same menu offering. The good news is that the food is fabulous. A sample three-course dinner menu included an appetizer of crab cakes with avocado, mango, and yuzu vinaigrette; a main entrée of duck breast with nectarine, bok choy, dicon radish, and cauliflower; and a dessert of funnel cake with popcorn ice cream and caramel. **Pros:** fabulous staff; variety of ranch activities to choose from; laundry service Wednesday and Saturday. **Cons:** very expensive; dining options are limited; no refund for cancellations 90 days prior to arrival date. ⊠ *Box 401, Crawford* ☎ *970/921–3454* ⊕ *www.smithforkranch.com* ⇝ *5 rooms, 4 cabins* ⌂ *In-room: no a/c, no phone. In-hotel: restaurant, bar, gym, children's programs ages 3 and up, Internet terminal, Wi-Fi* ⊟ *AE, MC, V* ⊘ *Closed Sept.–May* ⎟⎠⎢ *AI.*

OFF THE BEATEN PATH For spectacular views of wildflower meadows, evergreen mesa forests, and high-mountain lakes, take a relaxed two-hour tour through Grand Mesa, Uncompahgre, and Gunnison National Forests on the 63 mi **Grand Mesa Scenic and Historic Byway.** The "Alpine Oasis in the Sapphire Sky" follows Highway 64 from Cedaredge at the southern end to I–70 on the northern end. This route travels along the rim of the world's largest flat-top mountain, offering breathtaking views of Grand Valley more than a mile below. For more information, check out ⊕ *www.byways.org.*

10

LAKE CITY AND CREEDE

Lake City and Creede are in one of the most beautiful areas of Colorado. Both have colorful histories and excellent access to the many hiking and mountain-biking trails in the Gunnison National Forest and the Rio Grande National Forest. If you're driving through here, especially on the Silver Thread Scenic Byway or the Alpine Loop Scenic Byway, allow plenty of time, because you'll want to keep stopping to take pictures of the surrounding mountains.

LAKE CITY

45 mi from Ouray via Alpine Loop Scenic Byway (summer only); 55 mi southwest of Gunnison via U.S. 50 and Rte. 149; 49 mi northwest of Creede via Rte. 149.

Lake City—with its collection of lacy gingerbread-trim houses and false-front Victorians—claims to have the largest National Historic District in Colorado. But the history the town is perhaps best known for is the lurid story of a notorious rogue named Alfred Packer. Packer led a party of six prospectors who camped near Lake San Cristobal during the winter of 1874. That spring, only Packer emerged from the mountains, claiming that after he had been deserted by the rest he subsisted on roots and rabbits. Soon after, a Ute traveling near Lake San Cristobal came across a grisly pile of human flesh and crushed skulls. Packer protested his innocence and fled, but a manhunt ensued. He was caught nine years later and sentenced to life in prison.

Lake City is the point of departure for superb hiking and fishing in the Gunnison National Forest. A geological phenomenon known as the Slumgullion Earthflow occurred some 800 years ago, when a mountainside sloughed off into the valley, blocking the Lake Fork of the Gunnison River and creating Lake San Cristobal, the state's second-largest natural lake. There's a scenic overlook along Highway 149, just south of town, with a sign explaining how this happened.

GETTING HERE AND AROUND

Highway 149 turns into Gunnison Avenue as it passes through this tiny mountain town stretching seven blocks. The majority of the shops are on Gunnison Avenue and the parallel Silver Street and Bluffs Street lined with historic homes. Intersecting north–south streets are numbered from 2 to 8.

ESSENTIALS

Visitor Info Lake City/Hinsdale County Chamber of Commerce (✉ *800 N. Gunnison Ave.,* ☎ *970/944–2527 or 800/569–1874* ⊕ *www.lakecity.com*).

EXPLORING

Lake City is at the northern tip of the **Silver Thread Scenic Byway,** whose tail is 75 mi south in Southfork. The paved route, also called Highway 149, climbs over Slumgullion Pass from Lake City, overlooks the headwaters of the Rio Grande, and then drops down into the lush Rio Grande Valley.

The inspiring **Alpine Loop Scenic Byway** joins Lake City with Ouray and Silverton. This part of the route is only open in summer, and is not paved over Cinnamon Pass and Engineer Pass. However, this is heaven for four-wheelers, dizzily spiraling from 12,800-foot-high passes to gaping valleys.

SPORTS AND THE OUTDOORS

FISHING

Numerous high-alpine lakes and mountain streams make Lake City a fisherman's heaven. Lake San Cristobal is known around the region for its rainbow and brown trout. The Lake Fork of the Gunnison attracts anglers for rainbow and brook trout. For information about guided trips, fishing licenses, or renting gear, check with **Dan's Fly Shop** (✉ *723 N. Gunnison Ave.* ☎ *970/944–2281* ⊕ *www.dansflyshop.com*).

HIKING

There are lots of trails in this region, for varying abilities. Inquire locally for directions to the trailheads. Many follow logging roads, so it's best to get the latest scoop on conditions from a resident. Ambitious hikers often overnight in Lake City before attempting three of Colorado's easier Fourteeners. Sunshine and Redcloud are generally climbed together, and Handies is across the valley. This means it is fairly easy for fit hikers to bag three Fourteeners in just two days.

WHERE TO STAY

$–$$ ⬚ **Old Carson Inn.** This peaceful A-frame log cabin is nestled among stands of towering aspen and spruce. Seven rooms are brimming with rustic charm, and are nicely appointed with down comforters. The country breakfast, served family style, should get you off to a good start. **Pros:** beautiful setting; excellent food; comfortable rooms. **Cons:** not centrally located; extra charge for a single-night stay. ⌂ *Box 144, County Rd. 30,* ☎ *970/944–2511 or 800/294–0608* ⊕ *www.oldcarsoninn.com* ⟿ *7 rooms* ⌂ *In-room: no a/c, no TV* ▤ *AE, D, MC, V* ⦿ *BP.*

CREEDE

105 mi south of Gunnison via U.S. 50 and Rte. 149; 52 mi southeast of Lake City via Rte. 149.

Creede once earned a reputation as Colorado's rowdiest mining camp, and was immortalized in an evocative poem by the local newspaper editor, Cy Warman. "It's day all day in daytime," he wrote, "and there is no night in Creede." Every other building back then seems to have been a saloon or bordello. Bob Ford, who killed Jesse James, was himself gunned down here; other notorious residents included Calamity Jane and Bat Masterson. As delightful as the town is today, its location is even more glorious. About 96 percent of Mineral County is public land, including the nearby Weminuche Wilderness to the south and west and the Wheeler Geological Area to the west, where the unusual rock formations resemble playful abstract sculptures or M. C. Escher creations. The Colorado Trail and the Continental Divide Trail, two of the country's most significant long-distance recreational paths, pass through Mineral County.

GETTING HERE AND AROUND

Highway 149 turns into Main Street as passes through this mountain community stretching fifteen blocks.

ESSENTIALS

Visitor Info Creede–Mineral County Chamber of Commerce (✉ *904 S. Main St., Creede* ☎ *719/658–2374 or 800/327–2102* ⊕ *www.creede.com*).

EXPLORING

The **Underground Mining Museum** is housed in rooms that local miners blasted out of solid rock to commemorate the life of the hard-rock miner. Exhibits tracing the history of mining from 1892 to the 1960s teach you the difference between a *winze* (reinforced shaft leading straight down) and a *windlass* (hand-operated hoist). There are guided tours (at 10 and 3 daily), but you can also poke about on your own. After you've toured the mine, ask if you can look into the world's only underground firehouse, directly next door. If a volunteer firefighter is around, he'll gladly show you. Donations are welcome. ⊠ *503 Forest Service Rd. #9* ☎ *719/658–0811* ⏱ *June–Aug., daily 10–4; Sept.–May, weekdays 10–3* 💲 *$15 guided tour; $7 self-guided tour.*

The **Creede Historical Museum,** occupying the original Denver & Rio Grande Railroad Depot, paints a vivid portrait of those rough-and-tumble days. ⊠ *Main St. behind Basham Park* ☎ *719/658–2004* 💲 *$2* ⏱ *June–Aug., Mon.–Sat. 10–4, Sun. 1–4.*

WHERE TO EAT AND STAY

¢–$ ✕ **The Old Firehouse.** The style of this casual Italian restaurant, ice-cream

CAFE   parlor, and café with Wi-Fi reflects the building's heritage, with old-fashioned fire equipment, red ladders, and patches from fire departments around the country left by customers. Step up to the marble bar with its antique stained-glass back for a variety of ice-cream flavors. ⊠ *123 N. Main St.* ☎ *719/658–0212* ⊕ *www.theoldfirehouse.com* ⊟ *MC, V* ⏱ *Closed Oct.–mid-Apr.*

$ ⊞ **Antler's Rio Grande Lodge.** Dating to the late 1800s, this cozy lodge has rooms in the main building as well as rustic, secluded cabins along the river that are rented on a weekly basis ($900–$1,650). RV campsites ($32) are also available. The restaurant serves cuisine with a flamboyant flair—European dishes, island fare, and up to five nightly specials. The deck is a great place for fine views. **Pros:** mountain setting; solid restaurant; ability to cook your own meals in some cabins. **Cons:** off the beaten path; deposit is non-refundable if the reservation is cancelled within 60 days of the arrival date. ⊠ *26222 Hwy. 149, Creede* ☎ *719/658–2423* ⊕ *www.antlerslodge.com* ⇆ *9 rooms, 15 cabins* ⚐ *In-room: no a/c, no phone, kitchen (some), refrigerator, no TV. In-hotel: restaurant, bar, laundry facilities, Wi-Fi* ⏱ *Closed Oct.–Apr.* ⊟ *MC, V.*

$ ⊞ **Creede Hotel.** A relic of silver-mining days, this charming 1890s structure with a street-front balcony has been fully restored. Comfortable rooms are done up with the usual Victoriana. Excellent lunch and dinner, as well as complimentary breakfast, are served in the gracious dining room. **Pros:** in-town location. **Cons:** town can be noisy at night; closed in winter. ⊠ *120 N. Main St.,* ☎ *719/658–2608* ⊕ *www.creedehotel.com* ⇆ *4 rooms* ⚐ *In-room: no a/c, no phone, no TV. In-hotel: restaurant, bar* ⊟ *AE, D, MC, V* ⏱ *Closed Oct.–Apr.* ⏹ *BP.*

$ ⊞ **Wason Ranch.** Enjoy tranquillity in a spacious riverside cottage or cozy cabin, both with kitchens. The original ranch house, dating from the 1870s, is a local landmark. Set on the Rio Grande, this sprawling spread has miles of great fly-fishing. **Pros:** can cook your own food; beautiful river setting; great location. **Cons:** off the beaten path; deposit is non-refundable if the reservation is cancelled within 30 days of the arrival date. ⊠ *19082 Hwy. 149,* ☎ *719/658–2413 or 877/927–6626* ⊕ *www.wasonranch.com* ⇆ *9 cottages* ⚐ *In-room: no a/c, kitchen. In-hotel: Wi-Fi* ⊟ *D, MC, V.*

THE ARTS

★ **Creede Repertory Theatre** (✉ *Box 269, Creede* ☎ *866/658–2540* ⊕ *www. creederep.org*), housed in the beautifully restored 1892 Creede Opera House (✉ *124 N. Main St.*), has a summer season of up to five shows a week. The fall season is known for productions of works by new playwrights.

SHOPPING

San Juan Sports (✉ *102 S. Main St.* ☎ *719/658–2359 or 888/658–0851*) specializes in sales and rentals of outdoor gear for hiking, biking, backpacking, camping, and winter backcountry expeditions. There are also good selections of maps, books, and the ubiquitous Colorado T-shirts.

EN ROUTE

Continue along Route 149—the Silver Thread National Scenic Byway—on its beautiful journey east through South Fork. The road flirts with the Rio Grande and passes near the majestic North Clear Creek Falls.

You need a four-wheel-drive vehicle to navigate the 24 mi from Creede to the **Wheeler Geologic Area,** distinguished by dramatically eroded pinnacles of volcanic tuff, but it's worth the drive through subalpine terrain and open parks until you reach the magical-looking spires, pinnacles, and domes. Once there, exploring is on foot or horseback only.

TELLURIDE AND THE SAN JUAN MOUNTAINS

The San Juan Mountains cover more than 12,000 square mi of southwestern Colorado. This striking mountain range ranks as one of the most rugged in the country, and is defined by the hundreds of peaks rising to an elevation of 13,000 feet or more. This high mountain country is the perfect playground for laid-back camping and hiking, and extreme sports like ice climbing and heli-skiing.

TELLURIDE

66 mi south of Montrose, 125 mi north of Durango.

Tucked like a jewel in a tiny valley caught between azure sky and gunmetal mountains is Telluride, once so inaccessible that it was a favorite hideout for desperadoes like Butch Cassidy, who robbed his first bank here in 1889. The savage but beautiful terrain of the San Juan Mountains, with peaks like 14,157-foot Mount Sneffels and rivers like the San Miguel, now attracts mountain people of a different sort—alpinists, snowboarders, freestylers, mountain bikers, and freewheeling four-wheelers—who attack any incline, up or down, and do so with abandon.

Telluride is chic, which thrills some and dismays others. Many townies deplore the over-the-top Telluride Mountain Village development in the heart of the ski area, and some bitterly resent the construction of the glamorous Wyndham Peaks Resort. The ambivalence felt about the influx of wealth and new buildings brings into question whether development is inevitable, whether the pristine can be preserved in this fast-paced world. For better or worse, Telluride is gorgeous. The San Juans loom over town either menacingly or protectively, depending on the lighting.

10

The Spirit of Telluride

The town's independent spirit is shaped not only by its mining legacy, but by the social ferment of the 1960s and early '70s. Before the ski area opened in 1971, Telluride had been as remote as it was back in Cassidy's day. It was even briefly included on the "Ghost Town Club of Colorado" itinerary, but that was before countercultural types moved in, seeking to lose themselves in the wilderness. By 1974 the town's orientation had changed so radically that the entire council was composed of hippies. An enduring Telluride tradition called the Freebox (Pine Street and Colorado Avenue), where residents can sort through and take whatever used clothing and appliances they need, remains as a memento of those times. (One memorable day, just after a fur shop had the temerity to open in town, surprised residents found a wide selection of minks, sables, and chinchillas at the box. After the mysterious break-in, the furriers got the point and moved on.)

Despite such efforts at keeping visible signs of wealth away, more and more locals are finding they can no longer afford to live here. And thanks to the construction of the Telluride Regional Airport in the mid-1980s, it has drawn even more people. Today Telluride is an upscale alternative to Vail and Aspen, and celebrities who need only be identified by their first names (Arnold and Oprah, for example) have been spotted here.

GETTING HERE AND AROUND

Although the resort and the town are distinct areas, you can travel between them via a 2.5-mi, over-the-mountain gondola, one of the most beautiful commutes in Colorado. The gondola makes a car unnecessary for local transportation; both the village and the town are pedestrian friendly. This innovative form of public transportation operates summer and winter, from early morning until late at night, and unless you have skis or a snowboard, the ride is free.

The free Galloping Goose shuttle loops around Telluride every 15 minutes in summer and winter, less often in the off-season. Telluride Express serves Telluride Regional Airport.

Telluride magazine prints an excellent historic walking tour in its "Visitors' Guide" section. The town is made up of one pastel Victorian residence or frontier trading post after another. It's hard to believe that the lovingly restored shops and restaurants once housed gaming parlors and saloons known for the quality of their "waitressing." That party-hearty spirit lives on, evidenced by numerous annual summer celebrations.

WHEN TO GO

Telluride has two off-seasons, when most restaurants and many lodgings are closed. Nearly everyone flees town after the ski area shuts down in mid-April, to return in early or mid-June. (But with the growing renown of Mountainfilm, a Memorial Day celebration of mountain sports and mountain culture, more places are opening then.) Off-season rates in the summer attract visitors looking to enjoy the town's mountain charm. However, when the summer festivals are in fullswing, prices skyrocket and rooms book up fast. The biggies are the Telluride Bluegrass Festival in June, the Telluride Jazz Celebration in July, the Telluride Film Festival in August, and the Telluride Blues and Brews Festival in September. Whenever you decide to go, you should check ahead for upcoming events at least three months in advance. The town closes up from late September or early October until ski season gets going in late November to early December.

FESTIVALS Highly regarded wine and wild-mushroom festivals alternate with musical performances celebrating everything from bluegrass to jazz to chamber music. Displaying a keen sense of humor, the town even promotes the Nothing Festival, when nothing whatsoever is on the calendar.

NOTHING FEST

Telluride is famous for its seemingly endless stream of festivals—so much so that its nickname is "Festival City." In 1991 a resident wrote a tongue-in-cheek letter to the city requesting that a Nothing Festival be implemented to give the citizens a break. Much to everyone's surprise, it was. During the festival, as listed on the Web site ⊕ *www. telluridenothingfestival.com*, "Sunrises and sunsets as normal." T-shirts with a special logo are for sale each year and festival-goers are encouraged to tie a piece of string on their wrists to indicate nonparticipation.

★ The **Telluride Film Festival** (☎ *510/665–9494* ⊕ *www.telluridefilmfestival. com*) in early September is considered one of the world's leading showcases for foreign and domestic films. The **Telluride Bluegrass Festival** (☎ *800/624– 2422* ⊕ *www.bluegrass.com*) in June has gone far beyond its bluegrass roots and is now one of the premier acoustic folk–rock gatherings.

ESSENTIALS

Transportation Contacts Galloping Goose (☎ *970/728–5700*). **Telluride Express** (☎ *970/728–6000 or 888/212–8294* ⊕ *www.tellurideexpress.com*).

Visitor Info Telluride and Mountain Village Visitor Services (✉ *630 W. Colorado Ave., Box 653, Telluride* ☎ *970/728–3041 or 800/525–3455* ⊕ *www. visittelluride.com*). **Telluride Ski Resort** (✉ *565 Mountain Village Blvd.,* ☎ *970/728–6900 or 866/287–5015* ⊕ *www.tellurideskiresort.com*). **Telluride Snow Report** (☎ *970/728–7425*).

EXPLORING

William Jennings Bryan spoke at the **New Sheridan Hotel & Opera House** (✉ *231 W. Colorado Ave.* ☎ *970/728–4351 or 970/728–6363*) during his 1896 presidential campaign. The opera house, added in 1914 and completely redone in 1996, is now home to the thriving Sheridan Arts Foundation.

In the old Miner's Hospital, **Telluride Historical Museum** was constructed in 1888 and restored in 2000. Exhibits on the town's past, including work in the nearby mines and techniques used by doctors who once practiced here, are on display. ✉ *201 W. Gregory Ave.* ☎ *970/728–3344* ⊕ *www. telluridemuseum.org* 🎫 *$5* ⊘ *Tues., Wed., Fri., and Sat. 11–5, Thurs. 11–7, Sun. 1–5. Closed Thurs. evening and Sun. in winter.*

10

Operated by local thespian Ashley Boling, **Historic Tours of Telluride** (☎ 970/728–6639) provides humorous walking tours around the downtown streets, adding anecdotes about infamous figures such as Butch Cassidy and Jack Dempsey.

EN ROUTE
U.S. 550 and Route 62 fan out from Ridgway to form one of the country's most stupendously scenic drives, the **San Juan Skyway**. The roadway weaves through a series of Fourteeners (a Rockies term for peaks reaching more than 14,000 feet) and picturesque mining towns. U.S. 550 continues south to historic Ouray and over Red Mountain Pass to Silverton and Durango. Take Route 62 west and Route 145 south to see the extraordinary cliff dwellings of Mesa Verde National Park. U.S. 160 completes the San Juan Skyway circuit to Durango. In late September and early October this route has some of the most spectacular aspen viewing in the state.

Fodor's Choice
★
DOWNHILL SKIING AND SNOWBOARDING

Telluride is really two ski areas in one. For many years Telluride had a reputation for being an experts-only ski area. Indeed, the north-facing trails are impressively steep and long, and by spring the moguls are massive. The terrain accessed by Chairlift 9, including the famed Spiral Staircase and the Plunge, is for experts only (although one side of the Plunge is groomed so advanced skiers can have their turn).

But then there is the other side—literally—of the ski area, the gently sloping valley called Goronno Basin, with long runs excellent for intermediates and beginners. On the ridge that wraps around the ski area's core is the aptly named See Forever, a long cruiser that starts at 12,255 feet and seems to go on and on. Below that are numerous intermediate runs and a phenomenal terrain park called Sprite Air Garden, designed for snowboarders. Near Goronno Basin is another section that includes super-steep, double-diamond tree runs on one side and glorious cruisers on the other.

Slide through a Western-style gate and you come to Prospect Bowl, a 733-acre expansion that includes three chairlifts and a network of runs subtly cut around islands of trees. One cluster of intermediate runs is served by a swift high-speed quad. The terrain runs the gamut from almost flat, beginner terrain to double-diamond fall-away chutes, cliff bands, and open glades. ⊠ *565 Mountain Village Blvd.,* ☎ *970/728–6900 or 800/778–8581* ⊕ *www.tellurideskiresort.com* ☉ *Late Nov.–early Apr., daily 9–4.*

FACILITIES
3,530-foot vertical drop; 1,700 skiable acres; 24% beginner, 38% intermediate, 38% advanced/expert; 2 gondolas, 7 high-speed quad chairs, 2 triple chairs, 2 double chairs, 2 surface lifts, 1 moving carpet.

LESSONS AND PROGRAMS
The **Telluride Ski & Snowboard School** (⊠ *565 Mountain Village Blvd.* ☎ *970/728–7507 or 800/801–4832* ⊕ *www.tellurideskiresort.com*) has half-day group clinics beginning at $65. Lessons for first-timers are available for alpine and telemark skiers, as well as snowboarders. A five-hour clinic with rentals and restricted lift tickets costs $160. Children's programs (☎ *970/728–7545*) for ages 3 to 12 are $150 a day for lifts, lessons, and lunch. Telluride was a pioneer in creating Women's Week

CLOSE UP

Telluride Bluegrass Festival

Bluegrass may have evolved from country's "mountain music," with bands like Bill Monroe's Blue Grass Boys, but Colorado's Telluride Bluegrass Festival added another layer to the genre beginning in 1973.

Traditional bluegrass bands from across the nation played the festival from the start, but when contemporary Colorado bands that had never previously played bluegrass started adding the quintessential instruments—mandolin, fiddle, guitar, upright bass, and banjo—to their lineups, their adoption of the "high lonesome sound" garnered national attention. It forced bluegrass to undergo several transformations, sometimes right before audience's eyes in Telluride, as the bands' enthusiasm prompted more and more experimentation.

As the festival gained in popularity, it brought more artists to Colorado, who came for the music and stayed for the agreeable climate and focus on nature that tie in so well with bluegrass's folksy sensibilities. Crossover between rock and bluegrass and other musical styles became more common, and the festival began to earn the moniker "Woodstock of the West." Colorado bands such as String Cheese Incident, Leftover Salmon, and Yonder Mountain String Band performed regularly at the event, appealing to a younger audience and encouraging more experimentation.

Now the Telluride Bluegrass Festival in June draws such popular acts as Emmylou Harris, Alison Krauss, Los Lobos, and Counting Crows. It has also spawned other popular and successful gatherings, including its sister festival held each July at Planet Bluegrass Ranch in Lyons, a town of about 1,600 that has become a bluegrass artists' colony of sorts. In fact, most evenings throughout the summer you can wander the streets and hear impromptu porch jams, and the planned picking jams happen almost nightly at places such as Oskar Blues, where sometimes dozens of pickers will show up to play. The towns of Greeley and Pagosa Springs have gotten in on the act, too, both hosting bluegrass festivals in August.

10

programs, five days of skills-building classes with female instructors. Sessions are scheduled for January, February, and March.

LIFT TICKETS The one-day walk-up rate is $92. On multiday, advance-purchase tickets the daily rate can drop as low as $59.

RENTALS Equipment rentals are available at **Paragon Ski and Sport** (✉ *236 S. Oak St.* ☎ *970/728–4581* ⊕ *www.paragontelluride.com*). Beginner packages (skis, boots, and poles) are $44 a day, and top-of-the-line packages are $54 a day. Paragon also rents telemark and cross-country gear, as well as snowshoes and snowblades.

Ski rentals are available from the ubiquitous **Telluride Sports** (✉ *150 W. Colorado Ave.* ☎ *970/728–4477 or 800/828–7547* ⊕ *www.telluridesports. com*). Complete ski packages (skis, boots, and poles) start at around $42, and snowboard packages start at $33. There are 7 other locations in the area.

NORDIC SKIING

TRACK SKIING

Telluride Nordic Center (⊠ *Town park* ☎ *970/728–1144* ⊕ *www. telluridetrails.org [works seasonally])* gives you access to 10 mi of cross-country trails. The areas around Molas Divide and Mesa Verde National Park are extremely popular. The center also rents equipment for both adults and children.

The **Topaten Touring Center** (☎ *970/ 728–7517*), near the Chair 10 unload, has 6.25 mi of trails groomed for cross-country skiing and snowshoeing in a high-mountain setting.

OTHER SPORTS AND THE OUTDOORS

Telluride Outside (⊠ *121 W. Colorado Ave.* ☎ *970/728–3895 or 800/831–6230* ⊕ *www.tellurideoutside.com*) organizes a variety of summer and winter activities in the Telluride area, including 4WD tours, white-water rafting, snowmobile tours, mountain-biking trips, and even winter fly-fishing excursions.

FISHING

For an afternoon in some of the finest backcountry wilderness around, as well as a plethora of rainbow, cutthroat, brown, and brook trout, head for the beautiful San Miguel and Delores rivers.

Telluride Outside (⊠ *121 W. Colorado Ave.* ☎ *970/728–3895 or 800/831–6230* ⊕ *www.tellurideoutside.com*), Colorado's second-largest fishing-guide service, runs guided fly-fishing trips from its fly-fishing store, the Telluride Angler.

FOUR-WHEELING

The Tomboy Road, accessed directly from North Fir Street at the edge of town, leads to one of the country's most interesting mining districts. It went down in history in 1901 when the Western Federation of Miners organized a strike at Tomboy Mine. The state militia was eventually called in to put an end to the strike. The ruins of Tomboy Mine, Tomboy Mill, and parts of the town of Tomboy are all that remain of those turbulent times. The road has fabulous views of Bridal Veil Falls and passes through the Social Tunnel on its way to the high country. After 7.5 mi, the road crests over 13,114-foot-high Imogene Pass, the highest pass road in the San Juan Mountains. If you continue down the other side, you end up near Yankee Boy Basin near Ouray.

Dave's Mountain Tours (⊠ *Box 2736, Telluride* ☎ *970/728–9749* ⊕ *www. telluridetours.com*) conducts summer jeep tours over Imogene Pass and other historic areas. If you want an in-town adventure, go on the Segway historical tour. Dave's runs snowmobile tours in season.

GLIDER RIDES

Offering an unusual look at the San Juans, **Telluride Soaring** (☎ 970/209–3497) operates out of the Telluride Regional Airport. Rates are about $130 per half hour, $180 per hour; rides are daily, weather permitting.

HIKING

The peaks of the rugged San Juan Mountains around Telluride require some scrambling, occasionally bordering on real climbing, to get to the top. A local favorite is Mount Wilson, a roughly 4,000-vertical-foot climb for which only the last 400 vertical feet call for a scramble across steep, shale slopes. July and August are the most likely snow-free months on this 8-mi round-trip hike.

Sound a bit too grueling? An immensely popular 2-mi trail leads to **Bear Creek Falls.** The route is also used by mountain bikers. The 3-mi **Jud Wiebe Trail** begins as an excellent hike that is often passable from spring until well into fall. From here you have amazing views of Utah's LaSal Mountains. For more ambitious hikers, the Jud Wiebe Trail links with the 13-mi Sneffels Highline Trail. This route leads through wildflower-covered meadows. A 1.8-mi trail leads to 425-foot **Bridal Veil Falls,** the state's highest cascade. It tumbles lavishly from the head of a box canyon. A beautifully restored powerhouse sits beside the falls.

HORSEBACK RIDING

Roudy Roudebush rode through America's living rooms courtesy of a memorable television commercial in which he and his horse, Cindy, trotted right up to the bar at the New Sheridan Hotel. Roudy is now riding Cindy's son, Golly, and you can join them. His slogan has long been "Gentle horses for gentle people, fast horses for fast people, and for people who don't like to ride, horses that don't like to be rode." **Ride with Roudy** (☎ 970/728–9611 ⊕ *www.ridewithroudy.com*) is in a barn on an old ranch 6 mi from Telluride. Trail rides pass through aspen groves and across open meadows with views of the Wilson Range. Winter rides leave from Roudy's other ranch in Norwood. Hour-long rides cost about $45.

MOUNTAIN BIKING

Having a fully equipped hut awaiting at the end of a tough day of mountain-biking 35 mi makes the **San Juan Hut System** (✉ *770 N. Cora, Ridgway* ☎ *970/626–3033* ⊕ *www.sanjuanhuts.com*) the backcountry biker's choice. The system operates two 215-mi routes, one from Telluride to Moab, Utah, the other from Durango to Moab. Dirt roads, desert slick rock, and canyon country—the areas along the way where there are canyons to explore, such as in Moab and Grand Junction—are all part of the experience, and the huts supply the beds, blankets, wood-burning stoves, and cooking stoves, which cuts down on what you need to haul on your bike.

RAFTING

There are plenty of rapids around Telluride. **Telluride Outside** (✉ *121 W. Colorado Ave.* ☎ *970/728–3895 or 800/831–6230* ⊕ *www.tellurideoutside.com*) explores the Gunnison and San Miguel rivers.

WHERE TO EAT

$$$$ ✕ **221 South Oak Bistro.** In a pretty Victorian cottage, this elegant bistro
CONTINENTAL entices you to linger. Chef-owner Eliza Gavin, who trained in Paris, New
Orleans, and Napa Valley, creates such dishes as Muscovy duck breast
paired with duck confit, spinach, shiitakes, and pine nuts; elk short loin
with asparagus and Vermont cheddar–stuffed potato; and potato-crusted
halibut with asparagus and fennel. Sunday brunch draws visitors and
locals alike with a fabulous menu of breakfast offerings including a
spinach, leek, and chèvre frittata; New Orleans–style barbecued shrimp;
kiwi, strawberry, and Nutella–stuffed French toast; eggs Florentine; and
biscuits with spicy pork sausage gravy. Regulars come on Wednesday
evenings to sample special martinis. ⊠ *221 S. Oak St.* ☎ *970/728–9507*
⊕ *www.221southoak.com* ⊟ *AE, MC, V* ☉ *Closed early Apr.–May, and
mid-Oct.–mid-Dec. No lunch.*

$$$$ ✕ **Allred's.** After riding up in the gondola, diners are still astounded by the
AMERICAN views from this mountainside eatery. Choose from a selection of steaks,
lamb, elk, chicken, and seafood paired with a variety of mouth-watering
sauces such as leek and goat-cheese fondue, sage brown butter, and
paprika tomato broth. Sides include everything from chorizo and black-
bean casserole to potato-cauliflower gratin. A pianist lightens up the
mood in the lounge from 7 to 10 Wednesday through Sunday. The drink
menu is simple but elegant, with a selection of premium wines, cham-
pagnes, vintage cocktails, and modern martinis. ⊠ *Top of San Sophia
gondola* ☎ *970/728–7474* ⊕ *www.tellurideskiresort.com* ⊟ *AE, D, MC,
V* ☉ *Closed early Apr.–early June and Oct.–late Nov. No lunch.*

$ ✕ **Baked in Telluride.** Racks of fresh-baked breads, rolls, bagels, donuts,
CAFE and other pastries are on display everywhere in this bakery, which also
makes heavenly pasta sauces (check out the Alfredo), pizzas, calzones,
sandwiches, tacos, and huge, inexpensive salads. Get it to go or sit in one
of the tables in the back. The front porch is especially busy as locals meet
and greet at this inexpensive java joint. ⊠ *127 S. Fir St.* ☎ *970/728–4705*
⊟ *AE, D, MC, V.*

$$$ ✕ **Brown Dog Pizza.** This casual pizzeria serves a nice selection of salads,
PIZZA pastas, burgers, subs, and pizza in a sports bar facing the main drag.
★ Sports memorabilia covers any wall space not taken up with big-screen
TVs. The mouth-watering thin-crust pizza is the big draw, and is served
until 11 PM. In addition to the homemade crust and sauce, fresh specialty
toppings include artichoke hearts, broccoli, eggplant, green chilies, jalape-
ños, pickles, and sun-dried tomatoes. However, the most popular pizzas
on the menu are the barbecued chicken and the Boone's Meaty, which is
loaded with pepperoni, sausage, meatballs, bacon, and Canadian bacon.
⊠ *110 E. Colorado Ave.,* ☎ *970/728–8046* ⊕ *www.browndogpizza.com*
⊟ *AE, D, MC, V.*

$$$$ ✕ **Cosmopolitan.** Hotel Columbia, a sleek lodge at the base of the gondola,
AMERICAN is home to this elegant restaurant specializing in dishes such as barbecued
★ wild king salmon with fried sweet potatoes, crab-stuffed roasted chicken
breast with risotto and asparagus, and hickory-smoked duck pizza with
mango and goat cheese. Try the New Orleans–style beignets with a
cappuccino for dessert, cheekily listed as "coffee and donuts" on the
menu. The extensive wine list ranges from a 2007 Macon-Lugny for $33

to a 1996 Château Mouton Rothschild Pauillac for $605. Remodeled in 2009, the restaurant's contemporary style includes copper metallic accents and historic photos. ⊠ *300 W. San Juan Ave.* ☎ *970/728–1292* ⊕ *www.cosmotelluride.com* ⌕ *Reservations essential* ⊟ *AE, MC, V* ⊘ *Call for seasonal closings. No lunch.*

$$ **✕ Fat Alley BBQ.** Messy, mouthwatering ribs and Carolina-style pulled-
SOUTHERN pork sandwiches are complemented by delectable side dishes such as red beans and rice, baked sweet potatoes, and snap-pea and feta salad. More than a dozen beers, 30 bourbons, and a few wines are available, in addition to homemade sweet iced tea and pink lemonade. A few long tables flanked by benches let you dine family-style on the first floor of the small cream-and-green painted Victorian. ⊠ *122 S. Oak St.* ☎ *970/728–3985* ⌕ *Reservations not accepted* ⊟ *AE, MC, V.*

$$$ **✕ Honga's Lotus Petal & Tea Room.** A local favorite, this tearoom serves
ASIAN Japanese-, Thai-, and Balinese-influenced fare in contemporary elegance. The sushi bar is the best in town. Though the place caters mostly to vegetarians, it also puts free-range chicken and organic beef on the menu. Blackened tofu is the signature dish, and the crowds go wild for the crunchy shrimp roll and pineapple-coconut curry. Don't leave town without sampling the addictive pot stickers. Even locals stop by for Honga's specialty drinks, such as the pomegranate mojito and Tito's vodka strawberry-lemon mojito, at the patio bar, which is open from 4 to 6, weather permitting. ⊠ *135 E. Colorado Ave.* ☎ *970/728–5134* ⊕ *www.hongaslotuspetal.com* ⊟ *AE, DC, MC, V* ⊘ *Closed early Apr.– late May and mid-Oct.–late Nov.*

$$$$ **✕ La Marmotte.** With its rough brick walls, lacy curtains, and baskets
FRENCH overflowing with flowers or strings of garlic bulbs, this romantic bistro
Fodor's Choice would be right at home in Provence. Fish dishes, such as slow-baked
★ Scottish salmon and clams casino, are particularly splendid. For a truly delightful meal, chose from the prix-fixe three-course menu, which includes a choice of appetizer, entrée, and dessert for one standard price. Chef Mark Reggiannini delivers French country charm with his spectacular menu, stellar wine pairing, and homey dining experience. The menu changes nightly depending on the availability of fresh, local ingredients. ⊠ *150 W. San Juan Ave.* ☎ *970/728–6232* ⊕ *www.lamarmotte. com* ⌕ *Reservations essential* ⊟ *AE, MC, V* ⊘ *Closed Wed. No lunch.*

¢ **✕ Maggie's Bakery & Cafe.** A little spot with a blue awning and a couple
CAFE of tables set up outside, Maggie's often has the front door propped open and the smell of fresh-baked breads and oatmeal cookies lures customers in. You can grab breakfast and lunch here as well as a sweet treat (the sticky buns are the best), including piled-high sandwiches, Mexican food, and soup. ⊠ *217 E. Colorado Ave.* ☎ *970/728–3334* ⊟ *No credit cards* ⊘ *No dinner.*

$$$ **✕ New Sheridan Chop House.** Old meets new in this fabulous 2008 addi-
STEAKHOUSE tion to the Telluride dining scene and the best steak house in town.
★ Choose the toppings for your succulent steak from balsamic blue cheese, black truffle and lobster, crispy red onions, Australian red crab, and one of four delectable sauces. Sides include black-truffle creamed spinach, Parmesan pommes frites with truffle oil, and white polenta with goat cheese. There are also fabulous pastas, fish dishes, and rack of lamb. The

10

extensive wine list includes many by the glass. Mirrors aged with gold patina, dark wood, and oil lamps complement the contemporary red-leather booths and brightly colored murals. ⊠ *231 W. Colorado Ave.,* ☎ *970/728–4351 or 800/200–1891* ⊕ *www.newsheridan.com* ⊟ *AE, D, DC, MC, V* ⊘ *Closed mid-Apr.–mid-May and mid-Oct.–mid-Nov.*

WHERE TO STAY

$$$$ ⊡ **Camel's Garden.** In a curious contradiction, this ultramodern lodging that is all gleaming glass and sleek surfaces bears the name of one of the town's oldest mines. Fireplaces keep the rooms toasty on winter evenings, and a hot tub on the second floor is great for relaxing stiff muscles from a day on the slopes. There are plenty of nice touches, including CD players and chic leather furniture. The hotel is steps away from the Oak Street chairlift. **Pros:** convenient to lift; tasty breakfast; romantic. **Cons:** very modern; not especially kid-friendly. ⊠ *250 W. San Juan Ave.,* ☎ *970/728–9300 or 888/772–2635* ⊕ *www.camelsgarden. com* ⇌ *30 rooms, 4 condos* ♿ *In-room: no a/c (some), DVD, Wi-Fi. In-hotel: restaurant, spa, Wi-Fi* ⊟ *AE, D, DC, MC, V* ⦿| *CP.*

$$$$ ⊡ **Hotel Columbia Telluride.** It's hard to go wrong with views of the moun-
★   tains, the gondola, and the San Miguel River. The Victorian style has been replaced with cool contemporary. A 2009 remodeling completely changed the face of this Telluride favorite. Everything from the art on the walls to the flooring and the beds to the TVs has been replaced with pieces in a neutral palette of cool creams and toasty tans. Two of the suites even have hot tubs on their decks. The gracious staff will store your mountain bike or your skis, and with the gondola right there it's easy to access just about anything. The in-house Cosmopolitan restaurant ($$$$) is the town's best option for elegant American food, and the complimentary breakfast there is above average. **Pros:** stunning views; charming, spacious rooms; convenient to gondola. **Cons:** some street noise, must keep your shutters closed or gondola riders can see right in. ⊠ *301 W. San Juan Ave.,* ☎ *800/201–9505* ⊕ *www.columbiatelluride. com* ⇌ *21 rooms* ♿ *In-room: refrigerator, DVD, Wi-Fi. In-hotel: res-taurant, concierge, parking (fee)* ⊟ *AE, MC, V.*

$$$$ ⊡ **The Hotel Telluride.** The rooms are far more upscale than the pricing would suggest, and the building itself looks like an old stone mansion nestled against the mountain. All rooms have San Juan views from a patio or balcony, and a complimentary breakfast buffet is at the Bistro, a lodge-style eatery on-premises. The airy lobby has a large stone fireplace, comfy leather sofas, hand-carved wooden antiques, warm wool rugs, and curving iron and antler chandeliers. The fitness center has state-of-the-art machines, massages are offered in the spa, and the hot tubs on the roof are delightful when it's snowing. **Pros:** terrific value; abundant breakfast; guest shuttle. **Cons:** hot tubs often taken; hotel fills up in season. ⊠ *199 N. Cornet St.,* ☎ *866/468–3504* ⊕ *www.thehoteltelluride. com* ⇌ *59 rooms, 2 suites* ♿ *In-room: safe, refrigerator, Wi-Fi. In-hotel: restaurant, bar, gym, spa, concierge, laundry facilities, public Wi-Fi, some pets allowed* ⊟ *AE, D, MC, V* ⦿| *BP.*

$$$$ ⊡ **Inn at Lost Creek.** A grand stone-and-wood structure with the architec-ture of a European alpine lodge, this rambling five-story luxury lodge is next to the Mountain Village Gondola (which carries you to downtown

Telluride) and just two blocks from the conference center. You can literally ski out the front door. Most rooms are suites with balconies, ideal for a romantic getaway, and the rooftop spas are nice extras. Extra amenities include ski and boot storage, boot drying, ski waxing, in-room washers and dryers, and fabulous dining at 9545 Restaurant and Bar, which has a ski valet and a divine menu of seafood, duck, beef, pork, and vegetarian specialties. **Pros:** ski in ski out; romantic; convenient location. **Cons:** pricey; two-night minimum; rooftop spa usually crowded. ⊠ *119 Lost Creek La., Mountain Village* ☎ *970/728–5678 or 888/601–5678* ⊕ *www.innatlostcreek.com* ↩ *29 suites, 3 studios* ⚐ *In-room: kitchen (some), DVD, Wi-Fi. In-hotel: restaurant, room service, bar, gym, spa, laundry facilities, Internet terminal, Wi-Fi* ☰ *AE, D, DC, MC, V.*

$$$$ 🖼 **lumière.** "Lumière" means "light" in French, and this luxury lodge lives up to its name. Suites open to beautiful views of the mountain, and the airy decor brings the outside in with a warm color palette of orange, cream, and brown. To top it off, the personal service is out of this world: extremely polite and helpful staff even offer to fill the fridge and pantry ahead of time. Other personalized services include ski valet service, twice-daily maid service, and a fabulous spa menu. A European breakfast is served daily, and the bar at lumière serves signature cocktails, sushi, and appetizers in the afternoon and early evening. Lodgings include studio and one-, two-, and three-bedroom suites; two-, three-, and four-bedroom penthouses; and "The Tower," a 5-bedroom, 7,500-square-foot private residence. **Pros:** ski-in ski-out property; valet parking; fabulous, friendly staff. **Cons:** incredibly pricey; hotel layout can be a little confusing. ⊠ *118 Lost Creek La.* ☎ *907/369–0400* ⊕ *www.lumierehotels.com* ↩ *29 suites and residences, 1 5-bedroom home* ⚐ *In-room: safe, kitchen, DVD, Wi-Fi. In-hotel: room service, bar, gym, spa, laundry facilities, laundry service, Wi-Fi, parking (free)* ☰ *AE, D, DC, MC, V* ⦿ *BP.*

$$$ 🖼 **New Sheridan Hotel.** William Jennings Bryan delivered his rousing "Cross of Gold" speech here in 1896, garnering a presidential nomination in the process. This Telluride landmark underwent a major renovation in 2008, replacing the velvet furniture and kitschy decor with replica period pieces, historic black-and-white photos, and lovely rooms decorated with contemporary furnishings in various shades of green, red, and purple. The parlor, situated in the old lobby, serves breakfast, lunch, and dinner in a casual setting. For more formal fare, check out The Chop House, an elegant seafood and steak restaurant featuring Telluride's only nitrogen wine bar. The gorgeous Victorian-era bar, a favorite among locals, is the original. **Pros:** rooftop hot tubs; accommodating staff; free use of the gym down the street. **Cons:** narrow hallways; noise from the bar can drift upstairs at night; 100-percent deposit required 30 days prior to arrival. ⊠ *231 W. Colorado Ave.,* ☎ *970/728–4351 or 800/200–1891* ⊕ *www.newsheridan.com* ↩ *26 rooms, 2 suites* ⚐ *In-room: safe, Wi-Fi. In-hotel: 2 restaurant, bar, public Wi-Fi* ☰ *AE, D, DC, MC, V* ⦿ *Closed mid-Apr.–mid-May and mid-Oct.–mid-Nov.*

10

NIGHTLIFE AND THE ARTS

THE ARTS

The **Sheridan Arts Foundation** (✉ *110 N. Oak St.* ☎ *970/728–6363* ⊕ *www. sheridanoperahouse.com*) is a mentoring program that brings top actors and singers to town to perform alongside budding young artists in the Sheridan Opera House. The **Telluride Repertory Theatre Company** (☎ *970/728–4539* ⊕ *www. telluridetheatre.org*) gives free performances in the town park each summer.

NIGHTLIFE

Allred's (✉ *Top of San Sophia gondola* ☎ *970/728–7474*) is a divine après-ski location. Take in eye-popping views of the mountains and the lights twinkling in the town below as you enjoy an excellent selection of wines by the glass. Appetizers can make for an early dinner. **Excelsior Cafe** (✉ *200 W. Colorado Ave.* ☎ *970/728–4250* ⊕ *excelsiorcafe. net*) is the spot to hear the best folk–rock. The **Fly Me to the Moon Saloon** (✉ *132 E. Colorado Ave.* ☎ *970/728–6666*) has live music—jazz, blues, funk, ska, rock, you name it—most nights. The action gets wild on the spring-loaded dance floor. The **Last Dollar Saloon** (✉ *100 E. Colorado Ave.* ☎ *970/728–4800* ⊕ *www.lastdollarsaloon.com*) has a jukebox filled with old favorites. The century-old bar at the **New Sheridan Hotel** (✉ *231 W. Colorado Ave.* ☎ *970/728–4351 or 800/200–1891* ⊕ *www.newsheridan. com*) is a favorite hangout for skiers returning from the slopes. Prime time is between 4 PM and 8 PM. In summer, folks gather to socialize and watch the world go by. On July 4 a cowboy named Roudy is known to ride into the bar and enjoy his drink while astride his horse.

SHOPPING

BOOKS

Between the Covers Bookstore & Coffee House (✉ *224 W. Colorado Ave.* ☎ *970/728–4504*) is perfect for browsing through the latest releases while sipping a foam-capped cappuccino.

BOUTIQUES

The **Bounty Hunter** (✉ *226 W. Colorado Ave.* ☎ *970/728–0256* ⊕ *www. shopbountyhunter.com*) is the spot for leather items, especially boots and vests. It also has an astonishing selection of hats, among them Panama straw, beaver felt, and just plain outrageous.

CRAFT AND ART GALLERIES

Hell Bent Leather & Silver (✉ *215 E. Colorado Ave.* ☎ *970/728–6246* ⊕ *www.hellbentleather.com*) is a fine source for Native American arts and crafts.

SPORTING GOODS

Further Adventures (✉ *650 Mountain Village Blvd.,* ☎ *970/728–8954* ⊕ *www.bootdoctors.com/further*) will set you up with gear and guides for your whitewater-rafting, mountain-biking, and fly-fishing trip. They also operate as Boot Doctors for winter sports needs. **Telluride Sports** (⌧ *150 W. Colorado Ave.* ☏ *970/728–4477 or 800/828–7547* ⊕ *www. telluridesports.com*) has equipment and clothing for all seasons.

RIDGWAY

45 mi from Telluride via Rtes. 62 and 145; 26 mi south of Montrose via U.S. 550.

The 19th-century railroad town of Ridgway has been the setting for some classic Westerns, including *True Grit* and *How the West Was Won.* Though you'd never know it from the rustic town center, the area is also home to many swank ranches, including one belonging to fashion designer Ralph Lauren.

GETTING HERE AND AROUND

U.S. 550 runs along the eastern side of town heading north to Montrose and south to Ouray. Route 62 heads west right through the middle of town on its way to Telluride. The rest of the main part of town encompasses all of seven blocks, making side travel a breeze.

EXPLORING

The **Ridgway Railroad Museum** (⌧ *Junction U.S. 550 and CO 62* ☏ *970/626–5458* ⊕ *www.ridgwayrailroadmuseum.org* ⌧ *Free* ☉ *June–Sept., daily 9–4; Oct.–May, Mon.–Fri. 10–3*) celebrates the town's importance during the heyday of the railroad. The exhibits include a wooden boxcar built for the filming of *Butch Cassidy and the Sundance Kid.*

SPORTS AND THE OUTDOORS

BACKCOUNTRY SKIING

Among the better backcountry skiing routes is the **San Juan Hut System** (⌧ *770 N. Cora.,* ☏ *970/626–3033* ⊕ *www.sanjuanhuts.com*). It leads toward Telluride along the Sneffels Range. The five huts in the system are about 7 mi apart, and are well equipped with beds, blankets, wood-burning stoves, and cooking stoves. Previous backcountry experience is highly recommended. Reservations are recommended at least two weeks in advance.

GOLF

Divide Ranch and Club. This semi-private 18-hole, Byron Coker–designed course twists through a maze of high-mesa forest, complete with mountain views and wildlife. It's long and often demanding, but at 8,000 feet your drives might go a little farther and higher than at sea level. Course and driving range are open from May to October. Cart rental is $17.50 for 18 holes. ⌧ *151 Divide Ranch Circle* ☏ *970/626–5284* ⊕ *www. eqresorts.com* ⅃ *18 holes. Yards: 7,039. Par: 72. Green fee: $65/$75.*

WATER SPORTS

At the **Ridgway State Park & Recreation Area** (⌖ *28555 U.S. 550,* ☏ *970/626–5822* ⊕ *www.parks.state.co.us* ⌧ *Daily use fee $6*), 12 mi north of Ridgway, the 5-mi reservoir is stocked with plenty of rainbow trout, as well as the larger and tougher German brown. Anglers also pull up kokanee, yellow perch, and the occasional large-mouth bass. Other amenities include a swimming beach, picnic areas, playgrounds, a campground ($14 tent sites, $22 full hook-ups), and yurt rentals ($60).

10

WHERE TO EAT AND STAY

$$ ✕ **True Grit Cafè.** Scenes from *True Grit* were filmed here, and the local
AMERICAN　hangout is a shrine to the film and its star, John Wayne. This neigh-
borhood pub serves standard fare—burgers, steak, pasta, nachos, and
delicious chicken-fried steak. Those who feel like taking a walk on the
wild side can sample Rocky Mountain oysters or the homestyle buffalo
meatloaf. The huge stone fireplace, two-story balcony, and cozy inte-
rior would make even "the Duke" feel at home. ⊠ *123 N. Lena Ave.*
☎ *970/626–5739* ⊕ *www.truegritcafe.com* ⊟ *D, MC, V.*

$$ 🏨 **Chipeta Sun Lodge & Spa.** The dramatic Southwestern-style adobe's
rooms have rough-hewn log beds, hand-painted Mexican tiles, and
stunning views from the decks. For extended stays, there are eight condos complete with full kitchens; some with fireplaces, balconies, and
private hot tubs. The inn is a stone's throw from the year-round outdoor
activities in this stretch of the San Juan Mountains. When you're finished hiking or biking, return to the spa for a little pampering. The on-
site Four Corners Café is open daily for breakfast and dinner, and serves
Southwestern specialties such as huevos rancheros, Rocky Mountain
trout, and Colorado ranch rib eye. **Pros:** unique rooms; on-site restaurant; ideal location for outdoor activities in the area. **Cons:** across the
street from a park, which fills up on weekends; limited parking. ⊠ *304
S. Lena St.,* ☎ *970/626–3737 or 800/633–5868* ⊕ *www.chipeta.com*
⌨ *25 rooms* ⌂ *In-room: no a/c (some), kitchen (some), refrigerator, no
TV (some), Wi-Fi. In-hotel: restaurant, pool, gym, spa, laundry facilities, Wi-Fi, some pets allowed* ⊟ *AE, D, DC, MC, V.*

OURAY

*10 mi south of Ridgway via U.S. 50; 23 mi from Silverton via U.S.
550 north.*

The town of Ouray (pronounced *you-ray*) nestles in a narrow, steep-
walled valley in the shadows cast by rugged peaks of the San Juan
Mountains. It was named for the great Southern Ute chief Ouray,
labeled a visionary by the U.S. Army and branded a traitor by his
people because he attempted to assimilate the Utes into white society.
The former mining town is the proud owner of a National Historic
District, with lavish old hotels, commercial buildings, and residences.
The town's ultimate glory lies in its surroundings, and it has become an
increasingly popular destination for climbers (both the mountain and
ice varieties), mountain-bike fanatics, and hikers.

More than 25 classic edifices are included in the walking-tour brochure
issued by the Ouray County Historical Society. Among the points of
interest are the grandiose Wright's Opera House, the Western Hotel,
and the St. Elmo Hotel.

GETTING HERE AND AROUND

U.S. 550 runs straight through town and turns into Main Street for the
7 blocks from 3rd Avenue to 9th Avenue. The Visitors' Information
Center and the Hot Springs Park are on the north end of town, and the
historic landmark hotel, the Beaumont, is smack in the middle of town
between 5th and 6th avenues. The Uncompahgre River runs parallel

to Main Street just a couple blocks west of town, and Box Canyon is just southwest of Main Street at the confluence of Canyon Creek and the Uncompaghre River.

ESSENTIALS

Visitor Info Ouray County Chamber (⊠ *1230 Main St.,* ☎ *970/325–4746 or 800/228–1876* ⊕ *www.ouraycolorado.com*).

EXPLORING

TOP ATTRACTIONS

Fodor's Choice
★

Ouray is also the northern end of the Million Dollar Highway, the awesome stretch of U.S. 550 that climbs over **Red Mountain Pass.** As it ascends steeply from Ouray, the road clings to the cliffs hanging over the Uncompahgre River far below. This two-laner bears little resemblance to the image one usually has of U.S. highways. Guardrails are few, hairpin turns are many, and behemoth RVs often seem to take more than their share of road. It earned its nickname either because the crushed ore used for the roadbed was rumored to contain gold and silver, or because of the fortune that 19th-century road builder Otto Mears spent to create it. This priceless road is kept open all winter by heroic plow crews. The Ouray side, on the whole, is steeper and narrower than the Silverton side. It is the most spectacular part of the 236-mi **San Juan Skyway,** designated as an All-American Road for its scenic splendor and historic significance.

One particularly gorgeous jaunt is to **Box Cañon Falls.** The turbulent waters of Clear Creek thunder 285 feet down a narrow gorge. A steel suspension bridge and well-marked trails afford breathtaking vistas. Birders flock to the park, and a visitor center has interpretive displays. ⊠ *West end of 3rd Ave. off U.S. 550* ☎ *970/325–7080* ⊠ *$3* ☺ *Mid-Oct.–mid-May, daily 10–10; mid-May–mid-Oct., daily 8 AM–dusk.*

The **Historic Wiesbaden Hot Springs Spa & Lodge** is at the source of the springs. In an underground chamber you can soak in the steamy pools and inhale the pungent vapors. There's also an outdoor pool. Massage and mud wraps are offered at the spa. Note that they request that anyone who has smoked in the last three months not use their facilities because of guests' allergy issues. ⊠ *625 5th St.* ☎ *970/325–4347 or 888/846–5191* ⊕ *www.wiesbadenhotsprings.com* ⊠ *$15 for the public for three hours, guests use pool and caves free* ☺ *Daily 8 AM–9:45 PM.*

WORTH NOTING

On the **Bachelor-Syracuse Mine Tour,** a mine train hauls visitors down 3,500 feet into one of the region's great mines. Explanations of mining techniques, a visit to a blacksmith shop, and panning for gold are part of the experience. Tours depart every half-hour. ⊠ *1222 County Rd. 14* ☎ *970/325–0220 or 888/227–4585* ⊕ *www.bachelorsyracusemine.com* ⊠ *$16.95* ☺ *Aug.–June, daily 9–4; July, daily 9–5.*

One of the loveliest buildings in town is the **Beaumont Hotel** (⊠ *505 Main St.* ☎ *970/325–7000* ⊕ *www.beaumonthotel.com*), on the National Register of Historic Places. This 1887 landmark, a confection of French, Italian, and Romanesque Revival design, stood vacant for years before Dan and Mary King set about restoring it to perfection.

10

The **Ouray County Museum** preserves the history of ranching and mining in the San Juan Mountains and Ouray. Mining equipment, railroad paraphernalia, and commercial artifacts are carefully arranged in the former St. Joseph's Hospital, built in 1887. ⊠ *420 6th Ave.* ☎ *970/325–4576* ⊕ *www.ouraycountyhistoricalsociety.org* ✍ *$5* ♾ *Call for hrs.*

After a hike, immerse yourself in nature again at the area's various hot springs. At **Ouray Hot Springs Pool** it's hard to tell which is more refreshing, the pools brimming over with 96°F to 106°F water or the views of surrounding peaks. There's a fitness center in the bathhouse. ⊠ *1220 Main St.* ☎ *970/325–7073* ✍ *$10* ♾ *Summer, daily 10–10; winter, daily noon–9.*

SPORTS AND THE OUTDOORS
FOUR-WHEELING
Off-roaders delight in the more than 500 mi of four-wheel-drive roads around Ouray. Popular routes include the Alpine Loop Scenic Byway to the Silverton and Lake City areas, and Imogene Pass or Black Bear Pass to Telluride. Figure on the four-wheeling season running from May to September, but you'll have to keep an eye on the weather.

About the first 7 mi of the road to **Yankee Boy Basin** are accessible by regular cars, but it takes a four-wheel drive to reach the heart of this awesome alpine landscape. The route, designated County Road 361, veers off U.S. 550 just south of Ouray and climbs west into a vast basin ringed with soaring summits and carpeted with lavish displays of wildflowers. This is one of the region's premier day-trip destinations. For information, contact the **Ouray Ranger District** (⊠ *2505 S. Townsend Rd.* ☎ *970/240–5300* ⊕ *www.fs.fed.us/r2/gmug*).

If you have the skill and confidence but not the right vehicle, you can rent one from **Switzerland of America Tours** (⊠ *226 7th Ave.* ☎ *970/325–4484 or 866/990–5337* ⊕ *www.soajeep.com*). The company also operates guided tours in open-air six-passenger jeeps. Full-day tours cost $60–$130.

ICE CLIMBING
Ouray is known in ice-climbing circles for its abundance of frozen waterfalls. The Ouray Ice Festival, held each January, helped to cement ★ its reputation. The **Ouray Ice Park** (✉ *Box 1058, Ouray* ☎ *970/325–4288* ⊕ *www.ourayicepark.com*) is the world's first facility dedicated to ice climbing. In the Uncompahgre Gorge south of town, the Ice Park has three main climbing areas with more than 40 routes. **Ouray Mountain Sports** (⊠ *732 Main St.* ☎ *970/325–4284* ⊕ *www.ouraysports.com*) arranges lessons and guided climbs.

NORDIC SKIING
About 9 mi south of Ouray, Ironton Park is a marked trail system for Nordic skiers and snowshoers. Several interconnecting loops let you spend a day on the trails. Local merchants stock trail maps. For information, contact **Ouray County Nordic Council** (✉ *Box 469, Ouray* ☎ *970/325–4932*).

WHERE TO EAT
$$$ ✕ **Bon Ton Restaurant.** It might be in the basement, but once you get down
MEDITERRANEAN   the stairs of the historic St. Elmo Hotel you'll find yourself in the most elegant restaurant in town. Stone walls and the hardwood floor give the

Bon Ton a European feel, and the Mediterranean-inspired dishes add to the flavorful scene. In addition to salads and pastas, you'll find such specialties as beef Wellington, chicken piccata, grilled salmon, roast duckling, and eggplant Parmesan. Be sure to check out the extensive wine list or one of the bar's fabulous martinis. Dinner is served nightly starting at 5:30 PM, and the restaurant has a Sunday champagne brunch from 9:30 AM to 1 PM. ⊠ *426 Main St.* ☎ *970/325–4951 or 866/243–1502* ⊕ *www.stelmohotel. com* ⚱ *Reservations essential* ⊟ *AE, D, DC, MC, V* ☻ *No lunch*.

$$$
MEXICAN ✕ **Buen Tiempo.** Brick walls and sage-green wainscoting are paired with Southwestern-styled cactus-carved benches and brightly painted chairs to create a spicy backdrop at this creative Mexican restaurant. Menu selections include traditional Sonoran entrées such as tacos, enchiladas, chiles rellenos, tamales, and burritos. A comprehensive margarita menu adds to the casual experience. ⊠ *515 Main St.* ☎ *970/325–4544* ⊟ *AE, D, DC, MC, V*.

WHERE TO STAY

$$$
Fodor's Choice 🏨 **Beaumont Hotel and Spa.** No detail has been overlooked at this restored
★ 1887 hotel, a gold-rush era landmark that stood vacant for 34 years. Soundproofing, individually decorated rooms, deep soaking tubs, and a spa are among the thoroughly modern features that make this such a relaxing place to stay. Other luxurious touches include stained-glass chandeliers, papered ceilings, and lovely antiques. Suites come with kitchenettes and separate sitting areas. All room have turn-down service at 6 PM. The outdoor patio area has heated floors, so you can enjoy the stunning views of the Amphitheater Range on chilly mornings. Tundra Restaurant ($$$–$$$$) is grand, with a cathedral ceiling and a balcony where a classical guitarist plays in the evenings. Local ingredients, wild game, and fresh fish are well matched by the stellar wine list. Don't miss the to-die-for risotto. **Pros:** soundproof rooms mean a quiet stay; heated outdoor patio is a nice touch; good value and a delightful spot. **Cons:** restaurant is expensive. ⊠ *505 Main St.,* ☎ *970/325–7000 or 888/447–3255* ⊕ *www. beaumonthotel.com* ⇒ *10 rooms, 2 suites* ⚐ *In-room: DVD, Internet, Wi-Fi. In-hotel: 2 restaurants, bar, spa, public Wi-Fi* ⊟ *AE, MC, V.*

$$ 🏨 **Black Bear Manor Bed & Breakfast.** Hosts Phil and Lucie Mims (and their little Scottish terrier) make you feel right at home in their modern space, which has terrific view of the surrounding San Juan Mountains from its observatory. All nine suites have private baths and interior and exterior entrances, so you can walk through the house or not. Some rooms have fireplaces and jetted tubs, and all include chocolates and robes upon arrival. Breakfast includes fresh-baked pastries served in a sunny, cheerful room that looks out onto the mountains. **Pros:** very welcoming hosts; setup means you don't have to see other guests if you don't want to; generous amenities. **Cons:** not a typical antique-filled B&B. ⊠ *100 6th Ave.,* ☎ *970/325–4219 or 800/845–7512* ⊕ *www. blackbearmanor.com* ⇒ *9 rooms* ⚐ *In-room: no a/c, Wi-Fi. In-hotel: no kids under 16* ⊟ *AE, MC, V* ¶◎¶ *BP.*

10

$$ 🏨 **Box Canyon Lodge & Hot Springs.** If soaking with the masses at the local hot springs is not your cup of tea, opt for a private plunge at this friendly lodge. This mineral spring was used first by the Utes, and later by the Cogar Sanitarium. Soak away your cares in four redwood tubs full of steaming 103°F to 107°F water and with mountain views. The lodge has a great location off the main drag and near the stream. The rooms are nondescript but modern and comfortable, and there is a Continental breakfast included. **Pros:** proximity to hot springs; welcoming staff; off-the-beaten-path feel. **Cons:** no-frills rooms. ⊠ *45 3rd Ave.,* ☎ *970/325–4981 or 800/327–5080* ⊕ *www.boxcanyonouray.com* ➮ *33 rooms, 6 suites* ⌂ *In-room: no a/c, refrigerator, DVD, Wi-Fi* ⊟ *AE, D, MC, V* ⑩ *CP.*

$$$ ⊡ **China Clipper Inn.** In a departure from the typical Western- and Victorian-style inns in this area, the China Clipper is tastefully decorated with Asian antiques. Most rooms open onto a charming flower-filled patio with hot tub. The inn was built almost entirely—with great attention to detail—by a retired Navy commander from Louisville, Kentucky. Full breakfast and afternoon tea are included in the rate. **Pros:** small; romantic. **Cons:** can be noisy between rooms. ⊠ *525 2nd St.,* ☎ *970/325–0565 or 800/315–0565* ⊕ *www.chinaclipperinn.com* ➮ *13 rooms* ⌂ *In-room: Wi-Fi. In-hotel: public Wi-Fi, no kids under 16* ⊟ *AE, D, MC, V* ⑩ *BP.*

$$ ⊡ **St. Elmo Hotel.** This tiny 1898 hostelry was originally a haven for "miners down on their luck," or so the story goes. Its original owner was Kitty Heit, who couldn't resist a sob story. Family ghosts reputedly hover about protectively. The rooms are graced with stained-glass windows, marble-top armoires, brass or mahogany beds, and other antiques. A complimentary breakfast buffet is served in a sunny parlor. The Bon Ton ($$) restaurant serves Mediterranean cuisine. **Pros:** reasonable rates. **Cons:** can feel a bit cramped. ⊠ *426 Main St.,* ☎ *970/325–4951 or 866/243–1502* ⊕ *www.stelmohotel.com* ➮ *7 rooms, 2 suites* ⌂ *In-room: no a/c, no phone, no TV. In-hotel: restaurant, Wi-Fi, no kids under 10* ⊟ *AE, D, DC, MC, V* ⑩ *BP.*

SHOPPING

In the restored Beaumont Hotel, **Buckskin Booksellers** (⊠ *505 Main St.* ☎ *970/325–4044* ⊕ *www.buckskinbooksellers.com*) has books about such topics as mining, railroading, and ranching, as well as collectibles and Native American items. **North Moon Gallery** (⊠ *505 Main St.* ☎ *970/325–4885*) carries irresistible pieces of jewelry. **Ouray Glassworks & Pottery** (⊠ *619 Main St.* ☎ *970/325–0275 or 800/748–9421* ⊕ *www.ourayglassworks.com*) sells exquisite handblown glass created by Sam Rushing and pottery by Diane Rushing.

SILVERTON

23 mi south of Ouray via U.S. 550, 20 mi north of Purgatory via U.S. 550.

Glorious peaks surround Silverton, an isolated, unspoiled old mining community. It reputedly got its name when a miner exclaimed, "We ain't got much gold but we got a ton of silver!" Silverton is the county seat, as well as the only remaining town, in San Juan County. The last mine went bust in 1991 (which is recent as such things go), leaving Silverton to boom only in summer when the Durango & Silverton Narrow Gauge Railroad *(see the Durango section)* deposits four trainloads of tourists a day. The Silverton Mountain ski area has also helped the town to shake off its long slumber, and more businesses are finding it worthwhile to stay open year-round.

Silverton's hardy and spirited populace still commemorates its rowdy past. At 5:30 PM on Thursday through Sunday evenings a gunfight erupts at the corner of Blair and 12th streets. Unsurprisingly, the good guys always win. At 6 PM the town's much-ballyhooed brass band plays old favorites.

The downtown area has been designated a National Historic Landmark District. Be sure to pick up the walking-tour brochure that describes—among other things—the most impressive buildings lining Greene Street: Miners' Union Hall, Teller House, the Town Hall, the San Juan County Courthouse (home of the county historical museum), and the Grand Imperial Hotel. These structures have historical significance, but more history was probably made in the raucous red-light district along Blair Street.

GETTING HERE AND AROUND

U.S. 550 N and U.S. 550 S meet at a junction in front of the Silverton Chamber of Commerce and Visitor Center. At the intersection, Greene St—with the main stores, restaurants, hotels, and the only paved street in town—heads northeast from 6th Street to 15th Street before splitting into Country Road 110 heading to the Silverton Mountain Ski Area to the north and Country Road 2 heading to the Old Hundred Gold Mine and the Mayflower Mill to the east.

DISCOUNTS AND DEALS

Ask at the Silverton Chamber of Commerce about a Heritage Pass, good for savings on admission to the Silverton Jail and Museum, Old Hundred Gold Mine, and Mayflower Mill.

ESSENTIALS

Visitor Info Silverton Chamber of Commerce (✉ *414 Greene St.,* ☎ *970/387–5654 or 800/752–4494* ⊕ *www.silvertoncolorado.com* ⊗ *May–June and Sept., daily 9–4; July–Aug., daily 9–5; Oct.–Apr., daily 10–3).*

EXPLORING

The **San Juan County Historical Museum** is in the old San Juan County Jail. It was erected in 1902 from prefabricated parts that were shipped by train from St. Louis. The museum houses a mineral collection, mining memorabilia, and local artifacts. ✉ *1559 Greene St.* ☎ *970/387–5838* ⊕ *www.silvertonhistoricsociety.org* ⊘ *$5* ⊗ *June–mid-Oct., daily 9–5.*

10

A tram takes visitors 1,500 feet into the **Old Hundred Gold Mine** for a tour of one of the town's oldest mining facilities. Old Hundred operated for about a century, from the first strike in 1872 until the last haul in the early 1970s. Temperatures remain at a steady 48°F year-round, so be sure to bring a sweater or a jacket. Guided tours leave every hour on the hour. ✉ *5 mi north of Silverton on Hwy. 5500, which turns into Greene St. Then take a left on Country Rd. 2 for two miles to Country Rd. 4, turn right for a quarter-mile and turn right on County Rd. 4A* ☎ *970/387–5444 or 800/872–3009* ⊕ *www.minetour.com* ☜ *$17* ⊙ *May 16–Oct. 5, daily 10–4.*

The nearby **Mayflower Mill** has been designated a National Historic Landmark. Tours explain how precious metals are extracted from the earth. ✉ *5 mi north of Silverton on Hwy. 110* ☎ *970/387–0294* ⊕ *www. silvertonhistoricsociety.org* ☜ *$7* ⊙ *Memorial Day–late Sept.*

If you look north toward Anvil Mountain, you'll see the community's touching tribute to miners, the **Christ of the Mines Shrine** (✉ *Trailhead: On Anvil Mountain at the end of 10th St.*). It was built in 1959 out of Carrara marble. A moderately strenuous 1-mi hike leads to the shrine, which has memorable views of the surrounding San Juan Mountains.

SPORTS AND THE OUTDOORS
DOWNHILL SKIING AND SNOWBOARDING
Run by the town, **Kendall Mountain Recreation Area** (✉ *1 Kendall Mountain Pl. 81433* ☎ *970/387–5522* ⊕ *www.skikendall.com* ☜ *$15*) is a single-tow ski center open weekends during ski season, weather permitting. It's not a challenging slope, so it's perfect for beginners. Sledding and tubing are also permitted. About 6 mi north of town, **Silverton Mountain** is one of the country's simplest yet most innovative ski areas. With a single lift accessing the never-groomed backcountry steeps and a maximum of 475 people per day allowed on the vast and challenging terrain on unguided days and 80 on guided days (which kind of day it is depends on conditions and time of year), Silverton Mountain gained instant cult status with some of the country's best skiers. Fans say the experience is like heli-skiing without a chopper. From the 10,400-foot base the lift ascends to 12,300 feet, and you can hike up to 13,300 feet if you want an extra-long run. This is for advanced and expert skiers only, and reservations are mandatory for guided skiing and strongly suggested for unguided. ✉ *Rte. 110A* ☎ *970/387–5706* ⊕ *www.silvertonmountain.com* ☜ *$49–$129.*

FOUR-WHEELING
Silverton provides easy access to such popular four-wheel-drive routes as Ophir Pass to the Telluride side of the San Juans, Stony Pass to the Rio Grande Valley, and Engineer and Cinnamon passes, components of the Alpine Loop. With an all-terrain vehicle you can see some of Colorado's most famous ghost towns, remnants of mining communities, and jaw-dropping scenery. The four-wheeling season is May to mid-October, weather permitting. In winter these unplowed trails are transformed into fabulous snowmobile routes.

Silver Summit RV Park and Jeep Rentals (✉ *640 Mineral St.* ☎ *970/387–0240 or 800/352–1637* ⊕ *www.silversummitrvpark.com*) rents Jeeps for about $150–$180 per day.

ICE-SKATING

At the Kendall Mountain Recreation Area, the **Silverton Town Rink** (⊠ *1 Kendall Mountain Pl., off 14th St.* ☎*970/387–5522*) lets you skate for free, weather permitting. Rentals are $5.

NORDIC SKIING

The local snowmobile club grooms a cross-country skiing and snow-shoeing loop completely around Silverton, so the route is flat, easy, and safe. Molas Pass, 6 mi south of Silverton on U.S. 550, has a variety of Nordic routes, from easy half-milers in broad valleys to longer, more demanding ascents.

St. Paul Lodge and Hut (⊠ *511 Butte Cir., Durango* ☎*970/799–0785* ⊕ *www.skistpaul.com*) is an incredible find for anyone enchanted by remote high country. Above 11,000 feet and about a half-hour ski-in from the summit of Red Mountain Pass between Ouray and Silverton, the lodge (a converted mining camp) provides access to above–tree line skiing. Included in the lodge rates are guide service (essential in this area), ski equipment, and telemark lessons, along with meals and lodging. Be prepared for rather primitive facilities.

WHERE TO EAT AND STAY

$$ ✕ **Handlebars.** As much a museum as an eatery, the restaurant is crammed
SOUTHERN with mining artifacts, odd antiques, and mounted animals—including a full-grown elk. Don't pass up the huge platter of baby back ribs basted with the restaurant's own barbecue sauce (bottles of sauce are also for sale). The hearty menu also includes steaks, hamburgers, chicken, pasta, prime rib, and chicken-fried steak. ⊠ *117 E. 13th St.* ☎*970/387–5395* ⊕ *www.handlebarsco.com* ▤ *D, MC, V* ☉ *Closed Nov.–Apr.*

$$ ⊡ **Wyman Hotel & Inn.** Listed on the National Register of Historic Places, this wonderful red-sandstone building dates from 1902. It has 24-inch-thick walls, so the builders obviously expected it to last a while. Rooms are filled with period antiques, and many have beautiful arched windows. Four have whirlpool tubs, where you can soak after a morning on the slopes. In summer you can opt to stay in a romantically refurbished caboose with a private hot tub. Full breakfast, afternoon tea, and a wine and cheese social hour are included. **Pros:** quiet; centrally located; updated amenities. **Cons:** stairs are steep; the walls are so thick that sometimes it's too quiet. ⊠ *1371 Greene St.,* ☎*970/387–5372 or 800/609–7845* ⊕ *www.thewyman.com* ↻ *12 rooms, 6 suites* ♿ *In-room: no a/c, DVD (some), Wi-Fi* ▤ *D, MC, V* ⍾⍾ *BP.*

NIGHTLIFE AND THE ARTS

THE ARTS

In the Miners Union Theatre, **A Theatre Group** (⊠ *1069 Greene St.* ☎*970/ 387–5337* ⊕ *www.atheatregroup.org*) stages a summer repertory season running from May to October and a winter season lasting from December to April.

NIGHTLIFE

Check out **Silverton Brewery** (⊠ *1333 Greene St.* ☎*970/387–5033*), which serves a nice selection of handcrafted microbrews and a casual menu of brats, hot dogs, and chili.

10

SHOPPING

Remember that the majority of Silverton's retail establishments only operate in the months when the Durango & Silverton Narrow Gauge Railroad is operating, May to October.

Blair Street Emporium (✉ *1147 Blair St.* ☎ *970/387–5323* ✆ *Closed Nov.–Apr.*) specializes in all manner of Christmas ornaments, lights, and decorations.The gift shop **My Favorite Things** (✉ *1145 Greene St.* ☎ *970/387–5643* ⊕ *www.4my-favorite-things.com* ✆ *Closed Nov.–Apr.*) stocks porcelain dolls, antique jewelry, and romantic, lacy wearables.

EN ROUTE The tortuous route between Silverton and Purgatory includes a dizzying series of switchbacks as it climbs over Coal Bank Pass and Molas Pass and past splendid views of the Grand Turks, the Needles Range, and Crater Lake. This is prime mountain-biking and four-wheeling territory.

MESA COUNTRY

Discover the southern reaches of the San Juan Mountains and Mesa Verde National Park in the high country of southwestern Colorado. In addition to fine dining and boutique shopping, visitors can ride the rails on the Durango & Silverton Narrow Gauge Railroad, raft the Animas River, explore 2,000 mi of hiking and biking trails, and ski at the Durango Mountain Resort.

DURANGO

25 mi south of Purgatory via U.S. 550; 45 mi east of Cortez via U.S. 160; 62 mi west of Pagosa Springs via U.S. 160.

Wisecracking Will Rogers had this to say about Durango: "It's out of the way and glad of it." His statement is a bit unfair, considering that as a railroad town Durango has always been a cultural crossroads and melting pot (as well as a place to raise hell). Laid out at 6,500 feet along the winding Animas River, with the San Juan Mountains as backdrop, the town was founded in 1879 by General William Palmer, president of the all-powerful Denver & Rio Grande Railroad, when nearby Animas City haughtily refused to donate land for a depot. Within a decade Durango had completely absorbed its rival. The booming town quickly became the region's main metropolis and a gateway to the Southwest.

A walking tour of the historic downtown offers ample proof of Durango's prosperity during the late 19th century. The northern end of Main Avenue has the usual assortment of cheap motels and fast-food outlets, all evidence of Durango's present status as the major hub for tourism in the area.

North of the U.S. 160 and U.S. 550 junction are two well-known recreational playgrounds: the ravishing golf course and development at the Lodge at Tamarron, and Purgatory at Durango Mountain Resort. Purgatory, as everyone still calls this ski area despite its 2001 name change, is about as down-home as a ski resort can get. The clientele includes cowboys, families, and college students on break.

GETTING HERE AND AROUND

Durango Transit has regular bus service up and down Main Avenue, as well as to Purgatory during ski season. Durango Transportation will transport you between the airports and the resorts.

Purgatory isn't a proper town, but simply a collection of resorts, restaurants, and ski shops clustered around Purgatory Mountain on U.S. 550 some 25 mi north of Durango. The mountain is named for the nearby Purgatory Creek, a tributary of the River of Lost Souls.

ESSENTIALS

Transportation Contacts Durango Transit (☎ *970/259–5438* ⊕ *www.durangogov.org/transit*). **Durango Transportation** (☎ *970/259–4818*).

Visitor Info Durango Chamber Resort Association (✉ *111 S. Camino del Rio, Durango* ☎ *970/247–0312 or 800/525–8855* ⊕ *www.durango.org*).

EXPLORING

The intersection of 13th Avenue and Main Avenue (locals also refer to it as Main Street) marks the northern edge of Durango's **National Historic District.** Old-fashioned streetlights line the streets, casting a warm glow on the elegant Victorians now filled with upscale galleries, restaurants, and the occasional factory outlet store. Dating from 1887, the Strater Hotel is a reminder of the time when this town was a stop for many people headed west.

The **3rd Avenue National Historic District** (known simply as "The Boulevard"), two blocks east of Main Avenue, contains several Victorian residences, ranging from the imposing mansions built by railroad barons to more modest variations erected by well-to-do merchants.

Ⓒ
Fodor's Choice
★
The most entertaining way to relive the halcyon days of the Old West is to take a ride on the **Durango & Silverton Narrow Gauge Railroad,** a nine-hour, round-trip journey along the 45-mi railway to Silverton. You'll travel in comfort in lovingly restored coaches or in the open-air cars called gondolas as you listen to the train's shrill whistle as it chugs along. You get a good look at the Animas Valley, which in some parts is broad and green and in others narrow and rimmed with rock. The train runs from mid-May to late October, with four departures daily between June and August and once daily at other times. A shorter excursion—to Cascade Canyon—is available in winter. The **Durango Depot** (✉ *4th St. and Main Ave.*), dating from 1882, is connected to a full railroad museum. ✉ *479 Main Ave.* ☎ *970/247–2733 or 888/872–4607* ⊕ *www. durangotrain.com* ⌨ *$65.*

About 7 mi north of Durango, **Trimble Spa and Natural Hot Springs** is a great place to soak your aching bones, especially after some hiking. The complex includes an Olympic-size swimming pool (May through Oct.) and two natural mineral pools ranging from 83°F to 107°F. Massage and spa treatments are also available. ✉ *6475 County Rd. 203, off U.S. 550* ☎ *970/247–0212* ⊕ *www.trimblehotsprings.com* ⌨ *$15* ☼ *Sun.– Wed. 8* AM*–10* PM*, Thurs. 8* AM*–9* PM*, Fri.–Sat. 8* AM*–11* PM*.*

10

DOWNHILL SKIING AND SNOWBOARDING

★ **Purgatory at Durango Mountain Resort** (formerly known simply as Purgatory) has plenty of intermediate runs and glade and tree skiing. What's unique about Purgatory is its stepped terrain: lots of humps and dips and steep pitches followed by virtual flats. This trail profile makes it easier for skiers and snowboarders to stay in control (or simply get their legs back under them after they've conquered a section a little steeper than they might be accustomed to). A great powder day on the mountain's back side will convince anyone that Purgatory isn't just "Pleasant Ridge," as it's somewhat condescendingly known in Crested Butte and Telluride.

The truth is that Purgatory is just plain fun, and return visitors like it that way. The ski area is perfect for families and those who enjoy skiing or snowboarding but are open to other diversions. Purgatory's innovative Total Adventure Ticket lets you trade a portion of the multiday lift ticket for a guided snowshoe tour, a ride on the Durango & Silverton Narrow Gauge Railroad, an afternoon of cross-country skiing, an excursion to the Sky Ute Casino, a soak and massage at Trimble Hot Springs, or a horse-drawn dinner sleigh ride. For a gentler skiing diversion, there are 26 mi of machine-groomed cross-country trails just outside the main ski area. ✉ *1 Skier Pl.,off U.S. 550* ☎ *970/247–9000 or 800/568–3275* ⊕ *www. durangomountainresort.com* ☉ *Late Nov.–early Apr., daily 9–4.*

FACILITIES   2,029-foot vertical drop; 1,200 skiable acres; 23% beginner, 51% intermediate, 26% advanced; 1 high-speed 6-passenger chair, 1 high-speed quad chair, 4 triple chairs, 3 double chairs, 1 surface lift, and 1 moving carpet (beginners' lift).

LESSONS AND PROGRAMS   Durango Mountain Resort's **Adult Adventure School** (☎ *970/385–2149*) runs 2½-hour group lessons for everyone from newcomers to experts at 9:45 AM and 1:15 PM each day during the season. The cost is $50. First-timers can opt for a full-day lesson for $89. There are also daily lessons in snow biking and twice-monthly lessons in telemark skiing.

Teaching children to ski or snowboard is a cinch at **Kids Mountain Adventure** (☎ *970/385–2149*). There are three age-appropriate classes for kids 3 to 12 years old. There's also child care for tots between two months and three years. A full day costs $80–$89.

For a bit more money, skiers and snowboarders can explore 35,000 acres of untamed wilderness on a snowcat with the **San Juan Ski Company** (☎ *800/208–1780* ⊕ *www.sanjuanski.com*).

LIFT TICKETS   The at-the-window rates are $62 to $67 for a one-day lift ticket. A Guaranteed to Green ski package, which means that they promise you will be able to ski from top to bottom on a green run by the end of it, is a good deal for beginner skiers, as it combines a half-day morning lesson with an all-day lift ticket. The cost is $175.

RENTALS **Bubba's Boards** (⊠ *Village Plaza* ☎ *970/259–7377 or 866/860–7377*) is Durango Mountain Resort's full-service snowboard shop. Rentals begin at $35 per day.

Performance Peak (⊠ *Village Center* ☎ *970/247–9000*) rents top-of-the-line demo and retail skis and boots from K2, Salomon, Dynastar, Volkl, Nordica, Dolomite, and Rossignol; full packages (skis, boots, and poles) begin at $48. Snowshoe rentals are $17. The shop also does custom boot fitting, ski tuning, and equipment repair.

Purgatory Rentals (⊠ *Village Center* ☎ *970/385–2182*) has skis, boots, and poles, as well as other equipment. Rates begin at $26 per day for the basic package, rising to $36 for the high-performance package.

OTHER SPORTS AND THE OUTDOORS

The **San Juan Public Lands Center** (⊠ *15 Burnett Ct.,* ☎ *970/247–4874* ⊗ *Weekdays 8–5*) gives out information on hiking, fishing, and camping, as well as cross-country skiing, snowshoeing, and snowmobile routes. This office also stocks maps and guidebooks.

BIKING

With a healthy college population and a generally mild climate, Durango is extremely bike friendly and a destination for single-track enthusiasts. Many locals consider bikes to be their main form of transportation. The bike lobby is active, the trail system is well developed, and mountain biking is a particularly popular recreational activity.

Every Memorial Day weekend the **Iron Horse Bicycle Classic** (☎ *970/259–4621* ⊕ *www.ironhorsebicycleclassic.com*) celebrates the first train run of the spring with a steep 47-mi race that climbs over a mile in elevation from Durango to Silverton.

Get an overview of the scene at ⊕ *www.trails2000.org*, home of the very active local advocacy trail group. Although everybody in town seems to be an expert, a good place to go for advice and maps before you head off is **Mountain Bike Specialists** (⊠ *949 Main Ave.* ☎ *970/247–4066* ⊕ *www.mountainbikespecialists.com*), where you can also rent a bike, arrange a tour, or get hooked up with the trail of your dreams.

To get around town, start with the **Animas River Trail,** which parallels the river from North City Park to the south part of town along a 5-mi route. It is the main artery linking up with other trail systems. With its many access points, you might consider it rather than driving around town, especially on a busy weekend.

The **Hermosa Creek Trail** is an intermediate-to-difficult 20-mi jaunt. It has a couple of steep spots and switchbacks, but it rolls through open meadows, towering aspen and pine forests, and along the sides of mountains before dumping out in a parking lot in Hermosa, 9 mi north of Durango. Don't try it too early in the season while the snow is melting, because there are two creek crossings. Starting at the same spot as the Hermosa Creek Trail is the Lime Creek Trail, which will test you as it mostly follows the old stage road; it covers 11 mi from

10

Purgatory to Silverton. ⊠ *Trailhead: Take Hwy. 550 north 28 mi from Durango. Look for parking lot on right, north of Cascade Village near Purgatory.*

NEED A BREAK?

If you're looking for a little taste of France, stop by the **Jean-Pierre Bakery and Café** (⊠ *601 Main Ave.* ☎ *970/385–0122*) for fresh-baked palmier pastries, sugared strudels, or flaky croissants. The café also serves a delightful lunch and dinner in a historic brick building. The wine bar in the back is a great place for a little relaxation with a European flair.

FISHING

In business since 1983, **Duranglers** (⊠ *923 Main Ave.* ☎ *970/385–4081 or 888/347–4346* ⊕ *www.duranglers.com*) sells rods and reels, gives fly-fishing lessons, and runs custom trips to top fishing spots in the area, including the San Juan River in nearby northern New Mexico.

GOLF

Dalton Ranch Golf Club. About 6 mi north of Durango, Dalton Ranch is a Ken Dye–designed 18-hole championship course with inspiring panoramas of red-rock cliffs. Dalton's Grill has become a popular hangout for locals who like watching the resident elk herd take its afternoon stroll, especially in late fall and winter. The golf season here is early April to late October, weather permitting. ⊠ *589 County Rd. 252, off U.S. 550* ☎ *970/247–8774* ⊕ *www.daltonranch.com* ⚐ *Reservations essential* ⚑ *18 holes. Yards: 6,934/5,539. Par: 72/72. Green fee: $59–$90.*

Hillcrest Golf Course. Hillcrest is an 18-hole public course perched on a mesa near the campus of Fort Lewis College. The course is open from February to December, weather permitting. ⊠ *2300 Rim Dr.* ☎ *970/247–1499* ⚐ *Reservations essential* ⚑ *18 holes. Yards: 6,838/5,252. Par: 71/71. Green fee: $36.*

HIKING

Hiking trails are ubiquitous around Durango. Many trailheads around the edges of town lead to backcountry settings, and the San Juan Forest has plenty of mind-boggling walks and trails for those who want to backpack into wilderness. Before you go, check the local organization **Trails2000** (⊕ *www.trails2000.org*) for directions, information, and news about hiking in and around Durango.

If you're cramped for time, try the 0.66-mi **Animas View Overlook Trail** for spectacular views. It passes interpretive signs on geology, history, and flora before bringing you to a precipice with an unparalled view of the valley in which Durango sits and the Needle Mountains. It's the only wheelchair-accessible trail in the area, and you can picnic there, too.

The **Lion's Den Trail** hooks up with the **Chapman Hill Trail** west of Fort Lewis College for a nice moderate hike, climbing switchbacks that take you away from city bustle and hook up with the **Rim Trail.**

Fodor'sChoice
★ The **Colorado Trail** starts not far north of Durango and goes all the way to Denver. Though you're not obliged to go that far, just a few miles in and out will give you a taste of this epic trail, which winds through mountain ranges and high passes and some of the most amazing scenery in any mountains. ⊕ *www.coloradotrail.org.*

HORSEBACK RIDING

Southfork Riding Stables & Outfitters (⊠ *28481 U.S. 160* ☎ *970/259–4871*) has guided trail rides in summer and one-hour trips to view an elk herd in winter. You can also take part in cattle drives.

RAFTING

Durango Rivertrippers (⊠ *720 Main Ave.* ☎ *970/259–0289 or 800/292–2885* ⊕ *www.durangorivertrippers.com*) runs two- and four-hour trips down the Animas River, as well as 2- to 10-day wilderness expeditions on the Dolores River.

ROCK-CLIMBING

Contact rangers at the **San Juan National Forest** (⊠ *15 Burnett Ct.,* ☎ *970/247–4874* ⊕ *www.fs.fed.us/r2/sanjuan*) for information about rock climbing and other activities in the San Juan Mountains.

SouthWest Adventure Guides (⊠ *1205 Camino del Rio* ☎ *970/259–0370 or 800/642–5389* ⊕ *www.mtnguide.net*) is a climbing school that takes you to some of the area's most beautiful peaks. Other programs include rock climbing, ice climbing, Nordic skiing, snowshoeing, and mountaineering.

SNOWMOBILING

Snowmobile Adventures (⊠ *Village Center* ☎ *970/247–9000 or 970/385–2110*) runs guided tours on more than 60 mi of nearby trails.

WHERE TO EAT

$
AMERICAN
✕ **Brickhouse Cafe & Coffee Bar.** This popular little place may look like a bed-and-breakfast, but they take their coffee and tea seriously. Great lattes await at this restored historic house with wonderful landscaping. Don't miss the malted buttermilk waffles, pigs in a blanket, or big burgers. Breakfast and lunch are served all day. ⊠ *1849 Main Ave.* ☎ *970/247–3760* ⊕ *www.brickhousecafe.com* ▭ *AE, D, MC* ⊗ *No dinner. Closed Mon.*

$$
AMERICAN
✕ **Carver's Bakery & Brew Pub.** The "Brews Brothers," Bill and Jim Carver, have about eight beers on tap at any given time, including such flavors as Raspberry Wheat Ale, Jackrabbit Pale Ale, and Colorado Trail Nut Brown Ale. If you're feeling peckish, try one of the bread bowls filled with soup or salad. There's a patio out back where you can soak up the sun. From breakfast to the wee hours the place is always hopping. ⊠ *1022 Main Ave.* ☎ *970/259–2545* ⊕ *www.carverbrewing.com* ⤴ *Reservations not accepted* ▭ *AE, D, MC, V.*

$$
MEDITERRANEAN
✕ **Cyprus Cafe.** In warm weather, sit on the patio to listen to live jazz, and the rest of the time cozy up to your fellow diners in this tiny space. Mediterranean food receives upscale treatment here, from chicken breasts stuffed with artichokes, feta, and mint to rigatoni layered with shrimp, spinach, and ricotta to a salt-roasted duck that makes your mouth water when it hits the table. The wine list is small, eclectic, and reasonably priced. Lunch is also interesting; try the wild salmon with caramelized onions or chicken sausage with fresh mozzarella sandwiches. ⊠ *725 E. 2nd Ave.* ☎ *970/385–6884* ⊕ *www.cypruscafe.com* ▭ *AE, D, MC, V.*

$$$
JAPANESE
✕ **East by Southwest.** Pan-Asian food with a strong Japanese bent gets a bit of a Latin treatment in this snazzy but comfortable space. Steaks (using Kobe beef), sushi and sashimi, tempura, and other traditional dishes are elegantly presented and layered with complementary flavors; the seven-course tasting menu is a smart way to try it all. The sake,

10

beer, and wine selections are well varied, and the tea and tonic bar is fun, too. ✉ *160 E. College Dr.* ☎ *970/247–5533* ⊕ *eastbysouthwest. com* ☾ *No lunch Sun.* ☱ *AE, D, MC, V.*

$$
SOUTHWESTERN

✕ **Ken & Sue's Place.** Plates are big and the prices are reasonable at one of Durango's favorite restaurants. Locals are wild for the artfully prepared contemporary cuisine enlivened with a light touch of Asian and Southwestern accents. Try the pistachio nut–crusted grouper with vanilla-rum butter, or Aunt Lydia's meatloaf with red-wine gravy and mashed potatoes. If there's still room after that, try the bread pudding. ✉ *636 Main Ave.* ☎ *970/385–1810* ⊕ *www.kenandsues.com* ☱ *AE, D, MC, V* ☾ *No lunch weekends.*

$
AMERICAN

✕ **Olde Tymer's Cafe.** If you're longing to meet a local, look no farther than the bustling Olde Tymer's, in a beautiful old building with an inviting patio in the back. The hamburger is a huge specimen on a fat, fresh bun, and folks swear by the piled-high salads and sandwiches. When the weather's nice, take your chow to the patio. ✉ *1000 Main Ave.* ☎ *970/259–2990* ⊕ *www.otcdgo.com* ☱ *AE, D, MC, V.*

$$$$
STEAK

✕ **Ore House.** Durango is a meat-and-potatoes kind of town, and this is Durango's idea of a steak house. The aroma of beef smacks you in the face as you walk past, but there are chicken and seafood dishes available too. This local favorite serves enormous slabs of aged Angus that are hand cut daily. For a special occasion try the chateaubriand for two ($69.95). If you're watching your cholesterol, better "steer" clear. ✉ *147 E. College Dr.* ☎ *970/247–5707* ⊕ *www.orehouserestaurant.com* ☱ *AE, D, DC, MC, V.*

$$$$
CONTINENTAL

✕ **Red Snapper.** If you're in the mood for fresh fish, head to this congenial spot, which is full of saltwater aquariums. Try the drunken Hawaiian chicken or the tequila shrimp. Delicious steaks, prime rib, lobster, and king crab are also available. The salad bar is enormous. ✉ *144 E. 9th St.* ☎ *970/259–3417* ⊕ *www.redsnapperdurango.com* ☱ *AE, D, DC, MC, V* ☾ *No lunch weekends.*

$$$
STEAK
★

✕ **Sow's Ear.** It's a toss-up between the Ore House in downtown Durango and this watering hole in Purgatory's Silverpick Lodge for the area's "best steak house" award. The Sow's Ear has the edge, though, for its great views of the mountain. If you prefer more action, there's also an open kitchen in the dining area where you can watch your meal being prepared. The mouthwatering, fresh-baked jalapeño-cheese rolls and honey-wheat rolls, and creative entrées such as blackened filet mignon are a few more reasons Sow's Ear leads the pack. Complement your meal with a selection from their extensive domestic wine list. ✉ *48475 U.S. 550* ☎ *970/247–3527* ⚑ *Reservations essential* ☱ *AE, D, DC, MC, V* ☾ *Closed mid-Mar.–Memorial Day and Labor Day–mid-Dec.*

WHERE TO STAY

$$

▦ **Apple Orchard Inn.** About 8 mi from downtown Durango, this little B&B sits on 5 acres in the lush Animas Valley. The main house and six cottages surround a flower-bedecked pond, complete with geese. Cherrywood antiques, fluffy feather beds, and handcrafted armoires add a graceful touch to the handsome rooms. In the evening, relax on your cottage swing, enjoying views of the surrounding cliffs. The owners' experience at European cooking schools is evident in the breakfasts—and in the "train cookies" sometimes sent along with guests who make the journey to Silverton. **Pros:** inspiring views; off the beaten path; cottages are intimate and romantic. **Cons:** not right in town. ✉ *7758 County Rd. 203,* ☎ *970/247–0751 or 800/426–0751* ⊕ *www.appleorchardinn.com* ⇨ *4 rooms, 6 cottages* ⚅ *In-room: no a/c* ⊟ *AE, D, MC, V* ⏁ *BP.*

$ ⚏ **Durango Quality Inn.** This is one of the nicer budget properties along Durango's strip, because it's reliable, comfortable, and has sizable rooms. The hot tubs are nice after a day on the trails. **Pros:** spacious rooms; reasonable rates. **Cons:** typical chain feel. ✉ *2930 N. Main Ave.,* ☎ *970/259–5373 or 800/532–7112* ⊕ *www.qualityinn.com* ⇨ *48 rooms* ⚅ *In-room: refrigerators, Wi-Fi. In-hotel: pool, some pets allowed* ⊟ *AE, D, DC, MC, V* ⏁ *CP.*

$$ ⚏ **General Palmer Hotel.** Named after William Jackson Palmer, the owner of the Denver & Rio Grande Railroad and the founder of Durango, the 1898 building has been faithfully restored, giving it a clean, bright look. Period furniture and Victorian touches reinforce the historical feel, and the library and Teddy Bear Room are quiet areas for relaxing. The beds are four-posters, brass, or pewter, and the rooms are charming without being cutesy. Cookies, coffee, and tea are always available in the lobby, and Continental breakfast with homemade muffins is included. **Pros:** nicely restored lodging; rooms are quiet; turn-down service. **Cons:** pricey in season. ✉ *567 Main Ave.,* ☎ *970/247–4747 or 800/523–3358* ⊕ *generalpalmerhotel.com* ⇨ *39 rooms, 4 suites* ⚅ *In-room: refrigerator, Wi-Fi. In-hotel: concierge* ⊟ *AE, D, DC, MC, V* ⏁ *CP.*

$$ ⚏ **New Rochester Hotel.** This one-time flophouse is funky yet chic, thanks
★ to the mother-and-son team of Diane and Kirk Komick, who rescued some of the original furnishings. Marquee-lighted movie posters from Hollywood Westerns line the airy hallways, and steamer trunks, hand-painted settees, wagon-wheel chandeliers, and fluffy quilts in the rooms contribute to a laid-back retro vibe. Windows from Denver & Rio Grande Railroad carriages convert the back porch into a parlor car, and gas lamps add a warm glow to the courtyard. A full gourmet breakfast, with plenty of coffee and several varieties of tempting mini-muffins and scones, is included. The 10-room Leland House is a sister property across the street that offers more of a B&B experience. **Pros:** welcoming staff; large rooms; free use of bikes in town. **Cons:** can be noisy. ✉ *726 E. 2nd Ave.,* ☎ *970/385–1920 or 800/664–1920* ⊕ *www.rochesterhotel. com* ⇨ *13 rooms, 1 suite* ⚅ *In-hotel: restaurant, some pets allowed* ⊟ *AE, D, DC, MC, V* ⏁ *BP.*

$$ ⚏ **Purgatory Village Hotel at Durango Mountain Resort.** This comfortable slope-side lodging has generously proportioned rooms decorated with contemporary furnishings. If you want a bit of pampering, the one- and two-bedroom condos have wood-burning fireplaces and whirlpool baths. **Pros:** slope-side location; good restaurants; reasonable price considering locale. **Cons:** in season, the hotel is very chaotic. ✉ *1 Skier Pl.,* ☎ *970/385–2100 or 800/982–6103* ⊕ *www.durangomountainresort. com* ⇨ *133 rooms* ⚅ *In-room: no a/c, kitchen (some). In-hotel: 2 restaurants, bar, pool, public Wi-Fi* ⊟ *AE, D, MC, V.*

10

$$$
Fodor's Choice
★

🖫 **Strater Hotel.** Even though it opened more than a century ago, this hotel is still the hottest spot in town. The grande dame of Durango's hotels opened for business in 1887. Inside, the Diamond Belle Saloon glitters with crystal chandeliers, rustic oak beams, and plush velvety curtains. The individually decorated rooms are exquisite: after all, the hotel owns the country's largest collection of Victorian walnut antiques and has its own wood-carving shop to create exact period reproductions. Your room might have entertained Butch Cassidy, Louis L'Amour (he wrote *The Sacketts* here), Francis Ford Coppola, John Kennedy, or Marilyn Monroe (the latter two stayed here at separate times). **Pros:** location right in the thick of things; space has Old West feel; they will safely store your mountain bike for you. **Cons:** when the bar downstairs gets going, rooms right above it get no peace. ⊠ *699 Main Ave.,* ☎ *970/247–4431 or 800/247–4431* ⊕ *www.strater.com* ➪ *93 rooms* ⚭ *In-room: Internet, Wi-Fi. In-hotel: restaurant, room service, bar* ⊟ *AE, D, DC, MC, V* ⍟ *CP.*

GUEST RANCH
$$$$
☾

🖫 **Wilderness Trails Ranch.** It's only an hour's drive from Durango, but this family-owned and -operated guest ranch, nestled in the Upper Pine River valley, on the borders of the Piedra and Weminuche wilderness areas, might as well be a lifetime away. The riding programs are the main attraction here; you will be individually matched with horses to fit your experience and comfort level. Other activities include hiking, rafting, waterskiing, and fishing. Cozy log cabins complete with gas stoves, modern baths, and terry robes are arranged in a semicircle around the main lodge, campfire ring, and pool; Cordon Bleu–trained chefs are at the helm in the dining room, which has views of the mountains and busy hummingbird feeders through large picture windows. **Pros:** very friendly owners; family-friendly; gorgeous setting. **Cons:** minimum stay required. ⊠ *23486 County Rd. 501, Bayfield* ☎ *970/247–0722 or 800/527–2624* ⊕ *www.wildernesstrails.com* ➪ *10 cabins* ⚭ *In-room: no phone, refrigerator, no TV. In-hotel: bar, pool, children's programs (ages 3–17)* ⊟ *D, MC, V* ⍟ *Closed Oct.–May* ⍟ *FAP.*

NIGHTLIFE AND THE ARTS

THE ARTS

The **Diamond Circle Melodrama** (⊠ *802 E. 2nd Ave.* ☎ *970/247–3400*) stages rip-roaring melodramas all summer long. The **Durango Lively Arts Co.** (⊠ *802 2nd Ave.* ☎ *970/259–2606*) presents fine community theater productions. The **Fort Lewis College Community Concert Hall** is a modern 600-seat auditorium that hosts local, regional, and touring performers. The college's outdoor amphitheater is the setting for the **Durango Shakespeare Festival** (☎ *970/247–7657* ⊕ *www.durangoconcerts.com*).

BARS AND CLUBS

Awash in flocked wallpaper and lace, the **Diamond Belle Saloon** (⊠ *699 Main Ave.* ☎ *970/247–4431*) is dominated by a gilt-and-mahogany bar. The honky-tonk player piano and waitresses dressed as 1880s saloon girls pack them in to this spot in the Strater Hotel. **Lady Falconburgh's Barley Exchange** (⊠ *640 Main Ave.* ☎ *970/382–9664*) is a favorite with locals. The pub serves more than 140 types of beer. Taste many fine brews, including True Blonde Ale, Mexican Logger Octoberfest, and Pinstripe Red Ale, at **Ska Brewery & Tasting Room** (⊠ *255 Girard St.* ☎ *970/247–5792* ⊕ *www.skabrewing.com*). The brewery is open from noon to 7 PM weekdays and from noon to 3 PM on Saturday.

CASINOS

About 25 mi southeast of Durango, the **Sky Ute Casino & Lodge** (✉ *14324 Hwy. 172 N., Ignacio* ☎ *970/563–3000 or 888/842–4180* ⊕ *www.skyutecasino.com*) has limited-stakes gambling. There are 400 slot machines and tables for blackjack, poker, and bingo. Call for free shuttle service from Durango.

DINNER SHOWS

The **Bar D Chuckwagon** (✉ *8080 County Rd. 250, E. Animas Valley* ☎ *970/247–5753 or 888/800–5753* ⊕ *www.bardchuckwagon.com*) serves mouthwatering barbecued beef, beans, and biscuits. Many people head to this spot 9 mi from Durango to hear the Bar D Wranglers sing. Reservations are required.

SHOPPING

FOOD

Honeyville (✉ *33633 U.S. 550* ☎ *800/676–7690*), south of Durango Mountain Resort, sells jams, jellies (try the chokecherry), condiments, and honey. You can watch how the bees go about their work in glass hives and listen to a lecture by a fully garbed beekeeper.

BOOKS

Maria's Bookshop (✉ *960 Main Ave.* ☎ *970/247–1438* ⊕ *www.mariasbookshop.com*) specializes in regional literature and nonfiction.

BOUTIQUES

Appaloosa Trading Co. (✉ *501 Main Ave.* ☎ *970/259–1994* ⊕ *www.appaloosadurango.com*) is one of the best sources for all things leather, from purses to saddles, hats to boots. The exotic belts are especially nice when paired with sterling-silver buckles. They also sell locally produced weavings and other handicrafts.

GALLERIES

The selection of arts and crafts from Mexico and elsewhere is remarkable at **Artesanos Design Collection** (✉ *700 E. 2nd Ave.* ☎ *970/259–5755* ⊕ *www.artesanosdesign.com*). **Dietz Market** (✉ *26345 U.S. 160* ☎ *970/259–5811 or 800/321–6069* ⊕ *www.dietzmarket.com*) carries pottery, metalwork, candles, weavings, and foodstuffs, all celebrating the region. **Lime Berry Art Gallery** (✉ *925 Main Ave.* ☎ *970/375–9199* ⊕ *www.limeberryonline.com*) has an eclectic, fantastical mix of rugs, fine art, and home furnishings. **Toh-Atin Gallery** (✉ *145 W. 9th St.* ☎ *970/247–8277 or 800/525–0384* ⊕ *www.toh-atin.com*) is one of the best Native American galleries in Colorado, specializing in Navajo rugs and weavings. There's also a wide range of paintings, pottery, and prints.

10

PAGOSA SPRINGS

62 mi east of Durango via U.S. 160.

Although not a large town, Pagosa Springs has become a major center for outdoor sports. Hiking, biking, and cross-country skiing opportunities abound not far from the excellent ski area of Wolf Creek. It has no lodging facilities, so Pagosa Springs is a logical place to stay.

GETTING HERE AND AROUND

Highway 160 turns into Pagosa Avenue when it enters the town limits and doubles as the main drag, where the majority of restaurants, shops, and hotels are located. The town is 10 blocks long, and the other main thoroughfare, Lewis Avenue, runs parallel with Pagosa Avenue from 1st Street to 5th Street.

ESSENTIALS

Visitor Info Pagosa Springs Area Chamber of Commerce and Visitor Center (⊠ *402 San Juan St.,* ☎ *970/264–2360 or 800/252–2204* ⊕ *www.visitpagosasprings.com*). **Wolf Creek Snow Report** (☎ *800/754–9653*).

EXPLORING

With water ranging in temperature from 84°F to 114°F, **The Springs Resort** is a great place to relax. There are 23 outdoor tubs, a Mediterranean-style bathhouse, and a full-service spa. ⊠ *165 Hot Springs Blvd.* ☎ *800/225–0934 or 970/264–4168* ⊕ *pagosahotsprings.com* ⊡ *$20 lower deck, $25 premium pools 18 and older* ☉ *June 12–Sept. 6, daily 7 AM–1 AM; Sept. 7–June 11, Sun.–Thurs. 7 AM–11 PM, Fri. and Sat. 7 AM–1 AM* ⊟ *AE, D, DC, MC, V.*

DOWNHILL SKIING AND SNOWBOARDING

With more than 450 average inches of snow annually, **Wolf Creek Ski Area** is Colorado's best-kept white-powder secret. It's within 1,600 acres of Forest Service land in the San Juan Wilderness. The trails are designed to accommodate any level of ability and traverse every kind of ski terrain in ever-changing conditions, from wide-open bowls to steep glades, with a commanding view of remote valleys and towering peaks.

Because there are no overnight accommodations and it's a family-owned business, Wolf Creek has a reputation as a laid-back place for those with an aversion to lift lines and the faster-paced, better-known ski areas.

It's all skiing here, with the highest point at 11,904 feet, 1,604 feet from the base. At 2 mi, the longest run is Navajo Trail. Beginners can start on the Dickey Chairlift to the Snow Shoe or the Kelly Boyce Trail; both hook up with the Bunny Hop back down the hill.

Arguably the best area stretches back to Horseshoe Bowl from the Waterfall area, serviced by the Alberta Lift. The more intrepid will want to climb the Knife Ridge Staircase to the more-demanding Knife Ridge Chutes. Just below is the groomed Sympatico, which runs down a gentler ridge and through dense forest below the Alberta Lift. The 50 trails run the gamut from wide-open bowls to steep glades.

Lodging options from rustic log cabins, B&B, and motels in all price ranges are nearby along or off Highway 160: Creede, South Fork, and Monte Vista on the east and Pagosa Springs on the west. ⊠ *U.S. 160 at top of Wolf Creek Pass* ☎ *970/264–5629* ⊕ *www.wolfcreekski.com* ⊘ *Early Nov.–mid-Apr., daily 8:30–4.*

FACILITIES 1,604-foot vertical drop; 1,600 skiable acres; 20% beginner, 35% intermediate, 25% advanced, 20% expert; 1 quad, 2 triples, 2 doubles, 2 surface lifts.

LESSONS AND **Wolf Creek Ski School** holds group lessons—$55 for four hours and $40 PROGRAMS for two-hour sessions. First-day beginner packages (ages 9 and up) are $52 ($62 snowboard). Private one-hour lessons are $65 ($95 for two). Children over 4 can join the Wolf Pups program, which includes lift tickets and lunch. It's $50 for a half day, $60 for a full day.

LIFT TICKETS The walk-up rate is $52 for adults, $40 for half day, with three-day lift passes for $153.

RENTALS **Wolf Creek Ski Rental,** in the Sports Center Building across from the ticket office, rents skis and boards. Adult sets (skis, boots, poles) are $14–$31 and $18 for telemark. Boards are $26 with or without boots; boot rentals are $10.

OTHER SPORTS AND THE OUTDOORS
GOLF
Pagosa Springs Golf Club. The 27 championship holes here can be played in three combinations, essentially creating three 18-hole courses. A bonus is the gorgeous mountain scenery. The regular season runs from June 15 to September 15. Cart rental is $15 and club rental is $30 for 18 holes. Reservations are recommended during peak season. ⊠ *1 Pine Club Pl.* ☎ *970/731–4755* ⊕ *www.golfpagosa.com* ⚐ *27 holes. Yards: 5,074/7,228. Par: 71/72. Green fee: $45–$79.*

HIKING
Pagosa Springs sits in a wondrous landscape, and there's no better way to enjoy its isolated natural beauty than to experience it from a trail. Around here, trails pass through green forests and along cold mountain streams or mountain plateaus. Don't forget comfortable shoes, water, a map, and warm, wet-weather clothing—conditions can deteriorate quickly any month of the year.

If you aren't used to it, high altitude can catch you off guard. Drink plenty of water and slather on the sunscreen. And in summer an early morning start is best, as afternoon thunderstorms are frequent and a danger above the tree line.

The **Piedra Falls Trail** is a leisurely half-hour, 1.2-mi stroll through the scenic landscape of the San Juan Mountains to the falls, which tumble down a narrow wedge cut through volcanic rocks. Up close, the falls are quite wet, and from anywhere they are quite noisy. ⊠ *Pagosa Ranger District, San Juan National Forest, 180 Second St.* ☎ *970/264–2268* ⊕ *www.fs.fed.us/r2/sanjuan.*

For serious hikers and backpackers, the **Continental Divide Trail** (⊕ *www.cdtrail.org*) passes through 80 mi of the Weminuche Wilderness near the Wolf Creek summit.

10

WHERE TO EAT AND STAY

¢   ✕ **Elkhorn Cafe.** Filling and fiery Mexican fare (try the stuffed sopaipillas),
MEXICAN   as well as the usual burgers and chili fries, makes this a popular drop-in
spot for locals. Fill up on a breakfast burrito before attacking the Wolf
Creek bowls. ⊠ *438 Pagosa St.* ☎ *970/264–2146* ⊟ *AE, D, MC, V* ⊙ *No
dinner Sunday.*

$–$$ ⊡ **The Springs Resort and Spa.** Wrap yourself in a big white spa robe and
★   head directly for the pools. Multiple soaking pools are terraced on several levels overlooking the San Juan River, and as a hotel guests you'll
have 24-hour access. Pick your temperature (from Tranquility to Lobster
Pot), and relax. Rooms are standard but comfortable, and the larger
configurations have lots of space and kitchenettes. In 2009 the resort
added a green luxury hotel with 29 luxury suites with full kitchens and
sitting rooms. **Pros:** proximity to hot springs; can cook your own meals.
Cons: service can be indifferent. ⊠ *165 Hot Springs Blvd.,* ☎ *800/225–
0934* ⊕ *www.pagosahotsprings.com* ⤵ *46 rooms, 33 suites* ⌂ *In-room:
kitchen (some), Wi-Fi (some). In-hotel: bar, pool, spa, laundry facilities,
some pets allowed* ⊟ *AE, D, MC, V.*

CORTEZ

45 mi west of Durango via U.S. 160.

The northern escarpment of Mesa Verde and the volcanic blisters of the
La Plata Mountains to the west dominate sprawling Cortez. A series of
Days Inns, Dairy Queens, and Best Westerns, the town has a layout that
seems to have been determined by neon-sign and aluminum-siding sales-
men of the 1950s. Hidden among these eyesores, however, are fine galleries and a host of secondhand shops that can yield surprising finds.

GETTING HERE AND AROUND

Cortez sits at the junction of Highway 160 and Highway 491, making it a busy town for people heading north to Dolores and Telluride,
south into New Mexico and Arizona, and east to Durango. Highway
491 turns into Broadway heading north, and Highway 160 splits off,
turning into Main Street as it passes through the center of town and
heads east to Durango.

ESSENTIALS

Visitor Info Colorado Welcome Center (⊠ *Cortez City Park, 928 E. Main St.*
☎ *970/565–4048 or 800/253–1616* ⊕ *www.mesaverdecountry.com*). **Cortez
Area Chamber of Commerce** (⊠ *928 E. Main St., Cortez* ☎ *970/565–3414*
⊕ *www.cortezchamber.com*). **Mesa Verde Country** (⊡ *Box HH, Cortez*
☎ *800/253–1616* ⊕ *www.mesaverdecountry.com*).

EXPLORING

The exterior of the excellent **Cortez Cultural Center** has been painted to
resemble the cliff dwellings of Mesa Verde. Exhibits focus on regional
artists and artisans, the Ute Mountain branch of the Ute tribe, and
various periods of Ancestral Puebloan culture. The Cultural Park at
the Cortez Cultural Center contains an authentic Navajo hogan and a
Ute tepee. The park itself is open 9 to 5; admission is free. On summer
evenings there are Native American dances; sandpainting, rug weaving,
and pottery-making demonstrations; theatrical events; and storytelling.

✉ *25 N. Market St.* ☎ *970/565–1151* ⊕ *www.cortezculturalcenter.org* ⊠ *Free* ☉ *June–Aug., Mon.–Sat. 10–10; Sept.–May, Mon.–Sat. 10–5.*

Native American guides at **Ute Mountain Tribal Park** lead grueling hikes into this dazzling repository of Ancestral Puebloan ruins, including the majestic Tree House cliff dwelling and enchanting Eagle's Nest petroglyphs. Tours usually start at the Ute Mountain Pottery Plant, 15 mi south of Cortez, on U.S. 491. Overnight camping can also be arranged. ⌂ *Box 109, Towaoc* ☎ *970/565–3751 or 800/847–5485* ⊕ *www.ute-mountainute.com.*

Crow Canyon Archaeological Center promotes understanding and appreciation of Ancestral Puebloan culture by guiding visitors through excavations and botanical studies in the region. Also included in the weeklong programs are day trips to isolated canyon sites and hands-on lessons in weaving and pottery making with Native American artisans. ✉ *23390 County Rd. K,* ☎ *970/565–8975 or 800/422–8975* ⊕ *www.crowcanyon.org.*

A brass plaque set on a granite platform surrounded by four state flags marks the only spot where four states—Colorado, Arizona, Utah, and New Mexico—meet at a single point. **Four Corners Monument** (✉ *U.S. 160* ☎ *928/871–6647* ⊕ *www.navajonationparks.org* ⊠ *$3 per vehicle* ☉ *Sept.–May, daily 8–5; May–Sept., daily 7–8*) is photo-op country. Snacks and souvenirs are sold by Native Americans from rickety wood booths. To get here, travel south from Cortez on U.S. 160 for about 40 mi. You can't miss the signs.

OFF THE BEATEN PATH

Mud Creek Hogan. This endearing bit of classic American kitsch has more than a dozen enormous arrows stuck in the ground to mark the spot of a hokey trading post and museum, where you get the feeling that everything is for sale. The grounds are adorned with tepees and a giant plastic horse. Beside the shop is a re-creation of a frontier town, complete with saloon, hotel, bank, jail, and livery station. Don't breathe too hard, or you'll blow the town over: the paper-thin buildings are only facades. ✉ *East U.S. 160 from Mesa Verde National Park* ☎ *970/533–7117.*

WHERE TO EAT AND STAY

$$ **AMERICAN** ✗ **Nero's.** Chef Todd Halnier's menu has a spicy "Cowboy" steak, and exotic lasagna and shrimp dishes, the most popular being shrimp with artichoke hearts in lemon sauce. The menu is seasonal, and includes steak, veal, and seafood. Southwestern-color walls are accented with regional art. ✉ *303 W. Main St.* ☎ *970/565–7366* ⊟ *AE, D, MC, V.*

¢ ⌂ **Cortez Mesa Verde.** This is definitely the nicest motel on the strip, mostly because its air-conditioned rooms are spacious and pleasantly decorated with 1950s kitsch. The pool is a godsend after a long drive. **Pros:** reliable; reasonably priced. **Cons:** nothing fancy. ✉ *640 S. Broadway,* ☎ *970/565–3773* ⇆ *86 rooms* ⌕ *In-room: refrigerator (some), Wi-Fi. In-hotel: bar, pool* ⊟ *MC, V.*

NIGHTLIFE

At the base of the legendary Sleeping Ute Mountain, the state's largest casino rings with the sound of more than 500 slot machines. **Ute Mountain Casino Hotel Resort** (✉ *3 Weminuche Dr., Towaoc* ☎ *970/565–8800 or 800/258–8007* ⊕ *www.utemountainute.com*) also draws the crowds

10

for bingo, blackjack, and poker (both the live and the video versions). Near Four Corners, the casino is 11 mi south of Cortez on U.S. 160. If you're planning on staying awhile, Kuchu's restaurant, on-site hotel, and a full-service RV park are next door.

SHOPPING

Mesa Indian Trading Company and Gallery (⊠ *27601 U.S. Hwy. 160* ☎ *970/565–4492 or 800/441–9908* ⊕ *www.mesaverdepottery.com*) sells ceramics from most Southwestern tribes. **Clay Mesa Art Gallery and Studio** (⊠ *20 E. Main St.* ☎ *970/565–1902*) showcases original works by local artists Richard St. John and Lesli Diane. **Notah Dineh Trading Company and Museum** (⊠ *345 W. Main St.* ☎ *800/444–2024* ⊕ *www.notahdineh. com*) specializes in rugs, hand-carved kachinas, cradleboards, baskets, beadwork, and silver jewelry. Be sure to stop in the free museum to see relics of the Old West, as well as a noteworthy rug in the Two Grey Hills pattern. **Ute Mountain Pottery Plant** (⊠ *U.S. 160 at U.S. 491, Towaoc* ☎ *970/565–8548*) invites you to watch the painstaking processes of molding, trimming, cleaning, painting, and glazing pottery before adjourning to the showroom so that you can buy pieces straight from the source.

DOLORES

10 mi northeast of Cortez via U.S. 160 and Rte. 145.

On the bank of the Dolores River at the McPhee Reservoir, Colorado's second-largest body of water, Dolores is midway between Durango and Telluride on Highway 145. This sleepy little town in the San Juan Forest attracts visitors with its spectacular scenery, fabulous fly-fishing, water sports, mountain hiking, and outdoor adventure.

The gentle rising hump to the southwest of town is Sleeping Ute Mountain, which resembles the reclining silhouette of a Native American replete with headdress. The sacred site is revered by the Ute Mountain tribe as a great warrior god who, mortally wounded in a titanic battle with the evil ones, lapsed into eternal sleep, his flowing blood turning into the life-giving Dolores and Animas rivers.

EXPLORING

In 1968, state officials approved the construction of an irrigation dam across the Dolores River, forming the **McPhee Reservoir,** the second largest in the state. It draws fishermen looking to bag a variety of warm- and cold-water fish along its 50 mi of shoreline, which is surrounded by spectacular specimens of juniper and sage as well as large stands of pinyon pine. Camping, a boat ramp, and a generous fish-cleaning station add to the appeal. A relatively easy mountain-bike trail and hiking in the area, as well as a small marina and panoramic views off the mesa of the San Juan National Forest make this a popular recreation area.

★ The **Anasazi Heritage Center** houses the finest artifacts culled from more
☾ than 1,500 excavations in the region. A full-scale replica of an Ancestral Puebloan pit-house dwelling illustrates how the people lived around AD 850. The first explorers to stumble upon Ancestral Puebloan ruins were the Spanish friars Dominguez and Escalante, who set out in 1776 from Santa Fe to find a safe route west to Monterey. The two major ruins at

the Anasazi Heritage Center are named for the pair. The Dominguez site is the less impressive of the two, although it's of great archaeological interest because here scientists uncovered extremely rare evidence of a "high-status burial." The Escalante site is a 20-room masonry pueblo standing guard over the McPhee Reservoir. ☒ *27501 Rte. 184, 3 mi west of Dolores* ☎ *970/882–5600* ⊕ *www.co.blm.gov/ahc* ☒ *$3* ⊙ *Mar.–Oct., daily 9–5; Nov.–Feb., daily 9–4.*

In town, the enchanting **Galloping Goose Historical Society Museum** (☒ *5th St. at Rte. 145* ☎ *970/882–7082* ⊕ *www.gallopinggoose5.com*) is a replica of an 1881 train station that contains an original narrow-gauge railcar. This distinctive vehicle connected Telluride with the rest of the world in the declining years of rail travel.

Spread across 164,000 acres of arid mesa-and-canyon country, the **Canyons of the Ancients National Monument** holds more than 20,000 known archaeological sites, the greatest concentration anywhere in the United States. There are 40, 60, or sometimes even 100 sites per square mile. Some, like apartment-style cliff dwellings and hewn-rock towers, are impossible to miss. Others are as subtle as evidence of agricultural fields, springs, and water systems. They are powerful evidence of the complex and mystical civilization of the Ancestral Puebloan people (formerly known as the Anasazi, "the ancient ones") who inhabited the area between AD 450 and 1300 and are believed to have been the ancestors of today's Pueblo peoples.

The national monument includes several sites under federal protection: **Hovenweep National Monument** (⊕ *www.nps.gov/hove*), straddling the Colorado–Utah border, is known for distinctive square, oval, round, and D-shaped towers that were engineering marvels when they were built around AD 1200. **Lowry Pueblo,** in the northern part of the monument, is a 40-room pueblo. It has eight kivas (round chambers thought to have been used for sacred rituals). Its Great Kiva is one of the largest known in the Southwest. Also look for the Painted Kiva, which provides insight into Ancestral Puebloan decorative techniques.

In the vast and rugged backcountry area west of Mesa Verde National Park, the monument is a must if you're fascinated by the culture of the Ancestral Puebloans. The going may be rough, however. Roads are few, hiking trails are sparse, and visitor services are all but nonexistent. The Anasazi Heritage Center, 3 miles west of Dolores on Highway 184, serves as the visitor center for the Canyon of the Ancients National Monument. A brochure, which details the self-guided tour, is available at the entrance to the site. ☒ *From Dolores, take Hwy. 184 west to U.S. 491, then head west onto County Rd. CC for 9 mi* ☎ *970/562–5600* ⊕ *www.co.blm.gov/canm* ☒ *$6* ⊙ *Daily 8–5.*

SPORTS AND THE OUTDOORS
FISHING AND BOATING

McPhee Reservoir, filled in 1987, is popular with boaters and anglers. The Colorado Division of Wildlife stocks this large artificial lake with plenty of trout. Other species found here include bass, bluegills, crappies, and kokanee salmon. The most easily reached fishing access spot is at the end of Highway 145, west of downtown Dolores.

10

RAFTING

★ Beginning in the San Juan Mountains of southwestern Colorado, the Dolores River runs north for more than 150 mi before joining the Colorado River near Moab, Utah. This is one of those rivers that tend to flow madly in spring and diminish considerably by midsummer, and for that reason rafting trips are usually run between April and June. Sandstone canyons, Ancestral Puebloan ruins, and the spring bloom of wildflowers and cacti are trip highlights. The current's strength depends mostly on how much water is released from McPhee Reservoir, but for the most part this trip is a float interrupted by rapids that—depending on the flow level—can rate a Class IV.

Bill Dvořák's Kayak & River Rafting Expeditions (⊠ *17921 U.S. Hwy 285, Nathrop* ☎ *719/539–6851 or 800/824–3795* ⊕ *www.dvorakexpeditions. com*) will take you deep into the San Juan National Forest. This classic paddling experience and white-water rapids run is at its best from mid-April through mid-June. Trips range from 3 to 12 days.

WHERE TO EAT

$ ✕ **Dolores River Brewery.** This brewpub, which gleefully advertises itself AMERICAN   as "Dolores' Oldest Operating Brewery," is also the only one in town. Order an ale and a stout to wash down good pub grub in this fun spot. The usual pizzas, calzones, and sandwiches are matched on the menu with such lighter fare as salmon Caesar or yellowfin tuna salad. ⊠ *100 S. 4th St.* ☎ *970/882–4677* ⊕ *www.doloresriverbrewery.com* ▭ *AE, D, MC, V* ☉ *Closed Mon. No lunch.*

Mesa Verde National Park

WORD OF MOUTH

"Wetherill Mesa, which has some amazing cliff dwellings, is not open until Memorial Day. It isn't that hot here at that time; in fact, it is quite nice. Two nights in Mesa Verde is sufficient, it will give you plenty of time to see all the dwellings, do some hikes, and drive the loop."

—DebitNM

WELCOME TO MESA VERDE

TOP REASONS TO GO

★ **Cliff dwellings:** Built atop the pinyon-covered mesa tops and hidden in the park's valleys is a wondrous collection of 600 ancient dwellings, some carved directly into the sandstone cliff faces.

★ **Ancient artifacts:** Mesa Verde is a time capsule for the Ancestral Puebloan culture that flourished here 700 years ago; more than 4,000 archaeological sites and three million Puebloan objects have been unearthed at Mesa Verde.

★ **Geological marvels:** View the unique geology that drew the Ancestral Puebloan people to the area: protected desert canyons, massive alcoves in the cliff walls, thick bands of sandstone, continuous seep springs, and soils that could be used for both agriculture and architecture.

★ **Bright nights:** Mesa Verde's dearth of pollution makes for cloudless nights that provide a spectacular vision of the heavens punctuated by shooting stars, passing satellites, and—if the conditions are right—eerie lightning flashes from distant thunderheads.

1 **Morefield Campground.** Near the park entrance, this large campground includes a village area with a gas station and grocery store. The park's best-known sites are farther in, but some of the best hiking trails are close by.

2 **Far View Visitor Center.** Almost an hour's drive (but just 18 mi) from Mesa Verde's entrance, Far View is the park's center of gravity, with a visitor center, restaurants, and the park's only overnight lodge. The fork in the road here gives you access to the sites at Wetherill Mesa to the west and Chapin Mesa to the south. You can buy tickets for the popular ranger-led tours here.

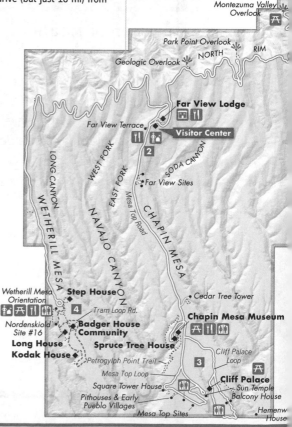

← TO CORTEZ

Montezuma Valley Overlook

Park Point Overlook   RIM

Geologic Overlook   NORTH

Far View Lodge

Far View Terrace

Visitor Center
2

Far View Sites

LONG CANYON

WEST FORK

EAST FORK

Mesa Top Road

SODA CANYON

CHAPIN MESA

NAVAJO CANYON

WETHERILL MESA

Cedar Tree Tower

Wetherill Mesa Orientation

Step House

Tram Loop Rd.
4

Nordenskiold Site #16

Badger House Community

Chapin Mesa Museum

Long House
Kodak House

Spruce Tree House

Petroglyph Point Trail

Cliff Palace Loop

Mesa Top Loop

Square Tower House

Cliff Palace
Sun Temple
Balcony House

Pithouses & Early Pueblo Villages

Mesa Top Sites
3

Hemenway House

Hopi eagle dancers at Spruce Tree House.

COLORADO

GETTING ORIENTED

3 Chapin Mesa. Home to the park's most famous cliff dwellings and archeological sites, Chapin Mesa includes the famous 150-room Cliff House dwelling and other man-made and natural wonders.

4 Wetherill Mesa. It's less visited than Chapin Mesa, but just as rewarding for visitors. Take the park tram and see Long House, Kodak House, and Badger House Community.

Perhaps no other area offers as much evidence into the Ancestral Pueblo's existence as Mesa Verde National Park. Several thousand archaeological sites have been found, and research is ongoing to discover more. The carved-out homes and assorted artifacts, displayed at the park's Chapin Mesa Archeological Museum, belonged to ancestors of today's Hopi, Zuni, and Pueblo tribes, among others. Due to the sensitive nature of these remnants, hiking in the park is restricted to designated trails, and certain cliff dwellings may only be accessed under accompaniment of a ranger during the peak summer season.

Petroglyphs

KEY	
👫	Ranger Station
⛺	Campground
🌲	Picnic Area
🍴	Restaurant
🏨	Lodge
🚶	Trailhead
🚻	Restrooms
☀	Scenic Viewpoint
......	Walking/Hiking Trails
......	Bicycle Path

MESA VERDE PLANNER

When to Go

The best times to visit the park are late May, early June, and most of September, when the weather is fine but the summer crowds have thinned. **Mid-June through August are Mesa Verde's most crowded months.** In July and August, lines at the museum and visitor center may last half an hour. Afternoon thunder showers are common in July and August.

The mesa gets as many as 100 inches of snow in winter. Snow may fall as late as May and as early as October, but there's rarely enough to hamper travel. In winter, the Wetherill Mesa Road and Far View Lodge are closed, but the sight of the sandstone dwellings sheltered from the snow in their cliff coves is spectacular.

AVG. HIGH/LOW TEMPS.

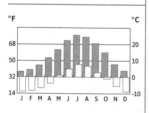

Flora and Fauna

Many areas of the park have extensive fire damage. In fact, wildfires here have been so destructive they are given names, just like hurricanes. The Bircher Fire in 2000 consumed 20,000 acres of brush and forest. It will take several centuries for the woodland to look as verdant as the area atop Chapin Mesa. But in the meantime, you'll have a chance to glimpse nature's powerful rejuvenating processes in action; the landscape is already filling in with vegetation specially adapted to thrive in a post-fire environment.

During warmer months you'll see brightly colored blossoms, like the yellow perky Sue, sage, yucca, and mountain mahogany. Sand-loving blue lupines are seen along the roadways in the higher elevations, and bright-red Indian paintbrushes are scattered throughout the rocky cliffs.

Drive slowly along the park's roads; mule deer are everywhere. You may spot wild horses grazing, and black bear encounters are not unheard of on the hiking trails. About 200 species of birds, including red-tailed hawks, golden eagles, and noisy ravens live here. Keep your eyes and ears open for the poisonous—but shy—prairie rattle snake. Animals are most active in the early morning and at dusk.

Getting Here and Around

The park has just one entrance, off U.S. 160, between Cortez and Durango in what's known as the Four Corners area. Durango, Colorado—35 mi east of the park entrance—has an airport.

Most of the scenic drives at Mesa Verde involve steep grades and hairpin turns, particularly on Wetherill Mesa. Vehicles over 8,000 pounds or 25 feet are prohibited on this road. Towed vehicles are prohibited past Morefield Campground. Check the condition of your vehicle's brakes before driving the road to Wetherill Mesa. For the latest road information, tune to 1610 AM, or call 970/529-4461. Off-road vehicles are prohibited in the park.

At less-visited Wetherill Mesa, you must leave you car behind and hike or ride the tram to Long House, Kodak House, and Badger House Community.

Updated by
Swain Scheps

11

Unlike most national parks of the west, Mesa Verde earned its status from its rich cultural history rather than its geological treasures. President Theodore Roosevelt established it in 1906 as the first national park to "preserve the works of man." The Ancestral Puebloan people, who lived in the region from roughly 600 to 1300, left behind more than 4,000 archaeological sites spread out over 80 square mi. Their ancient dwellings, set high into the sandstone cliffs, are the heart of the park.

Mesa Verde ("Green Table" in Spanish) is much more than an archaeologist's dreamland, however. It's one of those windswept places where man's footprints and nature's paintbrush—some would say chisel—meet. Rising dramatically from the San Juan Basin, the jutting cliffs are cut by a series of complex canyons and covered with green, from pines in the higher elevations down to sage and other mountain brush on the desert floor. From the tops of the smaller mesas, you can look across to the cliff dwellings in the opposite rock faces. Dwarfed by the towering cliffs, the sand-color dwellings look almost like a natural occurrence in the midst of the desert's harsh beauty.

PARK ESSENTIALS

ACCESSIBILITY

Accessibility to most of the archeological sites is limited within Mesa Verde as they require climbing ladders, squeezing through tunnels, and working your way up and down steep paths. Service dogs cannot be taken into Balcony House, Cliff Palace, or Long House because of ladders in those sites. None of these sites is accessible to those with mobility impairments. If you have heart or respiratory ailments, you may have trouble breathing in the thin air at 7,000 to 8,000 feet. Wheelchairs with wide-rim wheels are recommended on trails, some of which do not meet legal grade requirements. Mesa Top Loop Road provides the most comprehensive and accessible view of all the archaeological sites.

ADMISSION FEES AND PERMITS

Admission is $15 per vehicle for a seven-day permit. An annual pass is $30. Ranger-led tours of Cliff Palace, Long House, and Balcony House are $3 per person. Backcountry hiking and fishing are not permitted at Mesa Verde.

ADMISSION HOURS

The facilities open each day at 8 AM and close at sunset from Memorial Day through Labor Day. The rest of the year, the facilities close at 5. Wetherill Mesa, all the major cliff dwellings, and Morefield ranger station are open only from Memorial Day through Labor Day. Far View

Visitor Center, Far View Lodge, and Morefield Campground are open mid-April through mid-October.

ATM/BANKS

There are no ATMs in the park. The nearest bank is in Mancos, just 5 mi east of the park.

CELL-PHONE RECEPTION

Cellular reception in the park varies in quality depending on your location. Morefield Village and the north part of the park get better reception than the south. Public telephones can be found at Morefield Campground and Morefield Village, Far View Visitor Center, Far View Lodge, Far View Terrace, Spruce Tree Terrace, park headquarters (5 mi from the Far View Visitor Center), and the Wetherill Mesa snack bar. Far View Lodge has free Wi-Fi in the lobby.

EMERGENCIES

To report a fire or call for aid, dial 911 or 970/529–4465. First-aid stations are located at Morefield Campground, Far View Visitor Center, and Wetherill Mesa.

SHOPS AND GROCERS

Morefield Campground has a nicely stocked grocery store that is open 7 AM to 9 PM, mid-May to early October. The gift shops at Far View and on Mesa Top Loop Road have a small collection of essentials for sale as well.

PARK CONTACT INFORMATION

Mesa Verde National Park ⌂ Box 8, Mesa Verde, CO 81330 ☎ 970/529–4465 ⊕ www.nps.gov/meve.

SCENIC DRIVES

Mesa Top Road. This 12-mi drive skirts the scenic rim of Chapin Mesa, and splits into two loops—**Mesa Top Loop** and **Cliff Palace Loop**—that reach many of Mesa Verde's most important archaeological sites. Two of the parks' most impressive viewpoints are also on this road: Navajo Canyon Overlook and Sun Point Overlook, from which you can see Cliff Palace, Sunset House, and other dwellings. ☉ *Daily 8 AM–sunset.*

Park Entrance Road. The main park road leads you from the entrance off U.S. 160 to the Far View complex 18 mi away. You can stop at a couple of pretty overlooks along the way as a break from the switchbacks, but hold out for **Park Point,** which, at the mesa's highest elevation (8,572 feet), affords unobstructed 360-degree views.

WHAT TO SEE

HISTORIC SITES

Badger House Community. A self-guided walk takes you through a group of subterranean dwellings, called pit houses, and aboveground storage rooms. The community dates back to 650, the Basket Maker Period, and covers seven acres of land. Most of the pit houses and kivas—religious or ceremonial rooms—were connected by an intricate system

11

MESA VERDE IN ONE DAY

For a full experience, take at least one ranger-led tour of a major cliff dwelling site, as well as a few self-guided walks. Arrive early; it's about a 45-minute drive from the park entrance to your first stop, the **Far View Visitor Center**, where you can purchase tickets for Cliff Palace and Balcony House tours on Chapin Mesa. If it's going to be a hot day, you might want to take an early morning or late-afternoon tour. Drive to the **Chapin Mesa Museum** to watch a 25-minute film introducing you to the area and its history. Just behind the museum, hike the ½-mi-long **Spruce Tree House trail,** which leads to the best preserved cliff dwelling in the

park. Then drive to Balcony House for a ranger-led tour.

Have lunch at the Spruce Tree House cafeteria or the Cliff Palace picnic area. Afterward take the ranger-led tour of **Cliff Palace.** Use the rest of the day to explore the overlooks and trails off the two 6-mi loops of **Mesa Top Loop Road.** Take **Petroglyph Point Trail** to see a great example of Ancestral Puebloan rock carvings. A leisurely walk along the Mesa Top's **Soda Canyon Overlook Trail** gives you a beautiful bird's-eye view of the canyon below. On the drive back to the entrance stop and see the view from **Park Point.**

of tunnels, some up to 41 feet long. Allow about an hour to see all the sites. ⊠ *Wetherill Mesa Rd., 12 mi from the Far View Visitor Center* ⛽ *Free* ⊙ *June–Aug., daily 8–4:30.*

⊙ ★ **Balcony House.** The stonework of this 40-room cliff dwelling, which housed about 40 or 50 people, is impressive, but you're likely to be even more awed by the skill it took to reach this place. Perched in a sandstone cove 600 feet above the floor of Soda Canyon, Balcony House seems almost suspended in space. Even with the aid of modern steps and a partially paved trail, today's visitors must climb two wooden ladders (the first one 32 feet high) to enter. Surrounding the house is a courtyard with a parapet wall and the intact balcony for which the house is named. A favorite with kids, the dwelling is accessible only on a ranger-led tour. Youngsters love climbing the ladders, crawling through the tunnels, and clambering around its nooks and crannies. Purchase your ticket at the Far View Visitor Center. ⊠ *Cliff Palace Loop Rd., 8½ mi southeast of the Far View Visitor Center* ⛽ *$3* ⊙ *Late May–mid-Oct., daily 9–5.*

Fodor'sChoice ★ **Cliff Palace.** This was the first major Mesa Verde dwelling seen by cowboys Charlie Mason and Richard Wetherill in 1888. It is also the largest, containing about 150 rooms and 23 kivas on three levels. Getting there involves a steep downhill hike and four ladders. Purchase tickets at the Far View Visitor Center for the one-hour, ranger-led tour through this dwelling. From June to August, special Sunset Tour ranger-led evenings (⇨ *Ranger-Led Tours, in Educational Offerings*) offers a more in-depth look. ⊠ *Cliff Palace Loop Rd., 7 mi south of the Far View Visitor Center* ⛽ *Basic tour $3, Sunset Tour $10* ⊙ *Mid-May–mid-Oct., daily 9–5.*

Far View Sites Complex. This is believed to have been one of the most densely populated areas in Mesa Verde, comprising as many as 50 villages in a ½-square-mi area at the top of Chapin Mesa. Most of the sites here were built between 900 and 1300. Begin the self-guided tour at the interpretive panels in the parking lot, then proceed down a ½-mi, level trail. The ranger-led Far View Sites Walk takes place daily at 4. ⊠ *Park entrance road, 1½ mi south of the Far View Visitor Center* ⊠ *Free* ⊙ *Mid-May–mid-Oct., daily 8–6:30.*

Long House. Excavated in 1959 through 1961, this Wetherill Mesa cliff dwelling is the second largest in Mesa Verde. It is believed that about 150 people lived in Long

GOOD READS
Mesa Verde National Park: The First 100 Years, by Rose Houk, Faith Marcovecchio, and Duane A. Smith, captures the park as it celebrated its centennial.
Fire on the Mesa, by Tracey Chavis, discusses the wildfires that have been scarring Mesa Verde.
Mesa Verde: Ancient Architecture, by Jesse Walter Fewkes, tells the stories behind the park's dwellings.

House, so named because of the size of its cliff alcove. The spring at the back of the cave is still active today. The ranger-led tour begins a short distance from the parking lot and takes about 45 minutes. ⊠ *Wetherill Mesa Rd., 12 mi from the Far View Visitor Center* ⊠ *Tours $3* ⊙ *June–Aug., daily 10–4.*

☾
★ **Spruce Tree House.** This 114-room complex is the best-preserved site in the park, and the rooms and ceremonial chambers are more accessible to visitors. Here you can actually enter a kiva, via a short ladder, just as the original inhabitants did. It's a great place for kids to explore. Combined with its location in the heart of the most popular sites in the park, Spruce Tree House can resemble a playground during busy periods. Tours are self-guided, but a park ranger is on site to answer questions. The trail leading to Spruce Tree House starts behind the museum and leads you 170 feet down into the canyon. You may find yourself breathing hard by the time you make it back up to the parking lot. ⊠ *Park entrance road, 5 mi south of the Far View Visitor Center* ⊠ *Free* ⊙ *Mar.–Nov., daily 9–5.*

Triple Village Pueblo Sites. Three dwellings built atop each other from 750 to 1150 at first look like a mass of jumbled walls, but an interpretive panel helps identify the dwellings. The 325-foot trail from the walking area is paved and wheelchair accessible. ⊠ *Mesa Top Loop Rd., 8 mi south of the Far View Visitor Center* ⊠ *Free* ⊙ *Daily.*

SCENIC STOPS

Cedar Tree Tower. A self-guided tour takes you to, but not through, a tower and kiva built between 1100 and 1300 and connected by a tunnel. The tower-and-kiva combinations in the park are thought to have been either religious structures or signal towers. ⊠ *Park entrance road, 4 mi south of the Far View Visitor Center.*

Kodak House Overlook. Get an impressive view into Kodak House and its several small kivas from here. The house, closed to the public, was named for a Swedish researcher who absentmindedly left his Kodak camera behind here in 1891. ⊠ *Wetherill Mesa Rd., 12 mi from the Far View Visitor Center* ☉ *June–Aug.*

Soda Canyon Overlook. Get your best view of Balcony House here and read interpretive panels about the dwelling and canyon geology. ⊠ *Mesa Top Loop Rd., 9 mi south of the Far View Visitor Center.*

VISITOR CENTERS

There are two visitor centers at Mesa Verde, though one is called a museum (but in fact, it serves as the official visitor center when the other closes for the season in the middle of October).

★ **Chapin Mesa Archeological Museum.** This is an excellent first stop for park visitors for an introduction to Ancestral Puebloan culture as well as the area's development into a national park. Exhibits showcase original textiles and other artifacts and a theater plays a well-done movie every 30 minutes. Rangers are available to answer your questions and there's also a sign-in sheet for hiking trails. The museum sits at the south end of the park entrance rode and overlooks Spruce Tree House, nearby you'll find park headquarters, a research library, a gift shop, cafeteria, and bathrooms. ⊠ *Park entrance road, 5 mi south of the Far View Visitor Center* ☎ *970/529–4465* ⊠ *Free* ☉ *Apr.–mid-Oct., daily 8–6:30; mid-Oct.–Mar., daily 8–5.*

★ **Far View Visitor Center.** You can't miss the cylindrical brick building on the east side of the road in the Far View complex, but you actually must park across the street and walk through the tunnel under the road to get to the center. ■**TIP→ Stop here first and buy tickets for the Cliff Palace, Balcony House, and Long House ranger-led tours here.** Pick out a less-crowded tour if you want; computer screens show the number of available spaces left for each time. This center also acts as a mini-gift shop, viewing platform, and museum. An extensive selection of books, maps, and videos on the history of the park are available and rangers are on hand to answer questions and explain the history of the Ancestral Puebloans. ⊠ *15 mi south of the park entrance on main park road* ☎ *970/529–5036* ☉ *Mid-Apr.–mid-Oct., daily 8–5.*

SPORTS AND THE OUTDOORS

Outdoor activities are restricted due to the fragile nature of the archeological treasures here. Hiking is the best option, especially as a way to view some of the Ancestral Puebloan dwellings.

BIRD-WATCHING

Turkey vultures soar between April and October, large flocks of ravens hang around all summer, and ducks and waterfowl fly through Mesa Verde from mid-September through mid-October. Among the park's other large birds are red-tailed hawks, great horned owls, and a few golden eagles. The Steller's jay (the male looks like a blue jay with a dark hat on) frequently pierces the pinyon-juniper forest with its cries, and hummingbirds dart from flower to flower. Any visit to cliff dwellings late in the day will include frolicking white-throated swifts who make their home in rock crevices overhead.

HIKING

A handful of trails lead beyond Mesa Verde's most visited sites and offer more solitude than the crowded cliff dwellings. The best canyon vistas can be reached if you're willing to huff and puff your way through elevation changes and switchbacks. Bring more water than you think you'll need, wear sunscreen, and bring rain gear—cloudbursts can come seemingly out of nowhere. Certain trails are seasonal only, so check with a ranger before heading out. No backcountry hiking is permitted in Mesa Verde due to the fragile nature of the ancient dwellings and artifacts.

EASY

Farming Terrace Trail. This 30-minute, ½-mi loop beginning and ending on the spur road to Cedar Tree Tower meanders through a series of check dams the Ancestral Puebloans built in order to create farming terraces. ⊠ *Trailhead: Park entrance road, 4 mi south of the Far View Visitor Center.*

Soda Canyon Overlook Trail. One of the easiest and most rewarding strolls in the park, this little trail travels 1½ mi round-trip through the forest on almost completely level ground. The overlook is an excellent point from which to photograph the cliff dwellings. The trailhead is about ¼ mi past the Balcony House parking area. ⊠ *Trailhead: Cliff Palace Loop Rd., 8½ mi southeast of the Far View Visitor Center.*

MODERATE

Fodor'sChoice
★
Petroglyph Point Trail. Scramble along the narrow side of the canyon wall from Spruce Tree House to reach the largest and best-known petroglyphs in Mesa Verde. Older literature occasionally refers to the destination of this 2.8-mi loop hike as "Pictograph Point" but pictographs are painted onto the rock, petroglyphs are carved into it. If you pose for a photo just right, you can just manage to block out the gigantic DON'T TOUCH sign next to the rock art. The trail's 50¢ self-guide brochure—available at any ranger station—points out three dozen points of interest along the two-hour trail. ⊠ *Trailhead: Park entrance road, 5 mi south of the Far View Visitor Center* ☉ *Mar.–Nov., daily 9–5.*

Spruce Canyon Trail. Petroglyph Point Trail takes you along the side of the canyon, this trail ventures down into the canyon. It's only 2 mi long, but you can go down about 600 feet in elevation. Remember to save your strength; what goes down must come up again. ⊠ *Trailhead: Park entrance road, 5 mi south of the Far View Visitor Center* ☉ *Mar.–Nov., daily 9–5.*

DIFFICULT

Prater Ridge Trail. This 7.8-mi round-trip loop, which starts and finishes at Morefield Campground, is the longest hike you can take inside the park and affords fine views of Morefield Canyon to the south and the San Juan Mountains to the north. ⊠ *Trailhead: Morefield Campground, 4 mi from the park entrance.*

STARGAZING

Since there are no large cities in the Four Corners area, there is very little artificial light to detract from the stars in the night sky. Far View Lodge and Morefield Campground are great for sky-watching.

EDUCATIONAL OFFERINGS

BUS TOURS

ARAMARK Tours. If you want a well-rounded visit to the park's most popular sites, consider a group tour. The park concessionaire provides all-day and half-day guided tours of the Mesa Top Loop Road sites departing in air-conditioned busses from either Morefield Campground or Far View Lodge. Tour guides trade off with park rangers in educating you on history, geology, and excavation process in Mesa Verde. ☎ *970/564–4300 or 800/449–2288 ⊕ www.visitmesaverde.com ✆ $39–$65 ⊙ Mid-Apr.– mid-Oct., daily, tours depart at 8 AM and 1 PM.*

RANGER PROGRAMS

☾ **Evening Ranger Campfire Program.** A park ranger presents a different 45-minute program or slide presentation each night of the week. *⊠ Morefield Campground Amphitheater, 4 mi south of the park entrance ☎ 970/529–4465 ✆ Free ⊙ June–Aug., daily 9 PM–9:45 PM.*

☾ **Junior Ranger Program.** Children ages four through 12 can earn a certificate and badge for successfully completing a two-page questionnaire about the park. *⊠ Far View Visitor Center or Chapin Mesa Museum ☎ 970/529–4465.*

★ **Ranger-Led Tours.** Balcony House, Cliff Palace, and Long House can only be explored on a ranger-led tour; each lasts about an hour. Buy tickets for these at Far View Visitor Center the day of the tour, or at the Morefield Campground Ranger Station the evening before the tour, 5 PM to 8:30 PM. These are active tours; each requires climbing ladders without handrails and squeezing through tight spaces. If you have any concerns, you should ask the ranger ahead of time if the tour is right for you. During the summer, you can take a Sunset Tour of Cliff Palace, where a park ranger takes on the identity of an important figure in the park's history (such as archeologist Dr. J. Walter Fewkes, who led the restoration of many of the cliff dwellings in the 1920s). Anyone interested in a deeper knowledge of the site will love it, but kids may find it boring. Bring water, sunscreen, and bug spray. ☎ *970/529–4465 ✆ Tour $3, Sunset Tour $10 ⊙ Mid-Apr.–mid-Oct.*

Cliff Palace/Sun Temple Talks. Interpretive talks on park-related subjects are held twice daily at Cliff Palace Overlook near the Sun Temple parking area. Tours run about 30 minutes. *⊠ Cliff Palace Overlook, Mesa Top Loop Rd. ☎ 970/529–4465 ✆ Free ⊙ June–Aug., daily at 10 and 4.*

NEARBY TOWNS

A onetime market center for sheep and cattle ranchers 30 mi from the park, **Cortez** is now the largest gateway town to Mesa Verde and a base for tourists visiting the Four Corners region of Colorado. You can still see a rodeo and cattle drive here at least once a year. **Dolores,** steeped in a rich railroad history, is set on the Dolores River, 20 mi north of Mesa Verde. Neighboring both the San Juan National Forest and McPhee Reservoir, the second-largest lake in the state, Dolores is a favorite of outdoor enthusiasts. East of Mesa Verde by 36 mi, **Durango,** the region's main hub, comes complete with chain restaurants and hotels, shopping,

FESTIVALS AND EVENTS

JUNE

Mountain Ute Bear Dance. This traditional dance, held on the Tawaoc Ute reservation south of Cortez in June, celebrates spring and the legacy of the bear who taught the Ute people its secrets. ☎ *970/565-3751* ⊕ *www.utemountainute.com.*

JULY

Durango Fiesta Days. A parade, rodeo, barbecue, street dance, and pie auction come to the La Plata County Fair Grounds in Durango on the last weekend of the month. ☎ *970/247-8835* ⊕ *www.durangofiestadays.com.*

OCTOBER

Durango Cowboy Poetry Gathering. A parade and dance accompany art exhibitions, poetry readings, and storytelling to celebrate the traditions of the American West the first weekend in October. ☎ *970/749-2995 or 800/525-8855* ⊕ *www.durangocowboygathering.org.*

and outdoor equipment rental. Durango became a town in 1881 when the Denver and Rio Grande Railroad pushed its tracks across the neighboring San Juan Mountains.

WHERE TO EAT AND STAY

ABOUT THE RESTAURANTS

Dining options in Mesa Verde are limited inside the park, but comparatively plentiful and varied if you're staying in a nearby town. In surrounding communities, southwestern restaurants and steak houses are favored.

WHAT IT COSTS					
	¢	$	$$	$$$	$$$$
Restaurants	under $8	$8–$12	$13–$20	$21–$30	over $30
Hotels	under $70	$70–$100	$101–$150	$151–$200	over $200
Camping	under $10	$10–$17	$18–$35	$36–$50	over $50

Restaurant prices are per person for a main course at dinner. Hotel prices are per night for two people in a standard double room in high season, excluding taxes and services charges. Camping prices are for a standard (no hookups, pit toilets, fire grates, picnic tables) campsite per night.

ABOUT THE HOTELS

All 150 rooms of the park's Far View Lodge, open April through October, have private balconies and fill up quickly—so reservations are recommended, especially if you plan to visit on a weekend in the summer. Options in the surrounding area range from chain hotels to bed-and-breakfast inns. Durango in particular has a number of hotels in fine old buildings reminiscent of the Old West.

ABOUT THE CAMPGROUNDS

Morefield Campground is the only option within the park and is an excellent one. Reservations are accepted; it's open April through October. Nearby, Mancos has a campground with full amenities, while the San Juan National Forest offers backcountry camping.

WHERE TO EAT

¢–$ ✕**Far View Terrace.** This full-service cafeteria offers great views, plentiful choices, and reasonable prices. A coffee counter provides the requisite caffeine for the day's activities, and they'll cook your omelet and pancakes to order as you watch. Dinner options might include a Navajo taco piled high with all the fixings. Don't miss the creamy malts and homemade fudge. ⊠ *Mesa Top Loop Rd., across from the Far View Visitor Center* ☎ *970/529–4444* ▭ *D, MC, V* ☾ *Closed late Oct.–early Apr.*

¢ ✕**Knife's Edge Cafe.** An all-you-can-eat pancake breakfast is served every morning from 7:30 to 10, and at night there's an all-you-can-eat barbecue dinner from 5 to 8. ⊠ *4 mi south of the park entrance* ☎ *970/565– 2133* ▭ *AE, D, MC, V* ☾ *Closed Sept.–May. No lunch.*

$$–$$$ ✕**Metate Room.** The rugged high-desert terrain contrasts with this relaxing
★ space just off the lobby of the Far View Lodge. Tables in this southwestern-style dining room are candlelit and cloth covered, but the atmosphere remains casual. A wall of windows affords wonderful Mesa Verde vistas. Entrées include American staples like steak and seafood, or you can try one of the dishes centered on regional game such as elk, bison, quail, venison, and rabbit. Every table gets mesa bread and black bean hummus for starters. There's a solid array of wines and cocktails with kitschy names, like the "mesa-tini." ⊠ *Far View Lodge, across from the Far View Visitor Center, 15 mi southwest of park entrance* ☎ *970/529–4421* ▭ *AE, D, DC, MC, V* ☾ *Closed late Oct.–early Apr. No lunch.*

¢–$ ✕**Spruce Tree Terrace.** A limited selection of hot food and sandwiches is all you'll find at this cafeteria, but the patio is pleasant, and it's conveniently across the street from the museum. The Terrace is also the only food concession open year-round for lunch. ⊠ *Park entrance road, 5 mi south of the Far View Visitor Center* ☎ *970/529–4521* ▭ *AE, D, DC, MC, V* ☾ *No dinner Dec.–Feb.*

PICNIC AREAS **Park Headquarters Loop Picnic Area.** This is the nicest and largest picnic
☺ area in the park. It has 40 tables under shade trees and a great view into Spruce Canyon, as well as flush toilets and running water. ⊠ *6 mi south of the Far View Visitor Center.*

Wetherill Mesa Picnic Area. Ten tables placed under lush shade trees, along with drinking water and restrooms, make this a pleasant spot for lunch. ⊠ *12 mi southwest of the Far View Visitor Center.*

WHERE TO STAY

$ ▦**Far View Lodge.** Talk about a view—all rooms have a private bal-
★ cony, from which you can admire the neighboring states of Arizona, Utah, and New Mexico up to 100 mi in the distance. The spartan-meets-southwestern rooms don't have a lot of space to spare but the only other in-park lodging option is camping. Upgrade to a kiva room for a little

more space and a few more amenities (including air-conditioning). The staff is friendly and you can take in nightly talks by guest speakers on various park topics in the lobby. The hotel also offers enthusiastic guided tours of the park. The Metate Room (⇨ *Where to Eat*), the lodge's main dining room, is acclaimed for its fine steaks and excellent southwestern fare. Above it is a cocktail lounge that offers late night appetizers. **Pros:** close to the key sites; views are spectacular; nights are quiet and mystical; no television! **Cons:** no television?; simple rooms and amenities; walls are thin and less than soundproof. ⊠ *Across from the Far View Visitor Center, 15 mi southwest of park entrance* ✆ *Box 277, Mancos 81328* ☎ *970/564–4300 or 800/449–2288* ⊕ *www.visitmesaverde.com* ⌁ *150 rooms* ⚄ *In-room: no a/c (some), refrigerator (some). In-hotel: restaurant, bar, laundry facilities, Wi-Fi, some pets allowed* ▤ *AE, D, DC, MC, V* ⊘ *Closed Nov.–Mar.*

CAMPING

$$

Fodor's Choice

★

⚠ **Morefield Campground.** With more than 400 shaded campsites, access to trailheads, and plenty of amenities, the only campground in the park is an appealing mini-city for campers. It's a 40-minute drive to reach the park's most popular sites. Reservations are accepted only for tent and group sites. **Pros:** the village has a gas station and store; inside park boundaries. **Cons:** still far from key sites at the north end of the park. ⊠ *4 mi south of park entrance, Box 8, Mesa Verde* ☎ *970/564–4300 or 800/449–2288* ⊕ *www.visitmesaverde.com* ⌁ *365 tent/RV sites, 15 RV sites* ⚄ *Flush toilets, partial hookups (some), dump station, drinking water, guest laundry, showers, fire grates, grills, picnic tables, food service, electricity, public telephone, general store, ranger station, service station* ▤ *AE, D, DC, MC, V* ⊘ *Late Apr.–mid-Oct.*

South Central Colorado

COLORADO SPRINGS, ROYAL GORGE,
AND GREAT SAND DUNES

WORD OF MOUTH

"Pikes Peak is an astonishing life changing sight! You see, Denver, all the little cities, all the way into the Kansas, Nebraska, and New Mexico states. The highways look like webs drawn on a big glowing ball. If any one has ever thought that the Earth was flat, has never been to Pike's Peak. Denver is one mile above sea level, but Colorado Springs is far higher than that, and by the time you go up to the Peak, whew, 14,115 ft above sea level. The curve of the Earth is quite evident and dizzying!"
—BROADMOORBABY

Updated by
Lois Friedland

Stretching from majestic mountains into rugged high desert plains, south central Colorado has lots of 14,000-foot peaks, striking red-rock outcroppings, rivers that boil with white-water rapids in spring, and even the incongruous sight of towering sand dunes dwarfed by a mountain range at their back. It's worth a few days for white-water rafting, hiking in the backcountry, and exploring historic gold-mining towns. Colorado Springs is bustling, but other parts of the area have a barely discovered feel. If it's peace and quiet you're after, staying put in a cabin in the woods can make for an utterly relaxed week.

South central Colorado was first explored by the United States in 1806, three years after it made the Louisiana Purchase. Zebulon Pike took up the assignment of scout, but he never did climb the peak that is now named for him. Weaving through the southeastern section of the state are the haunting remains of the Santa Fe Trail, which guided pioneers westward beginning in the 1820s.

Framed by Pikes Peak, Colorado Springs is the region's population center and a hub for the military and the high-tech industry. The city has been a destination for out-of-towners since its founding in 1870, due to the alleged healing power of the local springwater and clean air. The gold rush fueled the city's boom through the early 20th century, as the military boom did following World War II. With more than 550,000 residents in the metro area, Colorado Springs offers a mix of history and modernity, as well as incredible access to the trails and red-rock scenery in this section of the Rockies.

Surrounding Colorado Springs is a ring of smaller cities and alluring natural attractions. To the west, between alpine and desert scenery, are the Florissant Fossil Beds, the Royal Gorge, and Cripple Creek, which offers gambling in casinos housed in historic buildings. You can go rafting near Cañon City, while Pueblo has a dash of public art and history museums. Outdoorsy types love the entire area: camping and hiking are especially superb in the San Isabel and Pike national forests. Climbers head to the Collegiate Peaks around Buena Vista and Salida (west of Colorado Springs) and the Cañon City area for a variety of ascents from moderate to difficult. Farther south, you can take the Highway of Legends Scenic Byway, which travels through the San Isabel National Forest and over high mountain passes. You can even take a day trip on the Rio Grande Scenic Railroad or the Cumbres & Toltec Scenic Railroad, which travels through a region not reachable by car.

12

TOP REASONS TO GO

Ride Up Pikes Peak: Katharine Bates wrote "America the Beautiful" after riding to the top of Pikes Peak. Today you can drive or ride the cog railway to the top for the same see-forever views.

Raft on the Arkansas: The Arkansas River is one of the most popular rivers for rafting and kayaking—from gentle floats to Class V rapids—in the United States.

Visit the U.S. Air Force Academy: Here you can learn more about the academy that trains future Air Force leaders and visit the stunning, non-denominational Cadet Chapel.

Hike a Fourteener: Coloradans collect hikes to the summit of Fourteeners—mountains that top 14,000 feet above sea level—like trophies.

Play on the Sand Dunes: At Great Sand Dunes, one of nature's most spectacular sandboxes, you'll feel like a kid again as you hike up a 750-foot dune then roll down the other side.

ORIENTATION AND PLANNNING

GETTING ORIENTED

This region, which encompasses the south-central section of Colorado, stretches from a collection of the state's 14,000-foot-high mountains in the heart of the Rockies eastward to Kansas, and from Colorado Springs south to the New Mexico state line. Pikes Peak, one of the most famous of Colorado's Fourteeners, forms the backdrop for Colorado Springs. Farther west, the Arkansas River towns of Buena Vista and Salida are within view of the Fourteeners of the Collegiate Peaks. Farther south, the Rio Grande runs through the flat San Luis Valley, which is lined by the Sangre de Cristo range. Cuchara Valley, just north of New Mexico, is framed by the Spanish Peaks.

Colorado Springs. About 70 mi south of Denver, Colorado Springs is a comfortable base camp for travelers headed for high altitude and high adventure. Colorado's second-largest city has natural attractions like Pike's Peak and Garden of the Gods, and more recent additions like the Broadmoor and the U.S. Air Force Academy.

Colorado Springs Side Trips. You could gamble or visit a gold mine and learn more about the gold rush in Cripple Creek. If you prefer outdoor adventures, take a walk among petrified tree trunks in Florissant Fossil Beds or go river rafting near Cañon City.

Collegiate Peaks. Buena Vista and Salida provide easy access to the largest collection of 14,000-foot-or-higher peaks in Colorado, perfect for hiking, boating, river rafting, horseback riding, and mountain biking in wilderness areas.

Southeast Colorado. If you're looking for a mountain drive with spectacular and diverse scenery, take the Highway of Legends Scenic Byway. Tiny towns along the way are in Cuchara Valley; Pueblo and Trinidad are larger hubs.

The San Luis Valley. You can play like a child rolling around the dunes at the Great Sand Dunes National Park and Preserve. Leave time for a drive through the tiny nearby towns or a ride on one of the two scenic railroads.

PLANNING

WHEN TO GO

Colorado Springs is a good year-round choice, because winters are relatively mild. Late spring or early summer is best if you want adrenaline-rush rafting, because the snowmelt is feeding the rivers. Summer is tourist season everywhere in south central Colorado. Early fall is another good time to visit, especially when the aspen leaves are turning gold. Some of the lodging properties in the smaller towns are closed in winter, although there are always some open for the cross-country skiers who enjoy staying in the small high-mountain towns.

GETTING HERE AND AROUND

AIR TRAVEL

Colorado Springs Airport (COS) is the major airport in the region, with a dozen nonstop destinations. Most south-central residents south of Colorado Springs drive to this city to fly out.

Alternatively, you can choose to fly to Denver International Airport (DEN), which has a lot more nonstop flights from other major cities to Colorado. It's a 70-mi drive from Denver to the Springs, but during rush hour it might take a solid two hours, whether you're in your own car or in one of the Denver–Colorado Springs shuttles. If you take the E–470 toll road for part of the drive, the ride will be faster.

Airports Colorado Springs Airport (COS) (☎ 719/550–1972 ⊕ www.flycos.com). **Denver International Airport (DEN)** (☎ 303/342–2000 ⊕ www.flydenver.com). **Pueblo Memorial Airport (PUB)** (☎ 719/553–2760 ⊕ www.pueblo.us/airport).

CAR TRAVEL

In Colorado Springs (whose airport has the typical lineup of car-rental agencies), the main north–south roads are Interstate 25, Academy Boulevard, Nevada Avenue, and Powers Boulevard, and each will get you where you want to go in good time; east–west routes along Woodmen Road (far north), Austin Bluffs Parkway (north central), and Platte Boulevard (south central) can get backed up.

Running north–south from Wyoming to New Mexico, Interstate 25 bisects Colorado and is the major artery into the area. Colorado Springs and Pueblo (which also has a pair of car-rental counters at the airport) are on Interstate 25. Florissant and Buena Vista are reached via U.S. 24 off Interstate 25; Cañon City and the Royal Gorge via U.S. 50. Salida can be reached via Highway 291 from either U.S. 24 or U.S. 50. Palmer Lake and Larkspur are accessible via Interstate 25 and Highway 105. Aside from Colorado Springs and Pueblo, most cities in south central Colorado lack car-rental service.

Car Contacts AAA Colorado (☎ 719/591–2222 for information or emergency road service). **Colorado Department of Transportation Road Condition**

Hotline (☎ *303/639–1111*). **Colorado State Patrol** (☎ *719/635–0385* ⊕ *www.cotrip.org*).

TRAIN TRAVEL

Amtrak's Southwest Chief stops daily in Trinidad and La Junta.

Train Contacts Amtrak (☎ *800/872–7245* ⊕ *www.amtrak.com*).

12

PARKS AND RECREATION AREAS

South central Colorado is chock-full of parks and recreational areas. Almost every chamber of commerce will have a list of trails in the near vicinity, so when you're asking for general information about the city, ask for a list of trails, too. The Arkansas River flows through this region, so every spring and summer people come here to raft through a mix of challenging white-water rapids interspersed with smoothly flowing sections. Pike, bass, and trout are plentiful in this region: popular fishing spots include Spinney Mountain Reservoir (between Florissant and Buena Vista), the Arkansas and South Platte rivers, and Trinidad Lake. Great Sand Dunes National Park and Preserve in the San Luis Valley is perfect for walking up (and sliding down) the dunes, hiking on mountain trails, kite flying, and wildlife viewing. Monarch, west of Salida, is the nearest ski area.

Arkansas Headwaters Recreation Area (✉ *Arkansas Headwaters Recreation Area, 307 W. Sackett Ave., Salida* ☎ *719/539–7289*) is unique because it follows a linear 150-mi stretch of the Arkansas River, from the mountains near Leadville to Lake Pueblo. The Arkansas River is popular for rafting and kayaking, and fisherman love it for its brown trout. There are six campgrounds along the river. The **Collegiate Peaks Wilderness Area** (✉ *Leadville Ranger District, San Isabel National Forest, 810 Front St., Leadville* ☎ *719/486–0749*), northwest of Buena Vista, includes 14 mountains above 14,000 feet and is known for superb hiking, mountain biking, and climbing. **Pike National Forest** (✉ *Forest Service Office, 601 S. Weber, Colorado Springs* ☎ *719/636–1602*) encompasses millions of acres of public land that stretch along the Front Range and go deep into the Rockies. Pikes Peak is the best-known 14,000-footer in Pike. **Ring of the Peak** (⊕ *www.ringthepeak.com*) is a collection of trails, four-wheel-drive roads, and a few roads that circle Pikes Peak. Altitudes range between 6,400 and 11,400 feet. Check the Web site for trail access.

RESTAURANTS

Many restaurants serve regional trout and game, as well as locally grown fruits and vegetables. In summer, look for cantaloupe from the town of Rocky Ford, dubbed the "Melon Capital of the World." Colorado Springs offers unique Colorado cuisine that zings taste buds without zapping budgets (plus the ubiquitous chain restaurants).

HOTELS

The lodging star is the Broadmoor resort in Colorado Springs, built from the booty of the late-19th-century gold-rush days, but there are also predictable boxy-bed motel rooms awaiting travelers at the junctions of major highways throughout the region. Interspersed are quaint mom-and-pop motels, as well as bed-and-breakfasts and small luxury hotels in tourist districts.

WHAT IT COSTS				
¢	$	$$	$$$	$$$$
Restaurants	under $8	$8–$12	$13–$18	$19–$25	over $25
Hotels	under $80	$80–$120	$121–$170	$171–$230	over $230

Restaurant prices are for a main course at dinner, excluding 7.4% tax. Hotel prices are for two people in a standard double room in high season, excluding service charges and 9.4%–11.7% tax.

COLORADO SPRINGS

The contented residents of the Colorado Springs area believe they live in an ideal location, and it's hard to argue with them. To the west the Rockies form a majestic backdrop. To the east the plains stretch for miles. Taken together, the setting ensures a mild, sunny climate year-round, and makes skiing and golfing on the same day feasible with no more than a two- or three-hour drive. You don't have to choose between adventures here: you can climb the Collegiate Peaks one day and go white-water rafting on the Arkansas River the next.

The state's second-largest city, it is known as a politically and socially conservative bastion, and the reputation is somewhat deserved (the evangelical group Focus on the Family has its headquarters here). The cultural scene is strong here, too, between the outstanding Colorado Springs Fine Arts Center, the Colorado Springs Philharmonic, and the variety of plays and musicals offered at several theaters.

The region abounds in natural and man-made wonders, from the red sandstone monoliths of the Garden of the Gods to the space-age architecture of the U.S. Air Force Academy's Cadet Chapel. The most indelible landmark is unquestionably Pikes Peak (14,115 feet); after seeing the view from the peak, Katharine Lee Bates penned "America the Beautiful." Pikes Peak is a constant reminder that this very contemporary city is still close to nature. Purple in the early morning, snow-packed after winter storms, capped with clouds on windy days, the mountain is a landmark for directions and, when needed, a focus of contemplation.

GETTING HERE AND AROUND

It's easiest to explore this region in a private car, because the attractions are spread out. If you're staying in the heart of town and don't intend to head out to Pikes Peak, the Air Force Academy or other attractions farther away, you could use the Mountain Metropolitan Transit bus system or grab a taxi. Gray Line offers tours of the Colorado Springs area, including Pikes Peak and Manitou Springs.

ESSENTIALS

Transportation Contacts City Cab (☎ 719/543–2525). **Colorado Springs Shuttle** (☎ 719/687–3456). **Mountain Metropolitan Transit** (☎ 719/385–7433). **Yellow Cab** (☎ 719/634–5000).

Tour Contacts Gray Line (☎ 719/633–1181 ⊕ grayline.com).

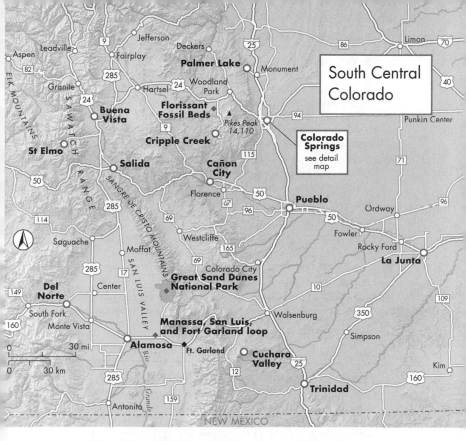

Visitor Info Colorado Springs Convention and Visitors Bureau
(✉ 515 S. Cascade Ave. ☎ 719/635–7506 or 800/888–4748 ⊕ www.
experiencecoloradosprings.com). **Colorado Springs Parks, Recreation and
Cultural Services Department** (☎ 719/385–5940). **Manitou Springs Chamber of Commerce** (✉ 354 Manitou Ave. ☎ 719/685–5089 or 800/642–2567
⊕ www.manitousprings.org). **Tri-Lakes Chamber of Commerce (Palmer Lake)**
(✉ 300 Hwy. 105, Monument ☎ 719/481-3282 ⊕ www.trilakes.net).

EXPLORING COLORADO SPRINGS

Pikes Peak is a must-do and pairs nicely with an afternoon of poking
around in the shops of Manitou Springs. The red rocks of Garden of the
Gods and Cheyenne Cañon Park are the other natural showstoppers—
mix and match them with exploring the surrounding neighborhoods
and tourist attractions. And don't forget the U.S. Air Force Academy,
just north of town.

*Numbers in the margin correspond to numbers on the Colorado Springs
Vicinity map.*

PIKES PEAK AND MANITOU SPRINGS

Access points for scaling the mighty Pikes Peak are in the Manitou Springs area, a quaint National Historic Landmark District that exudes an informal charm. Stop at the chamber for a free map of the 11 mineral-springs drinking fountains and historic sites. On your self-guided tour, stop by Soda Springs or Twin Springs during the day, or for an after-dinner spritz (it tastes and acts just like Alka-Seltzer).

TIMING   It takes a full day to visit Pikes Peak, explore Manitou Springs, and visit some of the attractions along Highway 24, if you want to enjoy each without doing a marathon sprint. Whether you head up Pikes Peak in a car and stop for lunch at the top or take the train (which includes a stop at the summit), plan at least four hours. Visiting the variety of shops, which sell souvenirs to antiques, along historic Manitou Springs' main street is a good way to stretch your legs after the journey to the peak. Heading underground into Cave of the Winds or visiting the Cliff Dwellings Museum will easily fill up the rest of the day.

TOP ATTRACTIONS

Pikes Peak. If you want to see the view from the top of Pikes Peak, the view that Katharine Bates described in "America the Beautiful," head up this 14,115-foot-high mountain on a train, in a car, or in a pair of hiking boots if you've got the stamina. Summit House is a casual café and trading post at the very top of the mountain. Whichever route you choose to take up the prominent peak, you'll understand why the pioneers heading West via wagon train used to say: "Pikes Peak or Bust."

Fodor's Choice
★

You can drive the 19-mi **Pikes Peak Highway** (⟐ *$10; $35 maximum per carload)*, which rises nearly 7,000 feet in its precipitous, dizzying climb; stop at the top for lunch and to enjoy the view; then be at the base again in approximately three hours. This is the same route that leading race-car drivers follow every year in the famed Pikes Peak Hill Climb, at speeds that have reached 123 mi per hour. The 12.6-mi hike up **Barr Trail** gains 7,510 feet in elevation before you reach the summit. Halfway up the steep trail is Barr Camp, where many hikers spend the night. ⊠ *U.S. 24 west to Cascade, 5 mi from Manitou Springs* ☎ *719/684–9383* ☉ *Summit House June–Aug., daily 7:30–7:20; Nov.–Apr., daily 9–3:30, weather permitting.*

❶ **Pikes Peak Cog Railway.** The world's highest cog railway departs from Manitou and follows a frolicking stream up a steep canyon, through stands of quaking aspen and towering lodgepole pines, before reaching the timberline, where you can see far into the plains until arriving at the 14,115-foot summit. Advance reservations are recommended in summer and on weekends. ⊠ *Depot, 515 Ruxton Ave.* ☎ *719/685–5401* ⊕ *www.cograilway.com* ⊰ *Reservations essential* ⟐ *$33.50* ☉ *Open year-round; check Web site or call for schedule.*

WORTH NOTING

❷ **Cave of the Winds.** Discovered by two boys in 1880, the cave has been exploited as a tourist sensation ever since. The entrance is through the requisite "trading post," but once inside the cave you'll forget the hype and commercialism. The cave contains examples of every major sort of limestone formation, from stalactites and stalagmites to delicate cave flowers, rare anthracite crystals, flowstone (rather like candle wax), and cave coral. Enthusiastic guides for the 45-minute tour also run more adventurous cave expeditions. A special lantern tour lasts 1½ hours. ☒ *100 Cave of the Winds Rd. off Hwy. 24,* ☎ *719/685–5444* ⊕ *www. caveofthewinds.com* ☒ *Discovery Tour $18, Lantern Tour $22* ⊙ *June– Aug., daily 9–9; Sept.–May, daily 10–5.*

❺ Manitou Cliff Dwellings Museum. Some Ancestral Puebloan cliff dwellings that date from the 1100s have been moved from other sites in southern Colorado to the museum. Two rooms of artifacts in the museum offer information on the history of the dwellings. Native American dance demonstrations take place several times a day in summer. ☒ *U.S. 24,* ☎ *719/685–5242 or 800/359–9971* ⊕ *www.cliffdwellingsmuseum.com* ☒ *$9.50* ⊙ *May–Sept., daily 9–6; Oct. and Nov., Mar. and Apr., daily 9–5; Dec.–Feb. 1, daily 9–4.*

❹ Manitou Springs. The town grew around the springs, so all 11 of them are in or near downtown. Competitions to design the fountains that bring the spring water to the public ensured that each fountain design is unique. It's a bring-your-own-cup affair; the water (frequently tested) is potable and free. The chamber of commerce publishes a free guide to the springs. ☎ *719/685–5089* ☒ *Free.*

❸ Miramont Castle Museum. Commissioned in 1895 as the private home of French priest Jean-Baptiste Francolon, the museum is still decorated, in part, as if a family lived here. More than 40 rooms offer a wide variety of displays and furnishings primarily from the Victorian era. Have lunch or high tea in the Queens Parlour Tea Room. ☒ *9 Capitol Hill Ave.* ☎ *719/685–1011* ⊕ *www.miramontcastle.org* ☒ *$6* ⊙ *June–Aug. Daily. 9–5; Sept.–May, Tues.–Sat. 10–4, Sun. noon–4*

THE BROADMOOR AND CHEYENNE CAÑON

Up in the Cheyenne Cañon section of town there are some terrific natural sites. Along the way you can view some of the city's exclusive neighborhoods and stop for lunch at the Broadmoor.

TIMING This is a good drive if there are kids in your group, because you can include stops at the Cheyenne Mountain Zoo and the Will Rogers Shrine of the Sun. Young ones can also blow off any extra energy racing up and down the paths at Seven Falls. Depending upon where you decide to stop, this could take a half to a full day.

TOP ATTRACTIONS

❻ The Broadmoor. This pink-stucco Italianate complex, which was built in
1918, is truly one of the world's great luxury resorts. Even if you don't
★ stay here, stop by for lunch on one of the restaurant patios in summer and to take a paddleboat ride on Lake Cheyenne, which anchors several of the resort's buildings. ☒ *1 Lake Circle* ☎ *719/634–7711 or 800/634–7711* ⊕ *www.broadmoor.com.*

❼ Cheyenne Mountain Zoo. America's highest zoo, at 6,800 feet, has more
 than 500 animals housed amid mossy boulders and ponderosa pines.
★ You can hand-feed the giraffe herd in the zoo's African Rift Valley and check out the animals living in Primate World, Wolves Alley, or the Asian Highlands. ☒ *4250 Cheyenne Mountain Zoo Rd.* ☎ *719/633–*

9925 ⊕ *www.cmzoo.org* ✉ *$14.25, includes admission to Will Rogers Shrine ⊙ June–Aug., daily 9–6; Sept.–May, daily 9–5. Gate closes at 4.*

⑩ **North Cheyenne Cañon Park.** This is Colorado Springs at its best. Nearby
Ⓒ Seven Falls has the hand of man all over its natural wonders, but the 1,600 acres of this city park, which is open year-round, manifest nature and natural history without a hint of commercialism—or charge. Start at **Starsmore Discovery Center** (⊙ *Apr.–Oct., daily. Call for hrs, which vary by season*) at the mouth of the canyon off Cheyenne Boulevard. The center is chock-full of nature exhibits and has a climbing wall where kids can try their hands and feet against gravity. The canyon's moderate hikes include the Lower Columbine and Mount Cutler trails, each less than a 3-mi round-trip. Both afford a view of the city and a sense of accomplishment. ✉ *2120 S. Cheyenne Cañon Rd.* ☎ *719/385–6086* ⊕ *www.springsgov.com* ✉ *Free ⊙ June–Aug., daily 9–5; Sept.–Oct. and Apr.–May, Wed.–Sun. 9–5.*

⑨ **Seven Falls.** The road up to this transcendent series of cascades is touted
★ as the "grandest mile of scenery in Colorado." That's an exaggeration, but the red-rock canyon *is* stunning—though no more so than the falls themselves, which plummet into a tiny emerald pool. A set of 224 steep steps leads to the top, but there's an elevator, too. Hours vary seasonally, so it may be wise to call ahead. ✉ *2850 Cheyenne Cañon Rd.* ☎ *719/632–0765* ⊕ *www.sevenfalls.com* ✉ *$9 before 5 PM; $10.50 after 5 PM ⊙ May–Sept., daily 8:30 AM–10:30 PM; Oct.–Apr., daily 9–4.*

WORTH NOTING

⑧ **Will Rogers Shrine of the Sun.** This five-story tower was dedicated in 1937, after the tragic plane crash that claimed Rogers's life. Its interior is painted with all manner of Western murals in which Rogers and Colorado Springs benefactor Spencer Penrose figure prominently, and is plastered with photos and homespun sayings of America's favorite cowboy. In the chapel are 15th- and 16th-century European artworks. ✉ *4250 Cheyenne Mountain Zoo Rd.* ☎ *719/578–5367* ✉ *$14.25, includes admission to Cheyenne Mountain Zoo ⊙ June–Aug., daily 9–5; Sept.–May, daily 9–5. Last entrance one hour before closing.*

GARDEN OF THE GODS AND URBAN COLORADO SPRINGS

This tour combines a chance to see some outstanding artworks, visit some unique museums, and stroll through one of the most beautiful city parks in the country.

TIMING Depending on which museums you decide to visit, a tour of Garden of the Gods and urban Colorado Springs could take from two-thirds of a day to a full day to take everything in, from learning how the pioneers struggled to survive and thrive to strolling through the stunning red-rock cliffs and visiting the Trading Post at Garden of the Gods.

QUICK BITES **Chef Ben Hofer's Café 36** (✉ *30 W. Dale St.* ☎ *719/477–4377* ⊕ *www. csfineartscenter.org ⊙ Lunch Tues.–Sun. Dinner Thurs.–Sat.*) is simply decorated and sited in the Colorado Springs Fine Arts Center, in such a way that diners have a spectacular view of greenery and trees and the mountains beyond. Lunch choices range from pan-seared pineapple halibut to house-made crispy falafel. The museum's Art Deco Lounge, with its tapas menu, is a popular gathering place. Live jazz on Fridays.

TOP ATTRACTIONS

⑬ **Colorado Springs Fine Arts Center.** This regional museum has a fine permanent collection of modern art and excellent rotating exhibits. Some highlight the cultural contributions of regional artists; others focus on famous artists such as the glassmaker Dale Chihuly. Enjoy the view of Pikes Peak and the mountains from the patio in the summer. ⊠ *30 W. Dale St.* ☎ *719/634–5581* ⊕ *www.csfineartscenter.org* ✉ *$7.50* ⊘ *Tues.–Sun. 10–5.*

⑰ **Garden of the Gods.** These magnificent, eroded red-sandstone formations—from gnarled jutting spires to sensuously abstract monoliths—were sculpted more than 300 million years ago. Follow the road as it loops past such oddities as the Three Graces, the Siamese Twins, and the Kissing Camels. High Point, near the south entrance, provides camera hounds with the ultimate photo op: a formation known as Balanced Rock and jagged formations that frame Pikes Peak. The visitor center has maps of the trails and several geological, historical, and hands-on displays, as well as a café. ⊠ *Visitor and Nature Center, 1805 N. 30th St., at Gateway Rd.* ☎ *719/634–6666* ⊕ *www.gardenofgods.com* ✉ *Free* ⊘ *May–Oct., daily 5 AM–11 PM; Nov.–May, daily 5 AM–9 PM.*

Fodor's Choice
★

⑫ **Pioneers Museum.** Once the Old El Paso County Courthouse, this repository has artifacts relating to the entire Pikes Peak area. The historic courtroom is absolutely elegant, and so perfectly appointed that it looks as if a judge will walk in any minute to start a trial. It's most notable for the special exhibits the museum puts together or receives on loan from institutions like the Smithsonian, such as the quilt competition that commemorated the 100th anniversary of the song "America the Beautiful." ⊠ *215 S. Tejon St.* ☎ *719/385–5990* ⊕ *www.cspm.org* ✉ *Free* ⊘ *June–Aug., Tues.–Sat. 10–4; call for Sept.–May hrs.*

⑳ **U.S. Air Force Academy.** The academy, which set up camp in 1954, is one of the most popular attractions in Colorado. Highlights include the futuristic design, 18,000 beautiful acres of land, and antique and historic aircraft displays. At the visitor center you'll find photo exhibits, a model of a cadet's room, a gift shop, a snack bar, and a 14-minute film designed to make you want to enlist on the spot. Other stops on the tour include a B-52 display, sports facilities, a parade ground, and the chapel. ■ **TIP→ The impressive cadet lunch formation usually takes place on Monday, Wednesday, and Friday at noon;** at other times of day, watch the freshmen square off their corners. The Air Force chapel, which can accommodate simultaneous Catholic, Jewish, and Protestant services, is easily recognized by its unconventional design, which features 17 spires that resemble sharks' teeth or billowing sails. ⊠ *Visitors can enter through North Gate, from Exit 156B off I–25, or South Gate, from Exit 150 off I–25* ☎ *719/333–2025* ⊕ *www.usafa.af.mil/* ✉ *Free* ⊘ *Daily 9–5.*

Fodor's Choice
★

⑪ **U.S. Olympic Training Center.** America's hopefuls come to train and be tested here, and depending on which teams are in residence at the time, you might catch a glimpse of some future Wheaties-box material. The hourly guided tours begin with a 12-minute video, followed by about a 30-minute

12

Colorado
Springs
Vicinity

walk around the facilities. ⊠ *1750 E. Boulder St.* ☎ *719/866–4618* ☞ *Free* ⊙ *June–Aug., Mon.–Sat. 9–4:30; Sept.–May, Mon.–Sat. 9–4.*

WORTH NOTING

⑭ ANA Money Museum. The American Numismatic Association's Money
Museum has a collection of old gold coins, mistakes made at the U.S.
Mint, and currency from around the world. ⊠ *818 N. Cascade Ave.*
☎ *800/367–9723* ⊕ *www.money.org* ☞ *$5* ⊙ *Tues.–Sat. 10:30–5. Tours available Tues.–Fri.*

⑮ Ghost Town. You can play a real player piano and a nickelodeon at this
Western town with a sheriff's office, general store, saloon, and smithy.
There's also gold panning in the summer. ⊠ *400 S. 21st St.* ☎ *719/634–
0696* ⊕ *www.ghosttownmuseum.com* ☞ *$6.50* ⊙ *June–Aug., Mon.–
Sat. 9–6, Sun. 11–6; Sept.–May, Mon.–Sat. 10–5, Sun. 11–5.*

⑱ Glen Eyrie. General William Jackson Palmer, the founder of Colorado
Springs, was greatly influenced by European architecture and lifestyle,
and lived in this evolving mansion-turned-castle from its beginnings in the
1870s until his death in 1909. Original gas lamps and sandstone structures
remain. Many of its rocks were hewn with the moss still clinging, to give
them an aged look. The grandiose estate is maintained by a nondenomi-
national fundamentalist Christian ministry called the Navigators, which
runs programs and seminars and publishes religious works. You can hike
on the grounds by pre-arrangement. An afternoon English tea is offered
daily in summer. ⊠ *3820 30th St.* ☎ *719/634–0808* ⊕ *www.gleneyrie.org*
☞ *$6* ⊙ *Tours: June–Aug., Tues.–Fri. at 11; Sept.–May, Fri.–Sun. at 1. Tea
Mon.–Sat. at 2:30, Sun. at 1:30. Reservations required for tours and tea.*

⑯ Old Colorado City. Once a separate, rowdier town where miners caroused,
today the stretch of Colorado Avenue between 24th Street and 28th Street,
west of downtown, is a National Historic Landmark District whose
restored buildings house galleries and boutiques as well as shops with
inexpensive souvenirs and restaurants. ⊠ *Colorado Ave. between 24th and
28th St., west of downtown* ⊕ *www.shopoldcoloradocity.com.*

⑲ Pro Rodeo Hall of Fame and Museum of the American Cowboy. Even a tenderfoot would get a kick out of this museum, which includes changing displays of Western art; permanent photo exhibits that capture
both the excitement of bronco-bustin' and the lonely life of the cowpoke; gorgeous saddles and belt buckles; and multimedia tributes to
rodeo's greatest competitors. ⊠ *101 Pro Rodeo Dr., Exit 148 off I–25*
☎ *719/528–4764* ⊕ *www.prorodeo.com* ☞ *$6* ⊙ *Summer, daily 9–5;
Nov.–Apr., Wed.–Sat. 9–5.*

㉑ Western Museum of Mining and Industry. The rich history of mining is represented through comprehensive exhibits of equipment and techniques
and hands-on demonstrations, including gold panning. The 27-acre
mountain site has several outdoor exhibits, and is a great spot for
a picnic. ⊠ *Exit 156A, off I–25* ☎ *719/488–0880* ⊕ *www.wmmi.org*
☞ *$8* ⊙ *Mon.–Sat. 9–4.*

⑬ FAC Modern. This satellite venue of the Colorado Springs Fine Arts Center in the downtown area focuses on contemporary art. ⊠ *Plaza of
the Rockies, South Tower, 121 S. Tejon St.,* ☎ *719/477–4308* ⊕ *www.
csfineartscenter.org* ☞ *Free* ⊙ *Mon.–Fri. 10–4.*

SPORTS AND THE OUTDOORS

A number of activities are available within an hour or two of Colorado Springs, including hot-air ballooning, white-water rafting, and access jeep tours. Riding in a jeep is one way to view the backcountry; a horseback ride on trails through meadows and along mountainsides is another.

Some of the best choices for hiking in this region are the Barr Trail, which heads up Pikes Peak (and is for hardy, well-conditioned hikers), and the array of trails in North Cheyenne Cañon Park

ADVENTURE TOURS

Adventures Out West (✉ *1680 S. 21st St.* ☎ *719/578–0935 or 800/755–0935* ⊕ *www.adventuresoutwest.com*) offers high-adventure trips through the Royal Gorge and gentler trips through Bighorn Sheep Canyon. They can also arrange other activities, such as ballooning, horseback riding, and jeep tours. **Echo Canyon River Expeditions** (✉ *45000 U.S. Hwy. 50, Cañon City* ☎ *800/755–3246* ⊕ *www.raftecho.com*) offers rafting on the Arkansas and Colorado rivers. A Raft and Rail trip includes a morning on the Arkansas River and a ride on the Royal Gorge Railroad in the afternoon. They will also customize trips.

GOLF

★ **The Broadmoor Golf Club.** The three courses here offer distinctly diverse challenges, in part because they travel over a variety of terrain on the resort's 3,000 acres in the Rocky Mountain foothills. Donald Ross designed the original resort course in 1918, but today the East Course is a mix including nine of the original holes and nine more designed by Robert Trent Jones Sr. in 1965. When the Broadmoor hosted the 2008 U.S. Senior Open, the course was toughened dramatically to fit PGA tournament standards. Some of the fairways were narrowed—one now has a landing area just 22 feet wide—and grass on the greens was tweaked so balls look like they're sliding over ice. The West Course is also a combination of holes designed by each golf-course architect, but it's at a higher elevation (6,800 feet above sea level), and has more-vicious doglegs, rolling fairways, and multilevel greens. The Mountain Course, which was redesign by Nicklaus Design in 2006, has some wide forgiving fairways and large greens, but there are major elevation changes that add special challenges while providing outstanding mountain views. (✉ *1 Lake Circle* ☎ *719/577–5790* ⊕ *www.broadmoor.com* ♧ *Reservations essential* ⚑. *East Course: 18 holes. Yards: 7,310. Par: 72. Mountain Course: 18 holes. Yards: 7,637. Par: 72. West Course: 18 holes. Yards: 7,016. Par: 72. Green fee: $95–$230, depending on season and course.*

HIKING

Red Rock Canyon (✉ *Trailhead: Just south of U.S. 24 near 31st St.*) is a Colorado Springs city park. You can ramble on trails among the red sandstone monoliths and spires, balanced by white limestone and yellow-brown sandstone hogbacks.

Red Rock Loop Trail, on Manitou Section 16, is a 5.5-mi, moderately difficult loop with an elevation gain of up to 1,100 feet. The topography varies from steep, mountainous terrain to moderate slopes, mesas, and

12

canyons. There are views of sandstone formations and old quarries, as well as a terrific perspective of Colorado Springs and Pikes Peak. ⊠ *Trailhead: From I–25, Exit 141, west on U.S. 24 (Cimarron). Turn left on Trail Ridge Rd.*

Pikes Peak Greenway Trail. This trail combines with the New Santa Fe Regional Trail for 34 mi of multi-surface trails for hiking and biking. The trails run from Tejon Street through Colorado Springs into the Air Force Academy and north to Palmer Lake. A 6.9-mi section goes through the Air Force Academy, but you are expected to stay on the 6-foot-wide trail. Helmets and ID are required on the academy grounds, which may be closed at times. Past the academy, the trail then flows over gently rolling hills and finally follows a straight line and level course over an abandoned railroad track for the last 6.5 mi into Palmer. ⊠ *El Paso County Parks or Colorado Springs Governments* ☎ *719/520–6375* ⊕ *www.elpasocountyparks.com.*

HORSEBACK RIDING

Academy Riding Stables (⊠ *4 El Paso Blvd.* ☎ *719/633–5667*) offers trail rides.

MOUNTAIN BIKING

Challenge Unlimited (☎ *800/798–5954* ⊕ *www.bikithikit.com*) offers bike tours throughout Colorado, including the daily 20-mi bike tour down Pikes Peak May through mid-October. The tours include helmets and bikes. **Pikes Peak Mountain Bike Tours** (☎ *888/593–3062* ⊕ *www. bikepikespeak.com*) will take you to the top of Pikes Peak, then let you ride all the way down on one of their lightweight mountain bikes. An alternative tour is the 20-mi tour on Upper Gold Camp Road, which is a self-paced downhill ride along an old railroad tract converted to a hiking–bicycling trail that cuts through the mountains.

WHERE TO EAT

$–$$
AMERICAN

✕ **Adam's Mountain Café.** Join the locals sitting at mismatched tables, viewing drawings by a regional artist, and mingle with regulars at the community table. The long dining room has tall windows overlooking the patio. The food still has an organic bent, with many vegetarian options. Smashing breakfasts include orange-almond French toast and huevos rancheros; dinners such as Thai prawns with mango and mint, Senegalese Vegetables, or Caribbean Jerk Chicken are hits as well. ⊠ *934 Manitou Ave.* ☎ *719/685–4370* ⊕ *www.adamsmountain.com* ▤ *AE, D, MC, V* ⊘ *No dinner Sun. and Mon.*

$$$$
NEW AMERICAN

★

✕ **Blue Star.** Perch on a high stool in the bar while enjoying a glass of wine and tapas such as flash-fried squid with sweet Thai chili sauce or spanakopita primavera, or head to the simple and elegant dining room for a leisurely dinner. Influences drift around the globe, from pan-Asian to Mediterranean. It's a place frequented by everyone from blue-haired ladies to college students, so it's best to make a reservation. Blue Star offers half-price wine on Sunday, half-price martinis on Monday, and half-price imperial beers on Thurday. ⊠ *1645 S. Tejon St.* ☎ *719/632–1086* ⊕ *wwwthebluestar.net* ▤ *AE, MC, V.*

$$$-$$$$ ✕**Briarhurst Manor.** One of the most exquisitely romantic restaurants
CONTINENTAL   in Colorado, Briarhurst Manor has several dining rooms, each with
its own look and mood. The rich decor includes cherrywood wain-
scoting, balustrades, and furnishings, Van Briggle wood-and-ceramic
fireplaces, tapestries, chinoiserie, and hand-painted glass. Dine in the
Garden Room, which has massive bow windows, or in the book-lined
Library. In the Drawing Room, with its ornate chandelier and fireplace,
the tables are nicely spaced for conversation. Choose from classic Euro-
pean entrées such as trout almondine and Chateaubriand to more mod-
ern dishes like bison short ribs. ☒ *404 Manitou Ave.* ☎ *719/685–1864*
⊕ *www.briarhurst.com* ▤ *AE, MC, V.*

$$$-$$$$ ✕**Carlos Bistro.** Although this chic spot with copper-and-black decor is
NEW AMERICAN   a ways from downtown, it's a local favorite thanks to both its casual
ambience and the quality of its food. Here you'll find patrons—some
wearing jeans, others in suits—dining in the dim light on what appear to
be pieces of art framed by triangular white plates. Start with fresh oys-
ters or a blue-lump crab cake. Then move on to seared filet mignon with
a black-peppercorn brandy sauce or Filet à la Oscar—lump blue-crab
meat on filet mignon, topped with a béarnaise sauce. If you're not full,
try the New Orleans chocolate bread pudding, or the white-chocolate
bread pudding with macadamia nuts. ☒ *1025 S. 21st St.* ☎ *719/471–
2905* ▤ *AE, MC, V* ☉ *Closed Sun. No lunch Sat.*

$$$$ ✕**Charles Court at the Broadmoor.** Charles Court's contemporary country-
NEW AMERICAN   manor decor lends warmth to a fine-dining setting in this large resort.
Many of the tables in the large open space have a wonderful view of the
hotel's interior grounds and Cheyenne Lake. Tabletop items such as nap-
kin rings and centerpieces made from handblown glass add a lovely touch.
The menu is American-oriented, with a Rocky Mountain flair. Try the
Colorado rack of lamb, the tenderloin of buffalo, or the Rocky mountain
rainbow trout during a leisurely dinner. The wine cellar has more than
3,000 bottles. ☒ *The Broadmoor West, 1 Lake Circle* ☎ *719/577–5733*
⊕ *www.broadmoor.com* ▤ *AE, D, MC, V* ☉ *Closed Tues. and Wed.*

$$$-$$$$ ✕**Craftwood Inn.** This intimate restaurant is a favorite with locals for
AMERICAN   celebrating special occasions. A delightful Old English feel is achieved
through wrought-iron chandeliers, stained-glass partitions, heavy wood
beams, and a majestic stone-and-copper fireplace. Craftwood focuses
on game, so try the Wild Grill, a trio of elk, antelope, and venison; wild
Blue Russian boar or buffalo Oscar. Accompany your dinner with a
selection from the well-considered wine list. ☒ *404 El Paso Blvd., Mani-
tou Springs* ☎ *719/685–9000* ⊕ *www.craftwood.com* ⌂ *Reservations
essential* ▤ *AE, D, MC, V* ☉ *No lunch.*

$$$-$$$$ ✕**La Petite Maison.** Pale pink walls, floral tracery, Parisian gallery posters,
FRENCH   and pots overflowing with flowers create the cozy atmosphere of a French
country home. The pretty 1894 Victorian cottage has two romantic din-
ing rooms. Chef–owner Henri Chaperont prepares imaginative dishes
such as the continually popular grilled magret de canard with ginger and
coriander sauce, and the lobster napoleon with vanilla sauce. ☒ *1015 W.
Colorado Ave.* ☎ *719/632–4887* ⊕ *www.lapetitemaisoncs.com* ⌂ *Reser-
vations essential* ▤ *AE, D, DC, MC, V* ☉ *Closed Mon. No lunch.*

12

$$–$$$
ECLECTIC

✕ **Nosh 121.** Small plates, or noshing, is the focus at this popular restaurant next to the FAC Modern. People often share the more than 25 "noshers," ranging from Kobe beef sliders to Thai fish-and-chips, to a Latin platter with guacamole, chimichurri beef, and fish tacos. The Koi murals on the wall represent the restaurant's flow of energy and good service. Specials include "nosh" deals Saturday to Monday and wine flights on Sunday and Monday nights. ⊠ *121 S. Tejon St.,* ☎ *719/635–6674* ⊕ *www.nosh121.com* ⊟ *AE, MC, V* ☉ *Daily, no lunch Sat. and Sun.*

$$$$
NEW AMERICAN
★

✕ **Penrose Room at the Broadmoor.** Whatever number of courses you chose from the prix-fixe menu, you're guaranteed a memorable culinary and visual experience here. Executive Chef Bertrand Bouquin varies the menu seasonally, offering fine dining without the constraints of continental, American, or any other single cuisine. Appetizers such as sautéed fois gras with caramelized apple butter, and entrées such as monkfish and lobster tail wrapped in country bacon with black-truffle risotto and baby fennel, are plated to look like edible works of art. The best choice is the seven-course meal with wine pairings ($158). Request a table in the small glassed-in area, and you can watch the sun set behind Cheyenne Mountain, or if you're with a group, ask about sitting at the 16-seat Chef's Table in the demonstration kitchen. ⊠ *The Broadmoor South, 1 Lake Circle* ☎ *719/577–5733* ⊕ *www.broadmoor.com* ≜ *Reservations essential* ⊟ *AE, D, MC, V* ☉ *Closed Sun. Mon.*

¢
AMERICAN
☺

✕ **Poor Richards.** This is a four-in-one store loved by locals of all ages. On one side there's a pizza parlor, where you stand in line to order hand-tossed pizza, salads, and sandwiches. Step through a doorway and you're in a toy store. Step through another door and you'll find yourself in Rico's Coffee, Chocolate, and Wine Bar, where the ambience is more upscale, with wood floors and simple tables, and the menu veers toward organic. Order a sandwich or a cheese plate, or try a wine and chocolate pairing. Step though another doorway and you've entered a used-book store. You can enter each store from outside or through inside doors. ⊠ *320–324½ N. Tejon St.* ☎ *719/632–7721 for restaurant, 719/630–7723 for wine bar* ⊕ *www.poorrichards.biz/* ⊟ *AE, D, MC, V.*

$$$–$$$$
NEW AMERICAN
Fodor'sChoice
★

✕ **Summit at the Broadmoor.** The ambience in the resort's "American Brasserie," along with the innovative contemporary American cuisine, is a successful blend of big-city elegance and Western casualness. The 14-foot wine tower revolving slowly behind the bar is impossible to miss within the Summit's curved room, with windows interspersed with wood columns. The menu includes year-round favorites and a seasonal section; you may enjoy the subtle blending in the roasted potato soup with Hungarian paprika cream, the pan-seared Maine diver scallops with cumin, or the hanger steak with Summit fries and red-wine shallot sauce. Thirty wines are served by the glass, and half the fun of dining here is the conversation with the sommelier or the knowledgeable waitstaff about pairing the wine to food. You can get a chef's tasting dinner paired with wine, beer, or cocktails. ⊠ *19 Lake Circle.* ☎ *719/577–5775 or 800/634–7711* ⊕ *www.broadmoor.com* ≜ *Reservations essential* ⊟ *AE, D, MC, V* ☉ *Closed Mon.*

WHERE TO STAY

$$-$$$ ⊞ **Antlers Hilton Colorado Springs.** The marble-and-granite lobby strikes an immediate note of class at this downtown hotel, whose location provides easy access to restaurants, shopping, and offices. Basic moderate-size Hilton-style rooms are nicely decorated; bathrooms are spacious. The atrium off the lobby holds a day spa, which is not part of the hotel. **Pros:** good service, convenient location. **Cons:** not enough ambience or amenities for a romantic getaway or a family trip. ⊠ *4 S. Cascade Ave., 80903* ☎ *719/955–5600 or 866/299–4602* ⊕ *www.antlers.com* ⟿ *292 rooms, 8 suites* ⚹ *In-room: Internet. In-hotel: 2 restaurants, room service, bar, pool, gym, public Wi-Fi, laundry service, parking (paid)* ⊟ *AE, D, DC, MC, V.*

$$$$ ⊞ **The Broadmoor.** The luxurious Broadmoor resort continues to redefine
Fodor's Choice itself with settings where guests can unwind and be pampered. While
★ the Old World ambience—including the signature pink building with the Mediterranean-style towers—is still strong, the overall feel is pure luxury. The Cottages, which opened in 2009, hark back to the days when wealthy Easterners and friends gathered in the Adirondacks to enjoy an unhurried lifestyle. If you're going to stay in the South Towers, where the rooms vary in size from snug to immense—request one with a lake-view balcony. In summer, families gather around the large infinity pool, which appears to flow into Cheyenne Lake, and enjoy paddleboats. The award-winning spa offers innovative treatments such as the Magic of the Silk Route Massage, which utilizes spices and techniques from Thailand, India, and China during a silk body wrap and massage, plus a range of other massages, including Thai, Swedish, hot stone, and Ashiatsu. The tennis center and its instructors are excellent. **Pros:** you'll be thoroughly pampered at this world-class resort; choosing where to eat may be difficult, because there are so many good options. **Cons:** very expensive; rooms in the original West building are the least desirable. ⊠ *1 Lake Circle,* ☎ *719/634–7711 or 800/634–7711* ⊕ *www.broadmoor.com* ⟿ *593 rooms, 107 suites, 44 cottages* ⚹ *In-room: safe (some), DVD (some), Internet. In-hotel: 11 restaurants, bars, golf courses, tennis courts, pools, gym, spa, concierge, children's programs (ages 3–12), laundry service, public Wi-Fi, concierge, parking (paid), some pets allowed* ⊟ *AE, D, DC, MC, V.*

$$ ⊞ **Cheyenne Mountain Resort.** At this 217-acre resort on the slopes of Chey-
★ enne Mountain, superb swimming facilities (including an Olympic-size pool), a variety of tennis courts, and a Pete Dye championship golf course tempt you to remain on-property, despite the easy access to the high country. The main lodge is an attractive setting for relaxing and dining, with a massive stone fireplace and thick wooden beams supporting the soaring ceiling. An elaborate Sunday brunch is delicious. The guest rooms, in eight separate buildings on the hillside, are simply but attractively decorated, with private balconies. Most have white walls and wood furniture with colorful spreads on the beds. **Pros:** resort ambience; outstanding views of nearby mountains, especially if you stay in a room that overlooks the golf course. **Cons:** you must walk outside to get to the main building; as host to many conferences, it can get crowded with businesspeople. ⊠ *3225 Broadmoor Valley Rd.,* ☎ *719/538–4000 or 800/428–8886* ⊕ *www. cheyennemountain.com* ⟿ *316 rooms, 5 suites* ⚹ *In-room: refrigerator,*

Wi-Fi. In-hotel: 3 restaurants, room service, bar, golf course, tennis courts, pools, gym, bicycles, concierge, children's programs (ages 5–12), laundry service, public Internet, parking (free) ☐ *AE, D, DC, MC, V.*

$$–$$$ 🖭 **Cliff House.** This Victorian-era jewel was built in 1874 as a Manitou Springs stagecoach stop between Colorado Springs and Leadville. Crown princes, U.S. presidents, and famous entertainers have been past guests, and their names live on as monikers for several distinctly different and extremely attractive suites: the Katharine Bates, the Teddy Roosevelt, and the Clark Gable are a few. The Cliff House is a special-occasion getaway plump with accoutrements that pamper: bathtubs for two, steam showers, and even heated towel racks and toilet seats. It's right off the main street, a two-minute walk from Manitou's shops and restaurants. In addition to the more formal dining room, the casual Red Mountain Bar & Grill opened in 2009. **Pros:** convenient location; old-fashioned charm. **Cons:** not a good choice for those who prefer contemporary ambience, or those who want nightlife nearby. ⊠ *306 Cañon Ave., Manitou Springs* ☎ *719/685–3000 or 888/212–7000* ⊕ *www. thecliffhouse.com* ⇆ *38 rooms, 17 suites* ⚜ *In-room: safe, refrigerator, Wi-Fi, DVD, Internet. In-hotel: 2 restaurants, room service, bar, gym, laundry service, public Wi-Fi, parking (paid)* ☐ *AE, D, MC, V.*

$$$–$$$$ 🖭 **Garden of the Gods Club.** The views are spectacular from this long-time private club that overlooks the red rocks in the Garden of the Gods park. But, you don't have to be a member to spend a night in the lodge or the golf cottages. Deluxe suites are actually spacious rooms with larger sitting areas. The rooms have double-sink vanities, oversize tubs, and separate showers. The one- and two-bedroom cottages with full kitchens are by the golf course. **Pros:** great views; access to great golf on the private Kissing Camels course. **Cons:** you'll have to drive to all of the attractions and downtown; only one restaurant on-site. ⊠ *3320 Mesa Rd., 80904* ☎ *719/632–5541 or 800/923–8838* ⊕ *www. gardenofthegodsclub.com* ⇆ *69 rooms, 18 golf cottages* ⚜ *In-room: safe, refrigerator. In-hotel: restaurant, room service, bar, gym, laundry service, public Wi-Fi* ☐ *AE, D, MC, V.*

$$

Fodor's Choice

★

🖭 **Holden House.** Innkeepers Sallie and Welling Clark realized their dream when they restored this 1902 home and transformed it into a B&B. Two rooms in the main house, two in the adjacent carriage house, and one in another Victorian next door are filled with family heirlooms and antiques. Guest rooms are cozy with fireplaces and down pillows and quilts; you feel well taken care of with turn-down service and triple sheeting. The staff knows the region well, and can be helpful as you decide what to do in Colorado Springs. A full breakfast is served in a dining room that looks like it's ready for Victorian ladies to walk in and have tea. **Pros:** good choice for travelers who want something a touch—but not overly—homey; excellent breakfasts. **Cons:** in a residential neighborhood, must drive to attractions and restaurants. ⊠ *1102 W. Pikes Peak Ave.,* ☎ *719/471–3980* ⊕ *www.holdenhouse.com* ⇆ *5 rooms* ⚜ *In-room: refrigerator, DVD, Wi-Fi. In-hotel: no kids under 12* ☐ *AE, D, DC, MC, V* ⊙l *BP.*

12

NIGHTLIFE AND THE ARTS

THE ARTS

Colorado Springs' **Pikes Peak Center** (✉ *190 S. Cascade Ave.* ☎ *719/520–7469*) presents a wide range of musical events as well as touring theater and dance companies.

NIGHTLIFE
BARS AND CLUBS

Cowboys East (✉ *5869 Palmer Park Blvd.* ☎ *719/596–1212*) is for country music lovers and two-steppers. The **Golden Bee** (✉ *International Center at the Broadmoor, 1 Lake Circle* ☎ *719/634–7711*) is a Colorado Springs institution. The gloriously old-fashioned bar, with pressed-tin ceilings and magnificent woodwork, features a piano player leading sing-alongs. Watch out for the bees—as part of a long-standing tradition, they flick bee stickers into the audience during the show. The **Ritz** (✉ *15 S. Tejon* ☎ *719/635–8484*), located downtown, fills up at cocktail hour and has a bistro-style menu for dining, but the action is on Wednesday, Friday, and Saturday, when the live music starts. Locals say to get there before 7 PM if you want to eat.

BREWPUBS

At **Bristol Brewing** (✉ *1647 S. Tejon St.* ☎ *719/633–2555* ⊙ *Weekdays 10–9, Sat. 9–9*) you can get fresh brews, like Laughing Lab, Red Rocket, and Beehive, in the tasting bar. **Judge Baldwin's** (✉ *Antlers Hilton, 4 S. Cascade Ave.* ☎ *719/473–5600*) is a brewpub in the Antlers Hilton Colorado Springs hotel. **Phantom Canyon Brewing Co.** (✉ *2 E. Pikes Peak Ave.* ☎ *719/635–2800*), in a turn-of-the-20th-century warehouse, has billiards in an upstairs hall. There's great pub grub, plus sinful black-and-tan brownies.

COMEDY AND SHOWS

Loonees Comedy Corner (✉ *1305 N. Academy Blvd.* ☎ *719/591–0707*) showcases live stand-up comedy Thursday to Saturday evenings; some

★ of the performers here are nationally known. The **Flying W Ranch** (✉ *3330*
⊙ *Chuckwagon Rd.* ☎ *719/598–4000 or 800/232–3599*), open mid-May–September, ropes them in for the sensational Western stage show and chuck-wagon dinner. The Winter Steakhouse indoors opens during the colder months. The **Iron Springs Chateau** (✉ *444 Ruxton Ave., across from Pikes Peak Cog Railway* ☎ *719/685–5104*) stages comedy melodramas along with dinner mid-April through October and December.

SHOPPING

Colorado Springs has a mix of upscale shopping in boutiques and major chain stores. Many boutiques and galleries cluster in Old Colorado City and the posh Broadmoor One Lake Avenue Shopping Arcade.

Manitou Springs, a small town between Garden of the Gods and Pikes Peak, has a historic district, and the Chamber of Commerce has free maps with a tasting guide that tells you what is in each of the 11 naturally effervescent springs around town. There's a large artists' population; walk along Manitou Avenue and Ruxton Avenue, where you'll find a mix of galleries, quaint shops, and stores selling souvenirs.

SHOPPING DISTRICTS AND MALLS

Chapel Hills Mall (⊠ *1710 Briargate Blvd.*), at the north end of town, has a Macy's and a Dick's Sporting Goods, plus many other stores. **Citadel** (⊠ *750 Citadel Dr. E*) counts Dillard's, Express, Footlocker, and American Eagle Outfitters among its more than 100 stores. Among the tenants at the **Shops at Briargate** (⊠ *1885 Briargate Pkwy., Exit 151 on I–25* ☎ *719/265–6264*) are clothiers Ann Taylor and Coldwater Creek, plus other retailers such as Pottery Barn and Williams-Sonoma.

12

SPECIALTY SHOPS

ANTIQUES AND COLLECTIBLES

The **Ruxton Trading Post** (⊠ *22 Ruxton Ave. Manitou Spring* ☎ *719/685–9024*) has cowboy-and-Indian antiques and collectibles, Native American art, and nostalgia items from old TV programs and movies.

CRAFT AND ART GALLERIES

Commonwheel Artists Co-Op (⊠ *102 Cañon Ave., Manitou Spring* ☎ *719/685–1008*) exhibits wall art in various mediums, jewelry, and fiber, clay, and glass art. Like the sweet sounds of a dulcimer? At the **Dulcimer Shop** (⊠ *740 Manitou Ave., Manitou Spring* ☎ *719/685–9655*) you can buy one, buy a kit to make one, or even get some lessons to start you off. **Flute Player Gallery** (⊠ *2511 W. Colorado Ave.* ☎ *719/632–7702*) carries southwest Native American art, jewelry, and pottery. **Michael Garman Museum** (⊠ *2418 W. Colorado Ave.* ☎ *719/471–9391*) offers Western-style paintings and contemporary sculpture.

FOOD

Patsy's Candies (⊠ *1540 S. 21st St.* ☎ *719/633–7215*) is renowned for its saltwater taffy and chocolate. Tours weekdays mid-May through mid-September.

SPORTING GOODS

Kinfolks Mountain Outfitters (⊠ *950 Manitou Ave., Manitou Spring* ☎ *719/685–4433*) is a unique operation. It's chock-full of gear and information for hikers, bikers, and climbers, but in the back they serve beer, wine, and coffee, so you can relax and swap stories while sitting creek-side. There's live music on Friday and Saturday evenings.

COLORADO SPRINGS SIDE TRIPS

Easy day trips from Colorado Springs can lead you to the gambling or mining heritage in Cripple Creek. Florissant Fossil Beds attracts geology buffs. If you like heights, head to Cañon City and walk over the Royal Gorge Bridge, or take a lunchtime ride on the train that runs on a track through the most dramatic part of the canyon.

CRIPPLE CREEK

46 mi west of Colorado Springs via U.S. 24 and Rte. 67.

Colorado's third legalized gambling town, Cripple Creek once had the most lucrative mines in the state—and 10,000 boozing, brawling, bawdy citizens. Today the main street is lined with casinos housed in Victorian buildings. Outside of the central area, old mining structures and the stupendous curtain of the Collegiate Peaks are marred by slag heaps and parking lots. Take a side trip to nearby Victor, walk down streets where hundreds of miners once took streetcars to the mines, and learn about their lives.

GETTING HERE AND AROUND

The town is tiny, so it's easy to walk around and explore. Drive here in a private car, or hitch a ride on one of Ramblin' Express casino shuttles from Colorado Springs to Cripple Creek. Ramblin' Express also runs between Cripple Creek and nearby Victor.

ESSENTIALS

Transportation Contacts Ramblin' Express (☎ 719/590–8687 ⊕ ramblinexpress.com).

Visitor Info Pikes Peak Heritage Center (✉ 9283 S. Hwy. 16 ☎ 877/858–4653 ⊕ www.visitcripplecreek.com).

TOP EXPERIENCE: CASINOS

Miners gathered around card games in most of the 100 saloons in Cripple Creek, which opened during the wild years after Bob Womack discovered gold in 1890. Today there's a lineup of casinos set into storefronts and buildings with exteriors meticulously maintained to retain the aura they had a century ago. But inside the 18 casinos and gambling parlors here today there's no question that these are gambling halls, chock-full of slot machines, video and live poker tables, and blackjack tables. Today there are even a few casinos in modern buildings, too. Since 2009 the maximum bet limit was raised to $100. You can play craps and roulette at many of the casinos, some of which stay open 24 hours a day.

Most of the casinos on East Bennett Avenue house predictable (albeit inexpensive) restaurants. Beef is the common denominator across all of the menus. The price goes up, along with the quality, at restaurants like the Steakhouse at Bronco Billy's Casino. Some casinos also have hotel rooms.

Peek into the mining era's high life at the **Imperial Hotel and Casino**, where you'll see antiques, chandeliers, and hand-painted wallpaper from France as you play the latest slot machines. There's no craps or roulette here. ✉ 123 N. 3rd St. ☎ 719/689–7777.

The Rocky Mountain Victorian look of the **Gold Rush Hotel & Casino** is fairly typical of the establishments that line historic East Bennett Avenue. The casino has embraced the 2009 gaming laws, offering craps and roulette, as well as blackjack, poker, and slot machines, and stays open 24/7. ✉ 209 E. Bennett Ave. ☎ 719/689–2646 or 800/235–8239.

12

EXPLORING

The **Cripple Creek District Museum** provides a glimpse into mining life at the turn of the 20th century. ⊠ *500 Bennett Ave.* ☎ *719/689–2634* ⊠ *$5* ☉ *June 1–Sept. 30, daily 10–5; Oct. 17–May 17, Sat.–Sun. 10–4.*

The **Cripple Creek and Victor Narrow Gauge Railroad** weaves over reconstructed trestles and past abandoned mines to the Anaconda ghost town, then comes back to Cripple Creek during the 4-mi, 45-minute ride. In the boom days of the 1870s through the silver crash of 1893, more than 50 ore-laden trains made this run daily. For years Victor has been a sad town, virtually a ghost of its former self. Walking the streets—past abandoned or partially restored buildings—has been an eerie experience that evokes the mining (and post-mining) days far more than tarted-up Cripple Creek. But there's a partial renewal of the town, because Victor is again home to a gold mine, the Cripple Creek and Victor Mining Company. ⊠ *520 E. Carr St., at Bennett Ave.* ☎ *719/689–2640* ⊕ *www.cripplecreekrailroad. com* ⊠ *$12.25* ☉ *Mid-June–Aug., daily 10–5; trains depart every 40 mins. Runs in spring and fall but less frequently; call for hrs.*

The **Mollie Kathleen Gold Mine Tour** descends 1,000 feet into the depths in a mine that operated continuously from 1892 to 1961. The tours are wonderful, usually led by a former miner, but definitely not for the claustrophobic. ⊠ *9388 Rte. 67, north of town* ☎ *719/689–2466* ⊠ *$15* ☉ *Mid-May–Mid-Sept., daily 10–5; late Apr.–mid-May and late Sept.–Oct., daily 10–4, weather permitting; tours every 15 or 30 mins depending upon the season*

WORD OF MOUTH

"You'll probably find you can 'do' Cripple Creek in less than a day. It's very small and basically revolves around the casinos. If gambling's your main focus, you'll enjoy the town." —Virgogirl

FLORISSANT FOSSIL BEDS

35 mi west of Colorado Springs via U.S. 24.

GETTING HERE AND AROUND

From Cripple Creek, take Teller County Road 1, which goes right through the monument. It's about 17 mi from town.

EXPLORING

Florissant Fossil Beds National Monument is a temperate rain forest that was perfectly preserved by volcanic ash 34 million years ago. This little-known site is a heaven for paleontologists. The visitor center offers a daily guided walk and ranger talks in the ampitheatre in summer, or you can follow the well-marked hiking trails and lose yourself in the Eocene epoch among the remnants of petrified redwoods. ⊠ *15807 Teller County 1, Florissant* ☎ *719/748–3253* ⊕ *www.nps.gov/flfo* ⊠ *$3* ☉ *Summer daily 8–6; rest of year daily 9–5.*

PALMER LAKE

25 mi north of Colorado Springs via I–25 and Hwy. 105.

Artsy, and very sleepy, Palmer Lake is a magnet for hikers who set out for the evergreen-clad peaks at several in-town trailheads. There are more good restaurants and working artists than one would expect from a population of about 1,700. The town developed around the railroad tracks that were laid here in 1871—the lake itself was used as a refueling point for steam engines.

EXPLORING

In a landmark Kaiser-Frazer building on the north fringe of town, the **Tri-Lakes Center for the Arts** hangs rotating exhibits in its auditorium-gallery that also serves as a venue for music and theater. Classes and workshops are offered, and several resident artists work from studios on-site. ⊠ *304 Hwy. 105* ☎ *719/481–0475* ⊕ *www.trilakesarts.org* ⊠ *Free* ☉ *Tues.– Sat. noon–4.*

Larkspur (7 mi north of Palmer Lake) is home to just a few hundred residents, but it knows how to throw a heck of a party—and a medieval ひ one at that. The **Colorado Renaissance Festival** annually throws open its ★ gates to throngs of families, chain mail–clad fantasy enthusiasts, tattooed bikers, and fun lovers of every other kind. Within the wooded 350-acre "kingdom" there are performers who deliver everything from juggling stunts and fire-eating to hypnotism and comedy. The big event happens three times a day, when knights square off in the arena for a theatrical joust. There are also more than 200 artisans selling their wares (from hammocks to stained-glass "Sunsifters"), games, rides, and myriad food and drink booths. It's a great way to while away a summer day, though it can be a bit much to handle in the hottest weather. To reach Larkspur from Denver, take Interstate 25 south to Exit 173; if you're coming from Colorado Springs, take Interstate 25 north to Exit 172. ☎ *303/688–6010* ⊕ *www.coloradorenaissance.com* ⊠ *$17.95* ☉ *Early June–early Aug., weekends 10–6:30.*

QUICK BITES
Rock House Ice Cream is a popular stop for hikers on their way home. Choose from among 24 different types, including cake batter, black raspberry, cookie dough, or rainbow sherbet, for your cone or milk shake. ⊠ *24 Hwy. 105* ☎ *719/488–6917* ▤ *MC, V.*

SPORTS AND THE OUTDOORS

FISHING

Palmer Lake is stocked with trout, but a more secluded angling spot, the **Upper Palmer Lake Reservoir** (☎ *719/481–3282*), has a mix of trout and bottom-feeders in a peaceful mountain setting. See ⊕ *www.wildlife. state.co.us/fishing* for more information on fishing licenses.

HIKING

The **New Santa Fe Regional Trail** goes from Palmer Lake along an abandoned railroad right-of-way, through the US Air Force Academy—where you must stay on the six-foot-wide trail—and links up with the Pikes Peak Greenway Trail in Colorado Springs. The trail is also popular with equestrians and bikers, as well as cross-country skiers and snowshoers. ✉ *El Paso County Parks* ☎ *719/520–6375* ⊕ *adm. elpasoco.com/Parks/New_Santa_Fe_Regional_Trail.htm.*

One of the most popular hiking trails between Denver and Colorado Springs, the **Palmer Lake Reservoirs Trail** (✉ *Trailhead: At bottom of Old Palmer Rd.* ☎ *719/481–3282*) begins near Glen Park. After a fairly steep incline, the 3-mi trail levels out and follows the shoreline of Upper and Lower Palmer Lake reservoirs between forested mountains. Bikes and leashed dogs are permitted.

WHERE TO EAT

$$ ╳ **B & E Filling Station.** Though it doesn't look like much from outside, casu-
ECLECTIC ally elegant dining is the name of the game at this eatery. With stained-glass windows, mountain views, and local art on the walls, the place is easy on the eyes—and the food is easy on the palate. Mouthwatering entrées include blue-crab chicken, bacon-wrapped beef tenderloin, and spicy seafood chipotle. ✉ *25 Hwy. 105* ☎ *719/481–4780* ⊕ *bandefillingstation. com/* ⚞ *Reservations essential* ▭ *D, MC, V* ⊙ *Closed Sun. and Mon. No lunch.*

NIGHTLIFE

A roadhouse eatery, **O'Malley's Steak Pub** (✉ *104 Hwy. 105* ☎ *719/488– 0321*) offers the most reliable nightlife in the area, with an upstairs poolroom, occasional bands, and plenty of local color. You can play chef here—cooking steaks to your liking on a communal grill. The outdoor deck has a great view of the nearby mountainside.

SHOPPING

The fun and eclectic **Finders Keepers** (✉ *91 Hwy. 105* ☎ *719/487–8020*) sells jewelry, antiques, homemade jams and jellies, and local arts and crafts.

CAÑON CITY AND ROYAL GORGE

59 mi east of Salida via U.S. 50; 45 mi southwest of Colorado Springs.

Cañon City is an undeniably quirky town. From its easy access to the nearby Royal Gorge, a dramatic slash in the earth, to its aggressive strip-mall veneer (softened, fortunately, by some handsome old buildings), you'd think Cañon City existed solely for tourism. Nothing could be further from the truth: Cañon City is in Fremont County, called "Colorado's Prison Capital" by some. In Cañon City and nearby Florence there are 13 prisons, including Supermax. While this may seem like a perverse source of income to court, the prisons have pumped more than $200 million into the local economy.

GETTING HERE AND AROUND

The route from Colorado Springs to Cañon City goes through Red Rock Canyon, with lovely views. You'll need a car to get to Cañon City, where there is no public transportation other than cab service.

ESSENTIALS

Visitor Info Cañon City Chamber of Commerce (✉ *403 Royal Gorge Blvd.* ☎ *719/275–2331 or 800/876–7922* ⊕ *www.canoncitycolorado.com*).

EXPLORING

Cañon City is the gateway to the 1,053-foot-deep **Royal Gorge,** which
Fodor's Choice was carved by the Arkansas River more than 3 million years ago. The
★ famed Royal Gorge War between the Denver & Rio Grande and Santa
Fe railroads occurred here in 1877. The battle was over the right-of-way
through the canyon, which could only accommodate one rail line. Rival
crews would lay tracks during the day and dynamite each other's work at
night. The dispute was finally settled in court—the Denver & Rio Grande
won. Today there's a commercially run site, the Royal Gorge Bridge and
Park, along one part of the gorge. ⊠ *12 mi west of Cañon City.*

The **Royal Gorge Bridge and Park** has the world's highest **suspension
bridge.** Never intended for traffic, it was constructed in 1929 as a tourist attraction. The 1,053-foot-high bridge sways on gusty afternoons,
adding to the thrill of a crossing. You can also ride the astonishing
aerial tram (2,200 feet long and 1,178 feet above the canyon floor) or
descend the steepest **incline rail line** in the world to stare at the bridge
from 1,000 feet below. A ride on the **Royal Rush Skycoaster** ensures
an adrenaline rush—you'll swing from a free-fall tower and momen-
tarily hang over the gorge. Also on hand are a theater that presents a
25-minute multimedia show, outdoor musical entertainment in summer,
and the usual assortment of food and gift shops. Visiting this attraction
can prove to be expensive for a family—and some Fodors.com readers
suggest that it is not worth the money. ⊠ *4218 Fremont County Rd.
3A* ☎ *719/275–7507 or 888/333–5597* ⊕ *www.royalgorgebridge.com*
⊠ *$24* ⊗ *Hrs vary seasonally; call ahead or check Web site.*

A ride on the **Royal Gorge Route Railroad** takes you under the bridge and
through one of the most dramatic parts of the canyon. From the Santa
Fe depot in Cañon City, the train leaves several times a day for the two-
hour ride. The lunch ride is pleasant, and the food is good, although
not exactly "gourmet" as advertised. For an extra fee you can ride in
the cab with the engineer driving the train. ☎ *888/724–5748* ⊕ *www.
royalgorgeroute.com* ⊠ *$32.95 coach, $57.95 Vista Dome and up.*

Not only is **Buckskin Joe Frontier Town** the largest Western-style theme
park in the region, but it's also an authentic ghost town that was moved
here from 100 mi away. Such famous films as *True Grit* and *Cat Ballou*
were shot in this place, which vividly evokes the Old West, especially
during the re-created gunfights and hangings that occur daily. Children
love the horse-drawn trolley rides and gold panning, while adults appreciate live entertainment in the Silver Dollar Saloon. ⊠ *Cañon City off
U.S. 50,* ☎ *719/275–5149* ⊕ *www.buckskinjoe.com* ⊠ *$20* ⊗ *May and
Sept., daily 10–5; mid-June–Aug., daily 9:30–6.*

Introduce yourself and your kids to what life is like behind bars at the
Museum of Colorado Prisons, which formerly housed the Women's State Cor-
rectional Facility and where many of the exhibits are housed in cells. The
museum exhaustively documents prison life in Colorado through old photos and newspaper accounts, as well as with inmates' confiscated weapons
and contraband and an exhibit covering the current gang situations in the
U.S. There's also a video room where you can view titles such as *Prisons
Ain't What They Used to Be* and *Cañon City,* the first (1948) documentary

12

in the U.S. that features a prison break. The gas chamber sits in the courtyard. Many parents bring their children to this museum, but some videos might be disturbing for young kids. ✉ *201 N. 1st St.* ☎ *719/269–3015* ⊕ *www.prisonmuseum.org* ✉ *$7* ✆ *June–Aug., daily 8:30–6; May, Sept.–mid-Oct., daily 10–5; mid-Oct.–Apr., Wed.–Sun. 10–5.*

OFF THE BEATEN PATH

Winery at Holy Cross Abbey. The Benedictine monks once cloistered in the Holy Cross Abbey came to Cañon City for spiritual repose. But for the faithful who frequent the winery on the eastern edge of the monastery's property, redemption is more easily found in a nice bottle of merlot reserve or the popular Riesling. Tours of the winery's production facility are possible by advance reservation in spring and summer. The

FLORENCE PRISONS
The tiny, main-street town of Florence chalks up just a few antique shops, galleries, and coffee shops. But when it comes to prisons, they have more than their share, with four correctional facilities, including the infamous ADX Supermax, where an unruly population passes time in 23-hour lockdown. The ADX is home to plenty of men with sinister claims to fame. Among the current and former residents are Ted Kaczynski, Timothy McVeigh, Ramsey Yusef, the alleged architect of the 1993 bombing of the World Trade Center, and Richard Reid, aka "The Shoebomber."

Tasting Room, in a historic building, is open year-round. ✉ *3011 E. Hwy. 50* ☎ *719/276–5191 or 877/422–9463* ⊕ *www.abbeywinery.com* ✉ *Free* ✆ *Spring and summer, Mon.–Sat. 10–6, Sun. noon–5; Jan.–Mar., Mon.–Sat. 10–5, Sun. noon–5.*

SPORTS AND THE OUTDOORS
HIKING

For a pleasant stroll, try the **Arkansas River Walk** (✉ *Trailhead:Go south on 9th St., and turn east immediately south of bridge over river. It's about 2 blocks to trailhead*). The 4-mi trail is virtually flat, and the elevation is only 5,320 feet. It follows the Arkansas River for 3 mi through woods, wetlands, and the riparian river environment.

Cañon City–owned **Red Canyon Park,** 12 mi north of town, offers splendid easy to moderate hiking among the rose-color sandstone spires.

RAFTING

OUTFITTERS AND EXPEDITIONS

With dozens of outfitters working from Salida, Buena Vista, and Cañon City, south-central Colorado is one of the top places in the country to go rafting. The **Colorado River Outfitters Association** (⊕ *www.croa.org*) is an organization of more than 50 licensed outfitters who run rafting trips on Colorado's 13 river systems. The Web site has descriptions of the river systems.

Echo Canyon River Expeditions (☎ *719/275–3154 or 800/748–2953* ⊕ *www.raftecho.com*) offers float trips with gentle rapids on the Arkansas for first-time rafters in Bighorn Sheep Canyon, family trips through Brown Canyon, and adrenaline-inducing rides through the Royal Gorge. Rafting through the Royal Gorge is not an experience for the faint of heart; you'll pass between narrow canyon walls through rolling Class IV and V waves, with hordes of tourists watching from the suspension bridge above. This company also runs combo trips including rafting-train ride, and paddle-saddle tours.

WHERE TO EAT AND STAY

$$$ ✕ **Merlino's Belvedere.** This Italian standby has ritzy coffee-shop decor,
ITALIAN with floral banquettes, centerpieces, and a rock grotto. Locals swear by the top-notch steaks, seafood, and pasta choices, which range from penne *vegetali* (with grilled vegetables) and manicotti to Angela's Combo, which has cavatelli and spaghetti with garlic and Romano cheese. There is live music some weekend nights. ✉ *1330 Elm Ave.* ⊕ *www.belvedererestaurant.com* ☐ *AE, D, DC, MC, V.*

$ ⌂ **Quality Inn and Suites.** Some of the famous people who have stayed here—John Belushi, Tom Selleck, Jane Fonda, John Wayne, Glenn Ford, and Goldie Hawn among them—now have their names emblazoned on the door of a hotel room. Spacious and ultracomfortable, basic accommodations are offered in the two wings. **Pros:** close to the Royal Gorge Bridge and Park. **Cons:** day trips to Pikes Peak and Colorado Springs require a solid hour of driving each way; Wi-Fi is only available in the business section. ✉ *U.S. 50 and Dozier St.,* ☎ *719/275–8676 or 800/525–7727* ⊕ *www.choicehotels.com* ⟿ *150 rooms* ♿ *In-room: Internet (some), Wi-Fi (some). In-hotel: restaurant, bar, pool, public Wi-Fi* ☐ *AE, D, MC, V.*

THE COLLEGIATE PEAKS

Buena Vista and Salida are comfortable base towns for vacationers who love hiking and mountain biking the trails that zigzag up and down the 14,000 footers called the Collegiate Peaks. These towns are also favorites for folks who want to stay in rustic cabins or small mom-and-pop motels, perhaps take a rafting trip on the Arkansas River, and come home with a wallet still intact.

BUENA VISTA

94 mi west of Colorado Springs on U.S. 24 and U.S. 285.

Skyscraping mountains, the most impressive being the Collegiate Peaks, ring Buena Vista (pronounced *byoo*-na *vis*-ta by locals). The 14,000-foot, often snowcapped peaks were first summited by alumni from Yale, Princeton, Harvard, and Columbia, who named them for their respective alma maters. A small mining town–turned–casual resort community, Buena Vista's main street is lined with Wild West–style historic buildings. On U.S. 24, which bisects the town, there are inexpensive roadside motels. The town is also a hub for the white-water rafting industry that plies its trade on the popular Arkansas River, and a great central location for hiking, fishing, rafting, and horseback riding.

GETTING HERE AND AROUND

You'll need your own car to explore this region. Everything outdoors from hiking and mountain biking to rafting on the Arkansas is an easy drive from Buena Vista.

12

ESSENTIALS

Visitor Info Buena Vista Chamber of Commerce (⊠ *343 Hwy. 24* ☎ *719/395–6612* ⊕ *www.buenavistacolorado.org*).

EXPLORING

Fodor'sChoice
★
Taking its own name from the many peaks named after famous universities, the 168,000 **Collegiate Peaks Wilderness Area** includes more 14,000-foot-high mountains (14) than any other wilderness area in the lower 48 states, and 6 more peaks with summits above 13,800 feet. Forty miles of the Continental Divide snake through the area as well. The most compelling reason to visit Buena Vista is for the almost unequaled variety of hikes, climbs, biking trails, and fishing streams here. Two ranger offices, one in Leadville and one in Salida, handle inquiries about this region. ⊠ *Leadville Ranger District, 810 Front St., Leadville* ☎ *719/486–0749.* ⊠ *Salida Ranger District, 325 W. Rainbow Blvd., Salida* ☎ *719/539–3591* ⊕ *www.fs.fed.us/r2/whiteriver/recreation/wilderness/collegiatepeaks/index.shtml.*

★
To relax sore muscles after your outdoor adventure, visit **Mount Princeton Hot Springs Resort,** 8 mi from Buena Vista, for a restorative soak. The resort has four pools at this writing plus several "hot spots in the creek"—the water temperature ranges between 85°F and 105°F. The resort here also has 9 rooms in the lodge, 40 others in two different buildings that are more basic, and 10 cabins ($$), which are quietly upscale in style and are underpriced for what they offer. The restaurant has a large stone fireplace and a dramatic view of the Chalk Cliffs. ⊠ *15870 County Rd. 162, 4½ mi west of Nathrop on County Rd. 162,* ☎ *719/395–2447* ⊕ *www.mtprinceton.com* ⊠ *$10 weekdays; $15 weekends* ☉ *Lower pools: daily 9–9; upper pool with waterslide: June–Sept., daily 11–6.*

Before leaving downtown, meander through the **Buena Vista Heritage Museum.** The falling-down miner's cabin and pretty carriage outside give a hint of what's in the building. Each room is devoted to a different aspect of regional history: one to mining equipment and minerals, another to fashions, and another to household utensils. There are working models of the three railroads that serviced the area in its heyday, a schoolroom, and historical photos in the archives. ⊠ *506 E. Main St.* ☎ *719/395–8458* ⊕ *www.buenavistaheritage.org* ⊠ *$5* ☉ *June–Sept., Mon.–Sat. 10–5, Sun. noon–5.*

SPORTS AND THE OUTDOORS

HIKING

The **Trailhead** (⊠ *707 Hwy. 24* ☎ *719/395–8001* ⊕ *www.thetrailheadco.com*) is an outdoor specialty shop where you can get maps, guidebooks, gear, and clothing for hiking or climbing in the region.

RAFTING

The rafting and kayaking on the **Arkansas River** can be the most challenging in the state, ranging from Class II to Class V, depending on the season.

OUTFITTERS
AND
EXPEDITIONS
Independent Whitewater (☎ *800/428–1479 or 719/539–7737* ⊕ *www.independentrafting.com*) is a family-owned company that's been running the Arkansas River for nearly 20 years. Trip sizes are small, and the take-out is at a private area after running Seidel's Suckhole and Twin

FodorśChoice
★

Falls on regular half-day trips. **River Runners** (☎ *800/723–8987* ⊕ *www.whitewater.net*) has been offering rafting trips on the Arkansas for more than 30 years. This group also runs the Royal Gorge stretch, which is classed expert, but there are choices on the river for families who want a gentler experience.

> ### RAFTING THE ARKANSAS
>
> Adrenaline-charging rapids range from Class II to Class V on Colorado's Arkansas River, one of the most commercially rafted rivers in the world. Among the most fabled stretches of the Arkansas are the Narrows, the Numbers, and Browns Canyon, but extreme paddlers tend to jump on trips through the Royal Gorge, which the river has carved out over aeons. Plan your trip for the early summer snowmelt for the biggest thrills.

WHERE TO EAT

$–$$
MEXICAN

✕ **Casa del Sol.** Housed in an old blacksmith's shop (1890), this stucco-clad restaurant has a quasi–tiki-hut feel inside and a nice outdoor seating area. The smothered burritos are tasty and hearty, the homemade salsa is hot, and the service is quick and friendly. Among the most popular entrées are the spicy Santa Fe, which has stacked corn enchiladas with meat sauce and cheddar cheese, and the Pechuga Suiza, a chicken breast rolled in a tortilla with Monterey Jack cheese and sour cream. The full-service bar here specializes in tart but potent margaritas. ✉ *333 U.S. 24* ☎ *719/395–8810* ▤ *D, MC, V.*

$–$$
AMERICAN

✕ **Eddyline Restaurant & Brewery.** The sleek decor at this casual new brewpub puts it in a different category than the other restaurants in Buena Vista. Kayaks, local art, ironwork details, and steel tables give the dining area and tiny bar sophistication. The pub is by the up and coming South Main River Park, so after dining on wood-fired pizzas, steaks, or seafood, washed down with ales brewed on-site, you can tackle the nearby miles of hiking and biking trails to use up the calories. Or you can just watch people on the climbing boulder from the patio. ✉ *926 S. Main St.* ☎ *719/966–6000* ⊕ *www.eddylinepub.com* ▤ *D, MC, V.*

¢–$
AMERICAN
FodorśChoice
★

✕ **mothers bistro.** Set in a historic former hotel, the tiny restaurant focuses on organic and regional foods. Midday meals such as a whole-wheat wrap stuffed with smoked turkey, fresh cilantro, curried mayo, cucumbers, and mango; or fig and Brie panini on fresh ciabatta. Small plates in the evening range from Mother's mac and cheese made with tortiglioni, sun-dried tomatoes, and Romano cheese, or quiche or meatloaf and freshly baked bread. There's a lovely outdoor patio and a full bar. ✉ *414 E. Main St.* ☎ *719/395–4443* ⊕ *www.mothersbistrobv.com* ☉ *June–Aug., daily; call for Sept.–May hrs* ▤ *AE, D, MC, V.*

WHERE TO STAY

$$

🏠 **Ghost Town Guest House.** Although it looks like one of the old buildings in this authentic ghost town, it's actually a solidly made new structure opened in 2009 by a couple who decided to get away from urban living. Inside, there's an attractive living room and dining area for guests, plus three bedrooms with gas-log fireplaces, claw-foot soaking tubs, and great views of the surrounding woods or the rickety structures on St. Elmo's tiny Main Street. There's a comfortable communal living room with a snack-filled refrigerator, TV and DVD, and a patio overlooking the woods. If you want to hike in the wilderness in the summer or snowshoe in the winter, just walk out the door and the trails are right there. Three-course breakfasts include hand-kneaded breads. Dinners are down-home cooking, often with soups and stews that have been simmering on the stove for hours. **Pros:** unique setting; friendly hosts. **Cons:** in the middle of the wilderness; must drive 30 minutes to

> **BUENA VISTA LODGING ALTERNATIVES**
>
> There are many cabins and some B&Bs in this region. For information about rental units in the Buena Vista area, contact the **Buena Vista Chamber of Commerce** (☎ 719/395–6612 ⊕ www.buenavistacolorado.org).

12

civilization some rooms up many stairs. ⊠ *25850 County Rd. 162* ☎ *719/395–2120* ⊕ *www.ghosttownguesthouse.com* ⮌ *3 rooms* ⌂ *In-room: Wi-Fi, no a/c, no phone, no TV, Internet (some). In-hotel: Wi-Fi, parking (free)* ▭ *No credit cards* ⦿⊣ *MAP.*

$$ ★ **Liar's Lodge.** Right on the banks of the Arkansas River, this rugged, rustic B&B is surrounded by 23 acres of woodland. The Great Room, under 25-foot-high ceilings, is centered around a huge river-rock fireplace, and the uniquely decorated rooms are named after landmarks in the river: the Pinball Room has a king bed, a sleeping loft, and a two-person hot tub (but alas, no pinball machine); the Frog Rock Room has a queen and a twin and opens onto a river deck. Larger groups might opt for the 1,200-square-foot house that overlooks the river. You'll hear the river gurgling from your room if you leave a window open. **Pros:** gorgeous setting; river views (and sounds). **Cons:** you'll have to go into Buena Vista for dinner; good choice for romantic getaways. ⊠ *30000 County Rd. 371,* ☎ *719/395–3444 or 888/542–7756* ⊕ *www.liarslodge. com* ⮌ *5 rooms, 1 house* ⌂ *In-room: no a/c, no phone, Wi-Fi. In-hotel: parking (free)* ▭ *MC, V* ⦿⊣ *BP.*

NIGHTLIFE

Head to the **Green Parrot** (⊠ *304 E. Main St.* ☎ *719/395–9046*), a long-standing Buena Vista watering hole with live music some weekends. The **Lariat** (⊠ *206 E. Main* ☎ *719/395–9494*) is another locals' hangout, where pool, video games, and darts are the main diversions. There are live DJs on some Friday nights.

SHOPPING

There are a few antiques shops right across the highway from the Buena Vista Visitors Center. **Rustic Woods** (⊠ *310 U.S. 24* ☎ *719/395–2561*) has attractive decorative items to heavy furniture, all centered around various wood, of course.

Global Garage (⊠ *222 Hwy. 24* ☎ *719/395–8092* ⊕ *www.globalgarage. org*) is a combination of an offbeat restaurant, an upscale resale shop, and a place where local artisans sell their work.

OFF THE BEATEN PATH

If you want to see an authentic ghost town, head off Highway 285/U.S. 24 up County Road 162 about 15 mi to the end of the road. The last part of the scenic ride is on a rough road winding through the Sawatch forest. **St. Elmo,** which was the supply center for the Mary Murphy Mine and dozens of smaller mines, including the Gold Queen and Boss

Tweed. Once a thriving place filled with saloons, a schoolhouse, and hotels, today, St. Elmo is the best-preserved ghost town in Colorado. It doesn't take long to walk along the main street and peer into some of the rickety old buildings, but it's worth the drive. There is a B&B, and the **St. Elmo General Store** (☎ 719/395–2117 ⊕ *www.st-elmo.com*) is open in the summer.

SALIDA

25 mi south of Buena Vista via U.S. 24 and 285 and Rte. 291; 102 mi southwest of Colorado Springs.

Imposing peaks, including 14,000-plus-foot Mount Shavano, dominate the town of Salida, which is on the Arkansas River. Salida draws some of the musicians who appear at the Aspen Music Festival—classical pianists, brass ensembles, and the like—for its Salida–Aspen Concerts in July and August. The town's other big event is the annual **Kayak and Rafting White-Water Rodeo** (⊕ *fibark.net/*) in June, on a section of river that cuts right through downtown. It's been taking place since 1949.

GETTING HERE AND AROUND
You need a private car to explore this area. There's a compact, walkable downtown area, but you'll need to drive to lodging, the trailheads in the mountains, rivers, and attractions.

ESSENTIALS
Visitor Info Heart of the Rockies Chamber of Commerce–Salida Chamber (✉ 406 W. Hwy. 50 ☎ 719/539–2068 or 877/772–5432 ⊕ www.salidachamber.org).

SPORTS AND THE OUTDOORS
BIKING
Absolute Bikes (✉ *330 W. Sackett Ave.* ☎ *719/539–9295*) rents cruisers and mountain bikes for $10 for two-hours up to $50 a day, and provides repair service, maps, advice, and equipment for sale.

DOWNHILL SKIING
Monarch is a small ski resort that tops out on the Continental Divide. The ski area has five chairlifts, 64 trails, 800 acres, and a 1,162-foot vertical drop. It's a family-friendly place with moderate pricing—one day lift tickets cost $54. The resort also offers snowcat skiing on steep runs off the Divide, plus the 130 acres of extreme terrain (accessible by hiking) in Mirkwood Basin. ✉ *22720 U.S. 50, 18 mi west of Salida* ☎ *719/530–5000 or 888/996–7669* ⊕ *www.skimonarch.com* ☜ *$54* ⊙ *Mid-Nov.–mid-Apr., daily 9–4.*

FISHING
The Arkansas River, as it spills out of the central Colorado Rockies on its course through the south-central part of the state, reputedly supports a brown-trout population exceeding 3,000 fish per mile. Some of the river's canyons are deep, and some of the best fishing locations are difficult to access, making a guide or outfitter a near necessity. See ⊕ *www.wildlife.state.co.us/fishing* for more information.

OUTFITTERS **ArkAnglers** (✉ *7500 W. Hwy. 50* ☎ *719/539–4223* ⊕ *www.arkanglers.com*) is a good fly shop with an experienced staff of guides, offering guided float and wade trips, fly-fishing lessons, and equipment rentals.

HORSEBACK RIDING

Mt. Princeton Hot Springs Stables (✉ *14582 County Rd. 162* ☏ *866/877–3630, 719/395–3630* ⊕ *www.mtprinceton.com*) offers trail rides along the dramatic Chalk Creek Cliffs. It's $35 per hour or $150 per day.

JEEP TOURS

12

High Country Jeep Tours (✉ *410 U.S. Hwy. 24, Buena Vista* ☏ *719/395–6111 or 866/458–6877* ⊕ *www.highcountryjeeptours.com*) takes customers on four-wheel-drive trips to old mines, ghost towns, and mountain vistas.

SNOW-MOBILING

Monarch Snowmobile Tours (✉ *22763 Hwy. 50, 18 mi west of Salida, Garfield,* ☏ *719/539–2572 or 800/539–2573* ⊕ *www.snowmobilemonarch.com*) takes customers on winter excursions around Monarch Park. Rentals start at $75 for a one-hour single rental and go up to $180 for six hours plus lunch.

RAFTING

The Salida area is a magnet for rafting aficionados, and there are dozens of outfitters. Salida is constantly jockeying with Buena Vista for the title of "Colorado's White-Water Capital." *For outfitters, see the Buena Vista section.*

WHERE TO EAT

$$$$
MODERN
AMERICAN

✕ **The Butcher's Table.** Kurt Boucher, the award-winning chef formerly with the Pine Creek Cookhouse near Aspen, owns this restaurant set in an 1881 building. His seasonal, high alpine cuisine has an emphasis on Colorado grown and raised, from local lamb to farm-raised striped bass. You can opt for a three-course prix-fixe menu that changes monthly or dine off the dinner menu. Leave room for dessert such as the chocolate lavacake or his rich version of s'mores. ✉ *228 F. St. 1* ☏ *719/530–9909* ⊕ *www.thebutcherstable.com* ▤ *AE, D, MC, V* ⌲ *Reservations essential* ⊙ *Closed Sun. and Mon.*

¢–$
MEXICAN

✕ **First Street Café.** This café in the historic district serves robust Mexican-American fare, sandwiches including an excellent Monte Christo, burgers, and some vegetarian dishes. The restaurant has original brick walls, pews from an old church, and bar tops and panel doors from an old stage at Denver's Red Rocks Ampitheatre. ✉ *137 E. 1st St.* ☏ *719/539–4759* ⊕ *www. firststreetcafesalida.com* ▤ *AE, D, MC, V.*

$$$
MODERN
AMERICAN
Fodor's Choice
★

✕ **Laughing Ladies.** Fine food is served in a relaxed atmosphere at a linen-covered table set on a century-old oak floor surrounded by exposed brick walls. Colorful oils, watercolors, and ceramics by local artists adorn the walls. The menu changes seasonally, but expect imaginative versions of classics, such as honey grilled pork chop with roasted sweet potatoes and candied bacon, or maple grilled salmon fillet with crispy polenta. Laughing Ladies has an excellent wine selection. ✉ *128 W. 1st St.* ☏ *719/539–6209* ⊕ *wwwtlaughingladiesrestaurant.com* ▤ *D, MC, V* ⌲ *Reservations essential* ⊙ *Closed Tues. and Wed.*

WHERE TO STAY

$

▦ **Tudor Rose.** Isolated, beautifully furnished, and idyllic—if you like a Victorian feel—this B&B sits on a 37-acre spread of pine forest and mountain ridges. The proprietors, John and Terré Terrell, redid the original private residence as a luxury mountain inn. An oak staircase with a waterfall cascading down the adjacent wall to the foyer is the centerpiece, but the deck overlooking the nearby Mosquito Range is a close second. The rooms are individually decorated, and there are also five chalets near the house that accommodate up to six people each. **Pros:** excellent choice for guests traveling with horses, because owners will stable horses in their barn. **Cons:** B&B rooms not an option for guests with young children; no pool ✉ *6720 County Rd. 104,* ☎ *719/539–2002 or 800/379–0889* 🌐 *www.thetudorrose.com* *4 rooms, 2 suites, 5 chalets* *In-room: no a/c, refrigerator (some), no TV (some). In-hotel: public Wi-Fi, parking (free), no kids under 10 except in chalets* *AE, D, MC, V* *BP.*

$ **Woodland Motel.** Since 1975, Steve and Viva Borbas have run this impeccable mom-and-pop motel on the outskirts of downtown Salida. Standard rooms are smallish but very clean, and have nice furnishings and amenities for the price. The more expensive rooms—two-bedroom condominium units and efficiency studios—are larger, and some have kitchens. Dogs receive royal treatment here: treats and freshly laundered doggie beds are included in the rate. **Pros:** reliable; inexpensive rooms. **Cons:** it's a 12-minute walk to the downtown area; rooms can be noisy. ✉ *903 W. 1st St.,* ☎ *719/539–4980 or 800/488–0456* 🌐 *www.woodlandmotel.com* *16 rooms, 2 condos* *In-room: kitchen (some), public Wi-Fi, Internet. In-hotel: some pets allowed, parking (free)* *AE, D, MC, V.*

THE ARTS

In a former power plant overlooking the Arkansas river, **Salida Steam Plant Events Center** (✉ *Sackett and G Sts.* ☎ *719/530–0933* 🌐 *www.steamplant.org*) has a theater that has put on several productions each summer, ranging from drama to comedy to music to cabaret.

SHOPPING

First Street and F Street are home to many antiques shops and art galleries, including specialists in contemporary art, photography, and jewelry. The annual **Salida ArtWalk** (🌐 salidaartwalk.org) takes place in late June. Ask the Chamber of Commerce for the *Art in Salida* or *Antique Dealers* brochures for information about the ArtWalk.

All Booked Up (✉ *134 E. 1st St.* ☎ *719/539–2344*) has Native American art and jewelry, mixed media artwork, and more. **cultureclash** (✉ *101 N. F St.* ☎ *719/539–3118*) has original artwork, glass, and intricately handcrafted jewelry. Brice Turnbill's wonderful blown-glass creations are at **Sunlight Studios** (✉ *1030 W. 1st St.* ☎ *719/539–5101*) has **Gallery 150** (✉ *150 W. 1st St.* ☎ *719/539–2971*) has jewelry and wearable art, plus blown glass and fiber art. **Spirit Mountain, Antler & Design** (✉ *223 E. 1st St.* ☎ *719/539–1500*) has stunning handcrafted tables inlaid with turquoise and other handmade furniture. The **Rock Doc at Prospectors Village** (✉ *17897 U.S. 285* ☎ *719/539–2019* 🌐 *www.therocdoc.net*), midway between Salida and Buena Vista, is an enormous rock shop with gold-panning equipment, metal detectors, and rock art. The shop also gives gold-panning lessons.

SOUTHEAST COLORADO

Pueblo is the biggest city along I–25 between Colorado Springs and the New Mexico border. South of Pueblo, Trinidad is close to the state border, and there are a few small towns sprinkled around the region. West of I–25 there's easy access to the mountains along picturesque routes such as the Highway of Legends, a scenic byway that runs through Cuchara Valley.

12

PUEBLO

40 mi east of Cañon City via U.S. 50; 42 mi south of Colorado Springs via I–25.

In 1842 El Pueblo trading post, on the bank of the Arkansas River, was a gathering place for trappers and traders. Today the trading post is an archaeological dig set in a pavilion next to the new El Pueblo History Museum. The thriving city of Pueblo surrounds the museum, and the Arkansas River runs through the city in a concrete channel, tamed by the Pueblo Dam.

To get a sense of the city and its offerings, start at the museum, stroll through the Union Avenue Historic District, and then take a ride on one of the tour boats leaving from the Historic Arkansas Riverwalk, an urban waterfront area that restored the Arkansas River channel to its original location. More than 110 parks, in addition to hiking and bicycling trails, help to define Pueblo as a sports and recreation center.

GETTING HERE AND AROUND

You can use the local bus system to move around during the day if you're staying near the Convention Center, but most of the buses you'll want stop running in the early evening. The local taxi is City Cab.

ESSENTIALS

Transportation Contacts Pueblo Transit (☎ 719/553–2727). **City Cab** (☎ 719/543–2525).

Visitor Info Pueblo Chamber of Commerce and Convention & Visitors Bureau (✉ 302 N. Santa Fe Ave. ☎ 719/542–1704 or 800/233–3446 ⊕ www.pueblochamber.org).

EXPLORING
TOP ATTRACTIONS

The **Union Avenue Historic District** is a repository of century-old stores and warehouses that make for a commercial district filled with a mix of stores ranging from kitschy to good. Among the landmarks are the glorious 1889 sandstone-and-brick Union Avenue Depot and Mesa Junction, at the point where two trolleys met, which celebrates Pueblo as a crossroads. Pitkin Avenue, lined with fabulous gabled and turreted mansions, attests to the town's more prosperous times. Walking-tour brochures are available at the visitors bureau.

El Pueblo History Museum is a nicely designed holding place for the city's history, but it extends its scope to chronicle life on the plains since the prehistoric era, as well as Pueblo's role as a cultural and geographic crossroads, beginning when it was a trading post in the 1840s. Remnants of the original trading post are now an archaeological dig enclosed in a pavilion next to the museum. ⊠ *301 N. Union Ave.* ☎ *719/583–0453* ✉ *$4* ⊘ *Tues.–Sat. 10–4.*

WORTH NOTING

Historic Arkansas Riverwalk of Pueblo is a 26-acre urban waterfront, where the Arkansas River channel has been restored to its original location. Stroll on the paths or take to the water on a boat tour or in a paddleboat (available at 101 South Union). ☎ *719/595–0242, 719/595–1589 boat reservations* ⊕ *www.puebloharp.com.*

Rosemount Victorian Museum is a splendid 37-room mansion, showplace of the wealthy Thatcher family. Exquisite maple, oak, and mahogany woodwork gleams throughout, with ivory glaze and gold-leaf trim. Italian marble fireplaces, Tiffany-glass fixtures, and frescoed ceilings complete the opulent look, and rooms seem virtually unchanged. The top floor—originally servants' quarters—features the odd Andrew McClelland Collection: objects of curiosity this eccentric philanthropist garnered on his worldwide travels, including an Egyptian mummy. ⊠ *419 W. 14th St.* ☎ *719/545–5290* ⊕ *www.rosemount.org* ✉ *$6* ⊘ *Tues.–Sat. 10–4; tours every half hr.*

☾ Rotating exhibits at the **Sangre de Cristo Arts Center** celebrate regional arts and crafts. The center also houses the superb Western art collection donated by Francis King; a performing-arts theater; and the highly rated **Buell Children's Museum**, which provides fun, interactive audiovisual experiences. ⊠ *210 N. Santa Fe Ave.* ☎ *719/295–7200* ⊕ *www.sdc-arts. org/bcc.html* ✉ *$4* ⊘ *Tues.–Sat. 11–4.*

☾ The fine **City Park** (⊠ *Pueblo Blvd. and Goodnight Ave.*) has fishing lakes, playgrounds, kiddie rides, tennis courts, a swimming pool, and the excellent **Pueblo Zoo** (☎ *719/561–9664* ⊕ *www.pueblozoo.org* ✉ *$8* ⊘ *June–Aug., daily 9–5; call for winter hrs*) —a biopark that includes an ecocenter with a tropical rain forest, black-footed penguins, ringtail lemurs, and pythons.

At the airport, the **Pueblo-Weisbrod Aircraft Museum** traces the development of American military aviation with more than two-dozen aircraft in mint condition, ranging from a Lockheed F-80 fighter plane to a Boeing B-29 Super Fortress of atomic-bomb fame. ⊠ *31001 Magnuson, Pueblo Memorial Airport* ☎ *719/948–9219* ⊕ *www.pwam.org* ✉ *$7* ⊘ *Weekdays 10–4, Sat. 10–2, Sun. 1–4.*

OFF THE BEATEN PATH

Bishop Castle. This elaborate creation, which resembles a medieval castle replete with turrets, buttresses, and ornamental iron, is the prodigious (some might say monomaniacal) one-man undertaking of Jim Bishop, a self-taught architect who began work in 1969. Once considered a blight on pastoral Highway 165, which winds through the San Isabel Forest, the castle is now a popular attraction; not yet complete, it is three stories high with a nearly 165-foot tower. Those who endeavor to climb into the structure must sign the guest book–cum–liability waiver. Bishop finances this enormous endeavor through donations and a gift shop. If you're lucky, he'll be there himself, perhaps railing against the Establishment. ⊠ *12705 Hwy. 165* ☎ *719/485–3040* ✉ *Free* ⊘ *Daily, hrs vary.*

SPORTS AND THE OUTDOORS

BIKING

The extensive **Pueblo Bike Trail System** loops the city, following the Arkansas River partway, and then goes out to the reservoir. There are popular in-line skating routes along these trails, too. You can get trail maps at the Chamber of Commerce.

BOATING, KAYAKING, AND FISHING

Along the stretch of the Arkansas River near the Pueblo Levee, there's a kayak course. The **Edge Ski, Paddle and Pack** (⊠ *107 N. Union Ave.* ☎ *719/583–2021* ⊕ *www.edgeskiandpaddle.com*) rents kayaks and gives lessons. There's excellent camping and fishing at **Lake Pueblo State Park** (⊠ *Off U.S. 50* ☎ *719/561–9320* ⊕ *www.parks.state.co.us/parks/ LakePueblo*), as well as many other outdoor activities. The **south shore marina** (☎ *719/564–1043*) rents pontoon boats. See ⊕ *www.wildlife. state.co.us/fishing* for more information on fishing licenses.

GOLF

Walking Stick Golf Course. This challenging links-style course is named after the native cholla, the cacti in the rugged terrain and arroyos that surround the rolling green fairways. ⊠ *4301 Walking Stick Blvd.* ☎ *719/584–3400* ⅄ *18 holes. Yards: 7,147/5,181. Par: 72/72. Green fee: $30–$32, plus $12 per person for cart.*

HIKING

You can bicycle, hike, and canoe along the 35 mi in the river trail system that follows the Arkansas River. For more information, call the **Greenway and Nature Center** (⊠ *Off 11th St., 5200 Nature Center Rd.* ☎ *719/549–2414* ⊕ *www.gncp.org*). A small interpretive center describes the flora and fauna unique to the area, and a **Raptor Rehabilitation Center,** part of the nature center, cares for injured birds of prey. You can hike in relative solitude on many trails threading the **San Isabel National Forest** (☎ *719/545–8737* ⊕ *www.fs.fed.us/r2/psicc/*), 20 mi southwest of Pueblo.

WHERE TO EAT

$$–$$$
AMERICAN

✕ **dc's on b street.** There are two dining areas in this restaurant, which is housed in the historic redbrick Coors building across from the Union Depot. At lunchtime you can get sandwiches, salads, and other light fare in a room with simple tables, brick walls, and a tin ceiling. For dinner in the more-elegant dining room, try poulet cordon bleu, a Santa Fe rubbed center pork chop complemented with a pomegranate reduction, or a seared bistro steak petit plate. ⊠ *115 B St.* ☎ *719/584–3410* 🖃 *AE, MC, V.*

$$$
CONTINENTAL

✕ **La Renaissance.** This converted church and parsonage is the most imposing and elegant space in town, and the impeccably attired, unfailingly courteous waitstaff completes the picture. Guests order five-course dinners (including sinful desserts), which are served with style. Standbys are prime rib, superb baby back ribs, and orange roughy. ⊠ *217 E. Routt Ave.* ☎ *719/543–6367* ⊕ *larenaissancerestaurant.com* 🖃 *AE, D, MC, V* ☾ *Closed Sun.*

$$
AMERICAN

✕ **Shamrock Brewing Company.** This consistently jam-packed hot spot is a bar and grill with a good kitchen. With dishes like corned beef and cabbage and Irish bangers, this is the place for authentic Irish pub grub. And

The Pueblo Levee

In 1978 a group of University of Southern Colorado art students headed out in the cover of night, set up lookouts, and lowered themselves over the wall of the Pueblo Levee. Outfitted with makeshift rope-suspension devices and armed with buckets of paint, the students spent the wee hours crafting a large blue cod on the levee's concrete wall, watching for police as they mixed up their acrylics. Overnight, the waterway—which directs the Arkansas River through the center of town—became home to a public art project that would eventually capture the imagination of the Pueblo community, as well as the attention of the art world and the *Guinness Book of World Records.* Pueblo Levee is a fantastic, colorful vision field that sprawls over 175,000 square feet, stretches for a mile, and is recognized as the largest mural in the world.

Organizers estimate that more than 1,000 painters have contributed to the mural—everyone from self-taught father-and-son teams who come to paint on weekends to the members of fire precincts, to classically trained muralists and art students from New York and Chicago. From time to time, a teacher and students at the Schools for Arts and Sciences will refresh some of the older murals. Witty graffiti, comic illustrations, narrative scenes, and cartoons line the levee, which is visible to passengers zooming along Interstate 25. Today, you can take the walking or biking path along the levee to look at the murals, or even take a kayak lesson below it.

of course they brew their own beer—there are usually six or seven varieties on tap. It's especially popular with the after-work crowd. ⊠ *108 W. 3rd St.* ☎ *719/542–9974* ⊕ *www.shamrockbrewing.com* ⊟ *AE, D, MC, V.*

WHERE TO STAY

$$–$$$
★
⚑ **Abriendo Inn.** This exquisite 1906 home, which is listed on the National Register of Historic Places, overflows with character. The house has original, restored parquet floors, stained glass, Minnequa oak wainscoting, and guest rooms that are richly appointed with antiques, oak armoires, quilts, crocheted bedspreads, and either brass or four-poster beds. Although all rooms have private bathrooms, one has a shower down the hall rather than en suite. Fresh fruit and cookies are left out for nibbling, and gourmet breakfasts are included in the rate. **Pros:** a classy place to stay, with an upscale feel; quiet residential neighborhood. **Cons:** some rooms have only showers, not bathtubs; need to drive to attractions and downtown. ⊠ *300 W. Abriendo Ave.,* ☎ *719/544–2703* ⊕ *www.abriendoinn.com* ➳ *10 rooms* ⚒ *In-room: Wi-Fi, refrigerator (some). In-hotel: public Wi-Fi* ⊟ *AE, MC, V* ⦿ *BP.*

$$
⚑ **Pueblo Convention Center Marriott.** A reliable brand-name hotel, the Marriott is geared for the convention crowd and offers good value and excellent service. The latest bedding from Marriott is known for its comfort. **Pros:** in the downtown area; connected to the Pueblo Convention Center; concierge floor. **Cons:** not much nearby for tourists; because it's a convention hotel, your neighbors may be early risers. ⊠ *110 W. 1st St.,* ☎ *719/542–3200 or 888/238–6507* ⊕ *www.marriott.com* ➳ *163 rooms*

12

⚒ In-room: refrigerator (some), Internet. In-hotel: restaurant, pool, gym, laundry service, public Wi-Fi, parking (free) ⊟ AE, D, MC, V.

NIGHTLIFE AND THE ARTS

THE ARTS

Broadway Theatre League (⊠ *Memorial Hall, No. 1 City Hall Place* ☎ *719/295–7222 for tickets*) presents three touring shows a year, such as Chorus Line, Wizard of Oz, and The Color Purple. The **Pueblo Symphony** (⊠ *301 N. Main St., Suite 106* ☎ *719/545–7967* ⊕ *pueblosymphony.net*) performs music, from pop to classical. Concerts are held at the Hoag Recital Hall on the CSU-Pueblo campus. **Sangre de Cristo Arts and Conference Center** (⊠ *210 N. Santa Fe Ave.* ☎ *719/295–7200*) presents visual exhibits in the Helen T. White galleries and has a performing-arts series that ranges from classical plays to ballets.

NIGHTLIFE

The **Shamrock Brewing Company** (⊠ *108 W. 3rd St.* ☎ *719/542–9974*) is always hopping after the workday.

SHOPPING

Pueblo's beautifully restored and renovated **Union Avenue Historic District** has a mixture of shops that range from places to buy interesting gifts to inexpensive clothing stores. Around the Union Avenue Depot—an elegantly restored building worth walking to—along Union Avenue and B Street, there are some art galleries, clothing stores, boutiques, and restaurants. You can get a map of galleries for the First Friday walks at the Chamber of Commerce or at many of the art galleries.

EN ROUTE

Heading east on U.S. 50 from Pueblo, leaving the Rockies far behind, you travel toward the eastern plains, where rolling prairies of the northeast give way to hardier desert blooms, and the land is stubbled with sage and stunted pinyon pines. One fertile spot—50 mi along the highway—is the town of **Rocky Ford,** dubbed the "Melon Capital of the World" for the famously succulent cantaloupes grown here.

LA JUNTA

60 mi east of Pueblo via U.S. 50; 105 mi southeast of Colorado Springs.

For an easy day trip from Pueblo into Colorado's past, head east to La Junta. The Koshare Indian Museum is in town, and Bent's Old Fort National Historic Site and the dinosaur tracks and ancient rock art of the canyonlands are nearby.

La Junta (which roughly translated from Spanish means "the meeting place") was founded as a trading post in the mid-19th century. It was a stop for the Santa Fe and Kansas Pacific railroads, and today is home to 7,600 residents.

GETTING HERE AND AROUND

Amtrak stops in La Junta but a private car is best to explore this remote area.

ESSENTIALS

Visitor Info La Junta Chamber of Commerce (⊠ *110 Santa Fe Ave.* ☎ *719/384–7411* ⊕ *www.lajuntachamber.com*).

EXPLORING

The **Koshare Indian Museum** contains extensive holdings of Native American artifacts and crafts (Navajo silver, Zuni pottery, Shoshone buckskin clothing), as well as pieces from Anglo artists, such as Remington, known for their depictions of Native Americans. The Koshare Indian Dancers—actually a local Boy Scout troop—perform regularly. ⊠ *115 W. 18th St.* ☎ *719/384–4411* ⊕ *www.koshare.org* ⊠ *$4* ⊙ *Daily noon– 5, call for extended summer hrs.*

QUICK BITES

For a food stop, try the watering hole with a quirky personality **Boss Hog's** (⊠ *808 E. 3rd St.* ☎ *719/384–7879*), a local institution.

★ **Bent's Old Fort National Historic Site,** 8 mi east of La Junta, is a perfect example of a living museum, with its painstaking re-creation of the original adobe fort. Founded in 1833 by savvy trader William Bent, one of the region's historical giants, the fort anchored the commercially vital Santa Fe Trail, providing both protection and a meeting place for the soldiers, trappers, and traders of the era. The museum's interior reveals daily life at a trading post, with recreations of a smithy, soldiers' and trappers' barracks, and more. Guided tours are offered daily during the summer ⊠ *35110 Hwy. 194* ☎ *719/383–5010* ⊠ *$3* ⊙ *June–Aug., daily 8–5:30; Sept.–May, daily 9–4.*

SPORTS AND THE OUTDOORS

Comanche National Grassland (⊠ *Office: 1420 E. 3rd St.* ☎ *719/384– 2181* ⊕ *www.fs.fed.us/r2/psicc/coma*) has a pair of canyon loops where there's a fair amount of rock art. Some of the largest documented sets of fossilized dinosaur tracks in the United States are in **Picket Wire Canyonlands,** a part of the grassland. There are picnic tables, but camping is prohibited. In addition to touring here by car, hiking, mountain biking, and horseback riding are popular.

TRINIDAD

80 mi south of Pueblo via I–25, Trinidad is just across the border from New Mexico; 127 mi south of Colorado Springs.

If you're traveling on Interstate 25 and want to stop for a night in a historic town with character instead of a motel on the outskirts of a bigger city, check out Trinidad. Walk around Corazon de Trinidad, the downtown area where some of the streets still have the original bricks— instead of pavement—and visit a few of the town's four superb museums, a remarkably large number for a town of about 11,000 residents. Trinidad was founded in 1861 as a rest-and-repair station along the Santa Fe Trail. Starting in 1878 with the construction of the railroad and the development of the coal industry, the town grew and expanded during the period from 1880 to 1910. But the advent of natural gas, coupled with the Depression, ushered in a gradual decline in population. During the 1990s there was a modest increase in the population and a major interest in the upkeep of the city's rich cultural heritage. Although newcomers are moving in and Trinidad is coming to life again, with restaurants, cafés, and galleries, the streets in the heart of town are still paved with brick, keeping a sense of the town's history alive.

12

GETTING HERE AND AROUND

Amtrak stops here. You'll need a private car or you can take the Trinidad Trolley from the Welcome Center around the downtown area.

TOURS

From Memorial Day to Labor Day you can take the free Trinidad Trolley, and the driver will give you an informal history of Trinidad between the stops at the and all of the museums.

ESSENTIALS

Visitor Info Colorado Welcome Center (✉ *309 Nevada Ave.* ☾ *10–3*). **Trinidad & Las Animas Chamber of Commerce** (✉ *136 W. Main, Trinidad* ☎ *719/846–9285* ⊕ *www. historictrinidad.com*).

SANTA FE TRAIL

Southern Colorado played a major role in opening up the West, through the Mountain Branch of the Santa Fe Trail. Bent's Fort was the most important stop between the route's origin in Independence, Missouri, and its terminus in Santa Fe, New Mexico. U.S. 50 roughly follows its faded tracks from the Kansas border to La Junta, where U.S. 350 picks up the trail, traveling southwest to Trinidad. If you detour onto the quiet county roads, you can still discern its faint outline over the dip of arroyos, and with a little imagination, conjure up visions of the pioneers.

EXPLORING

Downtown, called the **Corazon de Trinidad** *(Heart of Trinidad)*, is a National Historic Landmark District with original brick-paved streets, several Victorian mansions, churches, and the bright-red domes and turrets of Temple Aaron, Colorado's oldest continuously used Reform synagogue.

The **Trinidad History Museum,** a complex that includes three separate museums and a garden, represents the most significant aspects of Trinidad's history. Felipe Baca was a prominent Hispanic farmer and businessman whose 1870s residence, **Baca House,** has period furnishings. Displays convey a mix of Anglo (clothes, furniture) and local Hispanic (santos, textiles) influences. Next door, **Bloom Mansion** is an interesting contrast to the Baca House. Frank Bloom made his money through ranching and banking, and although he was no wealthier than Baca, his 1882 mansion represents a very different lifestyle. Using rail transportation, he was able to fill his ornate Second Empire–style Victorian—with mansard roof and elaborate wrought ironwork—with fine furnishings and fabrics brought from the East Coast and abroad. The adjacent **Santa Fe Trail Museum** is dedicated to the effect of the trail and railroad on the community. Inside are exhibits covering Trinidad's heyday as a commercial and cultural center up through the 1920s. Finish up with a stop in the **Heritage Gardens,** filled with native plants and century-old grapevines similar to those tended by the pioneers. ✉ *312 E. Main St.* ☎ *719/846–7217* ⊕ *www.coloradohistory.org* ✉ *$8* ☾ *May–Sept., daily 10–4. Call for winter hrs.*

The **A.R. Mitchell Memorial Museum and Gallery** celebrates the life and work of the famous Western illustrator, whose distinctive oils, charcoal drawings, and watercolors graced the pages of pulp magazines and ranch romances. The museum is in an old historic building with the original tin ceiling. Also on display are photos by the Aultman family;

dating from 1889, they offer a unique visual record of Trinidad. ⊠ *150 E. Main St.* ☎ *719/846–4224* ⌦ *$3, free on Sun.* ☉ *May–Oct., Tues.– Sat. 10–4; call for off-season hrs.*

On the other side of the Purgatoire River, the **Louden-Henritze Archaeology Museum** takes viewers back millions of years to examine the true origins of the region, including early geological formations, plant and marine-animal fossils, and prehistoric artifacts. ⊠ *Trinidad State Junior College, 600 Prospect,* ☎ *719/846–5508* ⊕ *historictrinidad.com/tour/ arc.html* ⌦ *Free* ☉ *Jan.–Nov., Mon.–Thurs. 10–3.*

SPORTS AND THE OUTDOORS

There's hiking, fishing in the reservoir, horseback riding, and camping in the Purgatoire River valley at the **Trinidad Lake State Park** (☎ *719/846– 6951* ⊕ *parks.state.co.us/parks/trinidadlake*), 3 mi west of Trinidad on Route 12.

GOLF

Cougar Canyon Golf Course. This Nicklaus Design course is a dramatic layout etched into arroyos and mesas, with views of the nearby Sangre de Christo Mountains. ⊠ *3700 E. Main* ☎ *719/422–7015* ⊕ *www. cougarcanyonliving.com* ⌦ *18 holes. Yards: 7,669/5,327. Par: 72. Green fee: $73–$83, plus $15 per person for cart.*

WHERE TO EAT

¢–$ ✕ **The Café.** Set in a downtown historic building, the Café serves imagi-
CAFE native and delicious sandwiches such as the Stonewall Gap, which has honey-smoked ham and melted Brie slathered with chutney in a ciabatta roll. This spot is usually crowded at breakfast and lunch, but you order at the counter, so things move quickly. Drop in for a muffin or pecan sticky bun and a cup of strong coffee or chai tea if you don't want a full meal. The Café is inside Danielson Dry Goods, and the other half of the building, which you can explore while waiting for your food, is an upscale-lifestyle store, with an eclectic array of humorous signs. ⊠ *135 E. Main St.* ☎ *719/846–7119* ⊟ *AE, MC, V* ☉ *No dinner.*

¢–$ ✕ **Nana and Nano's Pasta House.** The aroma of garlic and tomato sauce
ITALIAN saturates this tiny, unpretentious eatery. Pastas, including standards like homemade ravioli, gnocchi Bolognese, and rigatoni with luscious meatballs, are consistently excellent. If you don't have time for a sit-down lunch, stop at the deli counter for smashing heroes and gourmet sandwiches or takeouts of imported cheeses and olives. ⊠ *418 E. Main St.* ☎ *719/846–2696* ⊟ *AE, D, MC, V* ☉ *Closed Sun., Mon., and Tues.*

WHERE TO STAY

$–$$ ☷ **Black Jack's Saloon, Steak House & Inn.** Step inside this 1890s downtown building, where you can toss your peanut shells on the floor from your perch at the full-service antique bar downstairs from your room. Between this bar and the leafy-salad kind of bar is an open grill ($$) where the most succulent steaks on the Santa Fe Trail are prepared. Those avoiding red meat can go for salmon, swordfish, or chicken. The owners have also restored five rooms overhead, each named after some of the "ladies" who lived upstairs. Rooms are decorated in bordello style, as if the ladies just slipped outside for a break; bathrooms are similarly tricked up but have been modernized. In this quaint alternative

12

to motels, the rooms have robes and Wi-Fi, are air-conditioned, and come with a light Continental breakfast. **Pros:** these rooms take you back to another era; in the center of the historic district. **Cons:** it's over a colorful and popular saloon; small rooms. ✉ *225 W. Main St.,* ☎ *719/846–9501* ⊕ *www.blackjackssaloon.com* ⏎ *5 rooms* ⬧ *In-room: no phone, Wi-Fi.* ☐ *AE, MC, V* ⏹ *CP* ☺ *Restaurant closed Sun.*

$ 🏠 **Tarabino Inn.** This turn-of-the-20th-century Italianate–Victorian brick B&B in the Corazon de Trinidad National Historic District is the former abode of the Tarabino brothers, the proprietors of one of Trinidad's first department stores. The rooms are frilly, immaculate, and comfortable, with a dose of modern convenience. **Pros:** inn is filled with work by local artists, which is for sale; within walking distance of museums and downtown. **Cons:** feels like staying in someone's private home; no pets allowed. ✉ *310 E. 2nd St.,* ☎ *719/846–2115 or 866/846–8808* ⊕ *www.tarabinoinn.com* ⏎ *2 suites, 2 rooms without bath* ⬧ *In-room: refrigerator, Internet. In-hotel: Wi-Fi* ☐ *AE, D, MC, V* ⏹ *BP.*

NIGHTLIFE

Choose from a variety of lagers and ales, with names like La Fiesta and Ghost Town Brown Ale or one of the other traditional brews, at the **Trinidad Brewing Company** (✉ *516 Elm St.* ☎ *719/846–7069* ⊕ *www. trinidadbrewingcompany.com*).

SHOPPING

In the heart of the historic district there are some galleries and shops. **Purgatoire River Trading Company** (✉ *113 E. Main St.* ☎ *719/845–0202*) is the place to find authentic old Navajo rugs, Native American pottery, Pima baskets, and old-pawn jewelry. **Corazon Gallery** (✉ *149 E. Main St.* ☎ *719/846–0207*) is a local artists' co-op, with oils, handwoven clothing, and mixed-media artwork.

CUCHARA VALLEY

55 mi from Trinidad (to town of Cuchara) via Rte. 12; 117 mi south of Colorado Springs.

If you want a true mountain rural setting, head to Cuchara Valley. From here or La Veta you can go camping or hiking in the San Isabel National Forest, go horseback riding on trails through the woods, go fishing in streams, or play golf.

GETTING HERE AND AROUND

This is a tiny town along the Highway of Legends. You need a private car to get here and move around this region.

ESSENTIALS

Visitor Info Huerfano County Chamber of Commerce (✉ *400 Main St., Walsenburg* ☎ *719/738–1065* ⊕ *www.huerfanocountychamberofcommerce.com*). **La Veta–Cuchara Chamber of Commerce** (☎ *719/742–3676* ⊕ *www.laveta-cucharachamber.com*).

TOP EXPERIENCE: HIGHWAY OF LEGENDS

★ From Trinidad, Route 12—the scenic **Highway of Legends**—curls north through the Cuchara Valley. As it starts its climb, you'll pass a series of company towns built to house coal miners. The Highway of Legends takes you through some of the wildest and most beautiful scenery in southern Colorado. You can start the drive in Trinidad or La Veta. It takes you through dramatic scenery in the Spanish Peaks, and some of the oldest resort and vacation areas in this part of Colorado.

Cokedale is nestled in Reilly Canyon. The entire town is a National Historic Landmark District, and it's the most significant example of a turn-of-the-20th-century coal–coke camp in Colorado. As you drive through the area, note the telltale streaks of black in the sandstone and granite bluffs fronting the Purgatoire River and its tributaries, the unsightly slag heaps, and the spooky abandoned mining camps dotting the hillsides.

As you approach Cuchara Pass, several switchbacks snake through rolling grasslands and dance in and out of spruce stands whose clearings afford views of Monument Lake. You can camp, fish, and hike throughout this tranquil part of the **San Isabel National Forest,** which in spring and summer is emblazoned with a color wheel of wildflowers. Four corkscrewing miles later you'll reach a dirt road that leads to the twin sapphires of **Bear and Blue lakes.** The resort town of **Cuchara** is about 4 mi from the Highway 12 turnoff to the lakes. Nestled in a spoon valley (*cuchara* means "spoon"), the area became popular as a turn-of-the-20th-century camping getaway for Texans and Oklahomans because of its cool temperatures and stunning scenery.

In the Cuchara Valley you'll begin to see fantastic rock formations with equally fanciful names, such as Profile Rock, Devil's Staircase, and Giant's Spoon. With a little imagination you can devise your own legends about the names' origins. There are more than 400 of these upthrusts, which radiate like the spokes of a wheel from the valley's dominating landmark, the **Spanish Peaks.** In Spanish they are known as *Dos Hermanos,* or "Two Brothers"; in Ute, their name *Huajatolla* means "breasts of the world." The haunting formations are considered to be a unique geologic phenomenon for their sheer abundance and variety of rock types.

The Highway of Legends passes through the tiny, laid-back resort town of **La Veta** before intersecting with Highway 160 and going on to Walsenburg, another settlement built on coal and the largest town between Pueblo and Trinidad.

SPORTS AND THE OUTDOORS
GOLF
Grandote Peaks Golf Club. This Weiskopf Morrish–designed course is an underutilized gem that sits close to the base of the Spanish Peaks. On weekends you need reservations to play the classic 18-hole mountain course, but it might be easy to get on at the last minute weekdays. ⊠ *5540 Hwy. 12, La Veta* ☎ *719/742–3391 or 800/457–9986* ⊕ *www. grandotepeaks.com* ⌘ *18 holes. Yards: 7,085/5,608. Par: 72/73. Green fee: $55/$75 plus $15 for cart.*

HIKING
The **San Isabel National Forest** (⊠ *3028 E. Main St., Cañon City,* ☎ *719/ 269–8500*) has myriad hiking trails, not to mention campgrounds, fishing streams, and mountain-biking terrain. In winter it's a cross-country skiing destination.

WHERE TO STAY

$ ⭐ 🎴 **Inn at the Spanish Peaks Bed & Breakfast.** This Southwestern-style B&B is set in an adobe-style home with open beams and high ceilings. The attractive great room has a fireplace. Three themed guest suites all have decks with views of the surrounding mountains; the nicely done St. Andrews Suite focuses on golf, and the Colorado Suite has a handmade log bed. **Pros:** mountain views; friendly owners; good breakfasts. **Cons:** you are really in the outback of Colorado; no air-conditioning. ⊠ *310 E. Francisco St., La Veta* ☎ *719/742–5313* ⊕ *www.innatthespanishpeaks.com* ⊅ *3 suites* ⚘ *In-room: no a/c, no TV, In-hotel: public Wi-Fi* ➟ *MC, V* ⋔ *BP.*

$ 🎴 **La Veta Inn.** The shady courtyard, with its fireplace, is a selling point at this inn in the historic district of La Veta. There are some antiques in the guest rooms, but it's not a fancy place. The restaurant ($$) serves dinner only. **Pros:** next to galleries, a few blocks from Tom Weiskopf's Grandote Peaks Golf Course. **Cons:** not ideal for travelers who want a more urban atmosphere; closed January and February. ⊠ *103 W. Ryus Ave.* ⊡ *Box 300, La Veta* ☎ *719/742–3700, 888/806–4875 reservations* ⊕ *www.lavetainn.com* ⊅ *18 rooms* ⚘ *In-room; DVD, Wi-Fi. In-hotel: restaurant, bar, some pets allowed* ➟ *AE, D, MC, V.*

> **CUCHARA VALLEY LODGING ALTERNATIVES**
>
> The rental of condominiums, homes, and cabins is handled by **Cuchara Cabins and Condos** (☎ 719/742–3340).

THE SAN LUIS VALLEY

At 8,000 square mi, the San Luis Valley is considered to be the world's largest alpine valley, sprawling on a broad, flat, dry plain between the San Juan and La Garita mountains to the west and the Sangre de Cristo range to the east. But equally important is that the valley, like the Southwest, remains culturally rooted in the early Hispanic tradition rather than the northern European one that early prospectors and settlers brought to central and northern Colorado.

Despite its average elevation of 7,500 feet, the San Luis Valley's sheltering peaks help to create a relatively mild climate. The area is one of the state's major agricultural producers, with huge annual crops of potatoes, carrots, canola, barley, and lettuce. In many ways it's self-sufficient; in the 1950s local business owners threatened to secede to prove that the state couldn't get along without the valley and its valuable products. Half a century later, however, the reality is that the region is economically disadvantaged and contains two of the state's poorer counties. The large and sparsely populated valley contains some real oddities, including an alligator farm, a UFO-viewing tower, and the New Age town of Crestone, with its spiritual centers.

This area was settled first by the Ute, then by the Spanish, who left their indelible imprint in the town names and architecture. The oldest town (San Luis), the oldest military post (Fort Garland), and the oldest church (Our Lady of Guadalupe in Conejos) in the state are in this valley.

GREAT SAND DUNES NATIONAL PARK AND PRESERVE

Updated
by Martha
Connors

Created by winds that sweep the San Luis Valley floor, the enormous sand dunes that form the heart of Great Sand Dunes National Park and Preserve are an improbable, unforgettable sight. The dunes, as curvaceous as Rubens' nudes, stretch for more than 30 square mi. Because they're made of sand, the dunes' very existence seem tenuous, as if they might blow away before your eyes, yet they're solid enough to withstand 440,000 years of Mother Nature—and the modern stress of hikers and saucer-riding thrill-seekers.

GETTING HERE AND AROUND

Great Sand Dunes National Park and Preserve is about 240 mi from both Denver and Albuquerque, and roughly 180 mi from Colorado Springs and Santa Fe. The fastest route from the north is Interstate 25 south to U.S. 160, heading west to just past Blanca, to Highway 150 north, which goes right to the park's main entrance. For a more scenic route, take U.S. 285 over Kenosha, Red Hill, and Poncha Passes, turn onto Highway 17 just south of Villa Grove, then take County Lane 6 to the park (watch for signs just south of Hooper). When traveling from the south, go north on Interstate 25 to Santa Fe, then north on U.S. 285 to Alamosa, then U.S. 160 east to Highway 150. From the west, Highway 17 and County Lane 6 take you to the park. The park entrance station is about 3 mi from the park boundary, and it's about a mile from there to the visitor center; the main parking lot is about a mile farther.

ORIENTATION

The Great Sand Dunes Park and Preserve encompasses 150,000 acres (about 234 square mi) of land and mountains surrounding the dunes. Looking at the dunes from the west, your eye sweeps over the grassland and sand sheet, a vast expanse of smaller dunes and flatter sections of sand and knee-high brush. The Sangre de Cristo Mountains rear up in the east behind the dunes, forming a dramatic backdrop and creating a stunning juxtaposition of color and form.

Sand dunes. The 30-square-mi field of sand has no designated trails. The highest dune in the park—and, in fact, in North America—is 750-foot-high Star Dune.

Sangre de Cristo Mountains. Named the "Blood of Christ" Mountains by Spanish explorers because of their ruddy color—especially at sunrise and sunset—the range contains 10 of Colorado's 54 Fourteeners.

WHEN TO GO

About 300,000 visitors come to the park each year, most on summer weekends; they tend to congregate around the main parking area and Medano Creek. To avoid the crowds, hike away from the main area up to the High Dune. Or come in the winter, when the park is a place for contemplation and repose—as well as skiing and sledding.

Fall and spring are the prettiest times to visit, with the surrounding mountains still capped with snow in May, and leaves on the aspen trees turning gold in September and early October. In summer, the surface temperature of the sand can climb to 140°F in the afternoon, so climbing the dunes is best in the morning or late afternoon. Since you're at a high altitude—about 8,200 feet at the visitor center—the air temperatures in the park itself remain in the 70s most of the summer.)

EXPLORING
SCENIC DRIVE

★ **Medano Pass Primitive Road.** This 22-mi road connects Great Sand Dunes with the Wet Mountain Valley and Highway 69 on the east side of the Sangre de Cristo Mountains via a climb to Medano Pass (about 10,000 feet above sea level). It also provides access to campsites in the national preserve. It is a four-wheel-drive-only road that is best driven by someone who already has good driving skills on rough, unpaved roads. (Your four-wheel-drive vehicle must have high clearance and be engineered to go over rough roads, and you may need to drop your tires' air pressure.) The road has sections of deep, loose sand, and it crosses Medano Creek nine times. Before you go, stop at the visitor center for a map and ask about current road conditions. Drive time pavement to pavement is 2½ to 3 hours.

WHAT TO SEE

★ **Dune Field.** The more than 30 square mi of big dunes in the heart of the park is the main attraction, although the surrounding sand sheet does have some smaller dunes. You can start putting your feet in the sand 3 mi past the main park entrance.

High Dune. This isn't the park's highest dune, but it's high enough in the dune field to provide a view of all the dunes from its summit. It's on the first ridge of dunes you see from the main parking area.

VISITOR CENTER

Great Sand Dunes Visitor Center. View exhibits, browse in the bookstore, and watch a 20-minute film with an overview of the dunes. Rangers are on hand to answer questions. Facilities include restrooms and a vending machine stocked with soft drinks spring, summer, and fall, but no food. (The Great Sand Dunes Oasis, just outside the park boundary, has a café that is open May through late-September.) ✉ *Near the park entrance* ☏ *719/378–6399* ☼ *Late May–early Sept., daily 9–6; early Sept.–late May, hrs vary (call ahead).*

SPORTS AND THE OUTDOORS
BIRD-WATCHING

The San Luis Valley is famous for its migratory birds, many of which make a stop in the park. Great Sand Dunes also has many permanent feathered residents. In the wetlands, you might see American white pelicans and the American avocet. On the forested sections of the mountains there are goshawks, northern harriers, gray jays, and Steller's jays. And in the alpine tundra there are golden eagles, hawks, horned larks, and white-tailed ptarmigan.

FISHING

Fly fishermen can angle for Rio Grande cutthroat trout in the upper reaches of Medano Creek, which is accessible by four-wheel-drive vehicle. It's catch and release only, and a Colorado license is required (☏ *800/244–5613*). There's also fishing in Upper and Lower Sand Creek Lakes, but it's a very long hike (3 or 4 mi from the Music Pass Trailhead, located on the far side of the park in the San Isabel National Forest).

PARK ESSENTIALS

ACCESSIBILITY
The park has two wheelchairs with balloon tires (for the sand) that can be borrowed; someone must push them. You can reserve one by calling the visitor center. There is one accessible campsite.

ADMISSION FEES AND PERMITS
Entrance fees are $3 per adult above age 16 and are valid for one week. Pick up camping permits ($14 per night per site at Pinyon Flats Campground) and backpacking permits (free) at the visitor center.

ADMISSION HOURS
The park is open 24/7. It is in the mountain time zone.

ATMS/BANKS
The park has no ATM. The nearest bank is 35 mi away in Alamosa.

CELL-PHONE RECEPTION
Cell-phone reception in the park is sporadic. Public telephones are at the visitor center, dunes parking lot, and at the Pinyon Flats campground—you need a calling card (these aren't coin-operated phones).

PARK CONTACT INFORMATION
Great Sand Dunes National Park and Preserve ⊠ *11999 Hwy. 150, Mosca* ☎ *719/378–6399* ⊕ *www.nps.gov/grsa.*

HIKING
Visitors can walk just about anywhere on the sand dunes in the heart of the park. The best view of all the dunes is from the top of High Dune. There are no formal trails because the sand keeps shifting, but you don't really need them: There's no way you'd get lost out here.

■ TIP→ **Before taking any of the trails in the preserve, rangers recommend stopping at the visitor center and picking up the handout that lists the trails, including their degree of difficulty.** The dunes can get very hot in the summer, reaching up to 140°F in the afternoon. If you're hiking, carry plenty of water; if you're going into the backcountry to camp overnight, carry even more water and a water filtration system. A free permit is needed to backpack in the park. Also, watch for weather changes. If there's a thunderstorm and lightning, get off the dunes or trail immediately, and seek shelter. Before hiking, leave word with someone indicating where you're to hike and when you expect to be back. Tell that contact to call 911 if you don't show up when expected.

EASY **Hike to High Dune.** Get a panoramic view of all the surrounding dunes. Since there's no formal path, the smartest approach is to zigzag up the dune ridgelines. High Dune is 650 feet high, and to get there and back takes about 1½ to 2 hours. It's 1.2 mi each way, but it can feel like a lot longer if there's been no rain for awhile and the sand is soft. If you add on the walk to Star Dune, which is a few more miles, plan on another two hours and a strenuous workout up and down the dunes to get there. ⊠ *Start from main dune field.*

MODERATE **Mosca Pass Trail.** This moderately easy trail follows the route laid out
Fodor's Choice centuries ago by Native Americans, which became the Mosca Pass toll
★ road used in the late 1800s and early 1900s. This is a good afternoon

hike, because the trail rises through the trees and subalpine meadows, often following Mosca Creek. It is 3½ mi one way, with a 1,480-foot gain in elevation. Hiking time is two to three hours each way. ⊠ *Lower end of the trail begins at the Montville Trailhead, just north of the visitor center.*

DIFFICULT **Music Pass Trail.** This steep trail offers superb views of the glacially carved Upper Sand Creek Basin, ringed by many 13,000-foot peaks and the Wet Mountain Valley to the east. At the top of the pass you are about 11,000 feet above sea level and surrounded by yet higher mountain peaks. It's 3½ mi and a 2,000-foot elevation gain one way from the lower parking lot on the east side of the preserve, off Forest Service Road 119, and 1 mi from the upper parking lot (only reachable in a four-wheel-drive vehicle). Depending on how fit you are and how often you stop, it could take six hours round-trip. ⊠ *Trail begins on eastern side of park, reached via Hwy. 69, 4½ mi south of Westcliffe. Turn off Hwy. 69 to the west at the sign for Music Pass and South Colony Lakes Trails. At the "T" junction, turn left onto South Colony Rd. At the end of the ranch fence on the right you'll see another sign for Music Pass.*

EDUCATIONAL OFFERINGS
PROGRAMS AND TOURS
☾ **Bison Tour.** The Nature Conservancy, an international nonprofit conservation organization, owns a 103,000-acre ranch that includes a herd of roughly 2,000 bison in the 50,000-acre Medano Ranch section, in the southwest corner of the park. The conservancy offers a two-hour tour focused on the "Wild West" section of the park, where bison—along with coyotes, elk, deer, pronghorns, porcupines, and birds such as great horned owls and red-tailed hawks, roam in the grasslands and wetlands. Depending on the season, the tour will be led as a hayride or a four-wheel-drive vehicle drive. ⊠ *Tours begin at the Nature Conservancy's Zapata Ranch Headquarters, 5303 Hwy. 150, Mosca* ☎ *888/592–7282 or 719/378–2356* ⊕ *www.zranch.org* ⊠ *$50.*

RANGER PROGRAMS
Interpretive Programs. Terrace talks and nature walks designed to help visitors learn more about the park are scheduled most days from late May through September. (Contact the park in advance about any programs from October through April.) ⊠ *Programs begin at the visitor center* ☎ *719/378–6399* ⊠ *Free.*

☾ **Junior Ranger Programs.** During summer months, children ages 3 through 12 can join age-appropriate activities to learn about plants, animals, and the park's ecology, and they can become Junior Rangers by working successfully through an activity booklet. Ask for schedules and activity booklets at the visitor center. Youngsters can learn about the park prior to their trip via an interactive online program for kids at ⊕ *www.nps.gov/grsa/forkids/beajuniorranger.htm.* Sign up at the visitor center. ☎ *719/378–6399* ⊠ *Free.*

WHERE TO STAY

Great Sand Dunes has one campground that is open year-round. During weekends in the summer, it can fill up with RVs and tents by mid-afternoon. Black bears live in the preserve, so when camping there, keep your food, trash, and toiletries in the trunk of your car (or use bear-proof containers).

CAMPING   ♨ **Pinyon Flats Campground.** Set in a pine forest about a mile past the
¢ visitor center, this campground has a trail leading to the dunes. Sites are available on a first-come, first-served basis, although groups of 10 or more might be able to reserve in advance. (Register at the kiosk.) RVs are allowed, but there are no hookups. The campground can fill up on summer weekends, and tends to have lots of families when school is out. Quiet hours start at 10 PM. **Pros:** only campground in park; close to main dunes. **Cons:** can get crowded, especially on summer weekends; best for smaller RVs. ⊠ *On the main park road, near the visitor center* ☎ *719/378–6399* ♨ *88 tent/RV sites* ⚴ *Flush toilets, fire grates, picnic tables* ⊟ *D, MC, V.*

ALAMOSA

35 mi southwest of Great Sand Dunes via U.S. 160 and Rte. 150; 163 mi southwest of Colorado Springs.

Updated by
Lois Friedland

The San Luis Valley's major city is a casual, central base from which to explore the region and visit the Great Sand Dunes.

EXPLORING

Just 3 mi outside town is the **Alamosa National Wildlife Refuge.** These natural and man-made wetlands bordering the Rio Grande River—an anomaly amid the arid surroundings—are an important sanctuary for myriad migrating birds. ⊠ *9383 El Rancho La.* ☎ *719/589–4021* ⌨ *Free* ☉ *Daily sunrise–sunset.*

From late February to mid-March, birders flock to nearby Monte Vista to view the migration of the sandhill cranes at the **Monte Vista National Wildlife Refuge.** Nicknamed the Valley of the Cranes, you can see these interesting creatures at close range. Every morning during the Festival of the Cranes, buses shuttle visitors to the refuge from Alamosa. ⊠ *6140 Hwy. 15, Monte Vista* ⌨ *Free* ☉ *Daily sunrise–sunset.*

The **San Luis Valley Museum** showcases Indian artifacts, photographs, military regalia, and collectibles of early railroading, farming, and ranch life. Exhibits feature the multicultural influence of Hispanic, Japanese-American, Mormon, and Dutch settlers. ⊠ *401 Hunt* ☎ *719/587–0667* ⌨ *$2* ☉ *Tues.–Sat. 10–4.*

WHERE TO EAT

¢ ✕**East West Grill.** Noodles and teriyaki are on the menu at this casual
ASIAN fast-food-style place, where you order and get your food at the counter. Offerings include rice bowls, noodle bowls, salads, and bento boxes filled with wild salmon, sesame chicken, or soba noodles and steamed fresh veggies. The pad thai is tasty, and the sesame chop salad is nicely dressed. Dine in or carry out. ⊠ *408 4th St.* ☎ *719/589–4600* ⊕ *www. east-westgrill.com* ⊟ *AE, D, MC, V.*

12

$$
STEAK

✕ **True Grits.** At this steak house the cuts of beef are good, as are the burgers, but that's not the real draw. As the name implies, this locals' hangout is really just a shrine to John Wayne. It's worth a stop to see his portraits, which hang everywhere: the Duke in action; the Duke in repose; the Duke lost in thought. Reservations are suggested. ⌧ *Junction U.S. 160 and Rte. 17* ☎ *719/589–9954* ▭ *AE, D, MC, V* ☽ *No lunch.*

¢
CAFE
★

✕ **Milagro's Coffeehouse.** The coffee is full-bodied at this combination coffeehouse, Internet café, and used-book store, where all profits go to help local charities. The decor is secondhand basic, but the tuna salad sub and the Reuben are especially tasty. Free Wi-Fi makes this a popular spot for locals. The used-book selection is very eclectic, and includes some obscure titles. Dine in or carry out. ⌧ *Main and State Sts.* ☎ *719/589–9299* ▭ *MC, V.*

WHERE TO STAY

$
☺

▭ **Inn of the Rio Grande.** The city's largest hotel is a dog-friendly property with comfortable rooms and suites. It's a full-service hotel, and kids will love the indoor pool and 150-foot waterslide. It's also a good choice for businesspeople, because there are work desks and free Wi-Fi in the rooms and a conference center. The hotel's in-house resaurant, Clancy's, also does room service. The hotel is conveniently on Sante Fe Drive/Highway 160, about a mile from downtown. **Pros:** indoor water park; pet friendly. **Cons:** basic rooms. ⌧ *333 Santa Fe Dr.,* ☎ *719/589–5833* ⊕ *www.innoftherio.com* ⇌ *126 rooms* ᗜ *In-room: refrigerator (some), Wi-Fi. In-hotel: restaurant, pool, gym, public Wi-Fi, some pets allowed, parking (free)* ▭ *AE, D, MC, V.*

SHOPPING

Fireworks Gallery (⌧ *608 Main St.* ☎ *719/589–6064*) carries fine art, collectibles, jewelry, weavings, and prints.The San Luis Valley is noted for its produce. Mycophiles can take a tour of the **Rakhra Mushroom Farm** (⌧ *10719 Rd. 5 S* ☎ *719/589–5882*). Call ahead; mornings are preferred. **Treasure Alley** (⌧ *713 Main St.* ☎ *719/587–0878*) offers an eclectic mix of gifts, from jewelry and jewelry boxes to local artwork and clocks. **Vintage Garage Antiques Mall** (⌧ *420 Main St.* ☎ *719/587–5494*) is a renovated garage brimming with old stuff, jewelry, antiques, glassware, and much more.

MANASSA, SAN LUIS, AND FORT GARLAND LOOP

To get a real feel for this area, take an easy driving loop from Alamosa that includes Manassa, San Luis, and Fort Garland. In summer, take a few hours to ride one of the scenic railroads that take you into wilderness areas in this region.

TIMING

The driving distance for this loop, including a 7-mi jog down to Antonio if you want to take a ride on the Cumbres and Toltec Scenic Railroad, is about 100 mi. But, it's along secondary roads and goes through small towns, so don't expect to maintain highway speeds.

EXPLORING

The **Cumbres & Toltec Scenic Railroad** chugs through spectacular scenery in Colorado and New Mexico. The steam railroad is 64 mi long, and the depot is in Antonito. Several different itineraries are available with restored vintage tourist-class and parlor cars. ☎ *888/286–2737* ⊕ *www. cumbrestoltec.com* ⊠ *Coach class $74, tourist class $106, $139 in parlor car* ⊙ *Late May–mid-Oct., daily. Call or check Web site for times.*

The **Rio Grande Scenic Railroad** takes travelers from Alamosa up to La Veta pass. ☎ *888/726–7245* ⊕ *www.riograndescenicrailroad.com* ⊠ *Coach class $48* ⊙ *Late May–mid-Oct., daily. Hrs vary.*

The town of **Manassa** is about 23 mi from Alamosa, south on U.S. 285 and 3 mi east on Route 142. Known as the Manassa Mauler, one of the greatest heavyweight boxing champions of all time is honored in his hometown at the **Jack Dempsey Museum** (⊠ *412 Main St.* ☎ *719/843–5207* ⊙ *Memorial Day weekend–Labor Day weekend, Tues.–Sat. 10–5.*

San Luis, founded in 1851, is the oldest incorporated town in Colorado. Murals depicting famous stories and legends of the area adorn several buildings in the town. A latter-day masterpiece is the **Stations of the Cross Shrine,** created by renowned local sculptor Huberto Maestas. The shrine is formally known as La Mesa de la Piedad y de la Misericordia (Hill of Piety and Mercy), and its 15 stations illustrate the last hours of Christ's life. The trail leads up to a chapel called Capilla de Todos Los Santos. San Luis's Hispanic heritage is celebrated in the **San Luis Museum & Cultural Center** (⊠ *401 Church Pl.* ☎ *719/672–3611* ⊠ *$2* ⊙ *Summer, Mon.–Sat. 10–4, Sun. noon–4; winter, weekdays 10–4).* It has an extensive collection of artwork, *santos* (decorated figures of saints used for household devotions), *retablos* (religious paintings on wood), and *bultos* (carved religious figures).

One of Colorado's first military posts, **Fort Garland,** was established in 1858 to protect settlers. It lies in the shadow of the Sangre de Cristo Mountains. They were named the Blood of Christ Mountains because of their ruddy color, especially at dawn. The legendary Kit Carson commanded the outfit, and five of the original adobe structures are still standing. The **Fort Garland State Museum** features a re-creation of the commandant's quarters and period military displays. The museum is 16 mi north of San Luis via Route 159 and 24 mi east of Alamosa via U.S. 160. ⊠ *South of intersection U.S. 160 and Hwy. 159,* ☎ *719/379–3512* ⊠ *$5* ⊙ *Apr.–Oct., daily 9–5; Nov.–Mar., Thurs.–Mon. 10–4.*

DEL NORTE

31 mi west of Alamosa via U.S. 160; 194 mi southwest of Colorado Springs.

Del Norte is a tiny town, but there's an excellent honey shop on the main street, a regional history museum, and good hiking in nearby Penitente Canyon.

EXPLORING

The **Rio Grande County Museum and Cultural Center** celebrates the region's multicultural heritage with displays of petroglyphs, mining artifacts, early Spanish relics, and rotating shows of contemporary art. ⊠ *580 Oak St.* ☎ *719/657–2847* ☜ *$1* ☺ *Tues.–Sat. 10–5.*

Just north of town is the gaping **Penitente Canyon.** Once a retreat and place of worship for a small, fervent sect of the Catholic Church known as Los Hermanos Penitente, it is now a haven for rock climbers, hikers, and mountain bikers. Follow Route 112 about 3 mi from Del Norte, then follow the signs to the canyon.

In the nearby La Garita Wilderness is another marvel—the towering rock formation **La Ventana Natural Arch.**

SPORTS AND THE OUTDOORS

FISHING

The **Rio Grande River** (⊕ *www.wildlife.state.co.us/fishing*) between Del Norte and South Fork teems with rainbows, browns, and cutthroats. The area is full of "gold medal" waters, designated as great fishing spots by the Colorado Wildlife Commission.

SHOPPING

Elk Ridge (⊠ *616 Grand Ave.* ☎ *719/657–2322*) is the place for gourmet products and gift baskets overflowing with goodies. **Haefeli's Honey Farms** (⊠ *425 Grand Ave.* ☎ *719/657–2044*) sells delectable mountain-bloom honeys.

Travel Smart Colorado

GETTING HERE AND AROUND

Denver is Colorado's hub; all interstate highways intersect here, and most of the state's population lives within a one- or two-hour drive of the city. The high plains expand to the east from Denver, and the western edge of the metro area ends at the foothills of the Rocky Mountains. A corridor of cities along Interstate 25 parallels the foothills from Fort Collins to Pueblo, and most lonely stretches of highway are in the eastern portion of the state on the plains. Although scheduled air, rail, and bus service connects Denver to many smaller cities and towns, it is difficult to travel without a car.

▌ AIR TRAVEL

It takes about two hours to fly to Denver from Los Angeles, Chicago, or Dallas. From New York and Boston the flight is about 3½ hours. If you're traveling during snow season, allow extra time for the drive to the airport. If you'll be checking skis, arrive even earlier.

AIRPORTS

The major air gateway to the Colorado Rockies is Denver International Airport (DEN), 15 mi northeast of downtown Denver and 45 mi from Boulder. Flights to smaller, resort-town airports generally connect through it. During inclement weather, flights can be delayed or canceled. Although there are a few eateries in the airport, there are not any hotels on-site. Most hotels are several miles away toward Denver.

Some of the major airlines and their subsidiaries serve communities around the state: Grand Junction (GJT), Durango (DRO), Steamboat Springs (HDN), Gunnison–Crested Butte (GUC), Telluride (TEX), Aspen (ASE), Vail (EGE). Some major airlines have scheduled service from points within the United States to Colorado Springs Airport (COS); the relatively mild weather in Colorado Springs means that its airport is sometimes still functional when bad weather farther north and west affects the state's other airports. During ski season some of the major resort towns have increased service, and direct flights are available.

You might want to consider the time saved—or not saved—by flying to your resort destination versus renting a car at Denver International Airport and driving the same distance. A car trip from Denver to Vail can take 90 minutes to two hours in smoothly flowing traffic. Aspen is about four hours by car from Denver. Steamboat Springs' airport is actually 22 mi away in Hayden, and Vail's airport is 34 mi away in Eagle, requiring some travel by car or shuttle. In winter, flights in and out of mountain towns are frequently diverted, delayed, or canceled in bad weather. Weigh the possible time saving gained by flying against the time spent driving and enjoying the scenery along the way to your destination.

Airport Information Colorado Springs Airport (COS) (☎ 719/550–1972 ⊕ www. springsgov.com/airportindex.aspx). **Denver International Airport (DEN)** (☎ 303/342–2000, 800/247–2336, 303/342–2333 TTY, 800/688–1333 TTY ⊕ www.flydenver.com).

GROUND TRANSPORTATION

If you are driving, the best way from Denver International Airport to Denver, the ski resorts, or the mountains is along Peña Boulevard to Interstate 70 and then west. If you are traveling south from Denver, take Interstate 25. You can bypass some traffic by using the E–470 tollway, which intersects Peña a couple of miles west of the airport. It connects to Interstate 25 both south and north of Denver. When flying into Colorado Springs, take Interstate 25 north and south. Vail, Aspen, Telluride, and the surrounding towns are accessible on Highway 24 without going through Denver.

RTD has frequent bus service to Denver and Boulder; visit their booth in the main terminal for destinations, times, and tickets. There are taxis and various private airport shuttles to cities along the Front Range from the airport, and some offer door-to-door service. Many hotels and ski resorts have their own buses; check with your lodging or ski resort to see if they offer service. The Ground Transportation Information Center is on the fifth level of the main terminal, and can direct travelers to companies' service counters. All services depart from and arrive on level five of the main terminal building.

TRANSFERS BETWEEN AIRPORTS

Transferring between Denver International and Colorado Springs airports is easily done with your originating airline if you are flying Allegiant Airlines, American, Continental, Delta, Frontier, Northwest Airlines, United, or US Airways. If you choose, bus and shuttle services are available through Ramblin Express or Supershuttle.

Contacts Ramblin Express (☎ 877/726-2546 ⊕ www.ramblinexpress.com). **Supershuttle** (☎ 800/258-3826 ⊕ www.supershuttle.com).

FLIGHTS

Large airlines serve Denver International Airport (DEN) from many cities in the United States. A few international carriers serve Denver with nonstop flights from London, England; Frankfurt and Munich, Germany; as well as Vancouver, Calgary, Toronto, Winnipeg, and Montreal, Canada. Frontier Airlines and United Airlines are Denver's largest carriers, with the most flights and the longest list of destinations. United Express and Great Lakes Airlines connect Denver with smaller cities and ski resorts within Colorado.

Airline Contacts Aero Mexico (☎ 800/237-6639 ⊕ www.aeromexico.com). **Air Canada** (☎ 888/247-2262 ⊕ www.aircanada.com). **Air Tran Airways** (☎ 800/247-8726 ⊕ www.airtran.com). **Alaska Airlines** (☎ 800/252-7522 or 206/433-3100 ⊕ www.alaskaair.com). **Allegiant Airlines** (☎ 702/505-8888 ⊕ www.allegiantair.com). **American Airlines** (☎ 800/433-7300 ⊕ www.aa.com). **British Airways** (☎ 800/247-9297 ⊕ www.britishairways.com). **Continental Airlines** (☎ 800/523-3273 ⊕ www.continental.com).

Delta Airlines (☎ 800/221-1212 ⊕ www.delta.com). **Frontier** (☎ 800/432-1359 ⊕ www.frontierairlines.com). **Great Lakes** (☎ 800/554-5111 ⊕ www.flygreatlakes.com). **jetBlue** (☎ 800/538-2583 ⊕ www.jetblue.com). **Lufthansa** (☎ 800/645-3880 ⊕ www.lufthansa.com). **Mexicana** (☎ 800/531-7921 ⊕ www.mexicana.com). **Midwest Airlines** (☎ 800/452-2022 ⊕ www.midwestairlines.com). **Northwest Airlines** (☎ 800/225-2525 ⊕ www.nwa.com). **Southwest Airlines** (☎ 800/435-9792 ⊕ www.southwest.com). **United Airlines** (☎ 800/864-8331 ⊕ www.united.com). **USAirways** (☎ 800/428-4322 800/622-1015 ⊕ www.usairways.com).

▌ BUS TRAVEL

Traveling by bus within the Denver–Boulder region is fairly easy with RTD, since their coverage of the area is dense and most routes are not too circuitous. The free 16th Street MallRide and the light-rail routes within Denver make travel to and from downtown attractions easy.

Mountain Metropolitan Transit serves the Colorado Springs area. Colorado Mountain Express offers both shared-ride shuttles and private-car airport services from Denver International Airport (DEN) and Eagle County Regional Airport.

Bus Information Colorado Mountain Express (☎ 800/525-6363 or 970/926-9800 ⊕ www.ridecme.com). **Mountain Metropolitan Transit** (☎ 719/385-7433) **RTD** (☎ 303/299-6000 or 800/366-7433 ⊕ www.rtd-denver.com).

▌ CAR TRAVEL

Colorado has the most mountainous terrain of the American Rockies, and the scenery makes driving far from a tedious means to an end.

Car travel within the urban corridor north and south of Denver can be congested, particularly weekday mornings and afternoons. Congestion is not limited to the major highways; city arterials and smaller roads and streets can be slow during peak driving times. Weekends, too, can have quite a bit of traffic, particularly along I–70 between Denver and the high mountains. Heavy traffic is not limited to ski season or bad weather. It is nearly a matter of course now for eastbound I–70 to be heavily congested on Sunday afternoons. If you are returning to Denver International Airport for a Sunday-afternoon or evening flight, plan accordingly, and allow plenty of time to reach the airport.

GASOLINE

At this writing, gasoline costs between $2.12 and $2.79 a gallon. In major cities throughout Colorado, gas prices are roughly similar to the rest of the continental United States; in rural and resort towns prices are considerably higher. Although gas stations are plentiful in many areas, you can drive more than 100 mi on back roads without finding gas.

LICENSE PLATE TOLL

Denver's Eastern Beltway, the E–470, is a toll road. You are automatically a License Plate Toll customer on E–470 if you are not an EXpressToll customer with a transponder. No advance registration is required, and customers drive non-stop through the tolls. Cameras will photograph the front and rear license plates and a bill will be sent one month later to the registered owner of the vehicle for all the tolls incurred during that period.

Whether you have a Colorado or an out-of-state license plate, the billing process works the same for all vehicle registrations. You will receive your bill approximately one month after using E–470. Full payment must be received by the due date on the bill or each of the transactions listed on the statement will become toll violations. In that case, a toll violation citation for each toll will be sent to the vehicle's registered owner.

PARKING

On-street metered parking is available in larger cities. Meters take quarters, dimes, and nickels. Check the meter to see if any maximum time applies. Larger cities also have pay-by-the-hour lots and garages. Some require prepayment in cash, and others take payment at departure. A few resort towns have free parking lots and on-street parking. On-street parking in small towns is generally not difficult.

ROAD CONDITIONS

Colorado offers some of the most spectacular vistas and challenging driving in the world. Roads range from multilane blacktop to barely graveled backcountry trails; from twisting switchbacks considerately marked with guardrails to primitive campgrounds with a lane so narrow that you must back up to the edge of a steep cliff to make a turn. Scenic routes and lookout points are clearly marked, enabling you to slow down and pull over to take in the views.

One of the more unpleasant sights along the highway is roadkill—animals struck by vehicles. Deer, elk, and even bears may try to get to the other side of a road just as you come along, so watch out for wildlife on the highways. Exercise caution both for the sake of the animal in danger and your car, which could be totaled in a collision.

FROM	TO	DRIVE TIME
Denver	Boulder	40–60 mins
Denver	Fort Collins	60 mins
Denver	Colorado Springs	60–75 mins
Denver	Estes Park	1½–2 hrs
Denver	Glenwood Springs	2½–3 hrs
Glenwood Springs	Aspen	1 hr
Glenwood Springs	Crested Butte	3 hrs
Denver	Grand Junction	4 hrs
Grand Junction	Telluride	2–3 hrs
Denver	Durango	6–7 hrs

License Plate Toll EXpress Toll (☎ *303/537–3470* ⊕ *www.expresstoll.com*).

Road Condition Information Colorado (☎ *303/639–1111* ⊕ *www.cotrip.org*).

Emergency Services AAA of Colorado (☎ *303/753–8800*). **Colorado State Patrol** (☎ *303/239–4501 or *277 from a cell phone*). For police or ambulance, dial 911.

RULES OF THE ROAD

You'll find highways and national parks crowded in summer, and almost deserted (and occasionally impassable) in winter. Follow the posted speed limit, drive defensively, and make sure your gas tank is full. The law requires that drivers and front-seat passengers wear seat belts.

Always strap children under age 4 or under 40 pounds into approved child-safety seats. You may turn right at a red light after stopping if there's no sign stating otherwise and no oncoming traffic. When in doubt, wait for the green.

If your vehicle breaks down, or you are involved in an accident, move your vehicle out of the traffic flow, if possible, and call for help: 911 for emergencies and

*277 from a cell phone for the Colorado State Patrol.

The speed limit on U.S. interstates in Colorado is up to 75 MPH in rural areas and between 55 MPH and 65 MPH in urban zones. Mountain stretches of I–70 have lower limits—between 55 MPH and 70 MPH.

WINTER DRIVING

Modern highways make mountain driving safe and generally trouble-free even in cold weather. Although winter driving can occasionally present real challenges, road maintenance is good and plowing is prompt. However, in mountain areas tire chains, studs, or snow tires are essential. If you're planning to drive into high elevations, be sure to check the weather forecast and call for road conditions beforehand. Even main highways can close. It's a good idea to carry an emergency kit and a cell phone, but be aware that the mountains can disrupt service. If you do get stalled by deep snow, do not leave your car. Wait for help, running the engine only if needed, and remember that assistance is never far away. Winter weather isn't confined to winter months in the high country (it's been known to snow in July), so be prepared year-round.

Contacts Automobile Association (*AAA* ⊕ *www.aaa.com*).

CAR RENTAL

Rates in most major cities run about $58 a day and $230 a week for an economy car with air-conditioning, automatic transmission, and unlimited mileage. This does not include tax or fees on car rentals, which is as high as 24% in the Denver metro area. Keep in mind if you're venturing into the Rockies that you'll need a little oomph in your engine to get over the passes. If you plan to explore any back roads, an SUV is the best bet, because it will have higher clearance. Unless you plan to do much mountain exploring, a four-wheel drive is usually needed only in winter.

To rent a car in Colorado you must be at least 25 years old and have a valid driver's license; most companies also require a major credit card. Some companies at certain locations set their minimum age at 21, and then add a daily surcharge. In Colorado, child-safety seats or booster seats are compulsory for children under 5 (with certain height and weight criteria).

You'll pay extra for child seats ($5–$12 a day), drivers under age 25 (at least $25 a day), and usually for additional drivers (about $10 per day). When returning your car to Denver International Airport, allow 15 minutes (30 minutes during busy weekends and around the holidays) to return the vehicle and to ride the shuttle bus to the terminal.

Major Rental Agencies Alamo (☎ 800/462-5266 ⊕ www.alamo.com). **Avis** (☎ 800/331-1212 ⊕ www.avis.com). **Budget** (☎ 800/527-0700 ⊕ www.budget. com). **Hertz** (☎ 800/654-3131 ⊕ www.hertz. com). **National Car Rental** (☎ 800/227-7368 ⊕ www.nationalcar.com).

▌ TRAIN TRAVEL

Amtrak connects nine stations in Colorado to both coasts and all major American cities. The *California Zephyr* and the *Southwest Chief* pass once per day with east- and west-bound trains that stop in Denver, Winter Park, Granby, Glenwood Springs, Grand Junction, and Trinidad. The Ski Train connects Denver's Union Station and the Winter Park ski resort during ski season and in summer. There are also several scenic narrow-gauge sightseeing railroads all over the state.

Information Amtrak (☎ 800/872-7245 ⊕ www.amtrak.com). **Cumbres & Toltec Scenic Railroad** (☎ 719/376-5483 or 888/286-2737 ⊕ www.cumbrestoltec.com). **Durango & Silverton Narrow Gauge Railroad** (☎ 888/872-4607 ⊕ www.durangotrain. com). **Georgetown Loop Railroad** (☎ 888/456-6777 ⊕ www.georgetownlooprr. com). **Historic Royal Gorge Route Railroad** (☎ 719/276-4000 or 888/724-5748 ⊕ www. royalgorgeroute.com). **Leadville, Co. & Southern Railroad Company** (☎ 719/486-3936 or 866/386-3936 ⊕ www.leadville-train.com). **Rio Grande Scenic Railroad** (☎ 719/587-0520 or 877/726-7245 ⊕ www.riograndescenicrailroad.com).

ESSENTIALS

■ ACCOMMODATIONS

Accommodations in Colorado vary from the very posh ski resorts in Vail, Aspen, and Telluride to basic chain hotels and independent motels. Dude and guest ranches often require a one-week stay, and the cost is all-inclusive. Bed-and-breakfasts can be found throughout the state. Hotel rates peak during the height of the ski season, which generally runs from late November through March or April; although rates are high all season, they top out during Christmas week and in February and March. In summer months, a popular time for hiking and rafting, hotel rates are often half the winter price.

Properties are assigned price categories based on the cost of a standard double room during high season. Lodging taxes vary throughout the state.

Most hotels and other lodgings require you to give your credit-card details before they will confirm your reservation. However you book, get confirmation in writing and have a copy of it handy when you check in.

Be sure you understand the hotel's cancellation policy. Some places allow you to cancel without any kind of penalty—even if you prepaid to secure a discounted rate—if you cancel at least 24 hours in advance. Others require you to cancel a week in advance or penalize you the cost of one night. Small inns and B&Bs are most likely to require you to cancel far in advance. Most hotels allow children under a certain age to stay in their parents' room at no extra charge, but others charge for them as extra adults; find out the cutoff age for discounts.

Most hotels in Denver and Colorado Springs cater to business travelers, with facilities like restaurants, cocktail lounges, swimming pools, fitness centers, and meeting rooms. Many properties offer special weekend rates of up to 50% off regular prices. However, these deals are usually not extended during summer months, when city hotels are often full. In resort towns hotels are decidedly more deluxe; rural areas generally offer simple, sometimes rustic accommodations.

Ski towns throughout Colorado are home to dozens of resorts in all price ranges; the activities lacking at any individual property can usually be found in the town itself—in summer as well as winter. Off the slopes, there are both wonderful rustic and luxurious resorts, particularly in out-of-the-way spots near Rocky Mountain National Park and other alpine areas.

General Information Colorado Hotel and Lodging Association (☎ *303/297–8335* ⊕ *www.coloradolodging.com*).

■ TIP→ Assume that hotels operate on the European Plan (**EP**, no meals) unless we specify that they use the Breakfast Plan (**BP**, with full breakfast), Continental Plan (**CP**, Continental breakfast), Full American Plan (**FAP**, all meals), or Modified American Plan (**MAP**, breakfast and dinner), or are all-inclusive (**AI**, all meals and most activities).

APARTMENT AND HOUSE RENTALS

Rental accommodations are quite popular in Colorado's ski resorts and mountain towns. Condominiums and luxurious vacation homes dominate the Vail Valley and other ski-oriented areas, but there are scads of cabins in smaller, summer-oriented towns in the Rockies and the Western Slope. Many towns and resort areas have rental agencies. *For contact information, see the Where to Stay sections.*

With a direct home exchange you stay in someone else's home while they stay in yours. Some outfits also deal with vacation homes, so you're not actually staying in someone's full-time residence, just their vacant weekend place.

Exchange Clubs Forgetaway (⊕ *www.forgetaway.weather.com*). **Home Away**

(☎ 512/493–0382 ⊕ www.homeaway.com).
Home Exchange.com (☎ 800/877–8723
⊕ www.homeexchange.com); $99.95 for a one-
year online listing. **HomeLink International**
(☎ 800/638–3841 ⊕ www.homelink.org);
$115 yearly for Web-only membership; $175
includes Web access and two catalogs. **Inter-
vac U.S.** (☎ 800/756–4663 ⊕ www.intervacus.
com); $69.99 for Web-only membership for U.S.
homes; $99.99 includes Web access for U.S.
and abroad.

**Local Rental Agencies Colorado
Mountain Cabins & Vacation Home Rentals**
(☎ 719/636–5147 or 866/425–4974
⊕ www.coloradomountaincabins.com).
Colorado Vacation Directory (☎ 303/499–
9343 or 888/222–4641 ⊕ www.thecvd.com).

BED AND BREAKFASTS

Charm is the long suit of these establishments, which often occupy a restored older
building with some historical or architectural significance. They're generally small,
with fewer than 20 rooms. Breakfast is
usually included in the rates. The owners
often also manage the B&B, and you'll
likely meet them and get to know them
a bit. Breakfasts are usually substantial,
with hot beverages, cold fruit juices, and
a hot entrée. Bed & Breakfast Innkeepers
of Colorado prints a free annual directory
of its members.

Reservation Services Bed & Breakfast.com
(☎ 512/322–2710 or 800/462–2632
⊕ www.bedandbreakfast.com). **Bed & Breakfast Innkeepers of Colorado** (⊕ www.
innsofcolorado.org). **Bed & Breakfast Inns
Online** (☎ 310/280–4363 or 800/215–7365
⊕ www.bbonline.com). **BnB Finder.com**
(☎ 888/469–6663 ⊕ www.bnbfinder.com).

GUEST RANCHES

If the thought of sitting around a campfire
after a hard day on the range is your idea
of a vacation, consider playing dude on a
guest ranch. Wilderness-rimmed working
ranches accept guests and encourage them
to pitch in with chores and other ranch
activities; you might even be able to participate in a cattle roundup. Most dude

ranches don't require previous experience with horses, although a few working
ranches reserve weeks in spring and fall—
when the chore of moving cattle is more
intensive than in summer—for experienced
riders. Luxurious resorts on the fringes of
small cities offer swimming pools, tennis
courts, and a lively roster of horse-related
activities such as breakfast rides, moonlight rides, and all-day trail rides. Rafting,
fishing, tubing, and other activities are
usually available at both types of ranches.
In winter, cross-country skiing and snowshoeing keep you busy. Lodgings can run
the gamut from charmingly rustic cabins
to the kind of deluxe quarters you expect
at a first-class hotel. Meals may be gourmet or plain, but hearty. Many ranches
offer packages and children's and off-
season rates; ask when you book. No
special equipment is necessary, although
if you plan to do much fishing, you're
best off bringing your own tackle (some
ranches have tackle to loan or rent). Be
sure to check with the ranch for a list of
items you might be expected to bring. If
you plan to do much riding, a couple of
pairs of sturdy pants, boots, a wide-brim
hat to shield you from the sun, and outerwear that protects from rain and cold
should be packed. Nearly all dude ranches
in Colorado offer all-inclusive packages:
meals, lodging, and generally all activities.
Weeklong stays cost between $1,300 and
$3,600 per adult, depending on the ranch's
amenities and activities.

**Information Colorado Dude and Guest
Ranch Association** (☎ 866/942–3472
⊕ www.coloradoranch.com).

▌ BUSINESS SERVICES AND FACILITIES

Several cities throughout Colorado have
business services where you can print photographs, photocopy documents, send a
fax, and check your e-mail. The larger cities along the Interstate 25 corridor have
more selection and locations. A few are

locally owned, but most are franchises of FedEx Office.

Contacts FedEx Office (⊕ *www.fedex.com/ us/office*).

CHILDREN IN COLORADO

Colorado is tailor-made for family vacations, offering dude ranches, historic railroads, mining towns, rafting, and many outdoor activities. Places that are especially appealing to children are indicated by a rubber-duckie icon ⊙ in the margin.

▮ COMMUNICATIONS

INTERNET

Internet access is available throughout Colorado. Most lodgings have wireless access for laptops, and many have computers available for guests. Many cafés, coffee shops, and restaurants have Wi-Fi, though some charge a fee for access. Many municipal public libraries will allow patrons to use the Internet, either free or for a small fee. Cybercafes lists more than 4,000 Internet cafés worldwide

Contacts Cybercafes (⊕ *www.cybercafes.com*).

▮ EATING OUT

Dining in Colorado is generally casual. Dinner hours are typically from 6 PM to 10 PM, but many small-town and rural eateries close by 9 PM. Authentic ethnic food is hard to find outside the big cities and resort towns like Aspen.

MEALS AND MEALTIMES

Unless otherwise noted, the restaurants listed in this guide are open daily for lunch and dinner.

Although you can find all types of cuisine in Colorado's major cities and resort towns, don't forget to try native dishes like trout, elk, and buffalo (the latter two have less fat than beef and are just as tasty). Steak is a mainstay in the Rocky Mountains. Chile verde, also known as green chile, is a popular menu item at Mexican restaurants in Colorado. Many restaurants serve vegetarian items, and some are exclusively vegetarian. Organic fruits and vegetables are also readily available.

RESERVATIONS AND DRESS

Regardless of where you are, it's a good idea to make a reservation if you can. In some places it's expected. We only mention them specifically when reservations are essential (there's no other way you'll ever get a table) or when they are not accepted. For popular restaurants, book as far ahead as you can (often 30 days), and reconfirm as soon as you arrive. Large parties should always call ahead to check the reservations policy. We mention dress only when men are required to wear a jacket or a jacket and tie—which is almost never in the Rockies.

SMOKING

Smoking is prohibited in Colorado's public places, including restaurants and bars, as of 2006.

WINES, BEER, AND SPIRITS

The legal drinking age in Colorado is 21. Colorado liquor laws do not allow anyone to bring their own alcohol to restaurants. You'll find renowned breweries throughout Colorado, including, of course, the nation's second-largest brewer: Miller-Coors. There are dozens of microbreweries in Denver, Colorado Springs, Boulder, and the resort towns—if you're a beer drinker, be sure to try some local brews. Although the region is not known for its wines, the wineries in the Grand Junction area and along the Front Range have been highly touted recently.

▮ ECOTOURISM

Although neither the Bureau of Land Management (BLM) nor the National Park Service has designated any parts of Colorado as endangered ecosystems, many areas are open only to hikers; vehicles, mountain bikes, and horses are banned. It's wise to respect these closures, as well as the old adage **leave only footprints, take only pictures.** It is considered poor form to pick wildflowers while hiking, and it is illegal to pick columbine, the state flower

FOR INTERNATIONAL TRAVELERS

CURRENCY

The dollar is the basic unit of U.S. currency. It has 100 cents. Coins are the penny (1¢), nickel (5¢), dime (10¢), quarter (25¢), half-dollar (50¢), and the very rare golden $1 coin and even rarer silver $1. Bills are denominated $1, $5, $10, $20, $50, and $100, all mostly green and identical in size; designs and background tints vary. You may come across a $2 bill, but the chances are slim.

CUSTOMS

Information U.S. Customs and Border Protection (☎ 877/227–5511 ⊕ www.cbp.gov).

DRIVING

Driving in the United States is on the right. Speed limits are posted in miles per hour (usually between 55 MPH and 70 MPH). Watch for lower limits in small towns and on back roads (usually 30 MPH to 40 MPH). Most states require front-seat passengers to wear seat belts; many states require children to sit in the backseat and to wear seat belts. In major cities morning rush hour is between 7 and 10 AM; afternoon rush hour is between 4 and 7 PM. To encourage carpooling, some freeways have special lanes, ordinarily marked with a diamond, for high-occupancy vehicles (HOV)—cars carrying two people or more.

Highways are well paved. Interstates—limited-access, multilane highways designated with an "I–" before the number—are fastest. Interstates with three-digit numbers circle urban areas, which may also have other limited-access expressways, freeways, and parkways. Tolls may be levied on limited-access highways. U.S. and state highways aren't necessarily limited-access, but may have several lanes.

Gas stations are plentiful. Most stay open late (24 hours along major highways and in big cities) except in rural areas, where Sunday hours are limited and where you may drive for long stretches without a refueling opportunity. Along larger highways, roadside stops with restrooms, fast-food restaurants, and sundries stores are well spaced. State police and tow trucks patrol major highways. If your car breaks down on an interstate, pull onto the shoulder and wait for help, or have your passengers wait while you walk to an emergency phone (available in most states). If you carry a cell phone, dial *55, noting your location on the small green roadside mileage marker.

ELECTRICITY

The U.S. standard is AC, 110 volts/60 cycles. Plugs have two flat pins set parallel to each other.

EMBASSIES

Contacts Australia (☎ 202/797–3000 ⊕ www.austemb.org). **Canada** (☎ 202/682–1740 ⊕ www.canadianembassy.org). **UK** (☎ 202/588–7800 ⊕ www.britainusa.com).

For police, fire, or ambulance, dial 911 (0 in rural areas).

HOLIDAYS

New Year's Day (Jan. 1); Martin Luther King Day (3rd Mon. in Jan.); Presidents' Day (3rd Mon. in Feb.); Memorial Day (last Mon. in May); Independence Day (July 4); Labor Day (1st Mon. in Sept.); Columbus Day (2nd Mon. in Oct.); Thanksgiving Day (4th Thurs. in Nov.); Christmas Eve and Christmas Day (Dec. 24 and 25); and New Year's Eve (Dec. 31).

MAIL

You can buy stamps and send letters and parcels in post offices. Stamp-dispensing machines can occasionally be found in airports, bus and train stations, office buildings, drugstores, convenience stores, and in ATMs. U.S. mailboxes are stout, dark-blue steel bins; pickup schedules are posted inside the bin (pull the handle). Mail parcels over a pound at a post office.

A first-class letter weighing 1 ounce or less costs 44¢; each additional ounce costs 17¢. Postcards cost 28¢. Postcards or 1-ounce airmail letters to most countries cost 98¢; postcards or 1-ounce letters to Canada or Mexico cost 75¢. To receive mail on the road, have it sent c/o General Delivery to your destination's main post office. You must pick up mail in person within 30 days with a driver's license or passport for identification.

Contacts DHL (☎ *800/225–5345* ⊕ *www.dhl.com*). **FedEx** (☎ *800/463–3339* ⊕ *www.fedex.com*). **Mail Boxes, Etc.** (☎ *800/789–4623* ⊕ *www.mbe.com*). **UPS** (☎ *800/742–5877* ⊕ *www.ups.com*). **USPS** (☎ *800/275–8777* ⊕ *www.usps.com*).

PASSPORTS AND VISAS

Visitor visas aren't necessary for citizens of Australia, Canada, the United Kingdom, or most citizens of EU countries coming for tourism and staying for under 90 days. A visa is $131, and waiting time can be substantial. Apply for a visa at the U.S. consulate in your place of residence.

Visa Information **Destination USA** (⊕ *www.travel.state.gov*).

PHONES

Numbers consist of a three-digit area code and a seven-digit local number. Within many local calling areas, dial just seven digits. In others, dial "1" first and all 10 digits; this is true for calling toll-free numbers—prefixed by "800," "888," "866," and "877." Dial "1" before "900" numbers, too, but know they're very expensive.

For international calls, dial "011," the country code, and the number. For help, dial "0" and ask for an overseas operator. Most phone books list country codes and U.S. area codes. The country code for Australia is 61, for New Zealand 64, for the United Kingdom 44. Calling Canada is the same as calling within the United States (country code: 1).

For operator assistance, dial "0." For directory assistance, call 555–1212 or 411 (free at many public phones). To call "collect" (reverse charges), dial "0" instead of "1" before the 10-digit number.

Instructions are generally posted on pay phones. Usually you insert coins in a slot (usually 25¢–50¢ for local calls) and wait for a steady tone before dialing. On long-distance calls the operator tells you how much to insert; prepaid phone cards, widely available, can be used from any phone. Follow the directions to activate the card, then dial your number.

CELL PHONES

The United States has several GSM (Global System for Mobile Communications) networks, so multiband mobiles from most countries (except for Japan) work here. It's almost impossible to buy just a pay-as-you-go mobile SIM card in the U.S.—needed to avoid roaming charges—but cell phones with pay-as-you-go plans are available for well under $100. AT&T (GoPhone) and Virgin Mobile have the cheapest with national coverage.

Contacts Cingular (☎ *888/333–6651* ⊕ *www.cingular.com*). **Virgin Mobile** (⊕ *www.virginmobileusa.com*).

of Colorado. Recycling is taken seriously throughout Colorado, and you will find yourself very unpopular if you litter or fail to recycle your cans and bottles.

All archaeological artifacts, including rock etchings and paintings, are protected by federal law and must be left untouched and undisturbed.

For organized trips in the great outdoors, see the Sports and the Outdoors section below.

Contacts U.S. Bureau of Land Management (☎ 303/239–3600 ⊕ www.blm.gov/co). **National Park Reservation Service** (☎ 800/436–7275 ⊕ www.recreation.gov).

▌ HEALTH

You may feel dizzy and weak and find yourself breathing heavily—signs that the thin mountain air isn't giving you your accustomed dose of oxygen. Take it easy, and rest often for a few days until you're acclimatized. Throughout your stay, drink plenty of water and watch your alcohol consumption. If you experience severe headaches and nausea, see a doctor. It's easy—especially in a state where highways climb to 11,000 feet and higher—to go too high too fast. The remedy for altitude-related discomfort is to descend into heavier air.

▌ PACKING

For the most part, informality reigns in the Centennial State; jeans, sport shirts, and T-shirts fit in almost everywhere. If you plan to golf, a collared shirt may be required for men. No matter what your vacation plans are, don't forget to pack sunscreen, lip balm with SPF, sunglasses, and a cap or hat. No matter the season, the sunshine is intense at Colorado's altitude, and there are plenty of souvenirs available that you'll prefer over a sunburn.

If you plan to spend much time outdoors, and certainly if you go in winter, choose clothing appropriate for cold and wet weather. Cotton clothing, including denim, can be uncomfortable when it

gets wet or when the weather's cold. Better choices are clothing made of wool or any of a number of synthetics that provide warmth without bulk and maintain their insulating properties when wet. It's not a bad idea to save your shopping for Colorado, where you'll find a huge selection of suitable clothing and gear.

In summer you'll probably want to wear shorts during the day. Because early morning and night can be cold, particularly in the mountains, pack a sweater and a light jacket, and perhaps a wool cap and gloves. For walks and hikes, you'll need sturdy footwear. Boots should have thick soles and plenty of ankle support; if your shoes are new and you plan to do a lot of hiking, break them in at home. Bring a day pack for short hikes, along with a canteen or water bottle, and don't forget rain gear, a hat, sunscreen, and insect repellent.

In winter, prepare for subzero temperatures with good boots, warm socks and liners, long johns, a well-insulated jacket, and a warm hat and mittens. Layers are the best preparation for fluctuating temperatures.

▌ SAFETY

Although Colorado is considered to be generally safe, travelers should take ordinary precautions—unfortunate incidents can happen anywhere. At your hotel lock your valuables either in the hotel's safe or in the safe in your room, if one is available. Be aware of your surroundings, and keep your wallet and passport in a buttoned pocket, or keep your handbag in front of you where you can see it. At night, avoid dimly lighted areas and areas where there are few people. Consider a taxi ride to your hotel if it is a long walk or you are alone.

Regardless of the outdoor activity or your level of skill, safety must come first. When hiking or taking part in any other outdoor activity, it's best (and often more fun) to go in pairs or small groups. If you do hike, cycle, kayak, or backcountry ski alone, it is essential that you tell someone where you are going and when you plan to return, whether it's a park ranger or the host of your B&B. Let them know, of course, when you've returned safely.

Many trails are at high altitudes, where oxygen is scarce. They're also frequently desolate. Hikers and bikers should carry emergency supplies in their backpacks. Proper equipment includes a flashlight, a compass, waterproof matches, a first-aid kit, a knife, a space blanket, and a light plastic tarp for shelter. Backcountry skiers should add a repair kit, a blanket, an avalanche beacon, and a lightweight shovel to their lists. Always bring extra food and a canteen of water, as dehydration is a real danger at high altitudes. Never drink from streams or lakes, unless you boil the water first or purify it with tablets. Giardia, an intestinal parasite, may be present.

Although you may tan easily, the sun is intense even at mile-high elevations (which are relatively low for the state), and sunburn can develop in just a few hours of hiking or sightseeing. Coloradans slather on sunscreen as a matter of course. Be sure to pack plenty of it, and don't forget to put it on when skiing—there's nothing glamorous about a goggle tan. The state's dry climate and thin air can also dehydrate you quickly. Carry a couple of liters of water with you each day and sip frequently.

Flash floods can strike at any time and any place with little or no warning. The danger in mountainous terrain is heightened when distant rains are channeled into gullies and ravines, turning a quiet streamside campsite or wash into a rampaging torrent in seconds. Check weather reports before heading into the backcountry, and be prepared to head for higher ground if the weather turns severe.

One of the most wonderful parts of the Rockies is the abundant wildlife. And although a herd of grazing elk or a bighorn sheep high on a hillside is most certainly a Kodak moment, an encounter with a bear or mountain lion is not. To avoid such an unpleasant situation while hiking, make plenty of noise and keep dogs on leashes and small children between adults. While camping, be sure to store all food, utensils, and clothing with food odors far away from your tent, preferably high in a tree. If you do come across a bear or big cat, do not run. For bears, back away quietly; for lions, make yourself look as big as possible. In either case, be prepared to fend off the animal with loud noises, rocks, sticks, etc. And, as the saying goes, do not feed the bears—or any wild animals—whether they're dangerous or not.

When in any park, give all animals their space. If you want to take a photograph, use a long lens rather than a long sneak to approach closely. Approaching an animal can cause stress and affect its ability to survive the sometimes brutal climate. In all cases, remember that the animals have the right-of-way; this is their home, you are the visitor.

Safety Transportation Security Administration (TSA; ⊕ www.tsa.gov).

▮ SPORTS AND THE OUTDOORS

The Colorado Rockies are one of America's greatest playgrounds. Information about Colorado's recreational areas and activities is provided in each regional section; the following is general information. *Also see Outdoor Adventures in Experience Colorado.*

Outfitter Listings Colorado Outfitters Association (☎ 970/824–2468 ⊕ www.coloradooutfitters.org).

GROUP TRIPS

Group sizes for organized trips vary considerably, depending on the organizer and the activity. Often, if you're planning a trip with a large group, trip organizers or outfitters will offer discounts of 10% and more and are willing to customize trips. For example, if you're with a group interested in photography or in wildlife, trip organizers have been known to get professional photographers or naturalists to join the group. Recreating as a group gives you leverage with the organizer, and you should use it.

One way to travel with a group is to join an organization before going. Conservation-minded travelers might want to contact the Sierra Club, a nonprofit organization, which offers both vacation and work trips. Hiking trails tend to be maintained by volunteers (this is more often done by local hiking clubs). Park or forest rangers are the best resource for information about groups involved in this sort of work.

Individuals or groups wanting to test their mettle can learn wilderness skills through "outdoor schools."

Contacts Boulder Outdoor Survival School (⌂ Box 1590, Boulder, CO 80305☎ 303/444–9779 or 800/335–7404 ⊕ www.boss-inc.com). **Sierra Club** (✉ 1536 Wynkoop St., 4th Fl., Denver, CO80202 ☎ 303/861–8819 ⊕ rmc.sierraclub.org).

American Hiking Society (✉ 1422 Fenwick La., Silver Spring, MD20910 ☎ 800/972–8608 ⊕ www.americanhiking.org).

▮ TAXES

Colorado's state sales tax is 2.9%, but after that it gets a little tricky. City sales taxes around the state range from 0.25% to 4%. County sales tax is between 1% and 4.5%. On top of state, county, and city taxes, some areas have local sales and lodging taxes that range from 0.9% to 4%. Some jurisdictions do not impose sales tax on groceries, and in some areas alcohol served in bars is taxed at a different rate from alcohol served in restaurants or purchased at liquor stores. In Denver, sales tax adds up to 7.72%, you'll pay 8.1% on your bill at a restaurant, and lodging tax is 14.85%. In Colorado Springs you'll pay only the sales tax—7.4%—at a restaurant, but lodging tax is 9.4%. In Boulder, sales tax is 8.16%, restaurant tax is 8.31%, and lodging tax is 10.25%. *For regional tax ranges, see the What It Costs charts in each section.*

▮ TIME

All of Colorado is in the Mountain Time Zone. Mountain Time is two hours earlier than Eastern Time and one hour later than Pacific Time, so Colorado is one hour ahead of California, one hour behind Chicago, and two hours behind New York.

Time Zones Timeanddate.com (⊕ www.timeanddate.com/worldclock) can help you figure out the correct time anywhere.

▮ TIPPING

It's customary to tip 15% to 20% at restaurants in cities; in resort towns, 20% is increasingly the norm. For coat checks and bellmen, $1 per coat or bag is the minimum. Taxi drivers expect 10% to 15%. In resort towns, ski technicians, sandwich makers, coffee baristas, and the like also appreciate tips.

■ TOURS

GUIDED TOURS

Tour Colorado offers a wide range of comprehensive tours statewide. Multi-day themed tours include train rides, scenic drives, wildlife-watching, agriculture, the Wild West, adventure thrills, and shopping excursions.

Contacts Tour Colorado (☎ *888/311–8687* ⊕ *www.tourcolorado.com*).

SPECIAL-INTEREST TOURS

Colorado Wine Country Tours takes wine lovers on a sommelier-guided tour of Colorado wineries on the Front Range and the Western Slope. Culinary Connectors offers Denver-based culinary tours of the city's best restaurants as well as tours of ethnic, gourmet, and farmers' markets.

Field Guides takes birders on 10-day trips in search of Colorado's prairie chickens and grouse every April. OARS offers multiday rafting trips on the Yampa and Green rivers and hiking vacations in Chaco Canyon, Mesa Verde National Park, Ute Mountain Tribal Park, and National Bridges Monument. Victor Emanuel Nature Tours offers several Colorado-based birding tours in the spring and summer.

Contacts Colorado Wine Country Tours (☎ *303/777–9463* ⊕ *www.coloradowinecountrytours.com*). **Culinary Connectors** (☎ *303/495–5487* ⊕ *www.culinaryconnectors.com*). **Field Guides** (☎ *800/728–4953* ⊕ *www.fieldguides.com*). **OARS** (☎ *800/346–6277* ⊕ *www.oars.com*). **Victor Emanuel Nature Tours** (☎ *512/328–5221 or 800/328–8368* ⊕ *www.ventbird.com*).

■ TRIP INSURANCE

Comprehensive trip insurance is valuable if you're booking a very expensive or complicated trip (particularly to an isolated region) or if you're booking far in advance. Comprehensive policies typically cover trip-cancellation and interruption, letting you cancel or cut your trip short because of illness, or, in some cases, acts of terrorism in your destination. Such policies might also cover evacuation and medical care. (For trips abroad you should have at least medical-only coverage. *See Medical Insurance and Assistance under Health.*) Some also cover you for trip delays because of bad weather or mechanical problems as well as for lost or delayed luggage.

Another type of coverage to consider is financial default—that is, when your trip is disrupted because a tour operator, airline, or cruise line goes out of business. Generally you must buy this when you book your trip or shortly thereafter, and it's available to you only if your operator isn't on a list of excluded companies.

Always read the fine print of your policy to make sure that you're covered for the risks that most concern you. Compare several policies to be sure you're getting the best price and range of coverage available.

Insurance Comparison Info Insure My Trip (☎ *800/487–4722* ⊕ *www.insuremytrip.com*). **Square Mouth** (☎ *800/240–0369* ⊕ *www.squaremouth.com*).

Comprehensive Insurers Access America (☎ *800/284–8300* ⊕ *www.accessamerica.com*). **AIG Travel Guard** (☎ *800/826–4919* ⊕ *www.travelguard.com*). **CSA Travel Protection** (☎ *800/873–9855* ⊕ *www.csatravelprotection.com*). **Travelex Insurance** (☎ *888/228–9792* ⊕ *www.travelex-insurance.com*). **Travel Insured International** (☎ *800/243–3174* ⊕ *www.travelinsured.com*).

■ VISITOR INFORMATION

Almost every town, county, and resort area has its own tourist office. Contact information is provided in the Essentials section at start of each area.

Contact Colorado Tourism Office (✉ *1625 Broadway, No. 2700, Denver* ☎ *800/265–6723* ⊕ *www.colorado.com*).

INDEX

ABOUT OUR WRITERS

Barbara Colligan, a resident of metropolitan Denver since 1968, has made numerous trips to Rocky Mountain National Park and the surrounding areas, often going with her twin daughters and the family dog. A big fan of the National Park System, Barbara has explored several national parks in Colorado and the West and heads to the Colorado mountains as often as her work schedule will allow.

Martha Schindler Connors is a freelance writer in Evergreen, CO, where she lives with her husband and two dogs. Her writing has appeared in many national and regional magazines. For this edition, Martha updated the Boulder and North Central and Black Canyon of the Gunnison National Park section.

Jad Davenport, a freelance travel writer and photographer, grew up in Colorado where he lives with his wife and daughters. He enjoys backcountry skiing, ice climbing, white-water kayaking, and hiking. His work has appeared in *Outside, National Geographic Adventure,* and *Men's Journal* magazines. For this edition, Jad updated Summit County, Vail Valley, and Aspen.

Lois Friedland is a Colorado-based journalist and editor who specializes in travel, skiing, and golf. She is About.com's adventure travel guide. For this edition, Martha updated Rockies Near Denver and South Central Colorado.

Carrie Miner has wandered the wilds of the southwest for more than a decade. She has written hundreds of travel articles and updates Southwest Colorado and Travel Smart for this edition.

Kyle Wagner wrote about restaurants and food in Denver for 12 years, first for the alternative weekly *Westword* and then for the *Denver Post*, before being named travel editor for the Post in 2005. Her work also has appeared in the *Rocky Mountain News* and *Sunset* magazine. She lives in Denver with her two teenage daughters, who had their passports stamped before they started kindergarten and prefer sushi to McDonald's. For this edition, Kyle updated Experience Colorado, Denver, and Northwest Colorado.